THE INDIAN PENAL CODE

THE INDIAN PENAL CODE

AS ORIGINALLY FRAMED IN 1837

C. H. CAMERON T.
B. MACAULAY

GYAN

Published by

Gyan Publishing House
5, Ansari Road
Daryaganj, New Delhi-110002
Phone: 011-47034999, 9811692060
E-mail: books@gyanbooks.com

Distribution Network
gyanbooks.com
India, USA, Canada, UK, Australia

ISBN: 978-93-7225-276-7 (PB)

First Published, 1888

2nd Impression 2025

Printed at: Gyan Press, Delhi.

THE INDIAN PENAL CODE
Arthur: C. H. CAMERON, T. B. MACAULAY

THE

INDIAN PENAL CODE

AS ORIGINALLY FRAMED IN 1837

WITH NOTES

BY

T. B. MACAULAY, J. M. MACLEOD,
G. W. ANDERSON AND F. MILLETT,

AND THE

FIRST AND SECOND REPORTS THEREON
DATED 23RD JULY 1846 AND 24TH JUNE 1847

BY

C. H. CAMERON AND D. ELIOTT,
INDIAN LAW COMMISSIONERS.

A VERBATIM REPRINT.

MADRAS:
HIGGINBOTHAM AND CO.
By Appointment in India to His Royal Highness the Prince of Wales.
1888.

PREFACE.

At the suggestion of several members of the Legal profession and officials in this and in other presidencies, we collate and publish this volume containing the Indian Penal Code as originally drafted in 1837 and the First and Second Reports of the Indian Law Commissioners thereon. These are exceedingly rare; but are frequently sought for as helps to the elucidation of the law as it at present exists. We much regret that we have up to this time failed to procure from the Government of India the subsequent papers and minutes of discussion that took place immediately preceding the passing of the Code into Law by the Governor-General in Council in 1860. Should however these be hereafter obtained we will most likely publish them as a supplemental volume.

January 1888. H. & Co.

CONTENTS.

APPENDIX.

FIRST REPORT ON THE PENAL CODE.

POSTSCRIPT.

SECOND REPORT ON THE PENAL CODE.

A PENAL CODE

Prepared by the Indian Law Commissioners, and published by Command of the Governor-General of India in Council.

TO THE RIGHT HONOURABLE

GEORGE LORD AUCKLAND, G.C.B.,

Governor-General of India in Council.

MY LORD,

The Penal Code which, according to the orders of Government of the 15th of June 1835, we had the honour to lay before your Lordship in Council on the 2nd of May last, has now been printed under our superintendence, and has, as well as the Notes, been carefully revised and corrected by us while in the press.

The time which has been employed in framing this body of law will not be thought long by any person who is acquainted with the nature of the labour which such works require, and with the history of other works of the same kind. We should, however, have been able to lay it before your Lordship in Council many months earlier, but for a succession of unfortunate circumstances against which it was impossible to provide. During a great part of the year 1836, the Commission was rendered almost entirely inefficient by the ill-health of a majority of the members; and we were altogether deprived of the valuable services of our colleague Mr. Cameron, at the very time when those services were most needed.

It is hardly necessary for us to entreat your Lordship in Council to examine with candour the work which we now submit to you. To the ignorant and inexperienced the task in which we have been engaged may appear easy and simple. But the members of the Indian Government are doubtless well aware that it is among the most difficult tasks in which the human mind can be employed; that persons placed in circumstances far more favourable than ours have attempted it with very doubtful success; that the best Codes extant, if malignantly criticised, will be found to furnish matter for censure in every page; that the most copious and precise of human languages furnish but a very imperfect machinery to the legislator; that, in a work so extensive and complicated as that on which we have been employed, there will inevitably be, in spite of the most anxious care, some omissions and some inconsistencies; and that we have done as much as could reasonably be expected from us if we have furnished the Government with that which may, by suggestions from experienced and judicious persons, be improved into a good Code.

Your Lordship in Council will be prepared to find in this performance those defects which must necessarily be found in the first portion of a Code. Such is the relation which exists between the different parts of the law, that no part can be brought to perfection while the other parts remain rude. The Penal Code cannot be clear and explicit while the substantive civil law and the law of procedure are dark and confused. While the rights of individuals and the powers of public functionaries are uncertain, it cannot always be certain whether those rights have been attacked, or those powers exceeded.

Your Lordship in Council will perceive that the system of penal law which we propose is not a digest of any existing system, and that no existing system has furnished us even with a groundwork. We trust that your Lordship in Council will not hence infer that we have neglected to inquire, as we are commanded to do by Parliament, into the present state of that part of the law, or that in other parts of our labours we are likely to recommend unsparing innovation, and the entire sweeping away of ancient usages. We are perfectly aware of the value of that sanction which long prescription and national feeling give to institutions. We are perfectly aware that lawgivers ought not to disregard even the unreasonable prejudices of those for whom they legislate. So sensible are we of the importance of these considerations, that, though there are not the same objections to innovation in penal legislation as to innovation affecting vested rights of property, yet, if we had found India in possession of a system of criminal law which the people regarded with partiality, we should have been inclined rather to ascertain it, to digest it, and moderately to correct it, than to propose a system fundamentally different.

But it appears to us that none of the systems of penal law established in British India has any claim to our attention, except what it may derive from its own intrinsic excellence. All those systems are foreign. All were introduced by conquerors differing in race, manners, language and religion from the great mass of the people. The criminal law of the Hindoos was long ago superseded, through the greater part of the territories now subject to the Company, by that of the Mahomedans, and is certainly the last system of criminal law which an enlightened and humane Government would be disposed to revive. The Mahomedan criminal law has in its turn been superseded, to a great extent, by the British Regulations. Indeed, in the territories subject to the Presidency of Bombay, the criminal law of the Mahomedans, as well as that of the Hindoos, has been altogether discarded, except in one particular class of cases; and even in such cases, it is not imperative on the judge to pay any attention to it. The British Regulations, having been made by three different legislatures, contain, as might be expected, very different provisions. Thus in Bengal serious forgeries are punishable with imprisonment for a term double of the term fixed for perjury:* in the Bombay Presidency, on the contrary, perjury is punishable with imprisonment for a term double of the term fixed for the most aggravated forgeries:† in the Madras Presidency, the two offences are exactly on the same footing.‡ In the Bombay Presidency the escape of a convict is punished with imprisonment for a term double of the term assigned to that offence in the two other Presidencies;§ while a coiner is punished with little more than half the imprisonment assigned to his offence in the other two Presidencies.‖ In Bengal the purchasing of regimental necessaries from soldiers is not punishable, except at Calcutta, and is there

* Bengal Regulation XVII of 1817, section IX.

† Bombay Regulation XIV of 1827, sections XVI and XVII.

‡ Madras Regulation VI of 1811, section III.

§ Bombay Regulation XIV of 1827, section XXIV, and Regulation V of 1831, section I. Bengal Regulation XII of 1818, section V, clause 1. Madras Regulation VI of 1822, section V, clause 2.

‖ Bombay Regulation XIV of 1827, section XVIII. Bengal Regulation XVII of 1817, section IX. Madras Regulation II of 1822, section V.

punishable with a fine of only fifty rupees.* In the Madras Presidency it is punishable with a fine of forty rupees.† In the Bombay Presidency it is punishable with imprisonment for four years.‡ In Bengal the vending of stamps without a license is punishable with a moderate fine; and the purchasing of stamps from a person not licensed to sell them is not punished at all.§ In the Madras Presidency the vender is punished with a short imprisonment; but there also the purchaser is not punished at all.|| In the Bombay Presidency, both the vender and the purchaser are liable to imprisonment for five years, and to flogging.¶

Thus widely do the systems of penal law now established in British India differ from each other: nor can we recommend any one of the three systems as furnishing even the rudiments of a good Code. The penal law of Bengal and of the Madras Presidency is, in fact, Mahomedan law, which has gradually been distorted to such an extent as to deprive it of all title to the religious veneration of Mahomedans, yet which retains enough of its original peculiarities to perplex and encumber the administration of justice. In substance it now differs at least as widely from the Mahomedan penal law, as the penal law of England differs from the penal law of France. Yet technical terms and nice distinctions borrowed from the Mahomedan law are still retained. Nothing is more usual than for the Courts to ask the law officers what punishment the Mahomedan law prescribes in a hypothetical case, and then to inflict that punishment on a person who is not within that hypothetical case, and who by the Mahomedan law would be liable either to a different punishment, or to no punishment. We by no means presume to condemn the policy which led the British Government to retain, and gradually to modify, the system of criminal jurisprudence which it found established in these provinces. But it is evident that a body of law thus formed must, considered merely as a body of law, be defective and inconvenient.

* Calcutta Rule, Ordinance and Regulation, passed 21st August, registered 18th November 1821.

† Madras Regulation XIV of 1832, section II, clause 1.

‡ Bombay Regulation XXII of 1827, section XIX.

§ Bengal Regulation X of 1829, section IX, clause 2.

|| Madras Regulation XIII of 1816, section X, clause 10.

¶ Bombay Regulation XVIII of 1827, section IX, clause 1.

The penal law of the Bombay Presidency is all contained in the Regulations; and is almost all to be found in one extensive Regulation.* The Government of that Presidency appears to have been fully sensible of the great advantage which must arise from placing the whole law in a written form before those who are to administer and those who are to obey it; and, whatever may be the imperfections of the execution, high praise is due to the design. The course which we recommend to the Government, and which some persons may perhaps consider as too daring, has already been tried at Bombay, and has not produced any of those effects which timid minds are disposed to anticipate even from the most reasonable and useful innovations. Throughout a large territory, inhabited to a great extent by a newly-conquered population, all the ancient systems of penal law were at once superseded by a Code, and this without the smallest sign of discontent among the people.

It would have given us great pleasure to have found that Code such as we could with propriety have taken as the groundwork of a Code for all India. But we regret to say that the penal law of the Bombay Presidency has over the penal law of the other Presidencies no superiority, except that of being digested. In framing it, the principles according to which crimes ought to be classified and punishments apportioned have been less regarded than in the legislation of Bengal and Madras. The secret destroying of any property, though it may not be worth a single rupee, is punishable with imprisonment for five years.† Unlawful confinement, though it may last only for a quarter of an hour, is punishable with imprisonment for five years.‡ Every conspiracy to injure or impoverish any person is punishable with imprisonment for ten years;§ so that a man who engages in a design as atrocious as the gunpowder plot, and one who is party to a scheme for putting off an unsound horse on a purchaser, are classed together, and are liable to exactly the same punishment. Under this law, if two men concert a petty theft, and afterwards repent of their purpose and abandon it, each of them is liable to twenty times the

* Bombay Regulation XIV of 1827.
† Regulation XIV of 1827, section XLII, clause 2.
‡ Regulation XIV of 1827, section XXXIII, clause 1.
§ Regulation XVII of 1828.

punishment of the actual theft.* All assaults which cause a severe shock to the mental feelings of the sufferer are classed with the atrocious crime of rape, and are liable to the punishment of rape, that is, if the Courts shall think fit, to imprisonment for fourteen years.† The breaking of the window of a house, the dashing to pieces a china cup within a house, the riding over a field of grain in hunting, are classed with the crime of arson, and are punishable, incredible as it may appear, with death. The following is the law on the subject: "Any person who shall wilfully and wrongfully set fire to or otherwise damage or destroy any part of a dwelling-house or building appertaining thereto, or property contained in a dwelling-house, or building or enclosure appertaining thereto, or crops standing or reaped in the field, shall be liable to any of the punishments specified in Section III of this Regulation."‡ The section to which reference is made contains a list of the punishments authorized by the Bombay Code, and at the head of that list stands "Death."

But these errors, the effects probably of inadvertence, are not, in our opinion, the most serious faults of the Penal Code of Bombay. That Code contains enactments which it is impossible to excuse on the ground of inadvertence—enactments the language of which shows that when they were framed their whole effect was fully understood, and which appear to us to be directly opposed to the first principles of penal law. One of the first principles of penal law is this, that a person who merely conceals a crime after it has been committed ought not to be punished as if he had himself committed it. By the Bombay Code, the concealment after the fact of murder is punishable as murder; the concealment after the fact of gang-robbery is punishable as gang-robbery;§—and this, though the concealment after the fact of the most cruel mutilations, and of the most atrocious robberies committed by not more than four persons, is not punished at all.

If there be any distinction which more than any other it behoves the legislator to bear constantly in mind, it is the distinction between harm voluntarily caused and harm

* Regulation XIV of 1837, section XXXIX.
† Regulation XIV of 1827, section XXIX, clause 1.
‡ Regulation XIV of 1827, section XLII, clause 1.
§ Regulation XIV of 1827, section I, clause 1.

involuntarily caused. Negligence, indeed, often causes mischief, and often deserves punishment. But to punish a man whose negligence has produced some evil which he never contemplated, as if he had produced the same evil knowingly and with deliberate malice, is a course which, as far as we are aware, no jurist has ever recommended in theory, and which we are confident that no society would tolerate in practice. It is, however, provided by the Bombay Code that "the unintentional commission of any act punishable by that Code shall be punished according to the Court's judgment of the culpable disregard of injury to others evinced by the person committing the said act, but the punishment for such unintentional commission shall not exceed that prescribed for the offence committed."*

We have said enough to show that it is owing not at all to the law, but solely to the discretion and humanity of the judges, that great cruelty and injustice is not daily perpetrated in the Criminal Courts of the Bombay Presidency.

Many important classes of offences are altogether unnoticed by the Bombay Code; and this omission appears to us to be very ill supplied by one sweeping clause, which arms the Courts with almost unlimited power to punish as they think fit offences against morality, or against the peace and good order of society, if those offences are penal by the religious law of the offender.† This clause does not apply to people who profess a religion with which a system of penal jurisprudence is not inseparably connected. And from this state of the law some singular consequences follow. For example, a Mahomedan is punishable for adultery: a Christian is at liberty to commit adultery with impunity.

Such is the state of the penal law in the Mofussil. In the meantime the population which lives within the local jurisdiction of the Courts established by the Royal Charters is subject to the English Criminal Law, that is to say, to a very artificial and complicated system,—to a foreign system,—to a system which was framed without the smallest reference to India,—to a system which even in the country for which it was framed is generally considered as requiring extensive reform,—to a system finally which has just been

---

* Regulation XIV of 1827, section I, clause 3.
† Regulation XIV of 1827, section I, clause 1.

pronounced by a Commission composed of able and learned English lawyers to be so defective that it can be reformed only by being entirely taken to pieces and reconstructed.*

Under these circumstances we have not thought it desirable to take as the groundwork of the Code any of the systems of law now in force in any part of India. We have, indeed, to the best of our ability, compared the Code with all those systems, and we have taken suggestions from all; but we have not adopted a single provision merely because it formed a part of any of those systems. We have also compared our work with the most celebrated systems of Western jurisprudence, as far as the very scanty means of information which were accessible to us in this country enabled us to do so. We have derived much valuable assistance from the French Code, and from the decisions of the French Courts of Justice on questions touching the construction of that Code. We have derived assistance still more valuable from the Code of Louisiana, prepared by the late Mr. Livingston. We are the more desirous to acknowledge our obligations to that eminent jurist, because we have found ourselves under the necessity of combating his opinions on some important questions.

The reasons for those provisions which appear to us to require explanation or defence will be found appended to the Code in the form of Notes. Should your Lordship in Council wish for fuller information as to the considerations by which we have been guided in framing any part of the law, we shall be ready to afford it.

One peculiarity in the manner in which this Code is framed will immediately strike your Lordship in Council,—we mean the copious use of illustrations. These illustrations will, we trust, greatly facilitate the understanding of the law, and will at the same time often serve as a defence of the law. In our definitions we have repeatedly found ourselves under the necessity of sacrificing neatness and perspicuity to precision, and of using harsh expressions because we could find no other expressions which would convey our whole meaning, and no more than our whole meaning. Such definitions standing by themselves might repel and perplex the reader,

* Letter to Lord John Russell from the Commissioners appointed to inquire into the state of the Criminal Law, dated 19th January 1837.

and would perhaps be fully comprehended only by a few students after long application. Yet such definitions are found, and must be found, in every system of law which aims at accuracy. A legislator may, if he thinks fit, avoid such definitions, and by avoiding them he will give a smoother and more attractive appearance to his workmanship; but in that case he flinches from a duty which he ought to perform, and which somebody must perform. If this necessary but most disagreeable work be not performed by the lawgiver once for all, it must be constantly performed in a rude and imperfect manner by every judge in the empire, and will probably be performed by no two judges in the same way. We have therefore thought it right not to shrink from the task of framing these unpleasing but indispensable parts of a Code. And we hope that when each of these definitions is followed by a collection of cases falling under it, and of cases which, though at first sight they appear to fall under it, do not really fall under it, the definition and the reasons which led to the adoption of it will be readily understood. The illustrations will lead the mind of the student through the same steps by which the minds of those who framed the law proceeded, and may sometimes show him that a phrase which may have struck him as uncouth, or a distinction which he may have thought idle, was deliberately adopted for the purpose of including or excluding a large class of important cases. In the study of geometry it is constantly found that a theorem which, read by itself, conveyed no distinct meaning to the mind, becomes perfectly clear as soon as the reader casts his eye over the statement of the individual case taken for the purpose of demonstration. Our illustrations, we trust, will in a similar manner facilitate the study of the law.

There are two things which a legislator should always have in view while he is framing laws: the one is, that they should be as far as possible precise; the other, that they should be easily understood. To unite precision and simplicity in definitions intended to include large classes of things, and to exclude others very similar to many of those which are included, will often be utterly impossible. Under such circumstances it is not easy to say what is the best course. That a law, and especially a penal law, should be drawn in words which convey no meaning to the people who are to obey it is an evil. On the other hand, a loosely-worded law is no law, and to whatever extent a legislature uses vague expressions, to that extent it abdicates its functions, and resigns the power of making law to the Courts of Justice.

On the whole, we are inclined to think that the best course is that which we have adopted. We have, in framing our definitions, thought principally of making them precise, and have not shrunk from rugged or intricate phraseology when such phraseology appeared to us to be necessary to precision. If it appeared to us that our language was likely to perplex an ordinary reader, we added as many illustrations as we thought necessary for the purpose of explaining it. The definitions and enacting clauses contain the whole law. The illustrations make nothing law which would not be law without them. They only exhibit the law in full action, and show what its effects will be on the events of common life.

Thus the Code will be at once a Statute book and a collection of decided cases. The decided cases in the Code will differ from the decided cases in the English law books in two most important points. In the first place, our illustrations are never intended to supply any omission in the written law, nor do they ever, in our opinion, put a strain on the written law. They are merely instances of the practical application of the written law to the affairs of mankind. Secondly, they are cases decided not by the judges but by the legislature, by those who make the law, and who must know more certainly than any judge can know what the law is which they mean to make.

The power of construing the law in cases in which there is any real reason to doubt what the law is amounts to the power of making the law. On this ground the Roman jurists maintained that the office of interpreting the law in doubtful matters necessarily belonged to the legislature. The contrary opinion was censured by them with great force of reason, though in language perhaps too bitter and sarcastic for the gravity of a Code. "Eorum vanam subtilitatem tam risimus quam corrigendam esse censuimus. Si enim in præsenti leges condere soli imperatori concessum est, et leges interpretari solo dignum imperio esse oportet. Quis legum ænigmata solvere et omnibus aperire idoneus esse videbitur nisi is cui legislatorem esse concessum est? Explosis itaque his ridiculosis ambiguitatibus tam conditor quam interpres legum solus imperator juste existimabitur."*

The decisions on particular cases which we have annexed to the provisions of the Code resemble the imperial rescripts in this, that they proceed from the same authority from which the provisions themselves proceed. They differ from the imperial rescripts in this most important circumstance, that they are not made *ex post facto*, that they cannot therefore be made to serve any particular turn, that the persons condemned or absolved by them are purely imaginary persons, and that, therefore, whatever may be thought of the wisdom of any judgment which we have passed, there can be no doubt of its impartiality.

The publication of this collection of cases decided by legislative authority will, we hope, greatly limit the power which the Courts of Justice possess of putting their own sense on the laws. But we are sensible that neither this collection nor any other can be sufficiently extensive to settle every question which may be raised as to the construction of the Code. Such questions will certainly arise, and, unless proper precautions be taken, the decisions on such questions will accumulate till they form a body of law of far greater bulk than that which has been adopted by the legislature. Nor is this the worst. While the judicial system of British India continues to be what it now is, these decisions will render the law not only bulky, but uncertain and contradictory. There are at present eight chief Courts subject to the legislative power of your Lordship in Council, four established by Royal Charter, and four which derive their authority from the Company. Every one of these tribunals is perfectly independent of the others. Every one of them is at liberty to put its own construction on the law; and it is not to be expected that they will always adopt the same construction. Under so inconvenient a system there will inevitably be, in the course of a few years, a large collection of decisions diametrically opposed to each other, and all of equal authority.

How the powers and mutual relations of these Courts may be placed on a better footing, and whether it be possible

* Cod. Just., Lib. I., Tit. XIV. 12.

or desirable to have in India a single tribunal empowered to expound the Code in the last resort, are questions which must shortly engage the attention of the Law Commission. But whether the present judicial organization be retained or not, it is most desirable that measures should be taken to prevent the written law from being overlaid by an immense weight of comments and decisions. We conceive that it is proper for us, at the time at which we lay before your Lordship in Council the first part of the Indian Code, to offer such suggestions as have occurred to us on this important subject.

We do not think it desirable that the Indian legislature should, like the Roman emperors, decide doubtful points of law which have actually been mooted in cases pending before the tribunals. In criminal cases, with which we are now more immediately concerned, we think that the accused party ought always to have the advantage of a doubt on a point of law, if that doubt be entertained after mature consideration by the highest judicial authority, as well as of a doubt on a matter of fact. In civil suits which are actually pending, we think it on the whole desirable to leave to the Courts the office of deciding doubtful questions of law which have actually arisen in the course of litigation. But every case in which the construction put by a judge on any part of the Code is set aside by any of those tribunals from which at present there is no appeal in India, and every case in which there is a difference of opinion in a Court composed of several judges as to the construction of any part of the Code, ought to be forthwith reported to the legislature. Every judge of every rank whose duty it is to administer the law as contained in the Code should be enjoined to report to his official superiors every doubt which he may entertain as to any question of construction which may have arisen in his Court. Of these doubts, all which are not obviously unreasonable ought to be periodically reported by the highest judicial authorities to the legislature. All the questions thus reported to the Government might with advantage be referred for examination to the Law Commission, if that Commission should be a permanent body. In some cases it will be found that the law is already sufficiently clear, and that any misconstruction which may have taken place is to be attributed to weakness, carelessness, wrong-headedness or corruption on the part of an individual, and is not likely to occur again: in such cases it will be unnecessary to make any change in the Code. Sometimes it will be found that a case has arisen respecting which the Code is silent: in such a case it will be proper to supply the omission. Sometimes it may be found that the Code is inconsistent with itself: if so, the inconsistency ought to be removed. Sometimes it will be found that the words of the law are not sufficiently precise: in such a case it will be proper to substitute others. Sometimes it will be found that the language of the law, though it is as precise as the subject admits, is not so clear that a person of ordinary intelligence can see its whole meaning: in these cases it will generally be expedient to add illustrations, such as may distinctly show in what sense the legislature intends the law to be understood, and may render it impossible that the same question, or any similar question, should ever again occasion difference of opinion. In this manner every successive edition of the Code will solve all the important questions as to the construction of the Code which have arisen since the appearance of the edition immediately preceding. Important questions, particularly questions about which Courts of the highest rank have pronounced opposite decisions, ought to be settled without delay; and no point of law ought to continue to be a doubtful point more than three or four years after it has been mooted in a Court of Justice. An addition of a very few pages to the Code will stand in the place of several volumes of reports, and will be of far more value than such reports, inasmuch as the additions to the Code will proceed from the legislature, and will be of unquestionable authority; whereas the reports would only give the opinions of the judges, which other judges might venture to set aside.

It appears to us also highly desirable that, if the Code shall be adopted, all those penal laws which the Indian legislature may from time to time find it necessary to pass should be framed in such a manner as to fit into the Code. Their language ought to be that of the Code. No word ought to be used in any other sense than that in which it is used in the Code. The very part of the Code in which the new law is to be inserted ought to be indicated. If the new law rescinds or modifies any provision of the Code, that provision ought to be indicated. In fact the new law ought, from the day on which it is passed, to be part of the Code, and to affect all the other provisions of the Code, and to be affected by them as if it were actually a clause of the original Code. In the next edition of the Code, the new law ought to appear in its proper place.

For reasons which have been fully stated to your Lordship in Council in another communication, we have not inserted in the Code any clause declaring to what places and to what classes of persons it shall apply.

Your Lordship in Council will see that we have not proposed to except from the operation of this Code any of the ancient sovereign houses of India residing within the Company's territories. Whether any such exception ought to be made is a question which, without a more accurate knowledge than we possess of existing treaties, of the sense in which those treaties have been understood, of the history of negotiations, of the temper and of the power of particular families, and of the feeling of the body of the people towards those families, we could not venture to decide. We will only beg permission most respectfully to observe that every such exception is an evil; that it is an evil that any man should be above the law; that it is a still greater evil that the public should be taught to regard as a high and enviable distinction the privilege of being above the law; that the longer such privileges are suffered to last, the more difficult it is to take them away; that there can scarcely ever be a fairer opportunity for taking them away than at the time when the Government promulgates a new Code binding alike on persons of different races and religions; and that we greatly doubt whether any consideration, except that of public faith solemnly pledged, deserves to be weighed against the advantages of equal justice.

The peculiar state of public feelings in this country may render it advisable to frame the law of procedure in such a manner that families of high rank may be dispensed, as far as possible, from the necessity of performing acts which are here regarded, however unreasonably, as humiliating. But though it may be proper to make wide distinctions as respects form, there ought in our opinion to be, as respects substance, no distinctions except those which the Government is bound by express engagements to make. That a man of rank should be examined with particular ceremonies or in a particular place may, in the present state of Indian society, be highly expedient. But that a man of any rank should be allowed to commit crimes with impunity must in every state of society be most pernicious.

The provisions of the Code will be applicable to offences committed by soldiers, as well as to offences committed by other members of the community. But for those purely military offences which soldiers only can commit, we have made no provision. It appears to us desirable that this part of the law should be taken up separately, and we have been given to understand that your Lordship in Council has determined that it shall be so taken up. But we have, as your Lordship in Council will perceive, made provision for punishing persons who, not being themselves subject to martial law, abet soldiers in the breach of military discipline.

Your Lordship in Council will observe that in many parts of the Penal Code we have referred to the Code of procedure, which as yet is not in existence; and hence it may possibly be supposed to be our opinion that, till the Code of procedure is framed, the Penal Code cannot come into operation. Such, however, is not our meaning. We conceive that almost the whole of the Penal Code, such as we now lay it before your Lordship, might be made law, at least in the Mofussil, without any considerable change in the existing rules of procedure. Should your Lordship in Council agree with us in this opinion, we shall be prepared to suggest those changes which it would be necessary immediately to make.

In conclusion, we beg respectfully to suggest that, if your Lordship in Council is disposed to adopt the Code which we have framed, it is most desirable that the native population should, with as little delay as possible, be furnished with good versions of it in their own languages. Such versions, in our opinion, can be produced only by the combined labours of enlightened Europeans and natives; and it is not probable that men competent to execute all the translations which will be required would be found in any single province of India. We are sensible that the difficulty of procuring good translations will be great; but we believe that the means at the disposal of your Lordship in Council are sufficient to overcome every difficulty; and we are confident that your Lordship in Council will not grudge any thing that may be necessary for the purpose of enabling the people who are placed under your care to know what that law is according to which they are required to live.

We have the honour to be,
My Lord,
Your Lordship's most obedient humble Servants,

T. B. MACAULAY.

J. M. MACLEOD.

G. W. ANDERSON.

F. MILLETT.

Indian Law Commission,
14th October 1837.

PENAL CODE.

CHAPTER I.

GENERAL EXPLANATIONS.

1. **Throughout this Code every definition of an offence, every penal provision, and every illustration of every such definition or penal provision, shall be understood subject to the exceptions contained in the chapter entitled "General Exceptions," though these exceptions are not repeated in such definition, penal provision or illustration.**

Illustration.

Clause 294 contains the following definition of an offence. "Whoever does any act, or omits what he is legally bound to do, with the intention of thereby causing, or with the knowledge that he is likely thereby to cause, the death of any person, and does by such act or omission cause the death of any person, is said to commit the offence of voluntary culpable homicide." Here it is not expressed that a child under seven years of age cannot commit voluntary culpable homicide; but the definition of voluntary culpable homicide is to be understood subject to the general exception contained in clause 64, which provides that nothing shall be an offence which is done by a child under seven years of age.

2. **Every expression which is explained in any part of this Code is used in every part of this Code in conformity with the explanation.**

3. **Wherever the causing of a certain effect with a certain intention, or with a knowledge of certain circumstances, is an offence, it is to be understood that if more persons than one jointly cause that effect, every one of them who has that intention, or that knowledge, commits that offence.**

Illustrations.

(*a*) A digs a pit, intending or knowing it to be likely that he may thereby cause a person's death.. B puts turf over the mouth of the pit, intending or knowing it to be likely that he may thereby cause a person's death. Here, if Z falls in and is killed, both A and B have committed voluntary culpable homicide.

(*b*) A and B are joint gaolers, and as such have the charge of Z, alternately, for six hours at a time. Each of them, during his time of attendance, illegally omits to furnish Z with food, intending or knowing it to be likely that he may thereby cause Z's death. Z dies of hunger. Both A and B have committed voluntary culpable homicide.

4. **Wherever the causing of a certain effect by an act or by an omission is an offence, it is to be understood that the causing of that effect partly by an act and partly by an omission is the same offence.**

Illustration.

A voluntarily causes Z's death, partly by illegally omitting to give Z food, and partly by beating Z. A has committed voluntary culpable homicide.

5. **The pronoun "he" is used of any person, whether male or female.**

6. The word "man" denotes a male human being of any age: the word "woman" denotes a female human being of any age.

7. The word "party" denotes collections of persons as well as persons.

Illustrations.

The Government of India, the Bank of Bengal, the Union Bank, the Asiatic Society, are parties.

8. The word "King" denotes as well the Queen Regnant as the King of the United Kingdom of Great Britain and Ireland.

9. The words "Government of India" denote the Executive Government of India, unless it be otherwise expressed.

10. The words "Government of a presidency" denote the Governor in Council or Deputy Governor in Council of that presidency, if there be a council, but if there be no council, then the Governor or Deputy Governor alone.

11. The word "presidency" denotes all the territories subject to the Government of a presidency.

12. The word "judge" denotes not only every person who is officially designated as a judge, but also every person who is empowered by law to give in any legal proceeding, civil or criminal, a definitive judgment, or a judgment which, if not appealed against, would be definitive, or a judgment which, if confirmed by some other authority, would be definitive, or who is one of a body of persons, which body of persons is empowered by law to give such a judgment.

Illustrations.

(*a*) A collector sitting on a summary suit, under Regulation VIII of 1831 of the Bengal Presidency, is a judge.

(*b*) A magistrate sitting on a charge on which he has power to sentence to fine or imprisonment, with or without appeal, is a judge.

(*c*) A landholder empowered, by Regulation XV of 1827 of the Bombay Presidency, to try persons accused of certain offences, is a judge.

13. The words "Court of Justice" denote a judge who is empowered by law to act judicially alone, or a body of judges which is empowered by law to act judicially as a body, when such judge or body of judges is acting judicially.

14. The words "public servant" denote a person falling under any of the descriptions hereinafter following; namely,

First.—Every covenanted servant of the East India Company.

Second.—Every commissioned officer, military or naval, in the service of the East India Company.

Third.—Every commissioned officer of the King's army, while serving under the Government of India.

Fourth.—Every judge.

Fifth.—Every officer of a Court of Justice whose duty it is, as such officer, to investigate or report on any matter of law or fact, or to make, authenticate or keep any document, or to take charge of any property, or to execute any judicial process, or to administer any oath, or to interpret or to preserve order in the Court.

Sixth.—Every juryman.

Seventh.—Every arbitrator to whom any cause has been referred by any Court of Justice.

Eighth.—Every person who holds any office by virtue of which he is empowered to place or keep any person in confinement.

Ninth.—Every officer of police whose duty it is, as such officer, to prevent offences, to give information of offences, to bring offenders to justice, or to protect the public health, safety or convenience.

Tenth.—Every officer whose duty it is, as such officer, to take, receive, keep or expend any property on behalf of the Government, or to make any survey, assessment or contract on behalf of the Government, or to execute any revenue process, or to investigate or to report on any matter affecting the pecuniary interests of the Government, or to make, authenticate or keep any document relating to the pecuniary interests of the Government, or to prevent the infraction of any law for the protection of the pecuniary interests of the Government.

Eleventh.—Every officer whose duty it is, as such officer, to take, receive, keep or expend any property for any secular common purpose of any village, town or district, or to make, authenticate or keep any document for the ascertaining of the rights of the people of any village, town or district.

Twelfth.—Every person holding any situation the holders of which have been declared to be public servants by an order of the Government of India, or of the Government of the presidency under which such situation is held.

Explanations.—Persons falling under any of the above descriptions are public servants, whether appointed by the Government or not.

Wherever the words "public servant" occur, they shall be understood of every person who is in actual possession of the situation of a public servant, whatever legal defect there may be in his right to hold that situation.

15. "Wrongful gain" is the gain of property to which the party gaining is not legally entitled.

"Wrongful loss" is the loss of property to which the party losing it is legally entitled.

A party is said to gain wrongfully when such party retains wrongfully, as well as when such party acquires wrongfully. A party is said to lose wrongfully when such party is kept out of property wrongfully, as well as when such party is deprived of property wrongfully.

16. Whoever does any thing with the intention of causing wrongful gain to one party by means of wrongful loss or risk of wrongful loss to another party, is said to do that thing "fraudulently."

17. When property is put into the possession of a person's wife or servant, in trust for that person, it is put into that person's possession if it was not before in his possession, and continues in his possession if it was before in his possession.

18. Property in the possession of a child under twelve years of age, of a lunatic or of an idiot, if such child, lunatic or idiot be in the keeping

of a guardian or guardians, is in the possession of such guardian or guardians.

19. Property is not said to be in the possession of any party other than a person.

Illustrations.

Property is not said to be in the possession of the Government of India, of the Government of Madras, of the Bank of Bengal, of the Agra Bank, of the Asiatic Society, but of the persons who are in trust for those parties.

20. A person is said to "counterfeit" who causes one thing to resemble another thing, intending to deceive by means of that resemblance.

***Explanation.*—It is not essential to counterfeiting that the imitation should be exact.**

Illustration.

If the embellishment of a coin be a wreath of forty leaves, and the inscription be KING WILLIAM, a person counterfeits that coin who, with the intention to deceive by means of a resemblance, makes a coin with a wreath of thirty-nine leaves, and the inscription KING WILLIAM.

21. The word "document" is not used to denote any matter except matter the whole or part whereof is in handwriting, or is meant by the maker thereof to appear to be in handwriting. Therefore a printed hand-bill, or a lithographed letter, no part of which was meant by the engraver to be taken for manuscript, is not a document. But a single word, or a single letter, or significant mark, if that word, letter or mark be in handwriting, or be meant by the maker thereof so to appear, is a document, and is sufficient to make the whole of the matter connected therewith a document, and every part of that matter part of a document.

Illustration.

A promissory note, the whole of which is in print or copper-plate, excepting the signature, which is in handwriting, is a document, and the part of the note which is in print or copper-plate is part of a document.

22. The words "valuable security" denote a document which is or purports to be a document whereby any legal right is created, extended, transferred, restricted, extinguished or released, or whereby any party acknowledges that such party lies under legal liability, or has not a certain legal right.

23. A statement is said to be "made under a sanction which is tantamount to an oath" in each of the three cases hereinafter described:

***First.*—When it is made by one of the people called Quakers, on affirmation received according to law instead of an oath.**

***Secondly.*—When it is made under the sanction of a declaration made according to law by permission of an authority legally competent to require that an oath shall be taken to the same effect with such declaration.**

***Thirdly.*—When it is made after an admonition to speak the truth, which admonition has been given according to law by an authority legally competent to require that an oath to speak the truth shall be taken by the person so admonished.**

24. The words "to do a thing" denote omissions as well as acts.

Illustration.

Clause 67 contains the following general exception. "Nothing is an offence which a person does in consequence of being mad or delirious at the time of doing it." A, a gaoler, goes mad, and in consequence of his madness, omits to supply his prisoners with food. The words "thing done by a person" apply to A's omission, and he has committed no offence.

25. The word "act" denotes as well a series of acts as a single act: the word "omission" denotes as well a series of omissions as a single omission.

26. A person is said to cause an effect "voluntarily," when he causes it by means whereby he intended to cause it, or by means which, at the time of employing those means, he knew to be likely to cause it.

Illustration.

A sets fire by night to an inhabited house in a large town, for the purpose of facilitating a robbery, and thus causes the death of a person. Here A may not have intended to cause death, and may even be sorry that death has been caused by his act; yet if he knew that he was likely to cause death, he has caused death voluntarily.

27. The word "offence" denotes a thing made punishable by this Code.

28. The word "illegal" is applicable to every thing which is an offence, or which is contrary to any direction of the law, or which furnishes ground for a civil action; and a person is said to be "legally bound to do" whatever it is illegal in him to omit.

29. The word "injury" denotes any harm whatever illegally caused to any party in body, mind, reputation or property.

30. The words "free consent" denote a consent given to a party who has not obtained that consent by directly or indirectly putting the consenting party in fear of injury.

31. The words "intelligent consent" denote a consent given by a person who is not, from youth, mental imbecility, derangement, intoxication or passion, unable to understand the nature and consequences of that to which he gives his consent.

32. The words "a person of Asiatic blood" denote a person whose father or mother or grandfather or grandmother was of Asiatic birth, and, as far as can be discovered, of pure Asiatic extraction.

33. The word "death" denotes the death of a human being, unless it be otherwise expressed.

34. The word "animal" denotes any living creature other than a human being.

35. The word "vessel" denotes any floating thing used for the conveyance by water of human beings, or of property.

36. Wherever the word "year" or the word "month" is used, it is to be understood that the year or the month is to be reckoned according to the British calendar.

37. The word "clause" denotes one of those portions of this Code which are distinguished by prefixed numeral figures.

38. The word "hereinbefore" and the word "hereinafter" relate to matter contained within the same clause in which these words occur.

39. Nothing which falls within any definition of an offence shall be construed as not being an offence, because it does not fall within the title of the chapter containing that definition.

Illustration.

A illegally imports sugar from Bombay into Bengal. Here A is within the definition of the offence of smuggling, though A's act may not affect the public revenue, and though the chapter by which the offence of smuggling is made punishable is entitled "Of Offences relating to the Revenue."

CHAPTER II.*

OF PUNISHMENTS.†

40. The punishments to which offenders are liable under the provisions of this Code are,

First.—Death.

Secondly.—Transportation.

Thirdly.—Imprisonment, which is of two descriptions, viz.,

(1) Rigorous.

(2) Simple.

Fourthly.—Banishment from the territories of the East India Company.

Fifthly.—Forfeiture of property.

Sixthly.—Fine.

41. In every case in which sentence of death has been passed, the Government of the presidency within which the offender has been sentenced may, without the consent of the offender, commute the punishment for any other punishment provided by this Code.

42. In every case in which sentence of transportation for life has been passed, the Government of the presidency within which the offender has been sentenced may, without the consent of the offender, commute the punishment for imprisonment of either description, or for banishment from the territories of the East India Company, which imprisonment or banishment may be for life, or for any term.

43. In every case in which sentence of imprisonment for a term of seven years or upwards has been passed on any offender who is not both of Asiatic birth and of Asiatic blood, it shall be lawful for the Government of the presidency within which the offender has been sentenced, at any time within two years after the passing of such sentence, to commute the remaining imprisonment, without the consent of the offender, for transportation for a term not exceeding the unexpired term of imprisonment, to which may be added banishment for life, or for any term, from the territories of the East India Company.

44. In every case in which sentence of rigorous imprisonment for a term of one year or upwards, or of imprisonment of any description for a term of two years or upwards, has been passed on any person who is

---

* See Appendix, Note A.

† The mode of inflicting, commuting and remitting punishments belongs to the law of procedure.

not both of Asiatic birth and of Asiatic blood, it shall be lawful for the Government of the presidency within which the offender was sentenced, at any time before one-third of the imprisonment has been suffered, to commute the remaining imprisonment, without the consent of the offender, for banishment from the territories of the East India Company, which banishment may be either for life or for any term.

45. In every case the Government of the presidency within which an offender has been sentenced, may, with the consent of the offender, commute the punishment for any other punishment provided by this Code, except death.

46. In every case the Government of the presidency within which an offender has been sentenced may at any time remit the whole or any part of the punishment without conditions, or on any conditions to which the offender has agreed.

47. In every case in which it is provided that an offender shall be punished with imprisonment of either description, it shall be competent to the Court which sentences such offender to direct in the sentence that such imprisonment shall be wholly rigorous, or that such imprisonment shall be wholly simple, or that any part of such imprisonment shall be rigorous, and the rest simple.

48. In calculating fractions of terms of imprisonment, imprisonment for life shall be reckoned as equivalent to imprisonment for twenty-four years.

49. In every case in which an offender is sentenced to forfeiture of all property, the sentence renders that offender incapable of acquiring any property except for the benefit of the Government.

Illustration.

A, for waging war against the Government of India, is sentenced to forfeiture of all his property. After the sentence, A's father dies, leaving an estate which, but for the sentence of forfeiture, would become the property of A. The estate becomes the property of Government.

50. Where no sum is expressed to which a fine may extend, the amount of fine to which the offender is liable is unlimited.

51. In every case in which an offender is sentenced to a fine, unless he be also sentenced to death, to imprisonment for life, or to transportation for life, it shall be competent to the Court which sentences such offender, to direct by the sentence that, in default of payment of the fine, the offender shall suffer imprisonment for a certain term, which imprisonment shall be in excess of any other imprisonment to which he may have been sentenced.

52. The term for which the Court directs the offender to be imprisoned, in default of payment of a fine, shall not exceed one-fourth of the term of imprisonment which is the maximum fixed for the offence, if the offence be punishable with imprisonment as well as fine.

53. The imprisonment which the Court imposes in default of payment of a fine may be of any description to which the offender might have been sentenced for the offence.

54. If the offence be not punishable with imprisonment as well as fine, the term for which the Court directs the offender to be imprisoned in default of payment of fine shall not exceed seven days, and the imprisonment shall be simple imprisonment.

55. The imprisonment which is imposed in default of payment of a fine shall terminate whenever that fine is either paid or levied by process of law.

56. If, before the expiration of the term of imprisonment fixed in default of payment, such a proportion of the fine be paid or levied that the term of imprisonment suffered in default of payment is not less than proportional to the part of the fine still unpaid, the imprisonment shall terminate.

Illustration.

A is sentenced to a fine of one hundred rupees, and to four months' imprisonment in default of payment. Here, if seventy-five rupees of the fine be paid or levied before the expiration of one month of the imprisonment, A will be discharged as soon as the first month has expired. If seventy-five rupees be paid or levied at the time of the expiration of the first month, or at any later time while A continues in imprisonment, A will be immediately discharged. If fifty rupees of the fine be paid or levied before the expiration of two months of the imprisonment, A will be discharged as soon as the two months are completed. If fifty rupees be paid or levied at the time of the expiration of those two months, or at any later time while A continues in imprisonment, A will be immediately discharged.

57. The fine, or any part thereof which remains unpaid, may be levied at any time within six years after the passing of the sentence, and if under the sentence the offender be liable to imprisonment for a longer period than six years, then at any time previous to the expiration of that period; and the death of the offender does not discharge from the liability any property which would, after his death, be legally liable for his debts.

58. Whenever any person, by doing any thing whereby he commits an offence falling under one penal provision of this Code, also commits an offence under another penal provision of this Code, the punishment shall not be cumulative, unless it be so expressly provided.

Illustration.

A strikes Z with violence, knowing it to be likely that he may thereby break Z's arm, and does break Z's arm. Here A commits an assault. He also by the same act commits the offence of voluntarily causing grievous hurt. But A is not liable to punishment both for assault and for voluntarily causing grievous hurt.

59. Where it is provided that punishment shall be cumulative, that provision does not authorize the combining in any case of the punishments provided by more than two penal provisions of this Code.

60. Where any thing which is an offence is made up of parts, any of which parts is itself an offence, the offender shall not be punished with the punishment of more than one of such his offences, unless it be so expressly provided.

Illustrations.

(*a*) A gives Z fifty strokes with a stick. Here, A may have committed the offence of voluntarily causing hurt to Z by the whole beating, and also by each of the blows which make up the whole beating. If A were liable to punishment for every blow, he might be imprisoned for fifty years, one for each blow. But he is liable only to one punishment for the whole beating, that is to say, to imprisonment for a term not exceeding one year, if the hurt which he has voluntarily caused is not grievous, and for a term not exceeding ten years, nor less than six months, if the hurt which he has voluntarily caused is grievous.

(*b*) But if, while A is beating Z, Y interferes and A strikes Y, here, as the blow given to Y is no part of the act whereby A voluntarily causes hurt to Z, A is liable to one punishment for voluntarily causing hurt to Z and to another for the blow given to Y.

61. In all cases in which judgment is given in the manner prescribed in the law of procedure that a person is guilty of an offence, but that it is doubtful under which of certain penal provisions of this Code he is punishable, the offender shall be liable to be punished with whatever punishment is common to the penal provisions between which the doubt lies; and if imprisonment is common to the penal provisions between which the doubt lies, and any one of those provisions admits of simple imprisonment, the offender may be sentenced to simple imprisonment.

Illustrations.

(*a*) Judgment is given in the manner prescribed in the law of procedure that A is guilty either of murdering Z, or of previously abetting by aid the murder of Z. The punishment of murder, and that of previously abetting murder by aid, are the same. A is therefore liable to that punishment.

(*b*) Judgment is given in the manner prescribed in the law of procedure that A has committed an offence, but that it is doubtful whether that offence be theft or criminal breach of trust. Theft is punishable with rigorous imprisonment for three years, or fine, or both; criminal breach of trust is punishable with imprisonment of either description for the same term, or fine, or both. A is therefore liable to fine, which is common to both the penal provisions, and to rigorous imprisonment for three years, which is common to both the penal provisions. But he may be sentenced to simple imprisonment because one of the penal provisions admits of simple imprisonment.

(*c*) Judgment is given in the manner prescribed in the law of procedure that A has committed either theft or criminal misappropriation of property not in possession. Here, as the punishment of fine is common to theft and to criminal misappropriation of property not in possession, A is liable to fine. Theft is punishable with imprisonment for a term which may extend to three years; criminal misappropriation of property not in possession is punishable with imprisonment for a term which may extend to two years. Imprisonment for two years is therefore common to both, and A may be punished with imprisonment for a term not exceeding two years. The imprisonment in both cases may be rigorous. A's imprisonment may therefore be rigorous. But the imprisonment for criminal misappropriation of property not in possession may be simple. Therefore A is liable to imprisonment of either description.

CHAPTER III.*

GENERAL EXCEPTIONS.

62. Nothing is an offence which is done by a person who is, or in good faith believes himself to be, commanded by law to do it.

Illustrations.

(*a*) A, a soldier, fires on a mob, by the order of his superior officer, in conformity with the commands of the law. A has committed no offence.

---

* See Appendix, Note B.

(*b*) A, an officer of a Court of Justice, being ordered by that Court to arrest Y, and being led into a belief that Z is Y, arrests Z, believing in good faith that in arresting Z he is obeying an order which he is commanded by law to obey. Here A may, under certain circumstances, be liable to a civil action, but he has committed no offence.

63. Nothing is an offence which is done by a person in the exercise, to the best of his judgment exerted in good faith, of any power given to him by law.

Illustration.

A sees Z commit what appears to A to be a murder. A in the exercise, to the best of his judgment exerted in good faith, of the power which the law gives to all persons of apprehending murderers in the fact, seizes Z, in order to bring Z before the proper authorities. A has committed no offence.

64. Nothing is an offence which is done by a child under seven years of age.

65. Nothing is an offence which is done by a child above seven years of age and under twelve, who has not attained sufficient maturity of understanding to judge of the nature and consequences of his conduct on that occasion.

66. Nothing is an offence which is done by a person in a state of idiocy.

67. Nothing is an offence which a person does in consequence of being mad or delirious at the time of doing it.

68. Nothing is an offence which a person does in consequence of being, at the time of doing it, in a state of intoxication, provided that either the substance which intoxicated him was administered to him without his knowledge, or against his will, or that he was ignorant that it possessed any intoxicating quality.

69. Nothing which is not intended to cause death, and which is not known by the doer to be likely to cause death, is an offence by reason of any harm which it may cause, or be intended by the doer to cause, or be known by the doer to be likely to cause to any person above twelve years of age who has given a free and intelligent consent, whether express or implied, to suffer that harm, or to take the risk of that harm, such consent not having been obtained by wilful misrepresentation on the part of the person who does the thing.

Illustrations.

(*a*) A, a dentist, offers Z, a person of ripe age and sound mind, a price for Z's teeth, and, without any wilful misrepresentation, obtains Z's consent to the drawing of Z's teeth. A draws Z's teeth. Here, though A's act falls under the definition of the offence of voluntarily causing hurt, A has committed no offence.

(*b*) A converts Z, a person of ripe age and sound mind, to the Mahomedan religion, and, without any wilful misrepresentation, obtains Z's consent to be circumcised. A circumcises Z. A has committed no offence.

(*c*) A and Z agree to fence with each other for amusement. If this agreement implies the consent of each to suffer any harm which, in the course of such fencing, may be caused without foul play, then if A, while playing fairly, hurts Z, A has committed no offence.

(*d*) A, a friend of Z, calls at Z's house, in Z's absence, and writes and seals several letters there with Z's paper and wax without asking any person's permission. Here, if the acquaintance between A and Z be such that, according to the usages of society, the consent of Z to such use of his property must be implied thence, A has committed no offence.

70. Nothing which is not intended to cause death is an offence by reason of any harm which it may cause, or be intended by the doer to cause, or be known by the doer to be likely to cause, to any person for whose benefit it is done, in good faith, and who has given a free and intelligent consent, whether express or implied, to suffer that harm or to take the risk of that harm, such consent not having been obtained by wilful misrepresentation on the part of the person who does the thing.

Illustration.

A, a surgeon, knowing that a particular operation is likely to cause the death of Z, who suffers under a painful complaint, but not intending to cause Z's death, and intending in good faith Z's benefit, performs that operation on Z, by Z's free and intelligent consent, not having obtained that consent by misrepresentation. A has committed no offence.

71. Nothing which is done in good faith for the benefit of a person who is under twelve years of age, or of unsound mind, by that person's lawful guardian or guardians, or by the authority of such lawful guardian or guardians, is an offence by reason of any harm which it may cause to that person:

Provided,

First.—That this exception shall not extend to the intentional causing of death, or to the attempting to cause death.

Secondly.—That this exception shall not extend to the doing of any thing which the person doing it knows to be likely to cause death, for any purpose other than the preventing of death or grievous hurt.

Thirdly.—That this exception shall not extend to the voluntary causing of grievous hurt, or to the attempting to cause grievous hurt, unless it be for the purpose of preventing death or grievous hurt, or in the performance of the rite of circumcision.

Fourthly.—That this exception shall not extend to rape, or to the gratification of unnatural lust, or to the attempting to commit rape or to gratify unnatural lust.

Fifthly.—That this exception shall not extend to the abetment, either previous or subsequent, of any offence, to the committing of which offence it would not extend.

Illustrations.

(*a*) A, a parent, whips his child moderately, for the child's benefit. A has committed no offence.

(*b*) A confines his child, for the child's benefit. A has committed no offence.

(*c*) A, in good faith, for his daughter's benefit, intentionally kills her to prevent her from falling into the hands of Pindarries. A is not within the exception.

(*d*) A, in good faith, for his child's benefit, without his child's consent, has his child cut for the stone, knowing it to be likely that the operation will cause the child's death, but not intending to cause the child's death. A has committed no offence, inasmuch as his object was the preventing of death or grievous hurt to the child.

(*e*) A, in good faith, for his child's pecuniary benefit, emasculates his child. Here, inasmuch as A has caused grievous hurt to the child for a purpose other than the preventing of death or grievous hurt to the child, A is not within the exception.

(*f*) A, intending in good faith the pecuniary benefit of Z, his daughter, a child under twelve years of age, abets a rape committed by B on Z. Neither A nor B is within the exception.

72. Nothing is an offence by reason of any harm which it may cause to a person for whose benefit it is done in good faith, even without that person's consent, if the circumstances are such that it is impossible for that person to signify consent, or if that person is in such a state of mind as to be incapable of intelligent consent,* and has no legal guardian to whom it is possible to apply for authority:

Provided,

First.—That this exception shall not extend to the intentional causing of death, or to the attempting to cause death.

Secondly.—That this exception shall not extend to the doing of any thing which the person doing it knows to be likely to cause death, for any purpose other than the preventing of death or grievous hurt.

Thirdly.—That this exception shall not extend to the voluntary causing of hurt, or to the attempting to cause hurt for any purpose other than the preventing of death or hurt.

Fourthly.—That this exception shall not extend to rape, or to the gratification of unnatural lust, or to the attempting to commit rape or to gratify unnatural lust.

Fifthly.—That this exception shall not extend to the abetment, either previous or subsequent, of any offence to the committing of which offence it would not extend.

Illustrations.

(*a*) Z is thrown from his horse, and is insensible. A, a surgeon, finds that Z requires to be trepanned. A, not intending Z's death, but in good faith, for Z's benefit, performs the trepan before Z recovers his power of judging for himself. A has committed no offence.

(*b*) Z is carried off by a tiger. A fires at the tiger, knowing it to be likely that the shot may kill Z, but not intending to kill Z, and in good faith intending Z's benefit. The tiger drops Z. It appears that A's ball has given Z a mortal wound. Nevertheless, A has committed no offence.

(*c*) A, a surgeon, sees a child suffer an accident, which is likely to prove fatal unless an operation be immediately performed. There is not time to apply to the child's legal guardians. A performs the operation, in spite of the entreaties of the child, intending in good faith the child's benefit. A has committed no offence.

(*d*) A is in a house which is on fire, with Z, a child. People below hold out a blanket. A drops the child from the house-top, knowing it to be likely that the fall may kill the child, but not intending to kill the child, and intending in good faith the child's benefit. Here, even if the child is killed by the fall, A has committed no offence.

73. Nothing is an offence by reason that it causes, or that it is intended to cause, or that it is known to be likely to cause any harm, if that harm is so slight that no person of ordinary sense and temper would complain of such harm.

Illustrations.

(*a*) A gets into a public carriage in which Z is sitting, and in seating himself slightly hurts Z by pressing him against the side of the carriage. Here, though A's act falls within the definition in clause 316, yet if the whole harm

---

* For the definition of intelligent consent, see clause 31.

caused was so slight that no man of ordinary sense and temper would complain of such harm, A has committed no offence.

(*b*) A, a servant in Z's house, having occasion to write a letter, dips a pen in ink, the property of Z. Here, though the act of A may fall under the definition of theft, A has committed no offence.

Of the Right of Private Defence.

74. Every person has a right, subject to the restrictions contained in the next following clause, to defend,

First.—His own body and the body of every other person against every assault.

Secondly.—His own property and the property of every other person against every act which is an offence falling under the definition of theft, robbery, mischief or criminal trespass, or which is an attempt to commit theft, robbery, mischief or criminal trespass.

75. There is no right of private defence against an act done by a public servant who is legally competent, as such public servant, to do that act, though that act may be an offence in that public servant, or against an act done by the direction of a public servant, or body of public servants, legally competent, as such public servant, or as such body, to direct that act to be done, though the directing that act to be done may be an offence.

There is no right of private defence in cases in which there is time to have recourse to the protection of the public authorities, in the manner indicated in the Code of Criminal Procedure.

The right of private defence in no case extends to the inflicting of more harm than it is necessary to inflict for the purpose of defence.

Illustrations.

(*a*) Z, a public servant legally competent to arrest persons as being suspected of certain offences, arrests A maliciously, not having any ground to suspect A of any such offence. Here, Z commits an offence. But as Z is legally competent to arrest A, A has no right of private defence against Z.

(*b*) A, a powerful man, well armed, finds Z, an unarmed boy, breaking into his house at night. A knows that he can defend his property against Z without killing Z. A kills Z. A has exceeded the right of private defence.

76. The right of private defence of the body extends, under the restrictions mentioned in the clause last preceding, to the voluntary causing of death or of any other harm to the assailant, if the assault which occasions the exercise of the right be of any of the descriptions hereinafter enumerated; namely,

First.—Such an assault as may reasonably cause the apprehension that death will otherwise be the consequence of such assault.

Secondly.—Such an assault as may reasonably cause the apprehension that grievous hurt will otherwise be the consequence of such assault.

Thirdly.—An assault with the intention of committing rape.

Fourthly.—An assault with the intention of gratifying unnatural lust.

Fifthly.—An assault with the intention of kidnapping.

Sixthly.—An assault with the intention of wrongfully confining any person, under circumstances which may reasonably cause it to be apprehended that the wrongful confinement will be such as is punishable by this Code with imprisonment for a term exceeding one year.

77. If the assault be not of any of the descriptions enumerated in the clause last preceding, the right of private defence of the body does not extend to the voluntary causing of death to the assailant, but does extend, under the restrictions mentioned in clause 75, to the voluntary causing to the assailant of any harm other than death.

78. The right of private defence of the body commences as soon as the danger to the body commences, though no assault may yet have been committed, and continues as long as the danger to the body continues.

79. The right of private defence of property extends, under the restrictions mentioned in clause 75, to the voluntary causing of death or of any other harm to the wrong-doer, if the offence, the committing of which, or the attempting to commit which, occasions the exercise of the right, be an offence of any of the descriptions hereinafter enumerated; namely,

First.—Robbery.

Secondly.—House-breaking by night.

Thirdly.—Mischief by fire committed on any building, tent or vessel, which building, tent or vessel is used as a human dwelling.

Fourthly.—Theft, mischief or house-trespass, under such circumstances as may reasonably cause apprehension that death or grievous hurt would otherwise be the consequence of such theft, mischief or house-trespass.

80. If the offence the committing of which, or the attempting to commit which, occasions the exercise of the right of private defence, be theft, mischief or criminal trespass, not of any of the descriptions enumerated in the clause last preceding, that right does not extend to the voluntary causing of death, but does extend, subject to the restrictions mentioned in clause 75, to the voluntary causing to the wrong-doer of any harm other than death.

81. The right of private defence of property commences when the danger to the property commences.

The right of private defence of property against theft or robbery continues till either the offender has effected his retreat with the property, or the property has been recovered.

The right of private defence of property against criminal trespass or mischief continues as long as the offender continues in the commission of criminal trespass or mischief.

The right of private defence of property against house-breaking by night continues as long as the house-trespass which has been begun by such house-breaking continues.

82. When an act which would otherwise be a certain offence is not that offence by reason of the youth, the idiocy, the madness, the delirium, or the intoxication of the person doing that act, or by reason of any misconception on the part of that person, every person has the same right of private defence against that act which he would have if that act were that offence.

Illustrations.

(*a*) Z, under the influence of madness, attempts to kill A. Z is guilty of no offence. But A has the same right of private defence which he would have if Z were sane.

(*b*) A enters by night a house which he is legally entitled to enter. Z, in good faith taking A for a house-breaker, attacks A. Here Z, by attacking A under this misconception, commits no offence. But A has the same right of private defence against Z which he would have if Z were acting under no misconception.

83. In cases in which there is a right of private defence extending to the voluntary causing of death to the person whose act renders defence necessary, if the defender be so situated that he cannot effectually exercise that right without risk of harm to an innocent person, his right of private defence extends to the running of that risk.

Illustration.

A is attacked by a mob who attempt to murder him. He cannot effectually exercise his right of private defence without firing on the mob, and he cannot fire without risk of harming young children who are mingled with the mob. A has a right to fire.

84. Nothing is an offence which is an exercise of the right of private defence, or which would be an exercise of the right of private defence if the circumstances under which it is done were such as the person who does it believes in good faith that they are.

Illustration.

Z, intending to frighten A by way of jest, stops A in the highway, and demands his money. A, believing in good faith that Z is a robber, and not knowing that he may save himself from being robbed without killing Z, kills Z. A has committed no offence.

CHAPTER IV.

OF ABETMENT.

85. Abetment is of two kinds, previous abetment and subsequent abetment.

86. A person is said previously to abet the doing of a thing who,

First.—Instigates any person to do that thing; or,

Secondly.—Engages in any conspiracy for the doing of that thing; or,

Thirdly.—Aids by any act or by any illegal omission the doing of that thing; or,

Fourthly.—Conceals by any act or by any illegal omission the existence of a design to do that thing, intending or knowing it to be likely that he may, by such concealment, facilitate the doing of that thing.

Explanation.—A person may previously abet the doing of a thing in any one of the four ways hereinbefore mentioned, though the thing abetted be not done.

87. A person is said previously to abet an offence who previously abets the doing of a thing which is an offence, not being under any misconception such that if a person being under that misconception did that thing, the doing of that thing would not be an offence.

Illustration.

A aids B to take a horse out of Z's possession. Here, if B took the horse fraudulently, B is guilty of theft. But if A aided B, believing that B had a right to take the horse, A is not said to have abetted the theft committed by B, though he has abetted the taking of the horse.

88. Whoever previously abets any offence by instigating any person to commit that offence shall, if that offence is committed by that person in consequence of that instigation, be punished with the punishment provided for that offence.

Explanation.—Such instigation as is hereinbefore described being an offence, the successful instigating to such instigation is also an offence punishable in the same manner.

Illustration.

A instigates B to instigate C to commit a theft. C commits the theft in consequence of the instigation. A and B are liable to the punishment of theft.

89. If any person by doing any thing whereby he commits an offence under the last preceding clause, also commits an offence under any clause contained in any other chapter of this Code, the punishment shall be cumulative.

Illustration.

A, by putting B in fear of death, induces B to burn a stack of corn belonging to Z. Here A is liable both to the punishment provided for burning such a stack of corn, and to the punishment of criminally putting B in fear of death.

90. Whoever, by instigation attended with the actual delivery of a bribe, previously abets any offence punishable with imprisonment, shall be punished with imprisonment of any description provided for that offence, for a term which may extend to one-fourth part of the longest term provided for that offence, or such fine as is provided for that offence, or both.

Illustration.

A causes money to be paid to B, in order to induce B to give false evidence. Here, whether B gives the false evidence or not, A has committed the offence defined in this clause.

91. Whoever, by instigation attended with the threat of causing any injury, previously abets any offence punishable with imprisonment, shall be punished with imprisonment of any description provided for that offence, for a term which may extend to one-fourth part of the longest term provided for that offence, or such fine as is provided for that offence, or both.

92. If any person by doing any thing whereby he commits an offence under the last preceding clause, also commits an offence under any clause contained in any other chapter of this Code, the punishment shall be cumulative.

93. Whoever, being present while any offence punishable with rigorous imprisonment for a term of one year or upwards is committed, previously abets that offence by instigating the offender to persist in the commission of that offence, shall be punished with imprisonment of either description for a term which may extend to one-fourth part of the longest term provided for that offence, or fine, or both.

94. Whoever previously abets any offence by instigating the public generally, or any number or class of persons exceeding ten, to the commission of that offence, shall be punished with imprisonment of either description for a term which may extend to three years, or fine, or both.

Illustrations.

(*a*) A affixes in a public place a placard, exhorting the members of a sect to meet at a certain time and place, for the purpose of attacking the members of an adverse sect while engaged in a procession. A has committed the offence defined in this clause.

(*b*) A inserts in a newspaper an article advising soldiers to shoot every commanding officer who uses them harshly. A has committed the offence defined in this clause.

95. Whoever previously abets any offence, by engaging in any conspiracy for the commission of that offence, shall, if that offence is committed in pursuance of that conspiracy, be punished with the punishment provided for that offence.

Explanation.—It is not necessary to bring a person within this clause that he should have concerted the offence with the person who has committed the offence. It is sufficient that he was engaged in the conspiracy in pursuance of which the offence has been committed.

Illustration.

B concerts with C a plan for poisoning Z. It is agreed that C shall administer the poison. B then explains the plan to A without mentioning C's name. A agrees to procure the poison. C administers the poison. Z dies in consequence. Here, though A and C have not conspired together, yet A has been engaged in the conspiracy in pursuance of which Z has been murdered. A has therefore committed the offence defined in this clause, and is liable to the punishment of murder.

96. Whoever previously abets any offence punishable with imprisonment, by engaging in a conspiracy to commit that offence, shall, if any act or any illegal omission takes place in pursuance of that conspiracy, and in order to the committing of that offence, be punished with imprisonment of any description provided for that offence, for a term which may extend to one-fourth part of the longest term provided for that offence, or such fine as is provided for that offence, or both.

Illustration.

A and B conspire to poison Z. A, in pursuance of this conspiracy, and in order to the poisoning of Z, buys poison. Here, both A and B have committed the offence defined in this clause. If they had murdered Z, and had been sentenced to imprisonment for doing so, the imprisonment would have been rigorous, and for life. Therefore, under clause 48, each of them is liable to rigorous imprisonment for a term which may extend to six years.

97. Whoever previously abets any offence by doing any act, or omitting what he is legally bound to do, with the intention of aiding the commission of that offence, shall, if that offence is committed, be punished with the punishment provided for that offence.

Illustrations.

(*a*) A keeps watch in the street, with the intention of securing B from interruption while B breaks into a house by night. A has committed the offence defined in this clause.

(*b*) A, a servant hired to take charge of his master's plate, illegally omits to lock the plate up, with the intention of thereby rendering it easier for B to steal the plate. B steals the plate. A has committed the offence defined in this clause.

(*c*) A, a police officer, directed by law to prevent the commission of robberies, sees B committing a robbery, and passes by without interfering, intending to facilitate the robbery by thus illegally omitting to perform his duty. A has committed the offence defined in this clause.

98. Wherever in an attempt to commit an offence, or in the commission of an offence, or in consequence of the commission of an offence, a different offence is committed, then whoever by instigation, conspiracy or aid, was a previous abettor of the first-mentioned offence shall be liable to the punishment of the last-mentioned offence, if the last-mentioned offence were such as the said abettor knew to be likely to be committed in the attempt to commit the first-mentioned offence, or in the commission of the first-mentioned offence, or in consequence of the commission of the first-mentioned offence; and if both offences be actually committed, and the person who has committed them be liable to cumulative punishment, the abettor shall also be liable to cumulative punishment.

Illustrations.

(*a*) B, with arms, breaks into an inhabited house at midnight, for the purpose of robbery. A watches at the door. B being resisted by Z, one of the inmates, murders Z. Here, if A considered murder as likely to be committed by B in the attempt to rob the house, or in the robbing of the house, or in consequence of the robbing of the house, A is liable to the punishment provided for murder.

(*b*) A instigates B to resist a distress. B, in consequence, resists that distress. In offering the resistance, B voluntarily causes grievous hurt to the officer executing the distress. As B has committed both the offence of resisting legal process and the offence of voluntarily causing grievous hurt, B is liable to cumulative punishment for these offences; and if A knew that B was likely voluntarily to cause grievous hurt in resisting the distress, A will also be liable to cumulative punishment.

99. Whoever, by instigation, conspiracy or aid, previously abets an offence, if in consequence of that instigation, or in pursuance of that conspiracy, or with that aid, an offence is committed which would be a different offence but for some misconception on the part of the doer from which misconception the abettor is free, or but for some intention or knowledge on the part of the doer, which intention or knowledge the abettor does not know that the doer has, shall be liable to the same punishment to which he would have been liable if no such misconception, intention or knowledge had existed on the part of the doer.

Illustrations.

(*a*) A makes preparations for the burning of Z, a Hindoo widow, believing that she has given a free consent to be burned. Here, A previously abets by aid the offence of voluntary culpable homicide by consent. If the preparations which A has made are subsequently used, without A's knowledge, for the purpose of putting Z to death without her consent, those who so use them are guilty of murder. But A is liable only to the punishment to which he would have been liable if voluntary culpable homicide by consent had been committed.

(*b*) A instigates B to commit mischief on certain property which B believes to be worth less than five rupees, but which A knows to be worth more than one hundred rupees. Here, B is liable only to fine, which may extend to an amount equal to ten times the loss caused. But A is punishable with imprisonment for a term which may extend to two years, and with unlimited fine.

100. Whoever, by instigation, conspiracy or aid, previously abets the doing of a thing which is done in consequence of that instigation, or in pursuance of that conspiracy, or with that aid, shall, if that thing would be a certain offence but for the youth, the idiocy, the madness, the delirium, or the intoxication of the person doing that thing, or but for some misconception on the part of that person from which misconception the abettor is free, be punished with the punishment provided for that offence.

Illustrations.

(*a*) A instigates B, a child of four years old, to take property in a way which in a grown-up person would be the offence of theft. B takes the property in consequence. B has committed no offence, but A is liable to the punishment of theft.

(*b*) A instigates B, a madman, to set fire to a dwelling-house; B sets fire to the house in consequence. B has committed no offence, but A is liable to the punishment of setting fire to a dwelling-house.

(*c*) A tells B, a police officer, that Z is Y, knowing that B is charged to arrest Y and meaning to cause Z to be illegally confined. B in consequence arrests Z, believing in good faith that he is commanded by law to do it. Here, B has committed no offence; but A is liable to be punished as if he had himself illegally confined Z.

(*d*) A instigates B to take property out of Z's possession, and in order to such instigation induces B to believe that the property belongs to A. B takes the property out of Z's possession, intending thereby to cause loss to Z and gain to A, but believing that loss and gain to be rightful loss and rightful gain. B, acting under this misconception, does not take fraudulently, and therefore does not commit theft. But A is liable to the punishment to which he would have been liable if B had committed theft.

101. Whoever, being a public servant, conceals by any act or illegal omission the existence of a design to commit any offence, the commission of which offence it is his duty as such public servant to prevent, and thereby previously abets that offence, shall, if that offence be committed, be punished with imprisonment of either description for a term which may extend to one-half of the longest term of imprisonment provided for that offence, or fine, or both

Illustration.

A, an officer of police, being legally bound to give information of all designs to commit dacoity which may come to his knowledge, and knowing that B designs to commit dacoity, omits to give such information, knowing it to be likely that this omission will facilitate the commission of the dacoity. Here, A has, by an illegal omission, concealed the existence of B's design, and has thus previously abetted dacoity. If the dacoity be actually committed, A has committed the offence defined in this clause, and is liable to imprisonment of either description for a term which may extend, under clause 48, to twelve years.

102. Whoever conceals by any act or illegal omission the existence of a design to commit any offence punishable with rigorous imprisonment for a term of one year or upwards, and thereby previously abets that offence, shall, if that offence be committed, be punished with imprisonment of either description for a term which may extend to one-fourth part of the longest term of imprisonment provided for that offence, or fine, or both.

Illustration.

A, knowing that a widow is about to be burned with the corpse of her husband, tells the magistrate that the family are determined that she shall not be burned. A thus misinforms the magistrate, knowing it to be likely that the burning of the widow will thereby be facilitated. Here, A has by an act concealed the existence of a design to commit voluntary culpable homicide, and has thus previously abetted voluntary culpable homicide. If, therefore, voluntary culpable homicide be committed, A has committed the offence defined in this clause.

103. A person is said subsequently to abet the doing of a thing who, knowing that thing to have been done, assists or attempts to assist, by any act or illegal omission, the doer of that thing to avoid any evil consequence of doing that thing, or to derive from the doing of that thing any advantage, with a view to which advantage that thing was done.

104. A person is said subsequently to abet an offence who subsequently abets what he knows to be an offence, or what he would know to be an offence but for his ignorance of the law.

Illustrations.

(*a*) A subsequently abets B in sitting Dhurna at Z's door, not knowing that B, by sitting Dhurna, has committed what is by law an offence, but knowing that B sat Dhurna with the intention of causing it to be believed that by so sitting he rendered Z an object of divine displeasure. Here, A but for his ignorance of the law would know B's act to be an offence (see clause 283). Here, therefore, A is said to have subsequently abetted the offence which B has committed.

(*b*) A subsequently abets the taking of property by B out of Z's possession. B has taken the property fraudulently; and has therefore been guilty of theft. But if A does not know the taking to be fraudulent, then as A, even if he knows the law, cannot know that B has been guilty of theft, A, though he has subsequently abetted the taking, is not said to have subsequently abetted B's offence.

105. Whoever, knowing that an offence has been committed, and knowing himself to be directed by law to give information in any quarter of that offence, subsequently abets that offence by intentionally omitting to give such information, shall be punished with imprisonment of either description for a term which may extend to six months, or fine, or both.

106. Whoever, knowing that an offence has been committed which is punishable with rigorous imprisonment for a term of one year or upwards, subsequently abets that offence by causing any marks of the commission of that offence to disappear, shall be punished with imprisonment of either description for a term which may extend to one-twelfth part of the longest term of imprisonment provided for that offence, or fine, or both.

Illustration.

A, knowing that B has murdered Z, assists B to hide the body. A is liable to imprisonment of either description for one-twelfth part of the term of imprisonment provided for murder, that is to say, to two years' imprisonment. (See clause 48.)

107. Whoever, except as hereinafter excepted, subsequently abets any offence punishable with imprisonment for seven years or upwards, by harbouring the offender with the intention of screening such offender from legal punishment, shall be punished with imprisonment of either description for a term which may extend to six months, or fine which may extend to one thousand rupees, or both.

Exception.—This provision does not extend to the case in which the harbour is given by the husband, or wife, or relation in the direct ascending or descending line, or brother, or sister of the person to whom the harbour is given.

108. Wherever a thing is done which is an offence by reason that it is fraudulently done, whoever subsequently abets that offence by assisting the offender to retain or dispose of any property acquired by that offence, shall be punished with imprisonment of either description for a term which may extend to one year, or fine, or both.

CHAPTER V.*

OF OFFENCES AGAINST THE STATE.

109. Whoever wages war against the Government of any part of the territories of the East India Company, or attempts to wage such war, or by instigation, conspiracy or aid, previously abets the waging of such war, shall be punished with death, or transportation for life, or imprisonment of either description for life, and shall forfeit all his property.

Illustrations.

(*a*) A joins an army of a foreign power which has invaded the territories of the East India Company, and serves in that army. A has committed the offence defined in this clause.

(*b*) A conspires with other persons to cause an insurrection against the East India Company's Government in one of the presidencies. A has committed the offence defined in this clause.

(*c*) A instigates a native power to make war on the Government of India. A has committed the offence defined in this clause.

110. Whoever, by any act, or by any illegal omission, conceals the existence of a design to wage war against the Government of any part of the territories of the East India Company, intending or knowing it to be likely that he may, by such concealment, facilitate the waging of such war, and thereby previously abets the waging of such war, shall be punished with imprisonment of either description for a term which may extend to fourteen years, and must not be less than two years, and shall also be liable to fine.

111. Whoever, with the intention of inducing or compelling the Governor-General of India, or the Governor or Deputy-Governor of any presidency, or any member of the council of India or of the council of any presidency, to exercise or refrain from exercising in any manner any of the lawful powers of such Governor-General, Governor, Deputy-Governor or member of council, assaults or makes show of assaulting, or wrongfully restrains or attempts wrongfully to restrain, or overawes by means of a riotous assembly, or attempts so to overawe such Governor-General, Governor, Deputy-Governor or member of council, shall be punished with imprisonment of either description for a term which may extend to seven years, and must not be less than one year, and shall also be liable to fine.

---

* See Appendix, Note C.

112. If any person, by doing any thing whereby he commits an offence under the last preceding clause, also commits an offence under any other clause of this Code, the punishment shall be cumulative.

113. Whoever, by words either spoken or intended to be read, or by signs, or by visible representations, attempts to excite feelings of disaffection to the Government established by law in the territories of the East India Company, among any class of people who live under that Government, shall be punished with banishment for life, or for any term, from the territories of the East India Company, to which fine may be added, or with simple imprisonment for a term which may extend to three years, to which fine may be added, or with fine.

Explanation.—Such a disapprobation of the measures of the Government as is compatible with a disposition to render obedience to the lawful authority of the Government, and to support the lawful authority of the Government against unlawful attempts to subvert or resist that authority, is not disaffection. Therefore the making of comments on the measures of the Government, with the intention of exciting only this species of disapprobation, is not an offence within this clause.

114. Whoever wages war against the Government of any Asiatic power in alliance with the Government established by law in the territories of the East India Company, or attempts to wage such war, or by instigation, conspiracy or aid, previously abets the waging of such war, shall be punished with banishment from the territories of the East India Company, to which fine may be added, or with imprisonment of either description for a term which may extend to three years, to which fine may be added, or with fine.

115. Whoever uses any place within the territories of the East India Company for the purpose of making preparations to commit depredations on the territories of any power at peace with the Government of the said territories, or for the purpose of taking refuge after committing such depredations, shall be punished with imprisonment of either description for a term which may extend to fourteen years, and must not be less than two years, and shall also be liable to fine, and to forfeiture of any specific property.

CHAPTER VI.*

OF OFFENCES RELATING TO THE ARMY AND NAVY.

116. Whoever, by instigation, conspiracy or aid, previously abets the committing of mutiny by a soldier or sailor in the service of the King or of the East India Company, shall be punished with imprisonment of either description for a term which may extend to seven years, and must not be less than one year, and shall also be liable to fine.

117. Whoever, by instigation, conspiracy or aid, previously abets the committing of mutiny by a soldier or sailor in the service of the King or of the East India Company, shall, if mutiny be committed in consequence of that instigation, in pursuance of that conspiracy, or with that aid, be punished with transportation for life, or imprisonment of either descrip-

* See Appendix, Note D.

tion for a term which may extend to life, and must not be less than three years, and shall also be liable to fine.

118. Whoever, by instigation, conspiracy or aid, previously abets an assault by any soldier or sailor in the service of the King or of the East India Company, on any superior officer of such soldier or sailor, shall be punished with imprisonment of either description for a term which may extend to three years, and must not be less than six months, and shall also be liable to fine.

119. Whoever, by instigation, conspiracy or aid, previously abets an assault by any soldier or sailor in the service of the King or of the East India Company, on any superior officer of such soldier or sailor, shall, if such assault be committed in consequence of that instigation, in pursuance of that conspiracy, or with that aid, be punished with imprisonment of either description for a term which may extend to seven years, and must not be less than one year, and shall also be liable to fine.

120. Whoever, by instigation, conspiracy or aid, previously abets the desertion of any soldier or sailor in the service of the King or of the East India Company, shall be punished with imprisonment of either description for a term which may extend to one year, or fine, or both.

121. Whoever, by instigation, conspiracy or aid, previously abets the desertion of any soldier or sailor in the service of the King or of the East India Company, shall, if desertion be committed in consequence of that instigation, in pursuance of that conspiracy, or with that aid, be punished with imprisonment of either description for a term which may extend to three years, or fine, or both.

122. Whoever, by instigation, conspiracy or aid, previously abets the desertion of any soldier or sailor in the service of the King or of the East India Company to an enemy, shall be punished with imprisonment of either description for a term which may extend to seven years, and must not be less than one year, and shall also be liable to fine.

123. Whoever, by instigation, conspiracy or aid, previously abets the desertion of any soldier or sailor in the service of the King or of the East India Company to an enemy, shall, if desertion be committed in consequence of that instigation, in pursuance of that conspiracy, or with that aid, be punished with transportation for life, or imprisonment for a term which may extend to life, and shall also be liable to fine.

124. Whoever, except as hereinafter excepted, knowing that a soldier or sailor in the service of the King or of the East India Company has deserted, subsequently abets such desertion by harbouring such soldier or sailor, shall be punished with imprisonment of either description for a term which may extend to three months, or fine which may extend to five hundred rupees, or both.

Exception.—This provision does not extend to the case in which the harbour is given by the husband or wife, or relation in the direct ascending or descending line, or brother or sister of the person to whom the harbour is given.

125. Whoever, by instigation, conspiracy or aid, previously abets what he knows to be a breach of military or naval discipline by any soldier or sailor in the service of the King or of the East India Company, shall, if such breach of discipline be committed in consequence of that instigation, in pursuance of that conspiracy, or with that aid, be punished with imprisonment of either description for a term which may extend to six months, or fine, or both.

Illustration.

B, a soldier, offers his military accoutrements for sale to A. A buys them, knowing that it is a breach of military discipline in B to part with those accoutrements. A has committed the offence defined in this clause.

126. Whoever, not being a soldier in the service of the King or of the East India Company, wears any garb or carries any token resembling any garb or token used by such a soldier, with the intention that it may be believed that he is such a soldier, shall be punished with imprisonment of either description for a term which may extend to three months, or fine which may extend to five hundred rupees, or both.

CHAPTER VII.

OF OFFENCES AGAINST THE PUBLIC TRANQUILLITY.

127. An assembly of twelve or more persons is designated as "a riotous assembly," if it is the object of that assembly to overawe the legislative or executive Government of India, or the Government of any presidency, or any public servant, or any body of public servants in the exercise of the lawful powers of such public servant, or of such body; or to resist the execution of any law; or to commit any assault, mischief or criminal trespass; or wrongfully to restrain any person; or to put any person in fear of hurt or of assault; or wantonly to insult or annoy any person; or if that assembly is attended with circumstances which may reasonably excite apprehensions that its object is one of those aforesaid.

Explanation.—An assembly which was not riotous when it assembled, may subsequently become a riotous assembly.

128. Whoever, being aware of facts which render any assembly a riotous assembly, intentionally joins that assembly, or continues in it, is said to commit the offence of "rioting."

129. Whoever commits the offence of rioting shall be punished with imprisonment of either description for a term which may extend to six months, or fine, or both.

130. Whoever commits the offence of rioting by joining or continuing in a riotous assembly, knowing that such riotous assembly has been commanded to disperse in the manner prescribed in the Code of Procedure, shall be punished with imprisonment of either description for a term which may extend to two years, or fine, or both.

131. If any person commits the offence of rioting in such a manner that he commits an offence under the last preceding clause, and also commits an offence under either of the two next following clauses, the punishment shall be cumulative.

132. Whoever commits the offence of rioting, being armed with any weapon for shooting, stabbing or cutting, or having made preparation for committing the offence of rioting by arming himself with any weapon whatever, shall be punished with imprisonment of either description for a term which may extend to two years, or fine, or both.

133. If murder be committed by any rioter while committing the offence of rioting, every other person who at the time of the committing of the murder is committing the offence of rioting as a member of the same riotous assembly, shall be punished with imprisonment of either description for a term which may extend to five years, or fine, or both.

134. If any person, in committing the offence of rioting, commits an offence under any clause contained in any other chapter of this Code, the punishment shall be cumulative.

135. Whoever intentionally joins or continues in any assembly of twelve or more persons, knowing that such assembly has been commanded to disperse in the manner prescribed in the Code of Procedure, shall be punished with simple imprisonment for a term which may extend to one month, or fine, or both.

136. Whoever, malignantly and wantonly, or by doing any thing which is illegal, gives any provocation to any person, intending or knowing it to be likely that the effect of that provocation may be that the offence of rioting will be committed, shall, if the offence of rioting be committed in consequence of such provocation, be punished with imprisonment of either description for a term which may extend to one year, or fine, or both.

137. If any person, by doing any thing whereby he commits an offence under the last preceding clause, also commits an offence under any other clause of this Code, the punishment shall be cumulative.

Illustration.

A offers an insult to the religion of a class of persons, with the deliberate intention of wounding their feelings: he is punishable with imprisonment for a term not exceeding one year by clause 282. But if he also knows it to be likely that he shall cause rioting, and does so cause rioting, he will be liable to punishment, both under clause 282 and under clause 136; that is to say, he will be punishable with imprisonment for a term not exceeding two years.

CHAPTER VIII.*

OF THE ABUSE OF THE POWERS OF PUBLIC SERVANTS.

138. Whoever, being or expecting to be a public servant,† directly or indirectly accepts, obtains or attempts to obtain from any party, for himself or for any other party, any gratification whatever other than legal remuneration, as a motive or a reward for doing or forbearing to do any official act, or for showing or forbearing to show in the exercise of his official functions favour or disfavour to any party, or for rendering or attempting to render any service or disservice to any party with the legislative or executive Government of India, or with the Government of any presidency, or with any public servant, as such, or with any body

* See Appendix, Note E.

† For the definition of the words "public servant," see clause 14.

of public servants, as such, shall be punished with imprisonment of either description for a term which may extend to three years, or fine, or both.

Explanations.—"Expecting to be a public servant." If a person not expecting to be in office obtains money by deceiving others into a belief that he is about to be in office, and that he will then serve them, he may be guilty of cheating, but he is not guilty of the offence defined in this clause.

"Gratification." The word gratification is used to denote not only pecuniary gratifications, and gratifications estimable in money, but also all gratifications of appetite and all honorary distinctions.

"Legal remuneration." All remuneration is legal which is given to a public servant by the Government which he serves, or by any person thereunto authorized by that Government, or which a public servant is permitted to accept by the Government which he serves, or by any person thereunto authorized by that Government.

"A motive or a reward for doing." A person may receive a gratification as a motive for doing what he does not intend to do; or as a reward for doing what he has not done.

Illustrations.

(*a*) A, a public servant, obtains Z's consent that Z's sister shall live with A as A's mistress, as a motive to A for giving Z a place in A's gift. A has committed the offence defined in this clause.

(*b*) A, a public servant, obtains from Z, a banker, a situation in Z's bank for A's brother, as a reward to A for deciding a cause in favour of Z. A has committed the offence defined in this clause.

(*c*) A, holding the office of resident at the court of a subsidiary power, accepts a lac of rupees from the minister of that power. It does not appear that A accepted this sum as a motive or a reward for doing or forbearing to do any particular official act, or for rendering or attempting to render any particular service to that power with the British Government. But it does appear that A accepted the sum as a motive or a reward for generally showing favour, in the exercise of his official functions, to that power. A has committed the offence defined in this clause.

(*d*) A, a public servant, induces Z erroneously to believe that A's influence with the Government has obtained a title for Z, and thus induces Z to give A money as a reward for this service. A has committed the offence defined in this clause.

139. Whoever directly or indirectly accepts, obtains or attempts to obtain from any party, for himself or for any other party, any gratification whatever, as a motive or a reward for inducing, by the exercise of personal influence, any public servant to do or to forbear to do any official act, or to show, in the exercise of the official functions of such public servant, favour or disfavour to any party, or to render or attempt to render any service or disservice to any party with the legislative or executive Government of India, or with the Government of any presidency, or with any public servant, as such, or with any body of public servants, as such, shall be punished with simple imprisonment for a term which may extend to six months, or fine, or both.

Illustrations.

An advocate who receives a fee for arguing a case before a judge; a person who receives pay for arranging and correcting a memorial addressed to Government, setting forth the services and claims of the memorialists; a paid agent for a condemned criminal who lays before the Government statements tending to show that the condemnation was unjust; are not within this clause, inasmuch as they do not exercise personal influence.

140. Whoever, being a public servant, abets, either previously or subsequently, the offence defined in the last preceding clause, when that offence is committed by means of real or pretended influence over himself, shall be punished with simple imprisonment for a term which may extend to three years, or fine, or both.

Illustration.

A is a public servant. B, A's mistress, receives a present as a motive for soliciting A to give an office to a particular person. A abets her doing so. B is punishable with imprisonment for a term not exceeding six months, or fine, or both. A is punishable with imprisonment for a term which may extend to three years, or fine, or both.

141. Whoever, being a judge, directly or indirectly accepts, obtains or attempts to obtain, for himself or for any other party, a gift of any valuable thing other than refreshments, according to the common usages of hospitality, from any party whom he knows to be plaintiff or defendant in any proceeding which is pending in the said judge's court, shall be punished with simple imprisonment for a term which may extend to two years, or fine, or both.

Explanation.—By a gift is meant any thing which is in reality a gift, whatever colour may be given to the transaction.

Illustrations.

(*a*) A, a judge, hires a house of Z, who has a cause pending in A's court. It is agreed that A shall pay fifty rupees a month, the house being such that, if the bargain were made in good faith, A would be required to pay two hundred rupees a month. A has obtained a gift of a valuable thing from Z.

(*b*) A, a judge, buys of Z, who has a cause pending in A's court, Government promissory notes at a discount, when they are selling in the market at a premium. A has obtained a gift of a valuable thing from Z.

(*c*) A, a judge, sells to Z, who has a cause pending in A's court, shares in a bank at a premium, when they are selling in the market at a discount. A has obtained a gift of a valuable thing from Z.

142. Whoever, being a judge, pronounces on any question which comes before him in any stage of any judicial proceeding, a decision which he knows to be unjust, shall be punished with simple imprisonment for a term which may extend to two years, or fine, or both.

143. Whoever, being a judge, for any purpose of favour or disfavour to any party, disobeys any direction of the law of procedure, shall be punished with simple imprisonment for a term which may extend to one year, or fine, or both.

144. Whoever, being in any office which gives him legal authority to commit persons to confinement, or to keep persons in confinement, commits any person to confinement, or keeps any person in confinement, in the exercise of that authority, knowing that in so doing he is acting unjustly, shall be punished with simple imprisonment for a term which may extend to two years, or fine, or both.

145. Whoever, being a public servant, knowingly disobeys any direction of the law as to the way in which he is to conduct himself as such public servant, intending or knowing it to be likely that he may by such disobedience cause injury to any party, or save any person from legal punishment, shall be punished with simple imprisonment for a term which may extend to one year, or fine, or both.

Illustrations.

(*a*) A, being an officer directed by law to take property in execution in order to satisfy a decree pronounced in Z's favour by a court of justice, knowingly disobeys that direction of law with the knowledge that he is likely thereby to cause injury to Z. A has committed the offence defined in this clause.

(*b*) A, being a magistrate in the Bengal Presidency, and being directed by law to commit an offender for trial before the sessions judge, knowingly disobeys that direction of law with the intention of thereby saving that offender from legal punishment. A has committed the offence defined in this clause.

146. Whoever, being a public servant, and being, as such public servant, charged with the preparation of any document, frames that document in a manner which he knows to be incorrect, intending or knowing it to be likely that he may thereby cause injury to any party, or save any person from legal punishment, shall be punished with imprisonment of either description for a term which may extend to three years, or fine, or both.

147. Whoever, being a public servant, and being legally bound, as such public servant, not to engage in trade, engages in trade, shall be punished with simple imprisonment for a term which may extend to three months, or fine, or both.

148. Whoever, being a public servant, and being legally bound, as such public servant, not to purchase or bid for certain property, purchases or bids for that property, either directly or by means of an agent, shall be punished with simple imprisonment for a term which may extend to three months, or fine, or both.

149. Whoever, being a public servant, knowingly and without any reasonable excuse disobeys any lawful order issued by his official superior or superiors for his guidance in the discharge of his public functions, or offers any intentional insult to any of his official superiors, or knowingly and without any reasonable excuse neglects the discharge of his official duties, shall be punished with fine to an amount not exceeding his salary for three months, if he be paid by salary; but if he be paid by fees, not exceeding thrice the amount of legal fees received by him in some one month; and if he be paid in land, not exceeding one-fourth of the clear annual value of such land.

150. Whoever, not belonging to a certain class of public servants, wears any garb or carries any token resembling any garb or token used by that class of public servants, with the intention that it may be believed, or with the knowledge that it is likely to be believed, that he belongs to that class of public servants, shall be punished with imprisonment of either description for a term which may extend to three months, or fine which may extend to five hundred rupees, or both.

151. If any person, in doing any thing whereby he commits an offence under any clause in this chapter, also commits an offence under any clause contained in any other chapter of this Code, the punishment shall be cumulative.

Illustration.

A, a public servant, threatens to assess Z's land unjustly high unless Z will give him money, and thus obtains money from Z. Here, A has committed the offence defined in clause 138, inasmuch as he has obtained from Z a gratification as a motive for forbearing to show disfavour to Z in the exercise of A's official functions. A has also committed extortion, inasmuch as he has obtained property from Z by putting Z in fear of injury. Therefore A is liable to the punishment of extortion added to that provided by clause 138.

CHAPTER IX*

OF CONTEMPTS OF THE LAWFUL AUTHORITY OF PUBLIC SERVANTS.

152. Whoever absconds in order to avoid being served with a summons or notice proceeding from any public servant or body of public servants, legally competent, as such public servant or as such body, to issue such summons or notice, shall be punished with imprisonment of either description for a term which may extend to one month, or fine which may extend to five hundred rupees, or both.

153. Whoever in any manner intentionally prevents the serving on himself, or on any other, of any summons or notice proceeding from any public servant or body of public servants, legally competent, as such public servant or as such body, to issue such summons or notice, or intentionally prevents the lawful affixing to any place of any such summons or notice, or intentionally removes any such summons or notice from any place to which it is lawfully affixed, or intentionally prevents the lawful making of any proclamation, under the authority of any public servant or body of public servants, legally competent, as such public servant or as such body, to direct such proclamation to be made, shall be punished with imprisonment of either description for a term which may extend to one month, or fine which may extend to five hundred rupees, or both.

154. If any person, by doing any thing whereby he commits an offence under the last preceding clause, also commits an offence under any clause contained in any other chapter of this Code, the punishment shall be cumulative.

155. Whoever, being legally bound to attend in person or by an agent at a certain place and time, in obedience to an order proceeding from any public servant or body of public servants, legally competent, as such public servant or as such body, to issue such order, intentionally omits to attend at that place or time, or departs from the place where he is bound to attend before the time at which it is lawful for him to depart, shall be punished with imprisonment of either description for a term which may extend to one month, or fine which may extend to five hundred rupees, or both.

Illustrations.

(*a*) A, being legally bound to appear before the Supreme Court of Calcutta in obedience to a subpœna issuing from that court, intentionally omits to appear. A has committed the offence defined in this clause.

(*b*) A, being legally bound to appear before a Zillah judge as a witness, in obedience to a summons issued by that Zillah judge, intentionally omits to appear. A has committed the offence defined in this clause.

---

* See Appendix, Note F.

(*c*) A, a proprietor of lands ordered to be sold, receives an order from the collector to attend an ameen in person, or by an agent, in the manner prescribed by section 10, Regulation XLV of 1793, of the Bengal Presidency. A, being legally bound to obey this order, intentionally disobeys it. A has committed the offence defined in this clause.

(*d*) A, a ryot, is summoned by the tehsildar to attend at the annual settlement of revenue, in the manner prescribed by section 5, Regulation III of 1831, of the Madras Presidency. A, being legally bound to attend, intentionally omits to do so. A has committed the offence defined in this clause.

156. **Whoever, being legally bound to produce or deliver up any document to any public servant, as such, or to any body of public servants, as such, intentionally omits so to produce or deliver up the same, shall be punished with imprisonment of either description for a term which may extend to one month, or fine which may extend to five hundred rupees, or both.**

Illustrations.

(*a*) A, being legally bound to produce a document before a Zillah court, intentionally omits to produce the same. A has committed the offence defined in this clause.

(*b*) A, a putwarree, is ordered by the collector to attend with his accounts an officer deputed by the collector, in the manner prescribed by section 25, Regulation XII of 1817, of the Bengal Presidency. A, being legally bound to obey this order, intentionally disobeys it. A has committed the offence defined in this clause.

(*c*) A has a rowanna for salt, which rowanna he is legally bound, under clause 3, section 46, Regulation X of 1819, of the Bengal Presidency, to deliver up to a darogah of a salt chokee. A intentionally omits to deliver up the same. A has committed the offence defined in this clause.

157. **Whoever, being legally bound to give any notice or to furnish information on any subject to any public servant, as such, or to any body of public servants, as such, intentionally omits to give such notice, or to furnish such information in the manner and at the time required by law, shall be punished with imprisonment of either description for a term which may extend to one month, or fine which may extend to five hundred rupees, or both.**

Illustrations.

(*a*) A is holder of Lakheraj lands, and as such is legally bound to furnish information to the collector, in the manner prescribed by section 7, Regulation VIII of 1800, of the Bengal Presidency. A intentionally omits to do so. A has committed the offence defined in this clause.

(*b*) A succeeds to a Malgoozaree estate, and is legally bound to notify such succession to the collector, in the manner prescribed by section 21, Regulation VIII of 1800, of the Bengal Presidency. A intentionally omits to do so. A has committed the offence defined in this clause.

158. **Whoever, being legally bound to furnish information on any subject to any public servant, as such, or to any body of public servants, as such, furnishes information on that subject which he knows to be false, shall be punished with imprisonment of either description for a term which may extend to six months, or fine which may extend to one thousand rupees, or both.**

Illustration.

A is legally bound to furnish a true return of his assessable carriages and horses to the assessor for Bombay, in the manner prescribed by section 25,

Regulation XIX of 1827, of the Bombay Presidency. A makes a return which he knows to be false. A has committed the offence defined in this clause.

159. Whoever refuses to bind himself by an oath, or sanction tantamount to an oath, to state the truth, when required so to bind himself by a public servant or body of public servants, legally competent to require that he shall so bind himself, shall be punished with imprisonment of either description for a term which may extend to six months, or fine, or both.

160. Whoever, being legally bound by an oath, or sanction tantamount to an oath, to state the truth on any subject to any public servant or body of public servants, refuses to answer any question demanded of him touching that subject by such public servant or body, in the exercise of the legal powers of such public servant or body, shall be punished with imprisonment of either description for a term which may extend to six months, or fine, or both.

161. Whoever refuses to sign any statement made by him when required to sign that statement by a public servant or body of public servants, legally competent to require that he shall sign that statement, shall be punished with imprisonment of either description for a term which may extend to three months, or fine which may extend to one thousand rupees, or both.

162. Whoever, being legally bound by an oath, or sanction tantamount to an oath, to state the truth on any subject to any public servant or body of public servants, states to such public servant or body as true that which he knows to be false touching that subject, shall be punished with imprisonment of either description for a term which may extend to three years and must not be less than six months, and shall also be liable to fine.*

163. Whoever gives to any public servant, or body of public servants, any information which he knows to be false, intending or knowing it to be likely that such false information may cause such public servant or such body to use the lawful power of such public servant or of such body to the loss or annoyance of any person, shall be punished with imprisonment of either description for a term which may extend to six months, or fine which may extend to one thousand rupees, or both.

Illustration.

A falsely informs a public servant that A knows Z to have contraband salt in a secret place, knowing that it is likely that the consequence of the information will be a search of Z's premises attended with annoyance to Z. A has committed the offence defined in this clause.

164. In every case in which any public servant, as such, or any person authorized by any public servant, as such, or by any body of public servants, as such, is legally empowered to enter any place, or to remain in any place, or to make any search, or to examine any thing, or to put any mark upon any thing; whoever, either by any act or by any illegal omission, intentionally prevents or attempts to prevent such public servant or authorized person from exercising such lawful power, or intentionally causes annoyance to such public servant or authorized

---

* For cases in which the false statement amounts to false evidence, see clause 190.

person in the exercise of such lawful power, shall be punished with imprisonment of either description for a term which may extend to three months, or fine which may extend to five hundred rupees, or both.

Explanation.—"Examine any thing." The word "examine" extends to all operations whereby the quality or quantity of any thing is ascertained.

Illustrations.

(*a*) Gauging, measuring, surveying, weighing, are modes of examination.

(*b*) Z is an officer of a court of justice lawfully empowered to enter A's house for the purpose of making a search. A, by fastening the door, attempts to prevent Z from entering. A has committed the offence defined in this clause.

(*c*) Z is a Revenue officer lawfully empowered to measure A's land for the purpose of assessment. A intentionally prevents Z from measuring the land. A has committed the offence defined in this clause.

(*d*) Z is a Custom-house officer lawfully empowered to go on board of a ship on its arrival in port. A, the commander of the ship, refuses to admit Z on board. A has committed the offence defined in this clause.

(*e*) Z is a Custom-house officer lawfully empowered to stay on board of a ship in a port in Bengal, and entitled, during such stay, to be furnished by the commander of the ship with fresh water. (Act No. XVI of 1837.) A, the commander of the ship, illegally omits to furnish Z with fresh water, and by such his illegal omission intentionally causes annoyance to Z in the exercise of Z's lawful powers. A has committed the offence defined in this clause.

165. If any person, by doing any thing whereby he commits an offence under the last preceding clause, also commits an offence under any clause contained in any other chapter of this Code, the punishment shall be cumulative.

166. Whoever offers any resistance to the taking of any property by the lawful authority of any public servant, as such, or of any body of public servants, as such, shall be punished with imprisonment of either description for a term which may extend to six months, or fine, or both.

167. If any person, by doing any thing whereby he commits an offence under the last preceding clause, also commits an offence under any clause contained in any other chapter of this Code, the punishment shall be cumulative.

168. Whoever intentionally obstructs any sale of property offered for sale by the lawful authority of any public servant, as such, or of any body of public servants, as such, shall be punished with imprisonment of either description for a term which may extend to one month, or fine which may extend to five hundred rupees, or both.

169. If any person, by doing any thing whereby he commits an offence under the last preceding clause, also commits an offence under any clause contained in any other chapter of this Code, the punishment shall be cumulative.

170. Whoever bids for any property offered for sale by the lawful authority of any public servant, as such, or of any body of public servants, as such, on account of any person, whether himself or any other, whom he knows to be under any legal incapacity to purchase that property at that sale, or bids for such property not intending to perform the obligations under which he lays himself by such bidding, shall be punished with imprisonment of either description for a term which may extend to one month, or fine, or both.

171. Whoever offers any resistance to the taking into custody of himself, or of any other, under the lawful authority of any public servant, as such, or of any body of public servants, as such, shall be punished with imprisonment of either description for a term which may extend to six months, or fine, or both.

172. If any person, by doing any thing whereby he commits an offence under the last preceding clause, also commits an offence under any clause contained in any other chapter of this Code, the punishment shall be cumulative.

173. Whoever intentionally rescues or attempts to rescue any person from any custody in which that person is detained under the lawful authority of any public servant, as such, or of any body of public servants, as such, shall be punished with imprisonment of either description for a term which may extend to six months, or fine, or both.

174. If any person, by doing any thing whereby he commits an offence under the last preceding clause, also commits an offence under any clause contained in any other chapter of this Code, the punishment shall be cumulative.

175. Whoever escapes or attempts to escape from any custody in which he is detained under the lawful authority of any public servant, as such, or of any body of public servants, as such, shall be punished with imprisonment of either description for a term which may extend to three months, or fine, or both.

176. If any person, by doing any thing whereby he commits an offence under the last preceding clause, also commits an offence under any clause contained in any other chapter of this Code, the punishment shall be cumulative.

177. Whoever, except as hereinafter excepted, knowing that a public servant or body of public servants has, in the exercise of the lawful powers of such public servant or body, directed a certain person to be taken into custody, harbours that person, with the intention of preventing that person from being so taken into custody, shall be punished with imprisonment of either description for a term which may extend to one month, or fine which may extend to two hundred rupees, or both.

Exception.—This provision does not extend to the case in which the harbour is given by the husband or wife or relation in the direct ascending or descending line, or brother or sister of the person to whom the harbour is given.*

178. Whoever, except as hereinafter excepted, knowingly harbours any person who has escaped from custody in which he was detained by the lawful authority of some public servant or body of public servants, shall be punished with imprisonment of either description for a term which may extend to two months, or fine which may extend to five hundred rupees, or both.

Exception.—This provision does not extend to the case in which the

* For rescue, escape and harbour after sentence, see Chapter X.

harbour is given by the husband or wife or relation in the direct ascending or descending line, or brother or sister of the person to whom the harbour is given.

179. Whoever intentionally offers any insult, or causes any interruption to any public servant or body of public servants, while such public servant or body is in the discharge of the public functions of such public servant or body, shall be punished with imprisonment of either description for a term which may extend to three months, or fine which may extend to five hundred rupees, or both.

180. If any person, by doing any thing whereby he commits an offence under the last preceding clause, also commits an offence under any clause contained in any other chapter of this Code, the punishment shall be cumulative.

181. Whoever, knowing himself to be directed by law to give any assistance to any public servant or body of public servants in the execution of the public duty of such public servant or body, intentionally omits to give such assistance, shall be punished with imprisonment of either description for a term which may extend to one month, or fine which may extend to two hundred rupees, or both.

182. Whoever, knowing that by a local order promulgated by a public servant or body of public servants lawfully empowered to promulgate such order, he is directed to abstain from a certain act, or to take certain order with certain property in his possession, disobeys such direction, shall, if such his disobedience causes or tends to cause any danger to human life, health or safety, or any obstruction or annoyance, or risk of such obstruction or annoyance, to persons lawfully employed, or any rioting, or any risk of rioting, be punished with imprisonment for a term which may extend to one month, or fine which may extend to two hundred rupees, or both.

Explanation.—It is not necessary that the offender should intend to produce harm, or contemplate his disobedience as likely to produce harm. It is sufficient that he knows of the order which he disobeys, and that his disobedience produces or is likely to produce harm.

Illustrations.

(*a*) An order is promulgated by a public servant lawfully empowered to promulgate such order, forbidding the celebration of a Hindoo festival, accompanied with swinging in front of the houses of the English gentlemen at Chowringhee. A knowingly disobeys the order, and thereby causes annoyance, or risk of annoyance, to English families. A has committed the offence defined in this clause.

(*b*) An order is promulgated in the manner aforesaid, directing all persons to keep their dogs within doors for fear of hydrophobia. A knowingly disobeys the order. Here, if A's disobedience tends to cause danger to human life, health or safety, A has committed the offence defined in this clause.

(*c*) An order is promulgated in the manner aforesaid, directing that a religious procession shall not pass down a certain street. A knowingly disobeys the order, and thereby causes danger of riot. A has committed the offence defined in this clause.

183. If any person, by doing any thing whereby he commits an offence under the last preceding clause, also commits an offence under any clause contained in any other chapter of this Code, the punishment shall be cumulative.

184. Whoever directly or indirectly holds out any threat of any injury to any public servant, or to any person in whom he believes that public servant to be interested, for the purpose of inducing that public servant to do any act, or to forbear or delay to do any act, connected with the exercise of the public functions of such public servant, shall be punished with imprisonment of either description for a term which may extend to one year, or fine, or both.

185. If any person, by doing any thing whereby he commits an offence under the last preceding clause, also commits an offence under any clause contained in any other chapter of this Code, the punishment shall be cumulative.

186. Whoever directly or indirectly holds out any threat of any injury to any person for the purpose of inducing that person to refrain or desist from making any legal application for protection against any injury to any public servant or body of public servants legally empowered as such to give such protection, shall be punished with imprisonment of either description for a term which may extend to one year, or fine, or both.

187. If any person, by doing any thing whereby he commits an offence under the last preceding clause, also commits an offence under any other clause of this Code, the punishment shall be cumulative.

CHAPTER X.*

OF OFFENCES AGAINST PUBLIC JUSTICE.

188. Whoever, in any stage of any judicial proceeding, being bound by an oath, or by a sanction tantamount to an oath, to state the truth, states that to be true which he knows to be false, touching any point material to the result of such proceeding, is said "to give false evidence."

Explanations.—It is not necessary that the offender should intend to mislead the judge as to the general merits of the question at issue. It is sufficient if he intends to mislead the judge as to any point material to that question.

An interpreter bound by an oath, or by a sanction tantamount to an oath, to interpret truly to a court of justice, if he intentionally gives a false interpretation of any words which it is material that he should duly interpret, is guilty of giving false evidence.

A trial before a court-martial is a judicial proceeding.

An investigation directed by law preliminary to a proceeding before a court of justice is a stage of a judicial proceeding, though that investigation may not take place before a court of justice.

An investigation directed by a court of justice according to law, and conducted under the authority of a court of justice, is a stage of a judicial proceeding, though that investigation may not take place before a court of justice.

Illustrations.

(*a*) A, in support of a just claim which B has against Z for 1,000 rupees,

---

* See Appendix, Note G.

falsely swears on the trial that he heard Z admit the justice of B's claim. A has given false evidence.

(*b*) A, in an inquiry before a magistrate for the purpose of ascertaining whether Z ought to be committed for trial, makes on oath a false statement material to the question. As this inquiry is a stage of a judicial proceeding, A has given false evidence.

(*c*) A, in an inquiry before an officer deputed by a court of justice to ascertain on the spot the boundaries of land, makes on oath a false statement material to the question. As this inquiry is a stage of a judicial proceeding, A has given false evidence.

189. Whoever causes any circumstance to exist, intending that such circumstance may appear in evidence in some stage of a judicial proceeding, and that such circumstance so appearing in evidence may cause any person who, in such judicial proceeding, acts as a judge, magistrate, juryman or abitrator, or makes any investigation under the authority of a court of justice to entertain an erroneous opinion touching any point material to the result of such proceeding, is said "to fabricate false evidence."

Illustrations.

(*a*) A puts jewels into a box belonging to Z, with the intention that they may be found in that box, and that this circumstance may cause Z to be convicted of theft. A has fabricated false evidence.

(*b*) A, with the intention of causing Z to be convicted of a criminal conspiracy, writes a letter in imitation of Z's handwriting, purporting to be addressed to an accomplice in such criminal conspiracy, and puts the letter in a place which he knows that the officers of the police are likely to search. A has fabricated false evidence.

(*c*) A, having a just claim against Z for 1,000 rupees, forges Z's signature to a bond for 1,000 rupees, for the purpose of supporting that claim before a court of justice. A has fabricated false evidence.

190. Whoever gives or fabricates false evidence shall, except in the case hereinafter excepted, be punished with imprisonment of either description for a term which may extend to seven years and must not be less than one year, and shall also be liable to fine.

Exception.—A person who fabricates false evidence, intending thereby to save himself from conviction for an offence, and not intending nor knowing it to be likely that the false evidence so fabricated may cause any injury to any other party, is not within the penal provision of this clause.

Illustrations.

(*a*) A commits an offence; he then takes a horse and rides with great speed to a distant place, in order that he may, by appearing there in an incredibly short time after the commission of his offence, cause a court of justice to think him innocent. A is not liable to punishment as a fabricator of false evidence.

(*b*) A, after wounding a person with a knife, goes into the room where Z is sleeping, smears Z's clothes with blood, and lays the knife under Z's pillow, intending not only that suspicion may thereby be turned away from himself, but also that Z may be convicted of voluntarily causing grievous hurt. A is liable to punishment as a fabricator of false evidence.

191. Whoever gives or fabricates false evidence, intending or knowing it to be likely that he may thereby cause any person to be convicted of any offence which is capital by this Code, shall be punished with transportation for life, or with rigorous imprisonment for a term which may extend to life, and must not be less than seven years, and shall also be liable to fine.*

192. Whoever gives or fabricates false evidence, intending or knowing it to be likely that he may thereby cause any person to be convicted of an offence which by this Code is not capital, but punishable with imprisonment for a term of more than seven years, shall be punished as a person convicted of that offence would be liable to be punished.†

Illustration.

A gives false evidence before a court of justice, intending thereby to cause Z to be convicted of a dacoity. The punishment of dacoity is transportation for life, or rigorous imprisonment for a term which may extend to life, and must not be less than three years, with or without fine. A, therefore, is liable to such transportation or imprisonment, and to fine.

193. Whoever removes, conceals, delivers to any party, or causes to be transferred to any party any property, intending thereby to prevent that property from being taken as a forfeiture or in satisfaction of a fine, under a sentence which has been pronounced or which he knows to be likely to be pronounced by a court of justice, or from being taken in execution of a decree which has been made or which he knows to be likely to be made by a court of justice in a civil suit, shall be punished with imprisonment of either description for a term which may extend to one year, or fine, or both.

194. Whoever claims any property knowing that he has no rightful claim to such property, or practises any deception touching any right to any property, intending thereby to prevent that property from being taken as a forfeiture or in satisfaction of a fine, under a sentence which has been pronounced or which he knows to be likely to be pronounced by a court of justice, or from being taken in execution of a decree which has been made or which he knows to be likely to be made by a court of justice in a civil suit, shall be punished with imprisonment of either description for a term which may extend to one year, or fine, or both.

195. Whoever, in any declaration made and subscribed by him, which declaration any court of justice is bound by law to receive as evidence of any fact, states as true what he knows to be false, touching any point material to the effect of such declaration, shall be punished with imprisonment of either description for a term which may extend to two years, or fine, or both.

196. Whoever fraudulently, or for the purpose of annoyance, institutes any civil suit, knowing that he has no just ground to institute such suit, shall be punished with imprisonment of either description for a term which may extend to one year, or fine, or both.

Explanation.—It is not necessary that the party to whom the offender intends to cause wrongful loss or annoyance should be the party against whom the suit is instituted.

Illustration.

A, intending fraudulently to deprive Z of property to which A knows that A has no right, institutes a suit against B for that property by collusion with B. A has committed the offence defined in this clause.

---

* For the case in which death is voluntarily caused by false evidence, see the head of Voluntary Culpable Homicide.

† The subornation of false evidence falls under the head of Abetment.

197. Whoever intentionally offers any insult or causes any interruption to any public servant or body of public servants, while such public servant or body is sitting as a court of justice, shall be punished with imprisonment of either description for a term which may extend to six months, or fine which may extend to one thousand rupees, or both.

198. If any person, by doing any thing whereby he commits an offence under the last preceding clause, also commits an offence under any clause contained in any other chapter of this Code, the punishment shall be cumulative.

199. Whoever directly or indirectly holds out any threat of any injury to any person for the purpose of inducing that person to refrain or desist from instituting, prosecuting or defending any civil suit, or from taking any legal step incident to or consequent upon such institution, prosecution or defence, or from giving evidence in any stage of any judicial proceeding whatever, shall be punished with imprisonment of either description for a term which may extend to two years, or fine, or both.

200. If any person, by doing any thing whereby he commits an offence under the last preceding clause, also commits an offence under any other clause in this Code, the punishment shall be cumulative.

201. Whoever escapes or attempts to escape from any custody in which he is lawfully detained in pursuance of a sentence of a court of justice, or by virtue of a commutation of such sentence, shall be punished with imprisonment of either description for a term which may extend to two years, or fine, or both.

202. If any person, by doing any thing whereby he commits an offence under the last preceding clause, also commits an offence under any other clause contained in this Code, the punishment shall be cumulative.

203. Whoever, having been lawfully transported for a term not extending to life, returns from such transportation, the term of such transportation not having expired, and his punishment not having been remitted, shall be punished with transportation for life, and shall also be liable to fine.

204. Whoever, having been sentenced to a punishment which has been lawfully commuted for transportation for a term of years, and subsequent banishment for life, returns from such transportation or banishment, his punishment not having been remitted, shall be punished with transportation for life, and shall also be liable to fine.

205. Whoever, having been lawfully banished, returns from such banishment, his term of banishment not having expired, and his punishment not having been remitted, shall be punished with transportation for a term which may extend to seven years, to which banishment for life shall always be added.

206. Whoever, except as hereinafter excepted, knowing that any person has escaped from any custody in which such person was lawfully detained in pursuance of the sentence of a court of justice, or by virtue of a commutation of such sentence, or has returned from lawful transportation or banishment, the term of such transportation or banishment not having expired, and the punishment of such person not having been remitted, gives harbour, assistance or intelligence to such person, with the intention of saving such person from the legal consequences of such escape or return, shall be punished with simple imprisonment for a term which may extend to six months, or fine which may extend to one thousand rupees, or both.

Exception.—This provision does not extend to the case in which the harbour, assistance or intelligence is given by the husband or wife, or relation in the direct ascending or descending line, or brother or sister of the person to whom the harbour, assistance or intelligence is given.

207. Whoever, having accepted any conditional remission of punishment in the manner described in the Code of Procedure, knowingly violates any condition on which such remission was granted, shall be punished with the punishment to which he was originally sentenced, if he has already suffered no part of that punishment, and if he has suffered any part of that punishment, then with so much of that punishment as he has not already suffered.

CHAPTER XI.*

OF OFFENCES RELATING TO THE REVENUE.

208. Whoever imports or attempts to import any property into the territories of the East India Company, or exports or attempts to export any property from the said territories, or conveys or attempts to convey any property from place to place within the said territories, in contravention of any law by which such importation, exportation or conveyance is prohibited or regulated, is said to commit the offence of "smuggling."

Illustrations.

(*a*) A imports goods by landing them at a place at which the landing of them is prohibited by law. A has committed the offence of smuggling.

(*b*) A conveys goods through the territories of the East India Company without a permit, being forbidden by law so to convey them. A has committed the offence of smuggling.

(*c*) A exports goods without paying an export duty on them, being forbidden by law so to export them. A has committed the offence of smuggling.

209. Whoever commits the offence of smuggling shall be punished with imprisonment of either description for a term which may extend to three months, or with fine which may extend to an amount equal to five hundred rupees, added to five times the market value of the property smuggled, or with both.

210. Whoever fraudulently receives smuggled goods, knowing the same to have been smuggled, shall be punished with imprisonment of either description for a term which may extend to three months, or with fine which may extend to an amount equal to five hundred rupees, added to five times the market value of the property smuggled, or with both.

211. Whoever, being in charge of any vessel, places that vessel in any situation in which he is forbidden to place it by any public servant or body of public servants employed in the collection of the revenue, and

* See Appendix, Note H.

empowered by law, as such public servant or body, to forbid the placing of such vessel in such situation, shall be punished with fine which may extend to one thousand rupees.

212. Whoever cultivates, collects or manufactures any article in contravention of any law by which the cultivation, collection or manufacture of that article is prohibited or regulated, shall be punished with simple imprisonment for a term which may extend to three months, or fine which may extend to five hundred rupees, or both.

Illustrations.

(*a*) A, contrary to law, cultivates the poppy. A has committed the offence defined in this clause.

(*b*) A cultivates tobacco in a district in which such cultivation is prohibited by law. A has committed the offence defined in this clause.

(*c*) A, contrary to law, collects opium from the poppy. A has committed the offence defined in this clause.

(*d*) A, in the Bombay Presidency, contrary to law, collects toddy from the brab tree. A has committed the offence defined in this clause.

213. Whoever makes or has in his possession any implement, material or receptacle, in order to the doing of any thing which is an offence under the last preceding clause, shall be punished with simple imprisonment for a term which may extend to three months, or fine which may extend to five hundred rupees, or both.

Illustrations.

(*a*) A makes a saltpan for the purpose of collecting salt, contrary to law. A has committed the offence defined in this clause.

(*b*) A has in his possession a still for the purpose of distillation, contrary to law. A has committed the offence defined in this clause.

214. Whoever sells or offers for sale any article in contravention of any law by which the selling or offering for sale of such article is prohibited or regulated, shall be punished with imprisonment of either description for a term which may extend to three months, or fine which may extend to five hundred rupees, or both.

215. Whoever has in his possession any article in contravention of any law by which the possession of that article is prohibited or regulated, shall be punished with fine, which may extend to twice the value of that article.

216. Whoever, being bound by law to put any mark on any article in his possession, omits to put such mark on such article, shall be punished with fine which may extend to the value of such article.

217. Whoever performs any part of the process of counterfeiting any stamp from which the Government derives a revenue, shall be punished with imprisonment of either description for a term which may extend to seven years, and must not be less than one year, and shall also be liable to fine.

218. Whoever has in his possession any implement or material, intending or knowing it to be likely that the same may be used for the purpose of counterfeiting any stamp from which the Government derives a revenue, shall be punished with imprisonment of either description for a term which may extend to seven years, and must not be less than one year, and shall also be liable to fine.

219. Whoever makes any implement, intending or knowing it to be likely that the same may be used for the purpose of counterfeiting any stamp from which the Government derives a revenue, shall be punished with imprisonment of either description for a term which may extend to seven years, and must not be less than one year, and shall also be liable to fine.

220. Whoever sells or offers for sale any stamp which he knows to be a counterfeit of any stamp from which the Government derives a revenue, shall be punished with imprisonment of either description for a term which may extend to seven years and must not be less than one year, and shall also be liable to fine.

221. Whoever has in his possession any stamp which he knows to be a counterfeit of any stamp from which the Government derives a revenue, intending to sell or offer for sale such stamp, shall be punished with imprisonment of either description for a term which may extend to seven years and must not be less than one year, and shall also be liable to fine.

222. Whoever uses as genuine any stamp, knowing it to be a counterfeit of any stamp, from which the Government derives a revenue, shall be punished with imprisonment of either description for a term which may extend to six months, or fine, or both.

223. Whoever, intending to cause wrongful loss to the Government, effaces from any substance bearing a stamp any writing for which such stamp has been used, in order that such stamp may be used for a different writing, shall be punished with imprisonment of either description for a term which may extend to three months, or with a fine which may extend to an amount equal to five hundred rupees, added to five times the price of such stamp, or with both.

224. Whoever, intending to cause wrongful loss to the Government, uses for any writing, as a stamp which has not been used before, a stamp which he knows to have been before used for a different writing, shall be punished with imprisonment of either description for a term which may extend to three months, or with a fine which may extend to an amount equal to five hundred rupees, added to five times the price of such stamp, or with both.

225. Whoever establishes or maintains any illegal post for the purpose of conveying letters or packets from place to place for hire, or receives any letter or packet in order to the conveying of the same by such illegal post, or conveys the same by such illegal post, or delivers the same after the conveyance of the same by such illegal post, shall be punished with imprisonment of either description for a term which may extend to three months, or fine which may extend to one thousand rupees, or both.

226. Whoever, being in charge of any letter or packet which is on board of any vessel, and being legally bound to deliver such letter or packet into the keeping of any officer in charge of a post-office, intentionally omits so to deliver the same at the time and in the manner directed by law, shall be punished with fine.

227. Whoever, being in charge of any vessel, refuses to receive on board for the purpose of conveyance any letter or packet which he is required to receive on board by any public servant or any body of public servants, legally competent as such to require him so to receive the same, shall be punished with fine which may extend to five hundred rupees.

228. Whoever, being legally authorized by license from any public servant, as such, or from any body of public servants, as such, to cultivate, to collect, to manufacture, to import, to export, to convey from place to place, to sell, or to have in his possession any article, disobeys any direction of law, or any condition imposed by the lawful authority of the public servant or body of public servants from whom such license was obtained, as to the way in which he is to act as such licensed person, shall be punished with fine which may extend to two hundred rupees.

Illustrations.

(*a*) A, a licensed stamp vender, being bound, as such licensed stamp vender, to have the schedule of stamps affixed in a conspicuous situation in his shop, omits to have that schedule so affixed. A has committed the offence defined in this clause.

(*b*) A, a proprietor of salt covered by rowannah, being legally bound daily to certify on the back of his rowannah the quantity sold by him, omits to do so. A has committed the offence defined in this clause.

229. The punishments provided by this chapter are independent of any confiscation to which the property, with respect to which the offences defined in this chapter have been committed, is liable under any law.

CHAPTER XII.*

OF OFFENCES RELATING TO COIN.

230. Coin is metal used as money, and bearing some mark that it is issued by the authority of some Government in order to be so used.

Illustrations.

(*a*) Cowries are not coin, as not being metal.

(*b*) Lumps of unstamped copper, though used as money, are not coin, inasmuch as they bear no mark of the authority which issues them.

(*c*) An ancient denarius is not now coin, inasmuch as such pieces are not now used as money.

(*d*) Medals are not coin, inasmuch as they are not intended to be used as money.

(*e*) Bank tokens issued by a private bank are not coin, inasmuch as they are not put forth by the authority of any Government.

231. Coin first issued by the authority of the Government of India, or of the Government of any presidency, to be used as money within the territories of the East India Company, is designated as Company's coin.

232. Whoever counterfeits coin shall be punished with imprisonment of either description for a term which may extend to three years and must not be less than six months, and shall also be liable to fine.

Explanation.—A person may commit this offence by causing a genuine coin to appear like a different coin.

233. Whoever counterfeits the King's or the Company's coin shall be punished with imprisonment of either description for a term which

---

* See Appendix, Note I.

may extend to seven years and must not be less than two years, and shall also be liable to fine.

234. Whoever makes any die for the purpose of counterfeiting coin, or of enabling any other person to counterfeit coin, shall be punished with imprisonment of either description for a term which may extend to three years and must not be less than six months, and shall also be liable to fine.

235. Whoever makes any die for the purpose of counterfeiting the King's or the Company's coin, or of enabling any other person to counterfeit the King's or the Company's coin, shall be punished with imprisonment of either description for a term which may extend to seven years and must not be less than two years, and shall also be liable to fine.

236. Whoever is in possession of any implement or material, with the intention of employing the same for the purpose of committing any of the offences defined in any of the four clauses last preceding, shall be punished with imprisonment of either description for a term which may extend to three years, and must not be less than six months, and shall also be liable to fine.

237. Whoever previously abets, by instigation, conspiracy or aid, the counterfeiting, without the territories of the East India Company, of the King's or the Company's coin, shall be punished with imprisonment of either description for a term which may extend to seven years and must not be less than two years, and shall also be liable to fine.

238. Whoever imports into the territories of the East India Company, or exports from the said territories, any coin which he knows to be counterfeit, intending or knowing it to be likely that such coin may pass as genuine, shall be punished with imprisonment of either description for a term which may extend to three years and must not be less than six months, and shall also be liable to fine.

239. Whoever imports into the territories of the East India Company, or exports from the said territories, any coin which he knows to be a counterfeit of the King's or the Company's coin, intending or knowing it to be likely that such coin may pass as genuine, shall be punished with imprisonment of either description for a term which may extend to seven years and must not be less than two years, and shall also be liable to fine.

240. Whoever, having any counterfeit coin which at the time at which he became possessed of it he knew to be counterfeit, delivers the same to any other, or attempts to induce any other to receive it, with the intention that such counterfeit coin shall pass as genuine, shall be punished with imprisonment of either description for a term which may extend to three years and must not be less than six months, and shall also be liable to fine.

241. Whoever, having any counterfeit coin which is a counterfeit of the King's or the Company's coin, and which at the time at which he became possessed of it he knew to be a counterfeit of the King's or the Company's coin, delivers the same to any other, or attempts to induce any other to receive it, with the intention that such counterfeit coin shall pass as genuine, shall be punished with imprisonment of either description for a term which may extend to seven years and must not be less than two years, and shall also be liable to fine.

242. Whoever, knowing any coin to be counterfeit, delivers the same to any other person as genuine, or attempts to induce any other person to receive it as genuine, shall be punished with fine to an amount which may extend to ten times the value of the coin of which such counterfeit coin is a counterfeit.

Illustration.

A, a coiner, delivers counterfeit Company's rupees to his accomplice B for the purpose of uttering them. B sells the rupees to C, another utterer, who buys them knowing them to be counterfeit. C pays away the rupees for goods to D, who receives them not knowing them to be counterfeit. D, after receiving the rupees, discovers that they are counterfeit, and pays them away as if they were good. Here, A, B and C are guilty of the offence defined in the last preceding clause. D is guilty only of the offence defined in this clause.

243. Whoever is in possession of counterfeit coin, having known at the time when he became possessed thereof that such coin was counterfeit, and intending or knowing it to be likely that such counterfeit coin may pass as genuine, shall be punished with imprisonment of either description for a term which may extend to three years and must not be less than six months, and shall also be liable to fine.

244. Whoever is in possession of counterfeit coin which is a counterfeit of the King's or the Company's coin, having known at the time when he became possessed of it that it was counterfeit, and intending or knowing it to be likely that such counterfeit coin may pass as genuine, shall be punished with imprisonment of either description for a term which may extend to seven years and must not be less than two years, and shall also be liable to fine.

245. Whoever, being employed in any mint lawfully established within the territories of the East India Company, does any act, or omits what he is legally bound to do, with the intention of causing any coin issued from that mint to be of different weight or composition from the weight or composition fixed by law, shall be punished with imprisonment of either description for a term which may extend to seven years and must not be less than two years, and shall also be liable to fine.

246. Whoever performs on any coin any operation which diminishes the weight or alters the composition of that coin, with the intention that the said coin shall pass as if its weight had not been so diminished or its composition so altered, shall be punished with imprisonment of either description for a term which may extend to one year and must not be less than three months, and shall also be liable to fine.

Explanation.—A person who scoops out part of the coin and puts any thing else into the cavity, changes the composition of that coin.

247. Whoever performs on any of the King's or the Company's coin any operation which diminishes the weight or alters the composition of that coin, with the intention that the said coin shall pass as if its weight had not been so diminished, or its composition so altered, shall be punished with imprisonment of either description for a term which may extend to three years and must not be less than one year, and shall also be liable to fine.

248. Whoever is in possession of any implement or material, intending to employ the same for the purpose of committing any of the offences defined in either of the three last preceding clauses, shall be punished with imprisonment of either description for a term which may extend to one year and must not be less than three months, and shall also be liable to fine.

249. Whoever, having coin in his possession with respect to which the offence defined in clause 246 has been committed, and having known at the time when he became possessed of such coin that such offence had been committed with respect to it, delivers such coin to any other, or attempts to induce any other to receive the same, with the intention that such coin may pass as if no offence had been committed with respect to it, shall be punished with imprisonment of either description for a term which may extend to one year and must not be less than three months, and shall also be liable to fine.

250. Whoever, having coin in his possession with respect to which the offence defined in clause 247 has been committed, and having known at the time when he became possessed of such coin that such offence had been committed with respect to it, delivers such coin to any other, or attempts to induce any other to receive the same, with the intention that such coin may pass as if no such offence had been committed with respect to it, shall be punished with imprisonment of either description for a term which may extend to three years and must not be less than one year, and shall also be liable to fine.

251. Whoever is in possession of coin with respect to which the offence defined in clause 246 has been committed, having known at the time of becoming possessed thereof that such offence had been committed with respect to such coin, and intending to cause the same to be in circulation, shall be punished with imprisonment of either description for a term which may extend to one year and must not be less than three months, and shall also be liable to fine.

252. Whoever is in possession of coin with respect to which the offence defined in clause 247 has been committed, having known at the time of becoming possessed thereof that such offence had been committed with respect to such coin, and intending to cause the same to be in circulation, shall be punished with imprisonment of either description for a term which may extend to three years and must not be less than one year, and shall also be liable to fine.

CHAPTER XIII.

OF OFFENCES RELATING TO WEIGHTS AND MEASURES.

253. Whoever, in dealing, fraudulently uses any balance which he knows to be false, shall be punished with imprisonment of either description for a term which may extend to one year, or fine, or both.

254. Whoever, in dealing, fraudulently uses any false weight or false measure of length or capacity, or fraudulently uses any weight or any measure of length or capacity as a different weight or measure from what it is, shall be punished with imprisonment of either description for a term which may extend to one year, or fine, or both.

255. Whoever is in possession of any balance or of any weight, or of any measure of length or capacity, which he knows to be false, and which he intends to use fraudulently in dealing, shall be punished with imprisonment of either description for a term which may extend to one year, or fine, or both.

256. Whoever makes any balance or weight, or measure of length or capacity, which he knows to be false, intending the same to be fraudulently used in dealing, shall be punished with imprisonment of either description for a term which may extend to one year, or fine, or both.

CHAPTER XIV.

OF OFFENCES AFFECTING THE PUBLIC HEALTH, SAFETY AND CONVENIENCE.

257. Whoever malignantly or wantonly does any act which he knows to be likely to spread the infection of any disease dangerous to life, shall be punished with imprisonment of either description for a term which may extend to six months, or fine, or both.

258. Whoever knowingly disobeys any rule made and promulgated according to law by the Government of India, or by the Government of any presidency, for putting any vessel into a state of quarantine, or for regulating the intercourse of vessels in a state of quarantine with the shore or with other vessels, or for regulating the intercourse between places where an infectious disease prevails and other places, shall be punished with imprisonment of either description for a term which may extend to six months, or fine, or both.

259. Whoever adulterates any article of food or drink, so as to make such article noxious as food or drink, intending or knowing it to be likely that such article may be sold as wholesome food or drink, shall be punished with imprisonment of either description for a term which may extend to six months, or fine which may extend to five hundred rupees, or both.

260. Whoever sells or offers for sale, as wholesome, any food or drink, knowing the same to be noxious, shall be punished with imprisonment of either description for a term which may extend to six months, or fine which may extend to five hundred rupees, or both.

261. Whoever adulterates any drug or medical preparation in such a manner as to lessen the efficacy or change the operation of such drug or medical preparation, or to make it noxious, intending or knowing it to be likely that such drug or medical preparation may be sold or issued from any dispensary as if it had not undergone such adulteration, shall be punished with imprisonment of either description for a term which may extend to six months, or fine which may extend to one thousand rupees, or both.

262. Whoever, knowing any drug or medical preparation to have been adulterated in such a manner as to lessen its efficacy, to change its operation, or to render it noxious, sells the same, or offers it for sale, or issues it from any dispensary as unadulterated, shall be punished with imprisonment of either description for a term which may extend to six months, or fine which may extend to one thousand rupees, or both.

263. Whoever knowingly sells or offers for sale, or issues from any dispensary, any drug or medical preparation as a different drug or medical preparation, shall be punished with imprisonment of either description for a term which may extend to six months, or fine which may extend to one thousand rupees, or both.

264. Whoever, by any act, or by omitting to take order with property in his possession, voluntarily causes the atmosphere in any public way to be in a state noxious to health or offensive to the senses, shall be punished with imprisonment of either description for a term which may extend to one month, or fine which may extend to five hundred rupees, or both.

265. Whoever drives any vehicle or rides on any public way in a manner so rash or negligent as to indicate a want of due regard for human life, shall be punished with imprisonment of either description for a term which may extend to six months, or fine which may extend to two thousand rupees, or both.

266. Whoever navigates any vessel in a manner so rash or negligent as to indicate a want of due regard for human life, shall be punished with imprisonment of either description for a term which may extend to six months, or fine which may extend to two thousand rupees, or both.

267. Whoever, being in charge of any vessel, conveys for hire any person by water in that vessel, when that vessel is in such a state or so loaded as to endanger the life of that person, shall be punished with imprisonment of either description for a term which may extend to six months, or fine which may extend to two thousand rupees, or both.

268. Whoever does with any poisonous substance any act so rash or negligent as to indicate a want of due regard for human life, or omits to take such order with any poisonous substance in his possession as he believes to be sufficient to guard against any probable danger to human life from such poisonous substance, shall be punished with imprisonment of either description for a term which may extend to six months, or fine which may extend to two thousand rupees, or both.

269. Whoever does with fire or any combustible matter any act so rash or negligent as to indicate a want of due regard to human life, or omits to take such order with any fire or any combustible matter in his possession as he believes to be sufficient to guard against any probable danger to human life from such fire or combustible matter, shall be punished with imprisonment of either description for a term which may extend to six months, or fine which may extend to two thousand rupees, or both.

270. Whoever does with any explosive substance any act so rash or negligent as to indicate a want of due regard for human life, or omits to take such order with any explosive substance in his possession as he believes to be sufficient to guard against any probable danger to human life from that substance, shall be punished with imprisonment of either description for a term which may extend to six months, or fine which may extend to two thousand rupees, or both.

271. Whoever does with any machinery any act so rash or negligent as to indicate a want of due regard for human life, or omits to take such order with any machinery in his possession or under his care as he believes to be sufficient to guard against any probable danger to human life from such machinery, shall be punished with imprisonment of either description for a term which may extend to six months, or fine which may extend to two thousand rupees, or both.

272. Whoever, having such a right over any building as entitles him to pull down or repair that building, omits to take such order with that building as he believes to be sufficient to guard against any probable danger to human life from the fall of that building, or of any part thereof, shall be punished with imprisonment of either description for a term which may extend to six months, or fine which may extend to two thousand rupees, or both.

273. Whoever omits to take such order with any animal in his possession as he believes to be sufficient to guard against any probable danger to human life, or any probable danger of grievous hurt, from such animal, shall be punished with imprisonment of either description for a term which may extend to six months, or fine which may extend to two thousand rupees, or both.

274. Whoever, by doing any act in any public way or public line of navigation, or by omitting to take order with any property in his possession, which property is in any public way or public line of navigation, voluntarily causes danger, annoyance or obstruction to those who pass along that way or line of navigation, or who reside in the neighbourhood of that way or line of navigation, shall be punished with fine which may extend to two hundred rupees.

CHAPTER XV.*

OF OFFENCES RELATING TO RELIGION AND CASTE.

275 Whoever destroys, damages or defiles any place of worship, or any object held sacred by any class of persons, with the intention of thereby insulting the religion of any class of persons, or with the knowledge that any class of persons are likely to consider such destruction, damage or defilement as an insult to their religion, shall be punished with imprisonment of either description for a term which may extend to seven years and must not be less than one year, and shall also be liable to fine.

276. Whoever voluntarily causes disturbance to any assembly lawfully engaged in the performance of religious worship or religious ceremonies, if in causing such disturbance he assaults any person, or makes show of assaulting any person, or threatens to assault any person engaged in such worship or ceremonies, shall be punished with imprisonment of either description for a term which may extend to three years and must not be less than six months, and shall also be liable to fine.

---

* See Appendix, Note J.

277. If any person, by doing any thing whereby he commits an offence under the last preceding clause, also commits an offence under any clause contained in any other chapter of this Code, the punishment shall be cumulative.

278. Whoever, in any place of worship, does any thing whereby he voluntarily causes disturbance to any assembly lawfully met therein for the performance of religious worship or religious ceremonies, shall be punished with imprisonment of either description for a term which may extend to one year, or fine, or both.

279. If any person, by doing any thing whereby he commits an offence under the last preceding clause, also commits an offence under any clause contained in any other chapter of this Code, the punishment shall be cumulative.

280. Whoever, with the intention of wounding the feelings or insulting the religion of any person, commits any trespass on any place of sepulture, offers any indignity to any human corpse, or causes disturbance to any assembly assembled for the performance of funeral ceremonies, shall be punished with imprisonment of either description for a term which may extend to one year, or fine, or both.

281. If any person, by doing any thing whereby he commits an offence under the last preceding clause, also commits an offence under any clause contained in any other chapter of this Code, the punishment shall be cumulative.

282. Whoever, with the deliberate intention of wounding the religious feelings of any person, utters any word, or makes any sound in the hearing of that person, or makes any gesture in the sight of that person, or places any object in the sight of that person, shall be punished with imprisonment of either description for a term which may extend to one year, or fine, or both.

283. Whoever does any act with the intention of causing it to be believed in any quarter that, by doing that act, he renders some other person an object of divine displeasure, or of causing it to be believed that by doing that act he obliges some other person, on pain of the divine displeasure, to do any thing which that person is not legally bound to do, or to omit any thing which that person is legally entitled to do, or threatens any person with doing any act which would, in any quarter, be believed to render the person threatened an object of divine displeasure, shall be punished with imprisonment of either description for a term which may extend to one year, or fine which may extend to one thousand rupees, or both.

Illustrations.

(*a*) A sits Dhurna at Z's door, with the intention of causing it to be believed that by so sitting he renders Z an object of divine displeasure. A has committed the offence defined in this clause.

(*b*) A threatens Z that, unless Z performs a certain act, A will kill one of A's own children, under such circumstances that the killing would be believed to render Z an object of divine displeasure. A has committed the offence defined in this clause.

284. Whoever, with the intention of causing any person to lose caste, commits any assault which causes that person to lose caste, or induces that person to do ignorantly any thing whereby that person incurs loss of caste, shall be punished with imprisonment of either description for a term which may extend to six months, or fine which may extend to two thousand rupees, or both.

Illustration.

A, with the intention of causing Z, a Brahmin, to lose caste, mixes beef broth with Z's food. Z swallows it in ignorance, and thereby loses caste. A has committed the offence defined in this clause.

285. Whoever intentionally causes any food belonging to any person to be in a state in which that person, according to the rules of his religion or caste, cannot use it as food, shall be punished with fine which may extend to fifty rupees.

286. Whoever, having been convicted of the offence defined in the clause last preceding, again commits the offence defined in the clause last preceding, shall be punished with imprisonment of either description for a term which may extend to one month, or fine which may extend to two hundred rupees, or both.

CHAPTER XVI.*

OF ILLEGAL ENTRANCE INTO AND RESIDENCE IN THE TERRITORIES OF THE EAST INDIA COMPANY.

287. Whoever, being a subject of the King, and not a native of the territories of the East India Company, on his arrival by sea in any place within the said territories omits to make known in writing his name, place of destination, and object of pursuit in India, to the chief officer of Customs or other officer authorized for that purpose, at the place at which such subject of the King has arrived, shall be punished with fine which may extend to one thousand rupees.

288. Whoever, being a subject of the King, and not a native of the territories of the East India Company, enters the said territories by land not being legally authorized so to do, shall be punished with simple imprisonment for a term which may extend to three months, or fine which may extend to two thousand rupees, or both.

289. Whoever, being a subject of the King, and not a native of the territories of the East India Company, and not having such a license as is by law necessary to authorize such a subject of the King to reside in a certain part of the said territories, enters or resides in that part of the said territories, shall be punished with simple imprisonment for a term which may extend to three months, or fine which may extend to two thousand rupees, or both.

290. Whoever, having been convicted of the offence defined in the clause last preceding, again commits the offence defined in the clause last preceding, shall be punished with banishment for life, or for any term, or with simple imprisonment for a term which may extend to one year, to which banishment or imprisonment fine may be added.

---

* See Appendix, Note K.

CHAPTER XVII.*

OF OFFENCES RELATING TO THE PRESS.

291. Whoever keeps in his possession a press for the printing of books or papers, not having made and subscribed the declaration required by law to be made and subscribed by every person keeping such a press in his possession, shall be punished with simple imprisonment for a term which may extend to two years, or fine which may extend to five thousand rupees, or both.

292. Whoever prints or publishes any book or paper which has not printed legibly on it the name of the printer, the name of the publisher, and the place of the printing and publication, shall be punished with simple imprisonment for a term which may extend to two years, or fine which may extend to five thousand rupees, or both.

293. Whoever prints or publishes any periodical work whatever containing public news, or comments on public news, otherwise than in conformity to the rules of law whereby the printing and publishing of such works is regulated, shall be punished with simple imprisonment for a term which may extend to two years, or fine which may extend to five thousand rupees, or both.

CHAPTER XVIII.†

OF OFFENCES AFFECTING THE HUMAN BODY.

OF OFFENCES AFFECTING LIFE.

294. Whoever does any act, or omits what he is legally bound to do, with the intention of thereby causing, or with the knowledge that he is likely thereby to cause, the death of any person, and does by such act or omission cause the death of any person, is said to commit the offence of "voluntary culpable homicide."

Illustrations.

(*a*) A lays sticks and turf over a pit, with the intention of thereby causing death, or with the knowledge that death is likely to be thereby caused. Z, believing the ground to be firm, treads on it, falls in, and is killed. A has committed the offence of voluntary culpable homicide.

(*b*) A, with the intention or knowledge aforesaid, relates agitating tidings to Z, who is in a critical stage of a dangerous illness; Z dies in consequence. A has committed the offence of voluntary culpable homicide.

(*c*) A, with the intention or knowledge aforesaid, gives Z his choice whether Z will kill himself, or suffer lingering torture; Z kills himself in consequence. A has committed the offence of voluntary culpable homicide.

(*d*) A, with the intention or knowledge aforesaid, falsely deposes before a court of justice that he saw Z commit a capital crime. Z is convicted and executed in consequence. A has committed the offence of voluntary culpable homicide.

(*e*) A is hired to guide Z through a jungle. In the midst of the jungle, A, no circumstance having occurred to release him from his legal obligation to guide Z through the jungle, with such intention or knowledge as aforesaid, leaves Z. Z dies in consequence. A has committed the offence of voluntary culpable homicide.

---

* See Appendix, Note L. † See Appendix, Note M.

(*f*) A, being legally bound to furnish food to Z, who is the mother of a sucking child, omits to furnish her with food, intending or knowing it to be likely that Z's death may be the consequence of the omission. Z survives, but the child is starved to death in consequence of the failure of milk, which is caused by A's omission. Here, even if A did not know of the existence of the child, he has committed the offence of voluntary culpable homicide.

(*g*) A keeps Z in wrongful confinement, and is therefore legally bound (see clause 338) to furnish Z with what he knows to be necessary to prevent Z from being in danger of death. A, knowing that Z is likely to die if medical advice be not procured, illegally omits to procure such advice. Z dies in consequence. A has committed the offence of voluntary culpable homicide.

(*h*) A knows Z to be behind a bush. B does not know it. A, intending to cause, or knowing himself to be likely to cause, Z's death, induces B to fire at the bush. B fires and kills Z. Here, B may be guilty of no offence, or if his firing was, under the circumstances, a rash act, he may be guilty of the offence defined in clause 304. But A has committed the offence of voluntary culpable homicide.

295. Voluntary culpable homicide is "murder," unless it be of one of the three mitigated descriptions hereinafter enumerated; (that is to say)

First.—Manslaughter.

Secondly.—Voluntary culpable homicide by consent.

Thirdly.—Voluntary culpable homicide in defence.

296. If a person, by doing any thing which he intends or knows to be likely to cause death, commits voluntary culpable homicide on a person whose death he neither intends nor knows himself to be likely to cause, the voluntary culpable homicide committed by the offender is of the same description of which it would have been if he had caused the death which he intended or knew himself to be likely to cause.

297. Voluntary culpable homicide is "manslaughter," when it is committed on grave and sudden provocation, by causing the death of the person who gave that provocation.

Explanation.—Provocation is designated as "grave," when it is such as would be likely to move a person of ordinary temper to violent passion, and is not given by any thing done in obedience to the law, or by any thing authorized by the law of civil or criminal procedure, or by any thing done by a public servant in the exercise of the lawful powers of such public servant, or by any thing done by any person in the exercise of the right of private defence against the offender.

Illustrations.

(*a*) A, under the influence of passion excited by a provocation given by Z, intentionally kills Y, Z's child. This is not manslaughter, but murder.

(*b*) A is lawfully arrested by Z, a bailiff. A is excited to sudden and violent passion by the arrest, and voluntarily kills Z. This is not manslaughter, but murder.

(*c*) A appears as a witness before Z, a magistrate. Z says that he does not believe a word of A's deposition, and that A has perjured himself. A is moved to sudden passion by these words, and kills Z. This is not manslaughter, but murder.

(*d*) A attempts to pull Z's nose. Z, in the exercise of the right of private defence, strikes A. A is moved to sudden and violent passion by the blow, and kills Z. This is not manslaughter, but murder.

(*e*) Z strikes B. B is by this provocation excited to violent rage. A, a bystander, intending to take advantage of B's rage in order to cause Z's death, puts a knife into B's hand. B kills Z with the knife. Here, B may have committed only manslaughter, but A has committed murder.

(*f*) Y gives grave and sudden provocation to A. A, on this provocation, fires a pistol at Y, neither intending nor knowing himself to be likely to kill Z, who is near him, but out of sight. A kills Z. Here, A has committed manslaughter.

298. Voluntary culpable homicide is "voluntary culpable homicide by consent," when the person whose death is caused, being above twelve years of age, suffers death, or takes the risk of death, by his own choice:

Provided,

First.—That the offender does not induce the person whose death is caused to make that choice by directly or indirectly putting that person in fear of any injury.

Secondly.—That the person whose death has been caused is not, from youth, mental imbecility, derangement, intoxication or passion, unable to understand the nature and consequences of his choice.

Thirdly.—That the offender does not know that the person whose death is caused was induced to make the choice by any deception or concealment.

Fourthly.—That the offender does not conceal from the person whose death is caused any thing which the offender knew to be likely to cause that person to change his mind.

Explanation.—Voluntary culpable homicide committed by inducing a person voluntarily to put himself to death is voluntary culpable homicide by consent, except when it is murder.

Illustrations.

(*a*) Z, a Hindoo widow, consents to be burned with the corpse of her husband. A kindles the pile. Here, A has committed voluntary culpable homicide by consent.

(*b*) A, by instigation, voluntarily causes Z, a child under twelve years of age, to commit suicide. Here, on account of Z's youth, the offence cannot be voluntary culpable homicide by consent. A has therefore committed murder.

(*c*) A, by deceiving Z into a belief that Z's family have perished at sea, voluntarily causes Z to commit suicide. Here, on account of the deception practised by A, the offence cannot be voluntary culpable homicide by consent. A has therefore committed murder.

299. Voluntary culpable homicide is "voluntary culpable homicide in defence," when it is committed by causing death under such circumstances that such causing of death would be no offence if the right of private defence extended to the voluntary causing of death in cases of assault not falling under any of the descriptions enumerated in clause 76, or in cases of theft, mischief or criminal trespass not falling under any of the descriptions enumerated in clause 79.

Illustrations.

(*a*) Z attempts to horsewhip A, not in such a manner as to cause grievous hurt to A. A draws out a pistol. Z persists in the assault. A, believing in good faith that he can by no other means prevent himself from being horsewhipped, shoots Z dead. A has committed voluntary culpable homicide in defence.

(*b*) Z commits simple theft on A's horse, and rides away with it. Here, A has a right of private defence which lasts till either Z can effect his retreat with the property, or till A can recover his horse, but which does not extend to the infliction of death, inasmuch as A is in no danger of death or hurt. A pursues Z, and, not being able to overtake him, shoots him dead. A has committed voluntary culpable homicide in defence.

(*c*) Z commits an assault not of a dangerous description on A. A, knowing that he can defend himself from the assault without killing Z, kills Z. Here, as A's act would be an offence even if the right of private defence in cases of assault of the descriptions not enumerated in clause 76 extended to the voluntary infliction of death, A has committed voluntary culpable homicide which is not voluntary culpable homicide in defence, but which, according to the circumstances, will be manslaughter or murder.

300. Whoever commits murder shall be punished with death, or transportation for life, or rigorous imprisonment for life, and shall also be liable to fine.

301. Whoever commits manslaughter shall be punished with imprisonment of either description for a term which may extend to fourteen years, or fine, or both.

302. Whoever commits voluntary culpable homicide by consent shall be punished with imprisonment of either description for a term which may extend to fourteen years and must not be less than two years, and shall also be liable to fine.

303. Whoever commits voluntary culpable homicide in defence shall be punished with imprisonment of either description for a term which may extend to fourteen years, or fine, or both.

304. Whoever causes the death of any person by any act or any illegal omission, which act or omission was so rash or negligent as to indicate a want of due regard for human life, shall be punished with imprisonment of either description for a term which may extend to two years, or fine, or both.

305. If the act or illegal omission, whereby death is caused in the manner described in the last preceding clause, be, apart from the circumstance of its having caused death, an offence other than the offence defined in clause 327, or an attempt to commit an offence, the offender shall be liable to the punishment of the offence so committed or attempted, in addition to the punishment provided by the last preceding clause.

Explanation.—In cases in which the doing of a certain thing and the attempting to do that thing are distinct offences, if the offence defined in the last preceding clause be committed in the attempting to do that thing, the additional punishment to which the offender is liable is the punishment not of attempting to do that thing, but of doing that thing.

Illustration.

A uses force to Z, a woman, intending to ravish her. He does not ravish her, but commits the offence defined in clause 304. Here, the term of imprisonment to which A has made himself liable is to be regulated not by the term of imprisonment assigned to the offence of attempting to ravish, but by the term of imprisonment assigned to actual rape, that is to say, A is liable to rigorous imprisonment for a term of not more than sixteen nor less than two years.

306. If any child under twelve years of age, any insane person, any delirious person, any idiot or any person in a state of intoxication, commits suicide, whoever previously abets by aid the commission of such suicide shall be punished with death, or transportation for life, or rigorous imprisonment for life, and shall also be liable to fine.

307. If any person commits suicide, whoever previously abets by aid the commission of such suicide shall be punished with imprisonment of either description for a term which may extend to fourteen years and must not be less than two years, and shall also be liable to fine.

308. Whoever does any act, or omits what he is legally bound to do, with such intention or knowledge and under such circumstances that if he by that act or omission caused death he would be guilty of murder, and carries that act or omission to such a length as at the time of carrying it to that length he contemplates as sufficient to cause death, shall be punished with transportation for life, or with rigorous imprisonment for a term which may extend to life, and must not be less than seven years, and shall also be liable to fine.

Illustrations.

(*a*) A, intending to murder Z by means of a spring gun, purchases such a gun. A has not yet committed the offence defined in this clause. A sets the gun loaded in Z's path, and leaves it there. A has committed the offence defined in this clause.

(*b*) A, intending to murder Z by poison, purchases poison, and mixes the same with food which remains in A's keeping. A has not yet committed the offence defined in this clause. A places the food on Z's table, or delivers it to Z's servants to place it on Z's table. A has committed the offence defined in this clause.

309. Whoever does any act, or omits what he is legally bound to do, with such intention or knowledge and under such circumstances that if he by that act or omission caused death he would be guilty of voluntary culpable homicide, and carries that act or omission to such a length as at the time of carrying it to that length he contemplates as sufficient to cause death, shall be punished with imprisonment of either description for a term which may extend to three years, or fine, or both.

Illustrations.

(*a*) A, on grave and sudden provocation, fires a pistol at Z, under such circumstances that if he thereby caused death he would be guilty of manslaughter. A has committed the offence defined in this clause.

(*b*) A lights a pile prepared for a suttee, under such circumstances that if he thereby caused death he would be guilty of voluntary culpable homicide by consent. A has committed the offence defined in this clause.

(*c*) A pursues a thief, and fires at him, under such circumstances that if he killed the thief he would commit voluntary culpable homicide in defence. A has committed the offence defined in this clause.

310. Whoever belongs or has at any time belonged to any gang of persons associated for the purpose of gaining a livelihood by inveigling and murdering travellers in order to take the property of such travellers, is designated as a "thug."

311. Whoever is a thug shall be punished with transportation for life, or imprisonment of either description for life, and shall also be liable to fine.

Of the Causing of Miscarriage.

312. Every woman who, being with child, voluntarily causes herself to miscarry, and every person who voluntarily causes a woman with child to miscarry, shall, if such miscarriage be not caused in good faith for the purpose of saving the life of the woman, be punished with imprisonment of either description for a term which may extend to three years, or fine, or both.

313. If any person commits the offence defined in the last preceding clause without the free and intelligent consent of the woman, the punishment of causing the miscarriage shall be in excess of any punishment to which the offender may be liable by reason of any hurt which he may have caused or attempted to cause to the woman.

OF HURT.

314. All bodily pain, disease and infirmity is designated as "hurt."

315. The following kinds of hurt are designated as "grievous":

First.—Emasculation.

Secondly.—Permanent privation of the sight of either eye.

Thirdly.—Permanent privation of the hearing of either ear.

Fourthly.—Privation of any member or joint.

Fifthly.—Destruction or permanent impairing of the powers of any member or joint.

Sixthly.—Permanent disfiguration of the head or face.

Seventhly.—Fracture or dislocation of any bone other than a tooth.

Eighthly.—Such hurt that the sufferer is, during the space of twenty days, in bodily pain, diseased, or unable to follow his ordinary pursuits.

316. Whoever does any act or omits what he is legally bound to do, with the intention of thereby causing hurt to any person, or with the knowledge that he is likely thereby to cause hurt to any person, and does thereby cause hurt to any person, is said "voluntarily to cause hurt."

317. Whoever voluntarily causes hurt, if the hurt which he intends to cause, or knows himself to be likely to cause, is grievous hurt, and if the hurt which he causes is grievous hurt, is said "voluntarily to cause grievous hurt."

Explanation.—A person is not said voluntarily to cause grievous hurt except when he both causes grievous hurt, and intends or knows himself to be likely to cause grievous hurt. But he is said voluntarily to cause grievous hurt, if, intending or knowing himself to be likely to cause grievous hurt of one kind, he actually causes grievous hurt of another kind.

Illustration.

A, intending or knowing himself to be likely permanently to disfigure Z's face, gives Z a blow which does not permanently disfigure Z's face, but which causes Z to be diseased during twenty days. A has voluntarily caused grievous hurt.

318. Whoever, except in the case provided for in clause 325, voluntarily causes hurt, shall be punished with imprisonment of either description for a term which may extend to one year, or fine which may extend to one thousand rupees, or both.

319. Whoever, except in the case provided for in clause 326, voluntarily causes grievous hurt, shall be punished with imprisonment of either description for a term which may extend to ten years and must not be less than six months, and shall also be liable to fine.

320. Whoever voluntarily causes hurt in an attempt to commit murder shall be punished with transportation for life, or rigorous imprisonment for a term which may extend to life and must not be less than seven years, and shall also be liable to fine.

321. Whoever voluntarily causes hurt for the purpose of extorting from the sufferer, or from any person interested in the sufferer, any property, or of constraining the sufferer of the hurt, or some person interested in such sufferer, to give any information which may lead to a wrongful transfer of any property, or to do any thing illegal or disreputable, shall be punished with rigorous imprisonment for a term which may extend to fourteen years and must not be less than one year, and shall also be liable to fine.

322. Whoever voluntarily causes grievous hurt for the purpose of extorting any property, or of constraining the sufferer of the hurt, or some person interested in such sufferer, to give any information which may lead to a wrongful transfer of any property, or to do any thing illegal or disreputable, shall be punished with transportation for life, or rigorous imprisonment for a term which may extend to life and must not be less than seven years, and shall also be liable to fine.

323. Whoever, except in the case provided for in clause 325, voluntarily causes hurt by means of the edge or point of any sharp instrument, or by means of fire or any heated substance, or by means of any corrosive substance, or by means of any explosive substance, or by means of any substance which it is deleterious to the human body to inhale, to swallow, or to receive into the blood, or by means of any animal, shall be punished with imprisonment of either description for a term which may extend to three years, or fine, or both.

324. Whoever, except in the case provided for in clause 326, voluntarily causes grievous hurt by means of the edge or point of any sharp instrument, or by means of fire or any heated substance, or by means of any corrosive substance, or by means of any explosive substance, or by means of any substance which it is deleterious to the human body to inhale, to swallow, or to receive into the blood, or by means of any animal, shall be punished with imprisonment of either description for a term which may extend to fourteen years and must not be less than one year, and shall also be liable to fine.

325. Whoever voluntarily causes hurt, on grave* and sudden provocation, if he neither intends nor knows himself to be likely to cause hurt to any person other than the person who gave the provocation, shall be punished with imprisonment of either description for a term which may extend to one month, or fine which may extend to five hundred rupees, or both.

326. Whoever voluntarily causes grievous hurt on grave and sudden provocation, if he neither intends nor knows himself to be likely to cause grievous hurt to any person other than the person who gave the provo-

---

* For the definition of grave provocation, see clause 297.

cation, shall be punished with imprisonment of either description for a term which may extend to one year, or fine which may extend to two thousand rupees, or both.

327. Whoever causes grievous hurt to any person by any act or illegal omission, which act or omission is so rash or negligent as to indicate a want of due regard for the safety of others, shall be punished with imprisonment of either description for a term which may extend to six months, or fine which may extend to one thousand rupees, or both.

328. If the act or illegal omission, whereby grievous hurt is caused in the manner described in the last preceding clause, be, apart from the circumstance of its having caused grievous hurt, an offence, the punishment shall be cumulative.

329. Whoever does any act, or omits what he is legally bound to do, intending or knowing it to be likely that by such act or omission he may cause grievous hurt, the voluntary causing of which grievous hurt would be an offence other than the offence defined in clause 326, and carries that act or omission to such a length as, at the time of carrying it to that length, he contemplates as sufficient to cause grievous hurt, shall be punished with imprisonment of either description for a term which may extend to one-half of the term of imprisonment to which he would have been liable if he had actually caused the grievous hurt which he intended to cause, or knew himself to be likely to cause, or fine, or both.

Illustrations.

(*a*) A ties a rope across a road by night, intending or knowing it to be likely that Z's horse may stumble over it, and that grievous hurt to Z may be the consequence. Grievous hurt is not caused. Here, if grievous hurt had been caused, A would have been liable to imprisonment for a term not exceeding ten years. A, therefore, is liable to imprisonment for a term not exceeding five years.

(*b*) A lays a steel-trap in Z's path, intending or knowing it to be likely that he may thereby cause grievous hurt to Z. Here, if grievous hurt were actually caused to Z, A, as having caused grievous hurt by means of a sharp instrument, would be liable to imprisonment for a term not exceeding fourteen years. If therefore no grievous hurt is caused, A is liable to imprisonment for a term not exceeding seven years.

(*c*) A puts an explosive substance under the seal of a letter, intending or knowing it to be likely that he shall thereby cause grievous hurt to some person. While A keeps the letter in his own custody, he has not committed the offence defined in this clause. As soon as he sends it to the post, he has committed the offence defined in this clause. If he actually causes by these means grievous hurt to any person, as the hurt is caused by means of an explosive substance, he is liable to imprisonment for a term not exceeding fourteen years. If he does not actually cause grievous hurt to any person, he is liable to imprisonment for a term not exceeding seven years.

Of wrongful Restraint and wrongful Confinement.

330. Whoever by any act or by any illegal omission voluntarily obstructs any person so as to prevent that person from proceeding in any direction in which that person has a right to proceed, is said "wrongfully to restrain" that person.

Explanation.—A person may obstruct another by causing it to appear to that other impossible, difficult or dangerous to proceed, as well as by causing it actually to be impossible, difficult or dangerous for that other to proceed.

Illustrations.

(*a*) A builds a wall across a path along which Z has a right to pass. Z is thereby prevented from passing. A wrongfully restrains Z.

(*b*) A illegally omits to take proper order with a furious buffalo which is in his possession (see clause 273), and thus voluntarily deters Z from passing along a road along which Z has a right to pass. A wrongfully restrains Z.

(*c*) A threatens to set a savage dog at Z, if Z goes along a path along which Z has a right to go. Z is thus prevented from going along that path. A wrongfully restrains Z.

(*d*) In the last illustration, if the dog is not really savage, but if A voluntarily causes Z to think that it is savage, and thereby prevents Z from going along the path, A wrongfully restrains Z.

331. Whoever wrongfully restrains any person in such a manner as to prevent that person from proceeding beyond certain circumscribing limits, is said "wrongfully to confine" that person.

Illustrations.

(*a*) A causes Z to go within a walled space, and locks Z in. Z is thus prevented from proceeding in any direction beyond the circumscribing line of wall. A wrongfully confines Z.

(*b*) In the last illustration, if there is in some nook of the walled space a door which is not secured, but which may easily escape observation, as A had voluntarily caused it to appear to Z impossible to proceed beyond the line of wall, A has wrongfully confined Z.

(*c*) A places men with fire-arms at the outlets of a building, and tells Z that they will fire at Z if Z attempts to leave the building. A wrongfully confines Z.

332. Whoever wrongfully restrains any person shall be punished with imprisonment of either description for a term which may extend to one month, or fine which may extend to five hundred rupees, or both.

333. Whoever wrongfully confines any person shall be punished with imprisonment of either description for a term which may extend to one year, or fine which may extend to one thousand rupees, or both.

334. Whoever wrongfully confines any person for three days or more shall be punished with imprisonment of either description for a term which may extend to two years, or fine, or both.

335. Whoever wrongfully confines any person for ten days or more shall be punished with imprisonment of either description for a term which may extend to three years, in addition to three days for every day of such wrongful confinement, and must not be less than six months, in addition to one day for every day of such wrongful confinement, and shall also be liable to fine.

336. Whoever keeps any person in wrongful confinement, knowing that a writ for the liberation of that person has been issued in the manner described in the Code of Procedure, shall be punished with imprisonment of either description for a term which may extend to three years and must not be less than one year, in addition to any term of imprisonment to which he may be liable under the last preceding clause, and shall also be liable to fine.

337. Whoever wrongfully confines any person, for the purpose of extorting from the person confined, or from any person interested in the person confined, any property, or of constraining the person confined, or any person interested in the person confined, to give any information which may lead to a wrongful transfer of property, or to do any thing illegal or disreputable, shall be punished with imprisonment of either description for a term which may extend to three years and must not be less than one year, in addition to any term of imprisonment to which he may be liable under either of the two last preceding clauses, and shall also be liable to fine.

338. Whoever, while keeping any person in wrongful confinement, knowing a certain thing to be necessary to prevent the person confined from being in danger of death, or hurt, voluntarily omits to furnish that thing to the person confined, shall be punished with imprisonment of either description for a term which may extend to one year, or fine, or both.

Illustration.

Z's eyes are in such a state as to require constant medical care. A wrongfully confines Z, and knowing that without medical attendance Z is likely to lose his eye-sight, omits to procure such medical attendance. A has committed the offence defined in this clause. If Z loses his eye-sight, A has by an illegal omission voluntarily caused Z to lose his eye-sight, and has thus become liable to the punishment of having voluntarily caused grievous hurt to Z.

Of Assault.

339. A person is said to use force to another, if he causes motion or change of motion or cessation of motion to that other, or if he causes to any substance such motion or change of motion or cessation of motion as brings that substance into contact with any part of that other's body, or with any thing which that other is wearing or carrying, or with any thing so situated that such contact affects that other's sense of feeling:

Provided, that the person causing the motion or change of motion or cessation of motion, causes that motion, change of motion or cessation of motion in one of the three ways hereinafter described:

First.—By his own bodily power.

Secondly.—By disposing any substances in such a manner that the motion or change or cessation of motion takes place without any further act on his part, or on the part of any other person.

Thirdly.—By inducing any animal to move, to change its motion, or to cease to move.

340. Whoever intentionally uses force, or attempts to use force, to any person without that person's consent, in order to the committing of any offence, or intending or knowing it to be likely that, by such use of force, he may cause to the person to whom the force is used injury, fear or annoyance, is said to commit an assault.

Illustrations.

(*a*) Z is sitting in a moored boat on a river. A unfastens the moorings, and thus intentionally causes the boat to drift down the stream. Here, A intentionally causes motion to Z, and he does this by disposing substances in such a manner that the motion is produced without any other act on any person's part. A has therefore intentionally used force to Z; and if he has done so without Z's consent, in order to the committing of any offence, or intending or knowing it to be likely that this use of force may cause injury, fear or annoyance to Z, A has committed an assault.

(*b*) Z is riding in a chariot. A lashes Z's horses, and thereby attempts to cause them to quicken their pace. Here, A has attempted to cause change of motion to Z by inducing animals to change their motion. A has therefore attempted to use force to Z, and if A has done this without Z's consent, intending or knowing it to be likely that he may thereby injure, frighten or annoy Z, A has committed an assault.

(*c*) Z is riding in a palanquin. A, intending to rob Z, seizes the pole, and stops the palanquin. Here, A has caused cessation of motion to Z, and he has done this by his own bodily power. A has therefore used force to Z. And as A has acted thus, intentionally, without Z's consent, in order to the commission of an offence, A has committed an assault.

(*d*) A intentionally pushes against Z in the street. Here, A has by his own bodily power moved his own person so as to bring it into contact with Z. He has therefore intentionally used force to Z; and if he has done so without Z's consent, intending or knowing it to be likely that he may thereby injure, frighten or annoy Z, he has committed an assault.

(*e*) A throws a stone, intending or knowing it to be likely that the stone will be thus brought into contact with Z, or with Z's clothes, or with something carried by Z, or that it will strike water, and dash up the water against Z, or Z's clothes, or something carried by Z. Here, A has attempted to use force to Z, and if he has done so without Z's consent, intending thereby to injure, frighten or annoy Z, he has committed an assault.

(*f*) A intentionally pulls up a woman's veil. Here, A intentionally uses force to her, and if he does so without her consent, intending or knowing it to be likely that he may thereby injure, frighten or annoy her, he commits an assault.

(*g*) Z is bathing. A pours into the bath water which he knows to be boiling. Here, A intentionally by his own bodily power causes such motion in the boiling water as brings that water into contact with Z, or with other water so situated that such contact must affect Z's sense of feeling. A has therefore intentionally used force to Z, and if he has done this without Z's consent, intending or knowing it to be likely that he may thereby cause injury, fear or annoyance to Z, A has committed an assault.

(*h*) A attempts to incite a dog to spring upon Z without Z's consent. Here, if A intends to cause injury, fear or annoyance to Z, he commits an assault.

341. Whoever makes any gesture or any preparation, intending or knowing it to be likely that such gesture or preparation will cause any person present to apprehend that he who makes that gesture or preparation is about to assault that person, is said "to make show of assault."

Explanation.—Mere words do not amount to a show of assault; but the words which a person uses may give to his gestures or preparations such a meaning as may make those gestures or preparations amount to show of assault.

Illustrations.

(*a*) A shakes his fist at Z, intending or knowing it to be likely that he may thereby cause Z to believe that A is about to assault Z. A has made show of assault.

(*b*) A begins to unloose the muzzle of a ferocious dog, intending or knowing it to be likely that he may thereby cause Z to believe that he is about to assault Z. A has made show of assault.

(*c*) A takes up a stick, saying to Z, "I will give you a beating." Here, though the words used by A could in no case amount to show of assault, and though the mere gesture, unaccompanied by any other circumstances, might not amount to show of assault, it is nevertheless possible that the gesture explained by the words may be show of assault.

342. Whoever assaults any person, otherwise than on grave* and sudden provocation given by that person, shall be punished with imprisonment of either description for a term which may extend to three months, or fine which may extend to five hundred rupees, or both.

343. Whoever, in attempting to commit murder, assaults any person, shall be punished with transportation for life, or rigorous imprisonment for a term which may extend to life, and must not be less than seven years, and shall also be liable to fine.

344. Whoever, in attempting to commit the offence of kidnapping, assaults any person, shall be punished with imprisonment of either description for a term which may extend to half the term for which the offender would have been liable to be imprisoned if he had committed the kidnapping which he has attempted to commit, and must not be less than six months, and shall also be liable to fine.

345. Whoever assaults any person in attempting to cause grievous hurt to that person, otherwise than on grave and sudden provocation given by that person, shall be punished with imprisonment of either description for a term which may extend to one-third part of the term for which he might have been imprisoned if he had actually caused such hurt as he attempted to cause, or fine, or both.

346. Whoever assaults any woman in attempting to commit rape on her, shall be punished with imprisonment of either description for a term which may extend to three years and must not be less than six months, and shall also be liable to fine.

347. Whoever assaults any woman, intending thereby to outrage her modesty, shall be punished with imprisonment of either description for a term which may extend to two years, or fine, or both.

348. Whoever assaults any person, intending thereby to dishonour that person, otherwise than on grave and sudden provocation given by that person, shall be punished with imprisonment of either description for a term which may extend to two years, or fine, or both.

349. Whoever assaults any person in attempting to commit theft on any property which that person is then wearing or carrying, shall be punished with imprisonment of either description for a term which may extend to two years, or fine, or both.

350. Whoever assaults any person in attempting wrongfully to confine that person, shall be punished with imprisonment of either description for a term which may extend to one year, or fine which may extend to one thousand rupees, or both.

351. Whoever assaults any person, on grave and sudden provocation given by that person, shall be punished with imprisonment of either description for a term which may extend to one month, or fine which may extend to two hundred rupees, or both.

352. Whoever makes show of assault, except on grave and sudden provocation given by the person whom he makes show of being about to assault, shall be punished with imprisonment of either description for a

* For the explanation of grave provocation, see clause 297.

term which may extend to one month, or fine which may extend to two hundred rupees, or both.

Of Kidnapping.

353. "Kidnapping" is of two kinds, kidnapping from the territories of the East India Company, and kidnapping from lawful guardianship.

354. Whoever conveys beyond the limits of the territories of the East India Company, or takes on board of any vessel with the intention of conveying beyond the limits of the said territories, any person without the free and intelligent consent of that person, or of some person legally authorized to consent on behalf of that person, or with such consent, but knowing that such consent has been obtained by deception or concealment as to the place of destination, or the future treatment of that person, is said to "kidnap that person from the territories of the East India Company."

Whoever conveys any child under twelve years of age out of the keeping of the lawful guardian or guardians of such child, without the free and intelligent consent of such guardian or guardians, or with such consent, but knowing that such consent has been obtained by deception or concealment as to the place of destination or the future treatment of the child, or that such consent is the effect of collusion between himself and such guardian or guardians for any purpose of injury to the child, is said to "kidnap that child from lawful guardianship."

355. Whoever kidnaps any person shall be punished with imprisonment of either description for a term which may extend to seven years and must not be less than one year, and shall also be liable to fine.

356. Whoever kidnaps any person, intending or knowing it to be likely that murder may, in consequence of such kidnapping, be committed on that person, shall be punished with transportation for life, or rigorous imprisonment for a term which may extend to life, and must not be less than seven years, and shall also be liable to fine.

Illustration.

A kidnaps Z from the territories of the East India Company, intending or knowing it to be likely that Z may be sacrificed to an idol. A has committed the offence defined in this clause.

357. Whoever kidnaps any person, intending or knowing it to be likely that the consequence of such kidnapping may be grievous hurt to that person, or the rape of that person, or the subjecting of that person to unnatural lust, or the slavery of that person, shall be punished with imprisonment of either description for a term which may extend to fourteen years and must not be less than two years, and shall also be liable to fine.

358. Whoever, being in charge of any vessel, knowingly suffers any person, who cannot without a certain order or permit legally embark on board of such vessel for any place which is not within the territories of the East India Company, to embark on board of the said vessel for any such place, shall be punished with simple imprisonment for a term which may extend to one month for every person so suffered to embark, or fine which may extend to two hundred rupees for every person so suffered to embark, or both.

Of Rape.

359. A man is said to commit "rape" who, except in the case hereinafter excepted, has sexual intercourse with a woman under circumstances falling under any of the five following descriptions:

First.—Against her will.

Secondly.—Without her consent, while she is insensible.

Thirdly.—With her consent, when her consent has been obtained by putting her in fear of death, or of hurt.

Fourthly.—With her consent, when the man knows that her consent is given because she believes that he is a different man to whom she is or believes herself to be married.

Fifthly.—With or without her consent, when she is under nine years of age.

Explanation.—Penetration is sufficient to constitute the sexual intercourse necessary to the offence of rape.

Exception.—Sexual intercourse by a man with his own wife is in no case rape.

360. Whoever commits rape shall be punished with imprisonment of either description for a term which may extend to fourteen years and must not be less than two years, and shall also be liable to fine.

Of unnatural Offences.

361. Whoever, intending to gratify unnatural lust, touches for that purpose any person, or any animal, or is by his own consent touched by any person, for the purpose of gratifying unnatural lust, shall be punished with imprisonment of either description for a term which may extend to fourteen years and must not be less than two years, and shall also be liable to fine.

362. Whoever, intending to gratify unnatural lust, touches for that purpose any person without that person's free and intelligent consent, shall be punished with imprisonment of either description for a term which may extend to life and must not be less than seven years, and shall also be liable to fine.

CHAPTER XIX.

OF OFFENCES AGAINST PROPERTY.*

Of Theft.

363. Whoever, intending to take fraudulently any thing which is property, and which is not attached to the earth, out of the possession of any person, without that person's consent, moves that thing in order to such taking, is said to commit "theft."

Explanations.—All things fastened to any thing attached to the earth are said to be attached to the earth.

A thing which is attached to the earth becomes capable of being the subject of theft as soon as it is severed from the earth.

---

* See Appendix, Note N.

A moving effected by the same act which effects the severance may be a theft.

The words to "move a thing" include the cases in which a person causes a thing to move by removing an obstacle which prevented it from moving, or by separating it from any other thing.

A person who by any means induces an animal to move in a direction in which he intends to induce that animal to move, is said to move that animal, and to move every thing which in consequence of the motion so caused is moved by that animal.

The consent mentioned in the definition may be express or implied, and may be given either by the person in possession, or by any person having for that purpose authority, either express or implied, from the person in possession.

A person may commit theft, though he intends to restore the property after taking it.

Illustrations.

(*a*) A cuts down a tree on Z's ground, with the intention of fraudulently taking the tree out of Z's possession without Z's consent. Here, as soon as A has severed the tree in order to such taking, he has committed theft.

(*b*) A pulls a bung out of a hogshead of liquor in Z's possession, with the intention of fraudulently taking some of the liquor without Z's consent. As soon as the liquor begins to flow, A has committed theft.

(*c*) A puts a bait for dogs in his pocket, and thus induces Z's dog to follow A. Here, if A's intention be fraudulently to take the dog out of Z's possession without Z's consent, A has committed theft as soon as Z's dog has begun to follow A.

(*d*) A drives Z's sheep before him, with the intention of fraudulently taking them out of Z's possession without Z's consent. As soon as any sheep begins to move in the direction in which A intended that it should move, A has committed theft.

(*e*) A meets a bullock carrying a box of treasure. He drives the bullock in a certain direction in order that he may fraudulently take the treasure. As soon as the bullock begins to move in the direction in which A intends it to move, A has committed theft on the treasure.

(*f*) A, being Z's butler, and intrusted by Z with the care of Z's plate, fraudulently runs away with the plate without Z's consent. Here, the plate, till carried off by A, was still in Z's possession, though it was also in A's possession. A has therefore committed theft.

(*g*) Z, going on a journey, intrusts his plate to A, the keeper of a warehouse, till Z shall return. A carries the plate to a goldsmith, and sells it. Here, the plate was not in Z's possession. It could not therefore be taken out of Z's possession, and A has not committed theft, though he may have committed criminal breach of trust.

(*h*) A finds a ring belonging to Z on a table in the house which Z occupies. Here, the ring is in Z's possession, and if A fraudulently removes it, A commits theft.

(*i*) A finds a ring lying on the high road, not in the possession of any person. A by taking it commits no theft, though he may commit criminal misappropriation of property not in possession.

(*j*) A sees a ring belonging to Z lying on a table in Z's house. Not venturing to misappropriate the ring immediately, for fear of search and detection, A hides the ring in a place where it is highly improbable that it will ever be found by Z, with the intention of taking the ring from the hiding-place, and selling it when the loss is forgotten. Here, A at the time of first hiding the ring commits theft.

(*k*) A delivers his watch to Z, a jeweller, to be regulated. Z carries it to his shop. A, not owing to the jeweller any debt for which the jeweller might lawfully detain the watch as a security, enters the shop openly, takes his watch by force out of Z's hand, and carries it away. Here A, though he may have committed criminal trespass and assault, has committed no theft, inasmuch as what he did was not done fraudulently.

(*l*) But if A carries away the watch out of Z's possession, with the intention of also recovering the value of the watch from Z, A has acted fraudulently, and has therefore committed theft, though the watch is his own property.

(*m*) Again: if A owes money to Z for repairing the watch, and if Z retains the watch lawfully as a security for the debt, and A takes the watch out of Z's possession with the intention of keeping Z out of the money due to him, he commits theft, inasmuch as he takes it fraudulently.

(*n*) Again: if A, having pawned his watch to Z, takes it out of Z's possession without Z's consent, not having paid what he had borrowed on the watch, he commits theft, though the watch is his own property, inasmuch as he takes it fraudulently.

(*o*) A takes an article belonging to Z out of Z's possession, without Z's consent, with the intention of carrying it back to Z and of pretending to have found it, in the hope of thus obtaining a reward from Z. Here, A takes fraudulently; A has therefore committed theft.

(*p*) A being exasperated at a passage in a book which is lying on the counter of Z, a bookseller, snatches it up, and tears it to pieces. A has not committed theft, as he has not acted fraudulently, though he may have committed criminal trespass and mischief.

(*q*) A and Z are gardeners. Z has reared a pine-apple of extraordinary size in hope of obtaining a prize. A takes the pine-apple without Z's consent, produces it before the judges as his own, and obtains the prize. He then sends back the pine-apple to Z. Here, as A took the pine-apple fraudulently, A has committed theft, though he has restored the pine-apple.

(*r*) A takes a gold chain from a child of five years old, with that child's consent, but without the consent of the child's guardians. Here, the chain was in the possession of the child's guardians. A has therefore taken the chain out of the possession of the guardians without their consent, and if he has done this fraudulently, he has committed theft.

(*s*) A takes a rupee from a gentleman's child of twelve years of age, with the child's consent. Here, it is probable that A conceived the rupee to have been placed entirely at the child's disposal. If this was A's impression, A has not committed theft.

(*t*) A, being on friendly terms with Z, goes into Z's library, in Z's absence, and takes away a book without Z's express consent. Here, it is probable that A may have conceived that he had Z's implied consent to use Z's books. If this was A's impression, A has not committed theft.

(*u*) A asks charity from Z's wife. She gives A money, food and clothes, which A knows to belong to Z, her husband. Here, it is probable that A may conceive that Z's wife is authorized to give away alms. If this was A's impression, A has not committed theft.

(*v*) A is the paramour of Z's wife. She gives A valuable property which A knows to belong to her husband Z, and to be such property as she has not authority from Z to give. If A takes the property, he commits theft.

(*w*) A and Z are joint proprietors of a horse. A takes the horse out of Z's possession, intending to use it for a time. A has not committed theft. But if A takes the horse fraudulently out of Z's possession, intending to carry it away altogether, or to sell it and appropriate the whole price, A commits theft.

(*x*) A, having charge, in trust for the Government, of a public treasury, fraudulently appropriates some of the money to himself. Here, as A has not taken the money out of the possession of any person (see clause 19), he is not guilty of theft, but he has committed criminal breach of trust.

(y) A believing in good faith that Z owes him a thousand rupees, and only intending to repay himself what is due to him without injury to any party, takes property out of Z's possession without Z's consent. A, not acting fraudulently, is not guilty of theft. But he may have committed an offence under the provisions contained in the chapter entitled "Of the illegal Pursuit of legal Rights."

(z) But if A, in the last illustration, intended to take and appropriate more than sufficient to repay himself, or intended, after repaying himself, to prosecute Z for the debt, here, as such intention was fraudulent, A commits theft.

364. Whoever commits theft shall be punished with rigorous imprisonment for a term which may extend to three years, or fine, or both.

365. Whoever commits theft within any building, tent or vessel, which building, tent or vessel is used as a human dwelling, or within any building used for the custody of property, in pursuance of a conspiracy, in which conspiracy any person residing or employed within that building, tent or vessel, and also any person not residing nor employed within that building, tent or vessel, are engaged, shall be punished with rigorous imprisonment for a term which may extend to three years and must not be less than six months, and shall also be liable to fine.

366. Whoever commits theft on any letter or packet, which, at the time of the committing of the theft is in the possession of any officer of the Post-office, or on any thing contained in any such letter or packet, shall be punished with rigorous imprisonment for a term which may extend to three years and must not be less than six months, and shall also be liable to fine.

367. Whoever commits theft, having made preparation for causing death, or hurt or restraint, or fear of death, or of hurt or of restraint to any person, in order to the committing of such theft, or in order to retiring after the committing of such theft, or in order to the retaining of property taken by such theft, shall be punished with rigorous imprisonment for a term which may extend to seven years and must not be less than one year, and shall also be liable to fine.

Illustrations.

(a) A commits theft on property in Z's possession, and while committing this theft he has a loaded pistol under his garment, having provided this pistol for the purpose of hurting or terrifying Z in case Z should resist. A has committed the offence defined in this clause.

(b) A picks Z's pocket, having posted several of his companions near him, in order that they may hustle Z if Z should perceive what is passing, and should resist or should attempt to detain A. A has committed the offence defined in this clause.

Of Extortion.

368. Whoever intentionally puts any person in fear of any injury to that person, or to any other, and thereby fraudulently induces the person so put in fear to deliver any property to any person, or to consent that any person shall retain any property, or to affix a seal to any substance, or to make, alter or destroy the whole or any part of any document which is or purports to be a valuable security, is said to commit "extortion."

Illustrations.

(a) A threatens to publish a defamatory life of Z, unless Z gives him money. He thus induces Z to give him money. A has committed extortion.

(*b*) A threatens Z that he will keep Z's child in wrongful confinement, unless Z will sign a promissory note binding Z to pay certain monies to A. Z signs the note. A has committed extortion.

(*c*) A threatens to send bludgeon men to plough up Z's field, unless Z will sign a bond binding himself under a penalty to deliver certain produce to B. Z signs the bond. A has committed extortion.

(*d*) A has lent Z money. Z has repaid the money. A has given Z a receipt. A afterwards threatens Z with bearing false evidence against him on a trial, unless Z will burn the receipt. Z burns the receipt. A has committed extortion.

(*e*) A, by putting Z in fear of injury, fraudulently induces Z to affix his seal to a blank paper. A has committed extortion.

369. Whoever commits extortion shall be punished with imprisonment of either description for a term which may extend to three years, or fine, or both.

370. Whoever, in order to the committing of extortion, puts any person in fear, or attempts to put any person in fear, shall be punished with imprisonment of either description for a term which may extend to one year, or fine, or both.

371. Whoever commits extortion by putting any person in fear, for that person or for any other, of death or of grievous hurt, shall be punished with imprisonment of either description for a term which may extend to fourteen years and must not be less than two years, and shall also be liable to fine.

372. Whoever, in order to the committing of extortion, puts any person in fear, or attempts to put any person in fear, for that person or for any other, of death or of grievous hurt, shall be punished with imprisonment of either description for a term which may extend to seven years and must not be less than one year, and shall also be liable to fine.

373. Whoever commits extortion by putting any person in fear of being falsely accused or defamed as a person under the influence of unnatural lust, shall be punished with imprisonment of either description for a term which may extend to fourteen years and must not be less than two years, and shall also be liable to fine.

374. Whoever, in order to the committing of extortion, puts any person in fear, or attempts to put any person in fear, of being falsely accused or defamed as a person under the influence of unnatural lust, shall be punished with imprisonment of either description for a term which may extend to seven years and must not be less than one year, and shall also be liable to fine.

OF ROBBERY AND DACOITY.

375. In all robbery there is either theft or extortion.

Theft is "robbery" if, in order to the committing of the theft, or in committing the theft, or in carrying away or attempting to carry away property obtained by the theft, the offender for that end voluntarily causes or attempts to cause to any person death, hurt or wrongful restraint, or fear of instant death, of instant hurt, or of instant wrongful restraint.

Extortion is "robbery" if the offender, at the time of committing the extortion, is in the presence of the person put in fear, and commits the extortion by putting that person in fear of instant death, of instant hurt, or of instant wrongful restraint to that person, or to some other person present at the time of committing the extortion, and, by so putting in fear, induces the person so put in fear then and there to deliver up any property.

Illustrations.

(*a*) A holds Z down, and fraudulently takes Z's money and jewels from Z's clothes without Z's consent. Here, A has committed theft, and in order to the committing of that theft, has voluntarily caused wrongful restraint to Z. A has therefore committed robbery.

(*b*) A meets Z on the high road, shows a pistol, and demands Z's purse. Z surrenders his purse. Here, A has extorted the purse from Z by putting the person on whom the extortion has been committed in fear of instant hurt. A has therefore committed robbery.

(*c*) A meets Z and Z's child on the high road. A takes the child, and threatens to fling it down a precipice, unless Z delivers his purse. Z delivers his purse. Here, A has extorted the purse from Z, by causing Z to be in fear of instant hurt to the child who is there present. A has therefore committed robbery on Z.

(*d*) But if A obtains property from Z by saying, "Your child is in the hands of my gang, and will be put to death unless within a month you send us 10,000 rupees," this is extortion, punishable under clause 371, but it is not robbery.

376. Where six or more persons conjointly commit or attempt to commit a robbery, or where the whole number of persons conjointly committing or attempting to commit a robbery, and persons present and aiding such commission or attempt, amounts to six or more, every person so committing, attempting or aiding, is said to commit "dacoity."

377. Whoever commits robbery shall be punished with rigorous imprisonment for a term which may extend to fourteen years and must not be less than two years, and shall also be liable to fine.

378. Whoever attempts to commit robbery shall be punished with rigorous imprisonment for a term which may extend to seven years and must not be less than one year, and shall also be liable to fine.

379. Whoever commits dacoity shall be punished with transportation for life, or with rigorous imprisonment for a term which may extend to life and must not be less than three years, and shall also be liable to fine.

380. If any one of six or more persons, who are conjointly committing dacoity, commits murder in so committing dacoity, every one of those persons shall be punished with death or transportation for life, or rigorous imprisonment for a term which may extend to life, and must not be less than seven years, and shall also be liable to fine.

381. Whoever is one of six or more persons assembled for the purpose of committing dacoity, shall be punished with rigorous imprisonment for a term which may extend to seven years and must not be less than one year, and shall also be liable to fine.

382. If any person voluntarily causes hurt in committing or attempting to commit robbery, or in committing dacoity, the punishment shall be cumulative.

Illustration.

A, in robbing Z of his ear-rings, tears them from his ears, and in so doing causes grievous hurt to Z. A is liable both to the punishment of voluntarily causing grievous hurt and to the punishment of robbery.

Of Criminal Misappropriation of Property not in Possession.

383. Whoever fraudulently takes into his possession any property which is in no person's possession, is said, except in the case hereinafter excepted, "criminally to misappropriate property not in possession."

Exception.—If the person taking the property into his possession neither knows, nor has reason to believe, that any particular party has a better right than himself to the property, or that any particular person can direct him to any such party, he is not guilty of the offence above defined.

Illustrations.

(*a*) A finds a rupee on the high road, not knowing, nor having reason to believe, that the rupee belongs to any particular party, or that any particular person can direct him to the party to whom the rupee belongs. A takes the rupee. Here, A has not committed the offence defined in this clause.

(*b*) A finds a letter on the road containing a bank note. From the direction and the contents of the letter he learns to whom the note belongs. He appropriates the note. Here, he criminally misappropriates property not in possession.

(*c*) A finds a check payable to bearer. He can form no conjecture as to the person who has lost the check. But the name of the person who has drawn the check appears. A knows that this person can direct him to the party in whose favour the check was drawn. A appropriates the check. Here, he criminally misappropriates property not in possession.

384. Whoever criminally misappropriates property not in possession shall be punished with imprisonment of either description for a term which may extend to two years, or fine, or both.

385. Whoever criminally misappropriates property not in possession, knowing that such property was in the possession of a deceased person at the time of that person's decease, and has not since been in the possession of any person legally entitled to such possession, shall be punished with imprisonment of either description for a term which may extend to three years and must not be less than six months, and shall also be liable to fine.

Illustration.

Z dies in possession of furniture and money. His servant, A, before the money comes into the possession of any person entitled to such possession, fraudulently takes possession of it. A has committed the offence defined in this clause.

Of Criminal Breach of Trust.

386. Whoever, being intrusted with the keeping of any property, or with any dominion over any property, and intending fraudulently to cause wrongful loss or risk of wrongful loss to any party for whom he is in trust, disobeys any direction of law prescribing the mode in which such trust is to be discharged, or violates any legal contract express or implied which he has made touching the discharge of such trust with any party from whom such trust was derived, is said to commit "criminal breach of trust."

Illustrations.

(*a*) A, being executor to the will of a deceased person, fraudulently disobeys the law which directs him to divide the effects according to the will, and absconds with them. A has committed criminal breach of trust.

(*b*) A is a warehouse-keeper. Z, going on a journey, intrusts his furniture to A, under a contract that it shall be returned on payment of a stipulated sum for warehouse-room. Z on his return tenders the sum. A fraudulently retains the goods. A has committed criminal breach of trust.

(*c*) A, residing at Calcutta, is agent for Z, residing at Delhi. There is an express or implied contract between A and Z that all sums remitted by Z to A shall be invested by A according to Z's direction. Z remits a lac of rupees to A, with directions to A to invest the same in Company's paper. A fraudulently disobeys the directions, and employs the money in his own business. A has committed criminal breach of trust.

(*d*) But if A, in the last illustration, not fraudulently, but believing that it will be more for Z's advantage to hold shares in the Bank of Bengal, disobeys Z's directions, and buys shares in the Bank of Bengal for Z, instead of buying Company's paper, here, though Z should suffer loss, and should be entitled to bring a civil action against A on account of that loss, yet A, not having acted fraudulently, has not committed criminal breach of trust.

(*e*) A, a revenue officer, is intrusted with public money, and is either directed by law, or bound by a contract express or implied with the Government, to pay into a certain treasury all the public money which he holds. A fraudulently appropriates the money. A has committed criminal breach of trust.

387. Whoever commits criminal breach of trust shall be punished with imprisonment of either description for a term which may extend to three years, or fine, or both.

388. Whoever, being a public servant in the Post-office department, and being, as such, intrusted with the keeping of any letter or packet, commits criminal breach of trust by misappropriating such letter or packet, or any thing contained therein, shall be punished with imprisonment of either description for a term which may extend to three years and must not be less than six months, and shall also be liable to fine.

OF THE RECEIVING OF STOLEN PROPERTY.

389. Property, the possession whereof has been transferred by theft or by robbery, or by criminal misappropriation of property not in possession, or which, being specific property, and having been intrusted to the keeping of a public servant, as such public servant, has been so misappropriated by that public servant that he has thereby committed a criminal breach of trust, is designated as "stolen property." But if such property subsequently comes into the possession of a person legally entitled to the possession thereof, it then ceases to be stolen property.

390. Whoever fraudulently receives any stolen property, knowing the same to be stolen property, shall be punished with imprisonment of either description for a term which may extend to three years, or fine, or both.

391. Whoever fraudulently receives any stolen property, the possession whereof he knows to have been transferred in the commission of dacoity, shall be punished with transportation for life, or with rigorous imprisonment for a term which may extend to life and must not be less than three years, and shall also be liable to fine.

OF CHEATING.

392. Whoever, by intentionally deceiving any person, fraudulently induces the person so deceived to deliver any property to any person, or to consent that any person shall retain any property, or to affix a seal to

any substance, or to make, alter or destroy the whole or any part of any document which is, or purports to be, a valuable security, is said to "cheat."

Illustrations.

(*a*) A, by presenting to Z a bill of exchange which A knows to be forged, intentionally deceives Z, and thereby fraudulently induces Z to discount the bill. A cheats.

(*b*) A, by falsely pretending to be a civil servant of the East India Company, intentionally deceives Z, and thus fraudulently induces Z to let him have on credit goods for which he does not mean to pay. A cheats.

(*c*) A, by putting a counterfeit mark on an article, intentionally deceives Z into a belief that this article was made by a certain celebrated manufacturer, and thus fraudulently induces Z to buy and pay for the article. A cheats.

(*d*) A, by exhibiting to Z a false sample of an article, intentionally deceives Z into believing that the article corresponds with the sample, and thereby fraudulently induces Z to buy and pay for the article. A cheats.

(*e*) A, by tendering in payment for an article a bill on a house with which A keeps no money, and by which A expects that the bill will be dishonoured, intentionally deceives Z, and thereby fraudulently induces Z to deliver the article, intending not to pay for it. A cheats.

(*f*) A, by pledging ornaments of paste to Z as diamonds, intentionally deceives Z and thereby fraudulently induces Z to lend money. A cheats.

(*g*) A intentionally deceives Z into a belief that A means to repay any money that Z may lend to him, and thereby fraudulently induces Z to lend him money. A cheats.

(*h*) A intentionally deceives Z into a belief that A means to deliver to Z a certain quantity of indigo plant, and thereby fraudulently induces Z to advance money. A cheats.

(*i*) A intentionally deceives Z into a belief that A has performed A's part of a contract made with Z, and thereby fraudulently induces Z to pay money. A cheats.

(*j*) A intentionally deceives Z into a belief that A is attached to Z, and thereby induces Z to give him pecuniary assistance. Here, A has, by intentionally deceiving Z, induced Z to deliver up property, but he has not fraudulently induced Z to deliver up property, inasmuch as the property delivered by Z to A becomes, by the delivery, A's property, notwithstanding the deception by which it had been obtained. Therefore A does not cheat.

(*k*) A, by exaggerating the excellence of an article on sale, intentionally deceives Z, and induces Z to buy and pay for that article. Here A has, by intentionally deceiving Z, induced Z to deliver up property. The question whether A has cheated will depend on the question whether he acted fraudulently, that is to say, whether he intended to cause wrongful gain to himself, by means of wrongful loss to Z. If the deception practised by A were such that A has, notwithstanding the deception, a legal right to the price as soon as it has been delivered to him by Z, no gain which the law pronounces to be wrongful has been intended. A, therefore, has not acted fraudulently, and has not cheated. But if the deception practised by A were such that Z has a legal right to have back the price which he has paid, there is wrongful loss and wrongful gain; and if A intended to cause such wrongful loss and wrongful gain, he has acted fraudulently, and has cheated.

393. A person is said to "cheat by personation," if he cheats in any of the ways hereinafter enumerated; namely,

***First.*—By pretending to be some other person.**

***Second.*—By taking a name not his own.**

***Third.*—By taking any title or addition to which he has not a right.**

Fourth.—By dropping any title or addition to which he has a right, and which is ordinarily annexed to the names of those who have a right to it.

Fifth.—By pretending to be of a country of which he is not.

Sixth.—By pretending to be of a calling of which he is not.

Seventh.—By pretending to be of a family of which he is not.

Eighth.—By falsely pretending to hold or to have held any office, real or imaginary.

Ninth.—By falsely pretending to be related by blood or marriage to any person, real or imaginary.

Tenth.—By falsely pretending to be in the employ of any party, real or imaginary.

Illustrations.

(*a*) A cheats by pretending to be a certain rich banker of the same name. A cheats by personation.

(*b*) A cheats by pretending to be B, a person who is deceased. A cheats by personation.

(*c*) John Smith cheats by calling himself Thomas Brown. John Smith cheats by personation.

(*d*) A cheats by taking the title of Rajah, having no right to that title. He cheats by personation.

(*e*) John Smith cheats by falsely calling himself Lieutenant-Colonel John Smith. He cheats by personation.

(*f*) Doctor Smith cheats by dropping the addition of doctor. He cheats by personation.

(*g*) A, an East Indian, cheats by pretending to be an Afghan. He cheats by personation.

(*h*) A cheats by falsely pretending to be a clergyman. He cheats by personation.

(*i*) A cheats by falsely pretending to be a member of one of the sovereign houses of India. He cheats by personation.

(*j*) A cheats by falsely pretending to be, or to have been, Governor of Macao, which is a real office, or French Consul at Singapore, which is an imaginary office. A cheats by personation.

(*k*) A cheats by falsely pretending to be married to B, an heiress. A cheats by personation.

(*l*) A cheats by falsely pretending to be the agent of a great commercial house in Europe. He cheats by personation.

(*m*) A cheats by falsely pretending to be the Vakeel of a native prince. A cheats by personation.

394. Whoever cheats shall be punished with imprisonment of either description for a term which may extend to one year, or fine, or both.

395. Whoever cheats with the knowledge that he is likely thereby to cause wrongful loss to a party whose interest in the transaction to which the cheating relates he was bound, either by law or by legal contract, to protect, shall be punished with imprisonment of either description for a term which may extend to two years, or fine, or both.

396. Whoever cheats by personation shall be punished with imprisonment of either description for a term which may extend to two years, or fine, or both.

397. Whoever attempts to cheat by personation shall be punished with imprisonment of either description for a term which may extend to one year, or fine, or both.*

Of Fraudulent Insolvency.

398. Whoever, being an insolvent trader, or being a trader who contemplates it as likely that he may become insolvent, fraudulently removes, conceals, delivers to any party, or causes to be transferred to any party, any property, intending thereby to prevent, or knowing it to be likely that he may thereby prevent, the distribution of that property according to law among his creditors, shall be punished with imprisonment of either description for a term which may extend to seven years and must not be less than one year, and shall also be liable to fine.

Of Mischief.

399. Whoever causes the destruction of any property, or any such change in any property, or in the situation of any property as destroys or diminishes the value of such property, intending thereby to cause wrongful loss to any party, is said, except in the case hereinafter excepted, to commit "mischief."

Explanation.—A person may commit mischief on his own property.

Exception.—Nothing is mischief which a person does openly, and with the intention in good faith of thereby saving any person from death or hurt, or of thereby preventing a greater loss of property than that which he occasions.

Illustrations.

(*a*) A voluntarily burns a valuable security belonging to Z, intending to cause wrongful loss to Z. A has committed mischief.

(*b*) A introduces water into an ice-house belonging to Z, and thus causes the ice to melt, intending wrongful loss to Z. A has committed mischief.

(*c*) A voluntarily throws into a river a ring belonging to Z, with the intention of thereby causing wrongful loss to Z. A has committed mischief.

(*d*) A, knowing that his effects are about to be taken in execution in order to satisfy a debt due from him to Z, destroys those effects, with the intention of thereby preventing Z from obtaining satisfaction of the debt, and of thus causing wrongful loss to Z. A has committed mischief.

(*e*) A, having insured a ship, voluntarily causes the same to be cast away, with the intention of causing wrongful loss to the underwriters. A has committed mischief.

(*f*) A causes a ship to be cast away, intending thereby to cause wrongful loss to Z, who has lent money on bottomry on the ship. A has committed mischief.

(*g*) A, having joint property with Z in a horse, shoots the horse, intending thereby to cause wrongful loss to Z. A has committed mischief.

(*h*) A, in a storm, throws overboard property of Z, in spite of Z's prohibition, but intending in good faith to save the lives of the crew, or to save property of greater value than that which is thrown overboard. Here, A has not committed mischief.

(*i*) A, in a great fire, pulls down houses in order to prevent the conflagration from spreading. He does this openly, and with the intention in good faith of

---

* For some of the aggravated forms of cheating, see the chapters of offences relating to the coin, to weights and measures, to documents, and to property-marks.

saving human life, or of saving property of more value than the value of the property sacrificed. A has not committed mischief.

400. Whoever commits mischief shall be punished with fine which may extend to ten times the amount of the wrongful loss which he has caused by such mischief.

401. Whoever commits mischief, having taken precautions not to be detected, shall be punished with imprisonment of either description for a term which may extend to six months, or fine, or both.

402. Whoever commits mischief, and thereby voluntarily causes wrongful loss to the amount of five rupees or upwards, shall be punished with imprisonment of either description for a term which may extend to six months, or fine, or both.

403. Whoever commits mischief, and thereby voluntarily causes wrongful loss to the amount of one hundred rupees or upwards, shall be punished with imprisonment of either description for a term which may extend to two years, or fine, or both.

404. Whoever commits mischief, intending thereby to enhance the value of any article, or directly or indirectly to affect the event of any competition so as to cause gain to any person, shall be punished with imprisonment of either description for a term which may extend to two years, or fine, or both.

Illustrations.

(*a*) A and Z are competitors for an agricultural prize. A, knowing that a cow belonging to Z is the finest that is likely to be exhibited, poisons it, in order to secure the prize to himself. A has committed the offence defined in this clause.

(*b*) A, having an article to sell, intending to raise the price of that article, destroys a quantity of that article which belongs to Z. A has committed the offence defined in this clause.

405. Whoever commits mischief with the deliberate intention of thereby insulting or annoying the person to whom he intends to cause wrongful loss, shall be punished with imprisonment of either description for a term which may extend to two years, or fine, or both.

Illustration.

A, with the deliberate intention of insulting or annoying Z, destroys a book which Z values as a rarity, a picture which Z values on account of its resemblance to a friend, a keepsake, a family relic, an animal to which Z is attached. A has in each of these cases committed the offence defined in this clause.

406. Whoever commits or attempts to commit mischief by killing, wounding or poisoning any animal or animals to the value of ten rupees or upwards, shall be punished with imprisonment of either description for a term which may extend to three years, or fine, or both.

407. Whoever commits or attempts to commit mischief on any natural or artificial channel or reservoir of water, intending or knowing it to be likely that he may thereby cause a diminution of cultivation or of agricultural produce, or a failing of the supply of water required for purposes of food or drink by human beings, or by animals which are property, or for purposes of cleanliness, or for the carrying on of any manufacture, shall be punished with imprisonment of either description for a term which may extend to three years, or fine, or both.

408. Whoever commits or attempts to commit mischief on any road, bridge or navigable channel, natural or artificial, intending or knowing it to be likely that he may thereby render it less safe or easy to travel or to convey property by such road, bridge or navigable channel, shall be punished with imprisonment of either description for a term which may extend to three years, or fine, or both.

409. Whoever commits or attempts to commit mischief, intending or knowing it to be likely that such mischief may cause an inundation, attended with loss to the amount of one hundred rupees or upwards, shall be punished with imprisonment of either description for a term which may extend to three years, or fine, or both.

410. Whoever commits or attempts to commit mischief on any light-house, sea-mark or buoy, intending or knowing it to be likely that such mischief may render such light-house, sea-mark or buoy less useful, as such light-house, sea-mark or buoy, shall be punished with imprisonment of either description for a term which may extend to three years, or fine, or both.

411. Whoever commits or attempts to commit mischief on any land-mark, intending or knowing it to be likely that he may thereby render such land-mark less useful, as such, shall be punished with imprisonment of either description for a term which may extend to one year, or fine, or both.

412. Whoever commits or attempts to commit mischief by fire, intending or knowing it to be likely that he may thereby cause the destruction of any property which is not kept within any building, the value of which property amounts to one hundred rupees or upwards, shall be punished with imprisonment of either description for a term which may extend to seven years and must not be less than six months, and shall also be liable to fine.

413. Whoever commits or attempts to commit mischief by fire, intending or knowing it to be likely that he may thereby cause the destruction of any building which is ordinarily used as a human dwelling, or as a place for the custody of property, shall be punished with imprisonment of either description for a term which may extend to fourteen years and must not be less than one year, and shall also be liable to fine.

414. Whoever commits or attempts to commit mischief by fire, intending or knowing it to be likely that buildings ordinarily used as human dwellings, to the number of not less than five, may be consumed, shall be punished with transportation for life, or rigorous imprisonment which may extend to life, and must not be less than seven years, and shall also be liable to fine.

415. Whoever commits or attempts to commit mischief on any decked vessel, intending or knowing it to be likely that he may thereby destroy that decked vessel, or render that decked vessel unsafe, shall be punished with imprisonment of either description for a term which may extend to fourteen years and must not be less than two years, and shall also be liable to fine.

416. Whoever commits or attempts to commit mischief, having made preparation for causing to any person death or hurt or wrongful restraint, or fear of death or of hurt or of wrongful restraint, while committing or attempting to commit such mischief, or while retiring after committing it, shall be punished with imprisonment of either description for a term which may extend to three years and must not be less than six months, and shall also be liable to fine.

417. If any person, by doing any thing which is an offence under the last preceding clause, also commits an offence under any other clause of this Code, the punishment shall be cumulative.*

Of Criminal Trespass.

418. Whoever exercises any dominion over any property, not having a legal right, independent of the consent of any other party, to exercise such dominion, and not having the consent, express or implied, of any party legally entitled to give a consent which would authorize the exercise of such dominion, is said to "trespass."

Illustrations.

(*a*) A walks into a building, not having a right of entry there, and not having the consent of any person entitled to authorize such entry. A trespasses.

(*b*) A goes across Z's field, not having a right of way there, and not having the consent of any person entitled to authorize A so to do. A trespasses.

(*c*) A takes up a book belonging to Z, and reads it, not having any right over the book, and not having the consent of any person entitled to authorize A so to do. A trespasses.

(*d*) A throws rubbish into Z's garden, not having any right over the garden, and not having the consent of any person entitled to authorize A so to do. A trespasses.

(*e*) A climbs up behind Z's carriage, not having a right so to do, and not having the consent of any person entitled to authorize him so to do. A trespasses.

(*f*) A goes into Z's field with Z's consent, but remains in the field after he has been directed by Z to withdraw. A trespasses.

419. Whoever knowingly trespasses in order to the injuring by any offence, to the intimidating, to the insulting or to the annoying of any possessor of the property which is the subject of the trespass, or of any person who, by the permission, express or implied, of such possessor, is exercising any dominion over such property, is said to commit "criminal trespass."

420. Whoever commits criminal trespass by entering or remaining in any building, tent or vessel used as a human dwelling, or any building used as a place for worship, or as a place for the custody of property, is said to commit "house-trespass."

Explanations.—The introduction of any part of the criminal trespasser's body is entering sufficient to constitute house-trespass.

A person who enters not as a house-trespasser, may remain as a house-trespasser.

421. Whoever commits house-trespass, taking precautions to conceal such house-trespass from some person who has a right to exclude or

---

* For mischief to certain documents, see the chapter of offences relating to documents.

eject the trespasser from the building, tent or vessel which is the subject of the trespass, is said to commit "lurking house-trespass."

Explanation.—A person who enters not as a lurking house-trespasser, may remain as a lurking house-trespasser.

422. Whoever commits lurking house-trespass after sunset and before sunrise, is said to commit "lurking house-trespass by night."

Explanation.—A person who enters not by night, may remain as a lurking house-trespasser by night.

423. A person is said to commit "house-breaking" who commits house-trespass in any of the six ways hereinafter described; namely,

First.—If he enters through a passage made by himself, or by any previous abettor of the house-trespass, in order to the committing of the house-trespass.

Second.—If he enters through any passage not intended for human entrance.

Third.—If he enters through any passage which he or any previous abettor of the house-trespass has opened in order to the committing of the house-trespass by any means by which that passage was not intended to be opened.

Fourth.—If he enters by opening any lock with a key which he did not find in the lock, or with a key which was left in the lock, in order to the committing of the house-trespass.

Fifth.—If he effects his entrance by committing an assault, or by making show of assault, or by threatening any person with assault.

Sixth.—If he enters by any passage which he knows to have been fastened against such entrance, and to have been unfastened from within by a previous abettor of the house-trespass.

Illustrations.

(*a*) A commits house-trespass by digging through the wall of Z's house, and putting his hand through the aperture. This is house-breaking.

(*b*) A commits house-trespass by creeping into a ship at a port-hole between decks. This is house-breaking.

(*c*) A commits house-trespass by entering Z's house through a window. This is house-breaking.

(*d*) A commits house-trespass by entering Z's house through the door, having opened the door with a false key. This is house-breaking.

(*e*) A commits house-trespass by entering Z's house through the door, having lifted the latch by putting a wire through a hole in the door. This is house-breaking.

(*f*) A finds the key of Z's house-door, which Z had lost, and commits house-trespass by entering Z's house, having opened the door with that key. This is house-breaking.

(*g*) Z is standing in his door-way. A forces a passage by knocking Z down, and commits house-trespass by entering the house. This is house-breaking.

(*h*) Z, the porter of Y, is standing in Y's door-way. A commits house-trespass by entering the house, having deterred Z from opposing him by shaking a stick at Z. This is house-breaking.

424. Whoever commits house-breaking after sunset and before sunrise is said to commit "house-breaking by night."

425. Whoever commits criminal trespass shall be punished with imprisonment of either description for a term which may extend to one month, or fine which may extend to five hundred rupees, or both.

426. Whoever commits house-trespass shall be punished with imprisonment of either description for a term which may extend to one year, or fine which may extend to one thousand rupees, or both.

427. If any person commits house-trespass in order to the committing of any other offence, and actually commits that other offence, the punishment shall be cumulative.

428. Whoever commits house-trespass in order to the committing of any offence punishable with death, or of any offence punishable with transportation for life, shall be punished with transportation for life, or with rigorous imprisonment for a term which may extend to life, and must not be less than three years, and shall also be liable to fine.

429. Whoever commits house-trespass in order to the committing of any offence punishable with imprisonment, shall be punished with imprisonment of either description for a term which may extend to one year, added to a term which may extend to one-third of the longest time for which he would have been liable to be imprisoned if he had committed the offence in order to the committing of which he committed the house-trespass, or fine, or both.

430. Whoever commits house-trespass, having made preparation for causing hurt to any person, or for assaulting any person, or for wrongfully restraining any person, or for putting any person in fear of hurt or of assault, in order to the committing of such house-trespass, or during the continuance of such house-trespass, shall be punished with imprisonment of either description for a term which may extend to two years, or fine, or both.

431. Whoever commits lurking house-trespass or house-breaking shall be punished with imprisonment of either description for a term which may extend to two years, or fine, or both.

432. If any person commits lurking house-trespass or house-breaking, in order to the committing of any other offence, and actually commits that other offence, the punishment shall be cumulative.

433. Whoever commits lurking house-trespass or house-breaking, in order to the committing of any offence punishable with imprisonment, shall be punished with imprisonment of either description for a term which may extend to two years, added to a term which may extend to one-half of the longest time for which he would have been liable to be imprisoned if he had committed the offence in order to the committing of which he committed such lurking house-trespass or house-breaking, and must not be less than one-half of the shortest time for which he would have been liable to be imprisoned if he had committed that offence, and shall also be liable to fine.

434. Whoever commits lurking house-trespass or house-breaking, having made preparation for causing hurt to any person, or for assaulting any person, or for wrongfully restraining any person, or for putting any person in fear of hurt or of assault, in order to the committing of such lurking house-trespass or house-breaking, or during the continuance of the house-trespass which has been begun by such lurking house-trespass or house-breaking, shall be punished with imprisonment of either description for a term which may extend to three years and must not be less than three months, and shall also be liable to fine.

435. Whoever commits lurking house-trespass by night, or house-breaking by night, shall be punished with imprisonment of either description for a term which may extend to three years, or fine, or both.

436. If any person commits lurking house-trespass by night, or house-breaking by night, in order to the committing of any other offence, and actually commits that other offence, the punishment shall be cumulative.

437. Whoever commits lurking house-trespass by night, or house-breaking by night, in order to the committing of any offence punishable with imprisonment, shall be punished with imprisonment of either description for a term which may extend to three years, added to a term which may extend to two-thirds of the longest time for which he would have been liable to be imprisoned if he had committed the offence in order to the committing of which he committed such lurking house-trespass by night, or house-breaking by night, and must not be less than the shortest time for which he would have been liable to be imprisoned if he had committed that offence, and shall also be liable to fine.

438. Whoever commits lurking house-trespass by night, or house-breaking by night, having made preparation for causing hurt to any person, or for assaulting any person, or for wrongfully restraining any person, or for putting any person in fear of hurt or of assault, in order to the committing of such house-trespass, or during the continuance of the house-trespass which has been begun by such lurking house-trespass by night, or house-breaking by night, shall be punished with imprisonment of either description for a term which may extend to seven years and must not be less than six months, and shall also be liable to fine.

439. Whoever commits criminal trespass by opening any closed receptacle which contains or which he believes to contain property, by any means by which that receptacle or any fastening of that receptacle is damaged, or by opening any lock, shall be punished with imprisonment of either description for a term which may extend to two years, or fine, or both.

440. Whoever, being intrusted, either by law or in pursuance of a contract made by him, with the keeping of any closed receptacle which contains or which he believes to contain property, commits criminal trespass by opening with a fraudulent intention that receptacle by any means by which that receptacle or any fastening of that receptacle is damaged, or by opening any lock, shall be punished with imprisonment of either description for a term which may extend to three years, or fine, or both.

CHAPTER XX.

OF OFFENCES RELATING TO DOCUMENTS.

441. A person is said to commit forgery who,

First, Makes any document, or any part of any document, or any mark which may appear to identify or authenticate any document, intending that it may be believed, in any quarter, that such document, part or mark, was made by some other person, or at some other time, or by some authority by which it was not made:

Or, Secondly, Having engaged to make any document by the authority and according to the direction of another, voluntarily omits to insert therein any thing which he is directed by that other to insert, intending that it may be believed in any quarter that the document is made according to that other's direction:

Or, Thirdly, Cancels any document, or any part of any document, intending that it may be believed in any quarter that such cancellation was made by some other person, or at some other time, or by some authority by which it was not made:

Or, Fourthly, Causes any part of any document or any mark which may appear to identify or authenticate any document to disappear, intending that it may be believed in any quarter that such part or mark never existed, or was caused to disappear by some other person, or at some other time, or by some authority by which it was not caused to disappear:

Or, Fifthly, Makes any mark, not in handwriting, nor meant to be taken for handwriting, which mark at the time when it is made is not part of a document, intending that such mark may become part of a document, or may appear to identify or authenticate a document, and may be believed in any quarter to have been made by some other person, or at some other time, or by some authority by which it was not made.

Illustrations.

(*a*) A writes a letter, and signs it with Z's name, intending that it may be believed that Z wrote the same. A has committed forgery under the first head of the definition.

(*b*) A has a letter of credit for 10,000 rupees, written by Z. A adds a cipher to the 10,000, and makes the sum 100,000, intending that it may be believed that Z so wrote the letter. A has committed forgery under the first head of the definition.

(*c*) A affixes Z's seal to a document, intending that it may be believed that Z affixed the same. A has committed forgery under the first head of the definition.

(*d*) A signs his own name to a bill of exchange, intending that it may be believed that the bill was drawn by another person of the same name. A has committed forgery under the first head of the definition.

(*e*) A, a trader, in anticipation of insolvency, lodges effects with B, and, in order to give a colour to the transaction, writes a promissory note, binding himself to pay to B a sum for value received, and antedates the note, intending that it may be believed to have been made before A was on the point of insolvency. A has committed forgery under the first head of the definition.

(*f*) Z dictates his will to A. A writes down a different legatee from the legatee named by Z, intending that it may be believed that what he writes was written by Z's authority. A has committed forgery under the first head of the definition, inasmuch as he makes a part of a document, intending that it may be believed that such part was made by an authority by which it was not made.

(*g*) A, having engaged to write Z's will according to Z's direction, and being directed by Z to write that Z leaves the residuum of his property equally between J, K and L, omits the name of K, intending that it may be believed that the document is made according to Z's direction. A has committed forgery under the second head of the definition.

(*h*) Z's will contains these words—"I direct that all my remaining property be equally divided between A, B and C." A scratches out B's name, intending that it may be believed that the whole was left to himself and C. A has committed forgery under the fourth head of the definition.

(*i*) A makes an engraved border in imitation of the border of a Government promissory note, intending that the paper on which the border is engraved may afterwards, by the addition of handwriting, or of an imitation of handwriting, become a document, and that this document may be believed to be a Government promissory note. A has committed forgery under the fifth head of the definition.

442. A document made in whole or in part by forgery is designated as a "forged document."

A document altered by forgery, marked by forgery, or cancelled in whole or in part by forgery, is designated as a "document falsified by forgery."

443. Whoever, with the intention of causing any injury to any party, or of rendering any illegal act or omission easier or safer than it would otherwise be, or of obtaining for any person any employment either in the service of the public or of an individual, commits forgery, or uses as genuine any document which he knows to be forged or falsified by forgery, shall be punished with imprisonment of either description for a term which may extend to two years, or fine, or both.

Illustrations.

(*a*) A, a British-born subject of the King, forges a license to reside at Delhi, intending thereby to render it easier for him to violate the law which forbids him to reside there without a license. A has committed the offence defined in this clause.

(*b*) A presents to Z a certificate of character which A knows to be forged, intending thereby to obtain employment under Z. A has committed the offence defined in this clause.

444. Whoever, with the intention of causing any injury to any party, forges or falsifies by forgery any document which is or purports to be a valuable security, or uses as genuine any document which he knows to be forged or falsified by forgery, and which is or purports to be a valuable security, shall be punished with imprisonment of either description for a term which may extend to fourteen years and must not be less than two years, and shall also be liable to fine.

445. Whoever commits forgery, intending or knowing it to be likely that the document forged or falsified by such forgery may be used as genuine for the purpose of cheating, or uses as genuine for the purpose of cheating, any document which he knows to have been forged or falsified by forgery, shall be punished with imprisonment of either description for a term which may extend to seven years and must not be less than one year, and shall also be liable to fine.

446. Whoever commits forgery, intending or knowing it to be likely that the document forged or falsified by such forgery may harm the reputation of any party, or uses as genuine, for the purpose of harming the reputation of any party, any document which he knows to have been forged or falsified by forgery, shall be punished with imprisonment of either description for a term which may extend to three years and must not be less than six months, and shall also be liable to fine.

447. Whoever makes any apparatus or material for engraving, or any seal, intending or knowing it to be likely that the same may be used for the purpose of committing any forgery which it would be an offence under any clause of this chapter to commit, shall be punished with imprisonment of either description for a term which may extend to fourteen years and must not be less than two years, and shall also be liable to fine.

448. Whoever has in his possession any plate or material or implement for engraving, or any seal, intending or knowing it to be likely that the same may be used for the purpose of committing any forgery which it would be an offence under any clause of this chapter to commit, shall be punished with imprisonment of either description for a term which may extend to fourteen years and must not be less than two years, and shall also be liable to fine.

449. Whoever has in his possession any document which he knows to be forged or falsified by forgery, and which is or purports to be a valuable security, intending or knowing it to be likely that the same may be used as genuine to the injury of any party, shall be punished with imprisonment of either description for a term which may extend to fourteen years and must not be less than two years, and shall also be liable to fine.

450. Whoever has in his possession any thing which is not a document, but which has been marked by forgery, intending that the same may be made a document purporting to be a valuable security, and intending or knowing it to be likely that such document may be used as genuine to the injury of any party, shall be punished with imprisonment of either description for a term which may extend to fourteen years and must not be less than two years, and shall also be liable to fine.

451. Whoever fraudulently destroys or defaces, or fraudulently attempts to destroy or deface, or fraudulently secretes any document which is or purports to be a will, shall be punished with imprisonment of either description for a term which may extend to fourteen years and must not be less than two years, and shall also be liable to fine.

452. Whoever fraudulently destroys or defaces, or fraudulently attempts to destroy or deface, or fraudulently secretes any document which purports to be a valuable security, shall be punished with imprisonment of either description for a term which may extend to three years and must not be less than six months, and shall also be liable to fine.

453. Whoever, being a public servant in the post-office department, and being, as such, intrusted with the keeping of any fastened letter or any fastened packet containing any document, intentionally opens the same, knowing that he has not legal authority so to do, shall be punished with imprisonment of either description for a term which may extend to two years, or fine, or both.

454. Whoever opens any fastened letter or any fastened packet containing any document, knowing that it does not belong to him, and that he has not the consent, express or implied, of any party legally entitled to give a consent which would authorize such opening of such letter or packet, shall be punished with imprisonment of either description for a term which may extend to six months, or fine which may extend to five hundred rupees, or both.

CHAPTER XXI.

OF OFFENCES RELATING TO PROPERTY-MARKS.

455. Every mark put on any property for the purpose of distinguishing the property marked from other property, or for the purpose of indicating to what party the property marked, or any dominion over the property marked, belongs, or for the purpose of indicating that any payment is due or has been made in respect of the property marked, or that the property marked is entitled to any exemption, is designated as a "property-mark."

456. Whoever makes any counterfeit property-mark, intending or knowing it to be likely that such counterfeit property-mark may be used as genuine to the injury of any party, or uses as genuine any counterfeit property-mark knowing the same to be counterfeit, and intending or knowing it to be likely that, by so using that property-mark, he may cause injury to some party, shall be punished with imprisonment of either description for a term which may extend to one year, or fine, or both.

Illustration.

A marks Z's sheep with a mark which Y is in the habit of affixing to Y's sheep, intending or knowing it to be likely that Z's sheep may be confounded with Y's, and that injury may thus be caused to Z. A has committed the offence defined in this clause.

457. Whoever makes any counterfeit property-mark, which is a counterfeit of any property-mark affixed by the lawful authority of some public servant, as such, or some body of public servants, as such, intending or knowing it to be likely that such counterfeit property-mark may be used as genuine to the injury of any party, or uses as genuine any such counterfeit property-mark, knowing the same to be counterfeit, and intending or knowing it to be likely that, by so using that counterfeit property-mark, he may cause injury to some party, shall be punished with imprisonment of either description for a term which may extend to three years and must not be less than six months, and shall also be liable to fine.

Illustration.

A, intending to cause Z to believe that a threatening letter comes from a place from which it does not come, and thus to injure Z by annoying and terrifying him, counterfeits the post-mark of the post-office of that place. A has committed the offence defined in this clause.

458. Whoever makes any counterfeit property-mark, intending or knowing it to be likely that such counterfeit property-mark may be used as genuine for the purpose of cheating, or uses as genuine, for the purpose of cheating, any property-mark which he knows to be counterfeit, shall be punished with imprisonment of either description for a term which may extend to two years, or fine, or both.

Illustration.

A counterfeits the mark of a cutler at Sheffield on cutlery made by himself in India, intending thereby to cheat. A has committed the offence defined in this clause.

459. Whoever puts any property-mark on any property, intending or knowing it to be likely that such property-mark may be used for the purpose of cheating, or uses any property-mark for the purpose of cheating, shall be punished with imprisonment of either description for a term which may extend to one year, or fine, or both.

CHAPTER XXII.*

OF THE ILLEGAL PURSUIT OF LEGAL RIGHTS.

460. Whoever in good faith, believing a debt to be legally due, takes or attempts to take any property from the person whom he believes to owe that debt, not fraudulently, but in order to satisfy that debt, under such circumstances that if his intention were fraudulent he would be guilty of theft or robbery, shall be punished with imprisonment of either description for a term which may extend to one year, or fine, or both.

Illustrations.

(*a*) A, believing in good faith that Z owes him one hundred rupees, in order to satisfy the debt, takes property belonging to Z, not fraudulently, but under such circumstances that, if he took it fraudulently, he would be guilty of theft. A sells that property for one hundred and fifty rupees, and sends back fifty rupees to Z. A has committed the offence defined in this clause.

(*b*) But if A, at the time of taking, intended to keep the whole sum of one hundred and fifty rupees, he acted fraudulently, and has committed theft.

(*c*) If A meant, after repaying himself, to sue Z for the debt, A acted fraudulently, and has committed theft.

461. Whoever takes property in the manner described in the last preceding clause, and keeps that property or any part thereof fraudulently, shall be punished with the punishment to which he would have been liable if the taking had been fraudulent.

Illustration.

A takes property in the manner described in clause 460, intending to repay himself a debt due to him by Z, and to refund the surplus. A subsequently changes his mind, and fraudulently keeps the whole. A is liable to be punished as if he had taken the property fraudulently.

---

* See Appendix, Note O.

462. If any person voluntarily causes hurt in doing any thing which is an offence under any clause of this chapter, the punishment shall be cumulative.

CHAPTER XXIII.*

OF THE CRIMINAL BREACH OF CONTRACTS OF SERVICE.

463. Whoever, being bound by a lawful contract to convey or conduct any person or any property from one place to another place, illegally omits so to do, intending or knowing it to be likely that such illegal omission will cause injury to some party, shall be punished with imprisonment of either description for a term which may extend to one month, or fine which may extend to one hundred rupees, or both.

Illustrations.

(*a*) A, a palanquin bearer, being bound by legal contract to carry Z from one place to another, runs away in the middle of the stage. A has committed the offence defined in this clause.

(*b*) A, a cooly, being bound by lawful contract to carry Z's baggage from one place to another, throws the baggage away. A has committed the offence defined in this clause.

(*c*) A, a proprietor of bullocks, being bound by legal contract to convey goods on his bullocks from one place to another, illegally omits to do so. A has committed the offence defined in this clause.

464. Whoever, being a seaman, bound by a lawful contract to serve on board of a merchant vessel, illegally leaves that vessel, or illegally remains absent from that vessel, or illegally disobeys any order of any officer of that vessel, shall be punished with imprisonment of either description for a term which may extend to three months, or fine which may extend to one hundred rupees, or both.

465. Whoever, being bound by a lawful contract to attend on any person who, by reason of youth, or of unsoundness of mind, or of disease, is helpless or incapable of providing for his own safety, or to supply the wants of any such person, illegally omits so to do, shall be punished with imprisonment of either description for a term which may extend to six months, or fine which may extend to five hundred rupees, or both.

CHAPTER XXIV.†

OF OFFENCES RELATING TO MARRIAGE.

466. Every man who by deceit causes any woman, who is not lawfully married to him according to the law of marriage under which she lives, to believe that she is lawfully married to him according to that law, and to cohabit with him in that belief, shall be punished with imprisonment of either description for a term which may extend to fourteen years and must not be less than two years, and shall also be liable to fine.

---

* See Appendix, Note P. † See Appendix, Note Q.

467. Every woman who by deceit causes any man to believe that he is lawfully married to her according to the law of marriage under which he lives, and to cohabit with her in consequence of that belief, shall be punished with simple imprisonment for a term which may extend to one year, or fine, or both.

468. Whoever, with any fraudulent intention, goes through the ceremony of being married according to any law in force in the territories of the East India Company, knowing that he is not thereby lawfully married, shall be punished with imprisonment of either description for a term which may extend to three years and must not be less than six months, and shall also be liable to fine.

CHAPTER XXV.*

OF DEFAMATION.

469. Whoever, by words either spoken or intended to be read, or by signs, or by visible representations, attempts to cause any imputation concerning any person to be believed in any quarter, knowing that the belief thereof would harm the reputation of that person in that quarter, is said, except in the cases excepted in the nine clauses next following, to defame that person.

Explanations.—An imputation is not defamatory, unless it be such as, if believed in that quarter in which it is intended to be believed, would harm the reputation of the person concerning whom it is intended to be believed.

Hence an imputation, which is defamatory when directed against one person, is not necessarily defamatory when directed against another person; and an imputation which is defamatory when intended to be believed in one quarter is not necessarily defamatory when intended to be believed in another quarter.

Also, it may be defamation to repeat or circulate an imputation which it was not defamation originally to make; and it is not necessarily defamation to repeat or circulate an imputation which it was defamation originally to make.

A deceased person may be defamed.†

A collection of persons cannot, as such, be defamed. But an individual may be defamed by means of an imputation thrown on a collection of persons of whom he is one, or by means of an imputation made in the form of an alternative.

If the imputation be such that, if it were believed in the quarter in which it was intended to be believed, the reputation of the person concerning whom it is intended to be believed would not be harmed, then, though that person may suffer in his interest, he has not been defamed.

"Harm the reputation." No imputation is said to harm a person's reputation unless that imputation directly or indirectly lowers the moral or intellectual character of that person, or lowers the character of that person in respect of his caste or of his calling, or lowers the commercial

---

* See Appendix, Note R.

† The course of proceeding in such a case belongs to the law of criminal procedure.

credit of that person, if he is engaged in trade, or causes it to be believed that the body of that person is in a loathsome state, or in a state generally considered as disgraceful.

Illustrations.

(*a*) A says, "Z is an honest man; he never stole B's watch;" intending to cause it to be believed that Z did steal B's watch. This is defamation, unless it fall within one of the exceptions.

(*b*) A is asked who stole B's watch. A points to Z, intending to cause it to be believed that Z stole B's watch. This is defamation, unless it fall within one of the exceptions.

(*c*) A draws a picture of Z running away with B's watch, intending it to be believed that Z stole B's watch. This is defamation, unless it fall within one of the exceptions.

(*d*) A says of Z that Z drinks wine. Here the question whether A has defamed Z, may turn on the question whether Z is a Musulman or a Christian.

(*e*) It may be defamation to say of a Sheeah that he has turned a Soonee. It may also be defamation to say of a Soonee that he has turned a Sheeah.

(*f*) A says of Z that Z is a coward. The question whether this is defamation or not may depend on the question whether Z be a soldier or a woman.

(*g*) A says of Z a Hindoo, that it is highly probable that he will be converted to Mahomedanism. The question whether this is defamation or not may depend on the question whether the communication was made to the Hindoo relatives of Z, or to a Musulman.

(*h*) A journeyman printer who sets the types for printing defamatory matter, a bookseller who sells books containing defamatory matter, a person who lends a defamatory newspaper or repeats defamatory verses, does not commit defamation, unless he has the intention described in the definition of defamation.

(*i*) The Bank of Bengal, the Civil Service, the Army, cannot be defamed, as such. But it may be defamation of every judge of the Sudder to say, "The whole Sudder Court is corrupt."

(*j*) A says, "X, Y or Z must be a thief. I do not know which committed the theft; but it was one of the three." This may be defamation of every one of the three persons named.

(*k*) A falsely tells B, who is a public servant having an office at his disposal, that Z, to whom B intends to offer that office, will not accept it. B, in consequence, gives that office to another. Here Z, though he suffers in his interests, is not harmed in his reputation, and therefore is not defamed.

470. *First Exception.*—**It is not defamation to attempt to cause any thing which is true to be believed in any quarter concerning any person.**

471. *Second Exception.*—**It is not defamation to express in good faith any opinion whatever respecting the conduct of a public servant in the discharge of his public functions, or respecting his character, so far as his character appears in that conduct, and no further.**

472. *Third Exception.*—**It is not defamation to express in good faith any opinion whatever respecting the conduct of any person touching any public question, and respecting his character, so far as his character appears in that conduct, and no further.**

Illustrations.

It is not defamation in A to express in good faith any opinion whatever respecting Z's conduct in petitioning Government on a public question, in signing a requisition for a meeting on a public question, in presiding or attending at such a meeting, in forming or joining any society which invites the public support, in voting or canvassing for a particular candidate for any situation in the efficient discharge of the duties of which the public is interested.

473. *Fourth Exception.*—It is not defamation to express in good faith any opinion whatever respecting the merits of any case, civil or criminal, which has been brought before any court of justice, or respecting the conduct of any person as a party, witness or agent, in any such case, or respecting the character of such person, as far as his character appears in that conduct, and no further.

Illustrations.

(*a*) A says, "I think Z's evidence on that trial is so contradictory that he must be stupid or dishonest." A is within this exception if he says this in good faith; inasmuch as the opinion which he expresses respects Z's character as it appears in Z's conduct as a witness, and no further.

(*b*) But if A says, "I do not believe what Z asserted at that trial, because I know him to be a man without veracity," A is not within this exception, inasmuch as the opinion which he expresses of Z's character is an opinion not founded on Z's conduct as a witness.

474. *Fifth Exception.*—It is not defamation to express in good faith any opinion respecting the merit of any performance which its author has submitted to the judgment of the public, or respecting the character of the author, so far as his character appears in such performance, and no further.

Explanation.—A performance may be submitted to the judgment of the public expressly, or by acts on the part of the author which imply such submission to the judgment of the public.

Illustrations.

(*a*) A person who publishes a book submits that book to the judgment of the public.

(*b*) A person who makes a speech in public submits that speech to the judgment of the public.

(*c*) An actor or singer who appears on a public stage submits his acting or singing to the judgment of the public.

(*d*) A says of a book published by Z, "Z's book is foolish, Z must be a weak man. Z's book is indecent, Z must be a man of impure mind." A is within this exception if he says this in good faith, inasmuch as the opinion which he expresses of Z respects Z's character only so far as it appears in Z's book, and no further.

(*e*) But if A says, "I am not surprised that Z's book is foolish and indecent, for he is a weak man, and a libertine," A is not within this exception, inasmuch as the opinion which he expresses of Z's character is an opinion not founded on Z's book.

475. *Sixth Exception.*—It is not defamation in a person having over another any authority, either conferred by law or arising out of a lawful contract made with that other, to pass in good faith any censure on the conduct of that other in matters to which such lawful authority relates.

Illustrations.

A judge censuring in good faith the conduct of a witness, or of an officer of the court; a head of a department censuring in good faith those who are under his orders; a parent censuring in good faith a child in the presence of other children; a schoolmaster, whose authority is derived from a parent, censuring in good faith a pupil in the presence of other pupils; a master censuring a servant in good faith for remissness in service; a banker censuring in good faith the cashier of his bank for the conduct of such cashier, as such cashier, are within this exception.

476. *Seventh Exception.*—It is not defamation to prefer, in good faith, an accusation against any person to any of those who have lawful authority over that person with respect to the subject-matter of accusation.

Illustrations.

If A in good faith accuses Z before a magistrate; if A in good faith complains of the conduct of Z, a servant, to Z's master; if A in good faith complains of the conduct of Z, a child, to Z's father; A is within this exception.

477. *Eighth Exception.*—It is not defamation in a person giving directions for the management of his concerns to make an imputation on the character of another, provided that the imputation be made in good faith for the protection of the interests of the person making it.

Illustration.

A, a shopkeeper, says to B, his foreman, "Sell nothing to Z unless he pays you ready money, for I have no opinion of his honesty." A is within the exception, if he has made this imputation on Z in good faith, for the protection of his own interests.

478. *Ninth Exception.*—It is not defamation to convey a caution, in good faith, to one person against another, provided that such caution be intended for the good of the person to whom it is conveyed, or of some party in whom that person is interested.

479. Whoever defames another shall be punished with simple imprisonment for a term which may extend to two years, or fine, or both.

480. Wherever defamation is committed by means of any printed or engraved substance; whoever at the time of printing or engraving the defamatory matter was a possessor of the machinery whereby such defamatory matter was printed or engraved, shall, except in the case hereinafter excepted, be punished with simple imprisonment for a term which may extend to two years, or fine, or both.

Exception.—No person shall be liable to punishment as a possessor of the machinery by which defamatory matter was printed or engraved, if such defamatory matter were printed or engraved contrary to his directions, or if the printing or engraving were purposely concealed from him.

481. Wherever defamation is committed by means of any printed or engraved substance, whoever first sells or offers for sale that printed or engraved substance, shall be punished with simple imprisonment for a term which may extend to two years, or fine, or both.

CHAPTER XXVI.

OF CRIMINAL INTIMIDATION, INSULT AND ANNOYANCE.

482. Whoever deliberately threatens any person to murder that person or any other in whom that person is interested, or to commit the offence of voluntarily causing hurt to that person or to any other person in whom that person is interested, or to commit mischief by fire on that person's property, or to kill or wound any animal which is that person's property, or to commit the offence of house-breaking on any building, tent or vessel which is that person's property, or wherein that person resides, or to commit any mischief or trespass injurious to that person by means of a riotous assembly, or falsely to impute unnatural lust to that person, or falsely to impute unchastity to that person if that person be a woman, with the intention of causing, by such threat, distress or terror to the person to whom such threat is conveyed, or of inducing that person to do any act which that person is not legally bound to do, or to omit the doing of any act which that person has a legal right to do, is said to commit the offence of "criminal intimidation."

483. Whoever commits the offence of criminal intimidation, shall be punished with imprisonment of either description for a term which may extend to two years, or fine, or both.

484. Whoever commits the offence of criminal intimidation, having taken precaution to conceal the quarter from whence the threat comes, shall be punished with imprisonment of either description for a term which may extend to three years and must not be less than six months, and shall also be liable to fine.

485. Whoever utters any word, makes any sound, makes any gesture, or exhibits any object, intending that such word or sound shall be heard, or that such gesture or object shall be seen by any person, and intending thereby to insult that person, shall be punished with imprisonment of either description for a term which may extend to three months, or fine which may extend to one thousand rupees, or both.

Explanations.—A person may exhibit an object by sending it to another as well as by placing it before the eyes of another.

The making of an imputation which is not defamatory because it falls under one of the exceptions appended to the definition of defamation, may be an offence under this clause.

Illustrations.

(*a*) Z has been guilty of an offence, and has been punished for it. A follows him, reproaching him with that offence. Here, A is not guilty of defamation, inasmuch as he has imputed to Z only what was true. But if A has used words, intending them to be heard by Z, and intending thereby to insult Z, he has committed the offence defined in this clause.

(*b*) A forces himself into the presence of a magistrate, crying out that the magistrate is a tyrant. Here, though A is not guilty of defamation if in good faith he accuses a public servant of tyranny, yet if he uses those words intending that the magistrate may hear them, and intending thereby to insult the magistrate, A commits the offence defined in this clause.

486. Whoever utters any word, makes any sound, makes any gesture, or exhibits any object, intending that such word or sound shall be heard, or that such gesture or object shall be seen by any woman, and intending thereby to insult the modesty of that woman, shall be punished with imprisonment of either description for a term which may extend to two years, or fine, or both.

Illustration.

A, intending to outrage the modesty of a woman, exposes his person indecently to her, or uses obscene words intending that she should hear them, or sends to her obscene drawings by post. A has committed the offence defined in this clause.

487. Whoever utters any word, makes any sound, makes any gesture, or exhibits any object, intending that such word or sound shall be heard, or that such gesture or object shall be seen by any person, and malignantly and wantonly intending thereby to annoy that person, shall be punished with imprisonment of either description, which may extend to one month, or fine which may extend to one hundred rupees, or both.

Illustrations.

(*a*) A follows Z in the street, hooting him, malignantly and wantonly intending thereby to annoy Z. A has committed the offence defined in this clause.

(*b*) A beats a gong under Z's window by night, malignantly and wantonly intending to annoy Z. A has committed the offence defined in this clause.

488. Whoever, in a state of intoxication, appears in any public place, or in any place which it is a trespass in him to enter, and there conducts himself in such a manner as to cause annoyance to any person, shall be punished with simple imprisonment for a term which may extend to twenty-four hours, or fine which may extend to ten rupees, or both.

APPENDIX.

Note A.

ON THE CHAPTER OF PUNISHMENTS.

FIRST among the punishments provided for offences by this Code stands death. No argument that has been brought to our notice has satisfied us that it would be desirable wholly to dispense with this punishment. But we are convinced that it ought to be very sparingly inflicted, and we propose to employ it only in cases where either murder or the highest offence against the State has been committed.

We are not apprehensive that we shall be thought by many persons to have resorted too frequently to capital punishment; but we think it probable that many, even of those who condemn the English Statute book as sanguinary, may think that our Code errs on the other side. They may be of opinion that gang-robbery, the cruel mutilation of the person, and possibly rape, ought to be punished with death. These are doubtless offences which, if we looked only at their enormity, at the evil which they produce, at the terror which they spread through society, at the depravity which they indicate, we might be inclined to punish capitally. But atrocious as they are, they cannot, as it appears to us, be placed in the same class with murder. To the great majority of mankind nothing is so dear as life. And we are of opinion that to put robbers, ravishers and mutilators on the same footing with murderers is an arrangement which diminishes the security of life.

There is in practice a close connexion between murder and most of those offences which come nearest to murder in enormity. Those offences are almost always committed under such circumstances that the offender has it in his power to add murder to his guilt. They are often committed under such circumstances that the offender has a temptation to add murder to his guilt. The same opportunities, the same superiority of force, which enabled a man to rob, to mangle or to ravish, will enable him to go further, and to despatch his victim. As he has almost always the power to murder, he will often have a strong motive to murder, inasmuch as by murder he may often hope to remove the only witness of the crime which he has already committed. If the punishment of the crime which he has already committed be exactly the same with the punishment of murder, he will have no restraining motive. A law which imprisons for rape and robbery, and hangs for murder, holds out to ravishers and robbers a strong inducement to spare the lives of those whom they have injured. A law which hangs for rape and robbery, and which only hangs for murder, holds out, indeed, if it be rigorously carried into effect, a strong motive to deter men from rape and robbery, but as soon as a man has ravished or robbed, it holds out to him a strong motive to follow up his crime with a murder.

If murder were punished with something more than simple death; if the murderer were broken on the wheel or burned alive, there would not be the same objection to punishing with death those crimes which in atrocity approach nearest to murder. But such a system would be open to other objections so obvious that it is unnecessary to point them out. The highest punishment which we propose is the simple privation of life; and the highest punishment, be it what it may, ought not, for the reason which we have given, to be assigned to any crime against the person which stops short of murder. And it is hardly necessary to point out to his Lordship in Council how great a shock would be given to public feeling if, while we propose to exempt from the punishment of death the most atrocious personal outrages which stopped short of murder, we were to inflict that punishment even in the worst cases of theft, cheating or mischief.

It will be seen that, throughout the Code, wherever we have made any offence punishable by transportation, we have provided that the transportation shall be for life. The consideration which has chiefly determined us to retain that mode of punishment is our persuasion that it is regarded by the natives of India, particularly by those who live at a distance from the sea, with peculiar fear. The pain which is caused by punishment is unmixed evil. It is by the terror which it inspires that it produces good; and perhaps no punishment inspires so much terror in proportion to the actual pain which it causes as the punishment of transportation in this country. Prolonged imprisonment may be more painful in the actual endurance; but it is not so much dreaded beforehand; nor does a sentence of imprisonment strike either the offender or the bystanders with so much horror as a sentence of exile beyond what they call the Black Water. This feeling, we believe, arises chiefly from the mystery which overhangs the fate of the transported convict. The separation resembles that which takes place at the moment of death. The criminal is taken for ever from the society of all who are acquainted with him, and conveyed by means of which the natives have but an indistinct notion over an element which they regard with extreme awe, to a distant country of which they know nothing, and from which he is never to return. It is natural that his fate should impress them with a deep feeling of terror. It is on this feeling that the efficacy of the punishment depends, and this feeling would be greatly weakened if transported convicts should frequently return, after an exile of seven or fourteen years, to the scene of their offences, and to the society of their former friends.

We may observe that the rule which we propose to lay down is already in force in almost every part of British India. The Courts established by the Royal Charters and Courts Martial are at present the only Courts which sentence offenders to transportation for any term short of life. In the case of European offenders who are condemned to long terms of imprisonment, we allow the Government to commute imprisonment for transportation not perpetual. But in that case we are of opinion that in general the transported criminal ought not, after the expiration of the term for which he is transported, to be allowed to return to India. This rule and the reasons for it will be considered hereafter.

Of imprisonment we propose to institute two grades, rigorous imprisonment and simple imprisonment. But we do not think the Penal

Code the proper place for describing with minuteness the nature of either kind of punishment.

We entertain a confident hope that it will shortly be found practicable greatly to reduce the terms of imprisonment which we propose. Where a good system of prison discipline exists, where the criminal, without being subject to any cruel severities, is strictly restrained, regularly employed in labour not of an attractive kind, and deprived of every indulgence not necessary to his health, a year's confinement will generally prove as efficacious as confinement for two years in a gaol where the superintendence is lax, where the work exacted is light, and where the convicts find means of enjoying as many luxuries as if they were at liberty. As the intensity of the punishment is increased, its length may safely be diminished. As members of the committee which is now employed in investigating the system followed in the gaols of this country, we have had access to information which enables us to say with confidence that, in this department of the administration, extensive reforms are greatly needed, and may easily be made. The researches of that committee will, we hope, enable the Law Commission hereafter to prepare such a Code of prison discipline as, without shocking the humane feelings of the community, may yet be a terror to the most hardened wrongdoers. Whenever such a Code shall come into operation, we conceive that it will be advisable greatly to shorten many of the terms of imprisonment which we have proposed.

It will be seen that we have given to the Government a power of commuting sentences in certain cases without the consent of the offender. Some of the rules which we have laid down on this subject will be universally allowed to be proper. It is evidently fit that the Government should be empowered to commute the sentence of death for any other punishment provided by the Code. It seems to us also very desirable that the Government should have the power of commuting perpetual transportation for perpetual imprisonment. Many circumstances of which the executive authorities ought to be accurately informed, but which must often be unknown to the ablest judge, may, at particular times, render it highly inconvenient to carry a sentence of transportation into effect. The state of those remote provinces of the empire in which convict settlements are established, and the way in which the interest of those provinces may be affected by any addition to the convict population, are matters which lie altogether out of the cognizance of the tribunals by which those sentences are passed, and which the Government only is competent to decide.

The provisions contained in clauses 43 and 44 are more likely to cause difference of opinion. We are satisfied that both humanity and policy require that those provisions, or provisions very similar to them, should be adopted.

The physical difference which exists between the European and the native of India renders it impossible to subject them to the same system of prison discipline. It is most desirable, indeed, that in the treatment of offenders convicted of the same crime and sentenced to the same punishment there should be no apparent inequality. But it is still more desirable that there should be no real inequality, and there must be real inequality unless there be apparent inequality. It would be cruel to subject an European for a long period to a severe prison discipline, in a country in which existence is almost constant misery to an European who has not many indulgences at his command. If not cruel, it would be impolitic. It is unnecessary to point out to his Lordship in Council how desirable it is that our national character should stand high in the estimation of the inhabitants of India, and how much that character would be lowered by the frequent exhibition of Englishmen of the worst description, placed in the most degrading situations, stigmatized by the courts of justice, and engaged in the ignominious labour of a gaol.

As there are strong reasons for not punishing Europeans with imprisonment of the same description with which we propose to punish natives, so there are reasons equally strong for not suffering Europeans who have been convicted of serious crimes to remain in this country. As we are satisfied that nothing can add more strength to the Government, or can be more beneficial to the people, than the free admission of honest, industrious and intelligent Englishmen, so we are satisfied that no greater calamity could befall either the Government or the people than the influx of Englishmen of lawless habits and blasted character. Such men are of the same race and colour with the rulers of the country, they speak the same language, they wear the same garb. In all these things they differ from the great body of the population. It is natural and inevitable that in the minds of a people accustomed to be governed by Englishmen, the idea of an Englishman should be associated with the idea of Government. Every Englishman participates in the power of Government, though he holds no office. His vices reflect disgrace on the Government, though the Government gives him no countenance.

It was probably on these grounds that Parliament, at the same time at which it threw open a large part of India to British-born subjects of the King, directed the local legislature to provide against those dangers which might be expected from an influx of such settlers. No regulation can, in our opinion, promote more effectually, or in a more unexceptionable manner, the end which Parliament had in view than that which we now propose.

We recommend that, whenever a person, not both of Asiatic birth and of Asiatic blood, commits an offence so serious that he is sentenced to two years of simple imprisonment, or to one year of rigorous imprisonment, it shall be competent to the Government to commute that punishment for banishment from the territories of the East India Company.

If a person of unmixed European blood should commit an offence so heinous as to be visited with a sentence of imprisonment for seven years or more, we would give to the Government the power of substituting an equal term of transportation for that term of imprisonment, and of excluding the offender, after the expiration of the term of transportation, from the territories of the East India Company. The Government would, doubtless, make arrangements for transporting such offenders to some British colony situated in a temperate climate.

In the great majority of cases we believe that this commutation of punishment would be most welcome to an European offender. But however this may be, we are satisfied that it is for the interest both of the British Government and of the Indian people that the executive authorities should possess the power which we propose to confide to them.

The forfeiture of property is a punishment which we propose to inflict only on persons guilty of high political offences. The territorial possessions of such persons often enable them to disturb the public peace, and to make head against the Government; and it seems reasonable that they should be deprived of so dangerous a power.

Fine is one of the most common punishments in every part of the world, and it is a punishment the advantages of which are so great and obvious, that we propose to authorize the Courts to inflict it in every case, except where forfeiture of all property is necessarily part of the punishment. Yet the punishment of fine is open to some objections. Death, imprisonment, transportation, banishment, solitude, compelled labour, are not, indeed, equally disagreeable to all men. But they are so disagreeable to all men that the legislature, in assigning these punishments to offences, may safely neglect the differences produced by temper and situation. With fine, the case is different. In imposing a fine, it is always necessary to have as much regard to the pecuniary circumstances of the offender as to the character and magnitude of the offence. The mulct which is ruinous to a labourer is easily borne by a tradesman, and is absolutely unfelt by a rich zemindar.

It is impossible to fix any limit to the amount of a fine which will not either be so high as to be ruinous to the poor, or so low as to be no object of terror to the rich. There are many millions in India who would be utterly unable to pay a fine of fifty rupees; there are hundreds of thousands from whom such a fine might be levied, but whom it would reduce to extreme distress; there are thousands to whom it would give very little uneasiness; there are hundreds to whom it would be a matter of perfect indifference, and who would not cross a room to avoid it. The number of the poor in every country exceeds in a very great ratio the number of the rich. The number of poor criminals exceeds the number of rich criminals in a still greater ratio. And to the poor criminal it is a matter of absolute indifference whether the fine to which he is liable be limited or not, unless it be so limited as to render it quite inefficient as a mode of punishing the rich. To a man who has no capital, who has laid by nothing, whose monthly wages are just sufficient to provide himself and his family with their monthly rice, it matters not whether the fine for assault be left to be settled by the discretion of the Courts, or whether a hundred rupees be fixed as the maximum. There are no degrees in impossibility. He is no more able to pay a hundred rupees than to pay a lac. A just and wise judge, even if intrusted with a boundless discretion, will not, under ordinary circumstances, sentence such an offender to a fine of a hundred rupees. And the limit of a hundred rupees would leave it quite in the power of an unjust or inconsiderate judge to inflict on such an offender all the evil which can be inflicted on him by means of fine.

If, in imitation of Mr. Livingston, we provide that no fine shall exceed one-fourth of the amount of the offender's property, no serious fine will ever be imposed in this country without a long and often a most unsatisfactory investigation, in which it would be necessary to decide many obscure questions of right purposely darkened by every artifice of chicanery. And even if this great practical difficulty did not exist, we should see strong objections to such a provision in a very large class of cases. Take the case of a corrupt judge who has accumulated a lac of rupees by his illicit practices. A fine which should deprive such a man of the whole of his fortune would not appear to us excessive: and certainly we should think it most undesirable that he should be allowed to retain 75,000 rupees of his ill-gotten gains. Again, take the case of a man who has been suborned to commit perjury, and has received a great bribe for doing so. Such a man may have little or no property, except what he has received as a bribe; yet it is evidently desirable that he should be compelled to disgorge the whole. No man ought ever to gain by breaking the law; and if Mr. Livingston's rule were adopted in this country, many would gain by breaking the law. To punish a man for a crime, and yet to leave in his possession three-fourths of the consideration which tempted him to commit the crime, is to hold out at once punishments for crime, and inducements to crime. It appears to us that the punishment of fine is a peculiarly appropriate punishment for all offences to which men are prompted by cupidity; for it is a punishment which operates directly on the very feeling which impels men to such offences. A man who has been guilty of great offences arising from cupidity, of forging a bill of exchange, for example, of keeping a receptacle for stolen goods, or of extensive embezzlement, ought, we conceive, to be so fined as to reduce him to poverty. That such a man should, when his imprisonment is over, return to the enjoyment of three-fourths of his property, a property which may be very large, and which may have been accumulated by his offences, appears to us highly objectionable. Those persons who are most likely to commit such offences would often be less deterred by knowing that the offender had passed several years in imprisonment, than encouraged by seeing him, after his liberation, enjoying the far larger part of his wealth.

We have never seen any general rule for the limiting of fine, which we are disposed to adopt. The difficulty of framing a rule has evidently been felt by many eminent men. The authors of the Bill of Rights, with many instances of gross abuse fresh in their recollection, could devise no other rule than that excessive fines should not be imposed. And the authors of the Constitution of the United States, after the experience of another century, contented themselves with repeating the words of the Bill of Rights.

It will be seen that in cases which are not very heinous we propose to limit the amount of fine which the Courts may impose. But in serious cases we have left the amount of fine absolutely to their discretion; and we feel, as we have said, that, even in the cases where we have proposed a limit, such a limit will be no protection to the poor, who in every community are also the many. We feel that the extent of the discretion which we have thus left to the Courts is an evil, and that no sagacity and no rectitude of intention can secure a judge from occasional error. We conceive, however, that if fine is to be employed as a punishment, and no judicious person, we are persuaded, would propose to dispense with it, this evil must be endured. We shall attempt in the Code of Procedure to establish such a system of appeal as may prevent gross or frequent injustice from taking place.

The next question which it became our duty to consider was this: when a fine has been imposed, what measures shall be adopted in default of payment? And here two modes of proceeding, with both of which we were familiar, naturally occurred to us. The offender may be imprisoned till the fine is paid, or he may be imprisoned for a certain term, such imprisonment being considered as standing in place of the fine. In the former case, the imprisonment is used in order to compel him to part with his money; in the latter case, the imprisonment is a punishment substituted for another punishment. Both modes of proceeding appear to us to be open to strong objections. To keep an offender in imprisonment till his fine is paid is, if the fine be beyond his means, to keep him in imprisonment all his life; and it is impossible for the best judge to be certain that he may not sometimes impose a fine which shall be beyond the means of an offender. Nothing could make such a system tolerable except the constant interference of some authority empowered to remit sentences; and such constant interference we should consider as in itself an evil. On the other hand, to sentence an offender to fine and to a certain fixed term of imprisonment in default of payment, and then to leave it to himself to determine whether he will part with his money or lie in gaol, appears to us to be a very objectionable course. The high authority of Mr. Livingston is here against us. He allows the criminal, if sentenced to a fine exceeding one-fourth of his property, to compel the judge to commute the excess for imprisonment at the rate of one day of imprisonment for every two dollars of fine, and he adds, that such imprisonment must in no case exceed ninety days. We regret that we cannot agree with him; the object of the penal law is to deter from offences, and this can only be done by means of inflictions disagreeable to offenders. The law ought not to inflict punishments unnecessarily severe; but it ought not, on the other hand, to call the offender into council with his judges, and to allow him an option between two punishments. In general, the circumstance that he prefers one punishment raises a strong presumption that he ought to suffer the other. The circumstance that the love of money is a stronger passion in his mind than the love of personal liberty is, as far as it goes, a reason for our availing ourselves rather of his love of money than of his love of personal liberty for the purpose of restraining him from crime. To look out systematically for the most sensitive part of a man's mind, in order that we may not direct our penal sanctions towards that part of his mind, seems an injudicious policy.

We are far from thinking that the course which we propose is unexceptionable; but it appears to us to be less open to exception than any other which has occurred to us. We propose that, at the time of imposing a fine, the Court shall also fix a certain term of imprisonment which the offender shall undergo in default of payment. In fixing this term the Court will in no case be suffered to exceed a certain maximum, which will vary according to the nature of the offence. If the offence be one which is punishable with imprisonment as well as fine, the term of imprisonment in default of payment will not exceed one-fourth of the longest term of imprisonment fixed by the Code for the offence. If the offence be one which by the Code is punishable only with fine, the term of imprisonment for default of payment will in no case exceed seven days.

But we do not mean that this imprisonment shall be taken in full satisfaction of the fine. We cannot consent to permit the offender to choose whether he will suffer in his person or in his property. To adopt such a course would be to grant exemption from the punishment of fine to those very persons on whom it is peculiarly desirable that the punishment of fine should be inflicted, to those very persons who dislike that punishment most, and whom the apprehension of that punishment would be most likely to restrain. We therefore propose that the imprisonment which an offender has undergone shall not release him from the pecuniary obligation under which he lies. His person will, indeed, cease to be answerable for the fine; but his property will for a time continue to be so. What we recommend is, that at any time during a certain limited period the fine may be levied on his effects by distress. If the fine is paid or levied while he is imprisoned for default of payment, his imprisonment will immediately terminate, and if a portion of the fine be paid during the imprisonment, a proportional abatement of the imprisonment will take place.

It may perhaps appear to some persons harsh to imprison a man for non-payment of a fine, and, after he has endured his imprisonment, to take his property by distress in order to realize the fine. But this harshness is rather apparent than real; if the offender, having the means of paying the fine, chooses rather to lie in prison than to part with his money, his case is the very case in which it is most desirable that the fine should be levied, and he is the very convict who has least claim to indulgence. The confinement which he has undergone may be regarded as no more than a reasonable punishment for his obstinate resistance to the due execution of his sentence. If the offender has not the means of paying the fine while he continues liable to it, he will be quit for his imprisonment. There remains another case; that of an offender who, being really unable to pay his fine, lies in prison for a term, and within six years after his sentence acquires property. This case is the only case in which it can, with any plausibility, be maintained that the law, as we have framed it, would operate harshly. Even in this case, it is evident that our law will operate far less harshly than a law which should provide that an offender sentenced to a fine should be imprisoned till the fine should be paid. Under both laws imprisonment is inflicted, under both a fine is exacted. But the one law liberates the offender on payment of the fine, and also fixes a limit beyond which he cannot be detained in gaol, whether the fine be paid or no. The other law keeps him in confinement till the money is actually paid. It is, therefore, at least as severe as ours on his property, and is immeasurably more severe on his person.

In fact, we treat an offender who has been sentenced to fine more leniently than the law now treats a debtor either in England or in this country. By the English law, an insolvent not in trade is kept in confinement till he has surrendered all his property, till he has answered interrogatories respecting it, till the Court is satisfied that he has paid all that he can pay. Even when his person is liberated, his future acquisitions still continue to be liable to the claims of his creditors. The law throughout British India is in principle the same with the law of England: the offender who has been sentenced to fine must be considered as a debtor, and, as a debtor, not entitled to any peculiar lenity. It will be difficult to show on what principles a creditor ought to be allowed to employ, for the purpose of recovering a debt from a person who is perhaps only unfortunate, a more stringent mode of procedure than that which the State employs for the purpose of realizing a fine from the property of a criminal. If a temporary imprisonment for debt ought not to cancel the claim of the private creditor, neither ought a temporary imprisonment in default of payment of a fine to cancel the claims of public justice.

It is undoubtedly easy to put cases in which this part of the law will operate more severely than we could wish; and so it is easy to put cases in which every penal clause in the Code would operate more severely than we could wish. This is an evil inseparable from all legislation. General rules must be framed; and it is absolutely impossible to frame general rules which shall suit all particular cases. It is sufficient if the rule be, on the whole, more beneficial than any other general rule which can be suggested. Those particular cases in which a rule generally beneficial may operate too harshly must be left to the merciful consideration of the Executive Government. We are satisfied that the punishment of fine would, under the arrangement which we propose, be found to be a most efficacious punishment in a large class of cases. We are satisfied that if offenders are allowed to choose between imprisonment and fine, fine will lose almost its whole efficacy, and will never be inflicted on those who dread it most.

Closely connected with these questions respecting the punishment of fine is another question of the highest importance, which indeed belongs rather to the law of civil rights and to the law of procedure than to the penal law, but respecting which we are desirous to place on record the opinion which we have formed, after much reflection and discussion.

In a very large proportion of criminal cases there is good ground for a civil as well as for a penal proceeding. The English law, most erroneously in our opinion, allows no civil claim for reparation in cases where injury has been caused by an offence amounting to felony. Thus a person is entitled to reparation for what he has lost by petty fraud, but to none if he has been cheated by means of a forged bill of exchange. He is entitled to reparation if his coat has been torn, but to none if his house has been maliciously burned down. He is entitled to reparation for a slap on the face, but to none for having his nose maliciously slit, or his ears cut off. A woman is entitled to reparation for a breach of promise of marriage, but to none for a rape. To us it appears that of two sufferers, he who has suffered the greater harm has, *cæteris paribus*, the stronger claim to compensation; and that of two offences, that which produces the greater harm ought, *cæteris paribus*, to be visited with the heavier punishment. Hence it follows that in general the strongest claims to compensations will be the claims of persons who have been injured by highly penal acts; and that to refuse reparation to all sufferers who have been injured by highly penal acts is to refuse reparation to that very class of sufferers who have the strongest claim to it.

We are decidedly of opinion that every person who is injured by an offence ought to be legally entitled to a compensation for the injury. That the offence is a very serious one, far from being a reason for thinking that he ought to have no compensation, is *primâ facie* a reason for thinking that the compensation ought to be very large.

Entertaining this opinion, we are desirous that the law of criminal procedure should be framed in such a manner as to facilitate the obtaining of reparation by the sufferer. We are inclined to think that an arrangement might be adopted under which one trial would do the work of two. We conceive that, in every case in which fine is part of the punishment of an offence, it ought to be competent to the tribunal which has tried the offender, acting under proper checks, to award the whole or part of the fine to the sufferer, provided that the sufferer signifies his willingness to receive what is so awarded in full satisfaction of his civil claim for reparation. If the Criminal Court shall not make such an award, or if the sufferer shall not be satisfied with such an award, he must be left to his civil action. But if, in such an action, he recovers damages, the fine ought, in our opinion, to be employed, as far as the fine will go, in satisfying those damages.

The plan we propose would not be open to the strong and indeed unanswerable objections which Mr. Livingston has urged against the plan of blending a civil and criminal trial together. Yet we think it likely that our plan would in a great majority of cases render a civil proceeding unnecessary. We are happy to be able to quote the high authority of Mr. Livingston in favour of the doctrine that every fine imposed for an offence ought to be expended, as far as it will go, in paying any damages which may be due in consequence of injury caused by that offence.

This course seems to be the only course consistent with justice to either party. It is most unjust to the man who has been disabled by a wound, or ruined by a forgery, that the Government should take, under the name of fine, so large a portion of the offender's property as to leave nothing to the sufferer. In general, the greater the injury the greater ought to be the fine. On the other hand, the greater the injury the greater ought to be the compensation. If, therefore, the Government keeps whatever it can raise in the way of fine, it follows that the sufferer who has the greatest claim to compensation will be least likely to obtain it. By empowering the Courts to grant damages out of the fine, and by making the fine after it has reached the treasury of the Government answerable for the damages which the sufferer may recover in a Civil Court, we avoid this injustice.

Nor is this arrangement required only by justice to the sufferer, it is also required by justice to the offender. However atrocious his crime may have been, he ought not to be subjected to any punishment beyond what the public interest demands; and we depart from this principle if, when a single payment would affect all that is required both in the way of punishment and in the way of reparation, we impose two distinct payments, the one by way of punishment and the other by way of reparation.

The principles on which a Court proceeds in imposing a fine are quite different from those on which it proceeds in assessing damages. A fine is meant to be painful to the person paying it; but civil damages are not meant to cause pain to the person who pays them. They are meant solely to compensate the plaintiff for evil suffered. They cause pain undoubtedly to the person who has to pay them; but this pain is merely incidental, nor ought the amount of damages at all to depend on the degree of depravity which the wrong-doer has shown, except in so far as that depravity may have increased the evil endured by the sufferer. If A, by mere inadvertence, drives the pole of his carriage against Z's valuable horse, and thus kills the horse, A has committed an action infinitely less reprehensible than if he kills the horse by laying poison secretly in its food. The former act would probably not fall at all under the cognizance of the Criminal Courts. The latter act would be severely punished. But the payment to which Z has a civil claim is in both cases exactly the same, the value of the horse, and a compensation for any expense and inconvenience which the loss of the horse may have occasioned. That A has committed no offence is no reason for giving Z less than his full damages; that A has committed a most wicked and malignant offence is no reason for giving Z more than his full damages. If a mere inadvertence cause a great loss, the damages ought to be high. If the most atrocious crime cause a small loss, the damages ought to be low. They are fixed on a principle quite different from that according to which penal laws are framed and administered.

Here then are two payments required from one person on account of one transaction. The object of the one payment is to give him pain, and the amount of that payment must be supposed to be sufficient to give him as much pain as it is desirable to inflict on him in that form. The object of the other payment is not at all to give pain to the payer, but solely to save another person from loss. It does, indeed, incidentally give pain to the payer; but it is not imposed for that end, nor is it proportioned to the degree in which it may be fit that the payer should suffer pain. Surely under such circumstances justice to the payer requires that the former payment should, as far as it will go, serve both purposes, and that if in the very act of enduring punishment he can make reparation, he should be permitted to do so.

We have now said all that we at present think it necessary to say respecting the punishments provided in the Code. It may be fit that we should explain why some others are omitted.

We have thought it unnecessary to place incapacitation for office, or dismissal from office, in the list of punishments. It will always be in the power of the Government to dismiss from office and to exclude from office even persons against whom there is no legal evidence of guilt. It will always be in the power of the Government, by an act of grace, to admit to office even those who may have been dismissed. We therefore propose that the power of inflicting this penalty shall be left in form, as it must be left in reality, to the Government.

We also considered whether it would be advisable to place in the list of punishments the degrading public exhibition of an offender on a pillory, after the English fashion, or on an ass, in the manner usual in this country. We are decidedly of opinion that it is not advisable to inflict that species of punishment.

Of all punishments this is evidently the most unequal. It may be more severe than any punishment in the Code. It may be no punishment at all. If inflicted on a man who has quick sensibility, it is generally more terrible than death itself. If inflicted on a hardened and impudent delinquent, who has often stood at the bar, and who has no character to lose, it is a punishment less serious than an hour of the treadmill. It derives all its terrors from the higher and better parts of the character of the sufferer; its severity is therefore in inverse proportion to the necessity for severity. An offender who, though he has been drawn into crime by temptation, has not yet wholly given himself up to wickedness and discarded all regard for reputation, is an offender with whom it is generally desirable to deal gently. He may still be reclaimed. He may still become a valuable member of society. On the other hand, the criminal for whom disgrace has no terrors, who dreads nothing but physical suffering, restraint and privation, and who laughs at infamy, is the very criminal against whom the whole rigour of the law ought to be put forth. To employ a punishment which is more bitter than the bitterness of death to the man who has still some remains of virtuous and honourable feeling, and which is mere matter of jest to the utterly abandoned villain, appears to us most unreasonable.

If it were possible to devise a punishment which should give pain proportioned to the degree in which the offender was shameless, hard-hearted, and abandoned to vice, such a punishment would be the most effectual means of protecting society. On the other hand, of all punishments the most absurd is that which produces pain proportioned to the degree in which the offender retains the sentiments of an honest man.

This argument proceeds on the supposition that the public exposure of the criminal has no other terrors than those which it derives from his sensibility to shame. The English pillory, indeed, had terrors of a very different kind. The offender was, even in our own time, given up with scarcely any protection to the utmost ferocity of the mob. Such a mode of punishment is, indeed, free from one objection which we have urged against simple exposure; for it is an object of terror to the most hardened criminal. But it is open to other objections so obvious, that it is unnecessary to bring them to the notice of his Lordship in Council. That the amount of punishment should be determined, not by the law or by the tribunals, but by a throng of people accidentally congregated, among whom the most ignorant and brutal would always on such an occasion be the most forward, would be a disgrace to an age and country pretending to civilization. We take it for granted that the punishment which we are considering, if inflicted in any part of India subject to the British Government would consist in degrading exposure, and nothing more. That punishment, we repeat, while it would be a mere subject of mockery to shameless and abandoned delinquents, would, when inflicted on men who have filled respectable stations and borne respectable characters, be so cruel that it would become justly more odious to the public than the very offences which it was intended to repress.

We have not thought it desirable to place flogging in the list of punishments. If inflicted for atrocious crimes with a severity proportioned to the magnitude of those crimes, that punishment is open to the very serious objections which may be urged against all cruel punishments, and which are so well known that it is unnecessary for us to recapitulate them. When inflicted on men of mature age, particularly if they be of decent stations in life, it is a punishment of which the severity consists, to a great extent, in the disgrace which it causes; and to that extent the arguments which we have used against public exposure apply to flogging.

It has been represented to us by some functionaries in Bengal, that the best mode of stimulating the lower officers of police to the active discharge of their duties is by flogging, and that since the abolition of that punishment in this presidency, the magistrates of the lower provinces have found great difficulty in managing that class of persons.

This difficulty has not been experienced in any other part of India. We, therefore, cannot, without much stronger evidence than is now before us, believe that it is impracticable to make the police officers of the lower provinces efficient without resorting to corporal punishment. The objections to the old system are obvious. To inflict on a public servant, who ought to respect himself and to be respected by others, an ignominious punishment which leaves an indelible mark, and to suffer him still to remain a public servant, to place a stigma on him which renders him an object of contempt to the mass of the population, and to continue to intrust him with any portion, however small, of the powers of Government, appears to us to be a course which nothing but the strongest necessity can justify.

The moderate flogging of young offenders for some petty offences is not open, at least in any serious degree, to the objections which we have stated. Flogging does not inflict on a boy that sort of ignominy which it causes to a grown man. Up to a certain age, boys, even of the higher classes, are often corrected with stripes by their parents and guardians;

and this circumstance takes away a considerable part of the disgrace of stripes inflicted on a boy by order of a magistrate. In countries where a bad system of prison discipline exists, the punishment of flogging has in such cases one great advantage over that of imprisonment. The young offender is not exposed even for a day to the contaminating influence of an ill-regulated gaol. It is our hope and belief, however, that the reforms which are now under consideration will prevent the gaols of India from exercising any such contaminating influence; and, if that should be the case, we are inclined to think that the effect of a few days passed in solitude or in hard and monotonous labour would be more salutary than that of stripes.

Being satisfied, therefore, that the punishment of flogging can be proper only in a few cases, and not being satisfied that it is necessary in any, we are unwilling to advise the Government to retrace its steps, and to re-establish throughout the British territories a practice which, by a policy unquestionably humane and by no means proved to have been injudicious, has recently been abolished through a large part of those territories.

The only remaining point connected with this chapter, to which we wish to call the attention of his Lordship in Council, is the provision contained in clause 61. This provision is intended to prevent an offender whose guilt is fully established from eluding punishment, on the ground that the evidence does not enable the tribunals to pronounce with certainty under what penal provision his case falls.

Where the doubt is merely between an aggravated and mitigated form of the same offence, the difficulty will not be great. In such cases the offender ought always to be convicted of the minor offence. But the doubt may be between two offences, neither of which is a mitigated form of the other. The doubt, for example, may lie between murder and the aiding of murder. It may be certain, for example, that either A or B murdered Z, and that whichever was the murderer was aided by the other in the commission of the murder; but which committed the murder, and which aided the commission, it may be impossible to ascertain. To suffer both to go unpunished, though it is certain that both are guilty of capital crimes, merely because it is doubtful under what clause each of them is punishable, would be most unreasonable. It appears to us that a conviction in the alternative has this recommendation, that it is altogether free from fiction, that it is exactly consonant to the truth of the facts. If the Court find both A and B guilty of murder, or of aiding murder, the Court affirms that which is not literally true; and on all occasions, but especially in judicial proceedings, there is a strong presumption in favour of literal truth. If the Court finds that A has either murdered Z or aided B to murder Z, and that B has either murdered Z or aided A to murder Z, the Court finds that which is the literal truth; nor will there, under the rule which we have laid down, be the smallest difficulty in prescribing the punishment.

It is chiefly in cases where property has been fraudulently appropriated that the necessity for such a provision as that which we are considering will be felt. It will often be certain that there has been a fraudulent appropriation of property; and the only doubt will be, whether this fraudulent appropriation was a theft or a criminal breach of trust. To allow the offender to escape unpunished on account of such a doubt would be absurd. To subject him to the punishment of theft, which is the higher of the two crimes, between which the doubt lies, would be grossly unjust. The punishment to which he ought to be liable is evidently that of criminal breach of trust; but that a Court should convict an offender of a criminal breach of trust, when the opinion of the Court perhaps is, that it is an even chance, or more than an even chance, that no trust was ever reposed in him, seems to us an objectionable mode of proceeding. We will not, in this stage of our labours, venture to lay it down as an unbending rule that the tribunals ought never to employ phrases which, though literally false, are conventionally true. Yet we are fully satisfied that the presumption is always strongly in favour of that form of expression which accurately sets forth the real state of the facts. In the case which we have supposed, the real state of the facts is, that the offender has certainly committed either theft or criminal breach of trust, and that the Court does not know which. This ought, therefore, in our opinion, to be the form of the judgment.

The details of the law on this subject must, of course, be reserved for the Code of procedure; but the provision which directs the manner in which the punishment is to be calculated appears properly to belong to the Penal Code.

Note B.

ON THE CHAPTER OF GENERAL EXCEPTIONS.

This chapter has been framed in order to obviate the necessity of repeating in every penal clause a considerable number of limitations.

Some limitations relate only to a single provision, or to a very small class of provisions. Thus the exception in favour of true imputations on character (clause 470) is an exception which belongs wholly to the law of defamation, and does not affect any other part of the Code. The exception in favour of the conjugal rights of the husband (clause 359) is an exception which belongs wholly to the law of rape, and does not affect any other part of the Code. Every such exception evidently ought to be appended to the rule which it is intended to modify.

But there are other exceptions which are common to all the penal clauses of the Code, or to a great variety of clauses dispersed over many chapters. Such are the exceptions in favour of infants, lunatics, idiots, persons under the influence of delirium; the exceptions in favour of acts done by the direction of the law, of acts done in the exercise of the right of self-defence, of acts done by the consent of the party harmed by them. It would obviously be inconvenient to repeat these exceptions several times in every page. We have, therefore, placed them in a separate chapter, and we have provided that every definition of an offence, every penal provision, and every illustration of a definition or penal provision, shall be construed subject to the provisions contained in that chapter. Most of those explanations appear to us to require no explanation or defence. But the meaning and the ground of the rules laid down in clause 69 and in the three following clauses may not be obvious at first sight. On these, therefore, we wish to make a few observations.

We conceive the general rule to be, that nothing ought to be an offence by reason of any harm which it may cause to a person of ripe age who, undeceived, has given a free and intelligent consent to suffer that harm or to take the risk of that harm. The restrictions by which the rule is limited affect only cases where human life is concerned. Both the general rule and the restrictions may, we think, be easily vindicated.

If Z, a grown man, in possession of all his faculties, directs that his valuable furniture shall be burned, that his pictures shall be cut to rags, that his fine house shall be pulled down, that the best horses in his stable shall be shot, that his plate shall be thrown into the sea, those who obey his orders, however capricious those orders may be, however deeply Z may afterwards regret that he gave them, ought not, as it seems to us, to be punished for injuring his property. Again, if Z chooses to sell his teeth to a dentist, and permits the dentist to pull them out, the dentist ought not to be punished for injuring Z's person. So if Z embraces the Mahomedan religion, and consents to undergo the painful rite which is the initiation into that religion, those who perform the rite ought not to be punished for injuring Z's person.

The reason on which the general rule which we have mentioned rests is this, that it is impossible to restrain men of mature age and sound understanding from destroying their own property, their own health, their own comfort, without restraining them from an infinite number of salutary or innocent actions. It is by no means true that men always judge rightly of their own interest. But it is true that, in the vast majority of cases, they judge better of their own interest than any lawgiver, or any tribunal, which must necessarily proceed on general principles, and which cannot have within its contemplation the circumstances of particular cases and the tempers of particular individuals, can judge for them. It is difficult to conceive any law which should be effectual to prevent men from wasting their substance on the most chimerical speculations, and yet which should not prevent the construction of such works as the Duke of Bridgewater's canals. It is difficult to conceive any law which should prevent a man from capriciously destroying his property, and yet which should not prevent a philosopher, in a course of chemical experiments, from dissolving a diamond, or an artist from taking ancient pictures to pieces, as Sir Joshua Reynolds did, in order to learn the secret of the colouring. It is difficult to conceive any law which should prevent a man from capriciously injuring his own health, and yet which should not prevent an artisan from employing himself in callings which are useful and indeed necessary to society, but which tend to impair the constitutions of those who follow them, or a public-spirited physician from inoculating himself with the virus of a dangerous disease. It is chiefly, we conceive, for this reason, that almost all Governments have thought it sufficient to restrain men from harming others, and have left them at liberty to harm themselves.

But though in general we would not punish an act on account of any harm which it might cause to a person who had consented to suffer that harm, we think that there are exceptions to this rule, and that the case in which death is intentionally inflicted is an exception.

It appears to us that the reasons which render it highly inexpedient to inflict punishment in ordinary cases of harm done by consent of the person harmed do not exist here. The thing prohibited is not, like the destruction of property, or like the mutilation of the person, a thing which is sometimes pernicious, sometimes innocent, sometimes highly useful. It is always, and under all circumstances, a thing which a wise lawgiver would desire to prevent, if it were only for the purpose of making human life more sacred to the multitude. We cannot prohibit men from destroying the most valuable effects, or from disfiguring the person of one who has given his unextorted and intelligent consent to such destruction or such disfiguration, without prohibiting at the same time gainful speculations, innocent luxuries, manly exercises, healing operations. But by prohibiting a man from intentionally causing the death of another, we prohibit nothing which we think it desirable to tolerate.

It seems to us clear, therefore, that no consent ought to be a justification of the intentional causing of death. Whether such intentional causing of death ought or ought not to be punished as murder is a distinct question, and will be considered elsewhere.

The next point which we have here to consider is how far consent ought to be a justification of the causing of death, when that causing of death is, in our nomenclature, voluntary, yet not intentional, that is to say, when the person who caused the death did not mean to cause it, but knew that he was likely to cause it.

In general we have made no distinction between cases in which a man causes an effect designedly, and cases in which he causes it with a knowledge that he is likely to cause it. If, for example, he sets fire to a house in a town at night, with no other object than that of facilitating a theft, but being perfectly aware that he is likely to cause people to be burned in their beds, and thus causes the loss of life, we punish him as a murderer. But there is, as it appears to us, a class of cases in which it is absolutely necessary to make a distinction. It is often the wisest thing that a man can do to expose his life to great hazard. It is often the greatest service that can be rendered to him to do what may very probably cause his death. He may labour under a cruel and wasting malady which is certain to shorten his life, and which renders his life, while it lasts, useless to others and a torment to himself. Suppose that under these circumstances he, undeceived, gives his free and intelligent consent to take the risk of an operation which in a large proportion of cases has proved fatal, but which is the only method by which his disease can possibly be cured, and which, if it succeeds, will restore him to health and vigour. We do not conceive that it would be expedient to punish the surgeon who should perform the operation, though by performing it he might cause death, not intending to cause death, but knowing himself to be likely to cause it. Again; if a person attacked by a wild beast should call out to his friends to fire, though with imminent hazard to himself, and they were to obey the call, we do not conceive that it would be expedient to punish them, though they might by firing cause his death, and though when they fired they knew themselves to be likely to cause his death.

We propose, therefore, that it shall be no offence to do even what the doer knows to be likely to cause death if the sufferer being of ripe age has, undeceived, given a free and intelligent consent to stand the risk, and if the doer did not intend to cause death, but on the contrary, intended in good faith the benefit of the sufferer.

We have now explained the provisions contained in clauses 69 and 70. The cases to which the two next clauses relate bear a close affinity to those which we have just considered.

A lunatic may be in a state which makes it proper that he should be put into a strait waistcoat. A child may meet with an accident which may render the amputation of a limb necessary. But to put a strait waistcoat on a man without his consent is, under our definition, to commit an assault. To amputate a limb is, by our definition, voluntarily to cause grievous hurt, and, as sharp instruments are used, is a very highly penal offence. We have therefore provided, by clause 71, that the consent of the guardian of a sufferer who is an infant or who is of unsound mind shall, to a great extent, have the effect which the consent of the sufferer himself would have, if the sufferer were of ripe age and sound mind.

That there should be some provision of this sort is evidently necessary. On the other hand, we feel that there is a considerable danger in allowing people to assume the office of judging for others in such cases. Every man always intends in good faith his own benefit, and has a deeper interest in knowing what is for his own benefit than any body else can have. That he gives a free and intelligent consent to suffer pain or loss, creates a strong presumption that it is good for him on the whole to suffer that pain or loss. But we cannot safely confide to him the interest of his neighbours in the same unreserved manner in which we confide to him his own, even when he sincerely intends to benefit his neighbours. Even parents have been known to deliver their children up to slavery in a foreign country, to inflict the most cruel mutilations on their male children, to sacrifice the chastity of their female children, and to do all this declaring, and perhaps with truth, that their object was something which they considered as advantageous to the children. We have therefore not thought it sufficient to require that on such occasions the guardian should act in good faith for the benefit of the ward. We have imposed several additional restrictions which, we conceive, carry their defence with them.

There yet remains a kindred class of cases which are by no means of rare occurrence. For example, a person falls down in an apoplectic fit. Bleeding alone can save him, and he is unable to signify his consent to be bled. The surgeon who bleeds him commits an act falling under the definition of an offence. The surgeon is not the patient's guardian, and has no authority from any such guardian; yet it is evident that the surgeon ought not to be punished. Again, a house is on fire. A person snatches up a child too young to understand the danger, and flings it from the house-top, with a faint hope that it may be caught in a blanket below, but with the knowledge that it is highly probable that it will be dashed to pieces. Here, though the child may be killed by the fall, though the person who threw it down knew that it would very probably be killed, and though he was not the child's parent or guardian, he ought not to be punished.

In these examples there is what may be called a temporary guardianship justified by the exigency of the case and by the humanity of the motive. This temporary guardianship bears a considerable analogy to that temporary magistracy with which the law invests every person who is present when a great crime is committed, or when the public peace is concerned. To acts done in the exercise of this temporary guardianship, we extend by clause 72 a protection very similar to that which we have given to the acts of regular guardians.

Clause 73 is intended to provide for those cases which, though, from the imperfections of language, they fall within the letter of the penal law, are yet not within its spirit, and are all over the world considered by the public, and for the most part dealt with by the tribunals, as innocent. As our definitions are framed, it is theft to dip a pen in another man's ink, mischief to crumble one of his wafers, an assault to cover him with a cloud of dust by riding past him, hurt to incommode him by pressing against him in getting into a carriage. There are innumerable acts without performing which men cannot live together in society, acts which all men constantly do and suffer in turn, and which it is desirable that they should do and suffer in turn, yet which differ only in degree from crimes. That these acts ought not to be treated as crimes is evident, and we think it far better expressly to except them from the penal clauses of the Code than to leave it to the judges to except them in practice; for if the Code is silent on the subject, the judges can except these cases only by resorting to one of two practices which we consider as most pernicious, by making law, or by wresting the language of the law from its plain meaning.

We propose (clauses 74 to 84) to except from the operation of the penal clauses of the Code large classes of acts done in good faith for the purpose of repelling unlawful aggressions. In this part of the chapter we have attempted to define, with as much exactness as the subject appears to us to admit, the limits of the right of private defence. It may be thought that we have allowed too great a latitude to the exercise of this right; and we are ourselves of opinion that if we had been framing laws for a bold and high-spirited people, accustomed to take the law into their own hand, and to go beyond the line of moderation in repelling injury, it would have been fit to provide additional restrictions. In this country the danger is on the other side; the people are too little disposed to help themselves; the patience with which they submit to the cruel depredations of gang-robbers, and to trespass and mischief committed in the most outrageous manner by bands of ruffians, is one of the most remarkable, and at the same time one of the most discouraging symptoms which the state of society in India presents to us. Under these circumstances we are desirous rather to rouse and encourage a manly spirit among the people than to multiply restrictions on the exercise of the right of self-defence. We are of opinion that all the evil which is likely to arise from the abuse of that right is far less serious than the evil which would arise from the execution of one person for overstepping what might appear to the Courts to be the exact line of moderation in resisting a body of dacoits.

We think it right, however, to say that there is no part of the Code with which we feel less satisfied than this. We cannot accuse ourselves of any want of diligence or care. No portion of our work has cost us more anxious thought or has been more frequently re-written. Yet we are compelled to own that we leave it still in a very imperfect state; and though we do not doubt that it may be far better executed than it has been by us, we are inclined to think that it must always be one of the least exact parts of every system of criminal law.

We have now made such observations as appear to us to be required on the general exceptions which we propose. It is proper that we should next explain why we have not proposed any exception in favour of some classes of acts which, as some persons may think, are entitled to indulgence.

We long considered whether it would be advisable to except from the operation of the penal clauses of the Code acts committed in good faith from the desire of self-preservation; and we have determined not to except them.

We admit, indeed, that many acts falling under the definition of offences ought not to be punished when committed from the desire of self-preservation; and for this reason, that, as the Penal Code itself appeals solely to the fears of men, it never can furnish them with motives for braving dangers greater than the dangers with which it threatens them. Its utmost severity will be inefficacious for the purpose of preventing the mass of mankind from yielding to a certain amount of temptation. It can, indeed, make those who have yielded to the temptation miserable afterwards. But misery which has no tendency to prevent crime is so much clear evil. It is vain to rely on the dread of a remote and contingent evil as sufficient to overcome the dread of instant death, or the sense of actual torture. An eminently virtuous man indeed will prefer death to crime; but it is not to our virtue that the penal law addresses itself; nor would the world stand in need of penal laws if men were virtuous. A man who refuses to commit a bad action, when he sees preparations made for killing or torturing him unless he complies, is a man who does not require the fear of punishment to restrain him. A man, on the other hand, who is withheld from committing crimes solely or chiefly by the fear of punishment, will never be withheld by that fear when a pistol is held to his forehead or a lighted torch applied to his fingers for the purpose of forcing him to commit a crime.

It would, we think, be mere useless cruelty to hang a man for voluntarily causing the death of others by jumping from a sinking ship into an overloaded boat. The suffering caused by the punishment is, considered by itself, an evil, and ought to be inflicted only for the sake of some preponderating good. But no preponderating good, indeed no good whatever, would be obtained by hanging a man for such an act. We cannot expect that the next man who feels the ship in which he is left descending into the waves, and sees a crowded boat putting off from it, will submit to instant and certain death from fear of a remote and contingent death. There are men, indeed, who in such circumstances would sacrifice their own lives rather than risk the lives of others. But such men act from the influence of principles and feelings which no penal laws can produce, and which, if they were general, would render penal laws unnecessary. Again, a gang of dacoits, finding a house strongly secured, seize a smith, and by torture and threats of death induce him to take his tools and to force the door for them; here, it appears to us, that to punish the smith as a house-breaker would be to inflict gratuitous pain; we cannot trust to the deterring effect of such punishment. The next smith who may find himself in the same situation will rather take his chance of being, at a distant time, arrested, convicted and sentenced to imprisonment, than incur certain and immediate death.

In the cases which we have put, some persons may perhaps doubt whether there ought to be impunity; but those very persons would generally admit that the extreme danger was a mitigating circumstance to be considered in apportioning the punishment. It might, however, with no small plausibility be contended that if any punishment at all is inflicted in such cases, that punishment ought to be not merely death, but death with torture; for the dread of being put to death by torture might possibly be sufficient to prevent a man from saving his own life by a crime; but it is quite certain, as we have said, that the mere fear of capital punishment which is remote, and which may never be inflicted at all, will never prevent him from saving his life. And *à fortiori*, the dread of a milder punishment will not prevent him from saving his life. Laws directed against offences to which men are prompted by cupidity, ought always to take from offenders more than those offenders expect to gain by crime. It would obviously be absurd to provide that a thief or a swindler should be punished with a fine not exceeding half the sum which he had acquired by theft or swindling; in the same manner, laws directed against offences to which men are prompted by fear ought always to be framed in such a way as to be more terrible than the dangers which they require men to brave. It is on this ground, we apprehend, that a soldier who runs away in action is punished with a rigour altogether unproportioned to the moral depravity which his offence indicates. Such a soldier may be an honest and benevolent man, and irreproachable in all the relations of civil life; yet he is punished as severely as a deliberate assassin, and more severely than a robber or a kidnapper. Why is this? Evidently because, as his offence arises from fear, it must be punished in such a manner that timid men may dread the punishment more than they dread the fire of the enemy.

If all cases in which acts falling under the definition of offences are done from the desire of self-preservation were as clear as the cases which we have put of the man who jumps from a sinking ship into a boat, and of the smith who is compelled by dacoits to force a door for them, we should, without hesitation, propose to exempt this class of acts from punishment. But it is to be observed, that in both these cases the person in danger is supposed to have been brought into danger, without the smallest fault on his own part, by mere accident, or by the depravity of others. If a captain of a merchantman were to run his ship on shore in order to cheat the insurers, and then to sacrifice the lives of others in order to save himself from a danger created by his own villainy; if a person who had joined himself to a gang of dacoits with no other intention than that of robbing were at the command of his leader, accompanied with threats of instant death in case of disobedience, to commit murder, though unwillingly, the case would be widely different, and our former reasoning would cease to apply; for it is evident that punishment which is inefficacious to prevent a man from yielding to a certain temptation may often be efficacious to prevent him from exposing himself to that temptation. We cannot count on the fear which a man may entertain of being brought to the gallows at some distant time as sufficient to overcome the fear of instant death; but the fear of remote punishment may often overcome the motives which induce a man to league himself with lawless companions, in whose society no person who shrinks from any atrocity that they may command can be certain of his life. Nothing is more usual than for pirates, gang-robbers and rioters to excuse their crimes by declaring that they were in dread of their associates, and durst not act otherwise. Nor is it by any means improbable that this may often be true. Nay, it is not improbable that crews of pirates and gangs of robbers may have committed crimes which every one among them was unwilling to commit, under the influence of mutual fear; but we think it clear that this circumstance ought not to exempt them from the full severity of the law.

Again, nothing is more usual than for thieves to urge distress and hunger as excuses for their thefts. It is certain, indeed, that many thefts are committed from the pressure of distress so severe as to be more terrible than the punishment of theft, and than the disgrace which that punishment brings with it to the mass of mankind. It is equally certain that, when the distress from which a man can relieve himself by theft is more terrible than the evil consequences of theft, those consequences will not keep him from committing theft; yet it by no means follows that it is irrational to punish him for theft; for though the fear of punishment is not likely to keep any man from theft when he is actually starving, it is very likely to keep him from being in a starving state. It is of no effect to counteract the irresistible motive which immediately prompts to theft; but it is of great effect to counteract the motives to that idleness and that profusion which end in bringing a man into a condition in which no law will keep him from committing theft. We can hardly conceive a law more injurious to society than one which should provide that as soon as a man who had neglected his work, or who had squandered his wages in stimulating drugs, or gambled them away, had been thirty-six hours without food, and felt the sharp impulse of hunger, he might, with impunity, steal food from his neighbours.

We should therefore think it in the highest degree pernicious to enact that no act done under the fear even of instant death should be an offence. It would *à fortiori* be absurd to enact that no act under the fear of any other evil should be an offence.

There are, as we have said, cases in which it would be useless cruelty to punish acts done under the fear of death, or even of evils less than death. But it appears to us impossible precisely to define these cases. We have, therefore, left them to the Government, which, in the exercise of its clemency, will doubtless be guided in a great measure by the advice of the Courts.

We considered whether it would be desirable to make any distinction between offences committed against freemen and offences committed against slaves. We certainly entered on the consideration of this important question with a strong leaning to the opinion that no such distinction ought to be made. We thought it our duty, however, not to come to a decision without obtaining information and advice from those who were best qualified to give it. We have collected information on the subject from every part of India, and we have now in our office a large collection of documents containing much that is curious, and that in future stages of the work in which we are engaged will be useful. At present we have only to consider the subject with reference to the Penal Code.

These documents have satisfied us that there is at present no law whatever defining the extent of the power of a master over his slaves; that every thing depends on the disposition of the particular functionary who happens to be in charge of a district, and that functionaries who are in charge of contiguous districts, or who have at different times been in charge of the same district, hold diametrically opposite opinions as to what their official duty requires. Nor is this discrepancy found only in the proceedings of subordinate Courts. The Court of Nizamut

Adawlut at Fort William lay down the law thus: "A master would not be punished, the Court opine, for inflicting a slight correction on his legal slave, such as a tutor would be justified in inflicting on a scholar, or a father on a child." The Court of Nizamut Adawlut at Allahabad take a quite different view of the law: "Although," they say, "the Mahomedan law permits the master to correct his slave with moderation, the Code by which the magistrates and other criminal authorities are bound to regulate their proceedings does not recognize any such power, and as the regulations of the Government draw no distinction between the slave and the freeman in criminal matters, but place them both on a level, it is the practice of the Courts, following the principles of equal justice, to treat them both alike." The Court of Foujdarry Adawlut at Madras state, that it is not the practice of the Courts to make any distinction whatever in cases which come before them; that a circular order of the Foujdarry Adawlut recognizes the right of a master to inflict corrections in certain cases, but that in practice no such distinction is made. We own that we entertain some doubts whether the practice be universally such as is supposed by the Foujdarry Adawlut. We perceive that two magistrates in the western division of the Madras Presidency differ from each other in opinion on this subject. The magistrate of Canara says, that "the right of the master to inflict punishment has been allowed, but only to a very small extent." The magistrate of Malabar states, that "the relation of a master and slave has never been recognized as justifying acts which would otherwise be punishable, or as constituting a ground for mitigation of punishment." The Court of Foujdarry Adawlut at Bombay has given no opinion on the point, and there is a great difference of opinion among the subordinate authorities in the Bombay Presidency. One gentleman conceives that the imposing of personal restraint is the only act otherwise punishable which the Courts would allow a master to commit when a slave might be concerned. Another conceives that a master has a power of correction similar to that of a father. A third goes further, and is of opinion, that "all but cases of very aggravated nature would be considered as entitled to exemption from or mitigation of punishment on this account." On the other hand, several gentlemen are of opinion that the relation of master and slave would not be considered by the Courts as a plea for any act which would be an offence if committed against a freeman.

It is clear, therefore, that we find the law in a state of utter uncertainty; it is equally clear that we cannot leave it in that state; we must either withdraw from a large class of slaves a protection to which the Courts under the jurisdiction of which they live now think them entitled, or we must extend to a large class a protection greater than what they actually enjoy.

We have not the smallest hesitation in recommending to his Lordship in Council that the law throughout all British India should be conformable to what, in the opinion of the Court of Nizamut Adawlut at Allahabad, is now actually the law in the Presidency of Fort William, and to what, in the opinion of the Court of Foujdarry Adawlut at Fort St. George, is now actually the practice in the Madras Presidency. That is to say, we recommend that no act falling under the definition of an offence should be exempted from punishment because it is committed by a master against a slave.

The distinction which, in the opinion of many respectable functionaries, the law now makes between acts committed against a freeman and acts committed against a slave is in itself an evil, and an evil so great, that nothing but the strongest necessity, proved by the strongest evidence, could justify any Government in maintaining it. We conceive that the circumstances which we have already stated are sufficient to show that no such necessity exists. By removing all doubt on the subject, we shall not deprive the master of a power the right to which has never been questioned, but of a power which is and has for some time been, to say the least, of disputable legality, and which has been held by a very precarious tenure.

To leave the question undecided is impossible; to decide the question by putting any class of slaves in a worse situation than that in which they now are is a course which we cannot think of recommending, and which we are certain that the Government will not adopt. The inference seems to be, that the question ought to be decided by declaring that whatever is an offence when committed against a freeman shall be also an offence when committed against a slave.

It may perhaps be thought that, by framing the law in this manner, we do, in fact, virtually abolish slavery in British India; and undoubtedly, if the law as we have framed it should be really carried into full effect, it will at once deprive slavery of those evils which are its essence, and will insure the speedy and natural extinction of the whole system. The essence of slavery, the circumstance which makes slavery the worst of all social evils, is not in our opinion this, that the master has a legal right to certain services from the slave, but this, that the master has a legal right to enforce the performance of those services without having recourse to the tribunals. He is a judge in his own cause; he is armed with the powers of a magistrate for the protection of his own private interest against the person who owes him service. Every other judge quits the bench as soon as his own cause is called on. The judicial authority of the master begins and ends with cases in which he has a direct stake. The moment that a master is really deprived of this authority, the moment that his right to service really becomes, like his right to money which he has lent, a mere civil right, which he can enforce only by a civil action, the peculiarly odious and malignant evils of slavery disappear at once; the name of slavery may be retained, but the thing is no longer the same. It is evidently impossible that any master can really obtain efficient service from unwilling labourers by means of prosecution before the civil tribunals; nor is there any instance of any country in which the relation of master and servant is maintained by means of such actions. In some states of society the labourer works because the master inflicts instant correction whenever there is any disobedience or slackness; in a different state of society, the people labour for a master because the master makes it worth their while. Practically, we believe it will be found that there is no third way. A labourer who has neither the motive of the freeman nor that of the slave, who is actuated neither by the hope of wages nor by the dread of stripes, will not work at all. The master may indeed, if he chooses, go before the tribunals and obtain a decree; but scarcely any master would think it worth while to do so, and scarcely any labourer would be spurred to constant and vigorous exertion by the dread of such a legal proceeding. In fact, we are not even able to form to ourselves the idea of a society in which the working classes should have no other motives to industry than the dread of prosecution. We understand how the planter of Mauritius formerly induced his negroes to work; he applied the lash if they loitered. We understand how our grooms and bearers are induced to work at Calcutta; they are gainers by working, and by obtaining a good character; they are losers by being turned away; but in what other way servants can be induced to work we do not understand.

It appears to us, therefore, that if we can really prevent the master from exacting service by the use of any violence or restraint, or by the infliction of any bodily hurt, one of two effects will inevitably follow: either the master will obtain no service at all, or he will find himself under the necessity of obtaining it by making it a source of advantage to the labourer as well as to himself. A labourer who knows that if he idles, his master will not dare to strike him; that if he absconds, his master will not dare to confine him; that his master can enforce a claim to service only by taking more trouble, losing more time and spending more money than the service is worth, will not work for fear. It follows that if the master wishes the labourer to work at all, the master must have recourse to different motives, to the motives of a freeman, to the hope of reward, to the sense of reciprocal benefit. Names are of no consequence. It matters nothing whether the labourer be or be not called a slave. All that is of real moment is that he should work from the motives and feelings of the freeman.

This effect, we are satisfied, would follow if outrages offered to slaves were really punished exactly as outrages offered to freemen are punished. But we are far indeed from thinking that, by merely framing the law as we have framed it, we shall produce this effect. It is quite certain that slaves are at present often oppressed by their masters in districts where the magistrates and judges conceive that the law now is what we propose that it shall henceforth be. It is therefore evident that they may continue to be oppressed by their masters when the law has been made perfectly clear. To an ignorant labourer, accustomed from his birth to obey a superior for daily food, to submit without resistance to the cruelty and tyranny of that superior, perhaps to be transferred, like a horse or a sheep, from one superior to another, neither the law which we now propose, nor any other law, will of itself give freedom. It is of little use to direct the judge to punish unless we can teach the sufferer to complain.

We have thought it right to state this, lest we should mislead his Lordship in Council into an opinion that the law, framed as we propose to frame it, will really remove all the evils of slavery, and that nothing more will remain to be done. So far are we from thinking that the law, as we propose to frame it, will, of itself, effect a great practical change, that we greatly doubt whether even a law abolishing slavery would, of itself, effect any great practical change. Our belief is that even if slavery were expressly abolished, it might, and would, in some parts of India still continue to exist in practice. We trust, therefore, that his Lordship in Council will not consider the measure which we now recommend as of itself sufficient to accomplish the benevolent ends of the British Legislature, and to relieve the Indian Government from its obligation to watch over the interests of the slave population.

Note C.

ON THE CHAPTER OF OFFENCES AGAINST THE STATE.

His Lordship in Council will perceive that, in this chapter, we have provided only for offences against the Government of India, and that we have made no mention of offences against the General Government of the British Empire. We have done so because it appears to us doubtful to what extent his Lordship in Council is competent to legislate respecting such offences. The Act of Parliament which defines the legislative power of the Council of India especially prohibits that body from making any law "which shall in any way affect any prerogative of the Crown or the authority of Parliament, or any part of the unwritten laws, or constitution of the United Kingdom of Great Britain and Ireland, whereon may depend, in any degree, the allegiance of any person to the Crown of the United Kingdom, or the sovereignty or dominion of the said Crown over any part of the said territories."

It might be argued that these words relate only to laws affecting the rights of the Crown and of Parliament, and not to laws affecting the penal sanctions of those rights, and that, therefore, though the Governor-General in Council has no power to absolve the King's subjects from their allegiance, he has power to fix the punishment to which they shall be liable for violating their allegiance. It seems to us, however, that there is the closest connexion in this case between the right and the penal sanction, that a power to alter the sanction amounts to a power to abolish the right, and that Parliament, which withheld from the Indian Legislature one of those powers, cannot be supposed to have intended to grant the other.

If the Governor-General in Council has the legal power to fix the punishment of a subject who should, in the territories of the East India Company, conspire the death of the King, or levy war against the King, then the Governor-General in Council has the legal power to fix that punishment at a fine of one anna; and it is plain that a law which should fix such a fine as the only punishment of regicide and rebellion would be a law virtually absolving all subjects within the territories of the East India Company from their allegiance.

This part of the penal law, therefore, we have not ventured to touch. We leave it to the Imperial Legislature. But we trust that we may be permitted to suggest to his Lordship in Council that the early attention of the Home authorities should be called to this subject.

There is no doubt that the criminal statute law of England is not binding generally on a native of India in the mofussil. Whether the statute law relating to treason be binding on such a native is a question with respect to which we do not venture to give a decided opinion. It seems to us exceedingly doubtful whether that part of the statute law be binding on such a native. It is quite certain that no Court has ever enforced it against such a native; and that, in the opinion of many respectable and intelligent judicial officers in the service of the Company, it could not legally be enforced against such a native. Nor are the Company's judicial officers, by whom alone such a native can legally be tried, likely to be accurately acquainted with the statute law of England on the subject of treason, or with the mass of constructions and precedents by which that law has been overlaid. If such a native be not punishable under the English statute law of treason, it is difficult to say under what law he could be punished for that crime. The regulations contain nothing on the subject. The Council of India, we conceive, is not competent to legislate respecting it. The Mahomedan law might possibly be so violently strained as to reach it in Bengal and in the Madras Presidency; and in the Bombay Presidency it might possibly be brought within that clause which arms the Courts with an enormous discretion in cases in which they conceive that morality and social order require protection. But there are, in our opinion, strong reasons against retaining either the Mahomedan penal law, or the sweeping clause of the Bombay Regulations, to which we have referred.

It may be added that the provision of the Bombay Regulations, to which we have referred, applies only to persons who profess a religion with which a system of penal law is inseparably connected. Unless, therefore, the English statute law on the subject of treason applies to natives in the mofussil, a point respecting which we entertain great doubt, a native Christian who should, at Surat, assist the levying of war, not against the Company's Government, but against the British Crown, would be liable to no punishment whatever.

This anomalous state of things may be, in some degree, explained by the singular manner in which the British Empire grew up in India. The East India Company was, during a long course of years, in theory at least, under two masters. It was subject to the King of England; it was subject also to the Great Mogul. It derived its corporate existence from the British Parliament. It held its territorial possessions by a grant from the Durbar of Delhi. The situation of the native subjects of the Company bore some analogy to that of the inhabitants of Mindelheim, while that fief of the empire was held by the Duke of Marlborough. The inhabitants of Mindelheim were subjects of the Duke of Marlborough, but they owed no allegiance to the English Crown, though their sovereign was subject to that Crown. It was in this way that the British Empire in India originated. It was long considered as a wise policy to disguise the real power of the English under the forms of vassalage, and to leave to the Mogul and his Viceroys the empty honours of a sovereignty which was really held by the Company. This policy was abandoned slowly and by imperceptible degrees. The recognition of the supremacy of the King of Delhi appeared on the seal of the British Government down to a late period, and on its coin down to a still later period. A great change has indeed taken place since the grant of the Dewannee of the lower provinces to the Company, but it has taken place so gradually, that, though it would be absurd to deny that the natives of British India are now subjects of his Majesty, it would be impossible to point out the particular time when they became so.

To these circumstances we attribute most of the anomalies which are to be found in the legal relation subsisting between the natives of British India and the General Government of the empire. It seems highly desirable that the Imperial Legislature should do what cannot be done by the Local Legislature, and should pass a law of high treason for the territories of the East India Company. As far, indeed, as respects the royal person, the present state of the law, though in theory unseemly, is not likely to cause any practical evil. It is highly improbable that any English King will visit his Indian dominions, or that any plot, having for its object the death of an English King, will ever extend its ramifications to India. But it is by no means improbable that persons residing in the territories of the East India Company may be parties to the levying of war against the British Crown, without violating any local regulation. If any insurrection were to take place in any of the British dominions in the Eastern Seas, in Ceylon, for example, or in Mauritius, it is by no means improbable that persons residing within the Company's territories might furnish information and stores to the rebels. And if this were done by a person not subject to the jurisdiction of the Courts established by Royal Charter, we are satisfied that there would be the most serious difficulty in bringing the criminal to legal punishment.

We have, his Lordship in Council will perceive, made the abetting of hostilities against the Government, in certain cases, a separate offence, instead of leaving it to the operation of the general law laid down in the chapter on abetment. We have done so for two reasons. In the first place, war may be waged against the Government by persons in whom it is no offence to wage such war, by foreign princes and their subjects. Our general rules on the subject of abetment would apply to the case of a person residing in the British territories who should abet a subject of the British Government in waging war against that Government; but they would not reach the case of a person who, while residing in the British territories, should abet the waging of war by any foreign prince against the British Government. In the second place, we agree with the great body of legislators in thinking, that though in general a person who has been a party to a criminal design which has not been carried into effect, ought not to be punished so severely as if that design had been carried into effect, yet an exception to this rule must be made with respect to high offences against the state; for state-crimes, and especially the most heinous and formidable state-crimes, have this peculiarity, that if they are successfully committed, the criminal is almost always secure from punishment. The murderer is in greater danger after his victim is despatched than before. The thief is in greater danger after the purse is taken than before. But the rebel is out of danger as soon as he has subverted the Government. As the penal law is impotent against a successful rebel, it is consequently necessary that it should be made strong and sharp against the first beginnings of rebellion, against treasonable designs which have been carried no further than plots and preparations. We have therefore not thought it expedient to leave such plots and preparations to the ordinary law of abetment. That law is framed on principles which, though they appear to us to be quite sound, as respects the great majority of offences, would be inapplicable here. Under that general law, a conspiracy for the subversion of the Government would not be punished at all if the conspirators were detected before they had done more than discuss plans, adopt resolutions and interchange promises of fidelity. A conspiracy for the subversion of the Government, which should be carried as far as the gunpowder treason or the assassination plot against William the Third, would be punished very much less severely than the counterfeiting of a rupee, or the presenting of a forged check. We have, therefore, thought it absolutely necessary to make separate provision for the previous abetting of great state offences. The subsequent abetting of such offences may, we think, without inconvenience, be left to be dealt with according to the general law.

Note D.

ON THE CHAPTER OF OFFENCES RELATING TO THE ARMY AND NAVY.

A few words will explain the necessity of having some provisions of the nature of those which are contained in this chapter.

It is obvious that a person who, not being himself subject to military law, exhorts or assists those who are subject to military law to commit gross breaches of discipline, is a proper subject of punishment. But the general law respecting the abetting of offences will not reach such a person; nor, framed as it is, would it be desirable that it should reach him. It would not reach him, because the military delinquency which he has abetted is not punishable by this Code, and therefore is not, in our legal nomenclature, an offence. Nor is it desirable that the punishment of a person not military, who has abetted a breach of military discipline, should be fixed according to the principles on which we have proceeded in framing the law of abetment. We have provided that the punishment of the abettor of an offence shall be equal or proportional to the punishment of the person who commits that offence; and this seems to us a sound principle when applied only to the punishments provided by this Code. But the military penal law is, and must necessarily be, far more severe than that under which the body of the people live. The severity of the military penal law can be justified only by reasons drawn from the peculiar habits and duties of soldiers, and from the peculiar relation in which they stand to the Government. The extension of such severity to persons not members of the military profession appears to us altogether unwarrantable. If a person, not military, who abets a breach of military discipline, should be made liable to a punishment regulated, according to our general rules, by the punishment to which such a breach of discipline renders a soldier liable, the whole symmetry of the penal law would be destroyed. He who should induce a soldier to disobey any order of a commanding officer would be liable to be punished more severely than a dacoit, a professional thug, an incendiary, a ravisher or a kidnapper. We have attempted in this chapter to provide, in a manner more consistent with the general character of the Code, for the punishment of persons who, not being military, abet military crimes.

Note E.

ON THE CHAPTER OF THE ABUSE OF THE POWERS OF PUBLIC SERVANTS.

This chapter is intended to reach offences which are committed by public servants, and which are of such a description that they can be committed by public servants alone.

We have found considerable difficulty in drawing the line between public servants and the great mass of the community. We hope that the description which we have given in clause 14 will be found to comprehend all those whom it is desirable to bring under this part of the law, and we trust that, when the Code of procedure is completed, this description may be made both more accurate and more concise.

Those offences which are common between public servants and other members of the community, we leave to the general provisions of the Code. If a public servant embezzles public money, we leave him to the ordinary law of criminal breach of trust. If he falsely pretends to have disbursed money for the public, and by this deception induces the Government to allow it in his accounts, we leave him to the ordinary law of cheating. If he produces forged vouchers to back his statement, we leave him to the ordinary law of forgery. We see no reason for punishing these offences more severely when the Government suffers by them than when private people suffer. A Government, indeed, which does not consider the sufferings of private individuals as its own, is not only selfish but short-sighted in its selfishness. The revenue is drawn from the wealth of individuals, and every act of dishonest spoliation which tends to render individuals insecure in the enjoyment of their wealth is really an injury to the revenue. On every account, therefore, we think it desirable that the property of the state should, in general, be protected by exactly the same laws which are considered as sufficient for the protection of the property of the subject.

We are not without apprehension that we may be thought to have treated the transgressions of public servants too favourably, to have passed by without notice some malpractices which deserve punishment, and where we have provided punishments, to have seldom made those punishments sufficiently severe.

It is true that we have altogether omitted to provide any punishment for some kinds of misconduct on the part of public servants. It is true, also, that the punishments which we propose in this chapter are not generally proportioned either to the evil which the abuse of power produces, or to the depravity of a man who, having been intrusted with power for the public benefit, employs that power to gratify his own cupidity or revenge.

But it is to be remembered that there is a marked distinction between the penal clauses contained in this chapter and the other penal clauses of the Code. In general a penal clause sets forth the whole punishment which can be inflicted on an offender by any public authority. The penalty of theft, of breach of trust, of cheating, of extortion, of assault, of defamation, has been fixed on the supposition that it is the whole penalty which the criminal is to suffer, and that no power in the state can make any addition to it. But the penalty of an offence committed by a public functionary in the exercise of his public functions has been fixed on the supposition that it will often be only a part, and a small part, of the penalty which he will suffer. It is in the power of the Government to punish him for many acts which the law has not made punishable. It is in the power of the Government to add to any sentence pronounced by the Courts another sentence which will often be even more terrible. To a man whose subsistence is derived from official emoluments, whose habits are formed to official business, and whose whole ambition is fixed on official promotion, degradation to a lower post is a punishment; dismissal from the public service is a punishment sufficient even for a serious offence. The mere knowledge that his character has suffered in the opinion of those superiors on whom his advancement depends probably gives him as much pain as a heavy fine.

This is to a great degree the case in every country, and assuredly not less in India than in any other country. Indeed those servants of the Company by whom all the higher offices in the Indian Government are filled entertain a feeling about their situations very different from that which is found among political men in England. It is natural that they should entertain such a feeling; they are set apart at an early age as persons destined to hold offices in India; their education is conducted at home with that view; they are transferred when just entering on manhood to the country which they are to govern; they pass the best years of their lives in acquiring knowledge which is most important to men who are to fill high situations in India, but which in any other walk of life would bring little profit and little distinction, in mastering languages which, when they quit this country, are useless to them; in studying a vast and complicated system of revenue which is altogether peculiar to the East; in becoming intimately acquainted with the interests, the resources and the projects of potentates whose very existence is unknown even to educated men in Europe. To such a man, dismissal from the service of the Indian Government is generally a very great calamity. His life has been thrown away. It has been passed in acquiring information and experience which, in any pursuit to which he may now betake himself, will be of little or no service to him. There are therefore few covenanted servants of the Company who, even if they were men destitute of all honourable feeling, would not look on dismissal from the service as a most severe punishment. But the covenanted servants of the Company are English gentlemen, that is to say, they are persons to whom the ruin of their fortunes is less terrible than the ruin of their characters. There are few of them, we believe, to whom an intimation that their integrity was suspected by the Government would not give more pain than a sentence of six months' imprisonment for an offence not of a disgraceful kind, and to many of them death itself would appear less dreadful than ignominious expulsion from the body of which they are members.

Thus dismissal from the public service is a punishment exceedingly dreaded by public functionaries, and most dreaded in this country by the highest class of public functionaries. Nor is this all. It is not merely a severe punishment, but it is also a punishment which is far more likely to be inflicted than many punishments which are less severe. Those who are legally competent to inflict it are bound by no rules, except those which their own discretion may impose on them. For what kind and degree of delinquency they shall inflict it, by what evidence that delinquency shall be established, by what tribunals the inquiry shall be conducted; nay, whether there shall be any delinquency, any evidence, any tribunal, is absolutely in their breasts. They may inflict this punishment, and may be justified in inflicting it for transgressions which are not susceptible of precise definition, and which have not been substantiated by decisive proof. They may be justified in inflicting it, because many petty circumstances, each of which separately would be too trivial for notice, have, when taken together, satisfied them that a functionary is unfit for any public employment. They may be justified in inflicting it, because they strongly suspect him of guilt, which they cannot bring home to him by evidence to which a Zillah judge would pay any attention. Most of what we have said of the punishment of dismissal from office applies, though not in the same degree, to the slighter punishments of censure, suspension and removal from a higher to a lower post.

We have shown that public functionaries are liable not only to the punishments provided by this Code, but also to other peculiar punishments of great severity. It seems therefore to follow, that if those who possess the power of inflicting these peculiar punishments can be trusted, some malpractices of public functionaries may be safely left unnoticed in this Code, and that other malpractices need not be visited with legal punishment so rigorous as their enormity might seem to merit. The Executive Government, in our opinion, deserves to be trusted. At all events it must be trusted; for it is quite certain that no laws will prevent corruption and oppression on the part of the servants of the Indian Government, if that Government is inclined to screen the offenders. The Government, to say nothing of the vast influence which it can indirectly exert, appoints, promotes and removes judges at its discretion. It can remit any sentence pronounced by the Courts; it can, therefore, if it be not honestly disposed to correct official abuses, render any penal clauses directed against such abuses almost wholly inoperative. And if it be honestly disposed, as we firmly believe that it is, to correct official abuses, it will use for that purpose its power of rewarding and punishing its servants.

It will be seen that we propose, under clause 138, to punish with imprisonment for a term not exceeding three years, or with fine, or both, the corruption of public functionaries. The punishment of fine will, we think, be found very efficacious in cases of this description, if the judges exercise the power given them as they ought to do, and compel the delinquent to deliver up the whole of his ill-gotten wealth.

The mere taking of presents by a public functionary, when it cannot be proved that such presents were corruptly taken, we have made penal only in one particular case, to which we shall hereafter call the attention of his Lordship in Council. We have not made the taking of presents by public functionaries generally penal; because, though we think that it is a practice which ought to be carefully watched and often severely punished, we are not satisfied that it is possible to frame any law on the subject which would not be rendered inoperative either by its extreme severity or by its extreme laxity. Absolutely to prohibit all public functionaries from taking presents would be to prohibit a son from contributing to the support of a father, a father from giving a portion with a daughter, a brother from extricating a brother from pecuniary difficulties. No Government would wish to prevent persons intimately connected by blood, by marriage or by friendship, from rendering services to each other; and no tribunals would enforce a law which should make the rendering of such services a crime. Where no such close connexion exists, the receiving of large presents by a public functionary is generally a very suspicious proceeding; but a lime, a wreath of flowers, a slice of betel-nut, a drop of atar of roses poured on his handkerchief, are presents which it would in this country be held churlish to refuse, and which cannot possibly corrupt the most mercenary of mankind. Other presents, of more value than these, may, on account of their peculiar nature, be accepted, without affording any ground for suspicion. Luxuries socially consumed, according to the usages of hospitality, are presents of this description; it would be unreasonable to treat a man in office as a criminal, for drinking many rupees-worth of champagne in a year, at the table of an acquaintance; though if he were to suffer one of his subordinates to accept even a single rupee in specie, he might deserve exemplary punishment.

It appears to us, therefore, that the taking of presents where a corrupt motive cannot be proved, ought not in general to be a crime cognizable by the Courts. Whether in any particular case it ought to be punished or not will depend on innumerable circumstances, which it is impossible accurately to define, on the amount of the present, on the nature of the present, on the relation in which the giver and receiver stand to each other. Suppose that a wealthy English agent, who is interested in a young civil servant of the Company, were to pay the debts of that civil servant; or, suppose that a resident were to furnish money to enable his invalid assistant to proceed to the Cape. In these transactions there might be nothing which the most scrupulous could disapprove; but the case would be widely different if a wealthy native zemindar were to pay the debts of a collector of his district, or if any of the officers at the residency were to receive money from the minister of a foreign power. In such a case, though it might be impossible to prove a corrupt motive, we think that the Government would be inexcusable if it suffered the delinquent to remain in the public service.

We have hitherto put only extreme cases, cases in which it is clear that the taking of presents ought not to be punished, or cases in which it is clear that the taking of presents ought to be severely punished. But between the extremes lie an immense variety of cases, some of which call for severe punishment, some for milder punishment, some for censure, some for gentle admonition, while some ought to be tolerated. We have said that if a collector were to accept a large present of money from a wealthy native zemindar, he would deserve to be turned out of the service; but if the collector were to accept such a present from an English indigo planter, the case would be different. The indigo planter might be his uncle, his brother, his father-in-law, his brother-in-law; in that case there might be no impropriety in the transaction. Again, if a native in the public service were to accept a present from a zemindar who was connected with him by blood, marriage or friendship, there might be no impropriety in the transaction.

By the Act of Parliament to which the malpractices of the first British conquerors of India gave occasion, the servants of the Company were forbidden to receive presents from Asiatics, but were left at liberty to receive presents from Europeans. The legislators of that time appear to have proceeded on the supposition that the servants of the Company would all be Englishmen, and that no Englishman would ever have any such connexion with any native as would render the receiving of presents from that native unobjectionable.

Natives are now declared by law to be competent to hold any post in the Company's service. It would evidently be improper to interdict an Asiatic in the service of the Company from receiving pecuniary assistance from his Asiatic father, or from receiving a portion with an Asiatic bride. It seems to us therefore that the rule laid down by Parliament, though it will still be in many cases an excellent rule of evidence, ought not, under the altered circumstances of India, to continue to be a rule of law.

Again, it ought to be remembered that the European and native races are not at present divided from each other by so strong a line of separation as at the time when the British Parliament laid down the rule which we are considering. The interval is still wide, but it by no means appears to us as it appeared to the legislators of the last generation, to be impassable. It is evident, therefore, that the rule formerly laid down by Parliament is constantly becoming less and less applicable to the state of India. On these grounds we have thought it advisable to leave this matter to the Executive Government, which will doubtless promulgate from time to time such rules as it may deem proper, and will enforce submission to those rules by visiting its disobedient servants with censure, with degradation or with dismissal from the public service, according to the circumstances of every case.

We have thought it desirable to make one exception: we propose that a judge who accepts any valuable thing by way of gift from one whom he knows to be a plaintiff or a defendant in any cause pending in his Court shall be severely punished. This rule is not to extend to the taking of food in the interchange of ordinary civilities. It appears to us that the objections which we have made to a general law prohibiting the receipt of presents by public functionaries do not apply to this clause. The rule is clear and definite. The practice against which it is directed is not a practice which ought sometimes to be encouraged, and sometimes to be tolerated. It ought always, and under all circumstances, to be discouraged. It therefore appears to unite all the characteristics which mark out a practice as a fit object of penal legislation.

The only other penal provision of this chapter to which we think it necessary to call the attention of his Lordship in Council is that which is contained in clause 149.

We are of opinion that the preceding clauses, and the power which the Government possesses of suspending, degrading and dismissing public functionaries, will be found sufficient to prevent gross abuses. But there will remain a crowd of petty offences with which it is very difficult to deal, offences which separately are too slight to be brought before the criminal tribunals, which will sometimes be committed by good public servants, and which therefore it would be inexpedient to punish by removal from office, yet which will be very often committed if they can be committed with impunity, and which, if often committed, would impair the efficiency of all departments of the administration, and would produce infinite vexation to the body of the people.

By the existing laws of all the presidencies, a summary judicial power is given in certain cases to certain official superiors for the purpose of restraining their subordinates. We are inclined to believe that this is a wholesome power, and that it has, in the great majority of cases, been honestly employed for the protection of the public. We propose therefore to adopt the principle, and to make the system uniform through all the provinces of the empire, and through all the departments of the public service. We propose that a public functionary who is guilty of neglect of duty, who treats his superiors with disrespect, or who disobeys the lawful orders given by them for his guidance, shall be liable to a fine not exceeding the official pay which he receives in three months. In default of payment he will be liable (see clause 54) to seven days' imprisonment.

In the Code of procedure we think that it will be proper to provide that the power of awarding this penalty shall be given, not to the ordinary tribunals, but to the official superiors of the offender. Thus, if a subordinate officer employed in the collection of revenue should incur this penalty, it will be imposed by the collector, and the appeal will probably be to the Board of Revenue. If an officer employed to execute the process of a Zillah Court should neglect his duty, the fine will be imposed by the Zillah judge, and the appeal will probably be to the Sudder Court. If the offence should be committed by a tide-waiter, the collector of Customs for the port will probably impose the penalty, and the appeal will be to the Board of Customs. These instances we give merely as illustrations of what, at present, appears to us desirable. The details of this part of the law of procedure cannot be arranged without much consideration and inquiry.

One important question still remains to be considered. We are of opinion that we have provided sufficient punishment for the public servant who receives a bribe. But it may be doubted whether we have provided sufficient punishment for the person who offers it. The person who, without any demand express or implied on the part of a public servant, volunteers an offer of a bribe, and induces that public servant to accept it, will be punishable under the general rule contained in clause 88 as an instigator. But the person who complies with a demand, however signified, on the part of a public servant, cannot be considered as guilty of instigating that public servant to receive a bribe. We do not propose that such a person shall be liable to any punishment, and, as this omission may possibly appear censurable to many persons, we are desirous to explain our reasons.

In all states of society the receiving of a bribe is a bad action, and may properly be made punishable. But whether the giving of a bribe ought or ought not to be punished, is a question which does not admit of a short and general answer. There are countries in which the giver of a bribe ought to be more severely punished than the receiver. There are countries, on the other hand, in which the giving of a bribe may be what it is not desirable to visit with any punishment. In a country situated like England, the giver of a bribe is generally far more deserving of punishment than the receiver. The giver is generally the tempter, the receiver is the tempted. The giver is generally rich, powerful, well educated; the receiver, needy and ignorant. The giver is under no apprehension of suffering any injury if he refuses to give. It is not by fear, but by ambition, that he is generally induced to part with his money. Such a person is a proper subject of punishment. But there are countries where the case is widely different, where men give bribes to magistrates from exactly the same feeling which leads them to give their purses to robbers or to pay ransom to pirates; where men give bribes because no man can, without a bribe, obtain common justice. In such countries we think that the giving of bribes is not a proper subject of punishment. It would be as absurd, in such a state of society, to reproach the giver of a bribe with corrupting the virtue of public servants, as it would be to say that the traveller who delivers his money when a pistol is held to his breast corrupts the virtue of the highwayman.

We would by no means be understood to say that India, under the British Government, is in a state answering to this last description. Still we fear it is undeniable that corruption does prevail to a great extent among the lower class of public functionaries; that the power which those functionaries possess renders them formidable to the body of the people, that in the great majority of cases the receiver of the bribe is really the tempter, and that the giver of the bribe is really acting in self-defence.

Under these circumstances, we are strongly of opinion that it would be unjust and cruel to punish the giving of a bribe in any case in which it could not be proved that the giver had really by his instigations corrupted the virtue of a public servant, who, unless temptation had been put in his way, would have acted uprightly.

Note F.

ON THE CHAPTER OF CONTEMPTS OF THE LAWFUL AUTHORITY OF PUBLIC SERVANTS.

We were at first disposed to have one chapter for contempts of the lawful authority of Courts of Justice, another for contempts of the lawful authority of officers of revenue, and a third for contempts of the lawful authority of officers of police. But we soon found that these three chapters would be almost the same, word for word. It appeared to us also that, in the existing state of the civil administration of India, the separation which we were at first inclined to make would produce nothing but perplexity. The functions of magistrate and collector are very frequently united in the same person; and that person is perpetually called upon, both as magistrate and collector, to perform acts which are judicial in their nature, to try offenders, and to decide litigated questions of civil right. While the division of labour between the different departments of the public service is so imperfect, it would be idle to make nice distinctions between those departments in the Penal Code.

In order to frame this chapter, we went carefully through the existing regulations of the three presidencies, and extracted the numerous penal provisions which are intended to enforce obedience to the lawful authority of different classes of public servants. Having collected these provisions, and discarded a very few which we thought obviously unreasonable or superfluous, we proceeded to analyse the rest.

It is possible that our analysis may be imperfect; and it is highly probable that the punishments which we propose may require some modification. It will be seen that we propose the same punishment for all the offences which fall, in our analysis, under the same head. For example; one head is the omitting to obey the lawful summons of a public servant. For this offence we have only one punishment; and this punishment will be applicable alike to the witness who omits to obey the lawful summons of the Court of Sudder Dewanny Adawlut, to the witness who omits to obey the lawful summons of a moonsiff, to the putwarree who in Bengal omits to obey the lawful summons of the collector, to the ryot who in the Madras Presidency omits to obey the lawful summons of the collector, to the trader who in the same presidency omits to attend a meeting lawfully convened for the distribution of the Vizabuddy. In the same manner we propose one punishment for the captain of a ship in the Hoogly who illegally refuses to admit a custom-house officer on board, for a landholder who refuses to admit a surveyor lawfully commissioned by the collector to measure land, for a distiller who refuses to admit the proper officer to examine his distillery. Again, we propose the same punishment for the person who resists the taking of goods in execution under a decree of a Court of Justice, for the person who resists the taking of property by way of distress for arrears of revenue, for the person who resists the seizure of salt by lawful authority, for the person who resists the seizure of a boat in default of toll by lawful authority, for the person who resists the seizure of smuggled goods by lawful authority.

We are sensible that there may be reasons which have escaped us for making distinctions in punishment between offences which in our classification fall under the same head. But it is impossible to find in any single person, or in any small body of persons, so extensive and minute a knowledge of every province of India, and of every department of the public service, as would be a security against errors of this description. We have no doubt that if his Lordship in Council directs the Code to be published for general information, valuable suggestions will be received from servants of the Company in different parts of India, and that those suggestions will enable the Government to modify the provisions which we propose, by introducing proper aggravations and mitigations.

The only provision which appears to us to require any further explanation is that which is contained in clause 182.

We have, to the best of our ability, framed laws against acts which ought to be repressed at all times and places, or at times and places which it is in our power to define. But there are acts which at one time and place are perfectly innocent, and which at another time or place are proper subjects of punishment; nor is it always possible for the legislator to say at what time or at what place such acts ought to be punishable.

Thus it may happen that a religious procession which is in itself perfectly legal, and which, while it passes through many quarters of a town, is perfectly harmless, cannot without great risk of tumult and outrage be suffered to turn down a particular street inhabited by persons who hold the ceremony in abhorrence, and whose passions are excited by being forced to witness it. Again, there are many Hindoo rites which in Hindoo temples and religious assemblies the law tolerates, but which could not with propriety be exhibited in a place which English gentlemen and ladies were in the habit of frequenting for purposes of exercise. Again, at a particular season hydrophobia may be common among the dogs at a particular place, and it may be highly advisable that all people at that place should keep their dogs strictly confined. Again, there may be a particular place in a town which the people are in the habit of using as a receptacle for filth. In general this practice may do no harm, but an unhealthy season may arrive when it may be dangerous to the health of the population, and under such circumstances it is evidently desirable that no person should be allowed to add to the nuisance. It is evident that it is utterly impossible for the legislature to mark out the route of all the religious processions in India, to specify all the public walks frequented by English ladies and gentlemen, to foresee in what months and in what places hydrophobia will be common among dogs, or when a particular dunghill may become dangerous to the health of a town. It is equally evident that it would be unjust to punish a person who cannot be proved to have acted with bad intentions for doing to-day what yesterday was a perfectly innocent act, or for doing in one street what it would be perfectly innocent to do in another street, without giving him some notice.

What we propose, therefore, is to empower the local authorities to forbid acts which these authorities consider as dangerous to the public tranquillity, health, safety or convenience, and to make it an offence in a person to do any thing which that person knows to be so forbidden, and which may endanger the public tranquillity, health, safety or convenience. It will be observed that we do not give to the local authorities the power of arbitrarily making any thing an offence; for unless the Court before which the person who disobeys the order is tried shall be of opinion that he has done something tending to endanger the public tranquillity, health, safety or convenience, he will be liable to no punishment. The effect of the order of the local authority will be merely to deprive the person who knowingly disobeys the order of the plea that he had no bad intentions. He will not be permitted to allege that if he has caused harm, or risk of harm, it was without his knowledge.

Thus, if in a town where no order for the chaining up of dogs has been made, A suffers his dog to run about loose, A will be liable to no punishment for any mischief which the animal may do, unless it can be shown that A knew the animal to be dangerous. But if an order for confining dogs has been issued, and if A knew of that order, it will be no defence for him to allege, and even to prove, that he believed his dog to be perfectly harmless. If the Court think that A's disobedience has caused harm, or risk of harm, A will be liable to punishment. On the other hand, if the Court think that there was no danger, and that the local order was a foolish one, A will not be liable to punishment.

We see some objections to the way in which we have framed this part of the law; but we are unable to frame it better. On the one hand, it is, as we have shown, absolutely necessary to have some local rules which shall not require the sanction of the legislature. On the other hand, we are sensible that there is the greatest reason to apprehend much petty tyranny and vexation from such rules; and this although the framers of those rules may be very excellent and able men. There is scarcely any disposition in a ruler more prejudicial to the happiness of the people than a meddling disposition. Yet, experience shows us that it is a disposition which is often found in company with the best intentions, with great activity and energy, and with a sincere regard for the interest of the community. A public servant of more than ordinary zeal and industry, unless he have very much more than ordinary judgment, is the very man who is likely to harass the people under his care with needless restrictions. We have, therefore, thought it necessary to provide that no person should be punished merely for disobeying a local order, unless it be made to appear that the disobedience has been attended with evil, or risk of evil. Thus no person will be punished for disobeying an idle and vexatious order.

The mode of promulgating these orders belongs to the Code of procedure, which will of course contain such provisions as may be required for the purpose of enabling the Government to exercise a constant and efficient control over its local officers.

Note G.

ON THE CHAPTER OF OFFENCES RELATING TO PUBLIC JUSTICE.

Many offences which interfere with the administration of justice are sufficiently provided for in other chapters, particularly in the chapter relating to contempts of the lawful authority of public servants. There still remain, however, some offences of that description for which the present chapter is intended to provide.

The rules which we propose touching the offence of attempting to impose on a Court of Justice by false evidence differ from those of the English law, and of the Codes which we have had an opportunity of consulting.

It appears to us, in the first place, that the offence which we have designated as the fabricating of false evidence is not punished with adequate severity under any of the systems to which we refer. This may perhaps be because the offence, in its aggravated forms, is not one of very frequent occurrence in western countries. It is notorious, however, that in this country the practice is exceedingly common, and for obvious reasons. The mere assertion of a witness commands far less respect in India than in Europe, or in the United States of America. In countries in which the standard of morality is high, direct evidence is generally considered as the best evidence. In England assuredly it is so considered, and its value, as compared with the value of circumstantial evidence, is perhaps overrated by the great majority of the population. But in India we have reason to believe that the case is different. A judge, after he has heard a transaction related in the same manner by several persons who declare themselves to be eye-witnesses of it, and of whom he knows no harm, often feels a considerable doubt whether the whole, from beginning to end, be not a fiction, and is glad to meet with some circumstance, however slight, which supports the story, and which is not likely to have been devised for the purpose of supporting the story.

Hence, in England, a person who wishes to impose on a Court of Justice knows that he is likely to succeed best by perjury, or subornation of perjury. But in India, where a judge is generally on his guard against direct false evidence, a more artful mode of imposition is frequently employed. A lie is often conveyed to a Court, not by means of witnesses, but by means of circumstances, precisely because circumstances are less likely to lie than witnesses. These two modes of imposing on the tribunals appear to us to be equally wicked, and equally mischievous. It will indeed be harder to bring home to an offender the fabricating of false evidence than the giving of false evidence. But wherever the former offence is brought home, we would punish it as severely as the latter. If A puts a purse in Z's bag, with the intention of causing Z to be convicted as a thief, we would deal with A as if he had sworn that he saw Z take a purse. If A conceals in Z's house a paper written in imitation of Z's hand, and purporting to be a plan of a treasonable conspiracy, we would deal with A as if he had sworn that he was present at a meeting of conspirators at which Z presided.

The exception in clause 190 is in strict conformity with this principle. We propose to treat the giving of false evidence and the fabricating of false evidence in exactly the same way. We have no punishment for false evidence given by a person when on his trial for an offence, though we conceive that such a person ought to be interrogated. The grounds on which this part of the law is founded will shortly be submitted to Government in our report on the law of evidence. As we do not propose to punish a prisoner for lying at the bar in order to escape punishment, so we do not propose to punish him for fabricating evidence with the view of escaping punishment, unless he also contemplated some injury to others as likely to be produced by the evidence so fabricated. If A stabs Z, and afterwards on his trial denies that he stabbed Z, we do not propose to punish A as a giver of false evidence. And on the same principle, if A, after having stabbed Z, in order to escape detection, disposes Z's body in such a manner as is likely to lead a jury to think the death accidental, we do not propose to punish A as the fabricator of false evidence.

It appears to us that the offence of attempting to impose on a Court of Justice by false evidence is an offence of which there are numerous grades, some of which may be easily defined. The authors of the French Code have not overlooked these circumstances, though they have not, in our opinion, marked the gradations very successfully. The English law makes no distinction whatever between the man who has attempted to take away his neighbour's life by false swearing, and the man who has strained his conscience to give an undeserved good character to a boy accused of a petty theft. The former is punished far too leniently; the latter perhaps too severely.

The giving of false evidence must always be a grave offence. But few points in penal legislation seem to us clearer than that the law ought to make a distinction between that kind of false evidence which produces great evils, and that kind of false evidence which produces comparatively slight evils.

As the ordinary punishment of false evidence, we propose imprisonment for a term of not more than seven years, nor less than one year. If the false evidence is given or fabricated with intent to cause a person to be convicted of a grave offence not capital, we propose that the person who gives or fabricates such evidence may be punished with the punishment of the offence which he has attempted to fix on another. If the false evidence be given or fabricated with the intention of causing death, we propose to punish it in the same manner in which we propose to punish the worst attempts to murder. If such false evidence actually causes death, the person who has given or fabricated it falls under the definition of murder, and is liable to capital punishment. In this last point, the law, as we have framed it, agrees with the old law of England, which, though in our opinion just and reasonable, has become obsolete.

We think this the proper place to notice an offence which bears a close affinity to that of giving false evidence, and which we leave for the present unpunished, only on account of the defective state of the existing law of procedure,—we mean the crime of deliberately and knowingly asserting falsehoods in pleading. Our opinions on this subject may startle persons accustomed to that boundless license which the English law allows to mendacity in suitors. On what principle that license is allowed we must confess ourselves unable to discover. A lends Z money; Z repays it. A brings an action against Z for the money, and affirms in his declaration that he lent the money, and has never been repaid. On the trial A's receipt is produced; it is not doubted; A himself cannot deny that he asserted a falsehood in his declaration. Ought A to enjoy impunity? Again: Z brings an action against A for a debt which is really due. A's plea is a positive averment that he owes Z nothing. The case comes to trial; and it is proved by overwhelming evidence that the debt is a just debt. A does not even attempt a defence. Ought A in this case to enjoy impunity? If, in either of the cases which we have stated, A were to suborn witnesses to support the lie which he has put on the pleadings, every one of these witnesses, as well as A himself, would be liable to severe punishment. But false evidence in the vast majority of cases springs out of false pleading, and would be almost entirely banished from the Courts if false pleading could be prevented.

It appears to us that all the marks which indicate that an act is a proper subject for legal punishment meet in the act of false pleading. That false pleading always does some harm is plain. Even when it is not followed up by false evidence it always delays justice. That false pleading produces any compensating good to atone for this harm has never, as far as we know, been even alleged. That false pleading will be more common if it is unpunished than if it is punished appears as certain as that rape, theft, embezzlement, would, if unpunished, be more common than they now are. It is evident also that there will be no more difficulty in trying a charge of false pleading than in trying a charge of false evidence. The fact that a statement has been made in pleading will generally be more clearly proved than the fact that a statement has been made in evidence. The falsehood of a statement made in pleading will be proved in exactly the same manner in which the falsehood of a statement made in evidence is proved. Whether the accused person knew that he was pleading falsely, the Courts will determine on the same evidence on which they now determine whether a witness knew that he was giving false testimony.

We have as yet spoken only of the direct injury produced to honest litigants by false pleading. But this injury appears to us to be only a part, and perhaps not the greatest part, of the evil engendered by the practice. If there be any place where truth ought to be held in peculiar honour, from which falsehood ought to be driven with peculiar severity, in which exaggerations, which elsewhere would be applauded as the innocent sport of the fancy, or pardoned as the natural effect of excited passion, ought to be discouraged, that place is a Court of Justice. We object, therefore, to the use of legal fictions, even when the meaning of those fictions is generally understood, and we have done our best to exclude them from this Code. But that a person should come before a Court, should tell that Court premeditated and circumstantial lies for the purpose of preventing or postponing the settlement of a just demand, and that by so doing he should incur no punishment whatever, seems to us to be a state of things to which nothing but habit could reconcile wise and honest men. Public opinion is vitiated by the vicious state of the law. Men who, in any other circumstances, would shrink from falsehood, have no scruple about setting up false pleas against just demands. There is one place, and only one, where deliberate untruths, told with the intent to injure, are not considered as discreditable, and that place is a Court of Justice. Thus the authority of the tribunals operates to lower the standard of morality, and to diminish the esteem in which veracity is held; and the very place which ought to be kept sacred from misrepresentations, such as would elsewhere be venial, becomes the only place where it is considered as idle scrupulosity to shrink from deliberate falsehood.

We consider a law for punishing false pleading as indispensably necessary to the expeditious and satisfactory administration of justice, and we trust that the passing of such a law will speedily follow the appearance of the Code of procedure. We do not, as we have stated, at present propose such a law, because while the system of pleading remains unaltered in the Courts of this country, and particularly in the Courts established by Royal Charter, it will be difficult, or to speak more properly, impossible to enforce such a law. We have, therefore, gone no further than to provide a punishment for the frivolous and vexatious instituting of civil suits, a practice which, even while the existing systems of procedure remain unaltered, may, without any inconvenience, be made an offence. The law on the subject of false evidence will, as it appears to us, render unnecessary any law for punishing the frivolous and vexatious preferring of criminal charges.

No other part of this chapter appears to require comment.

Note H.

ON OFFENCES RELATING TO THE REVENUE.

In order to frame this chapter, we took a course similar to that which we took with the chapter relating to contempts of the lawful authority of public servants. We went carefully through the revenue laws of the three presidencies, extracted the penal clauses, analysed them, and reduced them to a small number of general heads.

His Lordship in Council will perceive that we have not thought it proper to insert in the Code any provision for the confiscation of property on the ground of a breach of the revenue laws, and that we leave the existing rules on that subject untouched. We have done so, because it does not appear to us that such confiscation is in strictness a punishment. It has indeed much in common with punishment; but it appears to us that there is a marked distinction, and that confiscation of the sort which is authorized in many parts of the regulations of the three presidencies would, considered in the light of a punishment, be anomalous and indefensible. It is a proceeding directed, not against the person who has broken the law, but against the thing with respect to which the law has been broken. It is not necessary that any misconduct should be proved, that any accusation should be brought, that any particular individual should be in the contemplation of the authority which directs the confiscation. Nay, the revenue laws authorize confiscation, not only in cases where misconduct is not proved, but in cases where it is proved that there has been no misconduct in any quarter; and, where there has been misconduct, those laws authorize the confiscation of the property of a person who is proved to have had no share in the misconduct.

To give a single example: if tobacco be found in the island of Bombay after the time at which it ought to be exported thence, it is confiscated, together with the receptacles which contain it, the substances in which it is packed, and the carriages and animals which are employed to convey it. This, which is a fair specimen of revenue laws respecting confiscation, is evidently objectionable, considered as a penal law. The carriages, the animals, the vessels, the tobacco itself, may all be the property of persons who are not in the least to blame. Indeed, we know that under this law the boxes of gentlemen have repeatedly been seized, because the servants who packed them had concealed tobacco in the baggage. Such a law, put into the form of a penal provision, would be too grotesque to be a subject of serious argument. It would, in the phraseology of our Code, run thus: "If any person places contraband tobacco in the baggage of any other person, the person in whose baggage such contraband tobacco is placed shall be punished with the confiscation of such baggage." And the following illustration would make the law, if possible, still more ridiculous: "Contraband tobacco is hidden in A's baggage, by A's servant, without A's knowledge, and contrary to A's express command. A has committed the offence defined in this clause."

It is evident, therefore, that this law, and many other laws of the same kind, must be defended on principles quite different from those on which penal legislation ought to be conducted. They must be defended, not as being penal laws directed against the guilty, but rather as being sharp and stringent laws of civil procedure which are intended to enable the Government to obtain its due with speed and certainty, at the cost whether of the guilty or of the innocent. Viewing them in this light, and knowing as we know that they are greatly mitigated in practice by the lenity of the Executive Government, we consider them as justifiable; but we are decidedly of opinion that they would be out of place in a Penal Code.

Note I.

ON THE CHAPTER OF OFFENCES RELATING TO COIN.

Most of the provisions in this chapter appear sufficiently intelligible without any explanation.

We have proposed that the Government of India should follow the general practice of Governments in punishing more severely the counterfeiting of its own coin than the counterfeiting of foreign coin. It appears to us peculiarly advisable, under the present circumstances of India, to make this distinction. It is much to be wished that the Company's currency may supersede the numerous coinages which are issued from a crowd of mints in the dominions of the petty princes of India. It has appeared to us that this object may be in some degree promoted by the law as we have framed it. That coinage, the purity of which is guarded by the most rigorous penalties, is likely to be the most pure; and that coinage which is likely to be the most pure will be the most readily taken in the course of business.

It is not very probable that any person in this country will employ himself in making counterfeit sovereigns or shillings; but should so improbable an event occur, we think that the King's coin should have the same protection which is given to the coin of the local Government. It may perhaps be thought that in proposing laws for the protection of the King's coin, we have departed from the principle which we laid down in our note on the law of offences against the State, and that we should have acted more consistently in leaving the British currency to the care of the British Legislature. It appears to us, however, that the offence of coining, though, in an arbitrary classification, it may be called by the technical name of treason, is in substance an offence against property and trade, that it is an offence of very nearly the same kind with the forging of a bank note, and that it would be an offence of exactly the same kind if the bank note, like the notes of the Bank of England formerly, were in all cases legal tender, or if the coin, like the Company's gold mohur at present, were not legal tender. We do not therefore conceive that in proposing a law for punishing the counterfeiting of the King's coin, we are proposing a law which can reasonably be said to affect any of the royal prerogatives.

The distinction which we propose to make (see clauses 241 and 242) between two different classes of utterers is marked in the French Code; and it is so obviously agreeable to reason and justice that we are surprised that, having been marked in that Code, it should not have been adopted by Mr. Livingston. We are glad to perceive that the Code of Bombay makes this distinction.

An utterer by profession, an utterer who is the agent employed by the coiner to bring counterfeit coin into circulation, is guilty of a very high offence. Such an utterer stands to the coiner in a relation not very different from that in which a habitual receiver of stolen goods stands to a thief. He makes coining a far less perilous and a far more lucrative pursuit than it would otherwise be. He passes his life in the systematic violation of the law, and in the systematic practice of fraud in one of its most pernicious forms. He is one of the most mischievous, and is likely to be one of the most depraved of criminals. But a casual utterer, an utterer who is not an agent for bringing counterfeit coin into circulation, but who, having heedlessly received a bad rupee in the course of his business, takes advantage of the heedlessness of the next person with whom he deals to pay that bad rupee away, is an offender of a very different class. He is undoubtedly guilty of a dishonest act, but of one of the most venial of dishonest acts. It is an act which proceeds not from greediness for unlawful gain, but from a wish to avoid, by unlawful means it is true, what to a poor man may be a severe loss. It is an act which has no tendency to facilitate or encourage the operations of the coiner. It is an occasional act, an act which does not imply that the person who commits it is a person of lawless habits. We think, therefore, that the offence of a casual utterer is perhaps the least heinous of all the offences into which fraud enters.

We considered whether it would be advisable to make it an offence in a person to have in his possession at one time a certain number of counterfeit coins, without being able to explain satisfactorily how he came by them. It did not, after much discussion, appear to us advisable to recommend this or any similar provision. We entertain strong objections to the practice of making circumstances which are in truth only evidence of an offence part of the definition of an offence; nor do we see any reason for departing in this case from our general rule.

Whether a person who is possessed of bad money knows the money to be bad, and whether, knowing it to be bad, he intends to put it in circulation, are questions to be decided by the tribunals according to the circumstances of the case, circumstances of which the mere number of the pieces is only one and may be one of the least important. A few bad rupees which should evidently be fresh from the stamp would be stronger evidence than a greater number of bad rupees which appeared to have been in circulation for years. A few bad rupees, all obviously coined with the same die, would be stronger evidence than a greater number obviously coined with different dies. A few bad rupees placed by themselves, and unmixed with good ones, would be far stronger evidence than a much larger number which might be detected in a large mass of treasure.

Note J.

ON THE CHAPTER OF OFFENCES RELATING TO RELIGION AND CASTE.

The principle on which this chapter has been framed is a principle on which it would be desirable that all Governments should act, but from which the British Government in India cannot depart without risking the dissolution of society: it is this, that every man should be suffered to profess his own religion, and that no man should be suffered to insult the religion of another.

The question whether insults offered to a religion ought to be visited with punishment does not appear to us at all to depend on the question whether that religion be true or false. The religion may be false, but the pain which such insults give to the professors of that religion is real. It is often, as the most superficial observation may convince us, as real a pain and as acute a pain as is caused by almost any offence against the person, against property or against character. Nor is there any compensating good whatsoever to be set off against this pain. Discussion, indeed, tends to illicit truth; but insults have no such tendency; they can be employed just as easily against the purest faith as against the most monstrous superstition. It is easier to argue against falsehood than against truth; but it is as easy to pull down or defile the temples of truth as those of falsehood; it is as easy to molest with ribaldry and clamour men assembled for purposes of pious and rational worship, as men engaged in the most absurd ceremonies. Such insults, when directed against erroneous opinions, seldom have any other effect than to fix those opinions deeper, and to give a character of peculiar ferocity to theological dissension: instead of eliciting truth they only inflame fanaticism.

All these considerations apply with peculiar force to India. There is perhaps no country in which the Government has so much to apprehend from religious excitement among the people. The Christians are numerically a very small minority of the population, and in possession of all the highest posts in the Government, in the tribunals and in the army. Under their rule are placed millions of Mahomedans, of differing sects, but all strongly attached to the fundamental articles of the Mahomedan creed, and tens of millions of Hindoos, strongly attached to doctrines and rites which Christians and Mahomedans join in reprobating. Such a state of things is pregnant with dangers which can only be averted by a firm adherence to the true principles of toleration. On those principles the British Government has hitherto acted with eminent judgment, and with no less eminent success; and on those principles we propose to frame this part of the Penal Code.

We have provided a punishment of great severity for the intentional destroying or defiling of places of worship, or of objects held sacred by any class of persons. No offence in the whole Code is so likely to lead to tumult, to sanguinary outrage, and even to armed insurrection. The slaughter of a cow in a sacred place at Benares in 1809 caused violent tumult, attended with considerable loss of life. The pollution of a mosque at Bangalore was attended with consequences still more lamentable and alarming. We have therefore empowered the Courts, in cases of this description, to pass a very severe sentence on the offender.

The provisions which we have made for the purpose of protecting assemblies held for religious worship, and of guarding from intentional insult the rites of sepulture and the remains of the dead, do not appear to require any explanation or defence.

The intentional depriving a Hindoo of his caste by assault or by deception is not at present an offence in any part of India, though it may be a ground for a civil action. It appears to us, however, that an injury so wanton, an injury which indicates so bad a feeling in the person who causes it, and which gives so much pain and excites so much resentment in the sufferer, is as proper a subject for penal legislation as most of the acts which are made punishable by this Code; we have, therefore, made it an offence. The rendering the food of a Hindoo useless to him by causing it to be in what he considers as a polluted state is an injury of the same kind, though comparatively venial. We propose to make it an offence, but not to deal with it severely, unless it should be repeatedly committed by the same person.

In framing clause 282, we had two objects in view; we wish to allow all fair latitude to religious discussion, and at the same time to prevent the professors of any religion from offering, under the pretext of such discussion, intentional insults to what is held sacred by others. We do not conceive that any person can be justified in wounding with deliberate intention the religious feelings of his neighbours by words, gesture or exhibitions. A warm expression dropped in the heat of controversy, or an argument urged by a person, not for the purpose of insulting and annoying the professors of a different creed, but in good faith for the purpose of vindicating his own, will not fall under the definition contained in this clause.

Clause 283 is intended to prevent such practices as those known among the natives by the names of Dhurna and Traga. Such acts are now punishable by law, and it is unnecessary to adduce any argument for the purpose of showing that they ought to be so.

Note K.

ON THE CHAPTER OF ILLICIT ENTRANCE INTO AN ILLICIT RESIDENCE IN THE TERRITORIES OF THE EAST INDIA COMPANY.

The Indian Legislature is required by the Act of Parliament 3 and 4 Wm. IV, cap. 85, section 84, "as soon as conveniently may be, to make laws or regulations providing for the prevention or punishment of the illicit entrance into or residence in the said territories of persons not authorized to enter or reside therein."

We have, therefore, thought it our duty to insert in the Penal Code provisions for the purpose of carrying the intentions of Parliament into effect.

Note L.

ON OFFENCES RELATING TO THE PRESS.

The penal provisions contained in this chapter are taken from the Act of the Governor-General of India in Council, No. 11 of 1835.

Sufficient provision appears to us to have been made in other parts of the Code, particularly by clause 195, for the punishment of the offence mentioned in the last section of the Act to which we have referred.

Note M.

ON OFFENCES AGAINST THE BODY.

The first class of offences against the body consists of those offences which affect human life; and highest in this first class stand those offences which fall under the definition of voluntary culpable homicide.

This important part of the law appears to us to require fuller explanation than almost any other.

The first point to which we wish to call the attention of his Lordship in Council is the expression "omits what he is legally bound to do" in the definition of voluntary culpable homicide. These words, or other words tantamount in effect, frequently recur in the Code. We think this the most convenient place for explaining the reason which has led us so often to employ them; for if that reason shall appear to be sufficient in cases in which human life is concerned, it will *à fortiori* be sufficient in other cases.

Early in the progress of the Code it became necessary for us to consider the following question: when acts are made punishable on the ground that those acts produce, or are intended to produce, or are known to be likely to produce, certain evil effects, to what extent ought omissions which produce, which are intended to produce, or which are known to be likely to produce, the same evil effects to be made punishable?

Two things we take to be evident; first, that some of these omissions ought to be punished in exactly the same manner in which acts are punished; secondly, that all these omissions ought not to be punished. It will hardly be disputed that a gaoler who voluntarily causes the death of a prisoner by omitting to supply that prisoner with food, or a nurse who voluntarily causes the death of an infant intrusted to her care by omitting to take it out of a tub of water into which it has fallen, ought to be treated as guilty of murder. On the other hand, it will hardly be maintained that a man should be punished as a murderer because he omitted to relieve a beggar, even though there might be the clearest proof that the death of the beggar was the effect of this omission, and that the man who omitted to give the alms knew that the death of the beggar was likely to be the effect of the omission. It will hardly be maintained that a surgeon ought to be treated as a murderer for refusing to go from Calcutta to Meerut to perform an operation, although it should be absolutely certain that this surgeon was the only person in India who could perform it, and that if it were not performed, the person who required it would die. It is difficult to say whether a Penal Code which should put no omissions on the same footing with acts, or a Penal Code which should put all omissions on the same footing with acts, would produce consequences more absurd and revolting. There is no country in which either of these principles is adopted. Indeed, it is hard to conceive how, if either were adopted, society could be held together.

It is plain, therefore, that a middle course must be taken; but it is not easy to determine what that middle course ought to be. The absurdity of the two extremes is obvious. But there are innumerable intermediate points; and wherever the line of demarcation may be drawn, it will, we fear, include some cases which we might wish to exempt, and will exempt some which we might wish to include.

Mr. Livingston's Code provides, that a person shall be considered as guilty of homicide who omits to save life, which he could save "without personal danger or pecuniary loss." This rule appears to us to be open to serious objection. There may be extreme inconvenience without the smallest personal danger, or the smallest risk of pecuniary loss, as in the case which we lately put of a surgeon summoned from Calcutta to Meerut to perform an operation. He may be offered such a fee that he would be a gainer by going. He may have no ground to apprehend that he should run any greater personal risk by journeying to the Upper Provinces than by continuing to reside in Bengal. But he is about to proceed to Europe immediately, or he expects some members of his family by the next ship, and wishes to be at the presidency to receive them; he, therefore, refuses to go; surely, he ought not, for so refusing, to be treated as a murderer. It would be somewhat inconsistent to punish one man for not staying three months in India to save the life of another, and to leave wholly unpunished a man who, enjoying ample wealth, should refuse to disburse an anna to save the life of another. Again, it appears to us that it may be fit to punish a person as a murderer for causing death by omitting an act which cannot be performed without personal danger or pecuniary loss. A parent may be unable to procure food for an infant without money; yet the parent, if he has the means, is bound to furnish the infant with food, and if, by omitting to do so, he voluntarily causes its death, he may with propriety be treated as a murderer. A nurse hired to attend a person suffering from an infectious disease cannot perform her duty without running some risk of infection; yet if she deserts the sick person, and thus voluntarily causes his death, we should be disposed to treat her as a murderer.

We pronounce with confidence, therefore, that the line ought not to be drawn where Mr. Livingston has drawn it. But it is with great diffidence that we bring forward our own proposition. It is open to objections: cases may be put in which it will operate too severely, and cases in which it will operate too leniently; but we are unable to devise a better.

What we propose is this, that where acts are made punishable on the ground that they have caused, or have been intended to cause, or have been known to be likely to cause, a certain evil effect; omissions which have caused, which have been intended to cause, or which have been known to be likely to cause, the same effect shall be punishable in the same manner, provided that such omissions were, on other grounds, illegal. An omission is illegal (see clause 28) if it be an offence, if it be a breach of some direction of law, or if it be such a wrong as would be a good ground for a civil action.

We cannot defend this rule better than by giving a few illustrations of the way in which it will operate. A omits to give Z food, and by that omission voluntarily causes Z's death. Is this murder? Under our rule it is murder if A was Z's gaoler, directed by the law to furnish Z with food. It is murder if Z was the infant child of A, and had therefore a legal right to sustenance, which right a Civil Court would enforce against A. It is murder if Z was a bedridden invalid, and A a nurse hired to feed Z. It is murder if A was detaining Z in unlawful confinement, and had thus contracted (see clause 338) a legal obligation to furnish Z, during the continuance of the confinement, with necessaries. It is not murder if Z is a beggar, who has no other claim on A than that of humanity.

A omits to tell Z that a river is swollen so high that Z cannot safely attempt to ford it, and by this omission voluntarily causes Z's death. This is murder, if A is a peon stationed by authority to warn travellers from attempting to ford the river. It is murder if A is a guide who had contracted to conduct Z. It is not murder if A is a person on whom Z has no other claim than that of humanity.

A savage dog fastens on Z. A omits to call off the dog, knowing that if the dog be not called off, it is likely that Z will be killed. Z is killed. This is murder in A, if the dog belonged to A, inasmuch as his omission to take proper order with the dog is illegal. (Clause 273.) But if A be a mere passer-by, it is not murder.

We are sensible that in some of the cases which we have put, our rule may appear too lenient; but we do not think that it can be made more severe without disturbing the whole order of society. It is true that the man who, having abundance of wealth, suffers a fellow-creature to die of hunger at his feet is a bad man, a worse man, probably, than many of those for whom we have provided very severe punishment. But we are unable to see where, if we make such a man legally punishable, we can draw the line. If the rich man who refuses to save a beggar's life at the cost of a little copper is a murderer, is the poor man just one degree above beggary also to be a murderer if he omits to invite the beggar to partake his hard-earned rice? Again, if the rich man is a murderer for refusing to save the beggar's life at the cost of a little copper, is he also to be a murderer if he refuses to save the beggar's life at the cost of a thousand rupees? Suppose A to be fully convinced that nothing can save Z's life unless Z leave Bengal and reside a year at the Cape; is A, however wealthy he may be, to be punished as a murderer because he will not, at his own expense, send Z to the Cape? Surely not. Yet it will be difficult to say on what principle we can punish A for not spending an anna to save Z's life, and leave him unpunished for not spending a thousand rupees to save Z's life. The distinction between a legal and an illegal omission is perfectly plain and intelligible; but the distinction between a large and a small sum of money is very far from being so; not to say that a sum which is small to one man is large to another.

The same argument holds good in the case of the ford. It is true that none but a very depraved man would suffer another to be drowned when he might prevent it by a word; but if we punish such a man, where are we to stop? How much exertion are we to require? Is a person to be a murderer if he does not go fifty yards through the sun of Bengal at noon in May in order to caution a traveller against a swollen river? Is he to be a murderer if he does not go a hundred yards?—if he does not go a mile?—if he does not go ten? What is the precise amount of trouble and inconvenience which he is to endure? The distinction between the guide who is bound to conduct the traveller as safely as he can, and a mere stranger, is a clear distinction. But the distinction between a stranger who will not give a halloo to save a man's life, and a stranger who will not run a mile to save a man's life, is very far from being equally clear.

It is, indeed, most highly desirable that men should not merely abstain from doing harm to their neighbours, but should render active services to their neighbours. In general, however, the penal law must content itself with keeping men from doing positive harm, and must leave to public opinion, and to the teachers of morality and religion, the office of furnishing men with motives for doing positive good. It is evident that to attempt to punish men by law for not rendering to others all the service which it is their duty to render to others would be preposterous. We must grant impunity to the vast majority of those omissions which a benevolent morality would pronounce reprehensible, and must content ourselves with punishing such omissions only when they are distinguished from the rest by some circumstance which marks them out as peculiarly fit objects of penal legislation. Now, no circumstance appears to us so well fitted to be the mark as the circumstance which we have selected. It will generally be found in the most atrocious cases of omission; it will scarcely ever be found in a venial case of omission; and it is more clear and certain than any other mark that has occurred to us. That there are objections to the line which we propose to draw, we have admitted; but there are objections to every line which can be drawn, and some line must be drawn.

The next point to which we wish to call the attention of his Lordship in Council is the unqualified use of the words "to cause death" in the definition of voluntary culpable homicide.

We long considered whether it would be advisable to except from this definition any description of acts or illegal omissions, on the ground that such acts or illegal omissions do not ordinarily cause death, or that they cause death very remotely. We have determined, however, to leave the clause in its present simple and comprehensive form.

There is undoubtedly a great difference between acts which cause death immediately, and acts which cause death remotely; between acts which are almost certain to cause death, and acts which cause death only under very extraordinary circumstances. But that difference, we conceive, is a matter to be considered by the tribunals when estimating the effect of the evidence in a particular case, not by the legislature in framing the general law. It will require strong evidence to prove that an act of a kind which very seldom causes death, or an act which has caused death very remotely, has actually caused death in a particular case. It will require still stronger evidence to prove that such an act was contemplated by the person who did it as likely to cause death; but if it be proved by satisfactory evidence that death has been so caused, and has been caused voluntarily, we see no reason for exempting the person who caused it from the punishment of voluntary culpable homicide.

Mr. Livingston, we observe, excepts from the definition of homicide cases in which death is produced by the effect of words on the imagination or the passions. The reasoning of that distinguished jurist has by no means convinced us that the distinction which he makes is well founded. Indeed, there are few parts of his Code which appear to us to have been less happily executed than this; his words are these: "The destruction must be by the act of another; therefore self-destruction is excluded from the definition. It must be operated by some act; therefore death, although produced by the operation of words on the imagination or the passions, is not homicide. But if words are used which are calculated to produce and do produce some act which is the immediate cause of death, it is homicide. A blind man or a stranger in the dark, directed by words only to a precipice, where he falls and is killed; a direction verbally given to take a drug that it is known will prove fatal, and which has that effect, are instances of this modification of the rule."

This appears to us altogether incoherent. A verbally directs Z to swallow a poisonous drug; Z swallows it, and dies; and this, says Mr. Livingston, is homicide in A. It certainly ought to be so considered. But how, on Mr. Livingston's principles, it can be so considered we do not understand. "Homicide," he says, "must be operated by an act." Where then is the act in this case? Is it the speaking of A? Clearly not, for Mr. Livingston lays down the doctrine that speaking is not an act. Is it the swallowing by Z? Clearly not, for the destruction of life, according to Mr. Livingston, is not homicide unless it be by the act of another, and this swallowing is an act performed by Z himself.

The reasonable course, in our opinion, is to consider speaking as an act, and to treat A as guilty of voluntary culpable homicide, if by speaking he has voluntarily caused Z's death, whether his words operated circuitously by inducing Z to swallow poison or directly by throwing Z into convulsions.

There will indeed be few homicides of this latter sort. It appears to us that a conviction, or even a trial, in such a case would be an event of extremely rare occurrence. There would probably not be one such trial in a century. It would be most difficult to prove to the conviction of any Court that death had really been the effect of excitement produced by words; it would be still more difficult to prove that the person who spoke the words anticipated from them an effect which, except under very peculiar circumstances, and on very peculiar constitutions, no words would produce. Still it seems to us that both these points might be made out by overwhelming evidence; and, supposing them to be so made out, we are unable to perceive any distinction between the case of him who voluntarily causes death in this manner, and the case of him who voluntarily causes death by means of a pistol or a sword. Suppose it to be proved to the entire conviction of a criminal court that Z, the deceased, was in a very critical state of health; that A, the heir to Z's property, had been informed by Z's physicians that Z's recovery absolutely depended on his being kept quiet in mind, and that the smallest mental excitement would endanger his life; that A immediately broke into Z's sick room, and told him a dreadful piece of intelligence, which was a pure invention; that Z went into fits, and died on the spot; that A had afterwards boasted of having cleared the way for himself to a good property by this artifice; these things being fully proved, no judge could doubt that A had voluntarily caused the death of Z; nor do we perceive any reason for not punishing A in the same manner in which he would have been punished if he had mixed arsenic in Z's medicine.

Again, Mr. Livingston excepts from the definition of homicide the case of a person who dies of a slight wound, which, from neglect or from the application of improper remedies, has proved mortal. We see no reason for excepting such cases from the simple general rule which we propose. It will, indeed, be in general more difficult to prove that death has been caused by a scratch than by a stab which has reached the heart; and it will, in a still greater degree, be more difficult to prove that a scratch was intended to cause death than that a stab was intended to cause death; yet both these points might be fully established. Suppose such a case as the following:—It is proved that A inflicted a slight wound on Z, a child who stood between him and a large property; it is proved that the ignorant and superstitious servants about Z applied the most absurd remedies to the wound; it is proved that under their treatment the wound mortified, and the child died. Letters from A to a confident are produced; in those letters, A congratulates himself on his skill, remarks that he could not have inflicted a more severe wound without exposing himself to be punished as a murderer, relates with exultation the mode of treatment followed by the people who have charge of Z, and boasts that he always foresaw that they would turn the slightest incision into a mortal wound. It appears to us, that if such evidence were produced, A ought to be punished as a murderer.

Again, suppose that A makes a deliberate attempt to commit assassination; in the presence of numbers he aims a knife at the heart of Z, but the knife glances aside, and inflicts only a slight wound. This happened in the case of Jean Chatel, of Damien, of Guiscard, and of many other assassins of the most desperate character. In such cases there is no doubt whatever as to the intention. Suppose that the person who received the wound is under the necessity of exposing himself to a moist atmosphere immediately afterwards, and that, in consequence, he is attacked with tetanus and dies. Here again, however slight the wound may have been, we are unable to perceive any good reason for not punishing A as a murderer.

We will only add, that this provision of the Code of Louisiana appears to us peculiarly ill-suited to a country in which, we have reason to fear, neglect and bad treatment are far more common than good medical treatment.

The general rule, therefore, which we propose is, that the question whether a person has by an act or illegal omission voluntarily caused death shall be left a question of evidence to be decided by the Courts, according to the circumstances of every case.

We propose that all voluntary culpable homicide shall be designated as murder, unless it fall under one of three heads. We are desirous to call the particular attention of his Lordship in Council to the law respecting the three mitigated forms of voluntary culpable homicide; and first to the law of manslaughter.

We agree with the great mass of mankind, and with the majority of jurists, ancient and modern, in thinking that homicide committed in the sudden heat of passion, on great provocation, ought to be punished; but that in general it ought not to be punished so severely as murder. It ought to be punished in order to teach men to entertain a peculiar respect for human life; it ought to be punished in order to give men a motive for accustoming themselves to govern their passions; and in some few cases for which we have made provision, we conceive that it ought to be punished with the utmost rigour.

In general, however, we would not visit homicide committed in violent passion, which had been suddenly provoked, with the highest penalties of the law. We think that to treat a person guilty of such homicide as we should treat a murderer would be a highly inexpedient course,—a course which would shock the universal feeling of mankind, and would engage the public sympathy on the side of the delinquent against the law.

His Lordship in Council will remark one important distinction between the law as we have framed it and some other systems. Neither the English law nor the French Code extends any indulgence to homicide which is the effect of anger, excited by words alone. Mr. Livingston goes still further: "No words whatever," says the Code of Louisiana, "are an adequate cause, no gestures merely showing derision or contempt, no assault or battery so slight as to show that the intent was not to inflict great bodily harm."

We greatly doubt whether any good reason can be assigned for this distinction. It is an indisputable fact, that gross insults by word or gesture have as great a tendency to move many persons to violent passion as dangerous or painful bodily injuries; nor does it appear to us that passion excited by insult is entitled to less indulgence than passion excited by pain. On the contrary, the circumstance that a man resents an insult more than a wound is any thing but a proof that he is a man of a peculiarly bad heart. It would be a fortunate thing for mankind if every person felt an outrage which left a stain upon his honour more acutely than an outrage which had fractured one of his limbs. If so, why should we treat an offence produced by the blamable excess of a feeling which all wise legislators desire to encourage, more severely than we treat the blamable excess of feelings certainly not more respectable?

One outrage which wounds only the honour and the affections is admitted by Mr. Livingston to be an adequate provocation. "A discovery of the wife of the accused in the act of adultery with the person killed is an adequate cause." The law of France, the law of England and the Mahomedan law are also indulgent to homicide committed under such circumstances. We must own that we can see no reason for making a distinction between this provocation and many other provocations of the same kind. We cannot consent to lay it down as an universal rule that in all cases this provocation shall be considered as an adequate provocation. Circumstances may easily be conceived which would satisfy a Court that a husband had in such a case acted from no feeling of wounded honour or affection, but from mere brutality of nature, or from disappointed cupidity. On the other hand, we conceive that there are many cases in which as much indulgence is due to the excited feelings of a father or a brother as to those of a husband. That a worthless, unfaithful and tyrannical husband should be guilty only of manslaughter for killing the paramour of his wife, and that an affectionate and high-spirited brother should be guilty of murder for killing, in a paroxysm of rage, the seducer of his sister, appears to us inconsistent and unreasonable.

There is another class of provocations which Mr. Livingston does not allow to be adequate in law, but which have been, and, while human nature remains unaltered, will be, adequate in fact to produce the most tremendous effects. Suppose a person to take indecent liberties with a modest female, in the presence of her father, her brother, her husband or her lover. Such an assault might have no tendency to cause pain or danger; yet history tells us what effects have followed from such assaults. Such an assault produced the Sicilian vespers; such an assault called forth the memorable blow of Wat Tyler. It is difficult to conceive any class of cases in which the intemperance of anger ought to be treated with greater lenity. So far, indeed, should we be from ranking a man who acted like Tyler with murderers, that we conceive that a judge would exercise a sound discretion in sentencing such a man to the lowest punishment fixed by the law for manslaughter.

We think it right to add that, though in our remarks on this part of the law we have used illustrations drawn from the history and manners of Europe, the arguments which we have employed apply as strongly to the state of society in India as to the state of society in any part of the globe. There is perhaps no country in which more cruel suffering is inflicted, and more deadly resentment called forth, by injuries which affect only the mental feelings.

A person who should offer a gross insult to the Mahomedan religion in the presence of a zealous professor of that religion; who should deprive some high-born rajpoot of his caste; who should rudely thrust his head into the covered palanquin of a woman of rank, would probably move those whom he insulted to more violent anger than if he had caused them some severe bodily hurt. That on these subjects our notions and usages differ from theirs is nothing to the purpose. We are legislating for them, and though we may wish that their opinions and feelings may undergo a considerable change, it is our duty, while their opinions and feelings remain unchanged, to pay as much respect to those opinions and feelings as if we partook of them. We are legislating for a country where many men, and those by no means the worst men, prefer death to the loss of caste; where many women, and those by no means the worst women, would consider themselves as dishonoured by exposure to the gaze of strangers; and to legislate for such a country, as if the loss of caste or the exposure of a female face were not provocations of the highest order, would, in our opinion, be unjust and unreasonable.

The second mitigated form of voluntary culpable homicide is that to which we have given the name of voluntary culpable homicide by consent. It appears to us that this description of homicide ought to be punished, but that it ought not to be punished so severely as murder. We have elsewhere given our reasons for thinking that this description of homicide ought to be punished.*

Our reasons for not punishing it so severely as murder are these: in the first place, the motives which prompt men to the commission of this

* See Note B, page 106.

offence are generally far more respectable than those which prompt men to the commission of murder. Sometimes it is the effect of a strong sense of religious duty, sometimes of a strong sense of honour, not unfrequently of humanity. The soldier who, at the entreaty of a wounded comrade, puts that comrade out of pain, the friend who supplies laudanum to a person suffering the torment of a lingering disease, the freedman who in ancient times held out the sword that his master might fall on it, the high-born native of India who stabs the females of his family at their own entreaty in order to save them from the licentiousness of a band of marauders, would, except in Christian societies, scarcely be thought culpable, and even in Christian societies would not be regarded by the public, and ought not to be treated by the law as assassins.

Again, this crime is by no means productive of so much evil to the community as murder. One evil ingredient of the utmost importance is altogether wanting to the offence of voluntary culpable homicide by consent. It does not produce general insecurity. It does not spread terror through society. When we punish murder with such signal severity, we have two ends in view; one end is, that people may not be murdered; another end is, that people may not live in constant dread of being murdered. This second end is perhaps the more important of the two. For if assassination were left unpunished, the number of persons assassinated would probably bear a very small proportion to the whole population; but the life of every human being would be passed in constant anxiety and alarm. This property of the offence of murder is not found in the offence of voluntary culpable homicide by consent. Every man who has not given his consent to be put to death is perfectly certain that this latter offence cannot at present be committed on him, and that it never will be committed unless he shall first be convinced that it is his interest to consent to it. We know that two or three midnight assassinations are sufficient to keep a city of a million of inhabitants in a state of consternation during several weeks, and to cause every private family to lay in arms and watchmen's rattles. No number of suicides, or of homicides committed with the unextorted consent of the person killed, could possibly produce such alarm among the survivors.

The distinction between murder and voluntary culpable homicide by consent has never, as far as we are aware, been recognized by any Code in the distinct manner in which we propose to recognize it; but it may be traced in the laws of many countries, and often, when neglected by those who have framed the laws, it has had a great effect on the decisions of the tribunals, and particularly on the decisions of tribunals popularly composed. It may be proper to observe that the burning of a Hindoo widow by her own consent, though it is now, as it ought to be, an offence by the regulations of every presidency, is in no presidency punished as murder.

The third mitigated form of voluntary culpable homicide is that which we have designated as voluntary culpable homicide in defence.

We have been forced to leave the law on the subject of private defence, as we have elsewhere said, in an unsatisfactory state; and, though we hope and believe that it may be greatly improved, we fear that it must always continue to be one of the least precise parts of every system of jurisprudence. That portion of the law of homicide which we are now considering is closely connected with the law of private defence, and must necessarily partake of the imperfections of the law of private defence. But wherever the limits of the right of private defence may be placed, and with whatever degree of accuracy they may be marked, we are inclined to think that it will always be expedient to make a separation between murder and what we have designated as voluntary culpable homicide in defence.

The chief reason for making this separation is that the law itself invites men to the very verge of the crime which we have designated as voluntary culpable homicide in defence. It prohibits such homicide indeed; but it authorizes acts which lie very near to such homicide; and this circumstance, we think, greatly mitigates the guilt of such homicide.

That a man who deliberately kills another in order to prevent that other from pulling his nose should be allowed to go absolutely unpunished, would be most dangerous. The law punishes and ought to punish such killing; but we cannot think that the law ought to punish such killing as murder; for the law itself has encouraged the slayer to inflict on the assailant any harm short of death which may be necessary for the purpose of repelling the outrage; to give the assailant a cut with a knife across the fingers which may render his right hand useless to him for life, or to hurl him down stairs with such force as to break his leg; and it seems difficult to conceive that circumstances which would be a full justification of any violence short of homicide should not be a mitigation of the guilt of homicide. That a man should be merely exercising a right by fracturing the skull and knocking out the eye of an assailant, and should be guilty of the highest crime in the Code if he kills the same assailant; that there should be only a single step between perfect innocence and murder, between perfect impunity and liability to capital punishment, seems unreasonable. In a case in which the law itself empowers an individual to inflict any harm short of death, it ought hardly, we think, to visit him with the highest punishment if he inflicts death.

It is to be considered also that the line between those aggressions which it is lawful to repel by killing, and those which it is not lawful so to repel, is in our Code, and must be in every Code, to a great extent an arbitrary line, and that many individual cases will fall on one side of that line which, if we had framed the law with a view to those cases alone, we should place on the other. Thus we allow a man to kill if he has no other means of preventing an incendiary from burning a house; and we do not allow him to kill for the purpose of preventing the commission of a simple theft. But a house may be a wretched heap of mats and thatch, propped by a few bamboos, and not worth altogether twenty rupees. A simple theft may deprive a man of a pocket-book which contains bills to a great amount, the savings of a long and laborious life, the sole dependence of a large family. That in these cases the man who kills the incendiary should be pronounced guiltless of any offence, and that the man who kills the thief should be sentenced to the gallows, or, if he is treated with the utmost lenity which the Courts can show, to perpetual transportation or imprisonment, would be generally condemned as a shocking injustice. We are, therefore, clearly of opinion that the offence which we have designated as voluntary culpable homicide in defence ought to be distinguished from murder in such a manner that the Courts may have it in their power to inflict a slight or a merely nominal punishment on acts which, though not within the letter of the law which authorizes killing in self-defence, are yet within the reason of that law.

We have hitherto been considering the law of voluntary culpable homicide; but homicide may be culpable, yet not voluntary. There will probably be little difference of opinion as to the expediency of providing a punishment for the rash and negligent causing of death. But it may be thought that we have dealt too leniently by the offender who, while committing a crime, causes death, which he did not intend to cause, or know himself to be likely to cause.

The law, as we have framed it, differs widely from the English law. "If," says Sir William Blackstone, "one intends to do another felony, and undesignedly kills a man, this is murder;" and he gives the following illustration of the rule: "If one gives a woman with child a medicine to produce abortion, and it operates so violently as to kill the woman, this is murder in the person who gave it."

Under the provisions of our Code, this case would be very differently dealt with according to circumstances. If A kills Z by administering abortives to her, with the knowledge that those abortives are likely to cause her death, he is guilty of voluntary culpable homicide, which will be voluntary culpable homicide by consent, if Z agreed to run the risk, and murder if Z did not so agree. If A causes miscarriage to Z, not intending to cause Z's death, nor thinking it likely that he shall cause Z's death, but so rashly or negligently as to cause her death, A is guilty of culpable homicide not voluntary, and will be liable to the punishment provided for the causing of miscarriage, increased by imprisonment for a term not exceeding two years. Lastly, if A took such precautions that there was no reasonable probability that Z's death would be caused, and if the medicine were rendered deadly by some accident which no human sagacity could have foreseen, or by some peculiarity in Z's constitution such as there was no ground whatever to expect, A will be liable to no punishment whatever on account of her death, but will of course be liable to the punishment provided for causing miscarriage.

It may be proper for us to offer some arguments in defence of this part of the Code.

It will be admitted that when an act is in itself innocent, to punish the person who does it because bad consequences, which no human wisdom could have foreseen, have followed from it would be in the highest degree barbarous and absurd.

A pilot is navigating the Hooghly with the utmost care and skill: he directs the vessel against a sand-bank which has been recently formed, and of which the existence was altogether unknown till this disaster. Several of his passengers are consequently drowned. To hang the pilot as a murderer on account of this misfortune would be universally allowed to be an act of atrocious injustice. But if the voyage of the pilot be itself a high offence, ought that circumstance alone to turn his misfortune into a murder? Suppose that he is engaged in conveying an offender beyond the reach of justice; that he has kidnapped some natives, and is carrying them to a ship which is to convey them to some foreign slave-colony; that he is violating the laws of quarantine at a time when it is of the highest importance that those laws should be strictly observed; that he is carrying supplies, deserters and intelligence to the enemies of the state. The offence of such a pilot ought, undoubtedly, to be severely punished. But to pronounce him guilty of one offence because a misfortune befel him while he was committing another offence,—to pronounce him the murderer of people whose lives he never meant to endanger, whom he was doing his best to carry safe to their destination, and whose death has been purely accidental,—is surely to confound all the boundaries of crime.

Again, A heaps fuel on a fire, not in an imprudent manner, but in such a manner that the chance of harm is not worth considering. Unhappily the flame bursts out more violently than there was reason to expect. At the same moment a sudden puff of wind blows Z's light dress towards the hearth. The dress catches fire, and Z is burned to death. To punish A as a murderer on account of such an unhappy event would be senseless cruelty. But suppose that the fuel which caused the flame to burst forth was a will, which A was fraudulently destroying: ought this circumstance to make A the murderer of Z? We think not. For the fraudulent destroying of wills, we have provided, in other parts of the Code, punishments which we think sufficient. If not sufficient, they ought to be made so. But we cannot admit that Z's death has, in the smallest degree, aggravated A's offence, or ought to be considered in apportioning A's punishment.

To punish as a murderer every man who, while committing a heinous offence, causes death by pure misadventure, is a course which evidently adds nothing to the security of human life. No man can so conduct himself as to make it absolutely certain that he shall not be so unfortunate as to cause the death of a fellow-creature. The utmost that he can do is to abstain from every thing which is at all likely to cause death. No fear of punishment can make him do more than this; and, therefore, to punish a man who has done this can add nothing to the security of human life. The only good effect which such punishment can produce will be to deter people from committing any of those offences which turn into murders what are in themselves mere accidents. It is in fact an addition to the punishment of those offences, and it is an addition made in the very worst way. For example, hundreds of persons in some great cities are in the habit of picking pockets. They know that they are guilty of a great offence; but it has never occurred to one of them, nor would it occur to any rational man, that they are guilty of an offence which endangers life. Unhappily one of these hundreds attempts to take the purse of a gentleman who has a loaded pistol in his pocket. The thief touches the trigger, the pistol goes off, the gentleman is shot dead. To treat the case of this pickpocket differently from that of the numerous pickpockets who steal under exactly the same circumstances, with exactly the same intentions, with no less risk of causing death, with no greater care to avoid causing death; to send them to the house of correction as thieves, and him to the gallows as a murderer, appears to us an unreasonable course. If the punishment for stealing from the person be too light, let it be increased, and let the increase fall alike on all the offenders. Surely the worst mode of increasing the punishment of an offence is to provide that, besides the ordinary punishment, every offender shall run an exceedingly small risk of being hanged. The more nearly the amount of punishment can be reduced to a certainty the better; but if chance is to be admitted, there are better ways of admitting it. It would be a less capricious, and therefore a more salutary course, to provide that every fiftieth or every hundredth thief selected by lot should be hanged, than to provide that every thief should be hanged who, while engaged in stealing, should meet with an unforeseen misfortune, such as might have befallen the most virtuous man while performing the most virtuous action.

We trust that his Lordship in Council will think that we have judged correctly in proposing that when a person engaged in the commission of an offence causes death by pure accident, he shall suffer only the punishment of his offence, without any addition on account of such accidental death.

When a person engaged in the commission of an offence causes death by rashness or negligence, but without either intending to cause death, or thinking it likely that he shall cause death, we propose that he shall be liable to the punishment of the offence which he was engaged in committing, superadded to the ordinary punishment of involuntary culpable homicide.

The arguments and illustrations which we have employed for the purpose of showing that the involuntary causing of death, without either rashness or negligence, ought, under no circumstances, to be punished at all, will, with some modifications, which will readily suggest themselves, serve to show that the involuntary causing of death by rashness or negligence, though always punishable, ought under no circumstances to be punished as murder.

It gives us great pleasure to observe, that Mr. Livingston's provisions on this subject, though in details they differ widely from ours, are framed on the principles which we have here defended.

We wish next to call the attention of his Lordship in Council to clauses 308 and 309.

These clauses appear to us absolutely necessary to the completeness of the Code. We have provided, under the head of bodily hurt, for cases in which hurt is inflicted in an attempt to murder; under the head of assault, for assaults committed in attempting to murder; under the head of criminal trespass, for some criminal trespasses committed in order to murder. But there will still remain many atrocious and deliberate attempts to murder which are not trespasses, which are not assaults, and which cause no hurt. A, for example, digs a pit in his garden, and conceals the mouth of it, intending that Z may fall in and perish there. Here A has committed no trespass, for the ground is his own, and no assault, for he has applied no force to Z. He may not have caused bodily hurt, for Z may have received a timely caution, or may not have gone near the pit; but A's crime is evidently one which ought to be punished as severely as if he had laid hands on Z with the intention of cutting his throat.

Again, A sets poisoned food before Z. Here A may have committed no trespass, for the food may be his own; and if so, he violates no right of property by mixing arsenic with it. He commits no assault, for he means the taking of the food to be Z's voluntary act. If Z does not swallow enough of the poisoned food to disorder him, A causes no bodily hurt; yet it is plain that A has been guilty of a crime of a most atrocious description.

Similar attempts may be made to commit voluntary culpable homicide in any of the three mitigated forms. A, for example, is excited to violent passion by Z, and fires a pistol intending to kill Z. If the shot proves fatal, A will be guilty of manslaughter; and he surely ought not to be exempted from all punishment if the ball only grazes the intended victim.

It is to meet cases of this description that clauses 308 and 309 are intended.

With respect to the law on the subject of abortion, we think it necessary to say only that we entertain strong apprehensions that this or any other law on that subject may, in this country, be abused to the vilest purposes. The charge of abortion is one which, even where it is not substantiated, often leaves a stain on the honour of families. The power of bringing a false accusation of this description is therefore a formidable engine in the hands of unprincipled men. This part of the law will, unless great care be taken, produce few convictions, but much misery and terror to respectable families, and a large harvest of profit to the vilest pests of society. We trust that it may be in our power in the Code of procedure to lay down rules which may prevent such an abuse. Should we not be able to do so, we are inclined to think that it would be our duty to advise his Lordship in Council rather to suffer abortion, where the mother is a party to the offence, to remain wholly unpunished, than to repress it by provisions which would occasion more suffering to the innocent than to the guilty.

Every one of those offences against the human body which remain to be considered falls under some one or more of the following heads: hurt, restraint, assault, kidnapping, rape, unnatural crimes.

Many of the offences which fall under the head of hurt will also fall under the head of assault. A stab, a blow which fractures a limb, the flinging of boiling water over a person, are assaults, and are also acts which cause bodily hurt. But bodily hurt may be caused by many acts which are not assaults. A person, for example, who mixes a deleterious potion, and places it on the table of another; a person who conceals a scythe in the grass on which another is in the habit of walking; a person who digs a pit in a public path, intending that another may fall into it, may cause serious hurt, and may be justly punished for causing such hurt; but they cannot, without extreme violence to language, be said to have committed assaults.

We propose to designate all pain, disease and infirmity by the name of hurt.

We have found it very difficult to draw a line between those bodily hurts which are serious and those which are slight. To draw such a line with perfect accuracy is, indeed, absolutely impossible; but it is far better that such a line should be drawn, though rudely, than that offences some of which approach in enormity to murder, while others are little more than frolics which a good-natured man would hardly resent, should be classed together.

We have, therefore, designated certain kinds of hurt as *grievous*.

We have given this name to emasculation,—to the loss of the sight of either eye,—to the loss of the hearing of either ear,—to the loss of any member or joint,—to the permanent loss of the perfect use of any member or joint,—to the permanent disfiguration of the head or face,—to the fracture and to the dislocation of bones. Thus far we proceed on sure ground. But a more difficult task remains. Some hurts which are not, like those kinds of hurt which we have just mentioned, distinguished by a broad and obvious line from slight hurts, may nevertheless be most serious. A wound, for example, which neither emasculates the sufferer, nor blinds him, nor destroys his hearing, nor deprives him of a member or a joint, nor permanently deprives him of the use of a member or a joint, nor disfigures his countenance, nor breaks his bones, nor dislocates them, may yet cause intense pain, prolonged disease, lasting injury to the constitution. It is evidently desirable that the law should make a distinction between such a wound, and a scratch which is healed with a little sticking plaster. A beating, again, which does not maim the sufferer or break his bones, may be so cruel as to bring him to the point of death. Such a beating, it is clear, ought not to be confounded with a bruise, which requires only to be bathed with vinegar, and of which the traces disappear in a day.

After long consideration we have determined to give the name of grievous bodily hurt to all hurt which causes the sufferer to be in pain, diseased or unable to pursue his ordinary avocations, during the space of twenty days.

This provision was suggested to us by article 309 of the French Penal Code. That article runs thus: "Sera puni de la peine de la réclusion, tout individu qui aura fait des blessures ou porté des coups, s'il est resulté de ces actes de violence une maladie ou incapacité de travail personnel pendant plus de vingt jours." *Réclusion*, it is to be observed, signifies imprisonment and hard labour for a term of not less than five nor more than ten years.

This law appears, from the *procès verbal* of Napoleon's Council of State, to have been adopted without calling forth a single* observation; but it has since been severely criticised by French jurists, and has been mitigated by the French legislature; indeed, it ought to have been completely recast, for it is undoubtedly one of the most exceptionable laws in the Code.

A man who means only to inflict a slight hurt may, without intending or expecting to do so, cause a hurt which is exceedingly serious. A push which to a man in health is a trifle may, if it happens to be directed against a diseased part of an infirm person, occasion consequences which the offender never contemplated as possible. A blow designed to inflict only the pain of a moment may cause the person struck to lose his footing, to fall from a considerable height, and to break a limb. In such cases, to punish the assailant with five years of strict imprisonment would be in the highest degree unjust and cruel. It is said, and we can easily believe it,† that, in such cases, the French juries have frequently refused, in spite of the clearest evidence, to pronounce a decision which would have subjected the accused to a punishment so obviously disproportioned to his offence.

We have attempted to preserve and to extend what is good in this article of the French Code, and to avoid the evils which we have noticed. It appears to us that the length of time during which a sufferer is in pain, diseased or incapacitated from pursuing his ordinary avocations, though a defective criterion of the severity of a hurt, is still the best criterion that

* Locré, Legislation de France, vol 30, page 362.

† Paillet, Manuel de Droit Français. Note on clause 309 of the Penal Code.

has ever been devised. It is a criterion which may, we think, with propriety be employed not merely in cases where violence has been used, but in cases where hurt has been caused without any assault, as by the administration of drugs, the setting of traps, the digging of pit-falls, the placing of ropes across a road. But though we have borrowed from the French Code this test of the severity of bodily injuries, we have framed our penal provisions on a principle quite different from that by which the authors of the French Code appear to have been guided. In apportioning the punishment, we take into consideration both the extent of the hurt and the intention of the offender.

What we propose is, that the voluntary infliction of simple bodily hurt shall be punished with imprisonment of either description, which may extend to one year, or fine, or both; the voluntary infliction of grievous bodily hurt with imprisonment of either description for a term which may extend to ten years and must not be less than six months, to which fine may be added.

These are the ordinary punishments; but there are certain aggravating and mitigating circumstances which make a considerable difference.

Where bodily hurt is voluntarily inflicted in an attempt to murder the person hurt, we propose to punish the offender with transportation for life, or with imprisonment for a term which may extend to life, and cannot be less than seven years. It does not appear to us that, where the murderous intention is made out, the severity of the hurt inflicted is a circumstance which ought to be considered in apportioning the punishment. It is undoubtedly a circumstance which will be important as evidence. A Court will generally be more easily satisfied of the murderous intention of an assailant who has fractured a man's skull, than of one who has only caused a slight contusion. But the proof might be complete. To take examples which are universally known:—Harley was laid up more than twenty days by the wound which he received from Guiscard; the scratch which Damien gave to Louis the Fifteenth was so slight that it was followed by no feverish symptoms. Yet it will be allowed that it would be absurd to make a distinction between the two assassins on this ground.

We propose that when bodily hurt is inflicted by way of torture, the punishment shall be very severe. In England, happily, such a provision would be unnecessary. But the execrable cruelties which are committed by robbers in this country for the purpose of extorting property, or information relating to property, render it absolutely necessary here. We propose that in such cases, if the hurt inflicted be what we have designated as *grievous*, the offender shall be punished with transportation for life, or with imprisonment for a term which may extend to life, and which shall not be less than seven years. Where the hurt is not grievous, we propose that the imprisonment shall be for a term of not more than fourteen years, nor less than one year.

Bodily hurt may be inflicted by means the use of which generally indicates great malignity. A blow with the fist may cause as much pain, and produce as lasting injury, as laceration with a knife, or branding with a hot iron. But it will scarcely be disputed that, in the vast majority of cases, the offender who has used a knife or a hot iron for the purpose of wreaking his hatred is a far worse and more dangerous member of society than he who has only used his fist. It appears to us that many hurts which would not, according to our classification, be designated as grievous, ought yet, on account of the mode in which they are inflicted, to be punished more severely than many grievous hurts. We propose, therefore, that where bodily hurt is voluntarily caused by means of any sharp instrument, of fire, of any heated substance, of any corrosive substance, of any explosive substance, of any poison internal or external, or of any animal, the maximum of imprisonment may be increased, in cases of grievous bodily hurt, to fourteen years, in other cases to three years.

In cases where bodily hurt is voluntarily caused on grave and sudden provocation, we propose to mitigate the punishment. This mitigation is common to cases of hurt and of grievous hurt. But the voluntary causing of grievous hurt on great and sudden provocation will still be punishable more severely than the voluntary causing of hurt not grievous on grave and sudden provocation. The provisions which we propose on this subject are framed on the same principles on which we have framed the law of manslaughter, and may be defended by the same arguments by which the law of manslaughter is defended.

Hitherto we have been considering cases in which hurt has been caused voluntarily; but hurt may be caused involuntarily, yet culpably. There may have been no design to cause hurt, no expectation that hurt would be caused; yet there may have been a want of due care not to cause hurt. For these cases of the involuntary yet culpable infliction of bodily hurt, we have provided rules which bear a close analogy to those which we have provided for cases of involuntary culpable homicide.

The provision contained in clause 329 bears, it will be seen, a close analogy to those contained in clauses 308 and 309. We have provided, under the head of assault, for cases in which an assault is committed in an attempt to cause grievous bodily hurt. But there may be most malignant and atrocious attempts to cause grievous bodily hurt without any assault. For example, Z is directed to use a lotion for his eyes. A substitutes for that lotion a corrosive substance, intending that it may destroy Z's eyesight. Again; A makes up a letter addressed to Z, and sends it to the post-office, having placed a strongly explosive substance under the seal, intending that the explosion may seriously injure Z. These are not assaults; yet they are evidently acts which deserve severe punishment, and that punishment is provided by clause 329.

By wrongful restraint, we mean, the keeping a man out of a place where he wishes to be, and has a right to be. Wrongful confinement, which is a form of wrongful restraint, is the keeping a man within limits out of which he wishes to go, and has a right to go.

The offence of wrongful restraint, when it does not amount to wrongful confinement, and when it is not accompanied with violence, or with the causing of bodily hurt, is seldom a serious offence, and we propose, therefore, to visit it with a light punishment.

The offence of wrongful confinement may be also a slight offence; but, when attended by aggravating circumstances, it may be one of the most serious that can be committed.

One aggravating circumstance is the duration of the confinement. Confinement for a quarter of an hour may sometimes be a mere frolic, which would deserve only a nominal punishment, which, indeed, might be so harmless as not to amount to an offence. (See clause 73.) But wrongful confinement continued during many days will always be a most serious offence. We have attempted to frame the law on this subject in such a manner as to give the offender a strong motive for abridging the detention of his prisoner. Another aggravating circumstance is the circumstance that the offender persists in wrongfully confining a person notwithstanding an order issued by a competent authority for the liberation or production of that person. The mode in which these orders are to be issued will be set forth in the Code of procedure. A third aggravating circumstance is the circumstance that the offender uses criminal confinement for purposes of extortion. For all these aggravated forms of wrongful confinement we have provided severe punishments.

We have also provided a separate punishment for a person who, while detaining another in wrongful confinement, omits to supply his prisoner with every thing necessary to health, ease and comfort. The effect of this provision is, that a person who wrongfully confines another will be answerable for any bodily hurt which he may cause by wrongfully omitting so to supply his prisoner.

We have found great difficulty in giving a definition of assault, and are by no means satisfied with that which we now offer. As, however, it at present appears to us to include all that we mean to include, and to exclude all that we mean to exclude, we have adopted it in spite of the objections which we feel to its harsh and quaint phraseology. We have adopted it with the less scruple, because we trust that the illustrations will render every part of it intelligible to an attentive reader.

A large proportion of the acts which we have designated as assaults will be offences falling under the heads of hurt and restraint. Thus, a stab with a knife is an offence falling under the head of hurt, and it is also an assault. The seizing a man by the collar, and thus preventing him from proceeding on his way, is unlawful restraint, and is also an assault. But there will be many assaults which it is absolutely necessary to punish, yet which cause neither bodily hurt nor unlawful restraint. A man who impertinently puts his arm round a lady's waist, who aims a severe stroke at a person with a horsewhip, who maliciously throws a stone at a person, squirts dirty water over a person, or sets a dog at a person, may cause no hurt and no restraint, yet it is evident that such acts ought to be prevented.

The ordinary punishment which we propose for assault is slight; but we propose to punish assaults which are committed in attempting murder with transportation for life, or with imprisonment for a term which may extend to life, and which cannot be less than seven years. We have also provided severe punishments for assault, when it is committed in an attempt to commit any grave offence against the person, when it is committed with the intention of dishonouring the sufferer, or when it is an outrage offered to female modesty.

The offence of kidnapping is sometimes committed by means of assault, and is sometimes attended with restraint; but this will not always be the case. A child, for example, who is decoyed from its guardians, who soon forgets its home, and who consents to remain with the kidnapper, cannot be said to have been assaulted or restrained. A labourer who has been induced to embark on board of a ship by false assurances that he shall be taken to a country where he shall have good wages, but whom the captain of the ship intends to sell for a slave, has not, as yet, been either assaulted or restrained.

The crime of kidnapping consists, according to our definition of it, in conveying a person without his consent, or the consent of some person legally authorized to consent on his behalf, or with such consent obtained by deception, out of the protection of the law, or of those whom the law has appointed his guardians.

This offence may be committed on a child by removing that child out of the keeping of its lawful guardian or guardians. On a grown man it can only be committed by conveying him beyond the limits of the Company's territories, or by receiving him on board of a ship for that purpose.

The carrying of a grown-up person by force from one place within the Company's territories to another, and the enslaving him within the Company's territories, are offences sufficiently provided for under the heads of restraint and confinement.

The enticing a grown-up person by false promises to go from one place in the Company's territories to another place also within those territories, may be a subject for a civil action, and, under certain circumstances, for a criminal prosecution ; but it does not appear to us to come properly under the head of kidnapping.

We propose to make the punishment of kidnapping peculiarly severe when it is committed with murderous intentions, as in the case of those subjects of the Company who were lately carried into the Jynteah country for purposes of human sacrifice.

We also propose to enhance the punishment of kidnapping in cases in which it is committed with the intention of inflicting grievous bodily harm on the person kidnapped, or of reducing that person to slavery, and when it is committed for purposes of rape or of unnatural lust.

We have placed under this head a provision for punishing persons who export labourers by sea from the Company's territories, in contravention of the Act recently passed by Government on that subject.

The provisions which we propose on the subject of rape do not appear to require any remark.

Clauses 361 and 362 relate to an odious class of offences respecting which it is desirable that as little as possible should be said. We leave, without comment, to the judgment of his Lordship in Council the two clauses which we have provided for these offences. We are unwilling to insert, either in the text or in the notes, any thing which could give rise to public discussion on this revolting subject ; as we are decidedly of opinion that the injury which would be done to the morals of the community by such discussion would far more than compensate for any benefits which might be derived from legislative measures framed with the greatest precision.

Note N.

ON THE CHAPTER OF OFFENCES AGAINST PROPERTY.

There is such a mutual relation between the different parts of the law that those parts must all attain perfection together. That portion, be it what it may, which is selected to be first put into the form of a Code, with whatever clearness and precision it may be expressed and arranged, must necessarily partake to a considerable extent of the uncertainty and obscurity in which other portions are still left.

This observation applies with peculiar force to that important portion of the Penal Code which we now propose to consider. The offences defined in this chapter are made punishable on the ground that they are violations of the right of property; but the right of property is itself the creature of the law. It is evident, therefore, that if the substantive civil law touching this right be imperfect or obscure, the penal law which is auxiliary to that substantive law, and of which the object is to add a sanction to that substantive law, must partake of the imperfection or obscurity. It is impossible for us to be certain that we have made proper penal provisions for violations of civil rights till we have a complete knowledge of all civil rights; and this we cannot have while the law respecting those rights is either obscure or unsettled. As the present state of the civil law causes perplexity to the legislator in framing the Penal Code, so it will occasionally cause perplexity to the judges in administering that Code. If it be matter of doubt what things are the subjects of a certain right, in whom that right resides, and to what that right extends, it must also be matter of doubt whether that right has or has not been violated.

For example, A, without Z's permission, shoots snipes on Z's ground, and carries them away: here, if the law of civil rights grants the property in such birds to any person who can catch them, A has not, by killing them and carrying them away, invaded Z's right of property. If, on the other hand, the law of civil right declares such birds the property of the person on whose lands they are, A has invaded Z's right of property. If it be matter of doubt what the state of the civil law on the subject actually is, it must also be matter of doubt whether A has wronged Z or not.

By the English law,* pigeons, while they frequent a dove-cote, are the property of the owner of the dove-cote. By the Roman law† they were not so. By the French law‡ they are his property at one time of the year, and not his property at another. Here it is evident that the taking of such a pigeon, which would in England be a violation of the right of property, would be none in a country governed by the Roman law, and that, in France, it would depend on the time of the year whether it were so or not.

A lends a horse to B; B sells the horse to Z, who buys it, believing in good faith that B has a right to sell it. A sees the horse feeding; he mounts it and rides away with it. Here, if the law of civil rights pro-

* Blackstone, Book II, Chapter 25.

† Columbarum fera natura est, nec ad rem pertinet, quod ex consuetudine evolare et revolare solent.—Inst. Lib. II. Tit. 1.

‡ Paillet Manuel de Droit Français.

vides that a thing sold by one who has no right to sell it shall nevertheless be the property of a *bonâ fide* purchaser, A has invaded Z's right of property. If, on the other hand, A's right is not affected by what has passed between B and Z, A does not commit an infraction of Z's right of property. If it be doubtful whether the right to the horse be in A or in Z, it must also be doubtful whether A has or has not committed an infraction of Z's right.

A path running across a field which belongs to Z has, during three years, been used as a public way. A, in spite of a prohibition from Z, uses it as such. Here, if, by the civil law, an usage of three years is sufficient to create a right of way, A has committed no infraction of Z's right; but if a prescription of more than three years, or an express grant, be necessary to create a right of way, A has committed an infraction of Z's right of property.

A discovers a mine on land occupied by him. Here, if the civil law assigns all minerals to the occupier of the land, A violates no right of property by appropriating the minerals; but if the civil law assigns all minerals to the Government, A violates the right of property by such appropriation.

The sea recedes, and leaves dry land in the immediate neighbourhood of Z's property. Z cultivates the land. A turns cattle on the land, and destroys Z's crops. Here, if the civil law assigns alluvial additions to the occupier of the nearest land, A is a wrong-doer. If it declares alluvial additions common, A is not a wrong-doer. If it assigns alluvial additions to the Government, both A and Z are wrong-doers. If it be uncertain to whom the law assigns alluvial additions, it must be also uncertain who is the wrong-doer, and whether there be any wrong-doer.

The substantive civil law, in the instances which we have given, is different in different countries, and in the same country at different times. As the substantive civil law varies, the penal law, which is added as a guard to the substantive civil law, must vary also. And while many important questions of substantive civil right are undetermined, the Courts must occasionally feel doubtful whether the provisions of the Penal Code do or do not apply to a particular case.

It would evidently be impossibe for us to determine in the Penal Code all the momentous questions of civil right which, in the unsettled state of Indian jurisprudence, will admit of dispute. We have, indeed, ventured to take for granted in our illustrations many things which properly belong to the domain of the civil law, because, without doing so, it would have been impossible for us to explain our meaning; but we have, to the best of our judgment, avoided questions respecting which, even in the present state of Indian jurisprudence, much doubt could exist. And in the text of the law we have, as closely as was possible, confined ourselves to what is in strictness the duty of persons engaged in framing a Penal Code. We have provided punishments for the infraction of rights, without determining in whom those rights vest, or to what those rights extend. We are inclined to hope that, even if the Penal Code should come into operation before the Code of civil rights has been framed, the number of cases in which the want of a Code of civil rights would occasion perplexity to the criminal tribunals will bear but a very small proportion to those in which no such perplexity will exist.

All the violations of the rights of property which we propose to make punishable by this chapter fall under one or more of the following heads:

1. Theft.
2. Extortion.
3. Robbery.
4. The criminal misappropriation of property not in possession.
5. Criminal breach of trust.
6. The receiving of stolen property.
7. Cheating.
8. Fraudulent bankruptcy.
9. Mischief.
10. Criminal trespass.

All these offences resemble each other in this, that they cause, or have some tendency, directly or indirectly, to cause some party not to have such a dominion over property as that party is entitled by law to have.

The first great line which divides these offences may be easily traced. Some of them merely prevent or disturb the enjoyment of property by one who has a right to it. Others transfer property to one who has no right to it. Some merely cause injury to the sufferer. Others, by means of wrongful loss to the sufferer, cause wrongful gain to some other party. The latter class of offences are designated in this Code as fraudulent. (See clause 16.)

Every offence against property may be fraudulently committed; but theft, extortion, robbery, the criminal misappropriation of property not in possession, criminal breach of trust, the receiving of stolen property, fraudulent bankruptcy and cheating, must be in all cases fraudulently committed. Fraud enters into the definition of every one of these offences; but fraud does not enter into the definition of mischief or of criminal trespass.

Theft, the criminal misappropriation of property not in possession, and criminal breach of trust, are in the great majority of cases easily distinguishable. But the distinction becomes fainter and fainter as we approach the line of demarcation, and at length the offences fade imperceptibly into each other. This indistinctness may be greatly increased by unskilful legislation; but it has its origin in the nature of things, and in the imperfection of language, and must still remain in spite of all that legislation can effect.

We believe it to be impossible to mark with precision, by any words, the circumstances which constitute possession. It is easy to put cases about which no doubt whatever exists, and about which the language of lawyers and of the multitude would be the same. It will hardly be doubted, for example, that a gentleman's watch lying on a table in his room is in his possession, though it is not in his hand, and though he may not know whether it is on his writing-table or on his dressing-table. As little will it be doubted that a watch which a gentleman lost a year ago on a journey, and which he has never heard of since, is not in his possession. It will not be doubted that when a person gives a dinner, his silver forks, while in the hands of his guests, are still in his possession; and it will be as little doubted that his silver forks are not in his possession when he has deposited them with a pawnbroker as a pledge. But between these extreme cases lie many cases in which it is difficult to pronounce, with confidence, either that property is or that it is not in a person's possession.

This difficulty, sufficiently great in itself, would, we conceive, be increased by laws which should pronounce that in a set of cases arbitrarily selected from the mass, property is in the possession of some party in whose possession, according to the understanding of all mankind, it is not. The rule of English law respecting what is called breaking bulk is an instance of what we mean. A person who has intrusted a hamper of wine to another to carry to a great distance is not in possession of that hamper of wine. But if the person in trust opens the hamper and takes out a bottle, the possession, according to the English law books, forthwith flies back to the distant owner. Mr. Livingston has laid down a rule of a similar kind, the effect of which, if we understand it rightly, is to annul the whole law of theft as he has framed it, and indeed to render it impossible that theft can be committed in Louisiana. Theft is defined by him to be "the fraudulently taking of corporal personal property having some assignable value, and belonging to another, from his possession and without his assent." But in a subsequent clause he says that "neither the ownership nor the legal possession of property is changed by theft alone, without the circumstances required in such case by the Civil Code, in order to produce a change of property; therefore, stolen goods, if fraudulently taken from the thief, are stolen from the original proprietor." But if stolen by the second thief from the original proprietor, they must, according to Mr. Livingston's definition of theft, be taken by the second thief out of the possession of the original proprietor; therefore, the first thief has left them in the possession of the original proprietor; that is to say, the first thief has not committed theft.

It will not be imagined that we refer to this inconsistency in the Code of Louisiana, for the purpose of throwing any censure on the distinguished author of that Code. To do so would be unjust, and in us especially most ungrateful, and also most imprudent; for we are by no means confident that inconsistencies quite as remarkable will not be detected in the Code which we now submit to Government. We note this error of Mr. Livingston for the purpose of showing how dangerous it is for a legislator to attempt to escape from a difficulty by giving a technical sense to an expression which he nevertheless continues to use in a popular sense.

For the purpose of preventing any difference of opinion from arising in cases likely to occur very often, we have laid down a few rules (see clauses 17, 18, 19,) which we believe to be in accordance with the general sense of mankind as to what shall be held to constitute possession. But, in general, we leave it to the tribunals, without any direction, to determine whether particular property is at a particular time in the possession of a particular person or not.

Much uncertainty will still remain. This we cannot prevent. But we can, as it appears to us, prevent the uncertainty from producing any practical evil. The provision contained in clause 61 will, we think, obviate all the inconveniences which might arise from doubts as to the exact limits which separate theft from misappropriation and from breach of trust.

The effect of that clause will be to prevent the judges from wasting their time and ingenuity in devising nice distinctions. If a case which is plainly theft comes before them, the offender will be punished as a thief. If a case which is plainly breach of trust comes before them, the offender will be punished as guilty of breach of trust. If they have to try a case which lies on the frontier, one of those thefts which are hardly distinguishable from breaches of trust, or one of those breaches of trust which are hardly distinguishable from theft, they will not trouble themselves with subtle distinctions, but, leaving it undetermined by which name the offence should be called, will proceed to determine what is infinitely of greater importance, what shall be the punishment.

In theft, as we have defined it, the object of the offender always is to take property which is in the possession of a person out of that person's possession; nor have we admitted a single exception to this rule. In the great majority of cases, our classification will coincide with the popular classification. But there are a few aggravated cases of what we designate as misappropriation and breach of trust, which bear such an affinity to theft that it may seem idle to distinguish them from thefts; and it certainly would be idle to distinguish such cases from thefts if the distinction were made with a view to those cases alone. But, as we have a line of distinction which we think it desirable to maintain in the great majority of cases, we think it desirable also to maintain that line in the few cases in which it may separate things which are of a very similar description.

One offence which it may be thought that we ought to have placed among thefts is the pillaging of property during the interval which elapses between the time when the possessor of the property dies, and the time when it comes into the possession of some person authorized to take charge of it. This crime, in our classification, falls under the head, not of theft, but of misappropriation of property not in possession.

The ancient Roman jurists viewed it in the same light. The property taken under such circumstances, they argued, being in no person's possession, could not be taken out of any person's possession. The taking, therefore, was not *furtum*, but belonged to a separate head, called the *crimen expilatæ hæreditatis*.* The French lawyers, however, long ago found out a legal fiction by means of which this offence was treated as theft in those parts of France where the Roman law was in force.† Mr. Livingston's definition of theft appears to us to exclude this species of offence, nor indeed do we think that it could be reached by any provision of his Code. That it ought to be punished with severity under some name or other is indisputable: by what name it should be designated may admit of some dispute; if we call it theft, we speak the popular language; if we call it misappropriation of property not in possession, we avoid an anomaly, and maintain a line which, in the great majority of cases, is reasonable and convenient. On the whole, we are inclined to maintain this line.

Again, a carrier who opens a letter intrusted to his charge, and takes thence a bank note, would be commonly called a thief. It is certain that his offence is not morally distinguishable from theft. Here, however, as before, we think it expedient to maintain our general rule; and we therefore designate the offence of the carrier not as theft, but as criminal breach of trust.

---

* Justinian Dig. Lib. XLVII. Tit. 19.

† Domat. Sup. III.

21

The illustrations which we have appended to the provisions respecting theft, the misappropriation of property not in possession, and breach of trust, will, we hope, sufficiently explain to his Lordship in Council the reasons for most of those provisions.

It may possibly be remarked, that we have not, like Mr. Livingston, made it part of our definition of theft, that the property should be of some assignable value. We would, therefore, observe that we have not done so only because we conceive that the law, as framed by us, obtains the same end by a different road. By one of the general exceptions which we have proposed (clause 73), it is provided, that nothing shall be an offence by reason of any harm which it may cause, or be intended to cause, or be known to be likely to cause, if the whole of that harm is so slight that no person of ordinary sense and temper would complain of such harm. This provision will prevent the law of theft from being abused for the purpose of punishing those venial violations of the right of property which the common sense of mankind readily distinguishes from crimes, such as the act of a traveller who tears a twig from a hedge, of a boy who takes stones from another person's ground to throw at birds, of a servant who dips his pen in his master's ink. It does not appear to us that any further rule on this subject is necessary.

The offence of extortion is distinguished from the three offences which we have been considering by this obvious circumstance, that it is committed by the wrongful obtaining of a consent. In one single class of cases, theft and extortion are in practice confounded together so inextricably, that no judge, however sagacious, could discriminate between them. This class of cases therefore has, in all systems of jurisprudence with which we are acquainted, been treated as a perfectly distinct class; and we think that this arrangement, though somewhat anomalous, is strongly recommended by convenience. We have therefore made robbery a separate crime.

There can be no case of robbery which does not fall within the definition either of theft or of extortion; but in practice it will perpetually be matter of doubt whether a particular act of robbery was a theft or an extortion. A large proportion of robberies will be half theft, half extortion. A seizes Z, threatens to murder him, unless he delivers all his property, and begins to pull off Z's ornaments. Z in terror begs that A will take all he has, and spare his life, assists in taking off his ornaments, and delivers them to A. Here, such ornaments as A took without Z's consent are taken by theft. Those which Z delivered up from fear of death are acquired by extortion. It is by no means improbable that Z's right-arm bracelet may have been obtained by theft, and left-arm bracelet by extortion; that the rupees in Z's girdle may have been obtained by theft, and those in his turban by extortion. Probably in nine-tenths of the robberies which are committed, something like this actually takes place, and it is probable that a few minutes later neither the robber nor the person robbed would be able to recollect in what proportions theft and extortion were mixed in the crime; nor is it at all necessary for the ends of justice that this should be ascertained. For though, in general, the consent of a sufferer is a circumstance which very materially modifies the character of the offence, and which ought, therefore, to be made known to the Courts, yet the consent which a person gives to the taking of his property by a ruffian who holds a pistol to his breast is a circumstance altogether immaterial.

His Lordship in Council will perceive that we have provided punishment of exemplary severity for that atrocious crime which is designated in the Regulations of Bengal and Madras by the name of Dacoity. This name we have thought it convenient to retain, for the purpose of denoting, not only actual gang-robbery, but the attempting to rob when such an attempt is made or aided by a gang.

The law relating to the offence of receiving stolen goods appears to require no comment.

The offence of cheating must, like that of extortion, be committed by the wrongful obtaining of a consent. The difference is, that the extortioner obtains the consent by intimidation, and the cheat by deception. There is no offence in the Code with which we have found it so difficult to deal as that of cheating. It is evident that the practising of intentional deceit for purposes of gain ought sometimes to be punished. It is equally evident that it ought not always to be punished. It will hardly be disputed that a person who defrauds a banker by presenting a forged check, or who sells ornaments of paste as diamonds, may with propriety be made liable to severe penalties. On the other hand, to punish every defendant who obtains pecuniary favours by false professions of attachment to a patron; every legacy hunter who obtains a bequest by cajoling a rich testator; every debtor who moves the compassion of his creditors by overcharged pictures of his misery; every petitioner who, in his appeals to the charitable, represents his distresses as wholly unmerited, when he knows that he has brought them on himself by intemperance and profusion, would be highly inexpedient. In fact, if all the misrepresentations and exaggerations in which men indulge for the purpose of gaining at the expense of others were made crimes, not a day would pass in which many thousands of buyers and sellers would not incur the penalties of the law. It happens hourly that an article which is worth ten rupees is affirmed by the seller to be cheap at twelve rupees, and by the buyer to be dear at eight rupees. The seller comes down to eleven rupees, and declares that to be his last word; the buyer rises to nine, and says that he will go no higher; the seller falsely pretends that the article is unusually good of its kind, the buyer that it is unusually bad of its kind; the seller that the price is likely soon to rise, the buyer that it is likely soon to fall. Here we have deceptions practised for the sake of gain, yet no judicious legislator would punish these deceptions. A very large part of the ordinary business of life is conducted all over the world, and nowhere more than in India, by means of a conflict of skill, in the course of which deception to a certain extent perpetually takes place. The moralist may regret this; but the legislator sees that the result of the attempts of the buyer and seller to gain an unfair advantage over each other is that, in the vast majority of cases, articles are sold for the prices which it is desirable that they should fetch; and therefore he does not think it necessary to interfere. It is enough for him to know that all this great mass of falsehood practically produces the same effect which would be produced by truth; and that any law directed against such falsehood would in all probability be a dead letter, and would, if carried into rigorous execution, do more mischief in a month than all the lies which are told in the making of bargains throughout all the bazaars of India produce in a century.

If, then, it be admitted that many deceptions committed for the sake of gain ought to be punished, and that many such deceptions ought not to be punished, where ought the line to run?

It appears to us that the line which we have drawn is correct in theory; that it is not more inconvenient in practice than any other line must be which can be drawn while the civil law of India remains in its present state, and that it will be unexceptionable whenever the civil law of India shall be ascertained, digested and corrected.

We propose to make it cheating to obtain property by deception in all cases where the property is fraudulently obtained; that is to say, in all cases where the intention of the person who has by deceit obtained the property was to cause a distribution of property which the law pronounces to be a wrongful distribution, and in no other case whatever. However immoral a deception may be, we do not consider it as an offence against the rights of property if its object is only to cause a distribution of property which the law recognizes as rightful. A few examples will show the way in which this principle will operate.

A intentionally deceives Z into a belief that he is strongly attached to Z. A thus induces Z to make a will, by which a large legacy is left to A. Here A's conduct is immoral and scandalous. But still A has a legal right on Z's death to receive the legacy. Even if the clearest proofs of A's insincerity are laid before a tribunal, even if A in open court avows his insincerity, the will cannot, on that account, be set aside. The gain, therefore, which A obtains under Z's will is not, in the legal sense of the expression, wrongful gain. He has practised deception; he has thus caused gain to himself and loss to others; but that gain is a gain to which the civil law declares him entitled, and which the civil law will assist him to recover if it be withheld from him; that loss is a loss with which the civil law declares that the losers must put up; A therefore has not committed the offence of cheating under our definition.

But suppose that the civil law should contain, as we think that it ought to contain, a provision declaring null a will made in favour of strangers by a testator who erroneously believed his children to be dead; and suppose that A intentionally deceives Z into a belief that Z's only son has been lost at sea, and by this deception induces Z to make a will by which every thing is left to A: here the case will be different. The will being null, any property which A could obtain under that will would be property which he had no legal right so to obtain, and to which another person had a legal right. The object of A has therefore been wrongful gain to himself, attended with wrongful loss to another party. A has, therefore, under our definition, been guilty of cheating.

Again, take the case which we before put, of a buyer and a seller. They have told each other many untruths, but none of those untruths was such as, after the article had been delivered and the price paid, would be held by a civil court to be a ground for pronouncing that either of them possessed what he had no right to possess. Though the buyer has falsely depreciated the article, yet when he takes it and pays for it, the legal right to it is transferred to him, as well as the possession; though the seller has falsely extolled the article, yet when he receives the price and delivers the article, the legal right to the price passes with the possession. However censurable, in a moral point of view, the deceptions practised by both may have been, yet those deceptions were intended to produce a distribution of property strictly legal.

Neither the buyer nor the seller, therefore, has been guilty of cheating; but if the seller has produced a sample of the article, and has falsely assured the buyer that the article corresponds to that sample, the case is different. If the article does not correspond to the sample, the buyer is entitled to have the purchase-money back. The seller has taken and kept the purchase-money without having a legal right to take or keep it, and it may be recovered from him by a legal proceeding. His gain is therefore wrongful, and is attended with wrongful loss to the buyer; he is therefore guilty of cheating under the definition.

So if the seller passes off ornaments of paste on the buyer for diamonds, the price which the seller receives is a price to which he has no right, and which the buyer may recover from him by an action. Here, therefore, the object of the seller has been wrongful gain attended with wrongful loss to the buyer; the seller is therefore guilty of cheating.

So if the buyer, intending to acquire possession of the goods without paying for them, induces the seller by deception to take a note which the buyer knows will be dishonoured, the buyer is guilty of cheating. His object is to retain in his own possession money which he is legally bound to pay to the seller. The gain which he makes by retaining the money is wrongful gain, and is attended with wrongful loss to the seller; he is, therefore, within the definition.

Whether the principle on which this part of the law is framed be a sound principle is a question which will be best determined by examining, first, whether our definition excludes any thing that ought to be included, and, secondly, whether it includes any thing that ought to be excluded.

It can scarcely, we think, be contended that our definition excludes any thing that ought to be included; for surely it would be unreasonable to punish, as an offence against the right of property, an act which has caused, and was intended to cause, a distribution of property which the law declares to be right, and refuses to disturb. If such an act be an offence, it must be an offence on some ground distinct from the effect which it produces on the state of property. Thus, if a person to whom a debt is due, thinking that he shall obtain payment more easily if he assumes the appearance of being in the public service, wears a badge of office which he has no right to wear when he goes to make his demand, he is guilty of the offence defined in clause 150; but if he gains only what he has a legal right to possess, if he deprives the debtor only of that which the debtor has no legal right to retain, he is not a wrong-doer as respects property, inasmuch as he has only rectified a wrong distribution of property.

Indeed, it appears to us that there is the strongest objection to punishing a man for a deception, and yet allowing him to retain what he has gained by that deception. What the civil law ought to say may be doubtful; but there can be no doubt that the civil and criminal law ought to say the same thing; that the one ought not to invite while the other repels; that the Code ought not to be divided against itself. To send a person to prison for obtaining a sum of money, and yet to suffer him to keep that sum of money, is to hold out at once motives to deter and motives to incite. Humanity requires that punishment should be the last resource, a resource only employed when no other means can be found of producing the desired effect. Penal laws clearly ought not to be made for the preventing of deception, if deception could be prevented by means of the Civil Code. To tempt men, therefore, to deceive by means of the Civil Code, and then to punish them for deceiving, is contrary to every sound principle.

We are, therefore, not apprehensive that we shall be thought to have granted impunity to any deception which ought to be punished as cheating.

But it is possible that our definition may be thought to include much that ought to be excluded. It certainly includes many acts which are not punishable by the law of England or of France. We propose to punish as guilty of cheating a man who, by false representations, obtains a loan of money, not meaning to repay it; a man who, by false representations, obtains an advance of money, not meaning to perform the service or to deliver the article for which the advance is given; a man who, by falsely pretending to have performed work for which he was hired, obtains pay to which he is not entitled.

In all these cases there is deception. In all, the deceiver's object is fraudulent. He intends in all these cases to acquire or retain wrongful possession of that to which some other person has a better claim, and which that other person is entitled to recover by law. In all these cases, therefore, the object has been wrongful gain, attended with wrongful loss. In all, therefore, there has, according to our definition, been cheating. We cannot see why such acts as these should be treated as mere civil injuries, why they should be classed with the mere non-payment of a debt, and the mere non-performance of a contract. They are infractions of a legal right effected by deliberate dishonesty. They are more pernicious than most of the acts which will be punishable under our Code. They indicate more depravity, more want of principle, more want of shame than most of the acts which will be punishable under our Code. We punish the man who gives another an angry push. We punish the man who locks another up for a morning. We punish the man who makes a sarcastic epigram on another. We punish the man who merely threatens another with outrage; and surely the man who, by premeditated deceit, enriches himself to the wrongful loss, perhaps to the utter ruin, of another is not less deserving of punishment.

That some deceptions of this sort ought to be punished is admitted; but almost every argument which can be urged for punishing any is an argument for punishing all. The line between wilful fraudulent deception and good faith is a plain line. If there is any difficulty in applying it, that difficulty will arise, not from any defect in the line, but from the want of evidence in particular cases. But we are unable to find any reason for distinguishing one sort of fraudulent deception from another sort. The French Courts apply a test which appears to us to be very objectionable. They have decided that it is not *escroquerie* to cheat by false promises, or by exciting chimerical hopes, unless the sufferer had reasons of weight for believing that the promises were sincere, and the hopes well grounded.* This rule seems to us to be a license for deception granted to cunning against simplicity. A weak and credulous person is more easily imposed on than a judicious and discerning person; and just so an infant is poisoned with a dose of laudanum which would hardly put a grown person to sleep; yet the poisoner is a murderer. A pregnant woman is grievously hurt by a blow which would make no impression on a boxer; yet the person who gives such a blow is punished with exemplary severity. The law in such cases inquires only whether the harm has been voluntarily caused or no; and why should the violation by deceit of the right of property be treated differently? The deceiver proportions his artifices to the mental strength of those whom he has to deal with, just as the poisoner proportions his drugs to their bodily strength; and we see no more reason for exempting the deceiver from punishment, because he has effected his purpose by a gross fiction which could have duped only a weak person, than for exempting the poisoner from punishment because he has effected his purpose with a few drops of laudanum, which could have been fatal only to a young child.

Some persons may be startled at our proposing to punish as a cheat every man who obtains a loan by making promises of payment which he does not mean to keep. But let it be considered that a debtor, though he may have contracted his debts honestly, though it may be from absolute inability that he does not pay them, though his misfortunes may be the effect of no want of industry or caution on his part, is now actually liable to imprisonment. Surely it is unreasonable to detain in prison the man who, by mere misfortune, has involuntarily violated the rights of property, and to leave unpunished the man who has voluntarily, and by wilful deceit, attacked those rights, if only he is lucky enough to have money to satisfy the demands on him.

For example: A and B both borrow money from Z. A obtains it by boasting falsely of his great means, of the large remittances which he looks for from England, of his expectations from rich relations, of the promises of preferment which he has received from the Government. Having obtained it, he secretly embarks on board of a ship, intending to abscond without repaying what he has borrowed. B, on the other hand, has obtained a loan without the smallest misrepresentation, and fully purposes to repay it. The failure of an agency house in which all his funds were placed renders it impossible for him to meet his engagements. Can it be doubted which of those two debtors ought rather to be sent to prison? Can it be doubted that A is a proper subject of punishment, and that B is not so? Yet at present A, if he is arrested before the ship sails, and lays down the money, enjoys entire impunity, while B may pass years in a gaol. It would be improper for us here to discuss at length the question of imprisonment for debt. But it seems clear that whether it be or be not proper that a debtor, as such, should be imprisoned, a distinction ought to be made between the honest and dishonest debtor. We are inclined to believe that the indiscriminate imprisonment of all debtors would be found to be unnecessary if this distinction were made; but while they are all put on the same footing, the law must be formed upon a rough calculation of the chances of dishonesty. All must be treated worse than honest debtors ought to be treated, because none are treated so severely as dishonest debtors ought to be treated. A respect-

* Paillet Manuel de Droit Français. Note on clause 408 of the Penal Code.

able man must be imprisoned for a storm, a bad season, or a fire, because his dishonest neighbour is not liable to criminal proceedings for cheating. We are satisfied that the only way to get rid of imprisonment for debt, as debt, is to extend the penal law on the subject of cheating in a manner similar to that in which we propose to extend it.

The provisions which we have framed on the subject of fraudulent bankruptcy are necessarily imperfect, and must remain so, until the whole of that important part of the law has undergone an entire revision.

The provisions which we propose on the subject of mischief do not appear to us to require any explanation.

We have given the name of trespass to every usurpation, however slight, of dominion over property. We do not propose to make trespass, as such, an offence, except when it is committed in order to the commission of some offence injurious to some person interested in the property on which the trespass is committed, or for the purpose of causing annoyance to such a person. Even then we propose to visit it with a light punishment, unless it be attended with aggravating circumstances.

These aggravating circumstances are of two sorts. Criminal trespass may be aggravated by the way in which it is committed. It may also be aggravated by the end for which it is committed.

There is no sort of property which it is so desirable to guard against unlawful intrusion as the habitations in which men reside, and the buildings in which they keep their goods. The offence of trespassing on these places we designate as house-trespass, and we treat it as an aggravated form of criminal trespass.

House-trespass, again, may be aggravated by being committed in a surreptitious or in a violent manner. The former aggravated form of house-trespass we designate as lurking house-trespass; the latter we designate as house-breaking. Again, house-trespass, in every form, may be aggravated by the time at which it is committed. Trespass of this sort has, for obvious reasons, always been considered as a more serious offence when committed by night than when committed by day. Thus we have four aggravated forms of that sort of criminal trespass which we designate as house-trespass, lurking house-trespass, house-breaking, lurking house-trespass by night, and house-breaking by night.

These are aggravations arising from the way in which the criminal trespass is committed. But criminal trespass may also be aggravated by the end for which it is committed. It may be committed for a frolic. It may be committed in order to a murder. It may also often happen that a criminal trespass which is venial, as respects the mode, may be of the greatest enormity as respects the end; and that a criminal trespass committed in the most reprehensible mode, may be committed for an end of no great atrocity. Thus A may commit house-breaking by night for the purpose of playing some idle trick on the inmates of a dwelling. B may commit simple criminal trespass by merely entering another's field for the purpose of murder or gang-robbery. Here A commits trespass in the worst way. B commits trespass with the worst object. In our provisions we have endeavoured to combine the aggravating circumstances in such a way that each may have its due effect in settling the punishment.

Note O.

ON THE CHAPTER OF THE ILLEGAL PURSUIT OF LEGAL RIGHTS.

This chapter is intended to prevent the enforcing of just claims by means which are so liable to be abused that, even when used for an honest end, they ought not to be tolerated. A creditor, for example, who has repeatedly in vain urged his debtor to pay him, finds that he has no chance of recovering his money without a troublesome and expensive law-suit. He accordingly seizes on property belonging to the debtor, sells it, keeps only just as much as will satisfy the debt, and sends back the surplus to the debtor. This act is distinguished from theft by one of the broadest lines of demarcation which can be found in the Code. It is not a fraudulent act. It is intended to correct a wrongful distribution of property, to do what the courts of law, if recourse were had to them, would order to be done. Public feeling would be shocked if such a creditor were called by the ignominious name of a thief.

At the same time it cannot be doubted that it would be most dangerous to allow men to pronounce judgment, however honestly, in their own favour, and to proceed to take property in execution for the purpose of satisfying that judgment. A specific thing, indeed, which a man has a right to possess, it is no offence in him to take wherever he finds it. He may commit other offences in order to take it; but the mere taking is no crime at all. If Z has borrowed A's horse, and illegally refuses to return it, it is no offence at all in A to take the horse if he sees it feeding by the roadside. If A enters Z's stable in order to take it, he may commit house-trespass, but he commits no theft. If A knocks Z down in order to take it, he may be guilty of assault, or of voluntarily causing bodily hurt, but he commits no robbery. This license, as it appears to us, must be confined to cases in which specific things are taken. In such cases the chance of abuse is very small. But where one thing is due, and another is taken, where a man seizes on another's furniture in satisfaction of a promissory note, or drives away another's cattle by way of paying himself for a suit of clothes, the case is very different. Honest men so often think themselves entitled to more than a court of justice would award to them, that it will be difficult to say, in cases in which the taker really has a plausible claim, and in which the value of what has been taken is not out of all proportion to the value of what is claimed, that the taker has acted dishonestly. In such cases, therefore, we think it absolutely necessary to provide a punishment for the illegal pursuit of legal rights. We observe that the French Courts have decided that the taking of property by a creditor in good faith, for the purpose of paying himself, is not theft; and this decision seems to us, as we have said, to be well grounded. But it does not appear to us that such an act is punishable under any clause of the French Code; and this we consider as a serious omission.

Note P.

ON THE CHAPTER OF THE CRIMINAL BREACH OF CONTRACTS OF SERVICE.

We agree with the great body of jurists in thinking that in general a mere breach of contract ought not to be an offence, but only to be the subject of a civil action.

To this general rule there are, however, some exceptions. Some breaches of contract are very likely to cause evil such as no damages or only very high damages can repair, and are also very likely to be committed by persons from whom it is exceedingly improbable that any damages can be obtained. Such breaches of contract are, we conceive, proper subjects for penal legislation.

In England it would be unnecessary to provide a punishment for a stage-coachman who should, however maliciously or dishonestly, drive on, leaving behiud a passenger whom he is bound to carry. The evil inflicted is seldom very serious; the country is everywhere well inhabited; the roads are secure. The means of conveyance can easily be obtained, and damages sufficient to compensate for any inconvenience or expense which may have been suffered can easily be recovered from the coach proprietors. But the mode of performing journeys and the state of society in this country are widely different. It is often necessary for travellers of the upper classes, even for English ladies, ignorant perhaps of the native languages, and with young children at their breasts, to perform journeys of many miles over uninhabited wastes, and through jungles in which it is dangerous to linger for a moment, in palanquins borne by persons of the lowest class. If, as sometimes happens, these persons should, in a solitary place, set down the palanquin and run away, it is difficult to conceive a more distressing situation than that in which their employer would be left. None but very high damages would be any reparation for such a wrong. But the class of people by whom alone such a wrong is at all likely to be committed can pay no damages. The whole property of all the delinquents would probably not cover the expense of prosecuting them civilly. It therefore appears to us that breaches of contract of this description may, with strict propriety, be treated as crimes.

The law which we have framed on this subject applies, it will be perceived, only to cases in which the contract with the bearers is lawful. The traveller, therefore, who resorts to the highly culpable, though we fear too common, practice of unlawfully compelling persons against their will to carry his palanquin or his baggage will not be protected by it. If they quit him, it is what they have a legal right to do, nor will they be punishable, whatever may be the consequence of their desertion.

Another species of contract which ought, we conceive, to be guarded by a penal sanction is that by which seamen are bound to their employers. The insubordination of seamen during a voyage often produces fatal consequences. Their desertion in port may cause evils such as very large damages only could repair; but they are utterly unable to pay any damages for which it would be worth while to sue. If a ship in the Hooghly, at a critical time of the year, is compelled by the desertion of some of the crew to put off its voyage for a fortnight, it would be mere mockery to tell the owners that they may sue the runaways for damages in the Supreme Court.

We also think that persons who contract to take care of infants of the sick and of the helpless lay themselves under an obligation of a very peculiar kind, and may with propriety be punished if they omit to discharge their duty. The misery and distress which their neglect may cause is such as the largest pecuniary payment would not repair; they generally come from the lower ranks of life, and would be unable to pay any thing. We therefore propose to add to this class of contracts the sanction of the penal law.

Here we are inclined to stop. We have indeed been urged to go further, and to punish as a criminal every menial servant who, before the expiration of the term for which he is hired, quits his employer. But it does not appear to us that in the existing state of the market for that description of labour in India, good masters are in much danger of being voluntarily deserted by their menial servants, or that the loss or inconvenience occasioned by the sudden departure of a cook, a groom, a hurkaru or a khidmutgar, would often be of a very serious description. We are greatly apprehensive that by making these petty breaches of contracts offences, we should give not protection to good masters, but means of oppression to bad ones.

Note Q.

ON THE CHAPTER OF OFFENCES RELATING TO MARRIAGE.

As this is a part of the law in which the English inhabitants of India are peculiarly interested, and which we have framed on principles widely different from those in which the English law on the same subject is framed, we think it necessary to offer some explanations.

The act which in the English law is designated as bigamy is always an immoral act. But it may be one of the most serious crimes that can be committed. It may be attended with circumstances which may excuse though they cannot justify it.

The married man who, by passing himself off as unmarried, induces a modest woman to become, as she thinks, his wife, but in reality his concubine, and the mother of an illegitimate issue, is guilty of one of the most cruel frauds that can be conceived. Such a man we would punish with exemplary severity.

But suppose that a person arrives from England, and pays attentions to one of his countrywomen at Calcutta. She refuses to listen to him on any other terms than those of marriage. He candidly owns that he is already married. She still presses him to go through the ceremony with her. She represents to him that if they live together without being married she shall be an outcast from society, that nobody in India knows that he has a wife, that he may very likely never fall in with his wife again, and that she is ready to take the risk. The lover accordingly agrees to go through the forms of marriage.

It cannot be disputed that there is an immense difference between these two cases. Indeed, in the second case the man can hardly be said to have injured any individual in such a manner as calls for legal punishment. For what individual has he injured? His second wife? He has acted by her consent, and at her solicitation. His first wife? He has certainly been unfaithful to his first wife. But we have no punishment for mere conjugal infidelity. He will often have injured his first wife no more than he would have done by keeping a mistress, calling that mistress by his own name, introducing her into every society as his wife, and procuring for her the consideration of a wife from all his acquaintance. The legal rights of the first wife and of her children remain unaltered. She is the wife; the second is the concubine. But suppose that the first wife has herself left her husband, and is living in adultery with another man. No individual can then be said to be injured by this second invalid marriage. The only party injured is society, which has undoubtedly a deep interest in the sacredness of the matrimonial contract, and which may therefore be justified in punishing those who go through the forms of that contract for the purpose of imposing on the public.

The law of England on the subject of bigamy appears to us to be in some cases too severe, and in others too lenient. It seems to bear a close analogy to the law of perjury. The English law on these two subjects has been framed less for the purpose of preventing people from injuring each other, than for the purpose of preventing the profanation of a religious ceremony. It therefore makes no distinction between perjury which is intended to destroy the life of the innocent, and perjury which is intended to save the innocent; between bigamy which produces the most frightful suffering to individuals, and bigamy which produces no suffering to individuals at all. We have proceeded on a different principle. While we admit that the profanation of a ceremony so important to society as that of marriage is a great evil, we cannot but think that evil immensely aggravated when the profanation is made the means of tricking an innocent woman into the most miserable of all situations. We have therefore proposed that a man who deceives a woman into believing herself his lawful wife when he knows that she is not so, and induces her, under that persuasion, to cohabit with him, should be punished with great severity.

There are reasons similar, but not exactly the same, for punishing a woman who deceives a man into contracting with her a marriage which she knows to be invalid. For this offence we propose a punishment which, for reasons too obvious to require explanation, is much less severe than that which we have provided for a similar deception practised by a man on a woman.

We also propose to punish every person who, with what we have defined as a fraudulent intention, goes through the forms of a marriage which he knows to be invalid.

We do not at present propose any law for punishing a person who, without practising any deception, or intending any fraud, goes through the forms of a marriage which he knows to be invalid. The difficulty of framing such a law in this country is great. To make all classes subject to one law would, evidently, be impossible. If the law be made dependent on the race, birthplace or religion of the offender, endless perplexity would arise. Races are mixed; religion may be changed or dissembled.

An East Indian, half English, half Asiatic by blood, may call himself a Mahomedan or a Hindoo; and there exists no test by which he can be convicted of deception. We by no means intend to express an opinion that these difficulties may not be got over. But we are satisfied that this part of the penal law cannot be brought to perfection till the law of marriage and divorce has been thoroughly revised.

We leave it to his Lordship in Council to consider whether, during the interval which must elapse before the necessary inquiry can be made, it might not be, on the whole, better to retain the existing law applicable to Christians in India, objectionable as that law is, than to allow absolute impunity to bigamy.

We considered whether it would be advisable to provide a punishment for adultery, and in order to enable ourselves to come to a right conclusion on this subject, we collected facts and opinions from all the three presidencies. The opinions differ widely; but as to the facts, there is a remarkable agreement.

The following positions we consider as fully established: first, that the existing laws for the punishment of adultery are altogether inefficacious for the purpose of preventing injured husbands of the higher classes from taking the law into their own hands; secondly, that scarcely any native of the higher classes ever has recourse to the courts of law in a case of adultery for redress against either his wife or her gallant; thirdly, that the husbands who have recourse in cases of adultery to the courts of law are generally poor men whose wives have run away; that these husbands seldom have any delicate feelings about the intrigue, but think themselves injured by the elopement; that they consider their wives as useful members of their small households; that they generally complain, not of the wound given to their affections, not of the stain on their honour, but of the loss of a menial whom they cannot easily replace, and that, generally, their principal object is that the woman may be sent back. The fiction by which seduction is made the subject of an action in the English Courts is, it seems, the real gist of most proceedings for adultery in the Mofussil. The essence of the injury is considered by the sufferer as lying in the "per quod servitium amisit." Where the complainant does not ask to have his wife again, he generally demands to be reimbursed for the expenses of his marriage.

These things being established, it seems to us that no advantage is to be expected from providing a punishment for adultery. The population seems to be divided into two classes—those whom neither the existing punishment, nor any punishment which we should feel ourselves justified in proposing, will satisfy, and those who consider the injury produced by adultery as one for which a pecuniary compensation will sufficiently atone. Those whose feelings of honour are painfully affected by the infidelity of their wives will not apply to the tribunals at all; those whose feelings are less delicate will be satisfied by a payment of money. Under such circumstances, we think it best to treat adultery merely as a civil injury.

Some who admit that the penal law now existing on this subject is in practice of little or no use, yet think that the Code ought to contain a provision against adultery; they think that such a provision, though inefficacious for the repressing of vice, would be creditable to the Indian Government, and that, by omitting such a provision, we should give a sanction to immorality. They say, and we believe with truth, that the higher class of natives consider the existing penal law on the subject as far too lenient, and are unable to understand on what principle adultery is treated with more tenderness than forgery or perjury.

These arguments have not satisfied us that adultery ought to be made punishable by law. We cannot admit that a Penal Code is by any means to be considered as a body of ethics, that the legislature ought to punish acts merely because those acts are immoral, or that, because an act is not punished at all, it follows that the legislature considers that act as innocent. Many things which are not punishable are morally worse than many things which are punishable. The man who treats a generous benefactor with gross ingratitude and insolence deserves more severe reprehension than the man who aims a blow in a passion, or breaks a window in a frolic; yet we have punishments for assault and mischief, and none for ingratitude. The rich man who refuses a mouthful of rice to save a fellow-creature from death may be a far worse man than the starving wretch who snatches and devours the rice; yet we punish the latter for theft, and we do not punish the former for hard-heartedness.

That some classes of the natives of India disapprove of the lenity with which adultery is now punished we fully believe, but this, in our opinion, is a strong argument against punishing adultery at all. There are only two courses which, in our opinion, can properly be followed with respect to this and other great immoralities; they ought to be punished very severely, or they ought not to be punished at all. The circumstance that they are left altogether unpunished does not prove that the legislature does not regard them with disapprobation; but when they are made punishable, the degree of severity of the punishment will always be considered as indicating the degree of disapprobation with which the legislature regards them. We have no doubt that the natives would be far less shocked by the total silence of the penal law touching adultery than by seeing an adulterer sent to prison for a few months while a coiner is imprisoned for fourteen years.

An example will illustrate our meaning. We have determined not to make it penal in a wealthy man to let a fellow-creature, whose life he could save by disbursing a few pice, die at his feet of hunger. No rational person, we are convinced, will suppose, because we have framed the law thus, that we do not hold such inhumanity in detestation; but if we had proposed to punish such inhumanity with a fine not exceeding fifty rupees, we should have offered a gross outrage to the feelings of mankind; that we do not think a certain act a proper subject for penal legislation, does not prove that we do not think that act a great crime; but that, thinking it a proper subject for penal legislation, we propose to visit it with a slight penalty, does seem to indicate that we do not think it a great crime.

Nobody proposes that adultery should be punished with a severity at all proportioned to the misery which it produces in cases where there is strong affection and a quick sensibility to family honour. We apprehend that among the higher classes in this country nothing short of death would be considered as an expiation for such a wrong. In such a state of society, we think it far better that the law should inflict no punishment than that it should inflict a punishment which would be regarded as absurdly and immorally lenient.

There is yet another consideration which we cannot wholly leave out of sight. Though we well know that the dearest interests of the human race are closely connected with the chastity of women and the sacredness of the nuptial contract, we cannot but feel that there are some peculiarities in the state of society in this country which may well lead a humane man to pause before he determines to punish the infidelity of wives. The condition of the women of this country is, unhappily, very different from that of the women of England and France; they are married while still children; they are often neglected for other wives while still young. They share the attentions of a husband with several rivals. To make laws for punishing the inconstancy of the wife, while the law admits the privilege of the husband to fill his zenana with women, is a course which we are most reluctant to adopt. We are not so visionary as to think of attacking, by law, an evil so deeply-rooted in the manners of the people of this country as polygamy. We leave it to the slow, but we trust the certain, operation of education and of time. But while it exists, while it continues to produce its never-failing effects on the happiness and respectability of women, we are not inclined to throw into a scale, already too much depressed, the additional weight of the penal law. We have given the reasons which lead us to believe that any enactment on this subject would be nugatory; and we are inclined to think that if not nugatory it would be oppressive. It would strengthen hands already too strong. It would weaken a class already too weak. It will be time enough to guard the matrimonial contract by penal sanctions when that contract becomes just, reasonable and mutually beneficial.

Note R.

ON THE CHAPTER OF DEFAMATION.

The essence of the offence of defamation consists in its tendency to cause that description of pain which is felt by a person who knows himself to be the object of the unfavourable sentiments of his fellow-creatures, and those inconveniences to which a person who is the object of such unfavourable sentiments is exposed.

According to the theory of the criminal law of England, the essence of the crime of private libel consists in its tendency to provoke breach of the peace; and, though this doctrine has not, in practice, been followed out to all the startling consequences to which it would legitimately lead, it has not failed to produce considerable inconvenience.

It appears to us evident that between the offence of defaming and the offence of provoking to a breach of the peace, there is a distinction as broad as that which separates theft and murder. Defamatory imputations of the worst kind may have no tendency to cause acts of violence. Words which convey no discreditable imputation whatever may have that tendency in the highest degree. Even in cases where defamation has a tendency to cause acts of violence, the heinousness of the defamation, considered as defamation, is by no means proportioned to its tendency to cause such acts: nay, circumstances which are great aggravations of the offence, considered as defamation, may be great mitigations of the same offence, considered as a provocation to a breach of the peace. A scurrilous satire against a friendless woman, published by a person who carefully conceals his name, would be defamation in one of its most odious forms. But it would be only by a legal fiction that the satirist could be said to provoke a breach of the peace. On the other hand, an imputation on the courage of an officer contained in a private letter, meant to be seen only by that officer and two or three other persons, might, considered as defamation, be a very venial offence. But such an imputation would have an obvious tendency to cause a serious breach of the peace.

On these grounds we have determined to propose that defamation shall be made an offence, without any reference to its tendency to cause acts of illegal violence.

We considered whether it would be advisable to make a distinction between the different modes in which defamatory imputations may be conveyed; and we came to the conclusion that it would not be advisable to make any such distinction.

By the English law, defamation is a crime only when it is committed by writing, printing, engraving or some similar process. Spoken words reflecting on private character, however atrocious may be the imputations which those words convey, however numerous may be the assembly before which such words are uttered, furnish ground only for a civil action. Herein the English law is scarcely consistent with itself. For if defamation be punished on account of its tendency to cause breach of the peace, spoken defamation ought to be punished even more severely than written defamation, as having that tendency in a higher degree. A person who reads in a pamphlet a calumnious reflection on himself, or on some one for whom he is interested, is less likely to take a violent revenge than a person who hears the same calumnious reflection uttered. Public men who have, by long habit, become callous to slander and abuse in a printed form, often show acute sensibility to imputations thrown on them to their faces. Indeed, defamatory words, spoken in the presence of the person who is the object of them, necessarily have more of the character of a personal affront, and are, therefore, more likely to cause breach of the peace than any printed libel.

The distinction which the English criminal law makes between written and spoken defamation is generally defended on the ground that written defamation is likely to be more widely spread and to be more permanent than spoken defamation. These considerations do not appear to us to be entitled to much weight. In the first place, it is by no means necessarily the fact that written defamation is more extensively circulated than spoken defamation. Written defamation may be contained in a letter intended for a single eye. Spoken defamation may be heard by an assembly of many thousands. It seems to us most unreasonable that it should be penal to say, in a private letter, that a man is dissipated, and not penal to stand up at the town-hall, and there, before the whole society of Calcutta, falsely to accuse him of poisoning his father.

In the second place, it is not necessarily the fact that the harm caused by defamation is proportioned to the extent to which the defamation is circulated. Some slanders,—and those slanders of a most malignant kind,—can produce harm only while confined to a very small circle, and would be at once refuted if they were published. A malignant whisper addressed to a single hearer, and meant to go no further, may indicate greater depravity, may cause more intense misery, and may deserve more severe punishment than a satire which has run through twenty editions. A person, for example, who, in private conversation, should infuse into the mind of a husband suspicions of the fidelity of a virtuous wife, might be a defamer of a far worse description than one who should insert the lady's name in a printed lampoon.

It must be allowed that, in general, a printed story is likely to live longer than a story which is only circulated in conversation. But, on the other hand, it is far easier for a calumniated person to clear his character, either by argument or by legal proceedings, from a charge fixed in a printed form, than from a shifting rumour, which nobody repeats exactly as he heard it. In general, we believe, a man would rather see in a newspaper a story discreditable to him which he had the means of refuting, than know that such a story, though not published, was current in society.

On the whole, we are so far from being able to discover any reason for exempting any mode of defamation from all punishment, that we have not even thought it right to provide different degrees of punishment for different modes of defamation. We do not conceive that on this subject any general rule can, with propriety, be laid down. We have, therefore, thought it best to leave to the courts the business of apportioning punishment, with due regard to the circumstances of every case.

We have thought it necessary, under the peculiar circumstances of this country, to lay down for the guidance of the courts a rule which, if we were legislating for a population among whom there was an uniform standard of morality and honour, might appear superfluous. India is inhabited by races which differ widely from each other in manners, tastes and religious opinions. Practices which are regarded as innocent by one large portion of society, excite the horror of another large portion. A Hindoo would be driven to despair if he knew that he was believed by persons of his own race to have done something which a Christian or a Mussulman would consider as indifferent or as laudable. Where such diversities of opinion exist, that part of the law which is intended to prevent pain arising from opinion ought to be sufficiently flexible to suit those diversities. We have, therefore, directed the judge not to decide the question whether an imputation be or be not defamatory, by reference to any particular standard, however correct, of honour, of morality, or of taste; but to extend an impartial protection to opinions which he regards as erroneous, and to feelings with which he has no sympathy.

There are nine excepted cases (see clauses from 470 to 478 inclusive) in which we propose to tolerate imputations prejudicial to character.

The exception which stands first in order will probably be thought by many persons objectionable. It is opposed to the rules of the English criminal law. It goes, we fear, beyond what even the boldest reformers of English law have proposed. It is at variance with the provisions of the French Code, and with the sentiments of the most distinguished French jurists. It is at variance also with the provisions of the Code of Louisiana. It is, therefore, with some diffidence that we venture to lay before the Governor-General in Council the results of a long and anxious consideration of this question.

The question is, whether the truth of an imputation prejudicial to character should, in all cases, exempt the author of that imputation from punishment as a defamer. We conceive that it ought to exempt him.

It will hardly be disputed, even by those who dissent from us on this point, that there is a marked distinction between true and false imputations, as respects both the degree of malignity which they indicate, and the degree of mischief which they produce. The accusing a man of what he has not done implies, in a vast majority of cases, greater depravity than the accusing him of what he has done. The pain which a false imputation gives to the person who is the object of it is clear, uncompensated evil. There is no set-off whatever. The pain which a true imputation gives to the person who is the object of it is in itself an evil, and, therefore, ought not to be wantonly inflicted. But there is often some counterbalancing good. A true imputation may produce a wholesome effect on the person who has, by his misconduct, exposed himself to it. It may deter others from imitating his example. It may set them on their guard against his bad designs.

Not only do true imputations generally produce some good to counterbalance the evil caused by them, but in many cases this counterbalancing good appears to us greatly to preponderate. However skilfully penal laws may be framed, however vigorously they may be carried into execution, many bad practices will always be out of reach of the tribunals. The state of society would be deplorable if public opinion did not repress much that legislators are compelled to tolerate. The wisest legislators have felt this, and have assigned it as a reason for not visiting certain acts with legal punishment, that those acts will be sufficiently punished by general disapprobation. It seems inconsistent and unwise to rely on the public opinion in certain cases as a valuable auxiliary to the law, and at the same time to treat the expression of that opinion in those very cases as a crime.

It is easy to put cases about which there could scarcely be any difference of opinion. A person who has been guilty of gross acts of swindling at the Cape comes to Calcutta, and proposes to set up a house of agency. A person who has been forced to fly from England on account of his infamous vices repairs to India, opens a school, and exerts himself to obtain pupils. A captain of a ship induces natives to emigrate, by promising to convey them to a country where they will have large wages and little work. He takes them to a foreign colony, where they are treated like slaves, and returns to India to hold out similar temptations to others. A man introduces a common prostitute as his wife into the society of all the most respectable ladies of the presidency. A person in a high station is in the habit of encouraging ruinous play among young servants of the Company. In all these cases, and in many others which might be named, we conceive that a writer who publishes the truth renders a great service to the public, and cannot, without a violation of every sound principle, be treated as a criminal.

There are undoubtedly many cases in which the spreading of true reports, prejudicial to the character of an individual, would hurt the feelings of that individual, without producing compensating advantage in any other quarter. The proclaiming to the world that a man keeps a mistress, that he is too much addicted to wine, that he is penurious in his house-keeping, that he is slovenly in his person; the raking up of ridiculous and degrading stories about the youthful indiscretions of a man who has long lived irreproachably as a husband and a father, and who has attained some post which requires gravity and even sanctity of character, can seldom or never produce any good to the public sufficient to compensate for the pain given to the person attacked, and to those who are connected with him. Yet we greatly doubt whether, where the imputations are true, it be advisable to inflict on the propagators of such miserable scandal any legal punishment, in addition to that general aversion and contempt with which their calling and their persons are everywhere regarded. Even in such cases, the question whether the imputation be true or false is not an unimportant question. Those who would not allow truth to be in such cases a justification, would admit that it ought generally to be a mitigating circumstance.* Indeed, we find it impossible to imagine any case in which we should punish a man who told no more than the truth respecting another, as severely as if what he told had been a lie invented to blast the reputation of that other.

These two propositions, then, we consider as established; first, that in some cases of prosecution for defamation, the truth of the imputations alleged to be defamatory ought to be a justification; secondly, that in the vast majority of such cases, if not in all, truth, if it be not a justification, ought to be a mitigation.

From these two propositions a third proposition necessarily follows: that in all cases of prosecution for defamation, if the defendant avers that the imputations complained of as defamatory are true, the court ought to go into the question of the truth of those imputations.

This ought to be done, not only in justice to the public and to the defendant, but in justice to the innocent complainant. It must not be forgotten, that one of the most important ends which a person proposes to himself in prosecuting a slanderer is the refuting of the slander. He generally considers the punishment of the offender as a secondary object; and, when there is no circumstance of peculiar aggravation in the case, is often willing to stay proceedings after obtaining a retractation and apology. To clear his fame is his first object. It is, we conceive, an object for the attaining of which he is entitled to the assistance of the law; but it is an object which cannot be attained unless the courts go into the question of truth.

The effect of a rule excluding evidence of the truth is to put on a par descriptions of persons between whom it is desirable to make the widest distinction. The public-spirited man who warns the mercantile community against a notorious cheat, or advises families not to admit into their intimacy a practised seducer of innocence, is placed on the same footing with the slanderer, who invents the most infamous falsehoods against persons of the purest character. On the other hand, a man who has, without the slightest reason, been held up to the world as a seducer or a swindler, is placed in exactly the same situation with one who well deserves those disgraceful names. So defective is the investigation that it leaves a suspicion lying on the most innocent, and no more than a suspicion lying on the most guilty.

We therefore think that in all cases of prosecution for defamation, the courts ought to allow the question of truth to be gone into. But if in all cases the courts allow the question of truth to be gone into, we are satisfied that no respectable person will venture to institute a prosecution for defamation in a case in which he knows that the truth of the defamatory matter is likely to be proved. He will feel that, by prosecuting, he should injure his own character far more deeply than any libeller can do. However disagreeable it may be to his feelings that a discreditable story concerning him should be repeated in society, and should furnish paragraphs for the newspapers, it must be much more disagreeable that such a story should be proved in open court by legal evidence; by prosecuting, he turns what was at most a strong suspicion into an absolute certainty. While he forbears to prosecute, many people will probably disbelieve the scandalous report; many will doubt about its truth. The mere circumstance that he abstains from prosecuting is no proof of guilt. It is notorious that slanders are often passed by with silent contempt by those who are the objects of them. Indeed, in a country where the press is free, a man whose station exposes him to remark would have nothing to do but to prosecute, if he should institute legal proceedings every time that he might be calumniated.

It seems to us, therefore, certain, that a man on whose character imputations have been thrown, which can be proved to be true, will, if he possess ordinary prudence and ordinary sensibility, abstain from having recourse to a court of law, which will fully investigate the truth of those imputations. By having recourse to a court of law, he would show that he belonged to a class of persons who are the last that a legislator would wish to favour, to that class of persons in whom the sense of shame is weak, and the malicious passions strong, and who are content to incur dishonour for the chance of obtaining revenge.

Being, therefore, of opinion, that in all cases of prosecution for defamation, evidence of the truth of the imputations alleged to be defamatory ought to be received, and being of opinion that practically there is no difference between receiving evidence of truth and allowing truth to be a justification, we have thought it advisable to provide, expressly, that truth shall always be a justification. By framing the law thus, we have not in the smallest degree diminished the real security of private character, or the real risk of detraction. We have merely made the language of the Code correspond with its virtual operation.

As we are satisfied that no practical mischief will be produced by the rule which we have proposed, we think that its perfect simplicity and certainty are strong reasons for adopting it.

If it be not adopted, it will be necessary to take one of two courses, either to provide that truth shall in no case be a justification, or to provide that truth shall be a justification in some cases and not in others. To the former course we feel, for reasons which we have already assigned, insurmountable objections. The effect of such a state of the law would be, that eminent public services would often be treated as crimes. If the latter course be taken, we are convinced that it would be found impossible to draw any line approaching to accuracy. We are convinced that it would be necessary to leave to the judges an almost boundless discretion, a discretion which no two judges would exercise in the same manner.

It has been suggested to us, from quarters entitled to great respect, that it would be a preferable course to admit in every case the truth of matter alleged to be defamatory to be given in evidence, for the purpose of proving that the accused person had not acted maliciously; but not to allow the proof of the truth to be a justification if it should appear that reputation had been maliciously assailed.

If a provision of this kind were adopted, it would, for the reasons which we have already given, be in practice nugatory; for no respectable person would prosecute the author of an imputation which could be proved to be true. And we take it for granted that the law of procedure will not be framed in so cruel and unreasonable a manner as to permit a prosecution for defamation to be instituted in opposition to the wishes of the person defamed. Such a power of prosecution would scarcely ever be used by a friend of the person defamed; it would never be used by a judicious friend; and it would be a most formidable weapon in the hands of a malignant enemy.

But if the provision which we are considering were not certain to be in practice nugatory, we should think it a highly objectionable provision. When an act is of such a description that it would be better that it should not be done, it is quite proper to look at the motives and intentions of the doer, for the purpose of deciding whether he shall be punished or not. But when an act which is really useful to society, an act of a sort which it is desirable to encourage, has been done, it is absurd to inquire into the motives of the doer, for the purpose of punishing him if it shall appear that his motives were bad.

If A kills Z it is proper to inquire whether the killing was malicious; for killing is *primâ facie* a bad act. But if A saves Z's life, no tribunal inquires whether A did so from good feeling, or from malice to some person who was bound to pay Z an annuity; for it is better that human life should be saved from malice than not at all. If A sets on fire a quantity of cotton belonging to Z, it is proper to inquire whether A acted maliciously; for the destruction of valuable property by fire is *primâ facie* a bad act; but if Z's cotton is burning, and A puts it out, no tribunal inquires whether A did so from good feeling or from malice to some other dealer in cotton, who, if Z's stock had been destroyed, would have been a great gainer; for the saving of valuable property from destruction is an act which it is desirable to encourage, and it is better that such property should be saved from bad motives than that it should be suffered to perish. Since, then, no act ought to be made punishable on account of malicious intention, unless it be in itself an act of a kind which it is desirable to prevent, it follows that malice is not a test which can with propriety be used for the purpose of determining what true imputations on character ought to be punished, and what true imputations on character ought not to be punished; for the throwing of true imputations on character is not *primâ facie* a pernicious act. It may, indeed, be a very pernicious act; but we are not prepared to say that in the majority of instances it is so. We are sure that it is often a great public service; and we are sure that it may be very pernicious when it is not done from malice, and that it may be a great public service when it is done from malice. It is perfectly conceivable that a person might, from no malicious feeling, but from an honest though austere and injudicious zeal for what he might consider as the interests of religion and morality, drag before the public frailties which it would be far better to leave in obscurity. It is also perfectly conceivable that a person who has been concerned in some odious league of villainy and has quarrelled with his accomplices, may, from vindictive feelings, publish the history of their proceedings, and may by doing so render a great service to society. Suppose that a knot of sharpers lives by seducing young men to the gaming-table and pillaging them to their last rupee. Suppose that one of these knaves, thinking himself ill-used in the division of the plunder, should revenge himself by printing an account of the transactions in which he has been concerned; he is prosecuted by the rest of the gang for defamation; he proves that every word in his account is true; but it is admitted that his only motives for publishing it were rancorous hatred and disappointed rapacity; it would surely be most unreasonable in the court to say: "You have told the public a truth which it greatly concerned the public to know; you have been the saving of many promising youths; you have been the means of ridding society of a dreadful pest; you have done, in short, what it was most desirable that you should do; but as you have done this, not from public spirit, but from dislike of your old associates, we pronounce you guilty of an offence, and condemn you to fine and imprisonment."

It is evident that society cannot spare any portion of the services which it receives. Far from scrutinizing the motives which lead people to render such services, and punishing such services when they proceed from bad motives, all societies are in the habit of offering motives addressed to the selfish passions of bad men for the purpose of inducing those men to do what is beneficial to the mass. We offer pardons and pecuniary rewards to the worst members of the community for the purpose of inducing them to betray their accomplices in guilt. That the quarrels of rogues are the security of honest men is an important truth which has passed into a proverb; and of that security we should to a certain extent deprive honest men if we were to make it an offence in one rogue to speak the truth about another rogue under the influence of passions excited in the course of a quarrel.

We have hitherto argued this point on the supposition that by malice is meant real malice, and not a fictitious, a constructive malice. We have the strongest objections to introducing into the Code such a kind of malice—a malice of which a person may be acquitted when it is clear that he has acted from the most deadly personal rancour, and found guilty when those who find him guilty are satisfied that he has acted only from the best feelings—a malice which may be only the technical name for benevolence.

On these grounds, we recommend to the Governor-General in Council that the first exception, as we have drawn it, be suffered to stand part of the Code.

The remaining exceptions will not require so long a defence; by clause 471 we allow the public conduct of public functionaries to be discussed, provided that such discussion be conducted in good faith. That the advantages arising from such discussion far more than compensate for the pain which it occasionally gives, will hardly be disputed by any English statesman.

But there are public men who are not public functionaries; persons who hold no office may yet, in this country, take a very active part in urging or opposing the adoption of measures in which the community is deeply interested. It appears clear to us that every person ought to be allowed to comment, in good faith, on the proceedings of these volunteer servants of the public, with the same freedom with which we allow him to comment on the proceedings of the official servants of the public. We have provided for this by clause 472.

By clause 473 we have allowed all persons freely to discuss in good faith the proceedings of courts of law, and the characters of parties, agents and witnesses as connected with those proceedings. It is almost universally acknowledged that the courts of law ought to be thrown open to the public; but the advantage of throwing them open to the public will be small indeed, if the few who are able to press their way into a court are forbidden to report what has passed there to the vast numbers who were absent, or if those who are allowed to know what has passed are not allowed to comment on what has passed. The only reason that the whole community is not admitted to hear every trial that takes place is that it is physically impossible that they should find room; and, by clause 473, we do our best to counteract the effect of this physical impossibility.

Whether public writers ought to be allowed to publish comments on trials while those trials are still pending is a question which, in the present state of India, it is hardly worth while to discuss. We have not thought it necessary to insert any provision on that subject in the chapter of offences against public justice; and such a provision, even if it were necessary, would evidently not belong to the head of defamation, for the harm done by such comments, as respects public justice, is exactly the same when the comments are laudatory as when they are abusive.

By clause 474 we allow every person to criticise, in good faith, published books, works of art which are publicly exhibited, and other similar performances.

By clause 475 we allow a person under whose authority others have been placed, either by their own consent or by the law, to censure, in good faith, those who are so placed under his authority, as far as regards matter to which that authority relates.

By clause 476 we allow a person to prefer an accusation against another, in good faith, to any person who has lawful authority to restrain or punish the accused.

By clause 477 we have excepted from the definition of defamation private communications which a person makes, in good faith, for the protection of his own interests; and by clause 478 we have excepted private communications which a person makes in good faith for the benefit of others.

It will be observed that in the eight last exceptions, we do not require that an imputation should be true; we require only that it should be made in good faith. For to require in these cases that the imputation should be true, would be to render these exceptions mere nullities. Whether a public functionary is or is not fit for his situation; whether a person who has bestirred himself to get up a petition in favour of a public measure ought to be considered as an enlightened and public-spirited citizen, or as a foolish meddler; whether a person who has been tried for an offence was or was not guilty; which of two witnesses who contradicted each other on a trial ought to be believed; whether a portrait is like; whether a song has been well sung; whether a book is well written;—these are questions about which honest and discerning men may hold opinions diametrically opposite; and to require a man to prove to the satisfaction of a court of law that the opinion which he has expressed on such a question is a right opinion is to prohibit all discussion on such questions. The same may be said of those private communications which we propose to allow. It is plainly desirable that a merchant should disclose to his partners his unfavourable opinion of the honesty of a person with whom the firm has dealings. It is desirable that a father should caution his son against marrying a woman of bad character. But if the merchant is permitted to say to his partners, if the father is permitted to say to his son, only what can be legally proved before a court, it is evident that the permission is worth nothing.

Whether an imputation be or be not made in good faith is a question for the courts of law. The burden of the proof will lie sometimes on the person who has made the imputation, and sometimes on the person on whom the imputation has been thrown. No general rule can be laid down. Yet scarcely any case could arise respecting which a sensible and impartial judge would feel any doubt. If, for example, a public functionary were to prosecute for defamation a writer who had described him in general terms as incapable, the court would probably require the prosecutor to give some proof of bad faith. If the prosecutor had no such proof to offer, the defendant would be acquitted. If the prosecutor were to prove that the defendant had applied to him for money, had promised to write in his praise if the money were advanced, and had threatened to abuse him if the money were withheld, the court would, probably, be of opinion that the defendant had not written in good faith, and would convict him.

On the other hand, if the imputation were an imputation of some particular fact, or an imputation which, though general in form, yet implied the truth of some particular fact which, if true, might be proved, the court would probably hold that the burden of proving good faith lay on the defendant. Thus if a person were to publish that a collector was in the habit of receiving bribes from the zemindars of his district, and were unable to specify a single case, or to give any authority for his assertion, the courts would probably be of opinion that the imputation had not been made in good faith.

Again: if a critic described a writer as a plagiarist, the courts would not consider this as defamation without very strong proof of bad faith. But if it were proved that the critic had, like Lauder, interpolated passages in old books in order to bear out the charge of plagiarism, the court would doubtless be of opinion that he had not criticised in good faith, and would convict him of defamation.

It will be necessary to provide in the Code of procedure rules for pleading in cases of defamation, which may give to an innocent man who has been calumniated the means of clearing his character. It will be proper to provide that a defendant who is accused of defamation, and who rests his defence on the truth of the imputation alleged to be defamatory, shall be held strictly to the proof of the substance of the imputation if the imputation be particular, and shall be compelled to descend to particulars in his plea if the imputation be general. It will not be expected that we should here go into any details respecting the law of criminal pleading. It is sufficient here to say, that the importance of framing that part of the law in such a manner as to give full protection to persons whose character has been unjustly aspersed has not escaped our attention.

We may here observe that an imputation which is not defamatory may, under certain circumstances, be punishable on other grounds. Such an imputation may be intended to excite disaffection. If so, though not punishable as defamation, it will be punishable as sedition. An attack made, in good faith, on the public administration of the Governor of a presidency, will in no case be a defamation. But if the author of it designed to inflame the people against the Government, he will be liable to punishment under clause 113.

Again: an imputation which is not defamatory may be intended to excite a mob to violence against an individual. If so, the author of the imputation is punishable under clause 94.

Again: an imputation which is not defamatory may be uttered in the hearing of the person who is the object of it, for the purpose of wantonly and maliciously annoying that person. If so, it is punishable under clause 485. There are many cases in which it is fit that unpleasant truth should be told respecting an individual. But there is no case in which it is desirable that such truth should be told in such a way that the telling of it is a gross personal outrage. A person who has detected, or thinks that he has detected, a dishonest misrepresentation in a book has a right to expose it publicly. But he cannot be allowed to intrude into the presence of the author of the book, and to tell him to his face that he is a liar. A person who knows the mistress of a female school to be a woman of infamous character deserves well of society if he states what he knows. But he cannot be allowed to follow her through the streets calling her by opprobrious names, though he may be able to prove that all those names were merited. A person who brings to notice the malversation of a public functionary deserves applause. But a person who hangs a public functionary in effigy at that functionary's door, with an opprobrious label, does what cannot be permitted, even though every word on the label, and every imputation which the exhibition was meant to convey, may be perfectly true.

We do not apprehend that the clauses relating to the printers and publishers of defamatory matter require any explanation or defence.

FIRST REPORT

ON THE

PENAL CODE

BY THE

INDIAN LAW COMMISSIONERS.

FROM

THE INDIAN LAW COMMISSIONERS,

To

THE HONORABLE THE PRESIDENT OF THE COUNCIL OF INDIA, IN COUNCIL.

Dated the 23rd July, 1846.

1. We have the honor to submit a Report on the Indian Penal Code, in pursuance of the instructions communicated to us in Mr. Secretary Bushby's letter, dated the 26th April 1845, as follows:—

Received 18th May 1845.

"The Governor-General in Council is desirous that "some step should be taken towards a revision of the "Code* with a view to its adoption with such amendments as may be "found necessary, or to its final disposal otherwise. For this purpose "I have been instructed to refer to you for examination, all the opinions "received from the several Presidencies as per enclosed list, and to "direct your attention to the 'Act of Crimes and Punishments' contained "in the Seventh Report of the Commissioners on the Criminal Law of "England, with a view to comparison, and the detection of any omis-"sions or other imperfections that may exist in the Code. With these "materials, the Governor-General in Council trusts that you will be "enabled to frame such a report as may assist the Government of India "in forming a judgment on the merits of the Code at no distant date."

2. We have with great pains and care examined, compared and digested, the voluminous papers containing commentaries and strictures on the Penal Code transmitted to us with Mr. Bushby's letter, and having reviewed the Code generally with reference thereto, we have directed our more particular attention to the Chapters of the greatest importance, namely, those treating "of offences affecting the human body," and "of offences against property," and to those of a general nature governing the whole, namely, the Chapter of "General Explanations," the Chapter of "General Exceptions," and the Chapter of "Abetment."

Chs. xviii, xix.

Chs. i, iii, iv.

3. Having studied the definitions of crimes and the rules and penal provisions contained in those chapters, with the aid of the lucid and able expositions of the principles upon which they are framed which are afforded in the valuable notes appended to the Code, we turned to the instructive reports of the Commissioners on the English Criminal Law, and to the Digest of crimes and punishments contained in their Seventh Report, and carefully compared the two systems, with reference occasionally to the Code Penal of France and Mr. Livingstone's Code for Louisiana, and with a constant regard to the Laws actually administered by the Company's Courts under the several Presidencies. Thus prepared, we proceeded to revise the Chapters, taking Clause by Clause,

---

*** The printed Draft of a Penal Code prepared by the Indian Law Commissioners, and submitted to the Government of India under date the 14th October 1837.**

and considering particularly the criticisms, objections, or suggested amendments, which we had previously noted as worthy of remark.

4. Our work performed in this manner has necessarily occupied a great deal of time, and the observations we have thought it proper to offer have extended to a greater length than we anticipated.

5. The following Report is a Record of those observations, prefaced by a general notice of the papers referred to us for examination, and some observations suggested by criticisms of a general nature contained therein. We submit it as affording a sample* from which your Honor in Council will be able to form a pretty fair judgment of the value of the whole Code.

REPORT.

Her Majesty's Supreme Courts—Judges and Law Officers.

6. The papers transmitted with Mr. Bushby's letter comprised Reports from the following Judges of Her Majesty's Supreme Courts :—

Calcutta...	The Hon'ble	Sir J. P. Grant, *Puisne Judge.*
	„	Sir H. W. Seton, *Puisne Judge.*
Madras ...	„	Sir R. B. Comyn, *Chief Justice.*
	„	Sir E. J. Gambier, *Puisne Judge, now Chief Justice.*
Bombay ...	„	Sir H. Compton, *Chief Justice.*
	„	Sir J. Awdry, *Puisne Judge, afterwards Chief Justice,*

a Report from the Advocate-General at Madras, Mr. G. Norton, and one from the Company's Standing Counsel at Calcutta, Mr. J. Cochrane.

Hon'ble Company's Courts. Judges of the Sudder Courts and Subordinate Judges and Magistrates, &c.

Also a Report from the Sudder Court for the North-Western Provinces under the Presidency of Fort William in Bengal, and separate Reports from two† of the Judges of the Sudder Court at Madras, and three‡ of the Judges of the Sudder Court at Bombay, accompanied by Reports from the Judges, Magistrates, &c., subordinate to the said Courts respectively, and a separate Report from Colonel Sleeman, Commissioner for the Suppression of Thuggee.

7. Of the Judges of Her Majesty's Courts whose reports are abovementioned, Sir J. P. Grant, Sir E. J. Gambier, and Sir H. Compton have not entered into a particular examination of the Code.

8. Sir J. P. Grant states that he considers it incompatible with his duties as a Judge to undertake the task of reviewing the Code and giving his opinion upon it, concluding with the following words, "I "confess that I cannot set a limit to the number of years which it would "be necessary for me to devote exclusively to the consideration and "study of such a Code, and of all the large and intricate and appall- "ing questions with which it must be of necessity surrounded, if I "could think it consistent with my judicial duties, and the measure of "my learning and capacity, to undertake so vast a task in so untried a "path of speculative jurisprudence and legislation."

---

* The whole Code consists of 488 Clauses, of which 233 Clauses are comprised in the Chapters reviewed in this Report.

† Mr. W. Hudleston and Mr. A. D. Campbell.

‡ Mr. Giberne, Mr. Pyne, and Mr. Greenhill.

9. Sir E. J. Gambier says, "I have always entertained the strongest "doubts of the propriety or expediency of promulgating any Code of "Law which professes to be more than a compilation and a better "arrangement of those enactments which have previously been in force, "and which former experience has sanctioned and approved; and I "have always thought that such a body of law should be modified by "those additions and alterations alone of which the same experience has "evinced the utility or the need. To do more than this, to put forth a "body of law which is not even founded upon any previously existing "system, and to clothe the enactments in language which is as new to "those who are to dispense the law as to those who are to live under it, "appears to me a mode of proceeding irreconcilable with the maxims of "practical wisdom, and one calculated to introduce a degree of confusion "and difficulty which has never yet been found in administering the "criminal justice of any civilized country."

"Such (he adds) being my general opinion on the Code in question, "I do not enter into the consideration of the different parts of it."

10. Sir H. Compton professes not to attempt a criticism of the work of the Law Commissioners, or of its arrangement, or particular provisions, but to state the grounds upon which *a priori* he is of opinion that the Code they have prepared should not be adopted. In the first part of his elaborate paper he endeavors to shew, that in preparing the Penal Code in the manner in which it has been prepared, as a general system of Criminal Law for India to be substituted for all the systems which now prevail, the Law Commissioners have done what was not intended by Parliament, while they have omitted to do "what was contemplated and commanded by Parliament," and that if in taking this course they were guided by instructions from the Governor-General in Council, such instructions were unwarranted, for "the Governor-General in Council had "not legal power to dispense with the directions contained in the Act of "Parliament, which in fact created their own authority."

11. Passing from this preliminary objection, and, for the purpose of discussion, supposing that all that has been directed by Parliament has been substantially done, and that the Law Commissioners have been instructed to prepare a Code, he proceeds to consider the three following questions:

1st. Whether it is expedient, if practicable, "at once to change the "penal jurisprudence of all British India"?

2nd. "Whether it is practicable to form one system of law that can, "or ought to be, applicable to every one in common"?

3rd. "Whether the Code which has been proposed is likely to pro"duce the benefits the Law Commissioners profess to expect from it"?

12. The first question he regards as decided already by Parliament, the language of the Act of Parliament plainly expressing, as he thinks, that "it was not the intention of the legislature, in short that it was not "*expedient* to change the whole penal jurisprudence of British India."

13. On the second question he refers to the experience of similar legislation in other countries, and averring that it has not produced the benefits expected from it "even with people who have long been subject to "the same form of Government, and who profess the same creed, and that "hitherto there has been found an inherent difficulty in framing any system "of written law," he concludes that "it may well be doubted whether it

"be *practicable*, if *expedient*, to make penal enactments that may be equally "applicable to every description of person in every part of British India," and intimates his opinion that "with due research and enquiry there "may be found in the systems of penal law which now prevail in British "India, sufficient and sound materials for making such alterations and "amendments in this branch of jurisprudence as the present form of "Government and the condition of the people may require."

14. Lastly, with respect to the Code prepared by the Law Commissioners, or rather (for he professes not to have examined the Code itself) to the description of it contained in their letter to the Governor-General in Council with which it is prefaced, and with reference particularly to their reasons for framing "illustrations of their definitions," and to their avowed desire to limit the power which Courts of Justice possess of putting their own sense on the laws, he argues that "similar attempts "to simplify Criminal Codes have utterly failed, and that it is no longer "considered useful to attempt to render them perfect by the introduction "of all possible cases, which after all is deemed an impossibility."

15. He insists on "the importance of procedure," in order "to shew "that until we know what system the Law Commissioners intend to "recommend, we cannot sufficiently examine or estimate the particular "provisions of the Code which has been framed."

16. Of the other Judges above named, the reports of Sir H. Seton and Sir R. Comyn contain comments upon details, as well as general remarks and criticisms upon the plan of the work and the principles laid down in it, and expounded in the Notes. The report of Sir J. Awdry consists of "general observations which respect the character of the whole work," which he intended to follow up with remarks upon the practical details, an intention which it is much to be regretted he did not fulfil.

17. Sir H. Seton speaking of the expediency of framing a Code for this country at the present time, observes that "the best justification of "it seems to be found in the necessity of some system, the absence of "any satisfactory one, and the hopelessness of constructing a more per-"fect one, except by means of successive improvements upon this," adding that "if the attempt were to be delayed until all the information "which theoretically might be considered desirable were obtained, it "could never be made."

18. Having submitted "a few observations respecting Codes generally," he proceeds to examine the one now under consideration. He remarks first the number of new offences created by it, and states his own views as to the desirableness of extending as far as possible the operation of compensation, and limiting that of punishment. These views he observes are not suggested as opposed to those contained in the Code, but he thinks it may fairly be questioned whether they are sufficiently kept in view in the multitude of new offences created by it.

19. He next adverts to the language of the Code, and more especially to the definitions of crimes contained in it. He observes that Criminal Legislation demands plain language and definite precepts, but how far this is supplied by the Code with all the assistance derived from its illustrations, he thinks questionable. He remarks that the object seems to have been to exclude judicial discretion, but that however desirable it may be to limit judicial discretion, it is in vain to attempt wholly to exclude it by definitions however illustrated.

20. He says generally that "the Code itself furnishes abundant "reasons why it should not be put into operation, until the whole sys- "tem is completed." This he adds, "will afford the means of extending "civil rights and remedies, and may be found to modify or supersede "many of the present provisions of it."

21. His observations upon the details of the Code are submitted in a separate paper.

22. Of these observations and the criticisms in his report, he says they "are made with freedom, but not in a hostile spirit, not without a "just sense of the great difficulty of the undertaking, of the pains be- "stowed upon the execution of it, and above all of the masterly manner "in which the principles connected with it are discussed and developed "in the notes."

23. Sir R. Comyn remarks, that "his own experience has been "almost exclusively confined to the administration of Criminal Law "at the Presidency of Fort Saint George under the English system," and observing of that system that "it is built up on notions not unfrequent- "ly inapplicable to the Native Society of India, and too often clogged by "technical subtleties, which, if intended to protect the innocent, occa- "sionally assist in the escape of the guilty," he says that "he certainly "should be very far from advocating the extension of it beyond the limits "of the several Presidencies, whilst he thinks it highly desirable that, "if the Mofussil is to be governed by regulations emanating from British "Authority, these should be assimilated throughout the territory as far "as the nature of things may permit," therefore "in reviewing the pro- "posed Code, he has endeavored to allow himself to be as little influ- "enced by the prejudices of education and professional habits as could "reasonably be expected, and to consider himself called upon to remark "upon an entirely new compendium of Law by which the persons and "property of those who reside in India, under the British dominion, "may be best protected."

24. He observes that he has found himself embarrassed in adverting to the various provisions of the Code by his ignorance of the manner in which it is proposed to carry them into effect, and expresses an opinion that under the system of criminal pleading now in force at the Presidencies, it would be difficult, if not impossible, to frame the accusations so as to meet many of them, adding that the very introduction of new Terms and new Definitions would be a great impediment.

25. Before adverting to the particular heads of enactment, he "points "out two or three imperfections which as a system of Criminal Law "seem to pervade the whole." His remarks refer, 1st, to the system of "Illustrations;" 2ndly, to the provisions by which "the commission or non-commission of an offence is made to depend upon what may be passing in the mind of the party offending at the time of committing the act laid to his charge;" 3rdly, to the provisions "treating acts which are really outrages on society as merely offences to individuals." After commenting on the above heads, he says "these are the chief general "observations which have occurred to me on an attentive perusal of the "text and the accompanying notes—many objections which had suggest- "ed themselves to me in the former have been entirely or in great "measure removed by the satisfactory reasoning of the latter." In reviewing the details he finds occasion for a few brief observations only, upon particular Chapters and Clauses. With regard to the two im-

portant Chapters treating of "offences affecting the human body" and of "offences against property," he says of the former that it contains only one provision which appears to him objectionable in substance, of the latter that "it strikes him as a very successful digest of Law for the protection of property."

26. Sir J. Awdry says he conceives that he is not consulted on the expediency or practicability of codification in general, or as regards the Penal Law of India in particular, but that assuming the necessity of framing a Penal Code as the only means of providing for the wants of a population which has no system of jurisprudence applicable to all, he is merely consulted as to the execution.

27. The first impression, he says, which was made upon him, by the perusal of an early draft of the Code without the preface or notes, was, how simple and practical the whole scheme seemed to be, how little (with certain grave exceptions) departing from the substantial principles of the Law of England. "This impression," he proceeds to say, "has "been confirmed by the perusal of the complete work, and to it has been "added a sense of the general comprehension of its plan and of the "sound reason of large classes of its enactments." Again he remarks, "the enactments are generally so conformable to the sound and univer-"sal principles of this branch of Law, which is or ought to be less artifi-"cial than the civil, that I should see no great inconvenience and no in-"justice in its introduction." Contrarily to Sir R. Comyn, he observes that "the procedure of the English Law seems fully adequate to the "general working of the Code," and that he could "easily leave to the "jury almost any charge it contains."

28. The above he observes, is "almost the highest praise of which "he conceives the draft of such a work capable, as long as it is not "matured by those amendments and interpretations which in the course "of time will supply its defects, correct its errors, and authenticate the "sense of every line. The present involves a bold, and to a certain "extent, a successful attempt to mitigate the unavoidable evils of the "sudden introduction of a mass of enacted Law."

29. On the whole he says, he "views this work as an admirable "attempt to comprise in a single statute, the definition of crimes and "their punishments, but no more; and considers that those who because "they can point out numerous and important defects in it, think they "shew that it is not entitled to that praise, only betray their own "ignorance of the extreme difficulty of sound legislation."

30. Mr. Norton, the Advocate-General at Madras, in a long report, offers objections to the Code "which not only extend throughout almost "all its details, but also to the legislative principles upon which it is "founded." In the conclusion of his report he says, "my objection to "the Code is to it as a *whole*. I conceive it framed on erroneous prin-"ciples. I deem it constitutionally defective, and that it requires recon-"struction throughout, and to be elaborated upon a different plan and "upon far more extensive data."

31. Mr. Cochrane, the Company's Standing Counsel at Calcutta, confines his observations to the Chapters under the heads of "Punishments," "General Exceptions," "Abetment," "Offences relating to the Army and Navy," and "Offences against Public Tranquillity," in all which he finds provisions that appear to him highly objectionable.

32. The Sudder Court for the North-Western Provinces of the Presidency of Fort William, while they express a doubt whether the plan followed in the preparation of the Code is the best that could have been adopted, yet "willingly recognize its comprehensiveness, and the general "success (as far as can be predicated of any production not submitted "to the test of practice) with which it has been executed." Referring to the opinions given by officers subordinate to the Court submitted with their own report, they observe that one only disapproves of the Code absolutely, and that the majority "approve of it with qualifications." A general approbation of the Code, we remark, is expressed by a considerable number.

33. Colonel Sleeman, Commissioner for the Suppression of Thuggee, whose opinion was specially called for by Government on account of his great practical experience, says "I have read the Code over several times "very carefully, and can honestly say that at every reading it has grown "more and more upon my esteem. I am persuaded that it might be "put immediately in force with great advantage to the people of India; "and that it would soon become all that could be desired under the "fostering care of the Legislative Council and Law Commission, in the "manner pointed out in the 25th para. of the letter of the Law Commis-"sion to the Governor-General of India." Colonel Sleeman suggests certain alterations and additions as likely to be useful. We may note in particular, that he proposes to add Clauses for the punishment of Seduction and Adultery, and making it penal to sell or buy human beings, in order to put an end to Slavery in India.

34. Of the Judges of the Sudder Court at Bombay and of the Officers subordinate to that Court whose opinions are recorded, not one disapproves of the Code absolutely; some express unqualified approbation of it; others express approbation with certain reserves and qualifications; and one or two, apparently approving in general, suggest additions and modifications by which they think it may be amended.

35. Of the two Judges of the Madras Sudder Court whose opinions are recorded,* one expresses unqualified disapprobation generally. The† other disapproves of the Code for the most part, but dissents from the adverse comments of his colleague in many places, and expresses approbation of particular portions. Of the subordinate Officers, a generally unfavorable opinion of the work is expressed by about a fourth part, and a generally favorable opinion by about one half; of the rest some may be taken as approving on the whole, but objecting to particular portions, and suggesting modifications, others as disapproving on the whole, but expressing approbation of particular portions, and a few as offering particular objections, but not giving a decided opinion on the whole.

36. We would draw attention especially to the able report of Mr. J. F. Thomas, a Judicial Officer of great experience (now Chief Secretary to the Government of Madras) referred to by the Judges of the Madras Sudder Court, as containing many important and judicious observations and suggestions.

37. We shall be found in the sequel to give due consideration to the valuable comments of Mr. Thomas, in reviewing the particular pro-

* Mr. W. Hudleston. † Mr. A. D. Campbell.

visions to which they apply. We shall now merely note the general opinion expressed by Mr. Thomas.

"Looking upon the Code as a whole, and as a substitute for the "existing Regulations, I consider it chiefly valuable as a compendium "of the latest, and most enlightened views of penal jurisprudence, ap-"plied with much judgment to the wants and circumstances of India. "The extensive use of pecuniary penalties, with the important object "of rendering them the means of indemnifying parties injured; the "Chapter on Abetment, and the introduction of the discriminating prin-"ciple of the French Code in cases of Perjury, are a few of the instances "of great and highly valuable improvements to which I allude. There "is also a comprehensiveness in the definitions of Offences which will, I "think, do much to remedy an evil of the present system under which "crimes may either be committed with impunity, or, are only brought "within the jurisdiction of the Courts, under some uncertain provisions "of the Mahomedan Law, (Section VII, Regulation X, 1816) unknown "to the Officers presiding in the Courts and which ordinarily annex "the arbitrary penalty of Ookoobut, leaving it therefore discretionary "with the Courts to adjudge any, or little, or no punishment. This "evil cannot exist under the new Code; whilst the comprehensiveness "of the definitions will also render the constant interference of the "legislature, and frequent additions to the penal Laws, unnecessary.

"The entire abrogation of the Mahomedan Law, relieving the Crim-"inal Jurisprudence of the country from a barbarous incumbrance, "will also be found a most important improvement, and I consider the "Code on the whole well calculated to form the basis of a greatly im-"proved system. It is, I am of opinion, capable of being at once made "Law in the Provinces, and substituted, with but little modification, for "the present Regulations of the Government."

38. Having thus briefly indicated the general tenor of the reports upon the Penal Code which have been referred to us for examination, we shall now notice particularly some of the objections that have been made to the plan of the work, and to the leading principles of the Code.

39. We conceive that we are not required on this occasion to discuss the reasonings which are to be found in several of these reports on the expediency of codification in general, or as regards the Penal Law of India in particular, but that, with Sir J. Awdry, "assuming the neces-"sity of a Penal Code as the only means of providing for the wants of "a population which has no one system of jurisprudence applicable to "all," and, with Sir H. Seton, deeming that "the best justification of it "is to be found in the necessity of some system, and the absence of any "satisfactory one," we are to consider, whether the Code which has been proposed is fitted in its principles and its substantive provisions for the purpose which it was designed to serve, and is capable, with or without modification, of being brought into practical operation as a general system—whether it may be advisable for the legislature to adopt it, not as a body of Law already perfect, which its authors never pretended it to be,* but as a systematically digested Statute of Crimes and Punish-

* NOTE.—They say, "in a work so extensive and complicated as that on which we have been employed, there will inevitably be, in spite of the most anxious care, some omissions, and some inconsistencies." "We have done as much as could reasonably be expected, if we have furnished the Government with that which may, by suggestions from experienced and judicious persons, be improved into a good Code."

ments based upon sound principles, and defined with a precision before unknown, sufficiently complete to be acted upon, and which when brought into operation may be reasonably expected to work immediately an important improvement in the administration of Criminal Justice, by methodizing it, and rendering it more easy, certain, and equal; looking to its being gradually matured and advanced towards perfection in the manner contemplated by the Commissioners, by which the legislature will be enabled easily to supply the defects, correct the errors, and reconcile the inconsistencies, discovered by experience.

40. In the prefatory letter to the Governor-General in Council, the Law Commissioners declare that the system of Penal Law contained in the Code is "not a digest of any existing system," and that no existing system had furnished "even the ground-work" for it. In another place in the same letter, after repeating that they had not thought it desirable, for reasons stated, "to take as the ground-work of the Code any of the "systems of Law now in force in any part of India," they say they had however "compared the Code with all those systems and taken sugges-"tions from all, though they had not adopted a single provision merely "because it formed a part of any of these systems," adding "we have "also compared our work with the most celebrated systems of Western "jurisprudence, as far as the very scanty means of information which "were accessible to us in this country enabled us to do so. We have "derived much valuable assistance from the French Code, and from the "decisions of the French Courts of Justice on questions touching the "construction of that Code. We have derived assistance still more "valuable from the Code of Louisiana, prepared by that eminent jurist, "the late Mr. Livingstone."

41. Upon the ground of the above declaration the Commissioners are severely censured in several of the reports. The course taken by them is denounced as "irreconcilable with the dictates of practical wisdom" and as leading almost inevitably to erroneous conclusions. The Code is spoken of slightingly as "an invention" "based upon theoreti-caunot practical principles," and this is said to be "a demerit fatal to "the hole work." But while the Commissioners are so much blamed for reacting all the syste s of Law at present in force in India, or, to speak more correctly, for not following any of them implicitly in laying the ground-work of their Code, those who find fault with them in this respect are not at all agreed as to what they ought to have done.

42. The Commissioners came to the determination to frame a new Code upon a plan of their own, because they found, as they thought, not "even the rudiments of a good Code" in any of the three systems contained in the Regulations of Bengal, Madras, and Bombay, and because they deemed the artificial and complicated system of the English Criminal Law which prevails within the local jurisdiction of Her Majesty's Courts to be unsuitable.

43. Now with respect to the former, we find that Mr. Norton, the Advocate-General at Madras, one of those who condemn the Commissioners for the course they have taken, is obliged to observe that "the rea-"sons assigned for rejecting the penal Laws prevailing in the *provinces* "of India as a ground-work for a systematic general Code of Criminal "Law for India are forcible and obvious. These Laws are incon-"sistent with each other, they are sometimes inconsistent with plain "justice, they are inadequate, and they are vague in point of expres-

"sion." But he takes a different view respecting the English Criminal Law, which in opposition to the Commissioners, he recommends "as sup-"plying a safe and firm ground-work and ample materials for construct-"ing a Penal Code for this country, subject to such modifications with "respect to the condition, habits, and usages of the people, as the statute "organizing the Indian Commission points out;" while on the contrary, as has been already shewn, Sir R. Comyn, the Chief Justice at the same Presidency, emphatically declares that the English system is one which he should be very far from advocating the extension of. There are some again who would have a body of Criminal Law for this country composed by a combination of the Regulations of Government with the principles of English Law administered by the Supreme Courts; while others eschewing English Law, would harmonize the Laws contained in the Regulations of the several Presidencies, and thereby construct a general system.

44. From the tenor of some of the animadversions upon the plan pursued by the Commissioners, it might be supposed that they had proceeded entirely upon theoretical views of their own, rejecting all the aids to be obtained from the Laws actually in force in India, whereas although they followed none implicitly, they took suggestions from all, so that Sir J. Awdry remarks how little (with certain grave exceptions) the Code departs from the substantial principles of the Law of England, and Mr. Norton, on the other hand, finds fault with it as paying too much deference in some parts to the body of Law contained in the Regulations for the guidance of the Company's Courts. The truth is, that the Commissioners not only took suggestions from the Laws actually in force in India, but borrowed also from the legislation of the most civilized countries of Europe, thus availing themselves of the practical wisdom embodied in many various Codes, while at the same time they sought instruction in the works of learned jurists, calling in the lights of science, or the "philosophy of jurisprudence," to use the phrase quoted by Mr. Norton, to help them in judging of the aptitude of the provisons contained in these Codes, and in devising new provisions where one of them supplied rules which they approved. Such new provisons the principles upon which they are founded, are in generalally expounded and defended in the notes to the Code, and the resonableness of the principles and the fitness of the provisions are to be considered impartially, without permitting the judgment to be influenced by prejudices against them as innovations and untried theories.

45. After all, the novelty which is so much animadverted upon is more imaginary than real, and is to be found more in form than in substance. On this point we find Sir J. Awdry remarking that although some beneficial principles are as far as he is aware newly developed in the Code, the amount of really new matter contained in it is not so great as to give the Commissioners a claim to originality, while he "thinks "them entitled to the far greater praise of having seldom much disre-"garded the experience and recorded moral sense of the world."

46. The system of definitions and illustrations of definitions which has been adopted in this Code, is much criticised and censured. The following are the explanations which the Commissioners have given of this leading feature of their plan: "One peculiarity in the manner in "which this Code is framed will immediately strike your Lordship in "Council. We mean the copious use of illustrations. These illustra-

"tions will, we trust, greatly facilitate the understanding of the Law, "and will at the same time often serve as a defence of the Law. In our "definitions we have repeatedly found ourselves under the necessity of "sacrificing neatness and perspicuity to precision, and of using harsh "expressions, because we could find no other expressions which would "convey our whole meaning, and no more than our whole meaning. "Such definitions standing by themselves might repel and perplex the "reader, and would perhaps be fully comprehended only by a few Stu-"dents after long application. Yet such definitions are found in every "system of Law which aims at accuracy. A legislator may, if he think "fit, avoid such definitions, and by avoiding them he will give a "smoother and more attractive appearance to his workmanship: but in "that case he flinches from a duty which he ought to perform, and "which somebody must perform. If this necessary, but most disagree-"able work be not performed by the Lawgiver once for all, it must be "constantly performed in a rude and imperfect manner by every Judge "in the Empire, and will probably be performed by no two Judges in "the same way. We have, therefore, thought it right not to shrink from "the task of framing these unpleasing, but indispensable parts of a "Code; and we hope that when each of these definitions is followed by a "collection of cases falling under it, and of cases which, though at first "sight they appear to fall under it, do not really fall under it, the defini-"tions and the reasons which led to the adoption of it will be readily "understood. The illustrations will lead the mind of the Student "through the same steps by which the minds of those who framed the "Law proceeded, and may sometimes shew him that a phrase which "may have struck him as uncouth, or a distinction which he may have "thought idle, was deliberately adopted for the purpose of including or "excluding a large class of important cases. In the study of geometry "it is found that a theorem which, read by itself, conveyed no distinct "meaning to the mind, becomes perfectly clear as soon as the reader "casts his eye over the statement of the individual case taken for the "purpose of demonstration. Our illustrations, we trust, will in a similar "manner facilitate the study of the Law."

"We have, in framing our definitions, thought principally of mak-"ing them precise, and have not shrunk from rugged and intricate "phraseology, when such phraseology appeared to us to be necessary to "precision. If it appeared to us that our language was likely to perplex "an ordinary reader, we added as many illustrations as we thought "necessary for the purpose of explaining it. The definitions and enact-"ing Clauses contain the whole Law. The illustrations make nothing "Law which would not be Law without them. They only exhibit the "Law in full action, and shew what its effect will be on the events of "common life."

"Thus the Code will be at once a Statute book and a collection of "decided cases. The decided cases in the Code will differ from the "decided cases in the English Law Books in two most important points. "In the first place, our illustrations are never intended to supply any "omission in the written Law, nor do they ever in our opinion, put a "strain on the written Law. They are merely instances of the prac-"tical application of the written Law to the affairs of mankind. Second-"ly, they are cases decided not by the Judges but by the Legislature, by "those who make the Law, and must know more certainly than any "Judge can know what the Law is which they mean to make."

47. The Commissioners on the Criminal Law of England "did not "think it expedient to illustrate the abstract rules and "propositions in the digest framed by them, by particu- "lar cases or examples, excepting in the few instances "where such illustrations were found already moulded into rules, and "therefore forming part of the existing Law." "It appears to us," they said, "that if an example falls clearly within the terms of the "rule, it is useless as an illustration, because the rule is explicit without "it; if on the other hand, the example borders upon the verge of the rule, "or does not fall clearly within its terms, it either renders the rule doubt- "ful, or the example itself constitutes the Law. An illustration cannot, "as is already observed, be of any use as a Law, except to remove some "doubt which would otherwise occur as to the proper application of the "Law to the case proposed, or to that and others of a similar kind. But "this very necessity proves the Law to be imperfect, and shews the "framer of the Law to have been aware of an imperfection which ought "to have been remedied by using terms which either plainly excluded or "included the proposed predicament. Laws must frequently be ambigu- "ous in their application, because it is impossible to foresee all the "various combinations of circumstances to which it may be necessary to "apply them; but it would argue great negligence not to use terms "which should clearly comprehend a case not only within the knowledge "of the law-maker, but even suggested by him."

4th Report, p. XVI.

48. The India Law Commissioners observe that "to unite precision "and simplicity in definitions intended to include large classes of "things, and to exclude others very similar to many of those which are "included, will often be utterly impossible." They thought that this difficulty might be best overcome by the use of illustrations. The English Commissioners apparently feeling the same difficulty, had recourse to the expedient of adding to the definitions expository clauses, where the definitions themselves are not sufficiently explicit, or where technical expressions are necessarily used, to "interpret them into popu- "lar language and give them a precise meaning." After giving their reasons, as above, for not resorting to illustrations, "in order to guard "against any misapprehension of their meaning," they say, "we do "not assert that illustrations are not useful as leading to a knowledge "and understanding of the Law, but that they ought not to form a part "of the Law, so as to supersede or vary it, or to be of concurrent au- "thority. There is, perhaps, no abstract rule or position in any science "to the understanding of which the mind may not conveniently be led "by the aid of familiar examples; they are indeed frequently the very "steps by which the rule was first discovered, and its truth or propriety "tested, and in either case must necessarily be included within it. It "is, however, to be remarked, that none but plain and obvious examples "are conducive even to the purposes of instruction; for predicaments "to which the application of the proposed rule was doubtful, would "serve to perplex rather than enlighten the mind." Here they appear to come pretty nearly to an agreement with the framers of the Indian Code, who in the passage above quoted in effect declare that they do not intend their illustrations "to form a part of the Law so as to supersede or vary it," "or to be of concurrent authority" so as to make anything Law which would not be Law without them, but simply to serve the same office as the expository Clauses in the digest of the English Commissioners, particularly those which are described in the following words,—"We have with a view to render the rules contained in the "Digest more generally intelligible, frequently applied the rules of Law "to a detail of facts, where a more general and abstract enunciation of "those rules would have been sufficient."

49. On this part of the plan of the Indian Law Commissioners Sir J. Awdry observes,—"Their method of illustration by examples "is excellent. It is the practice in other sciences, and the want of "it has been felt in Law. Mr. Livingstone occasionally uses it, but "in a manner confused between illustration and enactment. Here "it occupies its proper place, distinct from the enactment. They "truly say that precision could not always be made consistent with "neatness and perspicuity. They have preferred, and rightly, precision. "Their sentences are hardly more harsh, and are far less prolix and "involved, than those of legislation in general. But still they often *are* "and *must* be harsh, and at any rate the synthetical apprehension of "them is difficult to minds not accustomed to accurate thinking—but an "instance of the rule in action will lead the mind analytically to it. The "examples ought however, in my opinion, only to be looked at like those "in grammar, simply to lead the mind to apprehend the rule, not to "define its limits in doubtful cases, or the example becomes part of the "rule, and their statement that 'the definitions and enacting clauses "contain the whole Law' will be falsified. A fictitious example should "only illustrate; real examples like real history may instruct."

50. We understand the authors of the Code to have intended their illustrations to serve precisely the same purpose as examples in grammar, and as of examples in grammar or in any science it is not to be supposed that they ever "supersede or vary" the rule they are intended to illustrate, the same is in fairness to be presumed of the illustrations deliberately put forth to exemplify the intended action of the enactments contained in the Code. They shew as far as they go what the authors of the Code meant by the enactments. And it would be as unreasonable for a Judge to refuse to decide according to the illustration annexed to any enactment, in a case exactly parallel, as it would be in a student, in attempting to apply a rule of grammar, to refuse to follow the example set for the very purpose of guiding him in its application. Yet the example is not said to limit the rule. No more should the illustration be said to limit the enactment. Should it happen, accidentally, that the example is inapt, and such as, if followed, would "supersede or vary" the rule, in such a case, a most unlikely one, the student would exercise his reason, and finding the rule and example irreconcilable would properly follow the rule, concluding the example to have crept in by error. So also a Judge finding an illustration plainly at variance with the terms of the enactment, of the application of which it is exhibited as an example, would be at liberty to neglect it, and to apply the Law according to his own judgment of its meaning. He would not be justified however in neglecting the illustration if he found it reconcilable with the terms of the enactment, although it did not agree with his own understanding of their import, any more than the Judge sitting in an English Court in a case depending upon the construction of a statute* would be justified in neglecting an established precedent among the decided cases in the English Law books, though it did not square with his own notions.

* In a case depending upon the Common Law, Precedents are of more authority—they may be said to be the Law.

51. No more is the illustration a part of the enactment, than the example is a part of the rule in grammar, or a decided case upon the construction of a statute is a part of the statute, but each has a certain authority as a guide, and may not be unreasonably disregarded. For the purpose intended it seems to be a matter of indifference whether the examples be fictitious or real. The examples in grammar which Sir J. Awdry refers to as purely illustrative, are generally real examples. In geometry the cases taken for the purpose of demonstration are fictitious, invented for the occasion.

52. We have in the above remarks spoken of the examples in grammar as Sir J. Awdry has spoken of them, merely as illustrations, like examples in other sciences, but there is a material difference which it is proper to notice. The examples in grammar may indeed be *used* as illustrations. But they are the particular cases from which the rules in grammar are obtained by induction. They are the real authorities. The rules are merely what this or that grammarian has collected from them. In this view they resemble the decided cases in the Law books upon which rules of Common Law are founded.

53. It is of importance to ascertain what the authors of the Code really aimed at in framing it in the manner we have been considering, for it seems to have been greatly misunderstood, and some have been disposed to regard the work as a failure, because it is palpably incapable of effecting completely what they imagine to have been designed.

54. Sir H. Compton observes that "the object of the Law Com- "missioners seems to have been by definitions and by illustrations of "definitions to give to the new plan that simplicity, clearness, and cer- "tainty, which should render construction and analogical interpretation "unnecessary," and so "to expel from the penal jurisdiction of India what "has been called by Bentham *Judge-made Law;*" and without any attempt to test those definitions and illustrations, he labours, otherwise, to prove that the supposed object is impracticable, or as he expresses it, in words which he says were applied to the definitions and illustrations in the Code of Louisiana, that "the very attempt is founded on a radical "misconception of the duty of Law-makers and the degrees of clearness "attainable by them," concluding his observations to this effect with the remark, that "it will be consolatory to the Law Commissioners to find "that if they have failed, they have failed in common with legislators, "ancient and modern, of the most enlightened nations."

55. Again Sir H. Seton, who criticizes the Code generally in the most candid spirit, observes that "the object seems to have been to "exclude judicial discretion. But however desirable it may be (and to "none more than to Judges) to limit judicial discretion, it is in vain to "attempt wholly to exclude it by definitions, however illustrated." "The terms 'fraudulently,' 'unjustly,' &c. so frequently resorted to in "the Code, obviously because no other definitions were practicable, are so "many admissions of the fact, and must ever render the Code with all "its precautions mainly dependant for its practical operation upon the "discretion of those by whom it is administered." The same view of the design of the Commissioners is taken by others, whose animadversions are less moderate.

56. But in truth the Commissioners aimed at nothing more than what Sir H. Seton admits to be desirable, to *limit* judicial discretion.

They never entertained the fond idea that they could exclude it. Observing that the illustrations are meant to take the place of decided cases in the English Law books, with this difference that "they are cases decided "not by the Judges but by the Legislature, by those who make the Law, "and who must know more certainly than any Judge can know what "the Law is which they mean to make," they say "this collection of "cases decided by legislative authority will, we hope, greatly *limit* the "power which the Courts of Justice possess of putting their own sense "on the Laws. But we are sensible that neither this collection of cases "nor any other can be sufficiently extensive to settle every question "which may be raised as to the construction of the Code. Such ques-"tions will certainly arise, and unless proper precautions be taken, the "decisions on such questions will accumulate till they form a body of "Law of far greater bulk than that which has been adopted by the "Legislature." Here the exercise of judicial discretion is supposed; limited in some degree but not excluded; rendered unnecessary in cases to which the illustrations will apply, as it is unnecessary, in Courts governed by English Law, in cases to which applicable precedents are to be found in the English Law books, but still necessary in all other cases.

57. It is observed that there are at present eight Chief Courts subject to the Indian Legislature, every one at liberty to put its own construction on the Law; and as it is not to be expected that they will always adopt the same construction, there will be in the course of a few years a large collection of opposite decisions all of equal authority. This is an evil against which it is proper to provide, but it is not proposed to do so by excluding judicial interpretation. The suggestion is to narrow the field for the exercise of judicial discretion by frequent revisions of the Code, and making every successive edition of it solve all the important questions as to its construction which have arisen since the appearance of the last edition. Intermediately the Courts are intended to apply the written Law as well as they can on the grounds of reason, with this reserve, that the accused party shall have the advantage of a doubt, if that doubt be entertained after mature consideration by the highest judicial authority.

58. Sir J. Awdry supposes the Commissioners to assume that the office of interpretation essentially belongs to the Legislature, and argues against this doctrine as unphilosophical, inexpedient, and unconstitutional. But the Commissioners merely say that this doctrine was maintained by the Roman jurists, and that the contrary opinion was censured by them with great force of reason. They then explain how their illustrations differ from the imperial rescripts, in that they are not made *ex post facto*, and cannot therefore be made to serve any particular turn. They say expressly "we do not think it desirable that the Indian "Legislature should, like the Roman Emperors, decide doubtful points of "Law which have been mooted in cases pending before the tribunals."

59. This explanation seems to anticipate the objections urged by Sir J. Awdry, and manifests that there was no intention "to repeal that "rule of the British constitution which places interpretation and legisla-"tion in different hands, by which it ordinarily belongs to the Judges "(subject to correction) *jus dicere*, to pronounce what the Law is, to the "Legislature *jus dare*, to ordain what it shall be." Indeed Sir J. Awdry after arguing generally against the assumption by the Legislature "of the totally distinct office of interpretation," acknowledges that the

Commissioners do not in fact assign that office to the Indian Legislature, though he says "they claim it in principle." Even this assertion however is not warranted, pointed as it is to interpretation to be exercised in "reconsidering decided cases." At the utmost the Commissioners claim a right in the Legislature to pass declaratory Laws, such as Sir J. Awdry himself alludes to as exercised by Parliament, and of which he observes "such a power if it exist, is different from the ordinary power of interpretation."

60. In order to the proposed revisions of the Code the Commissioners suggest that the doubts or differences of opinion that may arise in the Courts as to the construction of its enactments should be reported to Government to be considered in the Legislative Department. "In some cases," the Commissioners observe, "it will be found that the Law is "sufficiently clear, and that any misconstruction which may have taken "place is to be attributed to weakness, carelessness, wrongheadedness, "or corruptions, on the part of an individual. In such cases it will be "unnecessary to make any change in the Code. Sometimes it will be "found that a case has arisen respecting which the Code is silent. In "such a case it will be proper to supply the omission. Sometimes it "may be found that the Code is inconsistent with itself. If so, the "inconsistency ought to be removed. Sometimes it will be found that "words of the Law are not sufficiently precise. In such a case it will "be proper to substitute others. Sometimes it will be found that the "language of the Law, though it is as precise as the subject admits, "is not so clear that a person of ordinary intelligence can see its whole "meaning. In these cases it will generally be expedient to add illustra-"tions such as may distinctly shew in what sense the Legislature intends "the Law to be understood, and may render it impossible that the same "question, or any similar question, should ever again occasion difference "of opinion."

61. The Commissioners remark that an addition of a very few pages to the Code in each successive edition, "will stand in the place "of several volumes of reports, and will be of far more value than such "reports, inasmuch as the additions to the Code will proceed from the "Legislature, and will be of unquestionable authority, whereas the reports "would only give the opinions of the Judges, which other Judges might "venture to set aside."

62. This remark obviously applies to the additional illustrations as well as to the alterations supposed to be made in "the definitions and enacting clauses," which, in the original edition of the Code, are, they say, to be regarded as "containing the whole Law," and seems to ascribe equal authority to both. Noticing this Sir J. Awdry observes that "the new illustration will, when introduced with the same author-"ity as the rest of the enactment, merely be an unusual form of enact-"ment, limiting, extending, or otherwise qualifying the provision. The "doctrine that the provision itself contains the whole Law will certainly "be falsified by giving, as the Commissioners propose, to this illustration "legislative authority. It will *therefore* not strain the Law, where it "is required to make language which is as precise as the subject admits "of, sufficiently intelligible, simply because it is a modifying part of "that Law. The method is new. I do not know where it is (contrary "to the view of the Commissioners) an avowed part of the Law, and "not retrospective, that it is inexpedient, nor when these are no longer "fictitious cases (as to which I have before expressed an opinion) but "the results of experience, can I say that in enacting that such and "such cases shall or shall not be deemed to be included may not be effec- "tual, at the same time that it is easier than amending the body of the "clause, as well as more authoritative than the judicial decision that "they are comprehended or not in its obscure terms."

63. Though it is not in terms so declared, it does indeed appear that the new illustrations in the successive editions of the Code are intended to be a part of the Law, and consequently absolutely binding upon those who have to administer it, and so to differ in character from the illustrations in the original edition. The hypothesis is that some definition or enactment has been misunderstood, and a wrong construction given of it. The illustration is authoritatively to extend, or limit, or otherwise qualify the construction. It is in effect a declaratory Law. Whereas the illustrations in the original Code are as has been observed merely examples, but examples clothed with an authority entitling them to the highest respect, though not absolutely binding. The difference however is of so little consequence practically that we are not sure that it would not be better to treat the illustrations in the original Code, as well as in the successive editions of it, as parts of the Law, of concurrent authority with the definitions and enactments.

64. With respect to the objection which has been made to the Code on the ground of the multitude of new offences created by it, we think that this will be best discussed in considering the particular provisions to which it applies. It will be found that exception is taken on this ground to some of the provisions in the chapter "of offences against property," upon which we have submitted our observations in the proper places.

65. Many persons have found fault with the composition of the Code as being in many places framed in a style very difficult to be understood, some indeed have pronounced parts of it to be unintelligible, and several have declared their opinion that it is incapable of being translated, and therefore useless for the general purpose for which it was intended. We have carefully considered the Clauses in the chapters we have reviewed which have been pointed out as affording grounds for this censure, and upon each we have given our opinion. The criticisms on this head are anticipated, and we think are sufficiently answered by the observations of the authors of the Code which we have already quoted. With respect to the "ruggedness of phraseology" which some have been offended with, in addition to what the authors of the Code have said for themselves, we submit the following concurrent remarks of the English Criminal Law Commissioners upon their own work:—"Elegance of diction must be regarded as a matter of inferior importance "in the declaration of abstract propositions and rules, and we have not "hesitated to use plain and even homely language in our Articles where "a neater construction of the sentences and more refined expressions "would have not contained so effectually the meaning of the Law." We would recommend attention generally to the observations of the English Criminal Law Commissioners on the manner in which the definitions and rules of the Criminal Law ought to be expressed, which are to be found in the 4th and 7th Reports.

4th Report, p. 13.

4th Report, p. 12 et seq.

7th Report, p. 6 et seq.

66. Sir J. Awdry as we have shewn has declared his opinion that "the sentences in the Code are hardly more harsh, and are far less "prolix and involved than those of legislation in general."

67. We apprehend that the opinions which some have expressed of the obscurity, almost unintelligibility, of particular Clauses, have been formed without such study as a Judge would be bound to bestow upon them, and we are strongly inclined to think that there is scarcely any one of those who, as we conceive, have somewhat rashly delivered such opinions, that being called upon as a Judge to construe the Clauses in question would feel himself at a loss to determine their meaning.

68. Mr. A. D. Campbell is one who has pronounced the Code to be "absolutely untranslatable," but the instance he adduces is not very convincing. "It will be no easy task," he says, "to convey in any of "the Native dialects the meaning even of No. 24, which "merely declares that 'to do a thing' denotes omissions "as well as acts; for in every language 'to do' must stand opposed to its "omission." We can only say that if there were no greater difficulty than this to be overcome the task of translation would in our estimation be an easy work. We do not however think that it will be an easy work; on the contrary we are of opinion with the authors of the Code that "the difficulty of procuring good translations will be great;" but we concur with them also in believing that the means at the disposal of the Government of India "are sufficient to overcome every difficulty" of this nature. Indeed when we consider what has been done in India by comparatively private means in the way of translating the scriptures, we are at a loss to understand how there can be a doubt on the subject. We may advert also to what has been actually accomplished in the translation of the Regulations of the several Presidencies and the Legislative Acts of the Government of India, in which we will venture to say are to be found as great difficulties as any that are to be met with in the Code. We would instance in the Acts the Preamble to 5 and 6 Victoria, Chapter 39, recited in Act XX of 1844, the Statute recited in Act IX of 1842, and Section 1 of Act XXX of 1839. In the Code of the Regulations for the Presidency of Fort William, not to multiply examples, we would point to the Preamble of Regulation I of 1821, and to the important Regulation VII of 1822.

He writes 42.

Prefatory address to the Governor-General in Council, p. vii.

69. The object we conceive should be "by the combined labour of enlightened Europeans and Natives" to make as good a translation as possible into one Native language, known more or less all over India, that is to say the Oordoo, to be used as an approved model in making versions into all the other languages into which it is usual to translate the Laws enacted by the Government of India. This we believe was the course taken lately in translating the new Articles of War.

70. We proceed to review the Chapters we have mentioned, in the order in which they stand in the Code.

CHAPTER I.

GENERAL EXPLANATIONS.

71. Mr. Norton says, "This Chapter appears to me to exemplify "vagueness and uncertainty in language," and "to contain many in-"correct positions, and some that are arbitrary and inconsistent."

72. Mr. Norton finds vagueness and uncertainty in what appears to us so explicit and definite, that, but for the instance he affords in his own case, we could not have supposed it possible to be misconceived by any instructed person endeavouring to understand it. Thus he says, he

Clause 4.

"cannot see clearly why (Clause 4) starving a man to "death is considered no act, but an omission." Now in the Clause referred to, it is laid down that "wherever the causing of a "certain *effect* by an *act* or by an *omission* is an offence, it is to be under-"stood that the causing of that effect partly by an act and partly by an "omission is the same offence." In the "illustration" the *effect* supposed is death, partly caused by an *act*, beating, partly by an *omission*, not supplying food. The word "starving" used by Mr. Norton, does not occur. As far as we know, Mr. Norton is singular in his inability to see the distinction between "act" and "omission" so illustrated, and we do not apprehend that there will be any difficulty generally in discerning it.

Clause 9.

Again it is declared in Clause 9 of this chapter that the words "Government of India" denote the Executive Government of India, unless it be otherwise expressed. Upon this Mr. Norton remarks,—"I do not know what is meant by the Executive Government as the explanation of the Government of India." Now of course Mr. Norton well knows that the constitution of the Government of India for legislative purposes is different from its constitution for all

3 and 4 Wm. IV, Cap. 85, Sec. XL.

other purposes; that for legislative purposes it consists of the Governor-General and a Council of four Ordinary Members, and for all other purposes, of the Governor-General and a Council of three Ordinary Members, the fourth Ordinary Member not being entitled to sit and vote in Council except at meetings for making Laws and Regulations; and that it is enacted that "all Laws

See XLVIII.

"and Regulations shall be made at some meeting of the "Council at which the said Governor-General and at "least *three* of the Ordinary Members of Council shall be assembled, and "that *all other functions* of the said Governor-General in Council may "be exercised by the said Governor-General and *one* or more Ordinary "Member or Members of Council." It is difficult to conceive that Mr. Norton knowing all this, can be in earnest in saying he does not know that the Governor-General in Council exercising "all other func-tions," except the function of legislation, is what is meant by the Executive Government of India.

73. Mr. Norton speaking of Clause 3, says, "I am unable to see

Clause 3.

"clearly what is meant by, or what is the reason of, "the limitation of a joint act to those specifically which "are said to consist of offences by causing a certain effect with a certain "intention or with a knowledge of certain circumstances." It might be replied, that Mr. Norton has not been very happy in expressing his own meaning. Perhaps he would have had a clearer view of the matter if, attending to the words of the clause, he had considered whether any case is excluded which ought to be included. It does not appear so to us.

74. In Clause 7, it is explained that the word "party" denotes collections of persons, as well as persons. Sir H. Seton questions "the use of 'party' for person." "The word party in a legal sense," he observes, "signifies a person who is party in "a cause or to a deed, &c. It implies the existence of some other party. "It is a person of a particular description." The intention however is not that the word "party" shall be used for "person" generally, but simply to explain that it may comprehend a body, such as the Government of India, the Bank of Bengal, &c., as well as an individual. It seems to be used in this Code only in some such particular sense as is indicated by Sir H. Seton, and as it is used in the Digest of the English Criminal Law Commissioners.

Clause 7.

75. Upon Clause 12, which explains the word "Judge," it has been asked whether a *Magistrate* or *Criminal Judge* investigating a case in which the party accused must be committed, if there is evidence against him, for trial by a Judge of superior jurisdiction, or a Judge trying a case in which the sentence rests with the Sudder Court, is comprehended in its terms. It is clear that every person "officially designated as a Judge" is included. The illustration (*b*) shews that a *Magistrate* sitting on a charge on which he has power to sentence to fine or imprisonment with or without appeal, is a Judge. A Magistrate conducting a preliminary investigation to ascertain whether there is ground to put an accused party on his trial by a Judge, it would seem, is not to be considered a Judge under this clause.

Clause 12.

76. Mr. Norton says he does not know if Arbitrators are included as Judges. Arbitrators "empowered by Law to give a definitive judgment," as for example under Regulation XVI of 1793 of the Bengal Code, and the corresponding Regulation XXII of 1802 of the Madras Code, we apprehend, are included.

77. Under Clause 14, Mr. Norton supposes that the first class of public servants therein described, viz., "every Covenanted Servant of the East India Company," may be taken to include Covenanters with Government by Charter-party. This is a mistake, which, considering the positive sense that the term "Covenanted Servant" bears in the Company's Territories, we deem to be most unlikely.

Clause 14.

78. Mr. Norton notices the comprehensiveness of some of the other descriptions of public servants, and observes on the whole, that he "can hardly tell what existing person may not be included under the term 'public servant.'" Supposing the several descriptions he specifies to be as comprehensive as he takes them to be, yet it does not appear to us that they are faulty in this respect, with reference to the provisions in the two chapters relating to public servants in the application of which recourse will be had to them. We think they will be found sufficiently distinct and definite for the purpose they are to serve. We have no apprehension that there will be any difficulty in determining who are positively excluded as not falling under any of the descriptions in Clause 14.

Chapters VII and VIII.

79. It is questioned by one Officer whether Juwabnevisses, Gomastahs, and other servants of that class, come under any of the descriptions in this clause so as to be subject to the provisions of Clause 138. It seems to us that as servants whose duty it is "to make" or "keep documents" they fall under the 5th, 10th, or 11th description, according to the Department in which they may be employed.

80. With reference to Clauses 15 and 16 Mr. Norton says,—"It "appears to me an incorrect position to include (as may "be) highway robberies among 'frauds' as by 'causing "wrongful gain to one party by means of wrongful loss to another "party.'" "Wrongful gain" and "wrongful loss" are explained in Clause 15; and in Clause 16 it is said,—"Whoever does any thing with "the intention of causing wrongful gain to one party, by means of "wrongful loss to another party, is said to do that thing fraudulently." In the definition of theft in Clause 363, a chief ingredient is the intention "to take fraudulently any thing which is property." It is said in Clause 375, that theft is "robbery" if attended with certain aggravations. Hence arises Mr. Norton's remark, that by the definition in Clause 16, highway robberies may be included among frauds. The remark we think does not affect the correctness of the definition of the term "fraudulently." The propriety of using this term in the definition of theft and robbery will be considered in the proper place.

Clauses 15 & 16.

81. With reference to these and other clauses in which the term "property" is used without a definition of it, an Officer observes that in discussing the Code with Natives the meaning of the term was questioned; and he suggests that it is a point on which disputes are likely to arise.

82. In the book of definitions annexed to Mr. Livingstone's Code, it is said that the term "property" conveys a compound idea composed of that which is its subject, and of the right to be exercised over it. We believe that the term "property" is everywhere used in this Code so as to be applicable exclusively to "that which is its subject," and we imagine that the expression so used was thought by the framers of the Code to be sufficiently intelligible by itself, and as clear as it could be made by the help of any set of words in the form of a definition. And so far as we have considered the provisions relating to "property" and the illustrations thereof, it does not appear to us that there is need for any explication of the term. In this view we are confirmed by finding that there is no question raised about it, in the papers referred to us, by any one but the individual whose observation we have noticed.

83. Referring to Clauses 17 and 18, Mr. Norton says, "It appears "both arbitrary and inconsistent to attribute possession "to cestuiqui trusts, and to guardians, of those things "which are put into a wife's or servant's possession in trust for the husband or master, or into an idiot's possession," as for instance, without "the consent or knowledge of the husband, master, or guardian." And Mr. Greenhill suggests that words should be added in Clause 18, specifying that the possession of the idiot, &c. is "with the knowledge of the guardian." The objection would have weight, we think, if such constructive possession could be charged against the party so possessing, as a criminal possession, in order to bring him within the definition of any offence, and to render him liable to a penal prosecution. But we are not

Clauses 17 & 18.

aware that the clauses in question are capable of being so perverted under any of the provisions of the Code; and they appear to be necessary with a view to precision in criminal charges affecting other parties in respect of property so situated, in which it may be material to declare in whom the possession rested at a certain time, as, for example, in charges of theft under Clause 363.

See Appendix, Note N, pages 159—161.

84. Upon Clause 19 which explains that "property is not said to be in the possession of any party other than a person," and upon the illustration which shews that property is not to be considered as in the possession of the Government of India, the Bank of Bengal, &c., but of the persons in trust for those parties, Sir H. Seton observes that "the sole object of this explanation seems to be to convert theft from a body of persons into criminal breach of trust," see Clause 363. "If so," he asks "whether it does not fall under the "rule as to General Exceptions, Note B,* viz., that it ought to be "appended to the rule which it is intended to modify." He asks again "why should not property in the possession of a body of persons be pro-"tected from theft? It is so by the Law of England." To these remarks and questions it may be answered that property belonging to a body of persons *is* protected from theft committed by any but the person who has possession of the property in trust for the owners. Such a person making away with the property committed to his keeping by a body of persons is not guilty of theft, but of a criminal breach of trust. See Illustration (x) under Clause 363. Any other person stealing such property will be guilty of theft, but of theft from the person who, according to the illustration under Clause 19, is considered to have possession in trust for the body to which the property belongs.

Clause 19.

85. Upon Clause 21 explaining the signification of the word "documents," Sir H. Seton puts the following questions:

Clause 21.

"Why should the term 'document' which in a popular sense has a "more extensive meaning, be limited to writing, which with the expla-"nation given, would exactly convey what is meant?"

"Why should a Gazette, a Proclamation, &c., cease to be documents? "they are usually classed among documentary evidence by the English "Law?"

"Whether the explanation has not reference solely to the chapter "relating to offences relating to documents and ought not therefore "to have been inserted in it?"

86. Mr. Norton also says it appears an arbitrary definition of a document to confine it to handwriting.

87. Mr. Greenhill observes that a printed or lithographed paper bearing the *seal* or *stamped signature* of a person unable to write would not be a document under the explanations given in this clause. He alludes to this, he says, as seals are used in India without handwriting.

88. The term "writing" which Sir H. Seton suggests to be used instead of "document" as conveying exactly what is meant, is defined in the Digest of the English Criminal Law Commissioners "to signify *any material* on which

Art. 3, Chapter XXIII.

* See Appendix, Note B, page 106.

"any words or figures, at length or abridged, are written, *printed*, or "*otherwise expressed*, or any map or plan is described." In Mr. Livingstone's book of definitions it is explained that "wherever the contrary "does not appear from the context the word writing means not only "words traced with a pen, or *stamped*, but *printed*, or *engraved*, or made "legible by *any other device*." It is obvious that these explanations of the term "writing" make it more comprehensive than the word "document" as it is defined by the Indian Law Commissioners, and they seem to be open to the objection that they give a meaning to the term more extensive than that which the word "writing" conveys in a popular sense, as the explanation of "document" in the clause under consideration, on the other hand, as Sir H. Seton remarks, comes short of the popular sense of its meaning. Another difference between the definition of "writing" in the Digest of the English Criminal Law Commissioners and that of "document" in this clause is that the former applies to the *material* on which words are written, &c., whereas the latter applies to the matter written, &c., Mr. Livingstone's definition of "writing" also applies to the words written, &c. Both the definitions referred to would embrace the seal used instead of a signature, or the stamped signature, alluded to by Mr. Greenhill, which the definition in this clause appears to exclude, but which we incline to think ought to be included. We are not aware indeed of any reason why the definition of "document" in this Code should not be as wide as that of "writing" in the Digest of the English Criminal Law. It is dangerous, however, so much to extend the terms of a definition lest what depends upon it in the sequel should be deranged. Perhaps Sir H. Seton's suggestion of placing the definition in the chapter "of Offences relating to Documents" for which it seems to have been framed might be adopted on the principle stated in the 2nd para. of Note B* in regard to Special Exceptions, altering it so as to include a paper bearing a seal intended to serve instead of the signature of a name, or the stamped signature of a name intended to serve instead of the same written with a pen.

89. With reference to Clause 22 which explains what is meant by the words "valuable security," Sir H. Seton asks "would not a cancelled instrument be 'a valuable security' under this clause?" We think not; for an instrument available for the purpose for which it was made is clearly what the clause intended; a cancelled instrument therefore, though by the cancelling of it a legal right may be "extinguished," inasmuch as the instrument upon which such right depended is thereby voided, does not fall within its scope.

Clause 22.

90. In Clause 26 it is explained that "a person is said to cause an "effect 'voluntarily' when he causes it by means where-"by he intended to cause it, or by means which, at the "time of employing those means, he knew to be likely to cause it." The latter part of this definition, which goes beyond the intention, to the obvious consequences of an action, is highly approved by Sir J. Awdry, but is disapproved by others. We shall consider the point in reviewing the chapter of General Exceptions.

Clause 26.

91. Colonel Sleeman objects to that part of Clause 28 which makes the term "illegal" applicable to every thing "which furnishes ground for a civil action." These appear wide

Clause 28.

* See Appendix, Note B, page 106.

words, but we think it would be difficult to restrict them without the risk of excluding something that ought to be included. Generally we apprehend it will be found unobjectionable to designate as illegal any thing done or omitted to be done by a man for which he is liable to a civil action.

92. Upon the explanation of "intelligent consent" in Clause 31 Sir H. Seton questions whether the word 'consent' does not necessarily import the capacity of the party giving it, implying that the definition is unnecessary. Mr. Norton observes that it is arbitrary and inconsistent to attribute to "intelligent consent" that consent "which may have been given under deception," implying that there ought to be a definition, but that the one which is given is too wide. Sir H. Seton we conceive would construe the word "consent," which he appears to consider sufficient by itself, to include consent given under deception, supposing the party to be capable of consenting at all, or able "to understand the nature and consequences of that to which he gives "his consent." Even supposing with Sir H. Seton that the definition is superfluous, which we do not think, it can do no harm. We do not think it would be proper to consider "a consent given under deception" as not an "intelligent consent."

Clause 31.

93. It has been suggested that it would be dangerous to put consent given under the influence of "passion" out of the pale of "intelligent consent," as in the definition, and we are rather inclined to that view.

94. It would seem that the definition of "a person of Asiatic blood" contained in Clause 32 has no relation to any provisions of the Code but those contained in Clauses 43 and 44 in the chapter of Punishments, and it appears to us that on a principle analogous to that stated in the 2nd para. of Note B* on the chapter of General Exceptions, it should be introduced as an explanation immediately after those clauses, in connection with which we shall examine it.

Clause 32.

---

* See Appendix, Note B, page 106.

CHAPTER III.

GENERAL EXCEPTIONS.

95. In Clause 26, as already noticed, it is explained that "a person "is said to cause an effect 'voluntarily' when he causes it by means "whereby he *intended* to cause it, or by means which at the time of em-"ploying those means he *knew to be likely* to cause it." In Clause 69 in this chapter it is declared that "nothing which is *not intended* to "cause death and which is not *known by the doer to be likely* to cause "death, is an offence by reason of any harm which it may cause," &c., if the sufferer has consented to suffer that harm, &c. In Clause 70, it is declared that "nothing which is *not intended* to cause death is an offence by reason of any harm which it may cause," &c., if the sufferer has consented to suffer that harm, &c. In Clause 294 in the chapter of offences affecting the human body, it is set forth that "whoever does any act "with the *intention* of thereby causing, or with the *knowledge that* "*he is likely thereby* to cause the death of any person, and does by "such act cause the death of any person, is said to commit the offence "of 'voluntary culpable homicide.'"

96. Sir J. Awdry observes with reference to the above explanation and the definitions corresponding with it, that "the general purpose "of avoiding fiction and adhering to strict truth is excellent. For "this reason I think the Commissioners have done well in subjoining "to 'intending,' the phrase 'or knowing that he was likely to produce "such an effect,' instead of leaving it to the legal presumption that "a man must be taken to intend the obvious consequences of his wilful "acts."

97. Mr. Norton on the other hand deems that the Commissioners have erred. He says, "It appears to me impossible to read as far as "this chapter* without suspecting that the Commissioners have some "peculiar object in distinguishing on so many occasions between the "doing an act 'with an intention' to effect a certain result, and the "doing it with a '*knowledge* that it is *likely*' to produce that result. "Now there appears to me an error in principle in legislating on any such "distinction, and I mention it the more pointedly at this opportunity, "because I think the present chapter will afford more than one instance "of the uncertainty, and even of the absurdity, which may arise from "the applications of such a distinguishing doctrine. The principle of "English Law is that a man's intentions and designs are to be judged of "by the quality of the act done, and that he shall be *presumed* to have "intended that which his act was naturally likely or calculated to effect. "But, if the Commissioners' distinction above noted is really intended, "and is to prevail, in estimating the substantive quality of an act, it "will follow that a man is to be supposed capable of designing a thing "by means not at all likely, and which he knows not to be likely, to "effect it, or, on the other hand, he is to be supposed capable of doing a "thing which he knows to be likely to cause a certain effect, and at the "same time not to intend that result."

98. Mr. A. D. Campbell makes the following remarks: "At Clause 26 "it is declared, that a person is said to cause an effect 'voluntarily' either

* Chapter XVIII.

"'when he causes it by means whereby he *intended* to cause it; or, *by* "*means which* at the time of employing these means *he knew to be likely* "to cause it;' I greatly doubt the propriety of the latter part of this "definition, especially with reference to the distinction subsequently "drawn by the Commissioners themselves in Note B,* between acts "which they there distinguish as '*voluntary, yet not intentional*,' that is "to say, when the person who caused death did not *mean* to cause it, "but *knew* that he was *likely* to cause it. They add, what appears to me "no less important than most appalling—'*in general*, we have made *no* "*distinction* between cases in which a man causes an effect *designedly*, "and cases in which he causes it with the *knowledge* that he is likely to "cause it.'"

"They then go on, in illustration of the cases of consent excepted from "this very extraordinary rule, in which on the contrary, they distinguish "the intent from the knowledge possessed of the likely result, to instance "a fatal operation by a Surgeon, and a shot fired at a wild beast, attack-"ing a man, which kills the latter; as exhibiting *no intent* whatever to "cause death, yet the possession of *knowledge* that the act *was likely* to "cause it. Now the only knowledge possessed, in both these instances, "seems to me to have been the very reverse of that which is here errone-"ously stated by the Law Commissioners, and to have coincided precisely "with the intent itself. The knowledge possessed was, that the act of "man was, in these instances, the sole means left to *prevent*, not to *cause*, "death; and the intent was the very same, not to *cause* but to *prevent* "death. The *likelihood* decidedly was the *prevention* of death by the act of "man, and the fatal alternative was *not* as the Law Commission errone-"ously state, any *likelihood* but the mere *improbable* result of the failure "of his best endeavors to prevent that death, which by the act of God, "was, otherwise, quite inevitable."

"But because the Law Commission, in these two instances, intend-"ing to give illustrations of the distinction between 'intent' and 'know-"ledge of likelihood' chance unfortunately to have here quoted two "cases, in which they happen on the contrary to coincide, instead of "differing from each other, there is no reason whatever thence to ques-"tion the correctness of the most important distinction here drawn by "the Law Commissioners themselves between crimes produced by 'in-"tent,' as contradistinguished from such as are caused 'without intent,' "yet are accompanied by a knowledge on the part of the causer of the "result '*likely*' to be produced, and there seems, on their own admission "of such distinction, the very strongest reason for doubting the propriety "of their having made no such distinction 'in general.' My decided "impression is that, throughout the Code, the glimmering here given by "the Law Commission of this highly important distinction is altogether "lost sight of, and that these two phrases, which, though they may occa-"sionally express the same, may also, as here admitted by the Law Com-"mission, often express very different, if not opposite, things, have been "nearly universally used in the Code, in the most dangerous manner, as "really convertible terms."

99. It appears to be necessary only to quote the words of the Commissioners* in the passage referred to by Mr. Campbell, in order to shew that there was no such confusion as he imagines in their views on this subject.

---

* See Appendix, Note B, page 108.

They say, "In general we have made no distinction between cases in "which a man causes an effect designedly, and cases in which he causes "it with a knowledge that he is likely to cause it. If, for example, he "sets fire to a house in a town at night, with no other object than that of "facilitating a theft, but being perfectly aware that he is likely to cause "people to be burned in their beds, and thus causes the loss of life, we "punish him as a murderer. But there is, as it appears to us, a class of "cases in which it is absolutely necessary to make a distinction. It is "often the wisest thing that a man can do to expose his life to great "hazard. It is often the greatest service that can be rendered to him to "do what may very probably cause his death. He may labor under a "cruel and wasting malady which is certain to shorten his life, and which "renders his life, while it lasts, useless to others and a torment to him-"self. Suppose under these circumstances he, undeceived, gives his free "and intelligent consent to take the risk of an operation which in a large "proportion of cases has proved fatal, but which is the only method by "which his disease can possibly be cured, and which, if it succeeds, will "restore him to health and vigor. We do not conceive that it would be "expedient to punish the Surgeon who should perform the operation, "though by performing it he might cause death, not intending to cause "death, but knowing himself to be likely to cause it. Again, if a person "attacked by a wild beast should call out to his friends to fire, though "with imminent hazard to himself, and they were to obey the call, we do "not conceive that it would be expedient to punish them, though they "might by firing cause his death, and though when they fired they knew "themselves to be likely to cause his death."

"We propose therefore that it shall be no offence to do even what "the doer knows to be likely to cause death if the sufferer being of ripe "age has, undeceived, given a free and intelligent consent to stand the "risk, and if the doer did not intend to cause death, but on the contrary "intended in good faith the benefit of the sufferer."

100. The Commissioners saw clearly the difference between "intent" and "knowledge of likelihood," and meant to express it distinctly, in order to avoid the necessity of fiction in laying a charge, as for example by imputing "intent" constructively where the circumstances imply only "a knowledge of likelihood," advisedly intending, as they did, that there should be no distinction in general, in respect of penal consequences, between cases in which a man causes an effect which is an offence designedly, and cases in which he causes it by doing what "he knows is likely to cause it." Advisedly intending this in general they worded the enactment so that the charge may be always expressed according to the truth. The exception which the Commissioners thought it necessary to make for the reasons stated in the passage we have cited, of cases in which a person does to another with his consent what he knows is likely to cause his death, intending not to cause his death, but to relieve him from suffering, is contained in Clause 70. It appears to us to be quite justified by the reasons stated.

101. We cannot agree with Mr. Norton that because in laying a charge against a man it is to be distinctly expressed according to the truth, as it is to be gathered from the circumstances, whether he intended the effect the causing of which is the offence imputed to him, or did the act from which such effect resulted not intending to cause such effect, but knowing it to be likely that such effect would result from his act, "it will follow that a man is to be supposed capable of designing a thing "by means not at all likely and which he knows not to be likely to "effect it."

102. The alternative deduction that "a man is to be supposed capable "of doing a thing which he knows to be likely to cause a certain effect "and at the same time not to intend that result," we do not dispute; on the contrary we hold it to be true; and therefore we think that the distinction in question is reasonable and proper.

103. The above definition of the term "voluntarily" in this Code agrees pretty nearly with the definition of the word "wilfully" in the Digest prepared by the Commissioners on the Criminal Law of England. In Article 2, Section 3, Chapter 1, it is laid down that "A hurt, damage, "or other evil consequence of an act, shall be deemed to have been "caused *wilfully* where the doer of the act *intended* such consequence to "result, or *knew or believed that it was likely* to result from his act, "or, where knowing or apprehending that such consequence would "*probably* result from his act, he wilfully incurred the risk of causing it."

104. It will be observed that this definition differs from that of the Indian Law Commissioners only in having a third branch or member besides the two contained in the latter, namely, the knowledge or apprehension that the effect or consequence in question would *probably* result from the act done.

105. It seems to us that the objections of Mr. Norton and Mr. Campbell, and of others to the same effect, are fully answered by the observations of the English Criminal Law Commissioners in explanation and defence of the above definition. We submit a few extracts. Upon the subject of "Wilful injuries" they say, "We now advert "to a large class of cases where, although the injurious "consequence which occurs be not that directly *intended* and to which "the offender has adapted his means, he yet clearly possesses the *mens* "*rea*, and where we think the act may properly be regarded as wilful. "This class includes all who, knowing or believing that the acts which "they do are *likely* to occasion an injurious result, or that hurt or damage will probably result, wilfully incur the risk of causing the injurious "consequences by doing those acts."

7th Report, p. 22.

"We have framed our definitions of crimes with reference to the "general principles above referred to; in so doing we have included "within the predicament of *wilful* offenders, not only such as directly "intend to inflict a particular injury, but also all such as wilfully and "knowingly incur the hazard of causing it."

106. In further explanation they say, "The proper test of guilt "in such cases is that of knowledge and consciousness "on the part of the malefactor that hurt or damage is "likely to result or will probably result, from what he does; his criminality consists in the wilfully incurring the risk of causing loss or "suffering to others. The case of a party so misconducting himself, "and so regardless of the interests of others seems to be undistinguishable in point of legal guilt and penal consequences from that "of a criminal who acts with the most direct intention to execute "an illegal purpose, and it seems to us that he may properly be

7th Report, p. 23.

"described as the voluntary author of the mischief produced. The "principle of exemption from criminal responsibility in respect of "a hurtful consequence is that of bonâ fide ignorance of the connexion "existing between the mere mechanical act and its consequence. That "principle ceases to operate where the connexion is known to be "either certain or probable. If the doer of an act know or believe "that a noxious consequence will result from that act, he is just as "culpable both in Law and Morals as if he had acted with the most "direct intention to hurt. Let it however be supposed that the con-"sequence is not* certain, but that it is a likely or probable con-"sequence, and that the likelihood or probability is known to the doer "of the act. Here again it is clear that the principle of exemption "above mentioned is unavailable to exempt the offender from liability "in respect of the consequence. All he can urge is, that he was not sure "that the hurtful consequence would follow; but he had no right to "incur the risk and danger of producing the mischief, and having done "so is justly responsible for it; he cannot reasonably complain that the "Law did not give him notice of the penalty annexed to the offence, or "that he did not wilfully offend, for the Law may justly, after due noti-"fication, doom such an offender to the penalties inflicted on those who "accomplish their purposes by more certain or direct means; the safety "of society is inconsistent with any distinction in this respect, and the "offender in truth acted wilfully, in wilfully incurring the risk and "danger of causing the injurious result."

107. The following is offered as an illustration—"Let it be sup-"posed that A was wilfully to mutilate the person of B, "not intending to kill him, but only to injure him from "a motive of revenge. Suppose also that he did this, knowing that "death, though not a certain result, was yet likely to result from what "he did, and that in fact death did result, it cannot we presume be "doubted, that the legal penalty ought to be just the same as if A had "directly intended to kill."

7th Report, p. 25.

108. The English Commissioners remark upon their definition of the term "wilful," (and the remark is equally applicable to the definition of the term "voluntary" in the Indian Code) that "although an act be wilful, its criminality must depend on "the definition of the particular crime which may make the wilful doing "of the act criminal either absolutely or subject to qualifications or excep-"tions." Applying this remark they say—"A party may put life itself "in peril and yet* be wholly innocent, whilst another who incurred "merely the same degree of peril would be highly criminal. A surgeon "may most innocently put the life of a patient in great peril in order to "avoid a still greater danger; a party may innocently shoot at a tiger "about to inflict deadly injury on some other person, although at the "risk of shooting him whom he wished to save; a person who incurred "precisely the same degree of risk and peril of life, but who incurred it "either with a positive evil intention, or wantonly without justification "or excuse would act criminally."

7th Report, p. 25.

* "In speaking of certainty, moral certainty is to be understood; there is in truth "no perfectly certain connexion between an act and its consequences; an accidental "circumstance may save an intended victim from the stab of the most expert "assassin."

109. It is to be observed that the two cases here stated by way of illustration are the same as are given for the same purpose in the Note of the Indian Law Commissioners, quoted above.

110. Sir R. Comyn notices as an objection to a variety of clauses "that the commission or non-commission of an offence is made too much "to depend upon what may be passing in the mind of the party offending "at the time of his committing the act laid to his charge."

111. Amongst other exceptions in this chapter, he remarks that by Clause 62 "the party's *belief in good faith* that he is commanded by "law to do an act exempts him from criminal liability; and in Clause 63 "the exemption arises from a man's exercising a power given him by "law; and *acting to the best of his judgment exerted in good faith*. So a "child above seven and under twelve cannot be guilty of an offence "unless he shall have attained sufficient maturity of understanding to "judge of the nature and consequences of his conduct on that occasion." Again by Clause 68 "a party will not be within the Code who commits "an offence under intoxication from a substance, of the *intoxicating* "*quality of which he may be ignorant*. In all these cases a most perplex- "ing question must be left to the Court, relative to the state of mind of "the party charged with the offence. In the first case, did he *in good* "*faith believe* he was commanded by Law? In the second case, did he "exert *the best of his judgment in good faith?* In the third, had the child "attained sufficient maturity, &c.? In the fourth, did the party *know* "the intoxicating nature of the means of his intoxication?"

112. "In these and other instances," he observes, "the mistake "seems to be in making the question of crime or no crime depend upon "the want of good faith, &c., so as to throw upon the prosecutor the "burthen of averring and proving the absence of good faith or miscon- "ception." After making these remarks, Sir R. Comyn himself antici- pates the answer to them by suggesting that, "the Code of procedure may "perhaps remove part of this difficulty by simply requiring averment "and proof of the supposed criminal act, and leaving the party accused "to satisfy the Court that he acted from such motives or impressions as "according to the Penal Code, may negative his being guilty at all."

113. Similar objections are made by Mr. Norton and others, who appear to forget that the exceptions in this chapter, in cases which come to trial, are to be alleged in defence, and proved by sufficient evidence. The detailed rules which may be necessary for governing the procedure of the Courts in trying such defences belong to the Code of procedure. It is to be presumed that they will be so framed that it will not serve a person accused of having done something which is an offence by this Code, merely to allege that he did it "in good faith, believing himself to be commanded by Law to do it" according to Clause 62, or that he did it "in the exercise, to the best of his judgment exerted in good faith, of a power given to him by Law" according to Clause 63, in either case no doubt he will be required to prove that his conduct was such as to lead fairly to the inference that he acted in good faith as alleged. It is true that he cannot prove directly what was in his mind, but he may be able to prove facts by which this may be sufficiently manifested.

114. Sir R. Comyn objects that "to permit a person who has "committed an injury to set up his *private intentions* as defence or "excuse, and to allege that he did the injury from *virtuous motives* or "from a wrongful impression of the Law or the fact, would frequently "produce a defect in justice, and allow offenders to escape." We do not find that it is permitted to any person to set up his private intentions, or to allege virtuous motives, simply, as defence or excuse under a criminal charge. We hold with the English Criminal Law Commissioners, that "to allow any man to substitute for Law his own notions of right would "be in effect to subvert the Law. To investigate the real motive in "each case would be impracticable, and even if that could be done a "man's private opinion could not possibly be allowed to weigh against "the authority of the Law." But no such thing is allowed by the two clauses above mentioned in which good faith is recognized to a certain extent as a ground of defence. Under both there must be a bonâ fide intention *to advance the Law*, manifested by the circumstances attending the act which is the subject of charge; and the party accused cannot allege generally that he had a good motive, but must allege specially that he believed in good faith that he was bound by Law to do as he did, or that being empowered by Law to act in the matter, he had acted to the best of his judgment exerted in good faith. To satisfy the Court of his good faith, he must shew at least that he acted advisedly, and that he had reasonable ground primâ facie for believing that he ought to do what he did.

115. Clause 62 has been generally construed, as it is construed by Sir R. Comyn, to mean that a person who has done a thing that is generally an offence shall be excused if he can prove to the satisfaction of the Court that he acted "from a wrongful impression of the Law or of the fact," causing him in good faith to believe that he was commanded by Law so to act. Ignorance or mistake of *facts* is an excuse under the Law of England; but this clause, in the extensive construction given to it, is considered to violate the maxim common to both English and Roman Law, "*ignorantia juris neminem excusat*," and great objection is made to it on that ground.

116. We feel satisfied that if the authors of the Code had intended to infringe a principle so generally established they would not have done so *sub silentio*, but would have drawn attention to it particularly in the Note upon the chapter. But while in that Note they carefully explain and vindicate some of the exceptions proposed, "the meaning and ground of which" they think "may not be obvious at first sight," they pass over the clause in question as one of those "which appear to require no explanation or defence." Although the words admit of a greater latitude of construction, we are assured that no more was meant than to excuse a person who has done what by Law is an offence, under a misconception of facts leading him to believe in good faith that he was commanded by Law to do it. This restriction being understood, the objections that have been made to the clause are obviated. To make it perfectly clear, we would suggest that the following proviso be subjoined to the clause—"Provided that this exception shall not extend to any "person who by reason of a misconception of Law, and not by reason of "a misconception of fact, believes himself to be commanded by Law to "do any thing."

See Appendix, Note B, page 106.

117. Clause 64 declares in conformity with the spirit of Article 3, Section 2, Chapter 1, of the Digest of the English Criminal Law, that nothing is an offence which is done by a child under seven years of age. In Clause 65, the same is declared in respect of "a child above seven "years of age and under twelve who has not attained sufficient maturity "of understanding to judge of the nature and consequence of his con-"duct on that occasion." It would seem from this that *maturity of understanding is to be presumed* in the case of such a child unless the negative be proved on the defence. By the English Law, in the case of a child from seven to fourteen years of age, *incapacity to commit a crime is to be presumed* until the contrary be proved. After fourteen years *capacity* is to be presumed until the contrary be proved. With reference to the precocity of children in the East, the rule of the Indian Code which fixes the age of twelve as the period after which the plea of immaturity of understanding shall not be allowed, appears to be proper.

Digest, Chapter I, Section 2, Art. 4.

Art. 5.

118. By Clause 67 "nothing is an offence which a person does in consequence of being mad or delirious at the time of doing it;" and by Clause 68 "nothing is an offence which a person does in consequence "of being, at the time of doing it, in a state of intoxication, provided "that either the substance which intoxicated him was administered to "him without his knowledge or against his will, or that he was ignorant "that it possessed any intoxicating quality." Mr. A. D. Campbell observes that delirium may be produced voluntarily by narcotic drugs; he proposes therefore to omit "delirious" in Clause 67, and to alter Clause 68 by omitting the words after "state" and substituting "of in-voluntary delirium or involuntary intoxication."

119. We apprehend that the word "delirious" is meant to distinguish the condition of a person labouring under a *transient* alienation of mind through the influence of some *unseen* cause, from that of one who is afflicted with *permanent* insanity, that is to say who is "mad," and that the delirium alluded to by Mr. Campbell arising *evidently* from the use of narcotic drugs, &c., is included under the term "intoxication" in Clause 68. This arrangement appears to be etymologically correct, and at the same time in accordance with the popular sense of the terms.

120. The authors of the Code have clearly explained the meaning and the ground of the rules laid down in Clause 69 and in the three following clauses. The general rule is, that "nothing "ought to be an offence by reason of any harm (in re-"spect of either person or property) which it may cause "to any person of ripe age who, undeceived, has given a free and intelli-"gent consent to suffer that harm or to take the risk of that harm. The "restrictions by which the rule is limited affect only cases where human "life is concerned." The general rule is contained in Clause 69, but this excludes acts either intended to cause death, or known to be likely to cause death. The three following clauses provide for cases where human life is concerned. Clause 70 justifies the causing of any harm even to death, when the person who caused it, did not mean to cause death, but knew that he was likely to cause death, by an act done in good faith for the benefit of the party suffering, with his consent, express or implied, as for example by a dangerous surgical operation. We have already noticed this clause, and expressed our opinion that it is fully vindicated by the reasons assigned by the Commissioners. Further, Clause 72 justifies,

See Appendix, Note B, page 106.

under certain restrictions, death or other harm resulting from acts done likewise in good faith for the benefit of a person, *without* his consent, when he is incapable of signifying or giving consent, as, for example, trepanning a person insensible from a fall. Again, Clause 71 justifies under similar restrictions the acts of guardians done in good faith for the benefit of their wards, notwithstanding any harm even to death arising therefrom.

121. Sir J. Awdry approves of the principles upon which these provisions are founded. He says, "A sound line seems to be drawn as "to trusting individuals with their own persons and properties, and in "certain cases with those of others. I agree no less to the exception "founded on the sanctity of human life." Sir R. Comyn on the other hand objects to Clause 69 as an instance in which the Code treats offences which are really outrages on society as merely offences to individuals. He says, "Clause 69 appears to proceed upon the maxim, *volenti non "fit injuria*, and it might be an answer to a civil action by an injured "person that the injury was inflicted by his own consent. But the public "are surely interested in the preservation of the limbs as well as the "lives of the Queen's subjects; and if such a state of society can be "imagined as that in which one may allow another to inflict upon him "any bodily injury short of death, it would well become the legislator "to step in and save persons from the consequences of their own free "and intelligent consent. In a country thoroughly civilized, a Law "such as is indicated by Clause 69 would in all probability be a dead "letter; but in India, where so much self-infliction and voluntary torture "are resorted to, it seems necessary to protect men from themselves, "rather than offer impunity to those who are assisting in their suffer-"ings." These objections we think are of little weight against the reasons of the Commissioners.

122. Mr. Norton says, "Clauses 69 to 73 are several of them adapted "to cases the very recital of which in the illustrations is calculated to "excite ridicule, and yet they exonerate others falling within such "exceptive clauses, which I imagine no one would wish so to be." He suggests that, "they may be found to authorize violations of the "peace in fighting, surgical operations of the most dangerous quality by "the most unqualified and ignorant quacks, selling for purposes of "prostitution, killing to prevent 'mischief' under some circumstances, "and any violence short of killing to prevent 'mischief' of any sort." The last two instances are obviously not in point with reference to the clauses here in question. The first instance we imagine refers to the Illustration (c) under Clause 69; but the exception of acts known to be likely to cause death would exclude dangerous fighting even with the consent required by the text, such as pugilistic prize fighting, and in a similar contest arising out of a sudden quarrel between two parties involving a breach of the peace, consent could hardly be implied. Whether an affray should be made an offence, independently of consequences, is a question to be considered in another place.

123. The second instance appears to refer to the illustrations of Clauses 70 and 72, in which operations performed by surgeons are given as examples. Under the former of these clauses we apprehend that "an unqualified and ignorant quack" could hardly be excused, for it is not to be conceived that such a one could obtain the free and intelligent consent of any person to his performing upon him an operation dangerous to life, but by misrepresentation; and such a one could hardly satisfy a Court of Justice that he had undertaken the operation in good faith under cl. 72, for good faith must surely be construed here to mean, a conscientious belief that he had skill to perform the operation and by it to benefit the party, while the supposition is that he was unskilled and ignorant. With respect to the instance of selling for prostitution, whether such a proceeding should be declared a substantive offence, is a question which will be considered in its proper place. If it be made penal it will be necessary to provide that the exception in cl. 71 shall not extend to it.

124. With reference to the Articles providing that the exceptions in Clauses 71 and 72 shall not extend to rape, &c., Mr. W. Hudleston and Mr. A. D. Campbell make strong observations upon the allusion to such acts "as within a rule respecting acts done in good faith for the benefit of a child or lunatic." The explanation of the Commissioners is that, "even parents have been known to deliver their children up to slavery "in a foreign country, to inflict the most cruel mutilations on their male "children, to sacrifice the chastity of their female children, and to do all "this, declaring, and perhaps with truth, that their object was something "which they considered as advantageous to the children. We have "therefore, (they say) not thought it sufficient to require that on such "occasions the guardians should act in good faith for the benefit of their "ward." The case given as an illustration (*f*), is a person abetting a rape on his daughter, intending in good faith her pecuniary benefit.

125. We regret that in the present state of moral feeling among large classes of the people of India we cannot regard this as a case out of all probability. We fear that parents in poor circumstances are too often to be found ready "to sacrifice the chastity of their female children" under circumstances very likely to involve a rape, in a belief that they will be benefited by the connection thus formed with persons able to provide for them. It seems to be proper therefore to guard the exception from abuse in this respect.

126. There is a difference between Clause 69 and Clause 70, in that the latter speaks of "any person" "who has given a free and intelligent consent," whereas in the former it is "any person above 12 years of age" who has given such consent. We have seen that in describing these clauses generally, the phrase used by the Commissioners is "a person of ripe age," which phrase is also used in describing Clause 70 particularly—"we propose therefore that it shall be no offence to do even "what the doer knows to be likely to cause death, if the sufferer, being "of ripe age, has, undeceived, given a free and intelligent consent "to stand the risk," &c. By Clause 31 "the words intelligent consent "denote a consent given by a person who is not from *youth*, &c., unable "to understand the nature and consequences of that to which he gives "his consent." In the case supposed in the illustration to Clause 70, if the child is under 12 years of age, and has a guardian, a surgeon ought not, we conceive, to act without the consent of the guardian according to Clause 71. If the child has not a guardian, but is, although under 12 years of age, capable of giving an intelligent consent, the surgeon would be justified under Clause 70 in acting upon that consent, and under Clause 72 even without that consent.

127. We may here notice a remark of Mr. A. D. Campbell—"With "reference to the very early age at which females reach the age of "puberty in India, it appears to me a mistake throughout the Code to "confound a person under 12 years of age with incapacitated infancy." From the observations we have just made it will be apparent that this remark is not strictly correct. We shall revert to the point when we come to consider the Clause 298 regarding "culpable homicide by consent," as applied to a case of Suttee where the widow is under 12, which Mr. Campbell had particularly in view.

128. Clause 73 has been objected to as superfluous. Sir H. Seton asks, "whether the subject is not one which might be left to the discre- "tion of those by whom the Law is to be administered? and whether "this clause affords any other security?" The answer is to be found in the Note of the Commissioners—"Clause 73 is intended to provide for "those cases which, though from the imperfections of "language they fall within the letter of the penal Law, "are yet not within its spirit, and are all over the world "considered by the public, and for the most part dealt "with by the tribunals, as innocent." After specifying instances, they say, "that these acts ought not to be treated as crimes is evident, and "we think it far better expressly to except them from the penal clauses "of the Code, than to leave it to the Judges to except them in practice. "For if the Code is silent on the subject the Judges can except these "cases only by resorting to one of two practices which we consider "most pernicious, by making Law, or by wresting the language of the "Law from its plain meaning."

See Appendix, Note B, pages 109 and 110.

129. Some of the objections to this clause seem to arise from misconception. Thus Sir R. Comyn observes upon it that "the criminality "of doing 'harm' depends upon whether the person harmed be of or- "dinary sense or temper, and likely to complain of such harm," and his comment is that "it seems straining the Criminal Law to suppose the "consumption of the time of the Court in ascertaining the sense and "temper of the party." Now all this is a mistake. There could be no question of the sense and temper of the person harmed under Clause 73. The only question there could be, is, how would men of ordinary sense and temper regard the harm of which he complained? was it so slight that no person of ordinary sense or temper would complain of it?

Clauses 74 to 84.

130. We come now to the provisions regarding the right of private defence, of which the Commissioners speak with great diffidence as the part of the Code the least satisfactory to themselves, at the same time observing that they are "inclined to "think it must always be one of the least exact parts of every system "of Criminal Law." They propose to except from the operation of the penal clauses of the Code large classes of acts done in good faith for the purpose of repelling unlawful aggressions. Of the definitions they have given of the limits of private defence, they observe as follows: "It may "be thought that we have allowed too great a latitude to the exercise of "this right; and we are ourselves of opinion, that if we had been framing "laws for a bold and high-spirited people, accustomed to take the law "into their own hand, and to go beyond the line of moderation in repel- "ling injury, it would have been fit to provide additional restrictions. In "this country the danger is on the other side. The people are too little "disposed to help themselves. The patience with which they submit to "the cruel depredations of gang robbers and to trespass and mischief "committed in the most outrageous manner by bands of ruffians, is one "of the most remarkable, and at the same time, one of the most discouraging symptoms which the state of society in India presents to us. "Under these circumstances we are desirous rather to rouse and encourage a manly spirit among the people than to multiply restrictions on "the exercise of the right of self-defence. We are of opinion that all the "evil which is likely to arise from the abuse of that right is far less "serious than the evil which would arise from the execution of one "person for overstepping what might appear to the Courts to be the "exact line of moderation in resisting a body of Dacoits."

131. Sir J. Awdry says, "I agree with the admission of the Commissioners that the line drawn as to the right of private defence is not "satisfactory, as well as that it is probably the least satisfactory part of "most Codes. I cannot suggest a better line. The difficulty is inherent. "A nicely graduated scale of urgency is impossible, because it depends "on a combination of so many circumstances wherein those which are "higher in their kind may exist in a lower degree, and because the rule "is to be applied by unlearned men, under circumstances likely to deprive them of self-possession. I do not see that the Commissioners have "erred from the line of moral right and wrong, and this is the true "guide—men cannot in general act in such cases from the knowledge of "their rights, but from the impulse of the moment acting on dispositions "ready or not ready to place others' safety in fair competition with their "own—upon this footing therefore, not on that of strict knowledge of "the law, must their responsibilities stand, though of course it is desirable to simplify the law, so as to obtain the largest possible amount "of knowledge."

132. Mr. Norton on the other hand says, "As to those 'General Exceptions' which exclude from criminality certain acts done in *private* "*defence*, a host of cases, as it appears to me, might be suggested falling "within the text which neither ought, nor perhaps were intended, to "be included, and as many more acts disallowed, which are justifiable! "Such terms as right of defending body or property against 'mischief' "or 'criminal trespass' are not indeed easy to be appreciated, and the "whole Clause 75 is, with reference to the vast variety of cases which "may possibly be pointed at, to me absolutely unintelligible. I know "not how to make Clause 76 square with the restrictions of Clause 75." He adds, "It would be too tedious a task to point out the doubts, and "difficulties, and incongruities which arise to my mind in the perusal of "the various vague and general expressions throughout this chapter."

133. Mr. W. Hudleston, one of the Judges of the Sudder Court at Madras, "thinks that the general principle of these rules respecting the "right of private defence contrasts disadvantageously with the plain "practical good sense of the Law of England on this subject." He views the several clauses as open to the objection that they would tend "to deter from exertion for the protection of person and property." It appears to him also that "the conditions enumerated are such as cannot be supposed to enter into the contemplation of the party assaulted." And he "regards the whole as a piece of legislation that savors of the "closet, and could not have emanated from practical knowledge and "experience."

134. Mr. A. D. Campbell, another Judge of the Sudder Court at Madras, and several other Judges of that Presidency, concur with

Mr. Hudleston in thinking that the subsequent qualifications of the right declared to be inherent in every person by Clause 74, are "calculated to "paralize those exertions in defence of their persons and property which "the Government has sought to encourage among the natives of this "country."

135. Mr. Giberne, a Judge of the Sudder Court at Bombay, makes observations to the same effect.

136. It will be seen from the quotation given above, that the Commissioners were fully alive to the danger of discouraging self-exertion on the part of the people by restrictions on the exercise of the right of self-defence, and apprehended that they might be thought to have gone too far the other way, and to have allowed too great a latitude to it. And so we find Officers of the Upper Provinces of the Bengal Presidency making this very objection. Thus Mr. Heyland anticipates that under colour of exercising the right of defence against mischief or criminal trespass, there will be endless affrays and breaches of the peace. "The "evil that is thus likely to arise," he observes, "is but too evident, and "there is doubtless a wide difference between this species of aggression "and that by a band of dacoits, and however little disposed the natives "of this country may be to oppose the latter, they are by no means "backward in opposing their neighbours in an act of trespass, or on any "slight provocation, and are only too ready to make use of their swords "and clubs on those occasions." Again, Mr. G. W. Bacon observes, that "nothing is more common than the defence that the deceased was sup-"posed to be a thief, when murdered in cool blood; and when really "suspected, the first thing done towards his apprehension is usually the "infliction of a sword cut. Whatever may be the case in Bengal, the "natives of these Provinces (North-Western Provinces) are ready enough "to slay, right or wrong, and require no further encouragement."

137. Before proceeding to notice the particular criticisms which we find in the papers referred to us upon the provisions of the Code on this subject, we shall shortly state for the purpose of comparison the rules set out in the Digest of the English Criminal Law Commissioners, which it is the more necessary to advert to, since "the plain practical good sense of the Law of England" is supposed to rebuke the theoretical contrivance which is attributed to the framers of the Code, in this, as in other parts of it.

138. First then with respect to *homicide*, it is laid down in the Digest that it is justifiable, 1stly, for the prevention of any felony, that is to say (Chapter I, Section 1) any offence punishable with death or transportation, against the *person*, *habitation*, or *property*, of the person killing or of *any other person;* 2ndly, for the defence of one's own *person* against *violence*, under reasonable *apprehension* of *immediate death* from the assailant; 3rdly, in repelling force by force in defence of one's own person, *using no more violence than is necessary;* 4thly, in defence of *moveable property*, repelling force by force, and *using no more violence than is necessary;* or under *fear of death* from the assailant; 5thly, in defence of *house or land*, resisting a person endeavouring by force to enter, using *no more violence than is necessary;* or under *fear of death;* 6thly, in *removing* from house or land a person who has *no right to be*

Chapter XV, Sec. 2, Art. 20.

Art. 22.

Art. 23.

Art. 24.

Art. 25.

Art. 26.

there, using *no more violence than is necessary*; or, under *fear of death.*
Sec. 5, Art. 51. And such justification extends to every person aiding or assisting another in the defence of his person or property.

139. By the Code every person has the right to defend *his own body*, and *the body of every other person* against *every assault*; and *his own property*, and *the property of every other person* against *theft*, *robbery*, *mischief*, or criminal trespass.

Clause 74.

140. Homicide, or "the voluntary causing of death," is justifiable in defence of *the body*, as above, against an assault likely to cause *death* (1) or *grievous hurt* (2), or with intent to commit rape (3), or an *unnatural offence* (4), or for the purpose of *kidnapping* (5), or of *confining wrongfully* (6): and in defence of *property*, against *robbery* (1), *house-breaking by night* (2), *mischief by fire* on any building, tent or vessel, used as a *human dwelling* (3), and against *theft*, *mischief*, or *house-trespass*, *under* circumstances causing *apprehension of death or grievous hurt* (4).

Clause 76.

Clause 79.

141. In cases not of any of the descriptions above enumerated, the right of self-defence extends to the causing of any harm other than death, in repelling assaults upon the person, or offences against property, subject to the general condition of inflicting *no more harm than it is necessary to inflict for the purpose of defence.*

Clause 77.

Clause 75.

142. The Digest does not expressly declare that every person has the right to defend his person and property, and for this end to repel force by force, and that where homicide may not under the circumstances be justifiable, any lesser degree of bodily harm may be justifiable, if no more violence was used than was necessary for the purpose of defence, but this appears to be implied in Article 44, Section 5 of Chapter XV in which it is laid down that "where violence is permitted to be used "in the defence of person or property, any excess beyond that which is "necessary and unavoidable is within the meaning of the last preceding "Article," which defines the offence of "Battery."

143. Comparing thus the provisions of the Code with the rules contained in the Digest of the English Criminal Law framed by Her Majesty's Commissioners, it is not easy to discover the contrast alluded to by Mr. Hudleston, and one is at a loss to conceive what Mr. Norton meant in his observation that "such terms as right of defending body or "property against mischief, or criminal trespass, are not easily appre-"ciated." The Code does not speak of defending the *body* against mischief or criminal trespass, but it does speak of defending *property* against such offences by resisting even to the death, if necessary; and so does the Law of England.

144. Coming now to the criticisms upon particular provisions, we shall notice first some observations of Mr. J. F. Thomas upon the declaration contained in Clause 75, that "the right of private defence in no "case extends to the inflicting of more harm than it is necessary to "inflict for the purpose of defence." Mr. Thomas says, "This I consider "too indefinite, and it is not aided by the illustration (*b*)—that A, a "powerful man well armed, defends his property by killing an unarmed "boy. The illustration shews, not merely that A inflicted 'more harm,' "it may be but little, or by some degrees, than was necessary, but such "as was obviously, and wantonly unnecessary, and the definition itself "should I think be confined to this class of cases. At present there is "too much uncertainty in the Law. Judges must differ greatly when "they have to determine the point, that no more harm than necessary "was done. I would make the line broader, and stronger; and would "suggest that the clause should run in these or similar terms—'The "right of private defence, in no case extends to the inflicting of harm "manifestly and clearly unnecessary to inflict for the purpose of defence.' "The illustration in the Code will then stand."

145. Mr. Giberne apprehends that this provision "will occasion "much doubt and difficulty, the opinion of the defender being acted upon "at the moment of danger with all his feelings enlisted in favor of "extreme measures, whereas the Judge quietly contemplating in his "Court the probable and distant danger, will naturally hold a very "different opinion, and the consequence will be, that people will be "discouraged from defending themselves and property from fear of the "consequences."

146. We have shewn that words substantially of the same import with those in question are used for the same purpose in the Digest of the English Law Commissioners, and we may take it upon the authority of the Commissioners that they are strictly in accordance with the present Law. We are not aware that it has been found in practice that they present any greater difficulty than is inherent in the nature of the case. The necessity for the degree of force used is a matter to be judged of "from the manner of the attack, the means used in the attack, or some "other manifestation of the criminal purpose." We doubt whether a stricter definition could be made without risking the consequence apprehended by Mr. Giberne from the present one.

147. Mr. Norton to explain his remark that he "knows not how to make Clause 76 square with the restrictions of Clause 75," observes that "taking the text of the two together, part of it may be read thus: "a female may defend herself against an assault, provided she ascertains "that the assault is with a view to rape, and provided she acts under "the restrictions of Clause 75, one of which is that she must not inflict "more harm than is necessary." We really cannot perceive any difficulty in this case, and we think that Mr. Norton would hardly be able to shew that the female would be in a more unfavorable position for defending herself in a Court of Justice, which it is to be remembered is the point in all the exceptions, under the clause in question, than under the English Law, as it is set forth in Article 20, coupled with Article 21, Section 2, Chapter XV of the Digest, which contain the provisions that apply to the case supposed. Under either law, the female being accused, let us say, of homicide, would confess the fact, but would justify it on the ground that she slew the man to save herself from violation, being unable to do so by any other means. Under either law she would have to give proof of circumstances evidencing the intent of the man, and the necessity of her act to prevent him from accomplishing his purpose.

148. We take it that Article 20, above mentioned, which justifies homicide for the prevention of any *felony*, includes all the cases in

Clause 76 of the Code, except the sixth, an assault with the intention of wrongfully confining any person, and this last we apprehend is covered by Article 23.

149. Referring to the case last mentioned under Clause 76, in connection with the first Article of Clause 75, Mr. Norton observes, that "a man may defend himself against an assault provided he ascertains "that the assault is with the intention of confining, and is aware that "the apprehended confinement is an offence punishable by more than a "year's imprisonment, and provided also, that the assailant does not "turn out to be a public servant authorized under circumstances to "confine *some* person though not the party assailed." This case is stated invidiously. Simply stated the proposed law is, that if a public servant, known to be one who is by his office competent to make arrests, shall attempt to confine a person, it may be wrongfully, that person will not be justified in resisting the attempt by force, but he will be justified in resisting by force any person not being a public servant, or not being legally competent, who shall attempt to confine him, and if from the circumstances there be reasonable cause to apprehend that the confinement is intended to be protracted, he will be justified in resisting even to death, if necessary.

Clause 75.

Clause 76.

150. We think, however, that there is reason in the exception that has been taken to the provision which justifies homicide in resisting an attempt at wrongful confinement likely to be continued for three days, that is to say, such a confinement as is punishable under Clause 334 with imprisonment for a term exceeding one year. Although it may be right to allow resistance even to death against an attempt to carry a person off to be kept a prisoner in a hill fastness, for example, where his captivity would be likely to continue for years, we cannot think it would be right to justify such an extremity to prevent a confinement which there was reason to apprehend might extend to three days, or a little more, even if it were quite certain that it could not be prevented by other means.

151. With reference to the second Article of Clause 76 and the fourth Article of Clause 79, Mr. Pyne, a Judge of the Sudder Court at Bombay, observes as follows: "Were 'grievous hurt' limited to the first "seven definitions of that offence, the right of private "defence against an assault by which it might reasonably be apprehended that such grievous hurt would take place, might "be taken as a justification for homicide, but, under the eighth designation of the offence, it is I think allowing too great latitude to the right "of private defence to suffer a person to resist to the death from a fear "of receiving an injury which may render him unable to follow his "ordinary pursuits for twenty days; the nature of the assault against "which a person in self-defence acts, must be taken into consideration, "in extenuation or aggravation of the homicide, and the intention of the "aggressor will always be much more clearly developed by the instrument "made use of, and other circumstances, when permanent bodily injury is "contemplated, than where the fear of the assaulted may magnify the "assault, into the apprehension of grievous hurt. It appears to me that "scarcely any assault can be committed, wherein the assailed may not "justify an act of homicide under the eighth definition of the offence."

Clause 314.

We shall revert to this observation in considering the definition of grievous hurt.

152. Upon the 3rd Article of Clause 79, Mr. T. Blane observes that "the restriction that the building, &c., should be used as a human dwell-"ing appears unnecessary and injurious. If I may kill a man while "attempting to rob my property from a godown or tent not used as a "dwelling, surely I ought to be allowed to do so if he attempts to destroy "the same property by fire. I might recover my property if robbed, "but not if destroyed by fire. By this rule the attempt to set fire to a "stable full of valuable horses, a warehouse, or even a public arsenal, "could not be resisted by killing the offender."

153. Mr. Blane appears to have overlooked that the definition of *robbery* in Clause 375 makes the causing or attempting to cause death, hurt, or unlawful restraint to any person, or fear of death, &c., a necessary ingredient of the offence. But we are on the whole inclined to concur in the opinion that the restriction to a human dwelling in the case of mischief by fire in defining the right of defence in Clause 79 is unadvisable. There is no such reserve with respect to house-breaking by night, which may be committed in a place for the custody of property as well as in a human dwelling.

Clause 424, which refers to Clause 420.

154. Mr. J. F. Thomas upon the same Article suggests that a distinction should be drawn between frail huts constructed of boughs, &c., and permanent dwellings. This is a point which will fall to be considered in examining the chapter on offences against property.

155. Upon Clause 81 Mr. T. Blane observes that the expression in the second para. "till the offender has effected his retreat" is very indefinite. The whole clause, with exception of the 1st para., he thinks is too much restricted. He remarks that the natives of this country seldom recover from the panic caused by an attack, or think of resistance, till a robbery has been completed, they cannot indeed assemble in sufficient numbers soon enough; if therefore a village has been attacked and robbed by a gang who have effected their retreat with the property to a neighbouring jungle, the villagers ought not to be precluded from attempting its recovery and the seizure of the robbers, even at the risk of killing any of them. Again he observes, that under this clause, if a man has broken into a house and carried off property only just outside the wall or door, the owner may not slay him in attempting to recover the property.

156. Mr. G. Casamajor offers remarks to the same effect. He and Mr. A. Elphinstone suggest that the privilege of this clause should operate till the offender is taken and delivered to an officer of Justice.

157. The rule of the Law of England is that "as homicide committed "in the prevention of forcible and atrocious crimes is "justifiable only upon the plea of necessity, it cannot "be justified unless the necessity continue to the time "when the party is killed. Thus though the person "upon whom a felonious attack is first made be not "obliged to retreat, but may pursue the felon till he finds himself out of "danger; yet if the felon be killed after he has been properly secured,

Russell 1.—552.

Art. 21, Sec. 2, Chapter XV of Digest.

"and when the apprehension of danger has ceased, such killing will be "murder; though perhaps, if the blood were still hot from the contest or "pursuit it might be held to be only manslaughter, on account of the high "provocation.

158. We think with Mr. Blane that the 2nd para. of Clause 81 is not sufficiently definite. We are not sure of the meaning intended by the expression "till the offender has effected his retreat with the property." We know not certainly when he is to be considered as having effected his retreat; probably it is when he has once got clear off, having escaped *immediate* pursuit, or pursuit not having been made; but the meaning should be made certain by an explanation or illustration. We presume that the protection of parties pursuing robbers, &c., for the recovery of property which they have succeeded in carrying off, or for bringing them to justice, was thought not to be within the scope of the provisions, touching the right of private defence. We apprehend that under the rules which will be laid down in the Code of procedure, parties will be protected on such occasions under Clauses 62 and 63.

Clause 82, Illustration (*b*).

Blackstone, 4—27.

159. Sir R. Comyn, speaking of Clause 82, says here misconception "is innocence." It does not appear however that in the instance given the proposed Law differs from the Law of England. Blackstone specifying ignorance or mistake of fact as one of the pleas or excuses which protect the committer of a forbidden act from the punishment which is otherwise annexed thereto, gives as an illustration the case of a man, who intending to kill a thief or house-breaker in his own house, by mistake kills one of his own family; "this," he observes, "is no criminal action." "Misconception" is not *expressly* mentioned as an excuse in any of the antecedent clauses; the reference we apprehend is to Clauses 62 and 63. The illustration appears to depend upon the latter. It is as follows: "A enters by night a house which he is legally entitled to enter. Z, in "good faith taking A for a house-breaker, attacks A. Here Z, by at"tacking A under this misconception, commits no offence. But A has "the same right of private defence against Z which he would have if Z "were acting under no misconception."

160. Mr. H. C. Tucker observes that it appears inconsistent in Clause 82 to allow A to kill Z making an attempt upon his life under the influence of madness, which under Clause 67* is no offence. The right of private defence holds against any assault causing the apprehension of death, and it matters not what is the mental condition of the assailant. *This* is to be considered only with respect to *his* responsibility.

161. Exception is taken by Mr. Hudleston, Mr. A. D. Campbell, Mr. T. Blane, and others to Clause 84. Mr. Blane observes, "a person's "simple belief in good faith that circumstances are so and so, ought not "to be sufficient—there ought also to be sufficiently strong and just "grounds for his belief. An instance has been known of a person shoot"ing his own servant who had come to his room at night mistaking him "for a robber, but he ought not to be held blameless, he ought to have "ascertained that he was a robber before he killed him." The party in such a case would have to satisfy the Court that he believed in good faith

---

* Mr. Tucker writes 68.

that the man was a robber, which must be taken we conceive to exclude a mere reckless conjecture or suspicion. Belief must have a foundation, and that must be shewn. The reference we have made above to the English Law in respect to "misconception," is in point here.

162. We have now finished our review of the provisions in the chapter of "General Exceptions" which appeared to call for remark. We proceed to notice some omissions, the reasons of which are given in the Note to the chapter.

163. By Article 30, Section 2, Chapter XV of the Digest of the English Criminal Law, it is laid down that "homicide is justifiable "whensoever a man is involuntarily placed in such a situation, that he is "under the necessity of exposing another person to certain death in order "to save his own life." In a note to this Article in the 4th Report of the Commissioners it is said, "the illustration commonly "applied in the text-books to this rule is the case supposed by Lord Bacon, (Maxims of the Law, Reg. 5) "where two persons being wrecked and getting on the "same plank which is insufficient to save them both, one thrusts the "other from it, whereby he is drowned."

Page 34.

Bacon v. Blackstone, 4—186.

164. Again by Article 6, Section 2, Chapter I of the Digest it is declared that, "Duress inducing just and well grounded fear of death, "or of grievous bodily harm, shall be sufficient to excuse a person acting "under such duress from penal consequences, except in case of treason "and homicide."

165. There are no corresponding rules in the Indian Code. The Commissioners say, "We long considered whether it would "be advisable to except from the operation of the penal "clauses of the Code, acts committed in good faith "from the desire of self-preservation, and we have determined not to "except them."

See Appendix, Note B, page 111.

166. They observe that, "it would be mere useless cruelty to hang a "man for voluntarily causing the death of others by "jumping from a sinking ship into an overloaded boat. "The suffering caused by the punishment is considered "by itself an evil, and ought to be inflicted only for the "sake of some preponderating good. But no preponderating good, in"deed no good whatever, would be obtained by hanging a man for such "an act." Again, "a gang of dacoits, finding a house strongly secured, "seize a smith, and by torture and threats of death induce him to take "his tools and to force the door for them. Here it appears to us that to "punish the smith as a house-breaker would be to inflict gratuitous pain. "We cannot trust to the deterring effect of such punishment." They then say, "If all cases in which acts falling under the definition of "offences are done from the desire of self-preservation were as clear as "the above, we should without hesitation propose to exempt this class "of acts from punishment. But in both these cases, the person in "danger is supposed to have been brought into danger, without the "smallest fault on his own part, by mere accident, or by the depravity "of others." On the other hand they remark that, "nothing is more "usual than for pirates, gang robbers, and rioters, to excuse their crimes "by declaring that they were in dread of their associates and could not "act otherwise. Nor is it by any means improbable that this may often

See Appendix, Note B, pages 111 and 112.

"be true. Nay it is not improbable that crews of pirates and gangs of "robbers may have committed crimes which every one among them was "unwilling to commit, under the influence of mutual fear." "But we "think it clear," they say, "that this circumstance ought not to exempt "them from the full severity of the law," and the reasons they give for "this opinion are that, "though we cannot count on the fear which a "man may entertain of being brought to the gallows at some distant "time as sufficient to overcome the fear of instant death, yet the fear of "remote punishment may often overcome the motives which induce a "man to league himself with lawless companions, in whose society no "person who shrinks from any atrocity that they may command is sure "of his life."

In fine they say, "We should think it in the highest degree perni-"cious to enact that no act done under the fear even of instant death "should be an offence. It would *a fortiori* be absurd to enact that no "act under the fear of any other evil should be an offence. There are "as we have said cases in which it would be useless cruelty to punish "acts done under the fear of death, or even of evils less than death. "But it appears to us impossible precisely to define those cases. We "have therefore left them to the Government, which in the exercise of "its clemency will doubtless be guided in a great measure by the advice "of the Court."

167. We think that a distinction may be drawn between cases in which a man does a thing which is an offence by law, spontaneously, to save his own life, and cases in which he does such a thing, from what is called duress, that is from the compulsion of others to save his life threatened by them.

168. With respect to the former, we agree with the authors of the Code that it is impossible to define precisely those cases in which it may be proper to excuse the parties, and that it is expedient to leave them to the discretion of the Government.

169. With respect to the latter, it seems to us that the following would be a safe definition with the explanation annexed:

"Nothing is an offence, except under Clause 294, which is done by a "person who is compelled to do it by threats, which may reasonably "cause the apprehension that instant death to that person will otherwise "be the consequence, the act being done in the presence of the person "using the threat, and the threat being continued to the time of doing "it, provided the party doing the act did not voluntarily place himself "in the situation by which he became subject to such constraint."

Explanation.—"A person who shall have voluntarily joined a gang "of dacoits, or a crew of pirates, or the like, knowing their character, "will not be entitled to the benefit of this exception, on the ground of "his having been compelled by his associates to do any thing that is an "offence by law.

"A person who shall have embarked ignorantly in a piratical vessel, "being compelled by the crew by threat of instant death to join in an "act of piracy, will be entitled to the benefit of the exception.

"So also a person seized by a gang of dacoits and forced by threat of "instant death to do a thing which is an offence by law, for example, a "smith compelled to take his tools and to force the door of a house for "the dacoits to enter and plunder it."

170. By the English Law according to the Digest, duress cannot be pleaded in excuse of treason or homicide; except, in cases of treason,

Articles 7 and 8.

the charge be for "levying war against the king," or "adhering to the king's enemies," or "supplying money, &c., to be used in furtherance of any treasonable design or purpose," when it may be pleaded under certain conditions.

171. The clause we have drawn relating to duress likewise excludes the plea in case of homicide, and it is expressed so as in effect to adopt the conditions above alluded to, not only in the case of persons compelled to join in waging war against the Government, &c., but generally, as we think they ought to be of general application.

172. We observe that duress is allowed as an excuse by the Code framed by Mr. Livingstone in case of the party having been threatened with loss of life or limb, or forced by actual violence, and the English Law allows it when the party was constrained by the fear of grievous bodily hurt as well as fear of death; we have thought it proper however to limit the excuse to cases in which the party acted under threat of instant death.

173. It is laid down in the Digest of the English Criminal Law that,

Chapter I, Section 2, Art. 9.

"a married woman charged with the commission of any "criminal act shall, in case her husband shall be pre-"sent at the time of the commission of such act, be "presumed to have acted under his coercion, and shall be entitled to an "acquittal, unless it appear that she did not so act. Provided that no

Art. 10.

"such presumption shall be made in case of any charge "of treason or homicide." By Mr. Livingstone's Code, "a married woman committing an offence by command or persuasion of "her husband shall suffer no greater punishment than simple imprison-"ment for one-half of the term to which she would have been sentenced "if she had committed the offence without such command or persuasion."

174. There is no provision in favor of the wife under such circumstances in the Code under review. The point is not adverted to in the Notes; we have therefore no explanation of the reasons upon which the framers of the Code determined not to allow the plea of coercion by the husband to avail in favor of the wife, either to the extent of excusing her, or in the way of extenuation. It seems to us, considering how much the women of India are under the power of their husbands, that such a plea may more properly be allowed in this country than in England.

CHAPTER IV.

OF ABETMENT.

175. Mr. J. F. Thomas considers the chapter of Abetment "a great and highly valuable improvement."

176. On the other hand, Mr. Norton says "This chapter appears to "me to confound and perplex the English Criminal Law of Principal "and Accessories, which law I conceive to be very clear and rational."

177. Mr. W. Hudleston likewise says "I am of opinion that these "rules are less worthy of adoption than the provisions of the Law of "England."

178. The Law of England on this subject is set forth in the Digest prepared by Her Majesty's Commissioners under the head of "Criminal Agency and Participation." In the first Article it is declared that "parties to a crime are either principals "in the first degree, or principals in the second degree, "or accessories before the fact."

Chapter I, Section 4, 7th Report, page 115.

179. "A principal in the first degree," according to Blackstone, "is he that is the actor or absolute perpetrator of the "crime," "in the second degree, he who is present aiding "and abetting the fact to be done." "An accessory is "he who is not the chief actor in the offence or present at its perform-"ance, but is some way concerned therein either before or after the fact "committed." The Digest explains that not only the absolute perpetrator of a criminal act is a principal in the first degree, but also he who causes it to be done, otherwise than by a guilty agent. An accessory is defined to be one who "not being present" at the doing of a criminal act "has procured or promoted the doing of it." And it is declared that "a party shall be deemed to procure or promote the "doing of a criminal act" "who shall by commandment, "counsel, advice, consent, aid, or otherwise, either directly or indirectly "cause, incite, or encourage any other offender to do such act or cause it "to be done."

Vol. 4, pages 34 and 35.

Art. 2, Chap. I, Sec. 4.

Art. 10.

Art. 11.

180. It is declared in Article 14, that "Every party to a crime within the meaning of Article 1 shall be deemed to be guilty of that crime," and that every penal provision in respect thereof shall be applicable to all parties within the meaning of the same. The effect of which, as explained in a Note, "is to make every one liable as the doer, who is "either the actual doer, or who aids in the doing, or procures or promotes "the doing of any criminal act."

181. There is no distinction of principals in the first degree and principals in the second degree in the Indian Code. In the 3rd clause of the chapter of General Explanations, it is laid down once for all that "Wherever the causing of a certain "effect with a certain intention, or with a knowledge of certain circum-"stances, is an offence, it is to be understood that if more persons than "one jointly cause that effect, every one of them who has that intention, "or that knowledge, commits that offence."

Chapter I, p. 1.

182. The definitions of substantive offences, construed with reference to this general explanatory clause, take in all who actually cause or assist in causing the effect which constitutes the offence, without distinction of leaders or followers, principals or subordinate agents. We apprehend that all are included whose acts are such as to bring them within the definition of principals in the first degree in Articles 3 and 4, Section 4, Chapter I of the Digest of the English Law, and all who as being actually present and assisting come directly within the definition of principals in the second degree in Article 7, but not such as are constructively regarded as principals in the second degree under the circumstances set forth in Article 8, though not present and not having any hand in causing the effect. The latter come under the third head in the definition of previous abetment in the Indian Code, and are made liable to the same punishment as the actual perpetrators. The effect is the same as by the English Law, but without that forced construction by which the English Law is strained for the purpose.

Clauses 86 and 97.

183. The provisions regarding "previous abetment," in the Indian Code, besides the offenders just mentioned, appear to apply to all who, as procuring and promoting the doing of criminal acts, in any of the ways set forth in the Article of the Digest quoted above, are liable to be dealt with by the English Law as accessories before the fact.

Previous abetment.

Art. 11, Sec. 4, Chapter I.

184. According to the definition in the Code previous abetment is the procuring and promoting the doing of a thing by instigation, conspiracy, or aid, or by concealment intended to facilitate the doing of the thing. The mode of abetment last mentioned is not in terms brought into the above Article in the Digest as rendering the offender liable to be dealt with as an accessory. The concealment of an intended offence by a party not consenting thereto is provided for as a misprision under the head of offences tending to defeat justice. If the concealment was wilful with the intention of facilitating the commission of the offence, we apprehend that it would be construed into such approbation or assent as would make the offender an accessory before the fact.

Art. 27, Sec. 5, Chapter V.

Russell 1, p. 29.

185. In the 8th Report of the Commissioners on the Criminal Law of England, lately published, this subject is again discussed. It is assumed to be impossible to make any distinction between accessories before the fact and principals, *as regards the degree of the offence*, and it is questioned whether there ought to be any distinction *in the mode of charging the offence*. "The main, and as it seems the "only reason for charging the procurement or participation of the offence "specially," say the Commissioners, "is the giving to the party charged "more accurate and circumstantial information as to the mode of partici- "pation intended to be proved." It is admitted that if the distinction were of easy practical application, it would be desirable to adopt it for this reason. But it is argued that it would be attended with great practical inconvenience.

Page 11.

186. After stating the difficulties, the Commissioners observe that there seem to be three modes of obviating them; "by admitting the "general charge to be sufficient, but requiring the prosecutor on applica- "tion by the accused and under the direction of the Court to supply the "accused with the names of the principals in the first degree, and such "particulars as would be necessary with a view to his defence; or second-

"ly, by allowing the charge to be stated in both ways by means of different "counts; thirdly, by allowing the charge to be made in the alternative," when it is doubtful whether the proof will show the party to have been an accessory before the fact or a principal in the second degree.

187. The authors of the Code, in framing the definitions of abetment, have made the distinction the propriety of which is here in question, and the provision in Clause 61, it seems to us, will obviate the difficulties apprehended by the English Commissioners. This clause directs that when a person is found guilty of an offence, but it is doubtful under which of certain penal provisions he is punishable, the offender shall be liable to whatever punishment is common to the penal provisions between which the doubt lies. The same result is aimed at by the suggestion which we find has been offered by Lord Denman, Lord Chief Justice of England, and other persons consulted by the Criminal Law Commissioners, namely, in the words of Lord Denman, that "when the train of circumstances makes it "perfectly clear that the accused is either principal or "accessory, but does not enable the Jury to see clearly "whether he is one or the other, the finding of that alternative by the "Jury ought to expose him to punishment."

Appendix A, 8th Report.

Page 212.

188. The above observations we conceive will be found to answer the question put by Sir. H. Seton, upon Clause 85, in this chapter, "why "omit abetment simply, viz., being present at and aiding?"

189. Mr. Norton, after the remark quoted above, objectingly observes that "those who *aid* and those who *conspire* and who may *also* be *pre-* "*sent* and substantively *co-operate* in the act, ought to all intents and "purposes to be considered as principals and not abettors." We have shewn that with respect to those who are "present" and "substantively co-operate" this is just what is intended, and Mr. Norton himself remarks that "Clause 3 of the 1st chapter enacts as much," "but that," says he, "is not so enacted by *this* chapter." We do not see why it should be again enacted in this chapter, the clause referred to being intended, as is clearly expressed, to govern the whole Code. With regard to "those who aid" and "those who conspire," though they are distinguished from the principal offenders for the sake of accuracy of definition, they are liable to be dealt with in the same manner, as we have already intimated.

190. As a specimen of Mr. Norton's criticisms we may notice his remarks upon abetment by concealment. "It may be asked," he says, "what is 'concealing'? probably 'not disclosing' is meant—A party "not disclosing the design of his friend or child to commit an offence is "himself criminally guilty, though he may afterwards prevent or dissuade "that very design from being effected." The inaptitude of this illustration will be obvious when on turning to the definition it is observed that concealment amounts to "abetment" only where the party *intends* or *knows* it *to be likely* that he may *thereby facilitate* the doing of the thing designed. This is the definition of what constitutes abetment: whether the abetment is criminal depends of course upon whether the thing is an offence or not.

Clause 86.

Clause 87.

191. "Luckily," Mr. Norton adds, "there is no punishment awarded in the Code for concealing a design not carried into effect." Is it to be believed that Mr. Norton sincerely thought that this happened by chance?

192. Again, in the very next paragraph of his Report, Mr. Norton mentions "as an example of very loose style of legislation, even in an "illustration" "that a person is declared (Clause 87) to steal a horse "who takes him fraudulently, and if another *aids* him in that act (say "by opening the stable door and leading the horse out) he *abets* that "*theft*, but is not a *principal thief*." This is an unaccountable misrepresentation, as will appear at once from the following quotation of the illustration to which he refers. "A aids B to take a horse out of Z's "possession. Here if B took the horse fraudulently, B is guilty of theft. "But if A aided B believing that B had a right to take the horse, A is "*not said to have abetted the theft* committed by B, though he has abetted "the taking of the horse." The illustration it will be perceived is the very reverse of what Mr. Norton represents it to be. His remarks are surely an example of an unhappily "loose style" of criticism.

193. Sir R. Comyn, adverting to the word "misconception" in Clause 87, refers to his remark on the same word in Clause 82, which we have already considered. Sir H. Seton, Mr. W. Hudleston, and Mr. A. D. Campbell, object to the passage in Clause 87 containing this word, as obscure. Sir H. Seton points to Clause 99 as liable to the same objection. The learned Judge doubts whether the misconception applies to the quality of the act in question as being an offence or not. In all the illustrations annexed to the clauses in which this word is used, for the purpose of shewing the sense in which it is to be taken, the misconception concerns the matter of fact. We understand, as we have said before, that in using this word there is a reference to Clauses 62 and 63. The misconception, it would seem, respects the circumstances, taking them wrongly to be such as would warrant the act done according to law. We beg to refer to the observations we have offered above upon the two clauses here adverted to.

Clauses 82, 87, 99 and 100.

194. The Code distinguishes between cases in which the abetment is successful and those in which the effect intended is not accomplished. When the offence is committed, if the abetment is by instigation, conspiracy, or aid, the punishment is the same as if the abettor had been a party in the commission of it. Otherwise, the punishment is limited to one-fourth of the longest term of imprisonment provided for the offence intended, or fine, or both, which however is to be inflicted only, in abetment by instigation, where the abetment was attended with the actual delivery of a bribe, or with the threat of causing injury, or was committed by a person present instigating the offender to persist in the commission of the offence, and in abetment by conspiracy, when some act takes place, in pursuance of the conspiracy, and in order to the committing of the offence. In abetment by concealment, if the offence be committed and the abettor be a public servant, the offender is liable to one-half of the longest term of imprisonment for the offence; if not a public servant, he is liable to one-fourth.

Clauses 88, 95 and 97.

Clauses 90, 91 and 93.

Clause 96.

Clauses 101 and 102.

195. The distinction here noticed having been overlooked by some of the officers who have offered observations on this chapter, they have been led to impute inconsistencies which do not exist. Another, Mr. Giberne, adverting to the distinction, expresses his disapproval of it, thinking that "the person who instigates another to commit an offence under any and every circumstance" has actually committed "his portion of the offence." He does not say however whether he would have the instigator always made punishable with the punishment of the offence which he abetted, or how he would determine the punishment. Mr. Cochrane (the Company's Standing Counsel) on this point says that he is not prepared to think that as a general principle equal punishment should be awarded to the man who abets as to the party committing an offence.

196. The English Law, as it is expressed in the Digest, makes every party to a crime, as principal, in the first or in the second degree, or as accessory before the fact, "guilty of that crime," and so far the Indian Code agrees with it. Instigations, &c., without effect are provided for separately by the English Law. In the Digest they are brought under the head of "Illegal solicitation." A specific penalty, viz., imprisonment not exceeding two years, or fine, or both, is prescribed, if the offence intended be a felony, if it be a misdemeanor the penalty is not to exceed one-half of that prescribed for the misdemeanor.

Art. 14, Sec. 4, Chapter I.

Chapter XXII, Art. 1.

197. The punishment is cumulative by the Indian Code when the person who instigates an offence (actually committed in consequence) does so by committing another offence, as when A by putting B in fear of death induces B to burn a stack of corn belonging to Z. Here A is punishable for the instigation under Clause 88, and the putting in fear of death under Clause 482. It is the same where the instigation is attended with the threat of causing any injury.

Clause 89.

Clause 91.

198. Mr. W. Hudleston and Mr. A. D. Campbell concur in objecting to the accumulation of punishment in this manner, the former expressing an opinion that the rule of punishing for the greater of two or more offences is preferable.

199. The principle of rendering the punishment cumulative when two offences are committed in one transaction, is followed to a considerable extent in this Code, but with discrimination; it is ordered in Clause 58, that punishments shall not be cumulative unless it be so expressly provided, and in Clause 59, that in no case shall be combined the punishments provided by more than two penal provisions of the Code. The question of the propriety of cumulative punishment will be more particularly considered in its proper place, in reviewing the chapter of Punishments.

200. We have said that we consider that all who, as being actually *present* and assisting in the commission of an offence, come directly within the definition of principals in the second degree in the English Law, are regarded by the Code as accomplices in the fact, or more strictly "accessories at the fact," and guilty of the offence, without distinction.

Russell 1, p. 21.

201. But Clause 93, which applies to a person "*present* while any offence is committed" and "instigating the offender to *persist* in the commission of *that* offence" is thought to militate against this view, as the punishment is limited, in regard to imprisonment, to one-fourth part of the longest term provided for the offence. We apprehend that *if the offence were persisted in or renewed*, the person implicated as above would be deemed an accomplice in the fact or "an accessory at the fact" liable to the punishment of the offence. We conceive that this clause is intended to meet a case in which the instigation has not had the effect intended. We infer this not only from its apparent tenor, but also from the position of the clause among other clauses providing for abetment by instigation when the offence appears not to have been committed.

202. The clause at first sight appears obscure from the reference to an offence *committed* as identical with that which is abetted in the manner stated. The meaning as we understand it, may be best illustrated by an example, as follows: A is casually present when a mob attacks a house with the intention of sacking it. A takes no part at first, but seeing the attack suspended he instigates the mob to persist; if the attack is renewed in consequence he is liable to punishment equally with the rioters; if his instigation is without effect, he is answerable for the instigation under this clause.

203. This clause is limited to cases in which the offence instigated is punishable with rigorous imprisonment for a term of one year or upwards. We do not understand that it is meant to apply exclusively to cases in which *rigorous* imprisonment is prescribed *positively*, but to all cases in which it *may* be inflicted, excluding cases in which *simple* imprisonment is prescribed positively. This remark applies also to Clause 102.

204. Simple instigation to commit an offence, without the effect intended, is not punishable except under the clause last noticed unless it be directed to the "public generally," or to "any number or class of persons exceeding ten," it is then punishable by imprisonment which may extend to three years, or fine, or both. Mr. Cochrane objects to the principle of this provision. Mr. J. F. Thomas thinks it will open the door to malicious prosecutions unless the instigation be confined to some overt acts like the illustrations. Mr. Hudleston adopts this objection, and adds that he thinks the provision needless. Mr. Campbell disagrees with Mr. Thomas and Mr. Hudleston.

Clause 94.

205. The suggestion of Mr. Thomas appears to us worthy of attention. Perhaps it may be most expedient to define the manner of instigation by the terms used in Clause 113, relating to attempts to excite feelings of disaffection to the Government, or such terms as may be settled when that clause comes under consideration.

206. The number ten is obviously fixed arbitrarily. By Clause 127, it requires twelve persons to constitute a riotous assembly. It would seem advisable to make the number the same in both clauses, if any number be specified. We are rather inclined to think it would be better not to specify a number. In that case the clause should be modified by substituting for the words "or any number or class of persons exceeding ten" the words "or any class of persons."

207. We do not find any observations upon the provisions regarding abetment by conspiracy which appear to require notice, except the remark of Mr. Norton that "the conspiracy to commit an offence, say murder, is an offence, though nothing is done," which we have to note as a mistake; and his objection to Clause 96 on the ground that the *same* punishment applies to the most trivial acts and to acts by which the object of the conspiracy may have been all but

Clauses 95 and 96.

effected. The weight of the objection will be easily estimated when it is perceived that there is purposely no minimum limit to the punishment, to admit of the Judge exercising a discretion, and applying "to the most trivial" acts the most trivial punishment. The objection holds, for as much as it is worth, in every instance in which a discretion is left to the Judge.

Clause 97.

208. We have stated above that we understand Clause 97, regarding abetment by aid, to comprehend persons who by the English Law are constructively considered to be principals in the second degree, though not present and not having any hand in causing the effect which constitutes the offence. Mr. Norton "presumes "that abetment by doing an act, or by illegal omission of an act, in "*actual substantive aid* of an offence, is really meant." We believe that he does not mean substantive aid by actual assistance *in the perpetration of the offence*, but some actual though not direct aid by which the perpetration of the offence has been facilitated, in contradistinction from what, he says, the literal construction of the clause imports, namely, that "a "person omitting a part of his duty, as by concealing any act with inten- "tion to aid it, although in fact he did not aid in the design at all, may "be punished as though he had aided in an offence (say a murder) "designed and committed." We apprehend that if the murder was committed, and the party omitted what it was his duty to do, with the *intention* of aiding the commission of the murder, he would be liable to punishment under this clause, whether by such omission he did or did not *in fact* aid the commission of the murder, and we have no doubt that he ought to be so punished as equally guilty whether his *intended aid* was effectual or not.

209. Mr. Norton complains of vagueness and uncertainty by the use of such words as "intention," &c., in this chapter, seeming to forget how language has been forced by the constructive interpretations given to the English Law on this very head, whereby to satisfy the terms "present" and "aiding" it is held that a person need not be actually present, and need not actually assist.

210. Mr. Norton says he cannot with every effort understand the distinction between the "*illegal omission*" of a Police officer which facilitates an offence under Clause 97, and the "*concealment*" of a Police officer which likewise facilitates an offence under Clause 101. The difference appears to us palpable. Under Clause 97, the omission respects what is either doing or is about to be done at the present time, and could not be done, in the case given as an illustration, but for the omission, which is all but a participation. In Clause 101, the concealment refers to *a design to commit* an offence at a *future* time, the commission of which the concealment may in a manner facilitate, by not exciting that attention which would probably prevent it: but this is a remote and precarious aid, which though deserving of punishment, is surely very different from that which is supposed to be rendered in the former case, conducing by an immediate influence and a positive efficacy to the commission of the offence.

Clause 101.

211. Upon Clause 97 Mr. J. F. Thomas observes that, as it is worded, it appears to include a case like that of the London Police officer, who by not interfering suffered the perpetration of a murder with the view to secure the reward called "blood money," by the after apprehension of the murderer. He remarks that "the officer, however indefensible his "conduct, and although his omission probably led to the murder being "actually perpetrated, yet was not in league with and had no intention "of favoring the offenders, which is the essence of the offence in this "clause, but his act nevertheless falls apparently within the definition "of 'aiding' by an illegal omission." We think that such an act or omission does fall, and properly so, within the definition, equally when it is prompted by the mercenary motive by which the London Police officer was actuated, as when it proceeds from the desire to favor the offender. The "*intention*" is the same in either case "to aid the commission of the offence," and that is what constitutes guilt under this clause, whatever may be the motive. It therefore appears that it would be unnecessary to modify the clause as Mr. Thomas suggests, even if there were any such a system in operation here as that to which he alludes, which we need hardly say there is not.

212. Clause 98 makes the previous abettor of an offence liable to the punishment of a different offence which may be committed in consequence of his abetment of the intended offence, if he knew that such different offence was likely to be committed in the attempt to commit the intended offence. This appears to us to agree substantially with Article 13, Section 4, Chapter I of the Digest of the English Criminal Law. It differs in making the abettor liable to cumulative punishment if the intended offence be also committed, according to the principle of this Code.

213. Many objections are made to this clause with reference to the condition that the abettor *knew* that the different offence was *likely* to be committed. Similar objections are made to other clauses which we need not particularly notice. They are sufficiently answered we conceive by the observations we have already offered in commenting upon the chapter of General Exceptions with respect to the definition contained in Clause 26.

Clause 99.

214. Upon Clause 99 Mr. W. Hudleston remarks that it "exhibits "refinement bordering upon unintelligibility wholly out "of place in a Criminal Code, and so worded that the "meaning would escape discovery without the illustrations." The clause appears to us also to be expressed somewhat obscurely, though certainly not to such a degree as to be unintelligible without the illustrations as Mr. Hudleston avers. These are however an important help.

Illustration (*b*).

215. The meaning we gather to be, first, that when a person abets the doing of a thing which he knows to be a certain offence, and it is done according to his intention, if from some misconception on the part of the doer his act does not fall within the definition of that offence, the abettor nevertheless shall be liable to the same punishment as if the doer could be convicted of that offence. Or if *in consequence* of the abetment, that is, in endeavouring to effect what the abettor intended, something is done which *is* an offence under one clause of the Code, but would be an offence under *another* clause, but for some misconception on the part of the doer which mitigates it, from which misconception the abettor is free, the abettor shall be liable to punishment under *that other* clause. Secondly, that if a person abets the doing of a thing which is an offence, for example by supplying means for the purpose, and through and in

Illustration (*a*).

consequence of such abetment, for example, by using the means supplied by him for committing the offence which he intended, a different and more heinous offence is committed intentionally, but without his knowledge, the abettor shall be liable only, to the punishment to which he would have been liable if the offence which he intended had been committed, or to the punishment to which the actual offender would have been liable, but for the intention entertained by him unknown to the abettor, by which his offence was aggravated so as to subject him to a higher penalty.

216. The principle of the second provision seems to be recognized in Articles 16 and 17, Section 4, Chapter I of the Digest.

217. If the scope of the clause be as we have understood it, the provisions contained in it would seem to be by no means an unnecessary refinement.

Clause 100.

218. The provision contained in Clause 100 appears to us clearly expedient.

Clauses 101 and 102.

219. Upon the clauses regarding abetment by concealment we see no occasion for remark in addition to what we have already submitted.

Subsequent abetment.

Clauses 103 to 108.

220. We come now to the clauses relating to "subsequent abetment," corresponding with what in the English Law hitherto has constituted the offence of an "accessory after the fact," an offence which does not appear in the Digest of the Criminal Law Commissioners. "There seems to be no reason," they say in their 7th Report, "for continuing the provisions as to accessories after the fact, the offences "of parties falling within this description at present being for the most "part referable to the class of offences against public justice, we have "dealt with them as such." So also in this Code acts by which according to the English Law a man would be liable to the punishment of an "accessory after the fact," as harbouring and concealing an offender with the intention of preventing him from being taken into custody, are provided for in the chapter "of contempts of the lawful authority of public servants."

Ch. IX, Clauses 177 and 178.

221. Mr. Norton sweepingly objects to the provisions under this head, on the ground that "so far from being applicable as *universal* rules "it appears to his mind impossible to read one of them which could not "be in the most obvious manner falsified by other cases than those specified by way of illustration;" he does not however support this allegation by any instances.

222. He further avers that "under some of these clauses, ignorance of the law and misconceptions of it form no excuse, under others "knowledge of the existing law in reference to the offences committed "and abetted, as clearly does form a substantive ingredient, and ignorance of that law an excuse. That knowledge of the law too required "as the criterion of guilt or innocence, has reference to *details* such as "the quantity of punishment (for instance) affixed to the crime abetted." Mr. Norton does not specify the particular clauses to which these remarks point, but he seems to refer to Clause 104, in which a person is said subsequently to abet an offence when he abets "what he would know to be an offence but for his ignorance of the law," as inconsistent with Clauses 105 and 106. He appears to think that under Clause 105 a man could not be convicted of subsequent abetment who did not know himself to be directed by law according to the words of the clause, and under Clause 106, who did not know positively that the offence was "punishable with rigorous imprisonment for one year or upwards."

223. To take the last instance first, it is obvious to remark that the reference to the punishment is merely a way of intimating that the rule is not to be applied to the lesser offences. In the Digest it is proposed to classify crimes other than treasons, as felonies and misdemeanors, not as heretofore, but with reference to the punishments to which they are liable. Felonies to consist of crimes punishable with death or transportation, misdemeanors, of crimes punishable otherwise, that is, all other crimes. According to the nomenclature of the Digest to say that a felony has been committed is in other words to say that an offence has been committed that is punishable with death or transportation.* This explanation applies also to Clause 107. It seems to us that the wording of Clause 106 and Clause 107 ought to correspond. We prefer the wording of Clause 107 as the more simple, "whoever subsequently abets any offence," &c., what is abetting an offence being already defined in Clauses 103 and 104.

224. With respect to Clause 105 we do not suppose that it was intended to allow a party to escape by pleading ignorance that he was "directed by law to give information, &c." But to prevent such a construction we would suggest the substitution of the word "being" for "knowing himself to be." There appears no more reason for these words importing that the party knew what the law required of him, in this clause, than in Clause 102, which makes concealment an offence.

225. Objection is made by officers of all the Presidencies to the punishment for subsequent abetment in Clause 106 as too lenient. The abetment here is assisting to conceal an offence "by causing any marks of the commission of the offence to disappear." The example is assisting a murderer to hide the body of his victim. The punishment may extend to one-twelfth part of the imprisonment for the offence. Murder is liable to the punishment of imprisonment for life, as alternative for death. By Clause 48 in calculating portions of terms of imprisonment, imprisonment for life is to be reckoned as equivalent to imprisonment for 24 years. The abettor is therefore liable to imprisonment for 2 years as the maximum term, with fine in addition at discretion. This punishment is considered too light for the case stated, and inadequate generally, on the ground that the subsequent abettor is in most cases a previous abettor also, though he may have kept himself free from any apparent complicity sufficient to convict him of that offence. It does appear to us that when a person previously abetting an offence by any act or omission intended to aid it, is punishable with the full penalty of the offence, a person so closely connected with the offence after its commission as to be within the definition in this clause by acts manifesting a sympathy with the offender and strongly indicative of assent to the offence, ought to be punishable more severely than by a twelfth part of the penalty of the offence. The receiver of stolen property may be considered as a subsequent abettor, but such an offender is

Clause 97.

* In Art. 28, Sec. 5, Chapter V of the Digest relating to concealment of offenders, the punishment to which the party concealing an offender is liable depends upon whether the offence committed was or was not punishable by transportation, or was or was not punishable with death.

Clauses 390 and 391. liable to imprisonment for three years, if the property has been obtained by theft, to transportation or imprisonment for life, if it has been obtained by dacoity.

226. There is an "exception" to Clause 107, relating to the harbouring of offenders, declaring that it does not extend to "harbour given by "the husband and wife, or relation in the direct ascending or descending "line, or brother or sister of the person to whom harbour is given."

227. A similar exception is annexed to Clause 177 and to Clause 206. It is objected to by several officers as giving too great a license. Mr. J. F. Thomas says "This provision taken from a Code enacted for a differ- "ent state of society is, I am inclined to think, only in part applicable to "this country. I would retain the exception as regards the husband and "the wife, the mother, the daughter, and the sister by whole blood. But "I would not retain it in the case of brothers or sisters by half blood, "nor even in the case of father and son, grandfather and grandson, nor "of brothers, unless it was satisfactorily established, that these relatives "were themselves wholly free from suspicion, not only in the special "case in which they harboured, but that their characters, and habits, "were at all times those of honest men. Constituted as society is in "India, where whole castes, (as Cullers and Marawars in our Southern "Provinces, Coorumburs, Cochawars, &c., elsewhere) are by birth, frater- "nities of thieves and plunderers, where each member of a family is at "all times ready to join his relation in robbery, or theft, if the father, "brother, &c., is allowed to render to his criminal relative this assistance "*ad libitum*, we shall greatly diminish the security of person and pro- "perty."

228. Mr. H. C. Tucker, of the Bengal Civil Service, thinks that the exception should only extend to husband and wife. Mr. E. H. Monckton, of the same Service, observes that "a man for example, who was in the "habit of harbouring thieves,* ought not to get off if it was proved he had "been in the habit of concealing his son under similar circumstances."

Russell 1, p. 36. Digest, Art. 11, Sec. 2, Chapter I. **229.** By the Law of England it is only the wife who is exempted from the penalty for receiving or harbouring an offender.

230. By the French Code Penal are excepted "Les ascendants et "descendants, epoux ou epouse, même divorcés, freres "ou sœurs des criminels recélés, ou leur alliés aux "mêmes degrés." Art. 248.

231. Mr. Livingstone's Code for Louisiana excepts the husband or wife of the offender; his relations in the ascending or descending line, either by affinity or consanguinity; his brothers or sisters; his domestic servants.

232. The exception in the Indian Code while it goes greatly beyond the narrow line of the Law of England it will be perceived falls short of both the other Codes referred to. We think it would be better to restrict it still more by excluding relations in the ascending or descending line beyond the first degree, and perhaps also brothers and sisters.

* This example is not exactly apt as the clause does not apply to thieves, who are not punishable with imprisonment for seven years, except under the aggravation described in Clause 367.

CHAPTER XVIII.

OF OFFENCES AFFECTING THE HUMAN BODY.

233. Sir R. Comyn, as we have already noticed, observes upon this important chapter that the only part of it which appears to him objectionable is Clause 298, touching "voluntary culpable homicide by consent."

234. Mr. Giberne, one of the Judges of the Sudder Court at Bombay, makes the following remarks: "Chapter XVIII may be considered one "of the most important of the Code. The first class of offences against "the body includes certain omissions as well as acts, the line denoting "which is admirably defined. The second mitigated form of murder, "voluntary culpable homicide by consent, is peculiarly adapted to cases "likely to occur in the country, such as Suttees, administering medicines "to procure abortion, &c., &c. In short all the different divisions and "definitions of the crimes provided for in this chapter have been "arranged with such accuracy and care, the principles and reasoning "in the Note M are so clearly and fully shewn, that it appears to me "that all that was required has been accomplished, and every remark "anticipated."

235. Mr. Norton says, "There is much in this chapter to assist an "effort as feasible as meritorious, that of a sound and distinctive digest "of the various crimes of wilful injury to the person. At the same time "I am compelled to the opinion that this effort has been too ill accom-"plished by the present chapter to admit of its being brought into prac-"tical operation."

236. Mr. W. Hudleston says, "I do not perceive the necessity for "the several novel designations of crime adopted in this chapter, and "with regard, generally, to the provisions for homicide, I am of opinion "that the Law of England on this subject suffices for all practical pur-"poses, and is every way preferable to the refinements of this Code."

237. We have already considered the remarks made by Mr. Norton upon the distinction between the doing an act with an intention to effect a certain result, and the doing it with a knowledge that it is likely to produce that result, and those of Mr. A. D. Campbell, upon the confounding, as he expresses it, of intent with mere knowledge of what is likely; and we have discussed this leading principle of the Code by which men are held to be responsible for the consequences which they know are likely to result from their acts, as well as for what they directly intend, so fully, that there appears to be no occasion for further remark in vindication of the definitions in this chapter which bring it prominently forward.

OF OFFENCES AFFECTING LIFE.

238. The Commissioners call attention to the expression "omits what he is legally bound to do" in the definition of voluntary culpable homicide, which words, or other words tantamount in effect, frequently recur in this and other parts of the Code.

See Appendix, Note M, page 138.

239. "What we propose," say the Commissioners, "is this, that "where acts are made punishable on the ground that "they have caused, or have been intended to cause, or "have been known to be likely to cause a certain evil "effect, omissions which have caused, or which have been intended to

See Appendix, Note M, page 139.

"cause, or which have been known to be likely to cause the same effect "shall be punishable in the same manner, provided that such omissions "were on other grounds *illegal*," according to the explanation of that term contained in Clause 28.

240. In the Digest of the English Criminal Law framed by Her Majesty's Commissioners it is declared that "the law "takes no cognizance of homicide unless death result "from bodily injury caused by some act or unlawful "omission," and it is explained that "the terms 'unlawful omission' "comprehend every breach of duty imposed by the law to do any act "or supply any thing necessary for the sustentation or preservation of "human life, or for the prevention of injury to the person."

Chapter XV, Sec. 1, Art. 1.

241. It seems to us that the line drawn in the Indian Code by the use of the adjectives "legal" and "illegal" applied to the duty and the omission respectively, is perfectly plain and intelligible, at the same time that it is just and right, and it does not appear to differ from the rule of the English law as laid down in the Digest. Nor do we see that the principle is excepted to expressly in any of the reports on the Code, though from the comments made upon some of the illustrations (by Mr. Hudleston* particularly) it would seem not to have been altogether approved, perhaps from not being perfectly understood.

242. The next point to which the Commissioners call attention in the Note on this chapter is the unqualified use of the words "to cause death" in the definition of voluntary culpable homicide. "We long considered," say they, "whether "it would be advisable to except from this definition any description of "acts or illegal omissions, on the ground that such acts or illegal omissions do not ordinarily cause death, or that they cause death very "remotely. We have determined however to leave the clause in its "present simple and comprehensive form."

See Appendix, Note M, page 141.

243. "There is undoubtedly a great difference between acts which "cause death immediately, and acts which cause death remotely; between "acts which are almost certain to cause death, and acts which cause "death only under very extraordinary circumstances. But that difference, we conceive, is a matter to be considered by the tribunals when "estimating the effect of the evidence in a particular case, not by the "Legislature in framing the general law. It will require strong evidence "to prove that an act of a kind which very seldom causes death, or an "act which has caused death very remotely, has actually caused death in "a particular case. It will require still stronger evidence to prove that "such an act was contemplated by the person who did it as likely to "cause death. But if it be proved by satisfactory evidence that death "has been so caused, and has been caused voluntarily, we see no reason "for exempting the person who caused it from the punishment of voluntary culpable homicide." After giving some illustrations of their views on the subject, and discussing the reasons for which Mr. Livingstone excepted certain cases which their definition includes, they say finally: "The general rule, therefore, which we propose is, that the question "whether a person has by an act or illegal omission voluntarily caused

* See remarks on the illustrations (*e*), (*f*) and (*g*) under Clause 294.

"death shall be left a question of evidence to be decided by the Courts "according to the circumstances of every case."

244. One of the cases alluded to as excepted by Mr. Livingstone is where death is produced by the effect of words on the imagination or the passions. This case is also excepted in the Digest of the English Criminal Law in which death resulting from "bodily injury" is "contradistinguished from death occasioned by any "influence on the mind, or by any disease arising from "such influence." The reason of this distinction is given by Her Majesty's Commissioners in the following quotation:—

Chap. XV, Section 1, Art. 1.

"If any man either by working upon the fancy of another, or possibly "by harsh or unkind usage puts another into such a passion of grief or fear that the party either dies suddenly, "or contracts some disease whereof he dies, though, as the circumstances "of the case may be, this may be murder or manslaughter in the sight "of God, yet *in foro humano* it cannot come under the judgment of "felony, because no external act of violence was offered whereof the "Common Law can take notice."—1 Hale's P. C. 429.

4th Report, p. 32.

245. The framers of the Indian Code say: "It would be most difficult "to prove to the conviction of any Court that death had "really been the effect of excitement produced by words. "It would be still more difficult to prove that the person who spoke the words anticipated from them an effect which, except "under peculiar circumstances, and on very peculiar constitutions, no "words would produce. Still it seems to us that both these points might "be made out by overwhelming evidence; and supposing them to be "so made out, we are unable to perceive any distinction between the case "of him who voluntarily causes death in this manner, and the case of "him who voluntarily causes death by means of a pistol, or a sword. "Suppose it to be proved to the entire conviction of a Criminal Court "that Z, the deceased, was in a critical state of health, that A, the heir "to Z's property, had been informed by Z's physicians that Z's recovery "absolutely depended on his being kept quiet in mind, and that the "smallest mental excitement would endanger his life, that A immediately broke into Z's sick room, and told him a dreadful piece of "intelligence which was a pure invention, that Z went into fits, and died "on the spot, that A had afterwards boasted of having cleared the way "for himself to a good property by this artifice. These things being "fully proved, no Judge could doubt that A had voluntarily caused the "death of Z; nor do we perceive any reason for not punishing A in the "same manner in which he would have been punished if he had mixed "arsenic in Z's medicine."

See Appendix, Note M, page 142.

246. Mr. Norton, Mr. Hudleston and Mr. A. D. Campbell all object to the illustration (*b*)* which is appended to Clause 294 to shew that the definition includes cases in which death is produced by the effect of words, on the principle above advocated, but it does not appear to us that any of them has given due consideration to the reasoning in support of it; certainly none of them has answered that reasoning.

247. Mr. Pyne however observes that such tidings (as supposed in

* A, with the intention or knowledge aforesaid, relates agitating tidings to Z, who is in a critical stage of a dangerous illness; Z dies in consequence. A has committed the offence of voluntary culpable homicide.

the illustration) may be communicated without a particle of malice, and still with the knowledge that the narrator is likely thereby to cause the death of his auditor. This he illustrates by a passage in the Memoirs of Sir Walter Scott, in which the publisher of his works is quoted as saying that to have made him aware of the condemnation of one of his works, in his then state, would have been his death-warrant. Upon which Mr. Pyne asks, supposing his friends to have done so, and the fatal event contemplated to have followed, should such a consummation have subjected them to be branded as murderers?

248. The case, it seems to us, would depend upon whether it could be alleged with truth, and satisfactorily proved, that the communication was made in good faith for the benefit of the party, in circumstances that his consent to suffer the consequences might be fairly considered as implied. The case being so would fall under the exception contained in Clause 70. In the instance of Sir W. Scott, if, for example, he were unduly relying on the value of the copyright of the work in question in making some arrangements of his affairs, we can conceive that it might be certainly for his benefit, within the meaning of the exception, to communicate the truth to him. It is hardly conceivable that his friends would make such a communication to him, knowing that it would probably be his "death-warrant," without some cause for which they believed it to be their indispensable duty to him to do so.

249. Having maturely considered the matter, we come to the same conclusion with the authors of the Code, that if death is certainly caused by words deliberately used by a person with the intention of causing that result, or with the knowledge that in the condition of the party to whom the words are spoken it is likely that they will make such an impression upon him as to cause his death, and without any such excuse as is admissible under any of the provisions in the chapter of General Exceptions, there is no sufficient reason why that person should be excepted from the penalty of culpable homicide, any more than one who has caused death by the infliction of a bodily injury which he knew to be likely to cause death. Here is the wilful doing of that which is known to be likely to produce evil, manifesting the *mens rea* essential to criminal responsibility; the evil produced is death; the efficient cause, the words spoken. It is scarcely agreeable to reason, that having traced the effect to its cause, the law should refuse to acknowledge it as an effective cause; or that the Judge should be obliged to say, it is true the effect was produced by the operation of words, but words in law are not an act, therefore the speaker is not criminally responsible.

250. Another case mentioned as excepted from the definition of homicide by Mr. Livingstone, but included in that given in this Code, is where "a person dies of a slight wound "which from neglect or from the application of im- "proper remedies has proved mortal."

See Appendix, Note M, page 148.

251. Two examples are given to illustrate the views of the authors of the Code on this point. The first case is as follows: "A inflicted a slight "wound on Z, a child who stood between him and a large property. It is "proved that the ignorant and superstitious servants about Z applied the "most absurd remedies to the wound, and that under their treatment the "wound mortified and the child died. Letters from A to a confidant are "produced. In those letters A congratulates himself on his skill, remarks "that he could not have inflicted a more severe wound without exposing "himself to be punished as a murderer, relates with exultation the mode "of treatment followed by the people who have charge of Z, and boasts "that he always foresaw that they would turn the slightest incision into a "mortal wound." Of this case we must say that it appears to us a most improbable one: though *if* such evidence were produced we could not but agree to the conclusion of the Commissioners that the party proved to have acted in the manner represented ought to be punished as a murderer, because it would be clear that in inflicting the slight wound he intended to cause the death of the person wounded. We can however scarcely imagine a person inflicting such a wound with the intention imputed, in the expectation that though it was but "the slightest incision" it would be so ill-treated by the ignorant and superstitious servants about the wounded person that it would certainly prove mortal. We can easily imagine a person with the feelings supposed congratulating himself on the result of his act so turned to his advantage, but it is difficult to conceive him contriving his act so astutely, and counting with such foresight, as is predicated, on the involuntary co-operation of others to effect his object while they meant to remedy the injury he had caused.

252. In the second case given by way of illustration there is, as observed by the Commissioners, no doubt whatever as to the intention, and therefore we agree with them that however slight the wound inflicted may have been, yet if it ultimately proves mortal, there is no reason for not punishing the person who inflicted it with the intention of murder, as a murderer.

253. It is because it is hardly possible to conceive murder to have been originally intended in the first of the two instances here adverted to, that we are doubtful of the propriety of putting it as a case within the definition in Clause 294, for fear of its leading to a latitude of construction which under some supposed analogy may include predicaments quite beyond its scope.

254. Mr. A. D. Campbell remarks that "though the Commissioners "in express terms state, that in India 'we have reason "to fear neglect and bad treatment are far more common "than good medical treatment,' instead of urging this as "the strongest possible reason why 'the case of a person who dies of "a *slight* wound, which *from neglect* or from the application of *im-"proper remedies* has proved mortal,' should, as in Mr. Livingstone's "Code, be excepted from homicide, they actually urge it as the very "reason why, in this country in particular, the inflicter of a mere "scratch, should in such cases, on the contrary, be constituted a mur-"derer."

See Appendix, Note M, page 143.

255. Mr. Campbell, it appears to us, has failed to apprehend the bearing of the remark which he quotes. The meaning of the Commissioners we conceive to be this, that whereas in countries in which good medical treatment is common it is difficult to suppose that a person inflicting a slight wound on another could contemplate his death as a probable result, such a result may be supposed to enter into his contemplation in a country where bad medical treatment is far more common than good, and therefore the definition of homicide ought not to exclude death resulting from a slight wound as the primary or original cause.

256. It is laid down in the Digest of the English Criminal Law that it is homicide if death be caused by bodily injury "although by proper remedies and skilful treatment death might have been prevented." So also, "although through neglect or ill-treatment, a fever or other disorder "ensue from the injury which is the immediate cause "of death." "But it is not homicide" "where the "death is not caused by the injury done, but by unskilful treatment or "other cause subsequent to the injury."

Chapter XV, Section 1, Art. 4.

Articles 5 and 6.

257. Russell says, "Upon this subject it has been ruled, that if a "man give another a stroke not in itself so mortal but "that with good care he might be cured, yet if the party "die of this wound within the year and day, it is murder, or other species "of homicide, as the case may be: though if the wound or hurt be not "mortal, and it shall be made clearly and certainly to appear that the "death of the party was caused by ill applications by himself or those "about him, of unwholesome salves or medicines, and not by the "wound or hurt, it seems that this is no species of homicide. But when "a wound not in itself mortal, for want of proper applications, or from "neglect, turns to a gangrene or a fever, and that gangrene or fever is "the immediate cause of the death of the party wounded, the party by "whom the wound is given is guilty of murder, or manslaughter, according to the circumstances. For though the fever or gangrene, and not "the wound, be the immediate cause of the death, yet the wound being "the cause of the gangrene or fever, is the immediate cause of the death, "*causa causati.* Thus, it was resolved that if one gives wounds to "another, who neglects the cure of them, or is disorderly and doth not "keep that rule which a person wounded should do, yet if he die it is "murder or manslaughter according to the circumstances; because if "the wounds had not been the man had not died: and, therefore, neglect "or disorder in the person who received the wounds shall not excuse the "person who gave them."

Vol. 1, p. 428.

258. The following case is given under Clause 294 as falling within the definitions of "voluntary culpable homicide." "A, "with the intention or knowledge aforesaid, falsely "deposes before a Court of Justice that he saw Z commit a capital crime. Z is convicted and executed in "consequence. A has committed the offence of voluntary "culpable homicide."

Death caused by false evidence in a Court of Justice.

Illustration (*d*).

259. The reason is stated in Note G, on the chapter of Offences against public justice. "The giving of false evidence "must always be a grave offence. But few points in "penal legislation seem to us clearer than that the law "ought to make a distinction between that kind of false evidence which "produces great evils, and that kind of false evidence which produces "comparatively slight evils."

See Appendix, Note G, page 131.

"As the ordinary punishment of false evidence, we propose imprisonment for a term of not more than seven years, nor less than one year. "If the false evidence is given or fabricated with intent to cause a person "to be convicted of a grave offence not capital, we propose that the "person who gives or fabricates such evidence may be punished with the "punishment of the offence which he has attempted to fix on another.

"If the false evidence be given or fabricated with the intention of causing death, we propose to punish it in the same manner in which we propose to punish the worst attempts to murder. If such false evidence actually causes death, the person who has given or fabricated it falls under the definition of murder, and is liable to capital punishment. In this last point, the law, as we have framed it, agrees with the old law of England, which though, in our opinion, just and reasonable, has become obsolete."

260. Mr. Livingstone seems to have proceeded on the same principle. By his Code it is provided that "if any one by means of perjury shall cause another to be convicted of a crime, he shall suffer the same punishment that is incurred by the commission of the crime of which such person has been convicted by means of the perjury."

Art. 191.

261. The following are the remarks of the English Criminal Law Commissioners on this subject: "The heinous crime here alluded to was punishable with death by the Roman Law as a species of assassination. See Digest, lib. 48. tit. 8, *Lex cornelia de sicariis*. Our earlier writers, adopting the doctrine of the Civil and Canon Law, speak of it as capital homicide by the law of England; but Sir Edward Coke declares 'that it was not holden for murder in his time,' 3 inst. 48; and Mr. J. Foster (Crown Cases, p. 132) says that 'the practice of many ages backwards doth by no means countenance the opinion' expressed by the old authorities. See Blackstone's Commentaries, Vol. IV, p. 196, and Mr. Christian's Note. Lord Mansfield, however, and several of the Judges in his time, appear to have entertained a contrary opinion.—See 1 East's P. C. 333. From the great number of facts, (some of them, such as the precise ground of the verdict, being very difficult of proof) which intervene between the act of the offender and the death of the object of his malice, it would be very difficult to prosecute such an offence effectually, and there are strong reasons of policy against admitting it to be murder, founded on the danger of deterring witnesses from giving evidence in capital cases, if it must be at the peril of their own lives. Besides, if causing sentence of death and execution by means of perjury be murder, the causing whipping or imprisonment by the same means would amount to the offence of assault and false imprisonment—a doctrine which it would be impossible to sustain. By the Bavarian Law, Art. 292, and also by the Prussian Law, Articles 1412, 1413, this crime, though punishable with death, is classed among fraudulent offences, and does not constitute homicide. The Code Penal places it under the head of false testimony." We may add that the Code Penal (Art. 361) in the case of a person being condemned upon false testimony to a more severe punishment than compulsory labour, makes the false witness liable to the same punishment.

4th Report, p. 34. See also Art. 8, Sec. 2, Cl. 15, of Digest. 7th Report, p. 224.

262. Mr. Hudleston takes up the objection to bringing this offence within the definition of "homicide" which is stated by Mr. Christian in his note upon Blackstone, Vol. IV, p. 196, and alluded to in the above remarks. "In this country," he adds, "the provision for making this perjury capital would involve the danger of conviction of such perjury upon false evidence. A new door would thus be opened to conspiracy."

263. His colleague, Mr. A. D. Campbell, differs from him and agrees with the Commissioners. Referring to Mr. Christian's observation quoted by Mr. Hudleston, that "few honest witnesses would venture to give "evidence against a prisoner tried for his life, if thereby they made them- "selves liable to be prosecuted as murderers," Mr. Campbell says, "This "appears to me a pure fallacy, by begging of the question. It first "wrongly assumes that capital punishment is to fall on the *honest* in- "stead of on the *dishonest* witness; and from these, evidently erroneous "premises, a deduction is drawn necessarily fallacious. Honest witnesses, "all over the world, give evidence against prisoners tried for their lives, "although they daily see the dishonest witness, who perjures himself, "punished by the pillory, or otherwise—why, I ask, should they not "equally continue so to do, though that punishment were increased, in "particular cases, even to death? The difference would be one in degree "alone, the principle would remain unaltered."

264. Mr. G. W. Bacon assents to what is said by the Commissioners in the Note on this point, and thinks it "quite just and right" to treat this offence as culpable homicide.

265. In their 5th Report the English Criminal Law Commissioners say: "In our last Report we remarked that the causing "of the death of an innocent man by means of perjury "is not punishable as murder by the English Law. There can however "be no doubt that any conspiracy to effect such an object is a crime which "is justly punishable with great severity." In the Digest they recommend that the latter offence shall be rendered liable to the penalties of the 7th class, viz., transportation for life, or for any term not less than seven years, or imprisonment for any term not exceeding three years.

Page 26.

Chap. IV, Section 5, Art. 26.

266. On the whole we are of opinion that the offence in question falls naturally within the definition of voluntary culpable homicide, which could not be expressed properly in terms that did not cover it; and but that we think it desirable to restrict rather than to extend capital punishment, and that it would be in effect an extension of it to make the perjurer liable to be convicted of homicide, which would be murder under Clause 295, when his false swearing has caused the condemnation and execution of an innocent person, we would not hesitate to recommend that this part of the Code be left untouched. For the reason last stated however we would advise that the illustration (*d*) be omitted under Clause 294, and that Clause 191 in the chapter of offences against public justice be declared applicable generally to the offence of giving false evidence with the intention of causing a person to be convicted of a capital crime, whether the object intended be effected or not. The punishment which may be awarded under this clause is transportation for life, or rigorous imprisonment for life, or for a term not less than seven years, and fine.

267. By Clause 295 it is declared that voluntary culpable homicide is "Murder" unless it be one of the three mitigated descriptions thereinafter enumerated, whereof the first is "Manslaughter." It is "Manslaughter" (Clause 297) "when it is "committed on grave and sudden provocation by causing "the death of the person who gave that provocation."

MURDER.

MANSLAUGHTER.

268. According to the Digest of the English Criminal Law, "Homi-"cide is manslaughter whensoever the killing is wilful, "but extenuated under certain circumstances." It is so extenuated when it is committed "under the influence of passion" excited by any act done or attempted or threatened "of an injurious or insulting character to the person of the party killing or of any other person," or "by any other grave cause of provocation" "to the party killing or any other person." By the Indian Code "provocation is designated as 'grave,' "when it is such as would be likely to move a person of ordinary temper "to violent passion."

Chapter XV, Sec. 3, Art. 2.

Sec. 2, Art. 32.

269. Under the English law the plea of provocation is not available when it has arisen from mere words or gestures. There is no such restriction in the Indian Code. The Commissioners observe on this point as follows: "Neither "the English law nor the French Code extends any indul-"gence to homicide which is the effect of anger, excited "by words alone. Mr. Livingstone goes still further: 'No words what-"ever,' says the Code of Louisiana, 'are an adequate cause, no gestures "merely shewing derision or contempt, no assault or battery so slight "as to shew that the intent was not to inflict great bodily harm.' We "greatly doubt whether any good reason can be assigned for this distinction. "It is an indisputable fact, that gross insults by word or gesture have as "great a tendency to move many persons to violent passion, as dangerous or "painful bodily injuries. Nor does it appear to us that passion excited by "insult is entitled to less indulgence than passion excited by pain."

Digest, Ch. XV, Sec. 2, Art. 34.

See Appendix, Note M, page 144.

270. With reference to these observations, Mr. Pyne makes the following remarks: "It is notorious that the most common mode of offering "insult among natives of all classes, is by the display of contemptuous "gestures and the use of irritating abuse, a habit so inveterate indeed as "to lose much of the offensiveness which would mark it when addressed "to communities more sensitive and alive to this description of annoy-"ance. An indignity offered to a person in a more civilized state by a "reflection upon his integrity, an imputation upon his courage, or a stain "upon his honor, might excite in the minds of such men sudden gusts of "passion which the law scarcely might control, but upon the mass of "Indian society, the refinement of feeling which barbs such attacks "is wanting, and no gestures, words or signs, could, I conceive, raise in "their minds that indignation of feeling at unmerited reflections, which "would justify the commission of voluntary culpable homicide under the "plea of 'grave' provocation emanating from such a cause; and I am "therefore disposed to think, from the obtuseness of feeling which per-"vades the community on this head, that the most grievous reproaches "would not exonerate the party offended from the guilt of murder, if in "resenting them he made use of any deadly weapon with the intention "of producing death, and it is moreover highly essential to the security "of life, that no such opening of committing murder under a mitigation "of punishment dependant upon contumelious gestures, contemptuous "actions, or insulting words, should be held out to the native community, "as from the inbred tendency, of the lower classes especially, to give "unrestrained freedom to the most indecent invectives, the deliberate "murderer may by the exercise of a little ingenuity reduce his offence to "the grade of manslaughter."

271. These remarks are deserving of attention, but it seems to us that Mr. Pyne has overlooked the discretion which is purposely left to the Court to judge whether the provocation be such as would be likely to move a person of ordinary temper to violent passion, not *any person*, it is to be understood, but a person of the same habits, manners, and feelings. A discreet Judge would of course take into consideration such points as are adverted to by Mr. Pyne, and would properly reject the plea of provocation by insulting words in one case, while he would as properly admit it in another, according as the party might be shewn to belong to a class sensitive to insults of this kind, or otherwise. The framers of the Code deemed it unadvisable to lay it down as a *rule* that insults by words or gestures should be considered an adequate cause of provocation, while, for the reason assigned, they thought it proper to *allow* the plea of provocation where it may be evident that such insults have as great a tendency as bodily injuries to excite violent passion. That there are many persons of such sensitive feelings among the higher ranks of the Natives of India is a truth which needs no proof, though unquestionably few of the great mass of the people would be much affected by words which to a European of the same rank and condition would cause the highest degree of irritation.

272. The English Commissioners make the following remark upon the article excluding the plea of provocation arising from mere words, &c. "We have framed the Article as nearly as we "could in conformity with the authorities, which, whilst "they, in many instances, recognize very slight causes of extenuation, "do not extend an express negative beyond the limits of our rule. It "seems to us, however, to be very questionable whether this rule, large "as it may seem, is strictly in accordance with principle, for words or "gestures may often be infinitely more irritating and provoking than a "personal injury of a trivial nature. It is extremely difficult, if not im-"possible, to define all the causes of provocation which ought to ex-"tenuate homicide, and we do not see any mode by which the object of "the law can be satisfactorily accomplished, unless it be by making the "existence of reasonable provocation, within certain limits, a matter of "fact to be decided by a jury. In France the difficulty has been in a "great degree evaded by the law introduced in 1832, enabling juries to "find 'attenuating circumstances,' and though we think a general law "of this kind is liable to serious objection, the occasional introduction of "a similar principle where precise definition is impracticable might per-"haps be desirable."

4th Report, p. 38.

273. The Indian Code does not allow the extenuation of "voluntary culpable homicide" to "manslaughter" on the plea of provocation, if that provocation be given by any thing done in obedience to the law, or authorized by the law of civil or criminal procedure, or done by a public servant in the exercise of his lawful powers, or by any person in the exercise of the right of private defence against the offender.

Clause 297, *Explanation.*

274. Mr. W. Hudleston, commenting on Clause 297, says generally, "the definition of manslaughter in the law of England appears to me "preferable to this—there it is clear and distinct, here it is vague and "liable to diversity of interpretation." He points particularly to the illustration (*d*) of provocation given in the exercise of the right of private defence, as contradicting the English law which he prefers. Mr. Norton adverting to the same illustration, "notices the construction given to "death caused by a party who in a sudden affray and in resentment of a "blow kills his antagonist—this is construed *murder* in case the blow re-"sented was given in self-defence following upon an assault by the killer. "Now, (he observes) this construction of guilt, depending on who was the "first actual personal aggressor and not on the suddenness and heat of "the affray, is quite as contrary to principle as it is to the English law." Mr. Norton concludes thus, "it is clear that the Commissioners have "not adverted to the doctrines and principles of the English law of self-"defence."

275. With all deference to Mr. Hudleston and Mr. Norton we are inclined to think that they are mistaken in averring that the illustration in question contradicts the law of England. The case is this—A attempts to pull Z's nose; Z in defence strikes A; whereupon A kills him. By the Penal Code this is not manslaughter but murder. What is it by the law of England? We apprehend that it is either "murder," or "homicide justifiable in self-defence." According to the Digest of the English Criminal law "homicide when necessary for self-defence is justifiable although the party using the plea was guilty of an assault" (as in this case) "which led to the fatal result," *provided*, among other things, that "he killed the assailant *from necessity in order to avoid immediate death.*" Now in the case supposed there is no appearance of any such necessity. It is therefore not "homicide justifiable in self-defence." We take it to be the alternative "murder." Mr. Norton thinks it is "manslaughter," "for "the actual first aggression *may* have been slight and the provocation to "it great, and the continuance of the affray and the heat and danger to "the killer arising out of it imminent and engrossing." But all this is contrary to the supposition. The aggression is supposed not to have been slight, but one extremely provocative, "A attempts to pull Z's nose," an aggression which if completed is viewed by the law as of so grave a character that if Z killed the aggressor he would not be guilty of murder but of manslaughter; no provocation whatever is alleged for the aggression; and there is no intimation that A was in any danger of further injury from Z if he had "retreated from conflict," which is another point to be proved in support of the plea of justification on the ground of self-defence. "It is agreed," it is said, "that if a man strike "another upon malice prepense and then fly to the wall, and there kill "him in his own defence, he is guilty of murder." See authorities quoted in Tomlin's Art. Homicide II. 2.

Chapter XV, Sec. 2, Art. 27.

276. Mr. A. D. Campbell says, "Contrary to my colleague, I think "under the reasons given in Note M, pages 144 and 145, that the principle "of this Clause (297) is right, but I entertain doubts of the propriety of "most of the virtual exceptions from its text, which are given under the "head of '*Explanation*.' I mean with regard to the words which follow "passion, for in what is done under cover of obedience to the law, and "still more under cover of its authority, or by public servants in the "lawful exercise of their powers, or even in self-defence, there may be "given such grave and such sudden provocation, as never, in justice, "ought to permit the death to amount to murder, but should confine it "to the lower crime of manslaughter. As well explained in the Notes, "the essence of extenuation from murder to this crime, consists entirely "in the provocation given."

277. We apprehend that grave provocation given by any thing done under *cover* of obedience to the law, or under *cover* of its authority, or by a public servant, or in defence, *in excess* of what is strictly warranted by the law, in point of violence, or as regards the means used, or the manner of using them, and the like, would be admissible in extenuation of homicide under this clause. For example, take the case of Wat Tyler referred to in the Note to this chapter. He was a public officer, a tax gatherer, who came to "exercise his lawful powers" in that capacity, but doing so in a manner unwarranted and highly offensive, Tyler was excited to "violent passion," and in his rage killed him on the spot. The Commissioners upon this say, "so far, indeed, should we "be from ranking a man who acted like Tyler with murderers, that we "conceive that a Judge would exercise a sound discretion in sentencing "such a man to the lowest punishment fixed by the law for man-"slaughter."

278. Under the above construction of the exceptions in respect to provocation subjoined to Clause 297, we see no valid objection to them, but if our construction be wrong, and we do not feel perfectly confident of its correctness, we should be disposed to think that some qualification is requisite.

279. We entirely agree with the authors of the Code in allowing such provocation as that which excited Wat Tyler to commit homicide, to be adequate in law, that is to say, in allowing the plea of provocation in cases in which the act done may have no tendency to cause pain or danger, or in any way to injure the person, and may wound only the honor or the affections; and it seems to us that this is allowed by the English law, by which, according to the Digest, passion excited by any act done "of an *insulting* character, to the person of the "party killing or of *any other person*," is sufficient to extenuate the guilt of killing.

Chapter XV, Sec. 2, Art. 32.

280. But manslaughter by the law of England includes not only cases in which homicide is wilful but extenuated, but "also where death is occasioned not wilfully, but culpa-"bly through want of reasonable care and caution, also "where death is occasioned not wilfully but in consequence of any un-"lawful violence or injury to, or endeavour to injure the person of any "other."

Chapter XV, Sec. 3, Art. 2.

281. We presume that Clause 304 of the Indian Code is intended to provide for such cases, among other cases of homicide described in Note M, page 148 as "culpable yet not voluntary." This clause will be considered in its proper place.

VOLUNTARY CULPABLE HOMICIDE BY CONSENT, Clause 298.

See Appendix, Note M, pages 145 and 146.

282. "The second mitigated form of voluntary culpable homicide," say the Indian Law Commissioners, "is that to which "we have given the name of 'voluntary culpable homi-"cide by consent.' It appears to us that this descrip-"tion of homicide ought to be punished, but that it "ought not to be punished so severely as murder." "Our reasons for not punishing it so severely as murder "are these: In the first place the motives which prompt "men to the commission of this offence are generally far more respect-"able than those which prompt men to the commission of murder. "Sometimes it is a strong sense of religious duty, sometimes a strong "sense of honor, not unfrequently of humanity. The soldier who, at "the entreaty of a wounded comrade, puts that comrade out of pain, "the friend who supplies laudanum to a person suffering the torment of "a lingering disease, the freedman who in ancient times held out the "sword that his master might fall on it, the high-born native of India "who stabs the females of his family at their own entreaty in order to "save them from the licentiousness of a band of marauders, would, "except in Christian societies, scarcely be thought culpable, and even in "Christian societies, would not be regarded by the public, and ought "not to be treated by the law as assassins."

"Again, this crime is by no means productive of so much evil to the "community as murder. One evil ingredient of the utmost importance "is altogether wanting to the offence of voluntary culpable homicide "by consent. It does not produce general insecurity. It does not "spread terror through society. When we punish murder with such "signal severity we have two ends in view. One end is that people may "not be murdered. Another end is that people may not live in constant "dread of being murdered. This second end is perhaps the more impor- "tant of the two. For if assassination were left unpunished the number "of persons assassinated would probably bear a very small proportion to "the whole population. But the life of every human being would be "passed in constant anxiety and alarm. This property of the offence of "murder is not found in the offence of voluntary culpable homicide by "consent. Every man who has not given his consent to be put to death "is perfectly certain that this latter offence cannot at present be com- "mitted on him, and that it never will be committed, unless he shall "first be convinced that it is his interest to consent to it. We know that "two or three midnight assassinations are sufficient to keep a city of a "million of inhabitants in a state of consternation during several weeks, "and to cause every private family to lay in arms and watchmen's rattles. "No number of suicides, or of homicides committed with the unextorted "consent of the person killed, could possibly produce such alarm among "the survivors."

"The distinction between murder and voluntary culpable homicide "by consent has never, as far as we are aware, been recognized by any "Code in the distinct manner in which we propose to recognize it. But "it may be traced in the Laws of many countries, and often, when neg- "lected by those who have framed the Laws, it has had a great effect on "the decisions of the tribunals, and particularly on the decisions of "tribunals popularly composed. It may be proper to observe that the "burning of a Hindoo widow by her own consent, though it is now, as "it ought to be, an offence by the regulations of every Presidency, is in "no Presidency punished as murder."

Chapter XV, Sec. 2, Art. 38.

283. In the Digest of the English Criminal Law it is declared that "homicide is neither justified nor extenuated by reason of any consent given by the party killed."

284. Of the clause in the Indian Code which recognizes "voluntary culpable homicide by consent" as a distinct offence less than murder, Sir R. Comyn observes, "the clause, it is true, is guarded by several "provisions, one of which relates to the state of mind of the party con- "senting to be killed, but, putting aside for argument's sake all religious "considerations of a future state, and merely adverting to man's strong "natural love of life, even in the most desperate circumstances, the mere "fact of a person consenting to be killed would indicate a morbid state "of mind sufficient to raise a doubt of his sanity. I cannot think that "in any country, or under any religion, *voluntary* homicide should be "leniently dealt with, or that any special circumstances, like those sup- "posed in the Note, would justify a law introducing the novel offence of "homicide by consent."

285. Sir J. Awdry, referring to the chapter of General Exceptions, says, "I agree to the exceptions grounded on the sanctity of human life, "and I wish that they (the Commissioners) had elsewhere followed up "the principle instead of providing that homicide by consent should not "be murder. The prerogative of mercy would much better be allowed "to apply when necessary to such cases, than a rule be laid down that a "man has to some extent a right to authorize its destruction."

286. Mr. Hudleston says, "It appears to me no alleviation of homicide that I have another's consent to kill him." Mr. A. D. Campbell on the other hand considers that the reasoning in pages 145 and 146 of Note M fully justifies the general principle.

287. Mr. Norton says, "I had imagined that the Clause 298 was "devised with a view mainly of punishing duels with a mitigated sen- "tence, and for distinguishing deaths by such a deliberate act from "murders. I was disposed under that impression to intimate my concur- "rence. But neither in the illustrations or the Notes is any such object "alluded to, and the only application of the clause seems to me to be to "cases of extraordinary local superstitions (better legislated upon speci- "fically) or to those which are almost or purely imaginary. The clause "in this view appears to me unnecessary and liable to ridicule."

288. Mr. Greenhill, a Judge of the Sudder Court at Bombay, understands this clause to include fatal duels.

289. The Judges of the Sudder Court, North-Western Provinces, observe that duelling is not specifically alluded to in the Code—but they conclude that it is provided for in Clause 294 and Clause 320 according as death or wounding may have ensued.

290. We observe that in the Draft of the Code first printed a duel was given as an illustration of "voluntary culpable homicide by consent." The wording of the definition was slightly altered on revision, but we think Clause 298 as it stands takes in the case of a person killed in a duel as one "who suffers death or takes the risk of death by his own choice." And if the clause be retained, if voluntary culpable homicide by consent be recognized as a distinct offence, we know not but it may be the best way of dealing with a species of crime which it has hitherto been found impossible to deter men from by the dread of capital punishment. It is in vain to denounce a penalty which is so contrary to the general sentiment, that except in cases marked by extreme malignity, or some special aggravation rousing indignation against the offender, it could not be executed without shocking the public sense. Yet this is just what must be said of the penalty of death threatened by the existing law to the person who kills another in what is called a fair duel—threatened but so rarely enforced, that it carries no terror with it, no terror at least of that which it threatens. It might be well worth a trial whether the certain expectation of punishment for culpable homicide by consent, the enforcement of which would surely be approved by the public mind, would not be more efficacious in preventing duels in which life is risked, than the present empty denunciation of the law. The penalty proposed is imprisonment of either description for a term which may extend to fourteen years, and must not be less than two years, which may be combined with fine at discretion.

291. It is probable that the authors of the Code were led to distinguish this form of voluntary culpable homicide, by the consideration of the case stated in the first illustration (*a*), of a Hindoo widow who with her own consent has been burned with the corpse of her husband. They were obliged to provide for this case which was already the subject of penal enactments in the Regulations for the Company's Courts. They found that "the burning of a Hindoo widow by her own consent though "it is now, as it ought to be, an offence by the Regulations of every "Presidency, is in no Presidency punished as murder." By Regulation XVII of 1829 of the Bengal Code, copied exactly in Regulation I of 1830 of Madras, and followed substantially in Regulation XVI of 1830 of Bombay, the offence is declared to be "culpable homicide," punishable in the Presidencies of Bengal and Madras by fine, or by imprisonment, or by both fine and imprisonment at the discretion of the Court, and in the same manner, except with a limitation of imprisonment to 10 years, in the Presidency of Bombay. This is not a case of "extraordinary *local* superstition" as Mr. Norton suggests, but a matter of national concern affecting a whole people, for which the Penal Code for India must legislate. The Commissioners had to consider whether they would rank this offence as murder, as falling within the definition thereof, or reduce it by a special exception to a lower grade of culpable homicide, following the existing law which had been enacted upon the most careful and solemn deliberation. They concluded that it ought not to be treated as murder. They had then to frame an exceptive definition, and the question would naturally arise whether the terms of the definition should be limited specifically to cases of Suttee, or be made general enough to comprehend other cases depending upon the same principle. This we presume was the process, the result we find in Clause 298, the terms of which are general, including all cases in which "the person whose death "is caused was above 12 years of age, and suffers death or takes the risk "of death, by his own choice."

292. We must here consider the remark of Mr. A. D. Campbell before alluded to, that the limitation as to age will, "contrary to what "is contemplated by the Code, make any one guilty of murder who in- "duces Suttee by a widow under 12 years of age." He conceives that the Commissioners meant merely to indicate the age at which persons may be taken generally to be capable of consenting, but with reference to the very early age at which females reach puberty in India and are married, he thinks that the above limitation will work differently from their intention, and exclude cases in which the party was capable of consenting and did give a free and intelligent consent to suffer death, which he supposes they did not mean to exclude.

293. We have before mentioned that there is a difference between Clause 69 and Clause 70 on this point. Under Clause 69 only a person above 12 years of age can give such a consent as will justify. Under Clause 70, construed as it must be with reference to Clause 31, a free and intelligent consent given by a person under 12 years of age will justify, if he were able to understand the nature and consequences of that to which he gave his consent. In the Note referring to these clauses there is no notice of this difference. In respect to both it is said indifferently that the consent required is the free and intelligent consent of a person "of ripe age." It seems however to be a condition of Clause 70, that the act in question should be proved to have been "bonâ fide for the benefit" of the party who has suffered by it, a condition which is not found in Clause 69.

See Appendix, Note B, page 108.

294. With respect to the case under consideration, we can hardly imagine that it was advisedly intended to make the difference between murder and culpable homicide by consent depend upon the circumstance of the widow at whose Suttee a person may have assisted, having been under or above 12 years of age, if she was "ripe" in both body and mind; supposing, for example, that she cohabited with her husband, and performed the ordinary duties of a wife with judgment and intelligence, and was one of whom there could be no doubt that she was able to "understand the nature and consequences of that to which she gave her consent." But it is clear that by Clause 298, if the widow be under 12, however ripe otherwise, any one assisting her to burn herself with the corpse of her husband must be found guilty of murder. We think this ought not to be. The obvious remedy is to reject the words "being above 12 years of age," and to substitute for them the words "being capable of making an intelligent choice," and to insert the same words in Clause 31 in addition to the words "intelligent consent."

295. Mr. Campbell further remarks with reference to the explanation annexed to Clause 298 that nothing is more common than for "native women of all ages to throw themselves into wells on the merest "momentary impulse of passion, excited generally by the most trifling "causes, such as an unexpected reprimand, a thwarted wish, the colic, &c., "and those who are afflicted by such female folly, are, as its alleged "instigators, too often harassed most unjustly by the Police, for fatal "consequences produced by the deceased alone." We are inclined to think that the explanation by which "inducing a person voluntarily to put himself to death" is declared to be voluntary culpable homicide by consent, would give an opening to a great deal of vexation and oppression in the manner suggested by Mr. Campbell. The word "inducing" is so comprehensive that it would afford ample verge and scope to malice and corruption to work safely in getting up pretended charges against innocent persons founded on circumstances in their domestic history which may be plausibly distorted, and in causing distressing inquiries thereupon into family matters. We are led to conclude that it will be better to omit the explanation. Cognizance would then be taken only of such cases of purposed inducement to suicide as clearly amount to murder. There may indeed arise cases in which it would be improper to treat the person who had induced another to commit suicide as guilty of murder, although the circumstances of the case might be clearly within the definition, and the purpose might be evident, as for example where the high-born native of India induces the females of his family to take poison in order to save themselves from pollution in an expected assault of a licentious soldiery, but such are cases to which, we agree with Sir J. Awdry, the prerogative of mercy would properly apply.

VOLUNTARY CULPABLE HOMICIDE IN DEFENCE. Clause 303.

296. The third mitigated form of voluntary culpable homicide designated as "voluntary culpable homicide in defence," is defined in Clause 299. The punishment proposed is the same as for manslaughter, viz., imprisonment of either description for a term which may extend to fourteen years, or fine, or both.

See Appendix, Note M, pages 146 and 147.

297. The Commissioners observe that this portion of the law is closely connected with the law of private defence, and must necessarily partake of its imperfections. But wherever the limits of the right of private defence may be placed, and with whatever degree of accuracy they may be marked, they are inclined to think that it will be always expedient to make a separation between murder and homicide falling within the definition in this clause. "The chief reason is that the law itself "invites men to the very verge of the crime designated as voluntary "culpable homicide in defence. It prohibits such homicide indeed; but "it authorizes acts which lie very near to such homicide, and this cir- "cumstance greatly mitigates the guilt of such homicide."

298. In cases in which it prohibits homicide, it authorizes the infliction of any harm short of death which may be necessary for the purpose of defence. "And it seems difficult (they observe) to conceive "that circumstances which would be a full justification of any violence "short of homicide should not be a mitigation of the guilt of homicide. "It is to be considered also (they say) that the line between those "aggressions which it is lawful to repel by killing, and those which it is "not lawful so to repel, is in this Code, and must be in every Code, to "a great extent an arbitrary line."

299. Referring to Clause 76 which authorizes the infliction of death in defence in certain cases of assault, and to Clause 79 which authorizes the same in certain cases of theft, mischief and criminal trespass, the definition declares that homicide committed in defence in *other* cases, under circumstances that would have justified it if the right of defence extended to the causing of death in such cases, is not murder, but voluntary culpable homicide in defence. An illustration (*c*) is given to shew that it is murder if the circumstances would not have justified the infliction of death, even if the right of defence extended so far. This appears clear enough. But Mr. Norton says, "With every effort to understand Clause 299, turning back to "the clauses therein referred to, and their explanations and illustrations, "applying the illustrations subjoined, and consulting the Notes on this "clause, which form no constituent part of the Code, I am obliged "to give it up in despair." He adds, "if I were to judge from my own "capacity, I should doubt whether this portion of the Code was intelli- "gible to any class." We need not point out the exaggeration which is so obvious in these remarks, as it is in Mr. Norton's criticisms on many other parts of the Code. We shall only observe, that among the many persons who have reviewed the Code, no other appears to have found it impossible to comprehend the definition in question, though several persons complain of it as obscure.

300. Mr. Hudleston is one of those who find fault with this definition. Having remarked that "it is not particularly intelligible, nor made so by the very peculiar illustrations;" he adds, regarding the substance of the enactment, "as observed by Mr. Blane, the natives of India could "never understand the subtleties of this part of the Code, nor in my "opinion those of any other country. The restrictions of the Code upon "the right of private defence seem little suited to encourage among the "people of India a manly spirit or energetic resistance to the attacks of "robbers." Mr. Blane, after the remark quoted by Mr. Hudleston as above, expresses his apprehension that the first case of punishment of this kind would have a disheartening effect. Upon similar grounds the same gentlemen and others object, as we have before noticed, to the rules regarding the right of private defence. It is surprising however that these gentlemen, particularly Mr. Hudleston, who pointedly observes that he has not overlooked the explanations in Note M, should not have perceived that the tendency of the enactment in question is to favor persons who have been led in an energetic exercise of the right of defence to step beyond the prescribed line. The law of England, of which Mr. Hudleston so often declares his preference, treats as murder what is here brought under the mitigated description of voluntary culpable homicide in defence, a mitigation introduced, say the Commissioners, "in order "that the Courts may have it in their power to inflict a slight or a merely "nominal punishment on acts which though not within the letter of the "law which authorizes killing in self-defence, are yet within the reason "of the law."

301. Mr. Norton it seems would adhere to the English law, of which he says—"the lines of separation of the various shades of guilt or of "justification may be narrow, but I conceive by the English law they "are clear and well founded in principle."

302. We think that the provision contained in Clause 299 is right in principle; and though at the first perusal the definition may appear somewhat obscure, yet it seems to us that it needs only to be deliberately analyzed to become perfectly clear, and we doubt whether it could be recast in a more lucid form.

PUNISHMENTS FOR OFFENCES AFFECTING LIFE.

303. With respect to the punishments for murder, viz., death, or transportation for life, or rigorous imprisonment for life to which fine may be added, Mr. Hudleston says—"I "prefer the provisions of our Regulations, which define "the grounds for mitigating the capital punishment." He does not specify the provisions which he had in his mind. In the general law relating to murder in the Madras Regulations, which Mr. Hudleston must be understood to refer to, there is no such definition: but a discretion is given to the Judges not to pass sentence of death, if there appear to them to be "alleviating circumstances" in the case—a discretion sufficiently arbitrary.

Reg. VIII of 1802, Sec. 15.

Madras Reg. VII of 1802, Section 15, Cl. 2, corresponding with Sec. 3, Reg. IV of 1797, and Sec. 15, Cl. 2, Reg. VII of 1803, of Bengal.

Beng. Reg. XII, 1825, Sec. 7, Cl. 1.

304. Mr. Hudleston objects to the punishment for manslaughter as too severe: but the maximum punishment for this offence by the Code is imprisonment for fourteen years, while the law of the Madras Presidency *authorizes* imprisonment for *life* in cases of culpable homicide not amounting to wilful murder, although seven years is the ordinary limit. The law was the same in Bengal till 1825, when seven years was fixed as the maximum limit. The law of Bombay limits the term of imprisonment to ten years, and Mr. Greenhill, one of the Judges of the Sudder Court at that Presidency, expresses his opinion that the extreme punishment proposed by the Code is unnecessarily severe. The Judges of the Sudder Court, North-Western Provinces, observe, that the penalties laid down for "culpable homicide by consent," and "in defence," are heavier than our Courts "have been accustomed to inflict for the same sort of offence," but that they are unwilling to designate them as too severe without having before them the Code of Procedure.

Sec. 27, Reg. XIV of 1827, of Bombay.

North-Western

Cls. 302 and 303.

305. Mr. A. D. Campbell, of the Madras Sudder Court, thinks the penalty in all the Clauses 301 to 303, but particularly in Clause 303, is too severe, and that too much discretion is left to the Judges.

306. Mr. J. F. Thomas, of the Madras Presidency, with reference to the same clauses, says, "It would be well I conceive if some rule were "laid down which should distinguish cases where persons guilty of "voluntary culpable homicide may be, comparatively, but little to blame, "from cases which come within a shade of murder. The provisions as "they now stand in the case of manslaughter and homicide in defence, "are, I think, open to the objection, that the same measure of penalty "may be inflicted on the least as on the most aggravated case, and all is "left to the discretion of the Judges. Is this latitude necessary or "expedient?"

307. Colonel Sleeman adverting to the provision of Clause 302, which prescribes two years as the minimum of imprisonment to which a person convicted of "voluntary culpable homicide by consent" shall be sentenced, advises that this restriction be omitted, and that the offence be put exactly upon the same footing as the other mitigated forms of voluntary culpable homicide in Clauses 301 and 303. It appears to us however, referring to the strong opinions against permitting the consent of the person who has suffered death to be a ground of mitigation at all, that the distinction which has been made, by prescribing the minimum above mentioned, is judicious.

308. The discretion to be vested in the Judges in meting the punishment for offences, and the fitness of the scale of penalties to be applied by them, are general questions which fall to be considered in treating of the chapter of punishments. We shall only say here that it does not appear to us that the penalties in the clause we have been considering are out of proportion with reference to the scale which seems to have been generally kept in view, or that a greater latitude of discretion has been given to the Judge in this than in other parts of the Code.

309. We come now to Clause 304, which provides for death caused by any act or illegal omission "so rash or negligent as to indicate a want of due regard for human life," described in the Note as homicide "culpable yet not voluntary." The next Clause 305 provides for cases in which the act or illegal omission which caused death is a distinct offence by itself. In such cases the punishment of the distinct offence is to be added to that prescribed by Clause 304 for the negligent causing of death. The definition in Clause 304 appears to include the cases

HOMICIDE CULPABLE YET NOT VOLUNTARY.

described in the 2nd* and 3rd† clauses of the Article which contains the definition of manslaughter in the Digest prepared by Her Majesty's Commissioners on Criminal Law, the cases in the 1st clause of that Article being those to which the definition of manslaughter is confined by Clause 297 of this Code.

Chap. XV, Section 3, Art. 2.

310. The Indian Law Commissioners observe that "there will prob-"ably be little difference of opinion as to the expediency "of providing a punishment for the rash and negligent "causing of death. But it may be thought that we have "dealt too leniently by the offender who, while committing a crime, "causes death, which he did not intend to cause or know himself to be "likely to cause."

See Appendix, Note M, page 148.

"The law as we have framed it differs widely from the English law. "'If,' says Sir William Blackstone, 'one intends to do another felony, "and undesignedly kills a man, this is murder,' and he gives the following "illustration of the rule: 'If one gives a woman with child a medicine "to produce abortion, and it operates so violently as to kill the woman, "this is murder in the person who gave it.'"

"Under the provisions of our Code, this case would be very differently "dealt with according to circumstances. If A kills Z by administering "abortives to her with the knowledge that those abortives are likely to "cause her death, he is guilty of voluntary culpable homicide, which "will be voluntary culpable homicide by consent, if Z agreed to run "the risk, and murder if Z did not so agree. If A causes miscarriage "to Z not intending to cause Z's death, nor thinking it likely that he "shall cause Z's death, but so rashly or negligently as to cause her death, "A is guilty of culpable homicide not voluntary, and will be liable to the "punishment provided for the causing of miscarriage, increased by im-"prisonment for a term not exceeding two years. Lastly, if A took such "precautions that there was no reasonable probability that Z's death "would be caused, and if the medicine were rendered deadly by some "accident which no human sagacity could have foreseen, or by some "peculiarity in Z's constitution such as there was no ground whatever "to expect, A will be liable to no punishment whatever on account of "her death, but will of course be liable to the punishment provided for "causing miscarriage."

311. The Commissioners offer arguments in defence of this part of the Code. Supposing "it will be admitted that, when an act is in itself "innocent, to punish a person who does it because bad consequences "which no human wisdom could have foreseen have followed from it, "would be in the highest degree barbarous and absurd," they ask, if the act be itself a high offence, ought that circumstance alone to make the person punishable for the consequences of his misfortune—to be liable, for example, to the punishment of murder if death was the issue of it? They argue that it ought not—that to pronounce a man guilty of an offence because a misfortune befell him while he was committing another offence, is to confound all the boundaries of crime. Proceeding

* "Where death is occasioned not wilfully but culpably through want of reasonable care and caution."

† "Where death is occasioned not wilfully, but in consequence of any unlawful violence, or injury to, or endeavour to injure the person of any other."

with their argument they observe, that "to punish as a murderer every "man who while committing a heinous offence causes death by pure "misadventure, is a course which evidently adds nothing to the security "of human life." "The only good effect which such punishment can "produce will be to deter people from committing any of those offences "which turn into murders what are in themselves mere accidents. It is "in fact an addition to the punishment of those offences, and it is an "addition made in the very worst way." They conclude "that when a "person engaged in the commission of an offence causes death by pure "accident, he should suffer only the punishment of his offence without "any addition on account of such accidental death."

312. Upon this subject the English Law Commissioners make the following remarks in their 4th Report: "It may be "very questionable whether, in point of principle, an "effect wholly unexpected, and unconnected with the intention and act "of the party, except by accident, can properly be made the foundation "of criminal responsibility; for as the object of punishment is the pre-"vention of crime, it ought properly to be annexed to such acts as are in "themselves culpable by reason of their mischievous tendency, and the "intention with which they are done, and not to such as are simply "accidental and unintentional. By the law of England this doctrine is "in many instances reversed, and the criminal intention incident to the "act intended but not perpetrated, or not in question, is supposed to be "transferred to the act which was the mere accidental consequence. "Thus a party doing the same act in the same manner, but who by mere "accident and not through want of caution, kills another, may be, accord-"ing to his intention in doing that act, though such intention be wholly "unconnected with the accidental result, guilty either of murder where "his intention was to commit a felony, or of manslaughter where his "intention was to commit a bare misdemeanor or trespass, or an act "*malum in se*, or purely innocent, where the act, although unlawful, was "merely *malum prohibitum*." After giving examples illustrative of the impropriety of the English law in this respect, they say in conclusion—"whilst we think that a mere accidental killing in the "endeavor to do an illegal or criminal act, wholly uncon-"nected with any danger or mischief to the person cannot on any just "principle be brought within the scope of the law of murder, it appears "to us that the same objections do not apply, or at all events, do not "apply with the same force, to the case where death is occasioned in the "endeavor to commit a crime with violence to the person or habitation of "another, and consequently is attended with some degree of risk to the "person, although it may not be so great as to constitute murder without "resorting to the consideration of the offender's intention. For here the "result is not a matter of pure accident wholly unconnected with the "criminal intent, and consequently the enhanced punishment is justified "by one of the main principles of Penal Laws, namely, the prevention "of crimes of violence attended with danger to the person." In the 7th Report however they retract this qualification, and express a positive opinion that "the intent to commit a minor crime ought "not in any case by reason of a purely accidental conse-"quence to be deemed equivalent for penal purposes to a wilful causing "of that consequence." Thus the English Commissioners arrived in the end at the same conclusion with the authors of the Indian Penal Code; and they modified their definition of wilful killing accordingly by omitting

Page 28.

Page 29.

Page 28.

after the words "to kill," the words "or do great bodily harm," which stood in the Draft contained in their 4th Report, according to the view *then* entertained by them, as expressed in the above quotation. The provisions on this subject in Mr. Livingstone's Code are also, as observed by the Indian Law Commissioners, framed on the same principles, though they differ in details from those under consideration.

313. Mr. Norton says of Clause 304, that he considers the provision contained in it to be just and expedient, but that he is quite unable to reconcile it with Clauses 69 to 72. He does not however point out any inconsistency, and we cannot conjecture what he alludes to.

314. Although he approves of Clause 304, Mr. Norton says, "when I "find under the next clause and its illustration that killing in the at- "tempt to commit a rape is a specimen of this rash and negligent way of "killing, and that such offence, with certain exceptions, is to be punished "as a combination of two offences, and either to be doubly punished, or "punished by substitution of the punishment attached to the commission "of the crime attempted, I am lost in confusion and uncertainty. I "have equal difficulty in learning what the law is, and how to apply "it." We think that Mr. Norton could hardly have been left in such perplexity, if he had considered the enactments here in question with due attention. He would have understood that Clause 304 provides for a case in which death has been caused by culpable rashness, or negligence, *not* in committing or attempting to commit an offence, while Clause 305 provides for the aggravated case of death so caused, in committing or attempting to commit an offence. In the latter case the punishment is to be that prescribed for the offence committed or attempted, with the punishment of involuntary culpable homicide (Clause 304) superadded. If the attempt be an offence by itself, it is explained that still the punishment of the *offence attempted*, and *not* the punishment *of the attempt* is to be awarded. We see no confusion or uncertainty here; but enactments so clear and intelligible as to leave no excuse for error in applying them.

315. Mr. Norton apparently finds fault with the illustration under Clause 305, namely, the case of a man attempting to commit a rape on a woman, and in the attempt involuntarily causing her death. Here the death of the woman being, to use the words of the English Commissioners, "an effect wholly unexpected and unconnected with the intention and act of the party, except by accident," is a homicide, which though culpable is not voluntary, and therefore does not fall under the definition of murder in this Code, nor under that proposed by the English Commissioners in their Digest; the homicide is culpable, because the circumstances evince on the part of the offender "a want of due regard for human life." On this ground the culprit is punishable, while he is punishable also for the crime which he intended to perpetrate, that is rape. Under this double liability he may be sentenced to rigorous imprisonment for a period extending to 16 years.

316. Mr. Norton does not explain particularly why he objects to the illustration, or how he thinks the case ought to be treated. Mr. Hudleston objects to the illustration "as a violation of all sound principle." "By the law of England," says he, "the act is murder, and so it ought to be." This objection founded on the authority of the law of England may be considered sufficiently answered by the observations we have quoted from the English Law Commissioners.

317. Mr. Pyne observes, "It is possible to conceive circumstances "under which the ravishment of a delicate woman would in all probability be attended with fatal consequences; and instances are not wanting where brutal excitement has led a plurality of ravishers to violate "a woman. To cause death by such means appears to me an offence "equally grave with culpable homicide. Take for example a rape committed on an infant 6 or 7 years of age from which death ensues; a "recent case of this kind has come before the Courts." It is clear that the case here last mentioned would fall under voluntary culpable homicide, because it would be a just inference from the circumstances that the offender knew he was likely by his brutal act to cause the death of the infant; and wherever the circumstances justified such an inference the offender ought to be charged with murder.

318. Referring to the words "an offence *other than the offence defined in Clause* 327," which appear in Clause 305, Sir H. Seton questions the propriety of "defining an offence by reference to another, not specifically, but as contained in a subsequent section of the Code," and Colonel Sleeman suggests that the words in italics should be omitted. They might be omitted without affecting the definition, for it is clear enough that the offence described in Clause 327 is but a lesser degree of that to which Clause 304 applies, and of course merges in the latter. The words appear to have been introduced to guard against even the semblance of inaccuracy.

319. Mr. G. W. Bacon thinks there are many cases of homicide in perpetration of another offence that have no connection with "pure accident," or "rashness or negligence," and taking such to be murder, as being attended with violence, he would punish them accordingly. Upon this we have to observe, that when homicide is committed in the perpetration of another offence, if it is not accidental nor attributable to rashness or negligence, it must fall within the definition of voluntary culpable homicide, and will be punishable as murder, as Mr. Bacon thinks it should be.

320. Mr. A. D. Campbell observes that he can nowhere discover in the Code the provision for death by pure accident alluded to in Note M. There is no such provision in the Code, and none is required. It is unnecessary to declare formally that an act purely accidental is not an offence, if the definitions are so framed, as we believe they are, that the effect of a mere accident cannot be charged as an offence.

321. Upon Clause 306, relating to the abetment of suicide committed by a child under 12 years of age and others incapable of rational judgment, Mr. J. F. Thomas says, "The inducement to commit the offence "here pointed out must be in the ordinary course of events so exceedingly "slight, that it scarcely seems necessary to place the offence on a level "with the most atrocious murder, and annex the penalty of death, &c. "It would in practice probably be found that a less penalty than death "would be sufficient to check the commission of the crime." Upon Clause 307 relating to the abetment of suicide in general, he says, "I "greatly doubt the necessity of such heavy penalties to repress the "offence. Five years' imprisonment where fine is imposed, I should consider ample, and better adapted to the character of the offence in the

"existing state of society. If the rule 'to do an act (Clause 24) denote "omission' is to be applied largely to this clause, it will require great "modification in my opinion, for the instances of suicide which might be "prevented by persons are numerous; and at present they have not the "most remote idea that they are acting criminally, and abetting a penal "act by such omission. They ought not therefore to be liable to the "heavy penalties here provided."

322. These clauses refer to abetment "by aid," the definition of which contained in Clause 97 shews that the offence consists in a person "doing any act or omitting what he is legally bound to do with the *in-"tention* of aiding," &c. The question to what extent *omissions* ought to be made punishable when they produce, are intended to produce, or are known to be likely to produce the same evil effects as *acts*, is discussed in the Note to the chapter under consideration. The conclusion is that such omissions, if they are illegal according to the explanation of that term in Clause 28, ought to be punished in the same manner as acts, and this is the rule of the Code. It seems to us that the rule would fall to be applied under these clauses chiefly in such a case as this, where a person legally bound to take care of the person of another has by an illegal omission of his duty *intentionally* given him the opportunity, or permitted him to obtain the means of killing himself.

323. It would apply also, we conceive, in the case of a person seeing another preparing to destroy himself, say by hanging, and allowing him to accomplish his purpose without any attempt to prevent him, if as may be expected, the law of procedure makes it a common duty incumbent upon all men to assist in preventing offences about to be committed in their presence. The intention here would be inferrible from the circumstances. In the former case collateral proof of the intention would be requisite. But we apprehend that it is *active* aid which is principally intended in these clauses, and to which the higher penalties are meant to be applied.

324. Clause 306 corresponds with Clause 298* inasmuch as the latter excepts from its provisions the same classes of persons as are mentioned in the former, and leaves the offence of causing the death of such persons, though with their consent, to be dealt with as murder; so Clause 306 attaches the penalties of murder to the offence defined therein. We have the same remarks to make here as are made upon Clause 298, as to the age of 12 years being fixed absolutely as that under which a child is to be taken as incapable of forming an intelligent judgment.

325. Clause 307, again, corresponds with Clause 298 in attaching to the offence defined in it, which is closely allied to 'culpable homicide by consent,' the same punishments as are applicable to the latter.

326. In concluding our review of the provisions regarding "offences affecting life," we think it proper to notice a point on which there is a difference of considerable importance between the law of England and the Indian Code.

Digest, Chapter XV, Section 1, Art. 7.

327. "The law" (of England) "takes no cognizance "of homicide unless the party injured die of the injury "within one year and a day thereafter." There is no such limitation in the Indian Code.

---

* 2nd Proviso.

328. In their 4th Report the English Criminal Law Commissioners observe upon the above rule, which they characterise as arbitrary, that "it cannot but be regarded as some sacrifice in point of principle, to allow a murderer to escape, merely because "the deceased, from natural strength of constitution, or from accidental "circumstances connected with the injury, happened to linger for "more than a year." They did not however "consider themselves to be "justified in suggesting any alteration of this ancient rule," remarking that they were not aware that any practical inconvenience had resulted from it.

Page 29.

329. We find that in an early Draft of the Indian Code there was a limitation. The reason for abandoning it is not recorded, but we may conjecture that it was deemed objectionable on account of "the sacrifice in point of principle" which it involves. Probably the English Criminal Law Commissioners would have thought this a sufficient reason for not admitting a limitation, if it had not been for the "ancient rule." There is no limitation in the Regulations of Bengal and Madras; but the law of Bombay bars the charge of murder if death does not take place within six months.

330. We are decidedly of opinion that it is not advisable to follow the English law in admitting a limitation which is confessedly objectionable in principle, and which would be new in India, except within the Presidency of Bombay and the jurisdiction of Her Majesty's Courts.

331. In explanation of the provisions contained in Clauses 308 and 309, the Commissioners make the following observations: "These clauses appear to us absolutely necessary to the "completeness of the Code. We have provided, under "the head of bodily hurt, for cases in which hurt is "inflicted in an attempt to murder; under the head of "assault, for assaults committed in attempting to murder; under the head of criminal trespass, for some criminal trespasses "committed in order to murder. But there will still remain many "atrocious and deliberate attempts to murder which are not trespasses, "which are not assaults, and which cause no hurt. A, for example, digs "a pit in his garden, and conceals the mouth of it, intending that Z may "fall in and perish there. Here A has committed no trespass, for the "ground is his own; and no assault, for he has applied no force to Z. "He may not have caused bodily hurt, for Z may have received a timely "caution, or may not have gone near the pit; but A's crime is evidently "one which ought to be punished as severely as if he had laid hands on "Z with the intention of cutting his throat."

ATTEMPTS to commit voluntary culpable homicide.

See Appendix, Note M, page 150.

332. Again they say, "similar attempts may be made to commit "voluntary culpable homicide in any of the three mitigated forms. A, "for example, is excited to violent passion by Z, and fires a pistol intending to kill Z. If the shot proves fatal, A will be guilty of manslaughter, and he surely ought not to be exempted from all punishment "if the ball only grazes the intended victim."

"It is to meet cases of this description that Clauses 308 and 309 are intended."

333. Sir R. Comyn, Mr. Norton, Mr. Hudleston, and Mr. James Thomas object to the phraseology of these clauses as vague and obscure Sir R. Comyn particularly observes "that carrying an act or omission to the length the offender *contemplates*, as sufficient to cause death," is a mode of expression utterly destitute of legal precision.

334. Mr. Hudleston says he cannot perceive the necessity of either of these provisions. His colleague Mr. A. D. Campbell, on the contrary, thinks them fully justified by the reasons given in the Note, but he considers it "desirable that they should if possible be made less obscure."

335. Colonel Sleeman proposes to substitute the word "considers" for "contemplates" in the passage referred to by Sir R. Comyn. And observing that "the door of repentance should be kept open as long as possible in law, as well as in religion," he suggests the addition of the following words—"and does not himself repent and interpose to save the intended victim from the consequences of that act or omission."

336. Mr. Greenhill observes with reference to Clause 309, that the terms "voluntary culpable homicide" used therein include murder, which the illustrations shew was not intended.

337. It is clear from the note as well as from the illustrations, that Clause 309 was meant to apply to attempts to cause death under circumstances which if death ensued would make the offence to be voluntary culpable homicide of one of the mitigated descriptions specified in Clause 295, attempts to commit murder being provided for expressly by Clause 308, and it appears to us to be advisable to declare this by introducing after the words "voluntary culpable homicide," the words "of one of the three mitigated descriptions enumerated in Clause 295," or inserting instead of "he would be guilty of voluntary culpable homicide," "he would be guilty of manslaughter or voluntary culpable homicide by consent," or "voluntary culpable homicide in defence."

338. As to the word "contemplates," which is thought not to be sufficiently precise, it does not appear to us that the meaning is at all doubtful, or that it would be made clearer by adopting Colonel Sleeman's suggestion. We do not think it necessary to alter this word or otherwise to change the phraseology of these clauses (except as above suggested in Clause 309,) with a view to elucidation and precision. It appears to us that with the aid of the illustrations the sense can scarcely be mistaken by any one of ordinary understanding giving his mind fairly to the consideration of the subject.

339. By Clause 308, a person attempting to commit murder though he fail in his purpose, if he shall have taken all the steps, which according to his plan were necessary to accomplish it, will be punishable with transportation for life, or imprisonment for life, or for a term not less than seven years, and also by fine. This clause is applicable to cases in which no harm is done. Where bodily hurt is inflicted in such an attempt, the offence will be liable to the same punishment, but under a different clause,* and so in cases of assault† and trespass.‡

340. Under the law of England as it stands at present, attempts to commit murder, although no bodily injury be inflicted, are punishable with transportation for life, or for any term not less than fifteen years, or imprisonment for any term not exceeding three years. The Criminal Law Commissioners have recommended that the minimum of transportation be reduced to seven years.

Digest, Chapter XV, Section 5, Art. 3.

* Clause 320. † Clause 343. ‡ Clause 429.

341. By Clause 309, attempts to cause death under circumstances which would reduce the offence, if the object were accomplished, to one of the mitigated forms of voluntary culpable homicide, carried to the same point as specified in Clause 308, will render the offender liable to be punished with imprisonment for a term which may extend to three years, or fine, or both. If killing a person in a duel fall under Clause 298, then any person shooting at another in a duel, we apprehend, will be within this clause, whether the other be wounded or not.

342. In the Digest of the English Criminal Law Commissioners it is proposed that whoever shall by any means whatever wilfully endanger the life of any person shall be liable to imprisonment for a term not exceeding three years, or fine, or both.

343. "Although no evil effect be produced" (say Her Majesty's Commissioners) "yet criminal endeavors consisting in manifest overt acts ought justly to be dealt with as penal." This is the principle upon which the provisions in question are founded.

344. With respect to the amendment proposed by Colonel Sleeman with the view of saving a person who having laid a plan of murder repents, as in the example of A intending to murder Z by means of a spring gun (in the illustration (*a*) subjoined to Clause 308), if A after setting the gun repents and removes it, we are of opinion that it is unnecessary, for in the case supposed we apprehend that without the words proposed to be added, A would not be chargeable under Clause 308. The last act undoing the previous act, he could not, we conceive, be charged with that previous act as an offence, unless for anything he knew it might have had effect in the mean time. For example, if A set the spring gun in the morning expecting that Z would pass the place in the afternoon and knowing that he could not pass before noon—in this case if A repenting of his purpose removed the spring gun before noon, that is, before it was possible it could have effect, it appears to us that the last act would exonerate him; not so, if he only knew that Z was to pass sometime in the course of the day, it might be the same hour, and that it was a mere accident that he did not pass before he removed the spring gun. In the former case he kept it in his power to prevent the mischief intended and did take the necessary step to prevent it in time.

Clauses 310 and 311. THUGGEE.

345. The act of the Indian Legislature No. XXX of 1836, made it an offence punishable with imprisonment for life with hard labour to have belonged to a gang of *Thugs*. In the first of these two clauses it is explained that "whoever "belongs or has at any time belonged to any gang of persons associated "for the purpose of gaining a livelihood by inveigling and murdering "travellers in order to take the property of such travellers, is designated "as a 'Thug.'" In Clause 311 it is prescribed that a Thug shall be punished with transportation for life, or imprisonment of either description for life, and shall be also liable to fine.

346. Mr. Greenhill thinks that the words "gaining a livelihood" in Clause 310 are "unnecessary and objectionable," and it seems to us that their introduction imposes a restriction not within the intention of the Legislature in the laws passed on this subject just before and after the date of the Code. It appears therefore to be a question for the consideration of Government whether they should be retained. It may be better to insert the word "habitually" before "associated" and to omit the words between "of" and "inveigling." We are not aware why transportation for life was not authorized in Act XXX of 1836, and no reason occurs to us for excepting "Thugs" in particular from this mode of punishment which is prescribed generally for offences of the same degree.

OF THE CAUSING OF MISCARRIAGE.

347. Clauses 312 and 313 contain provisions on the subject of abortion. By the former the woman herself if she voluntarily cause herself to miscarry, and every person who voluntarily causes a woman to miscarry, except for the purpose of saving her life, is liable to punishment. The law of England does not punish the woman; and she is not punishable by Mr. Livingstone's Code. The woman is punishable by the French Code.

See Appendix, Note M, page 151.

348. The framers of the Indian Code themselves express apprehensions that their provisions, or any other provisions on this subject, may be abused in this country to the vilest purposes, and they say that if they cannot in the Code of Procedure lay down rules to prevent such abuse they are inclined to think it would be their duty to advise that the offence of abortion, where the mother is a party to it, should be left wholly unpunished, rather than it should be repressed by provisions which would occasion more suffering to the innocent than to the guilty.

349. Mr. J. F. Thomas says of Clause 312: "This clause appears to "me to confound offences distinct in themselves, and which should not be "visited by a like measure of punishment."

"The high caste young widow, who, to hide her shame, should at the "risk of life cause herself to miscarry does not, under the peculiar "circumstances in which she is placed by the institutions of society, "commit an offence in any respect of like criminality with the seducer "of a young girl, or married woman, who to cover her crime should "cause such woman to miscarry. The offences are so distinct that I think "separate and special provisions should be made for them. In the one "instance a penalty of not less than two years would only meet the case; "in the other a trifling punishment in addition to the degradation of a "criminal trial would be ample. I much doubt the policy of providing "heavy penalties for the repression of the offence of causing miscarriage "by the woman herself, whilst the barbarous institutions of the country "create the offence. My experience would also lead me to propose that "miscarriage should be defined. I have known groundless and false "charges of this nature brought and the parties exposed to the pain of a "criminal investigation, when there was no evidence whatever as to the "existence of the fœtus, and it was not established therefore that the "woman was with child, or that there had been an abortion. 'Every "woman being with child' may open the door to vexatious accusations. "I would throw on the accuser the *onus* of establishing *in limine* that "the fœtus was distinctly formed and manifest on its abortion, before "the charge of causing miscarriage should be entertained. If this was "not alleged in the charge it should not be held that 'the woman was "with child';—an explanation might be added that to be with child in "the eye of the law, the charge must allege the abortion of a fœtus "fully formed."

350. Mr. Hudleston observes that the remarks of Mr. Thomas appear to deserve consideration, in which Mr. A. D. Campbell concurs.

Mr. Sharkey and Mr. Greenhill suggest that it should be specified that the woman was "quick with child." Mr. Sharkey opposes Mr. Thomas's views generally and particularly in regard to the punishment proposed, which he thinks by no means sufficient, as the offence is often little short of murder.

351. Mr. James Thomas also considers the punishment inadequate. Mr. Pyne says, "This is one of those offences which if death takes place "it is difficult to distinguish from murder. I do not consider that the "combined penalties provided in Clause 312 and in Clause 304 are sufficient to ensure that degree of caution which the preservation of human "life demands." Referring to Clause 313, he observes that "the offence "here is of a deeper dye, and yet if not aggravated by hurt is not liable "to greater punishment. It might without undue harshness be doubled."

352. We apprehend that an attempt to procure abortion issuing in the death of the woman may sometimes fall under "homicide by consent" and sometimes under "murder" according to the circumstances, where it appears that the party making the attempt knew from the condition of the woman or otherwise that it was likely to cause her death.

See Appendix, Note M, page 148.

353. As to the Clause 313, we conceive that generally some hurt will be caused which will afford ground for enhancing the punishment.

354. Colonel Sleeman says: "The evils inflicted upon society in India "by the police under the power invested in them by this law are so very "great, and must unavoidably continue to be so if it remains in force, "that I should certainly expunge it from the Code. I would merely "enact Clause 312: 'Whoever voluntarily causes a woman with child to "miscarry without her free and voluntary consent, except in good faith for "the purpose of saving her life, shall be punished with imprisonment "of either description for a term which may extend to three years, or "to fine, or both.' To this should be added the cumulative clause."

355. We are on the whole inclined to support Colonel Sleeman's suggestion, but it seems to us that it will be sufficient to omit from Clause 312 the words before "every person" and to let the rest stand. The next Clause 313 may be left unaltered.

Of Hurt.

356. By Clause 314 it is explained that "all bodily pain, disease, and infirmity, is designated as 'hurt.'"

357. "We have found it," say the authors of the Code, "very difficult to draw a line between those bodily hurts which "are serious and those which are slight. To draw such "a line with perfect accuracy is indeed absolutely impossible; but it is far better that such a line should be drawn though "rudely, than that offences some of which approach in enormity to "murder, while others are little more than frolics which a good-natured "man would hardly resent, should be classed together."

See Appendix, Note M, page 151.

"We have therefore designated certain kinds of hurt as 'grievous.'"

"We have given this name to emasculation,—to the loss of the sight "of either eye,—to the loss of the hearing of either "ear,—to the loss of any member or joint,—to the permanent disfiguration of the head or face,—to the fracture or dislocation "of bones." And "after long consideration, we have determined to give

Clause 315.

"the name of grievous bodily hurt to all hurt which causes the sufferer "to be in pain, diseased, or unable to pursue his ordinary avocations, "during the space of 20 days.".

"What we propose is, that the voluntary infliction of simple bodily "hurt shall be punished with imprisonment of either "description which may extend to one year, or fine, or "both; the voluntary infliction of grievous bodily hurt "with imprisonment of either description for a term "which may extend to ten years and must not be less than six months, "to which fine may be added."

See Appendix, Note M, page 153.

Clauses 318, 319.

"These are the ordinary punishments. But there are certain aggra-"vating and mitigating circumstances which make a considerable differ-"ence."

358. The aggravated cases are hurt, in an attempt to murder; hurt, simple and grievous for the purpose of extortion; hurt, simple and grievous by means the use of which generally indicates great malignity, as by a sharp instrument, fire, or any heated substance, or by any corrosive or explosive substance, or by poison, or by means of any animal. There is no distinction of simple and grievous hurt in the case of an attempt to murder. "It does not appear to us," say the Commissioners, "that where the murderous "intention is made out the severity of the hurt inflicted "is a circumstance which ought to be considered in "apportioning the punishment, though it is undoubtedly "a circumstance which will be important as evidence."

Clauses 320, 321, 322, 323 and 324.

See Appendix, Note M, page 153.

359. Referring to Clauses 321 and 322 they say, "We propose that "when bodily hurt is inflicted by way of torture the punishment shall "be very severe. In England happily such a provision would be un-"necessary. But the execrable cruelties which are committed by robbers "in this country for the purpose of extorting property, or information "relating to property, render it absolutely necessary here."

360. The cases of mitigation are those in which the hurt is caused on grave and sudden provocation. The principles on which the clauses providing for such cases are framed are the same as those on which the law of manslaughter is framed.

Clauses 325, 326.

361. For hurt caused involuntarily, but culpably, the rules provided bear a close analogy to those provided for cases of involuntary culpable homicide.

Clauses 327, 328.

362. And there is a provision corresponding in principle with that contained in Clause 308, for attempts to cause hurt not punishable as assaults, by which the offender is made liable to imprisonment for half the term to which he would have been liable if he had actually caused the hurt intended.

Clause 329.

363. Mr. Hudleston observes of Clause 314 that it "is open to the objection of giving to a word a meaning not its own." The word of which this is said is "hurt." Mr. Hudleston appears to object to its including "*all* bodily pain, disease, and infirmity;" and it must be acknowledged that this is a very wide definition, comprehending pain, disease, and infirmity resulting from natural causes, or from "the visitation of God in a natural way," as well as pain, &c., caused by the act of man. But there can be no misapprehension in consequence, as in defining subsequently the offences which consist of hurt, the application of the term is practically limited to hurt caused by the act or omission of man.

364. Of Clause 315 Mr. Hudleston says, "I consider this clause as "marked by needless particularity; it is a part of the system adopted "in this work to which I have stated my objections of attempting to "define every possible act of criminality. Mr. J. F. Thomas points out "omissions in the specifications which are instances of the mischief of "the principle." He adds—"The provisions connected with his clause "appear to me also to overload the Code with unprofitable verbiage in "amplification and particularization quite uncalled for. I allude to the "clauses to 329 inclusive."

365. It is to be regretted that Mr. Hudleston did not, like Mr. J. F. Thomas, apply himself to the consideration of the specifications contained in Clause 315 with a view to point out such defects as he could discover in order that the clause should be made as perfect as possible, rather than content himself with suggesting the possibility of mischief occurring in practice from some undetected omission, without, as far as appears, having found any ground for the surmise. This remark applies to many of the general observations of Mr. Hudleston. It would have been better also, we think, if, instead of generally condemning the clauses to 329 inclusive as quite uncalled for, Mr. Hudleston had shewn how they might have been dispensed with, without leaving those offences which fall under the definition of hurt, and do not also fall under the head of assault, exempt from punishment. The reasons for introducing these clauses into the Code, which are stated in the Note to this chapter, are not noticed by Mr. Hudleston.

366. Mr. Norton says, "I concur in the definitions of what shall be grievous hurt and the expediency of making them." But speaking of the provisions regarding personal injuries in general, which compose the remainder of this chapter, he makes the following remarks: "When "abstract rules of qualification of all sorts of offences against the person "by assault, imprisonment, or by other injury, only to be understood and "applied by reference to explanations and illustrations, shall be attempt-"ed to be put in practical operation, I can surmise all sorts of difficulties "and misconceptions and arbitrary constructions as likely to arise." "I might expend pages in exhibiting instances," he says, but he exhibits not one; and with the above summary remark he passes over all the detailed provisions regarding "hurt," (316 to 329) the definitions of "wrongful restraint and wrongful confinement," "assault," "kidnapping," "rape," and "unnatural offences," and the provisions for the punishment thereof, (330 to 362).

367. The following are the observations of Mr. J. F. Thomas referred to by Mr. Hudleston. Upon the first head in Clause 315, he says, "to "emasculation I would add, or injury to the *membra privata*. In this "country the enormities which appear in cases where dancing girls have "been parties, and in robberies where the object has been not to injure "so much as to force through fear confession of concealed property, "appear to me to require this addition. For whether the wounds, or the "injury actually received, are trifling and do not amount to hurt, as de-"fined under "eighthly," this act ought still, I think, to be repressed by "severe penalties, as peculiarly offensive to the feelings of the party "injured, as well as most dangerous—the slightest excess causing the "severest suffering." Upon the words "dislocation of any bone other "than a tooth," in the seventh head, he says, "This would not provide "for a class of cases which came before me in the Northern Division, "where the sufferers had the *whole* of their teeth forcibly removed; and "I am not clear that the offence could be brought under any of the prior "provisions."

"To meet the case I would suggest an explanation to the effect that "the removal of the whole, or the greater part of the teeth, permanently "weakening the powers of the jaw, does not come within the provision "for fracture or dislocation of a bone other than a tooth; but under the "preceding head, the sixth."

368. Mr. A. D. Campbell supports the suggestion of Mr. Thomas regarding the first head in this clause, observing that some horrible cases occur to his recollection evincing the propriety of it. Mr. Campbell also supports the suggestion of Mr. Thomas regarding the seventh head, remarking that it is the native mode of depriving a conjuror of his art to knock out all his front teeth, deemed indispensable to the due pronunciation of his incantations.

369. We are inclined to think that the addition to the first head proposed by Mr. Thomas is unnecessary, seeing that when this barbarous kind of hurts is caused for the purpose of extortion, &c., as in the cases alluded to by Mr. Thomas, it is punishable severely under Clause 321; and there being no ground, as far as we know, to believe that it is an offence of which there has been such experience under other circumstances as to call for its being distinguished specially.

370. With respect to the seventh head which excepts the fracture or dislocation of a tooth, we observe that "striking out the *fore tooth*" is included in the definition of maiming in the Digest of the English Criminal Law Commissioners, which also includes the kinds of hurt described under the first, second, fourth, fifth and seventh heads. We apprehend that the case stated by Mr. Thomas of the forcible removal of the *whole* of the teeth falls under the fifth head as "permanently impairing the powers of a member or joint," that is to say, the jaw, and that the fracture or dislocation of several teeth would properly be treated as an offence under the same head; but it seems to us that it would be better to specify this kind of hurt under the seventh head. We would not designate the fracture or dislocation of a single tooth, even the fore tooth, as grievous hurt, but when more than one tooth is removed by violence the case may be considered as aggravated as the fracture or dislocation of one of the small bones. We would therefore add to the seventh head the words "or of two or more teeth."

Chapter XV, Sec. 5, Art. 6.

371. The Commissioners have taken some pains to explain the grounds upon which they framed the definition under the eighth head in this clause, by which a hurt whereby the sufferer is in pain, or diseased, or unable to follow his ordinary pursuits, during the space of twenty days, is designated as grievous. The provision they state was suggested by Article 309 of the French Code. Thinking that the length of time during

See Appendix, Note M, pages 152, 153.

which a sufferer is in pain, diseased, or incapacitated from pursuing his ordinary avocation, though a defective criterion of the severity of a hurt, is still the best criterion that has ever been devised, they adopted it from the above Article, but they framed their penal provisions on a principle quite different from that by which the authors of the French Code appeared to have been guided, taking into consideration both the extent of the hurt and the intention of the offender. This will be found explicitly declared in the explanation to Clause 317.

372. Mr. Pyne objects to the definition of grievous hurt with reference to the second head in Clause 76 relating to the right of private defence, thinking that it allows too great a latitude to suffer a person to resist to the death from fear of receiving an injury which may render him unable to follow his ordinary pursuits for twenty days. Again he observes that a very trifling injury to hand or foot may prevent a clerk or laborer from following his ordinary pursuits for twenty days. Mr. Boldero also remarks that the provision is likely to work unequally, as one may from the nature of his pursuit be more easily disabled than another. Mr. Sharkey observes that the specification of twenty days is likely to lead to arbitrary sentences. Mr. H. Frere thinks that making the time of incapacity from work the test of whether a hurt is grievous, is inapplicable to India, where artificial means are constantly resorted to to disguise the real state of the case, and where medical assistance to find out the truth is frequently not procurable.

373. The words "grievous bodily harm" are used in the English Statutes and in the Digest of the English criminal law along with "maim," "disfigure" and "disable," but while the term "maim," as before noticed, is explained in the Digest, no explanation is given of the other expressions. But it seems to be understood that "to disfigure" is to do a man some external injury which detracts from his personal appearance, but does not weaken him; so the cutting off a man's ear or nose comes under this term by the English law, as it does, we apprehend, by this Code. Again "to disable" is to do something creating a permanent disability and not a mere temporary injury. It is not requisite, it appears, that "a grievous bodily harm" within the meaning of the law, should be either permanent or dangerous. Grievous bodily harm neither permanent nor dangerous is but a vague definition, yet it seems to be the closest that has been given by authority; probably in the practical administration of the law there is a pretty near approach to the rule laid down in this Code.

See Authorities referred to in Tomlin's Dictionary under the head "Mayhem."

374. We cannot but think that there is reason in the exceptions taken to estimating the severity of a hurt by the time during which the sufferer is unable to follow his ordinary pursuits, as a rule which will operate unequally. The man who lives by daily labour suffers far more by being kept from his work for twenty days, than he who has independent means, and whose ordinary pursuits may be intermitted for that time without causing him any material privation. Again an injury to the right hand may in the case of a clerk keep him from his work for twenty days, which if it happened to the left hand would be of no consequence. An injury to the foot may prevent one man from following his business, in which walking is necessary, which if it happened to another man in a sedentary employment would not interrupt him at all. The proposed criterion is therefore unsatisfactory, but some criterion is necessary and it will be difficult to devise a better. The following may perhaps be convenient—"such hurt as from the pain or disease it has caused, or the time it has prevented the sufferer from following his ordinary pursuits, is equivalent to the fracture or dislocation of a bone."

375. Upon Clauses 316 and 317, which define what it is "voluntarily to cause hurt" and "voluntarily to cause grievous hurt" respectively, Mr. G. W. Bacon makes the following remarks: "The intention "may be easily proved from the previous conduct of the offender, but "how we are to get at what degree of hurt he knew himself likely to "inflict, I know not. We will take the illustration (*a*) to Clause 329. "A intends to hurt Z, but it is impossible that he should have known it "to be likely that the hurt would be grievous under any of the first "seven definitions of Clause 315; or that Z would in consequence of it "be confined to his room for twenty days, under the eighth. Hurt not "at all grievous is received by Z. Is A to be punished under Clause 318, "or 329, or both? It is clear that hurt of both degrees may be the "consequence of A's conduct, but that's no reason for our inferring that "it was his intention to cause grievous hurt, or that he knew it to be "likely that the hurt would be of a grievous kind. Instead of troubling "ourselves with what the offender thought was likely to happen, we "ought to enquire and decide whether his act was such, as would by its "nature more probably cause grievous than simple hurt, and whether "from previous enmity there was reason to conclude that the offender "intended the former rather than the latter."

376. Now in the case put by Mr. Bacon it appears to us not only possible that A should know, but inconceivable that he should not know it to be likely that Z would sustain grievous hurt, perhaps a fracture or dislocation, by his horse falling over the rope intentionally tied by A across the road by night for the purpose of causing him to fall. If Z suffered hurt, but not grievous hurt by the fall, A might be arraigned either under Clause 318 for "voluntarily causing hurt," or under Clause 329 for the *attempt* to cause *grievous* hurt, but not under both.

377. We agree with Mr. Bacon in what we conceive to be his meaning as to the duty of the Judge, that is to say, that he is not to trouble himself with seeking for direct proof of what the offender thought was likely to happen, but is to infer it from the nature of his act, taking him to have intended grievous hurt, or at least to have contemplated grievous hurt as likely to occur, when he did what every body knows is likely to cause grievous hurt, and the more certainly drawing this conclusion where there is evidence of previous enmity against the party who has suffered. If the act was such that nothing more than simple hurt could reasonably be thought likely to ensue from it, then although grievous hurt may unexpectedly have ensued, it would be his duty to convict the offender of simple hurt only under Clause 316, judging that grievous hurt was not in his contemplation; for according to Clause 317 a person can be convicted of grievous hurt only when the result and the intention correspond, or when grievous hurt has been suffered from an act which was intended to cause grievous hurt, though it may be of a different kind.

378. Mr. Greenhill suggests that the minimum term of imprisonment should be omitted in Clauses 319 and 321, which define the punishments for "grievous hurt," and "hurt for the purpose of extortion," giving instances of cases which seem to fall within the definitions of those offences respectively, but which it would be improper to visit with the least degree of punishment therein prescribed. "Where the range is so great and the degrees so indefinite, he thinks it would be enough to fix the maximum;" an opinion in which we agree. On the same ground we agree with Mr. Pyne in thinking that the minimum term of imprisonment under Clause 322, viz., seven years, is likely to be found too severe a punishment in some cases, when the injury which has been sustained, although it may fall within one of the definitions of grievous hurt, is really not of an aggravated nature.

379. Mr. Greenhill asks whether Clause 320, which punishes hurt in an attempt to commit murder with transportation for life as the maximum, and imprisonment for seven years as the minimum, "is not inconsistent with Clause 309 whereby a person firing at another with intent to murder, but misses his aim, is only liable to three years." Mr. Greenhill appears to have made a mistake on this point, for Clause 309 does not apply to an attempt to commit *murder*, but an attempt to cause the death of a person, which if it had succeeded would have rendered the offender guilty of voluntary culpable homicide not amounting to murder. The punishment for an attempt to commit murder (Clause 308) is the same as that laid down in Clause 320.

380. Upon Clause 323 which provides for the punishment of hurt caused by means of the edge or point of any sharp instrument, &c., Mr. Greenhill asks if this would include a pointed piece of wood, and suggests, if it is intended to confine the penalty to an instrument the point or edge of which is metal, that it should be so expressed. The same suggestion he offers with respect to Clause 324. The instrument must be a *sharp* instrument with an *edge* which will cut, or a *point* which will stab; any instrument which answers to this description we apprehend will be within the definition whether made of metal or not.

381. The Sudder Court for the North-Western Provinces observe that "the Code does not seem to make provision for the offence of "administering poisonous or deleterious drugs in victuals or drink with "the view to stupify and rob persons, reckless whether death may be the "consequence of the act or not."

382. In making this remark the Court must have overlooked Clauses 323 and 324, which provide among other things for "hurt" and "grievous hurt" caused by means of "any substance which it is deleterious to the human body to inhale or swallow." The maximum punishment for grievous hurt so caused is imprisonment for fourteen years. The Court recommend transportation for life.

383. We think with Mr. Pyne that it is advisable to omit the minimum under Clause 324, as under Clauses 319 and 321, for the reason above stated.

384. We observe that in the provisions of the English law for the punishment of cutting, &c., with intent to maim, disfigure, or disable, or to do some other grievous bodily harm, attempting to murder by poison, &c., there is no minimum limit to the imprisonment to which the offender may be sentenced.

385. We have remarked that the term "maim" in the English criminal law includes the hurt designated as "grievous" under the 1st, 2nd, 4th, 5th and 7th heads of Clause 315. *Attempts* to maim, disfigure, or disable, or to cause some other grievous bodily harm, are classed together in the English law, and are punishable by transportation for life, or for any term not less than fifteen* years, or imprisonment for any term not exceeding three years. By this Code the maximum punishment for grievous hurt comprehending disfiguration and temporary disabling, as well as the hurts which come under the description of maiming, as above, is imprisonment for ten years, but this cannot be inflicted for an attempt to cause hurt unless the hurt has been actually caused. An *attempt to hurt* when the hurt intended has not been produced, is punishable by imprisonment for half the term to which the offender would have been liable if his attempt had succeeded.

Art. 5, Sec. 5, Chap. XV.

Clause 329.

386. While by this Code hurt caused in an attempt to murder is punishable with transportation for life or rigorous imprisonment for not less than seven years, the same offence by the law of England is capital, and attempts to murder, although no bodily injury be effected, are punishable with transportation for life as the maximum.

OF WRONGFUL RESTRAINT AND WRONGFUL CONFINEMENT.

387. We find Mr. Hudleston alone objecting generally to the rules regarding wrongful restraint and wrongful confinement contained in Clauses 330 to 339. He says—"This part "of the Code appears to me to be over-legislation. "The illustrations are remarkable for perverted in-"genuity not unfrequently displayed in this work." Referring to the explanations under Clause 330 and to the illustration (*d*) he observes, that "voluntarily causing a man to believe a dog savage, "who is not savage, and threatening to set him at the said man, so "preventing the man from going along a path, does not appear a very "simple description of wrongful restraint." "To the clauses which "follow to 338 inclusive," he adds "I prefer the English law of False "imprisonment."

388. It is to be wished that Mr. Hudleston had explained what he understood to be the English law on this point, and in what respect he preferred it. It seems that in the administration of the law of England the forcible detention of a person in the street is held to be *imprisonment*. Does Mr. Hudleston think it better that there should be a necessity for such a forced construction to bring the wrongful detention of a man under the law, than that there should be a distinct provision for that offence and another provision for the more aggravated offence of wrongful confinement? Mr. Hudleston objects to the Code in some places as giving to words a meaning not their own; on this ground he surely ought to object to the English law in the instance here given, for saying that to detain a man forcibly in the street is to *imprison* him. Clause 330 of the Code lays it down that to prevent a person from proceeding in any direction in which he has a right to proceed, that is, for example, to detain him forcibly in the street, is wrongful restraint, while wrongful confinement, obviously an aggravated form of wrongful restraint, is by Clause 331 defined to be preventing a "person from proceeding beyond certain circumscribing limits," or, as it is explained in the Note, "keeping a man within limits out of which he wishes to go and has a right to go."

Russell 1, p. 606.

See Appendix, Note M, page 154.

* Proposed in the Digest to be reduced to seven years.

389. Mr. Hudleston does not expressly object to the explanation subjoined to Clause 330, though he says of the example by which it is illustrated that it is not a very simple description of wrongful restraint. Let us take another example. Suppose that A presents a pistol at Z and threatens to fire at him if he goes in a certain direction in which he has a right to go, and thereby prevents him from going in that direction. Would Mr. Hudleston say that A does not wrongfully restrain Z, though in truth the pistol is not loaded?

390. Mr. Greenhill proposes a verbal alteration in Clause 334, that is, to substitute the definite words, "and less than ten days," instead of "or more," with reference to Clause 335, which provides for a confinement extending to ten days or more. As Clause 334 is obviously intended to apply to cases of confinement for three or more days less than ten, it may be as well to express this distinctly.

391. Upon Clause 335, which provides that confinement aggravated by duration for ten days or more, shall be punished with imprisonment for a term which may extend to three years with additional imprisonment of from one to three days for every day of such wrongful confinement, Sir H. Seton questions the principle on which the punishment is enhanced, observing that retaliatory punishment is a relique of barbarism, and has always the appearance of vindictiveness. The remark applies equally to Clauses 336 and 337.

392. We admit the objection in general; but in these cases, while the punishment is enhanced according to the duration which constitutes the aggravation, "we have attempted to frame the law on this subject," say the Commissioners, "in such a manner as to give the offender a strong motive for abridging the detention of his prisoner."

393. One cannot conceive of a wrongful confinement continued for ten days or more without deliberation and reflection and a special regard to the penal consequences, and when a man sees that by persisting in his offence he is every day becoming liable to a certain additional punishment, the motive to set his prisoner free will grow stronger daily. This reason we think obviates the general objection in these instances.

Clauses 336 and 337.

394. The other aggravations are when a person persists in wrongfully confining another notwithstanding a writ has been issued for his liberation; and when the confinement is for the purpose of extortion. The special provisions for these aggravated cases appear to us to be proper, except in prescribing a minimum of punishment. We would not fetter the discretion of the Judge further than by fixing the maximum in the three Clauses 335 to 337. The punishment for imprisonment according to the Digest of the law of England is imprisonment for *any* term not exceeding three years, *or* fine at discretion, or both. In the aggravated cases of confinement provided for by Clauses 335 to 337, imprisonment is prescribed peremptorily, and fine may be added at discretion.

See Appendix, Note M, p. 155.

395. With reference to Clause 338, the Commissioners say, "We "have also provided a separate punishment for a person "who, while detaining another in wrongful confinement, "omits to supply his prisoner with every thing neces- "sary to health, ease and comfort." The clause more definitely says, with any thing he knows to be "necessary to prevent the person confined from being in danger of death or hurt." The punishment is imprisonment for a term which may extend to one year, or fine, or both. We understand that the offender may be sentenced to punishment under this clause, and also for the offence of wrongful confinement under one or other of the clauses relating thereto. Here are two offences committed not by doing one thing, but by an illegal act and an illegal omission distinct from each other and each constituting a distinct offence, and therefore not within the scope of Clause 58, which at first sight may appear to apply. It is said in the Note that "the effect of this "provision is, that a person who wrongfully confines "another will be answerable for any bodily hurt which "he may cause by wrongfully omitting so to supply his prisoner." It would seem rather that he is made answerable for any hurt which his omission is likely to cause, though such hurt may not be caused. The illustration intimates that if hurt is caused the offender will be liable to punishment for the hurt in addition, as we understand, to the punishment for the confinement, the punishment for the omission under Clause 338 merging therein.

See Appendix, Note M, page 155.

396. In their Note upon the provisions regarding assault the authors of the Code say, "We have found great difficulty in "giving a definition of assault, and are by no means "satisfied with that which we now offer. As, however, "it at present appears to us to include all that we mean "to include, and to exclude all that we mean to exclude, we have adopt-"ed it in spite of the objections which we feel to its harsh and quaint "phraseology. We have adopted it with the less scruple because we "trust the illustrations will render it intelligible to an attentive reader."

OF ASSAULT.

See Appendix, Note M, page 155.

397. The definition of assault is contained in Clause 340 as follows: "Whoever intentionally uses force, or attempts to use force to any person, "without that person's consent, in order to the committing of any offence, "or intending or knowing to be likely that by such use of force he may "cause to the person to whom the force is used injury, fear, or annoyance, "is said to commit an assault."

398. The definition of assault in the Digest of the English criminal law runs thus: "An assault consists in an attempt or "offer, by a person having present ability, with force to "do any hurt or violence to the person of another." The definition in the Code appears to include what is termed "Battery" in the English law, which is defined in the Digest to be "any the least *hurt* or *violence* unlawfully and wilfully or culpably done to the person of another." The Commissioners remark that "a large proportion of the acts designated as as-"saults will be offences under the heads of hurt and "restraint. But there will be many assaults which it is "absolutely necessary to punish, yet which cause neither bodily hurt nor "unlawful restraint." To cover *these* offences, the definition is necessarily framed in terms which include the former also.

Chapter XV, Sec. 5, Art. 48.

Art 43.

See Appendix, Note M, page 155.

399. Where there is real hurt the charge we may suppose will be laid usually under the more appropriate head.

400. It is not we apprehend to the definition of assault in Clause 340 that the observations above quoted as to the harshness and quaintness of the phraseology apply, but to the elaborate explanation given in the preceding Clause 339 of what is meant by the essential words "uses force" in that definition.

401. There is no such explanation in the Digest of the English Criminal law. But Mr. Livingstone thought it necessary in giving his definitions of assault and battery, which he observes do not materially differ from those contained in the English law, to explain, both by definition and illustration, what is meant by the term "violence" which he uses instead of force.

402. Upon the explanation in Clause 339 of this Code, Sir H. Seton suggests for consideration, "whether the meaning of actual force might not be left to common sense, and constructive force only defined." Mr. Hudleston says he "cannot bring himself to believe that a definition "so artificial as this will be adopted in preference to the sort of definition "of assault and battery used in the law of England." "For the sake of "maintaining 'literal truth,'" "in which it might be questioned whether "or not the Law Commissioners have succeeded, common sense appears "to me to be sacrificed." "It would require an Army of Magistrates to "dispose of the complaints invited as it were by the illustrations to "Clause 340, which moreover seem below the dignity of law." Mr. A. D. Campbell, colleague of Mr. Hudleston, dissents from the latter remarks, but concurs in the former.

403. In defining the term "violence," Mr. Livingstone uses the words "physical force," as words intelligible by themselves. He explains that "by violence is meant any physical force applied either immediately by "any part of the body of the person using it, or by the instrumentality "or intervention of any other matter, whether animate or inanimate, and "it comes within the definition (of battery) whether the violence be pro-"duced by secondary means intentionally prepared by the offender, or be "caused by his immediate act." This explanation is followed by illustrations exemplifying each of the modes of applying physical force.

404. It appears to us that it is unnecessary to define what is meant by using force directly, and that all that is required is to define the mode in which force may be used indirectly. We think therefore that Clause 339 may be omitted, and that it will be sufficient to subjoin to Clause 340 a simple explanation that a person may use force to another within the meaning of the definition, not only by his bodily power directly affecting or acting upon that other person, but by means of any person, or of any animal, or of any inanimate substance, disposed or moved by him so as to affect or act upon that other person.

405. Illustrations may be given to exemplify force used by the instrumentality or intervention of other persons, or of animals or inanimate substances. In some of the cases there may be hurt, in others not, but this makes no difference. And although the party intended to be affected may not be affected, yet under the definition the attempt will be sufficient to constitute assault if it was made in order to the committing of any offence, or with the intention of causing or the knowledge that it was likely to cause injury, fear, or annoyance to the person against whom the attempt was aimed.

406. Upon Clause 341 which defines what it is "to make shew of assault," Mr. J. F. Thomas makes the following observations, in which Mr. W. Hudleston and Mr. A. D. Campbell express their concurrence. "It deserves, I conceive, much consideration whether this enactment is "adapted to the existing state of society; unless some special damage or "injury has been sustained, in consequence of this shew of assault, it "would be better to leave such acts unpunished, than to open so wide a "door, as this clause must, to frivolous and vexatious accusations."

"Every bazaar fracas, where the parties are loud and angry, is accom- "panied with abundant gestures and shew of assault, but it appears to "me nevertheless, on principles of general policy, inexpedient to encour- "age a resort to the Criminal Courts in these and similar cases, unless "some special hurt or injury has ensued. If a party is of that rank "and estimation in society, that any preparation or shew of assault "degrades him, he may have his remedy by civil action. This I am in- "clined to believe a better course, than to make the act of shew of "assault, as it now is, in all cases a crime."

407. What is here classed as a distinct offence less than assault, amounts to assault by the law of England, as laid down by Russell, "Drawing a sword or bayonet, or even hold- "ing up a fist in a menacing manner, &c., &c., at a person who is within "reach, or any other similar act, accompanied with such circumstances "as denote at the time an intention coupled with a present ability of "using actual violence against the person of another, will amount to an "assault."

Russell 1, p. 604.

408. The explanation subjoined to Clause 341 intimating that mere words do not amount to a shew of assault is conformable to the law of England. And we conceive that the further intimation that words may however be taken as circumstances giving a meaning to the gesture or act which they accompany, so as to make it amount to shew of assault, is also consonant to the English law.

409. Mr. W. Hudleston says, "I do not perceive why special provision for 'assault' should be made in Clauses 343 to 345 inclusive," viz., in attempting to murder, to commit the offence of kidnapping, and to cause grievous hurt. An answer is supplied by his colleague Mr. A. D. Campbell—"I deem 343 to 345 necessary in cases where proof may "be forthcoming to nothing but the 'assault' accompanied by attempt to "commit the specified crimes." He should have said, and perhaps he meant, where the attempt in fact was not carried beyond the assault. An attempt at murder carried beyond assault to such a length as the offender contemplates as sufficient to cause death falls under Clause 308. The punishment is the same in both cases, on the principle that "where "the murderous intention is made out the severity of "the hurt inflicted is not a circumstance which ought "to be considered in apportioning the punishment."

See Appendix, Note M, page 153.

410. By Clause 346 an assault on a woman in an attempt to commit rape on her, is punishable with imprisonment of either description for a term which may extend to three years, and must not be less than six months, and fine at discretion. The Sudder Court for the North-Western Provinces are of opinion that if this clause contemplates provision for all acts short of penetration, the punishment is inadequate. Mr. W. Hudleston observes that in many cases seven or fourteen years would not be excessive, to which Mr. A. D. Campbell assents. We apprehend that in the law of England this offence falls under the general head of "an assault with intent to commit a felony," which is punishable by fine and imprisonment. By the Article in the Digest which provides for such an assault it is declared to be punishable with imprisonment not exceeding two years, or fine at

Art. 49, Sec. 5, Chapter XV.

discretion, or both. But another Article provides that whosoever shall attempt to commit a felony by any assault, &c., done with the immediate intent to accomplish the criminal object, shall, though he fail in such attempt, be liable to imprisonment for any term not exceeding three years, or fine at discretion, or both. This, which probably would be applied to the case in question, it will be observed, agrees with Clause 346 of the Code, except that by the latter the imprisonment is not to be less than six months.

Art. 8, Chapter XXII.

See Appendix, Note M, page 155.

411. It is observed in the Note that severe punishments are provided for assault, when it is committed with intention of dishonouring the sufferer, or when it is an outrage to female modesty. Clause 347 applies to an assault of the latter description, and Clause 348 to one of the former description. The punishment is imprisonment not exceeding two years, or fine, or both. The law of England appears not to provide for such assaults specially.* But they are specially provided for in Mr. Livingstone's Code. The punishment denounced therein for the former offence is imprisonment not exceeding one year or less than two months, and fine not exceeding 2,000 dollars nor less than 200, and for the latter double the punishment assigned to the species of assault that is committed, but with a proviso that the fine shall not be less than 200 dollars, nor the imprisonment less than sixty days.

Articles 433 and 434.

412. Mr. W. Hudleston thinks that these clauses, and the rest to 352 inclusive, "might advantageously be omitted," while Mr. A. D. Campbell on the contrary deems the distinctions made by them judicious and proper.

413. Sir H. Seton questions the use of so vague a term as "dishonor" in a Criminal Code. Mr. Greenhill observes, "To dishonor does not "appear sufficiently definite, and if intended to apply to mere insult, "such as pulling a man's nose or laying a whip across his shoulders, the "punishment seems disproportionate to the penalties of the preceding "clauses." Mr. E. Monckton remarks that it would be an outrage to the modesty of one woman to do to her what would be thought nothing of by another. A kiss that would be highly resented by a lady might be no affront to the maid. He thinks illustrations would be useful.

414. When it is considered that such an insult as that mentioned by Mr. Greenhill will, by reason of the provocation arising from it, extenuate the act of killing the offender by the person insulted so as to make him guilty of manslaughter instead of murder, it may be thought fitting to visit it with a severe punishment. The same reason applies to assault outraging the modesty of a woman, "such an assault, (for example), as called forth the memorable blow of Wat Tyler."

415. There is a sufficient discretion allowed as to the extent of punishment to admit of a due regard being paid to variety of condition and circumstances, making the same act less offensive to one person than to another.

Clause 349.

416. An assault in attempting to commit a theft of property which a person is actually wearing or carrying is punishable by imprisonment of either description which may extend to two years, or two-thirds of the term of imprisonment which may be

---

* Taking indecent liberties with females, it appears, is a common assault.—Russell 1, pages 605, 606.

inflicted for the offence of theft, but in the latter case the imprisonment is to be rigorous. An assault in attempting wrongfully to confine a person is punishable by imprisonment of either description which may extend to one year, with fine limited to 1,000 rupees. The Sudder Court, North-Western Provinces, say they do not perceive why the punishment for the latter offence should be less than that for assault in an attempt to steal according to Clause 349. They appear to have overlooked that the punishment in Clause 349 exceeds that provided for "wrongful confinement." The punishment for assault in attempting to confine wrongfully is the same as for wrongful confinement.

Clause 350.

Clause 333.

417. Mr. G. W. Bacon suggests that confinement and assault to confine, under false pretence of lunacy, ought to be particularly noticed and severely punished. It does not appear to us that it is necessary to distinguish such cases. The maximum punishments authorized may be considered sufficient to meet the aggravation mentioned by Mr. Bacon.

418. Assault upon grave and sudden provocation is not wholly excused, but the punishment is limited to imprisonment for one month as the maximum, or a fine not exceeding 200 rupees, or both. "Shew of assault" is liable to the same punishment.

Clauses 351 and 352.

419. Of kidnapping the Commissioners observe, "The crime consists, according to our definition of it, in conveying a "person without his consent, or the consent of some "person legally authorized to consent on his behalf, or "with such consent obtained by deception, out of the "protection of the law, or of those whom the law has appointed his "guardians." "This offence may be committed on a child by removing "that child out of the keeping of its lawful guardian or guardians. On "a grown man it can only be committed by conveying him beyond the "limits of the Company's territories, or by receiving him on board of a "ship for that purpose." These definitions are contained in Clauses 353 and 354.

OF KIDNAPPING. See Appendix, Note M, page 156.

420. The punishment for simple kidnapping is imprisonment of either description not exceeding seven years and not less than one year, also fine.

Clause 355.

421. The punishment is enhanced in cases in which the kidnapping is committed with murderous* intentions, or with the intention of inflicting grievous bodily hurt, or of reducing the sufferer to slavery, or for the purpose of rape, or of unnatural lust.†

422. The offence of child-stealing simply by the law of England is punishable with transportation for seven years, or imprisonment not exceeding two years, proposed in the Digest to be extended to three years. The child must be under the age of ten years. The age specified in the Code is twelve years.

Chapter XV, Sec. 5, Art. 34.

423. Upon the provisions in the Code regarding this offence, Mr. Pyne makes the following remarks: "Kidnapping is a crime so injurious

---

* Clause 356. Transportation or rigorous imprisonment for life, or imprisonment for not less than seven years, also fine.

† Clause 357. Imprisonment of either description not exceeding fourteen and not less than two years, also fine.

"to society under either of the definitions given in Clause 353, but more "particularly from the territories of the East India Company, that I am "inclined to think the punishment here provided is too mild for the "magnitude of the offence, the object of which may be perpetual impri- "sonment, an aggravation of crime unprovided for. The facility with "which persons may be made away with without exciting observation "among their relations or the police has been lamentably exemplified in "the recent discovery of Thuggee, and once across the boundary of the "British Territory the succour of the law will rarely be extended to them."

"With reference to kidnapping being made for the purpose, or liable "to the consequence of subjecting the person to unnatural lust, the "utmost penalty of the law, short of capital punishment, does not ap- "pear to me too rigorous for the offence—the punishment provided in "Clause 362 is, I am of opinion, both as to its minimum and maximum "proportions more appropriate than the limited period of imprisonment "set forth in this clause."

424. The Sudder Court, North-Western Provinces, propose to add to Clause 357 the words "or the dedicating that person to prostitution." They observe that "cases are of common occurrence in this country in "which children are left at fairs, or abandoned in times of famine and "distress, and provision is required for the punishment of persons ap- "propriating such children with evil intentions."

425. We are not prepared to advise any alteration of the punishments proposed in the Code.

Vide Extract from Major Sleeman's Report on Megpunnaism at p. 347. Report of Indian Law Commissioners on Slavery in India.

426. It seems to us to be worthy of consideration whether the definition of kidnapping a child may not be enlarged, so as to include the illegal taking and detaining of a child not *actually* in the keeping of his lawful guardian at the time of such taking, for example, a child who has strayed and been left behind at a fair, still more a child whose parents have been murdered in order that the murderers may obtain possession of the child.

See Appendix, Note M, page 156.

427. While we think with the Sudder Court, North-Western Provinces, that it is a serious aggravation of kidnapping when it is committed with the intention of devoting a child to prostitution, yet we do not conceive it to be necessary to provide for that aggravation specially, considering that the offence may be punished under Clause 355 with imprisonment extending to seven years, and fine at discretion, which we deem to be sufficient.

428. It is explained that Clause 358 was intended for the punishment of persons exporting laborers by sea from the Company's territories, in contravention of the Act recently passed on that subject. The Act referred to must have been V of 1837, afterwards repealed. The Acts on this subject at present in force are XV of 1842 and XXI of 1843 for the Island of Mauritius, and XXI of 1844 for Jamaica, &c.

429. It seems to us that if provision is to be made in this Code for the punishment of acts contravening the said laws, it should be in exact correspondence with what is therein enacted on the subject, and this would be best done by adopting in the Code, with such verbal alterations as may be necessary in order to uniformity of expression, the definitions of the offences and the penalties to be inflicted contained in Sections IX, X and XIII of Act XV of 1842, with which those contained in Sections X, XI and XIV of Act XXI of 1844 are identical.

430. We have now to notice the suggestion of Colonel Sleeman to introduce in this place a declaration that the right of parents over their children does not extend to the disposing of them by sale, and provisions for the punishment of persons who shall sell or buy human beings within the Company's territories, or shall import human beings into the Company's territories for sale.

Letter to Secy. to Govt. of India, dated 18th February 1840, and Notes of Colonel Sleeman upon the Penal Code.

Letter from Secy. to Govt. of India, dated 9th March 1840, enclosing an Extract from the above letter, dated 18th Feb. 1840.

431. The Law Commissioners had this suggestion under consideration in preparing their Report upon Slavery in India.

432. The subject is treated in the portion of that Report entitled "Observations," p. 345 to 353. The recommendations of the Commissioners in which they were unanimous, are stated at p. 365-6. We quote the following remarks from p. 353 :—

"The prohibitory part of our recommendations is in conformity, it "will be seen, with those which Major Sleeman has made upon the same "subject. But in the permissive part we have ventured to go beyond "what he thinks expedient. He dreads the consequences of allowing "contracts for the services of infants terminating at the age of maturity. "'Who shall say' he asks 'into what hands or into what country such "children shall be transferred before that time comes?'"

"This is undoubtedly an evil to be guarded against, but we think "that the system of registration which we recommend may be so or- "ganized as to accomplish that purpose. We have the high authority of "Major Sleeman himself for asserting that in seasons of calamity the "permission to purchase and sell children saves no doubt a great number "from starvation. We could not therefore make up our minds to take "away altogether this resource from the starving poor, unless we were "prepared to suggest some other. But we are afraid that it would not "be possible in this country to set up any tolerably safe and economical "machinery for the distribution of public charity. We therefore propose "to permit these apprenticeships."

433. It was proposed to declare it to be lawful for the parents or guardians of minors to apprentice them till majority, or for any shorter period, and to punish any other person who should pretend to apprentice or sell a minor, and any person who should purchase or receive as an apprentice any minor from any person whom he had not good reason to believe to be the parent or guardian of such minor, and any person having in his possession one or more minors with the intention of selling or apprenticing them, not being the parent or guardian of such minors.

434. The views of the authors of the Penal Code on the subject of Slavery are stated in Note B.* By Section IV, Act V of 1843 it is enacted, according to their opinion, that any act which would be a penal offence if done to a free man, shall be equally an offence if done to any person on the pretext of his being in a condition of slavery.

* See Appendix, Note B, pages 113—116.

435. The private sale of a free person for the purpose of being dealt with as a slave is not prohibited by this law, but as under Section IV of the Act no person so sold could be dealt with as a slave against his will, it amounts to a virtual prohibition, which may be effectual as regards adults who can avail themselves of the protection of the law, without any further provision.

436. But with respect to children a further provision appears to be requisite. We think it should be made penal to sell or purchase a child under any circumstances.

437. The existing law of Bombay makes it an offence to sell a child under ten years of age, although already in a state of slavery, and to sell a free child of any age into slavery, except in time of famine; in the case of a free child the power of selling in such an emergency is confined to the parent.

Regulation XIV of 1827, Sec. 31.

438. We think that the sale of children by their parents, even in time of famine, should be prohibited. It does not appear to us to be right to permit it for the sake of the parents, that is, to enable the parents to get something for themselves besides being relieved from the burden of supporting the child, and it appears to be unnecessary for the sake of the child in order to save it from starvation, for we apprehend that it will not be more difficult to find a person willing to take the charge of a child in such extremity where nothing is to be paid to the parents, than to find one to purchase it for a price. The latter would have no greater power to retain the child in his service than the former.

OF RAPE. Clause 359.

439. We do not find any objections to the definition of rape except with regard to the 3rd and 4th descriptions.

440. The 3rd description of rape is when it is committed with the consent of the woman, but "when her consent has been obtained by putting her in fear of death or of hurt." Mr. A. D. Campbell and Mr. Pyne recommend that the words "or of hurt" be omitted, on the ground, as stated by Mr. Pyne, that "when the fear of the most trivial hurt produces consent, the woman's reluctance or chastity cannot be over great "or rigid." Mr. D. Greenhill proposes the words "grievous hurt" instead of "hurt." We concur in this suggestion. The words of the English law on this point as given in the Digest are "grievous bodily harm."

Art. 21, Sec. 5, Chapter XV.

441. The 4th description of rape is when it is committed with the consent of the woman, but "when the man knows that her consent is "given because she believes that he is a different man to whom she is or "believes herself to be married."

442. Mr. J. F. Thomas suggests that this protection should not be restricted to the case of *married* women alone. He thinks that slave girls and other women, who from the institutions of the country may not be married, but who cohabit with one man, and whose children are recognized as his by the father, are equally entitled to protection; he proposes to add after the words "to whom she is or believes herself to be married" the words "or with whom she cohabits."

443. We rather incline to the opinion of Mr. Thomas that it is desirable to give to females in the circumstances which he indicates the same protection in the case in question as is given to married women; but an obvious objection to such an extension of the provision is that it would give occasion to a troublesome collateral inquiry, likely sometimes to be turned into a trial of the complainant's conduct. Should the suggestion of Mr. Thomas be adopted we think it would be advisable to subjoin to the words, "or with whom she cohabits," the words following, "in such a manner that children born of her during the cohabitation will be entitled by the law of the parties to claim a maintenance from him," or words to that effect.

444. Again Mr. Thomas objects to the "exception which declares that sexual intercourse by a man with his own wife is in no case rape." He says, "I doubt the propriety of this exception. The early age at "which children are married and are in the eye of the law wives, makes "it necessary that protection should be given to them by the law till "they are of age to reside with their husbands. I remember a case of "forcible violation and great injury to a child where the offender was "the husband." Mr. Hudleston and Mr. A. D. Campbell concur with Mr. Thomas.

445. Although marriages are commonly contracted among Mahomedans and Hindoos before the age of puberty on the part of the female, yet usually the bride remains in the house of her parents till she is of a fit age for the consummation of the marriage, and it may be fairly presumed that the parents, her natural guardians, will in general take care to prevent abuse in this respect. There may however be cases in which the check of the law may be necessary to restrain men from taking advantage of their marital right prematurely. To meet such cases it may be advisable to exclude from the exception cases in which the wife is under nine years of age. Instances of abuse by the husband in such cases will then fall under the 5th description of rape.

446. We may observe that by the Statute 9 Geo. IV, Cap. 74, which governs the administration of Criminal Justice by Her Majesty's Courts in India, the age under which the carnal knowledge of a girl is a crime of the same degree with rape, is eight years; by the law in force in England it is ten years.

Section 65.

447. By the law at present in force in England the punishment for the crime last mentioned as well as for rape is transportation for life: by the Statute for India the punishment for both is death. The punishment prescribed by the Code is imprisonment not exceeding fourteen years and not less than two years, with fine in addition at the discretion of the Court.

Sections 64 and 65.
Clause 360.

448. Mr. J. F. Thomas thinks that both the maximum and minimum are fixed too low by the Code. He observes that "it would not be rare "to find women of caste by whom death would be considered a less evil "than the violation of their persons by some low caste fellow. In a "society so constituted the offence of rape should be visitable with the "higher penalty of imprisonment for life." "I can perceive," he proceeds to say, "no good reason for so low a penalty as two years. If rape "at all it must merit a higher penalty. This large range of two to "fourteen years in the case of an offence not capable scarcely of degrees, "for either there was or there was not a forcible violation, goes rather "to meet cases of doubt as to the fact than degrees in the offence. If "the fact of forcible violation was fully established I can perceive no "ground, even if the woman was without character, for lessening the "security of person. If not established then there was no rape, and let it "be dealt with as an assault if it be thought proper, or acquittal is prefer-"able if there is the slightest doubt of the fact." Mr. A. D. Campbell agrees with Mr. Thomas; Mr. Hudleston is of opinion that the punishment should not be less than imprisonment for seven years.

449. We cannot admit that this offence is not capable of degrees. Mr. Thomas has himself suggested cases differing very greatly in degree. On the one hand let us take the case of the chaste high caste female, who would sacrifice her life to save her honor, contaminated by the forcible embrace of a man of low caste, or of one who is below caste, say a Chandala or a Pariah. On the other hand that of the woman without character, or any pretension to purity, who is wont to be easy of access. In the latter case if the woman, from any motive, refuses to comply with the solicitation of a man and is forced by him, the offender ought to be punished; but surely the injury is infinitely less in this instance than in the former.

450. The punishment at present inflicted by the Company's Courts is ordinarily limited to imprisonment for seven years, and we suppose that in the worst cases the term of fourteen years is not exceeded. We think it advisable to allow the wide discretion permitted by the Code.

UNNATURAL OFFENCES.

451. The Law Commissioners observe that Clauses 361 and 362 relate to an odious class of offences respecting which it is desirable that as little as possible should be said. They therefore leave the provisions proposed therein without comment to the judgment of the Governor-General in Council. Mr. A. D. Campbell in concurrence with Mr. Blane censures the false delicacy which has in their opinion caused a most improper ambiguity in these clauses, leaving it uncertain whether they apply to mere indecent liberties, or extend to the actual commission of an offence of the nature indicated.

452. It appears to us clear enough that it was meant to strike at the root of the offence by making the first act tending to it liable to the same punishment, if the Judge shall deem it proper, as the offence actually accomplished. This is a new principle, and it would have been better if the Commissioners had explained for what reason they adopted it, in respect to the offences here contemplated in particular. We conceive that there is a very weighty objection to the clauses in question, in the opening which they will afford to calumny, if for an act so slight as may come within the meaning of the word "touches," a man may be exposed to such a revolting charge and suffer the ignominy of a public trial upon it.

453. Colonel Sleeman advises the omission of both these clauses, deeming it most expedient to leave offences against nature silently to the odium of society. It may give weight to this suggestion to remark that the existing law on the subject is almost a dead letter, as appears from the fact that in three years only six cases came before the Nizamut Adawlut at Calcutta, although it is but too true we fear that the frequency of the abominable offences in question "remains," as Mr. A. D. Campbell expresses it, "a horrid stain upon the land."

Statement from Sept. 1841 to July 1844.

454. Mr. Livingstone, we observe, makes no mention of offences of this nature in his Code for Louisiana, and they are omitted in the revised Statutes of Massachusetts, of which the chapter "of offences against the lives and persons of individuals"

No. 7.

is appended to the 2nd Report of the English Criminal Law Commissioners. By the French Penal Code offences of this description do not come within the scope of the law unless they are effected or attempted by violence, except the sufferer be under the age of ten years.

Articles 331 and 332.

455. The English Law Commissioners stated in their 2nd Report that it was their intention to enter upon the consideration of the laws relating to offences of this description, but in their 4th Report they observed that as the mitigation of capital punishment had since the 2nd Report was made been maturely considered by Parliament without leading to any alteration of the law relating to these offences, they for the present thought it unnecessary to make remarks upon them, and it does not appear that they afterwards resumed the subject.

CHAPTER XIX.

OF OFFENCES AGAINST PROPERTY.

See Appendix, Note N, pp. 157—159.

456. In their Note upon this chapter the authors of the Code advert to the peculiar difficulties that oppose the efforts of the Legislator to define with clearness and precision the offences which are the subject of it. "The offences defined in this chapter," they observe, "are made "punishable on the ground that they are violations of the right of pro-"perty. But the right of property is itself the creature of the law. It "is evident, therefore, that if the substantive civil law touching this "right be imperfect and obscure, the penal law which is auxiliary to that "substantive law, and of which the object is to add a sanction to that "substantive law, must partake of the imperfection or obscurity. It is "impossible for us to be certain that we have made proper penal provi-"sions for violations of civil rights till we have a complete knowledge "of all civil rights; and this we cannot have while the law respecting "those rights is either obscure or unsettled. As the present state of the "civil law causes perplexity to the Legislator in framing the Penal Code, "so it will occasionally cause perplexity to the Judges in administering "that Code. If it be matter of doubt what things are the subject of a "certain right, in whom that right resides, and to what that right ex-"tends, it must also be matter of doubt whether that right has or has "not been violated."

"It would, evidently," they continue, "be impossible for us to deter-"mine in the Penal Code all the momentous questions of civil right "which, in the unsettled state of Indian jurisprudence, will admit of "dispute. We have, indeed, ventured to take for granted in our illus-"trations many things which properly belong to the domain of the civil "law, because, without doing so, it would have been impossible for us "to explain our meaning. But we have, to the best of our judgment, "avoided questions respecting which, even in the present state of Indian "jurisprudence, much doubt could exist. And in the text of the law we "have, as closely as was possible, confined ourselves to what is in strict-"ness the duty of persons engaged in framing a Penal Code. We have "provided punishment for the infraction of rights, without determining "in whom those rights vest, or to what those rights extend. We are "inclined to hope that, even if the Penal Code should come into operation "before the Code of civil rights has been framed, the number of cases in "which the want of a Code of civil rights would occasion perplexity to "the criminal tribunals will bear but a very small proportion to those "in which no such perplexity will exist."

"All the violations of property proposed to be made punishable by "this chapter," it is remarked, "fall under one or more of the following "heads:—

" 1. Theft.
" 2. Extortion.
" 3. Robbery.
" 4. The criminal misappropriation of property not in possession.
" 5. Criminal breach of trust.
" 6. The receiving of stolen property.
" 7. Cheating.

" 8. Fraudulent bankruptcy.
" 9. Mischief.
" 10. Criminal trespass."

457. The Commissioners observe that "all these offences resemble "each other in this, that they cause, or have some tendency, directly or "indirectly, to cause some party not to have such a dominion over pro- "perty as that party is entitled by law to have."

458. They remark that "every offence against property may be fraud- "ulently committed. But theft, extortion, robbery, the criminal mis- "appropriation of property not in possession, criminal breach of trust, "the receiving of stolen property, fraudulent bankruptcy, and cheating, "must be in all cases fraudulently committed. Fraud enters into the "definition of every one of these offences. But fraud does not enter "into the definition of mischief, or of criminal trespass."

459. After stating that they believe it to be impossible to mark with precision by any words the circumstances which constitute possession, and giving instances illustrative of the difficulty, the Commissioners say, "For the purpose of "preventing any difference of opinion from arising in cases likely to "occur very often, we have laid down a few rules (see Clauses 17, 18, "19) which we believe to be in accordance with the general sense of "mankind as to what shall be held to constitute possession. But, in "general, we leave it to the tribunals, without any direction, to deter- "mine whether particular property is at a particular time in the posses- "sion of a particular person, or not."

See Appendix, Note N, page 160.

460. The chapter begins with the definition of "Theft." Between this head and that of "Robbery" is interposed the definition of "Extortion," an arrangement suited to the definition of "Robbery," in which it is declared that to constitute the offence so designated there must be either theft or extortion.

Clauses 363, 375 and 368.

461. In theft, as it is defined in this chapter, the object is to take property which is in the possession of a person out of that person's possession. This renders it necessary to introduce separate provisions under the head of "Criminal misappropriation of property not in possession," Clause 383. After this is the head of "Criminal breach of trust," Clause 386. Then that of "Receiving stolen property," Clause 389, which includes cases in which property is transferred by the last two offences as well as by theft and robbery. Last of the offences classed as fraudulent is "Cheating."

Clause 363.

462. We have already noticed Mr. Norton's comment upon the definition of the term "fraudulently" in Clause 16, as including highway robberies among frauds.* Here with reference to the definition of theft in Clause 363, after offering a definition of his own, regarding which he says, "whether it be clearer than "that in the Code, or whether it be more or less comprehensive than it "ought to be, or than that in the Code, I shall not argue;" he adds, "it "appears to me at all events that the ingredient of the crime expressed

OF THEFT.

* Mr. A. Bogbie makes remarks somewhat to the same effect, but apparently overlooking the definition in Clause 16.

"by the terms whoever *intending* to take *fraudulently* a thing which is "*property*, moves that thing in order to such taking, is vague enough to "lead to various constructions and to various difficulties in the way of "proof." Mr. Norton's definition of course omits the term "fraudulently." His objection to the use of this term is the more remarkable as he professes to follow the law of England, and it is employed in the more ancient definitions of theft or larceny according to that law, as well as in the modern work of Sir E. H. East, "which," say the English Criminal Law Commissioners, "has in practice been very much used as a substitute "for a Digest." In their 4th Report the English Criminal Law Commissioners proposed a general definition as follows: "A "fraudulent intention to appropriate that which belongs to another is an "ingredient common to the offences of

Bracton and Glamoil, cited by Russell 2, p. 93.

Russell, ut sup.

"Theft, including robbery;

"Extortion by threats;

"Obtaining by false pretences;

"Cheating;

"Embezzlement."

See also Prefatory remarks, p. 52, 4th Report.

463. We subjoin for the sake of easy comparison the definitions of theft in the Code and in the Digest:

Indian Penal Code, Clause 363—"Whoever, intending to take fraudulently any thing which is property, and which is not attached to the "earth, out of the possession of any person, without that person's con-"sent, moves that thing in order to such taking is said to commit "'theft.'"

7th Report.

Digest of the English Criminal Law, Chapter 18, Section 1, Article 1—

"Theft consists in,

"1st. A taking and removing of something;

"2nd. Being of the property of some other person and of some value;

"3rd. Without consent to transfer the right of property given by a "person authorized so to consent, or notwithstanding consent so given, "if such consent shall be obtained by intimidation;

"4th. And also without consent to part with the possession given "by a person authorized so to consent, or, notwithstanding consent so "given, if such consent shall be obtained by intimidation or fraud;

"5th. With intent to despoil the owner and fraudulently appropriate "the thing taken and removed."

464. In comparing these definitions, it is to be remembered, that to take fraudulently in the phraseology of the Code means to take a thing "with the intention of causing wrongful gain to one "party by means of wrongful loss to another party."

Clause 16.

465. According to the Code Penal, Article 369, "Quiconque a soustrait frauduleusement une chose qui ne lui appartient pas, est coupable de vol."

466. The following is Mr. Livingstone's definition, Article 645, "Theft is the fraudulently taking of corporal personal property, having "some assignable value and belonging to another, from his possession, "and without his assent."

467. "Explanations" and numerous "illustrations" are subjoined to the definition of theft in the Code, in order to explicate and elucidate as far as possible what is abstruse in it. So also the definition in the Digest is followed by expository Articles, which correspond in many points with the explanations in the Code.

468. In the Code for example in explanation of the words of the definition, "a thing not attached to the earth," it is declared that "a thing "which is attached to the earth becomes capable of being the subject of "theft as soon as it is severed from the earth," and again, "a moving "effected by the same act which effects the severance may be a theft."

Art. 6, Sec 1, Chapter XVIII.

In like manner in the Digest, after an explanation that the law of theft extends to all moveable property, it is declared that it extends "also to property severed from "the realty, although it be severed at the time and for the purpose of "taking and removing the same."

469. Referring to the explanations in the Code Mr. Norton says, "the "*moving* any thing *attached to the earth* in order to such taking (such a "taking as is contemplated in the definition) and the mere *severing* it "from the earth, are distinguished, the latter being a theft, and the "former not, but that distinction seems to me peculiarly subtle, to say "the least of it." Mr. Norton perhaps forgot that the distinction here noticed, by which a severance is necessary to make that a theft which else would not be a theft, is the rule of the English Criminal law in cases of ordinary theft of moveables, for though it be "well settled "that the felony lies in the very first act of removing "the property and therefore that the least removing of "the thing taken from the place where it was before with an intent to "steal it, is a sufficient asportation, though it be not quite carried away," yet there must be a *severance*. Thus "in a case where goods in a shop "were tied to a string which was fastened by one end to the bottom of "the counter, and a thief took up the goods and carried them to the door "as far as the string would permit, and was there stopped, this was "holden not to be a felony, because there was no severance."

Russell 2, p. 96.

470. The rule is different in regard to things *severed from the realty*. There must be a severance, but the severance and the *instant* taking of the thing severed do not constitute a theft. The following are the observations of the English Criminal Law Commissioners on this point: "We have already had occasion to observe upon the dis- "tinction which the law makes between mere moveables "and adherents to the realty. This gives rise to the rule that one who "severs property from the realty and forthwith carries it away, is not "guilty of theft, but of a trespass only. This rule is, in many respects, "opposed to reason and convenience, the more especially as it has been "extended by means of a very fanciful doctrine to mere moveables, not "because they are adherents to, but because they 'savour of the realty.' "The effect of the rule has been to leave a considerable class of property "without adequate protection from the Criminal law, and to induce the "necessity of making many supplementary laws for partially remedying "the defect. The rule itself is one of vague and indefinite operation,

4th Report, p. 53.

"leaving it wholly uncertain what length of time must intervene between "the severance and the taking to constitute the guilt of theft."

Art. 6, Sec. 1, Chapter XVIII.

471. The remedy proposed is to abolish the rule, and this is the object of the article we have quoted above, whereby the English law will be brought into conformity on this point with that proposed in the Code.

472. It is proposed also to abolish the rule as to severance in the case of moveables,* so that on this point likewise the Digest agrees with the Code.

First Report, page 9.
Vol. 4, p. 229.
Chapter XVIII, Section 1, Art. 1.

473. The English Criminal Law Commissioners in their Digest of the Common law relating to theft as actually in force, adopted the definition given by Blackstone:—"Theft is the felonious taking and carrying away of the personal goods of another." In the definition proposed in the Digest submitted in their 7th Report which we have transcribed above, they use the word "removing" instead of the phrase of "carrying away." This alteration is intended to obviate the necessity of an explanation that by "carrying away" is not meant what the words import, but "merely a removal to any distance, however small."

4th Report, p. 57.

474. According to the explanation in the Digest the taking and removing together constitute the same thing as is expressed in the Code by the single word "moving," as that is illustrated by the examples subjoined to Clause 363. The "taking" of the Digest is comprehended in the "moving" of the Code. The taking is said to be the act by which the offender has such possession of the thing that he is enabled to remove it. The "removing" is the essential act. The one can scarcely be distinguished from the other, more particularly in the case of driving an animal, where there is in reality no taking, no actual *prehension* or laying hold of the subject of theft prior to its removal. The word "taking" therefore appears to be mere surplusage.

Art. 3.
Art. 4.

475. By Mr. Livingstone's Code, "Taking alone without carrying "away is sufficient within the definition," and "taking "may be either by a removal, or simply by laying hold "upon the article."

Article 645. Clauses 6, 7.

476. Other alterations of the English law relating to theft, of considerable importance, are proposed by the Commissioners, particularly in respect of the *possession* of property the subject of theft. As it stands, the law, say the Commissioners, makes "possession by the proprietor essential to the offence," and it makes "a constructive possession by the proprietor sufficient to satisfy the rule, "though it be contrary to the fact, and even although the offender had "the actual possession by delivery from the proprietor."

4th Report, p. 54.

477. The Commissioners consider the doctrine in respect of possession by the proprietor to be wrong in principle, and they show how the Courts of Criminal law have endeavoured to escape from it and "to "enlarge the boundaries of the law of theft by forced and subtle constructions, in order to reach offenders guilty of fraudulently appropriating

* See Art. 5, which explains that it is not essential that the thing taken "be completely freed from all impediment to further removal."

4th Report, p. 52. "goods entrusted to their possession." They argue that "in principle possession by the proprietor of the article "stolen is not essential to the offence. For the essence of the offence is "the fraudulent appropriation or attempt to appropriate that which belongs "to another; and if the offender fraudulently take what belongs to "another, it is immaterial, except for mere technical purposes, who had, "or whether any one had actual possession of the property at the time of "the taking, so as the offender himself had not possession." "It is only "for the mere purpose of technical description that it is "necessary in a prosecution for such an offence to state "whose property was stolen; even this cannot be invariably required, "inasmuch as it may frequently happen that although the guilt of the "offender can clearly be proved, the owner cannot be discovered, and it "would be absurd that an offender should derive impunity from a circum-"stance not essential to the offence. Such a description of the property "is to be given where circumstances admit of it, as serves to particularize "the offence, and afterwards identify it if need be; but it is obvious that "for this purpose the naming the person from whose actual possession "the property was taken, though he were not the owner, would as well, "or even better serve the purpose intended, than if the owner himself "were to be named."

Page 53.

478. The Commissioners propose "to make possession by the owner "in all cases immaterial to the offence of theft, and to "embrace at once, by a direct substantive law, offenders "who having lawful possession of property, are guilty of fraudulent em-"bezzlements;" and their definitions are framed according to this view.

Page 54.

479. It will be observed that the definition of theft in the Code does not render it necessary to ascribe the property to any person as owner; the person to be named is "the person from whose actual possession the property was taken" or attempted to be taken; the matter to be charged is that the offender intending to take fraudulently a particular thing which is property, that is to say a thing over which some person has a right of property, out of the possession of A B without the consent of A B, moved that thing in order to such taking. In the Digest it is expressly declared that "theft may be committed by taking "and removing the property of another although the "actual owner be unknown." It appears to us that the definition in the Code with the separate provision for the fraudulent misappropriation of property *not in possession*, is likely to give rise to fewer difficulties in practice on the points in question than that which is proposed in the Digest.

Digest, Chapter XVIII, Section 1, Art. 12.

480. Sir H. Seton considers that in Clause 363 "an attempt" has been made "to incorporate all the subtleties of the English law of larceny in a single definition," and thinks the propriety of the attempt questionable; as also "the adoption of that part of the law of England which converts the attempt to commit a theft into constructive theft," by the use of the words "moves that thing" in order to the taking thereof.

481. Mr. W. Hudleston observes that the definition describes "an attempt at that which is theft by the law of England," appearing not to be aware that such an attempt as the definition describes is, as Sir H. Seton remarks, constructive theft by that law. He says "I do not "see any good reason for the alteration involving the abandonment of a "definition to which the people of India have long been accustomed and "perfectly understand, 'the felonious taking and carrying away the "personal goods of another.'"

482. We know not how Mr. Hudleston conceives this definition to have been given to the *people of India*, or how it can be said that they have long been accustomed to it.

483. Mr. Hudleston proceeds to say, "The illustrations (*a*) and (*b*) are not instances of theft according to any Code that I have seen." With respect to the former illustration, which applies to the "Explanations" (2nd and 3rd) notifying that things attached to the earth by being severed become capable of being the subject of theft, and that a moving within the meaning of the definition may be effected by the act which severs, the instance being the cutting down a tree, we have shewn that by the Digest as well as by the Code, such a case will fall under theft.

484. With respect to the illustration (*b*) Mr. A. D. Campbell well observes, that Mr. Hudleston must have forgotten Lapier's Case cited by Mr. Christian, the Editor of Blackstone, to shew that any the least removal of a thing is a sufficient "carrying away" within the definition given by Blackstone, or to use Mr. Campbell's words, is "with the stretch of "language necessary to justice so usual with the English law quoted by "him (Mr. Hudleston), absurdly strained by it into the falsity of "'carrying away.'"

4 Blackstone, page 231, Note of the Editor.

485. Mr. Hudleston again remarks of the illustration (*m*) that it is "questionable," of (*u*) that it is "absurd," (*y*) "bad," (*z*) "worse;" to which Mr. Campbell aptly replies, "these may be extreme cases, but I do "not think they deserve the epithets he (Mr. Hudleston) bestows on "them,—they clearly explain the principle of the new law."

486. The Code differs from the Digest in the "explanation" that "a person may commit theft though he intends to restore the property "after taking it," whereas by Article 30, Section 1, Chapter XVIII of the Digest, it is declared that "it is not theft where the intent is to "deprive the owner of the temporary possession only and not of his "absolute property in the thing taken." Thus the intent expressed in the definition given in the Digest is "to despoil the owner and fraudulently *appropriate* the thing taken and removed;" while the intent expressed in the definition in the Code is merely to "take fraudulently," that is to say, to take with the purpose of causing wrongful gain to the party taking or some other, by means of wrongful loss to the party from whom the thing is taken, or by depriving him of the benefit which he would have enjoyed from it if it had not been taken from him.

487. This is illustrated by the following example: "A and Z are "gardeners. Z has reared a pine-apple of extraordinary "size, in hope of obtaining a prize. A takes the pine-"apple without Z's consent, produces it before the Judges as his own "and obtains the prize. He then sends back the pine-apple to Z. Here, "as A took the pine-apple fraudulently, A has committed theft, though "he has restored the pine-apple." A is held guilty of theft because he took the pine-apple from Z with the fraudulent intention of gaining for himself a benefit which Z would have gained by it, if it had not been taken from him, or, in the words of the definition in Clause 16, "with the intention of causing a wrongful gain to himself by means of a wrongful loss to Z." Mr. Norton finds fault with this illustration on the

Illustration (*q*).

ground that to construe such a *use* of an article as "theft," involves the meaning of the terms in the text, "intending to take fraudulently," in inexplicable confusion. We think that the illustration, though it is somewhat quaint, sufficiently serves the purpose for which it was intended, and is necessary for that purpose, namely, to shew the application of the principle ennunciated in the explanation just adverted to. But we are not agreed as to this principle. One of us is inclined to concur in the opinion of the authors of the Code, conceiving that when a man fraudulently takes and uses as his own, that which does not belong to him, thereby wrongfully depriving another person of the benefit to which he was lawfully entitled from the use thereof, and wrongfully gaining that benefit for himself, he does all that is essential to the offence of theft, and that it is immaterial whether the wrongful possession and wrongful privation be, or were intended to be, temporary or otherwise. The offender in such a case actually "deprives the owner of the thing taken, and has and deals with it as his own property in fraud of the owner," and with "intent to despoil him," to use the words of the Digest, (Chapter XVIII, Section 1, Article 27); and it seems to make no essential difference whether he meant to appropriate the thing permanently or not. The other of us is disposed to think that the English Criminal Law Commissioners are right in preserving the restriction which is expressed in the article of their Digest quoted above.

488. Objection has been taken to another illustration (*o*) under this clause on the ground that the case stated is an attempt to get money by false pretences, or by "cheating" according to this Code, and not theft. The case is stated as follows :—"A takes an article belonging to Z out "of Z's possession, without Z's consent, with the intention of carrying it "back to Z and of pretending to have found it, in the hope of thus "obtaining a reward from Z." This indeed seems to fall within the definition of cheating in Clause 392, viz., "Whoever by intentionally "deceiving any person fraudulently induces the person so deceived to "deliver any property to any person." Here A takes an article the property of Z out of his possession, and bringing it back intentionally deceives Z into the belief that he had found it, and thereby fraudulently induces Z to give him a reward. A cheats Z because Z is led to give the reward by A's false representation that he had done him a service—that there was a *quid pro quo*. But the case also falls within the definition of theft, because A takes the article fraudulently, that is, with the intention of procuring a wrongful gain to himself by means of a wrongful loss to Z, namely, with the intention of fraudulently obtaining a reward from Z as for a service rendered to him which was not rendered.

489. Sir H. Seton observes with reference to the illustration (*w*), shewing how joint property may be taken fraudulently by one of the joint proprietors from the other so as to be within the definition of theft, that "by the English law theft cannot be committed by a joint proprietor." This is true, except as provided in a late Statute, in the case of members of Banking Co-partnerships, as noted in Article 8, Section 1 and Section 8, Chapter XVIII of the Digest. The principle of the exception here referred to we conceive to be the same as that which induced the Indian Law Commissioners to frame their definition of theft so as to include cases in which one of two or more joint proprietors fraudulently takes the common property out of the possession of the other or others, intending to appropriate it to his own sole use, or to sell it and appropriate the whole price. The Statute referred to applies when one member of a Co-partnership steals money, &c., belonging to the Co-partnership with intent to injure or defraud such Co-partnership.

490. Among the illustrations of theft in the Code are several, (*l*) (*m*), (*n*), in which the article stolen is the property of the person who commits the theft. By the law of England* at present it is theft where the owner takes and carries away a chattel "with a design to despoil the "person having lawful possession of it of all his interest therein by reason "of such possession." "This rule," it is stated, "includes amongst "others, cases where the owner steals from his own "bailee, agent or servant, if either they or any other "person would be liable to himself for the loss." We apprehend that the cases stated in the illustrations abovementioned would be construed as theft by the law of England, because in each case the person who had possession would be regarded as vested with that special property under which the thing taken might be laid in the indictment as of the goods and chattels of such person. "A bailee, a pawnee, and the like," says Russell, "have such special property."

Russell 2, p. 155.

Russell 2, p. 157.

491. But the Criminal Law Commissioners propose to alter the law on this point, considering that "this is one instance "among many of extending the law of theft beyond "the proper limits for the sake of reaching an offender." Therefore in the Digest of the law of theft submitted in their 4th Report, they introduced an article declaring that "theft cannot be committed by one who is either "the sole, or a joint, or a part-owner of the thing taken."

4th Report, Note to Art. 22, page 65.

Article 22, p. 65.

492. This is modified in the Digest submitted in the 7th Report, by omitting the words "the sole," retaining "a joint or a part-owner." We do not conceive that any difference was intended by this omission, as the Commissioners refer without remark to the note to the article we have quoted from the Digest in the 4th Report, as explaining the new rule. We suppose it was thought to be perfectly clear that their definition of the offence did not admit of a charge of theft being brought against a person being the sole owner of the thing taken.

Article 8, p. 244.

493. Under the definition in the Code, as the ownership does not come into question, it requires no straining to bring within its terms cases such as are exemplified in the illustrations (*l*), (*m*), (*n*); and we think that cases of the kind fall properly under the description of theft, as we find in them what is commonly recognized as the essential characteristic of that offence, namely, a fraudulent taking with intent to despoil, and it matters not, in our view, that the offender is the owner of the thing taken, if he took it fraudulently according to the hypothesis, with intent to despoil the possessor of the interest which he had by reason of his possession, or to cause wrongful loss to him and wrongful gain to himself by such taking.

494. The Commissioners explain in the notes that they have not made it a part of their definition that the property taken should be of some assignable value, because of the general provision in Clause 73, by which they conceive that the same end is obtained by a different road.

See Appendix, Note N, page 162.

495. Observing that the distinction between "theft," "criminal

* Digest of the Common Law relating to theft in the First Report of the Commissioners on Criminal Law, page 16.

See Appendix, Note N, page 159. misappropriation," and "breach of trust," "becomes fainter and fainter as we approach the line of demarcation and at length the offences imperceptibly fade into each other," the Commissioners point to the provision contained in Clause 61 as calculated to obviate all the inconveniences which might Page 161. arise from doubts as to the exact limits which separate them. Thus, if a case which is plainly theft comes before a Judge the offender will be punished as a thief. If it is plainly breach of trust the offender will be punished as guilty of breach of trust. If the case be one of those thefts which are hardly distinguishable from breaches of trust, or one of those which are hardly distinguishable from theft, the Judge will not trouble himself with subtle distinctions, but will proceed to sentence the offender under Clause 61 to a punishment common to the penal provisions between which the doubt lies.

496. This meets the objection of Mr. Norton to the illustration (*f*) under Clause 363, there presented as a case of theft, which Mr. Norton says is "to all intents and language" a case of "criminal breach of trust" as defined in Clause 386.

497. The reason why it is brought under "theft" is stated in the illustration, namely, that the plate of Z taken by his butler A, was still in Z's possession, though also in A's possession. And another illustration is given to point out the difference between "theft" and "breach of trust" in circumstances nearly similar. Illustration (*g*).

Page 245, Article 24. Illustration (*f*).

498. In the Digest of the English Law Commissioners there is an article containing a provision to the same effect as the illustration to which Mr. Norton excepts.

499. The framers of the Code observe upon the offence defined in Clause 383, under the designation of "Criminal misappropriation of property not in possession," that it is one which it may be thought they ought to have placed among thefts:—"If we call it theft," they say, "we "speak the popular language, if we call it misappropriation of property "not in possession, we avoid an anomaly, and maintain a line which, in "the great majority of cases, is reasonable and expedient. On the whole "we are inclined to maintain this line."

500. Mr. Norton remarks:—"It is quite impossible to calculate the "limits to which arbitrary constructions may carry the provision of "Clause 383, making it a crime *fraudulently* to take into a party's pos-"session property in no person's possession, except he may be altogether "ignorant of the superior claims of another person, or of the means of "discovering him. It seems to me one of those clauses suggested by the "specific cases exemplified in the illustrations to the clause." In another place he says, "Few I believe, will concede to the propriety of consider-"ing all property which may have been fraudulently taken into possession "from no person's possession (except he may be ignorant of any other "person's superior claim,) as 'stolen property,' (Clause 383) under what-"ever circumstances so fraudulently taken into possession." It is strange that Mr. Norton should refer to Clause 383 as treating property so taken into possession as "*stolen* property." To his other remarks we shall simply oppose the provisions in the Digest of the English Criminal Law Commissioners which regard cases of this description as falling under the law of theft. By Article 12, Section 1 of Chapter XVIII under the general head of "*Fraudulent* appropriation," it is declared that "theft may be committed by the taking and removing of the property of another although the actual owner be unknown." By Article 14 it is declared that "where the taking is upon a finding or other casualty, the "quality of the act depends on the intention of the party at the time, "and it is not theft unless the party took and removed the property with "intent to despoil the owner, and fraudulently to appropriate the thing "taken, although such owner be unknown."

501. The aggravations of theft of a general nature expressly provided for, are 1st, when it is committed within any building, tent, or vessel, used as a human dwelling, or within any building used for the custody of property, in pursuance of a conspiracy in which a person residing or employed within, and one not residing nor employed within, are engaged; 2nd, by a person having made preparation for causing death, or hurt, &c. There is a special provision also for theft on a letter or packet in the possession of an officer of the Post office.

Clause 365.

Clauses 366 and 367.

502. It is remarked by Mr. A. D. Campbell, who expresses a general opinion that much contained in this chapter is a great improvement on the English law, especially as regards the more correct definition of offences, and the discrimination of the various degrees of aggravation in the same offence, that it differs from the existing Regulations in not proportioning punishment in offences against property, with reference to the value of the property, and he concludes that this is because it contemplates sentence of restitution or fine equivalent to it, as part of the punishment. Other officers remark the same difference and object to it as a defect, considering, as one of them expresses it, that it puts the thief of lacs and the thief of a few rupees for want, on the same footing. In making this objection the officers last referred to appear to have overlooked the provision authorizing the imposition of a *fine without* any *limitation* of the amount *in addition to* imprisonment which may extend to three years.

503. Mr. W. Hudleston and Mr. W. Anderson are of opinion that the term of imprisonment ought to be extended. The latter suggests that the limit should be seven years, which is that which now obtains by the Regulations of Bengal and Madras in cases of theft to an amount exceeding 300 rupees, and in the Presidency of Bombay in cases which, with reference to the amount stolen, fall under the head of "robbery."

Bengal, 4 of 1820, Sec. 4. Madras, 1 of 1825, Sec. 9. Bombay, 14 of 1827, Sec. 37, Clause 4.*

504. It is to be observed that when theft is attended with any of the aggravations defined in Clauses 420 to 424, the punishment is cumulative, admitting of additional imprisonment for one year, two years, or three years, as the case may be.

Clauses 426-7, 431-2, 435-6.

505. Upon this arrangement Mr. Strange remarks that "whatever "is gained by it in critical accuracy, in practice is "risked by attempting to legislate separately for what "in effect are integral crimes. To punish a common "act of night burglary, besides making reference to "definitions, recourse must be had to four different "clauses, three of which are far removed from the first "(365,) and an account must be summed up, before it "can be ascertained to what punishment the burglar "may be sentenced." There is an appearance of diffi-

Sir H. Seton also questions the propriety of "the "separation of "house-trespasses "from theft, "which in so large "a majority of "cases is the sole "object of them."

* By Section 39 of this Regulation "thefts" are such "robberies" as from the *smallness of the amount stolen* and other reasons may be considered trivial.

culty as the case is here put, but we do not think it likely that there will be any real inconvenience in practice after the new way is once perfectly understood.

506. Referring to Clause 365, Mr. W. Hudleston says, "I agree with "Mr. J. F. Thomas that a distinction ought to be made between houses "of different descriptions." The following are the observations of Mr. Thomas: "'Any building or tent used as a human dwelling,' includes "thousands of mud or bamboo huts, with nothing but a grass, or mat "door—wholly insecure and unprotected. I think a distinction should be "drawn between such dwellings, and others of greater solidity, and duly "secured."

"Theft in the one by two or more persons, ought not to be subjected "to long and severe imprisonment, unless the thieves are old offenders. "I have known several criminal cases where two persons have committed "theft of some trifling article in one of these insecure huts, where I "should consider rigorous imprisonment uncalled for, especially in the "case of females; and even a month's imprisonment ample for a first "offence, in consequence of the manner in which the property has been "left unguarded, tempting to the commission of the crime."

"I should limit the clause to buildings used as human dwellings and "for the custody of property, *well* and *properly* secured, and add an illus-"tration, pointing out, that an open shed, or hut, with a grass or bamboo "mat for a door, is not a building properly secured."

507. The Sudder Court, North-Western Provinces, observe that as "tents or vessels" may be used for the custody of property, it does not appear why they are omitted after "building," in the second branch of this definition. They recommend that those words be inserted.

508. We observe that in the Draft of the Code first printed, the words were "any enclosed or covered place used as a human dwelling, or as a place for the custody of property," and in an "Explanation" of "enclosed and covered space" in a manuscript copy of the Draft in the office, and also written in pencil by the Secretary on the said printed copy, it is notified that "a tent, that part of a ship which lies under deck, and the cabins of a boat, are within the description." We have not found any note of the reason for the alteration in the revised Draft. We are inclined to think it would be better to insert "tent or vessel" after "building," in the second branch of the clause as well as in the first, as suggested by the Sudder Court.

509. With regard to the observations of Mr. J. F. Thomas, it is worthy of note that he does not object to "tent" being included in the definition; now the mat or bamboo huts he describes are not of less "solidity" nor less firmly "secured" than tents; and it seems that it would scarcely be consistent to exclude the former for an objection common to both, without excluding the latter also, which no one has recommended. If any distinction were to be made between the huts described by Mr. Thomas and buildings of more solid construction, it would seem that Clause 420 which defines "house-trespass" is the proper place for it. In the clause under consideration, the gravamen of the offence is the conspiracy of a person residing within the building, &c., with another person without, and this does not seem to be affected by any consideration touching the solidity of the building, &c.

510. In Clause 367, the aggravation is having made preparation for causing *death*, or hurt, or restraint, &c. In the analogous provision in Clauses 430, 434 and 438, it is preparation for causing not death but hurt, or restraint, &c. We think that Clause 367 is right, and we do not perceive why it should not be followed in the other clauses abovementioned. We observe that in the Draft first printed "death" was omitted in the clause corresponding with 367. We are inclined to think it should have been added on revision in the other clauses as well as in this.

Clause 384.

511. It is pertinently asked by Mr. Pelly, why *rigorous* imprisonment is prescribed positively for "theft" while "extortion" is punishable under Clause 369 by imprisonment of *either* description, as is "criminal misappropriation of property not in possession," an offence which is distinguished from theft merely for the sake of accuracy of definition.

Clauses 368 to 374

512. As extortion always involves "putting in fear of injury," while theft may be committed, and very often, indeed generally, is committed without any aggravating circumstances, we do not see reason for limiting the discretion of the Court as to the description of imprisonment in the one case more than in the other. In Clause 364 therefore we would substitute "imprisonment of either description" for "rigorous imprisonment." In the case of aggravated theft to which the other clauses apply, it seems to be proper to prescribe "rigorous imprisonment" absolutely. In the aggravated cases of "extortion" described in Clauses 371 and 373, we think that "rigorous imprisonment" should be likewise prescribed.

EXTORTION. Clause 368.

Chapter XVIII, Sec. 3, Art. 1. See 7 and 8, Geo. IV, c. 29, Sec. 8, and for India 9, Geo. IV, c. 74, Sec. 82.

513. The definition of "extortion" in the Code does not differ substantially from the general description of the class of offences brought under this head in the Digest of the English law, which is given by the Commissioners in their 4th Report, signifying that their distinguishing feature is "the obtaining of property by means of such threats of injury as do not amount to robbery." But the 1st Article in the chapter under this head does not agree with that general description, inasmuch as the offence therein provided for may be committed by merely sending a threatening letter to a person, with intent to obtain property from him, *although the object may not be effected*. By the Code in every case the person must be "put in fear of injury," and the object must be accomplished, to bring the offence within the definition of "extortion."

See Appendix, Note N, page 162.

514. Mr. Hudleston says of the definition of extortion in the Code, that "the first part appears to describe robbery." Mr. Norton observes, "I believe it will be in vain to seek the distinction intended between "'extortion' and 'robbery,' each offence consisting (at least in many "instances) in the putting in fear of personal injury and thereby accom-"plishing a theft." The authors of the Code remark that, "There can "be no case of robbery, which does not fall within the "definition either of theft or extortion. But in practice "it will perpetually be matter of doubt whether a par-"ticular act of robbery was a theft or an extortion." Here Clause 61 will be found of use. In practice in doubtful cases the offence will be charged in the alternative as "extortion" or "robbery," and the Judge, if the party is convicted, will proceed to pass judgment as directed in the said clause.

515. According to the Digest it is extortion where property is obtained by one person from another "by threat of violence to the person of any other," "where such offence shall not amount to robbery." According to the Code it is extortion when the object is effected "by putting any person in fear, for that person or for any other, of death or of grievous hurt" unless the offence shall amount to robbery; and it does amount to robbery "when the offender at the time of committing "the extortion *is in the presence of the person put in fear*, "and commits the extortion by putting that person in fear of instant "death," &c., "to that person or some other person present at the "time," &c.

Page 254, Art. 6.

Clause 371.

Clause 375.

Clauses 370-372 and 374.

516. It is an offence, but not "extortion," when a person puts another in fear in order to extortion, and specific provisions are made for the punishment of it.

517. Mr. H. C. Tucker observes upon the definition of extortion in Clause 368, that the putting in *fear* must be clear, the injury sufficient to compel the act with reference to the age, sex and situation of the person threatened, otherwise complaints of extortion will be continually brought forward. He thinks the cases in illustrations (*c*) and (*d*) not sufficient. Extortion he conceives should be confined to threats of personal injury for which no subsequent civil proceedings would afford an adequate remedy. Mr. Sharkey is of opinion that there should be a qualification, that the party had no alternative but to comply with the demand, or suffer the threatened consequence. We conceive that it will be a question for the Court whether the injury threatened was such as was likely to produce the effect intended, and whether under the circumstances the party was really put in fear, believing the injury to be inevitable if he did not comply.

518. Colonel Sleeman proposes an additional clause as follows:— "Whoever puts any person in fear of any annoyance to that person or to "any member of his family, by obscenity in language, gesture, or dress, "or by inflicting disgusting wounds on his own person with a design "to extort money, food, or clothing, is said to commit extortion." If it be thought proper to introduce any such provision in the Code, it appears to us that it would come more properly into the chapter "of criminal intimidation, insult, and annoyance."

Chapter XXVI.

519. It is remarkable that by the law of England, as represented in the Digest, the punishment for an attempt at extortion by sending a threatening letter is punishable with transportation, which may be for life, while the punishment for extortion actually effected by threat, is imprisonment for any term not exceeding three years.

Article 1, Sec. 3, Chapter XVIII.

Articles 5 and 6.

520. By the Code the highest punishment for aggravated extortion actually effected by putting in fear of death, &c., and by putting in fear of false accusation of an infamous character, is imprisonment of either description for a term which may extend to fourteen years. We have suggested above that the imprisonment should be "rigorous" in these cases.

Clauses 371, 373.

521. The punishment for the attempt to commit extortion by so putting in fear is imprisonment, which may extend to seven years.

522. The punishment for "extortion" is the same as in the law of England, namely, imprisonment not exceeding three years.

523. The definition of robbery is contained in Clause 375. It is "theft" aggravated by actual violence, or by causing fear of *instant* death, &c., or "extortion" aggravated by putting in fear of *instant* death, &c.

OF ROBBERY & DACOITY.

524. Mr. Hudleston says he thinks the definition in the law of England preferable, quoting that given by Blackstone. His Colleague, Mr. Campbell, expresses his dissent from this opinion.

Volume 4, p. 244.

525. The definition recommended by Mr. Hudleston has not been thought worthy of adoption by the English Criminal Law Commissioners. Their definition is more comprehensive in its terms, but still they have found it necessary to add several explanatory articles.

Chap. XVIII, Sec. 2, Art. 1.

526. As the law is exhibited in the Digest it agrees in substance pretty nearly with the first part of the definition in the Code "regarding robbery as an aggravation of theft." The Commissioners observe that "the limits of the offence of robbery have been rendered indefinite by constructive extensions." They propose to render it more definite "by limiting the crime of robbery to a taking "by personal violence, or threats of personal violence to the party robbed, "or some other person; and by making the existing law respecting extor-"tion more extensive." We conceive that the arrangement adopted in the Indian Code is preferable.

4th Report, p. 67.

527. Mr. Giberne, a Judge of the Sudder Court at Bombay, adverting to the definition of robbery in Clause 375, submits that under its terms a gang carrying away property to any amount from a house, if the family have quitted the house on their approach, or have remained quiet within it, so as to render violence unnecessary, would be punishable only under 365, the gang not having caused or attempted to cause death, or hurt, &c., or fear of instant death, &c. But in the case supposed it is to be presumed that the family quitted the house, or remained passive, from fear of the gang, knowing their purpose, and apprehending violence if they remained, or, if remaining, they did not rest quiet, and such fear, doubtless, falls within the definition, as caused by the gang.

Mr. Pyne, another Judge of the Sudder Court at Bombay, makes remarks nearly to the same effect.

528. The Indian Law Commissioners observe that they have provided punishment of exemplary severity for that atrocious crime which is designated in the Regulations of Bengal and Madras by the name of "dacoity." This name they say they have thought it convenient to retain for the purpose of denoting not only gang robbery, but the attempting to rob when such an attempt is made or aided by a gang. The definition of this crime is contained in Clause 376 as follows: "Where six or more persons conjointly commit "or attempt to commit a robbery, or where the whole number of persons "conjointly committing or attempting to commit a robbery, and persons "present and aiding such commission or attempt, amount to six or more, "every person so committing, attempting, or aiding, is said to commit "'dacoity.'"

See Appendix, Note N, page 163.

529. Several of the Bombay Officers object to the use of the term "dacoity" as being little known in that Presidency. It is not in common use in the Madras Presidency, where, as in that of Bombay, gang robbery is the designation ordinarily applied, and we are inclined to prefer it.

530. The Judges of the Sudder Court, North-Western Provinces, and Mr. Hudleston and Mr. Campbell, Judges of the Sudder Court at Madras, object to the definition of a gang as consisting of "six or more." Mr. Hudleston suggests three or more. He prefers the definition of robbery by open violence in the Regulations.

531. Mr. Giberne thinks the number of four which constitutes a gang by the law of Bombay is preferable to that here proposed; he observes that the offence is more frequently committed by five than any other number.

532. Mr. R. N. C. Hamilton referring to the definition of dacoity in Clause 376, observes, "There can be no reason why the union of six "persons for illegal acts when proved should not be punished as severely "as requisite, but that *that* number assembled unattended with aggra-"vating circumstances should constitute the crime of dacoity does seem "unnecessary." This remark as applied to Clause 376 seems to be founded on some misapprehension, for the six persons according to the definition must conjointly *commit*, or *attempt* a robbery; the offence of robbery must be complete, or there must have been overt acts committed plainly manifesting the intention of robbery, and the union of six persons for the commission of the crime is "the aggravating circumstance" which raises the offence to dacoity. The remark is more applicable to Clause 381, which provides for the punishment of persons assembled for the purpose of committing dacoity, a provision which answers to that contained in Clause 4, Section 4, Regulation LIII of 1803 of Bengal, and the corresponding Regulation of the Madras Code.

533. Mr. J. F. Thomas offers the following observations:—"It is, "I conceive, an omission in the enactments on this head, that a distinc-"tion is not drawn between the leaders, those also who are regular "members of an organized gang, and take the active part in dacoities, "and the low tools who are hired for a quarter of a rupee or a few "annas for the night, to swell the numbers of the gang. I was credibly "informed, that in several instances of gang robbery, or dacoity, brought "before the Criminal Tribunals in Tanjore, the majority of the prisoners "were low cultivating serfs, got together at a day's notice, unarmed, "who would receive no share of the plunder, or but some refuse article, "and a few annas."

"In lieu of the provisions in the Code, I would propose, and I would "not leave it discretional with the Courts, transportation, or imprison-"ment for life, or fourteen years, in the case of every leader, every "regular member of the gang, every person armed with a weapon capable "of inflicting death, and all who use personal violence in a dacoity, but, "for the great body of the gang, who, in some of our provinces are often "mere coolies, six or twelve months' rigorous imprisonment, and security "from the head of their village on release. The dacoities of Southern "India are not ordinarily like those in Northern India. For instance, "the robbery of guards with treasure, or of treasuries, and similar daring "outrages, are not known. If an accurate comparison is made between "the dacoities which come before the Nizamut Adawlut in Calcutta, and "the Foujdarry Adawlut in Madras, the distinction between the offence "in the two Presidencies will be clearly seen. The only exception I am "aware of, is in the case of the Hill gangs in the Northern Circars; for "it is rarely in other districts, and only in the special case of leaders (as "Appoo and Canten) that dacoities assume in this Presidency the same "character as in Bengal, and become the scourge of the country."

"I would also not only recommend a distinction as to the persons who "commit dacoity, but proportion the penalties to the nature of the dacoity "itself. A dacoity in Tanjore was often effected by a body of men, of "whom even the leaders had only sticks in their hands, the others "nothing."

"I would draw a distinction between gang robberies by such means, "when the offenders are not prepared to offer resistance to any armed "person, nor to the Police, and those atrocious cases in which a gang "came well armed, prepared for murder and every violence, and both "purpose, and do resist any force brought at the moment against them."

"Again, I would exclude from dacoity all robberies of grain by gangs "exceeding six, in periods of great scarcity or famine, and treat such "cases as theft, unless committed by an organized gang, and not by a body "congregated on the spur of the occasion in the hope of obtaining food."

"I would not, further, treat such cases as dacoity, although other "property than grain was taken, if it was clear, that the *main* object of "the great body of plunderers, or of the gang was grain, though they "might be led on to take other things."

534. Mr. A. D. Campbell says, "I agree with Mr. J. F. Thomas that "leaders, or heads of gangs, should be liable to punishment higher than "inflicted on the mere members of the gang."

535. Mr. Giberne would make the heads of gangs of dacoits liable to the punishment of death. He describes the proceedings of such a gang committing a succession of atrocities, and terrifying the population of a whole district:—"At length (he says) the gang is caught, tried and "convicted and punished by the new Code with transportation for life. "Surely in all such cases death is desirable as an example to the country."

536. Colonel Sleeman proposes an additional clause, as follows: "Whoever shall be convicted of having been habitually a leader or lead-"ing member of a gang of dacoits, shall be liable to a sentence of im-"prisonment for life, or for such limited period as the Court may deem "proper."

537. Lately the law has been altered, and made more stringent even than Colonel Sleeman proposed. By Act XXIV of 1843, "Whoever "shall be proved to have belonged to any gang of dacoits shall be punish-"ed with transportation for life, or with imprisonment for any less term "with hard labour."

538. The intention was to apply to dacoity the law in force for the prevention of Thuggee, but it differs in the punishment, as transportation for life is not authorized in cases of Thuggee.

539. If this very stringent law be continued,—and it may be presumed that the grounds upon which it was so recently deemed to be necessary are such as will justify its continuance for the present, though it may be hoped that eventually it may be mitigated,—we would suggest, with reference particularly to the observations of Mr. Thomas as to the constitution of these gangs, that some definition be given of what is meant by a person belonging to a gang of dacoits. The preamble to

Act XXIV of 1843 shews that the phrase is intended to designate, not a person who ordinarily lives by honest labour and who on some occasion has been tempted to join himself to a gang and to take a subordinate part in a robbery committed by such gang in the manner described by Mr. Thomas, but one who has habitually associated with a gang of "professional dacoits," "systematically employed in carrying on their lawless pursuits in different parts of the country," accompanying them in their expeditions, and actively participating in their operations.

540. According to the definition of dacoity in the Regulations of Bengal and Madras, which are identical in this point, it seems that the offence may be committed by a single person going forth *with an offensive weapon* with intent to rob, and actually perpetrating or attempting to perpetrate a robbery, or by a gang with or *without offensive weapons* doing the same. In practice, we apprehend, it is only gang robbery that is accounted dacoity. What number of persons constitutes a gang is not determined. By the law of Bombay robbery "committed by a number of persons greater than four is gang robbery." By the Code, under the definition of dacoity, and for the purposes thereof, six persons constitute a gang, including any persons present and aiding. In other respects, the definition appears to contain all that is essential in that of the Bengal and Madras Regulations.

Bengal Regulation LIII of 1803, Section 3.
Madras Regulation XV of 1803, Section 3.
Reg. XIV of 1827, Section 36.

541. The punishment of dacoity without murder, by those Regulations, is transportation for life; but "leaders of gangs or other "heinous offenders convicted of a repetition of the crime, or without such "repetition of a degree of cruelty, violence, or other aggravating crim- "inality, which under the discretion allowed by the Mahomedan Law "may be punishable with death, and which may appear to the Nizamut "Adawlut to render such heinous offenders liable to capital punishment, "shall be liable to a sentence of death." By the Bombay Regulation, gang robbery accompanied with force is punishable "in any of the modes specified in Section 3" thereof, which includes death.

Reg. XIV of 1827, Section 37.

542. By Clause 380 of the Code, if murder is committed by any one of a gang of dacoits, every one of the gang is liable to be punished with death. It does not appear to us to be advisable to extend the punishment of death to any other case. We agree with Mr. Thomas, that there ought to be a great distinction in adjudging punishment between persons proved to be leaders, or regular or habitual members of a gang of dacoits, following the practice of robbery as a profession, and poor coolies enticed to swell the number of the gang occasionally; but we do not think that such persons ought to escape with so slight a punishment as he suggests. We are of opinion that the minimum term of imprisonment may be properly reduced from three years to two years to meet such cases. At the same time we would recommend that the minimum be raised in the case of leaders and persons proved to be habitual members of a gang, and perhaps all who are armed with deadly weapons, from three to seven years.

543. It does not appear to us advisable to exclude from the class of offences designated by the term "dacoity," the gang robberies of grain to which Mr. Thomas refers. Certainly the term "dacoity" is not very apt as applied to them, but they clearly fall within the definition, and though the higher punishments would be excessive, yet there is a wide enough discretion, especially if the minimum be reduced to two years, to admit of the Judge generally adapting the penalty suitably to the circumstances.

544. It is not a light offence the plunder of grain by mobs, though sometimes there may be circumstances which dictate a lenient dealing with it. Such cases we think ought to be reported, after sentence passed according to the law, for the consideration of those whose prerogative it is to temper the ordinances of the law with mercy.

545. We are disposed to prefer the provision of the Bombay Regulation, by which four or more persons are held to constitute a gang, to that of the Code, by which there must be six or more persons present at a robbery to make it amount to dacoity. We observe that four was the number stated in the Draft of the Code first printed. We do not know why it was altered, but it appears by a note of the President that the alteration first proposed, was to reduce the number four to three.

546. Mr. B. Hutt observes that assisting in murder in dacoity, may be visited, under Clause 380, with less punishment than where simple murder is committed, the *minimum* in the former case being rigorous imprisonment for seven years, in the latter imprisonment for life.

Clause 97.

547. By the provisions under the head of "abetment" any one aiding the commission of an offence is liable, if that offence be committed, to the punishment provided for that offence; and if in an attempt to commit any offence, a different offence is committed, any person aiding the commission of the offence first mentioned, is liable to the punishment of the offence actually committed, if he knew it to be likely that such offence would be committed. Under these rules a person aiding a dacoity, if murder were committed by one of the gang of dacoits in committing the dacoity, would be liable to imprisonment for life, at the least; and we see no reason why any one, under the circumstances described in Clause 380, should escape with imprisonment for seven years. We think the penalties should be the same as in Clause 300.

548. It has been observed that Clause 382 will be nugatory in cases of dacoity when the sentence for that offence is transportation or imprisonment for life. It appears to us that it is not required at all as regards dacoity, as the clause relating to that offence sufficiently provides for the aggravation contemplated in Clause 382. In determining whether the offence shall be visited with transportation for life, or imprisonment for life, or for any shorter term down to the minimum prescribed by Clause 380, the Judge will of course take into consideration whether any person has been hurt or not, or whether there has been any other aggravation, and will pass sentence accordingly. We would suggest therefore, that the words "or in committing dacoity" be struck out of Clause 382 and that the clause itself be transposed, so as to follow immediately after Clause 378.

CRIMINAL MISAPPROPRIATION OF PROPERTY NOT IN POSSESSION.

Clauses 383 to 385.

549. We have already* noticed the reasons for separating the offence under this head from theft, and the remarks of Mr. Norton upon "the provision of cl. 383." Mr. Sharkey contends that the offence "is clearly theft," and considers the reasons given in the note for not so designating it as "more fanciful than substantial." It does not appear to us that his objections are well founded.

* Vide paras. 499 and 500.

550. Mr. Greenhill appears to us to be right in thinking that a person appropriating part of a wreck, or goods washed ashore, would commit an offence under these clauses.

CRIMINAL BREACH OF TRUST. Clauses 386 to 388.

551. Sir H. Seton questions "the expediency of multiplying offences "to the extent that they would be created by this "Clause 386." "The effect of it," he observes, "would "be to convert a large portion of what has hitherto "been equitable jurisdiction into criminal." "It was the mixture of equitable and criminal jurisdiction," he adds, "that led to the abolition of the Star Chamber."

552. The principle of the provisions under this head appears to be approved, on the other hand, by the Sudder Court for the North-Western Provinces, and by those Judges* of the Sudder Court of Bombay who have noticed it, and is not objected to by any of the Judicial officers of the Company.

553. The title of "criminal breach of trust" in this Code takes the place of "embezzlement" in the Digest of the English Criminal Law Commissioners.

See para. 478.

554. We have mentioned above the reasons of the English Commissioners for "embracing at once by a direct substantive law, offenders who having lawful possession of property are guilty of fraudulent embezzlement."

Chapter XVIII, Sec. 6, Art. 1.

555. According to the Digest,—"Whosoever being intrusted with the "possession of any moveable property or fixture, being of "the property of any other person, on any contract of "hiring, or as deposit, pledge or security, or for the "purpose of keeping, carrying, or repairing, or other purpose whatsoever, "under an obligation to return, deliver up, or specifically apply the same, "shall, with intent to defraud the owner, and in violation of such trust, "embezzle such property or fixture," shall be liable to the punishment for embezzlement. The term "embezzle" is explained "to comprehend any actual appropriation by the offender "of the property to his own use, or otherwise, to the despoiling, and in "fraud of the owner."

Art. 2.

556. By the Code, "criminal breach of trust" is committed by a person who "intending fraudulently to cause wrongful loss or risk of "wrongful loss to any party for whom he is in trust, disobeys any direc-"tion of law prescribing the mode in which such trust is to be discharged, "or violates any legal contract express or implied which he has made "touching the discharge of such trust with any party from whom such "trust was derived."

Arts. 1 to 13.

557. There would not be a material difference between the law of "embezzlement" in the Digest, and that relating to "criminal breach of trust" in the Code, but for a special provision in the former which declares that it shall "not affect any trustee in and under any instrument whatever." This provision is taken from the Statute 7 and 8, Geo. IV, Chapter 29, Section 50, corresponding with 9 Geo. IV, Chapter 74, Section 103, for India, which Sir H. Seton probably had in view in making the observation above quoted.

Art. 14.

---

* Messrs. Giberne and Greenhill.

558. We are unable to perceive any good reason for exempting trustees, so called technically, from penal responsibility for acts done by them fraudulently for their own gain to the despoiling of the party for whom they are in trust, or, in the phraseology of the Code, with the intention of causing wrongful gain to themselves by means of wrongful loss to the party for whom they are in trust, more than such parties as are described in Article 13 of the section of Embezzlement in the Digest, and Section 49 of the Statute abovementioned, (also 9 Geo. IV, Chapter 74, Section 102) who being intrusted with property as agents, convert such property to their own use or benefit.

559. With reference to Sir H. Seton's remark that "it was the mixture of equitable and criminal jurisdiction that led to the abolition of the Star Chamber," we may notice what Hallam says of the origin of this part of the jurisdiction of the Star Chamber. "Every misdemeanor" he states "came within the proper "scope of its enquiry, those especially of public impor- "tance, and for which the law, as then understood, had "provided no sufficient punishment. For the Judges interpreted the law "in early times with too great narrowness and timidity; defects which, "on the one hand, raised up the overruling authority of the Court of "Chancery as the necessary means of redress to the civil suitor who "found the gates of justice barred against him by technical pedantry; "and on the other, brought this usurpation and tyranny of the Star "Chamber upon the kingdom by an absurd scrupulosity about punishing "manifest offences against the public good. Thus corruption, *breach of* "*trust*, and malfeasance in public affairs, or attempts to commit felony, "seem to have been reckoned not indictable at common law, and came in "consequence under the cognizance of the Star Chamber."

Constitutional History, vol. 1, page 442-3.

560. Blackstone observes that "into the Court of King's Bench hath reverted all that was good and salutary of the jurisdiction of the Court of Star Chamber." But it seems that the observation requires to be qualified, since from a "*scrupulosity*" touching matters which civilly belong to the domain of equity, "offences manifestly against the public good" have been suffered to go unpunished, that beneficial part of the Criminal Jurisdiction of the Star Chamber relating to breaches of trust not having been assumed by or vested in the Court of King's Bench. There is no reason for such scrupulosity in India, where except within the limited sphere of the Queen's Courts the distinction between equitable and legal rights is unknown.

561. It is strange that Mr. Greenhill objects to the introduction of the term "fraudulently," which is intended to stamp the character of the transactions embraced by the clause in question, as "weakening the whole." Another officer, Mr. T. Blane, proposes to "include the *mali-* "*cious* intention of causing loss as well as the *fraudulent* intention, as "where a servant to injure his master suffers his property to be spoilt "although he gains nothing by it."

562. We need hardly say that neither the omission nor the addition proposed appears to us advisable.

563. Mr. Giberne observes that hitherto the offence defined in Clause 386 has been punishable by imprisonment for seven years, and that the proposed penalty of imprisonment which may extend to three years, appears to him insufficient. The punishment is that prescribed for simple theft, except that for the latter the imprisonment is ordered to be rigorous. We have suggested that it be left to the discretion of the judge to determine whether the imprisonment should be simple or rigorous in cases of theft, as it is with regard to this offence. By the Digest the punishment for embezzlement, where the property is worth less than 1£, is imprisonment not exceeding two years, where the value amounts to 1£ the offender may be sentenced to transportation of seven years, or imprisonment not exceeding three years.

564. The Sudder Court for the North-Western Provinces suggest that provision should be made for a severer punishment in certain instances of common occurrence in the mofussil, such as that of confidential persons employed by bankers to convey remittances in specie, appropriating the money to their own use, and alleging that it has been taken from them by robbers. This mode of sending remittances, they observe, is very general, and the offence is of so serious a complexion as to demand a heavier penalty than that contemplated. We incline to the same opinion, and would advise that the maximum term of imprisonment be not reduced below that which may be inflicted under the existing laws of the Company's Courts, namely, seven years.

565. Mr. Bacon referring to Clauses 366 and 388, observes that any person stealing a letter from the Post office, and a clerk of the Post office misappropriating the contents of a letter in his charge, are made liable to the same punishment, though there is no comparison between the degrees of criminality. The punishment awarded in Clause 388, he says, "must be allowed to be quite inadequate." We observe that by the Digest servants of the Post office are made liable to transportation for seven years, or imprisonment not exceeding three years, for stealing a letter, and to transportation for life, or for a term not less than seven years, or imprisonment not exceeding three years, for stealing money out of such letter. And that the latter punishment may be inflicted on any person stealing money out of a post letter, or stealing a post letter from a post letter bag or a Post office. It seems to us proper that there should be a distinction, as suggested by Mr. Bacon, between persons stealing post letters, not being servants of the Post office, and persons being servants of the Post office, misappropriating letters, &c., entrusted to their keeping.

Chapter XIV, Sec. 6, Art. 3.

Art. 4.

Art. 5.

566. For the latter offence the term of imprisonment might be extended to seven years.

OF THE RECEIVING OF STOLEN PROPERTY. Clauses 389 to 391.

567. Upon Clauses 389 and 390 Mr. J. F. Thomas makes the following observations:—

"These provisions I consider to be wholly inadequate to the offence, "when it has been committed by an habitual or professional receiver, by "an officer of Police, by a servant of the party robbed, by persons who "keep houses of ill fame, or for the sale of spirituous liquors, when the "amount is large, or by a party who is known to organize and originate "plans for robbery, and habitually lives on plunder. In such cases the "interests of society require heavier penalties than those provided, and "they should be made imperative."

568. Mr. W. Hudleston and Mr. A. D. Campbell, Judges of the Madras Sudder Court, concur in opinion that the aggravations of *receiv-*

ing recognized in Regulation VI of 1822 of the Madras Code are proper, and should be provided for. Mr. Campbell particularly refers to habitual and professional receivers.

569. Upon Clause 390 the Sudder Court, North-Western Provinces, observe, that the punishment does not appear sufficient to meet cases in which the stolen property may have been obtained by highway robbery, or theft attended with murder or poisoning, in respect to which the Court are of opinion that a higher measure of punishment is required.

570. Mr. Giberne and Mr. Pyne, Judges of the Bombay Sudder Court, think the proposed punishments too lenient.

571. Mr. Greenhill, another Judge of that Court, suggests that in Clause 391 "Thuggee" should be introduced before or after "Dacoity." Mr. A. Bell thinks the punishments too lenient, and suggests that the receiver should be punished equally with the thief.

572. The principle which Mr. Bell recommends appears to have been followed in Clause 391 in regard to dacoity, the punishment for "receiving property stolen in the commission of dacoity" being the same as for dacoity, and we think the application of it may properly be extended to robbery.

573. It seems to us advisable also to make a special provision for the punishment of common receivers of stolen property, upon a second conviction of receiving specific property known to have been stolen, &c., with imprisonment to seven years.

Chapter XVIII, Sec. 7, Art. 1. By the Statute for India, Sec. 107, fourteen years. Art 2. Stat. for India, Section 108, seven years.

574. The punishment proposed in the Digest for receiving property known to have been fraudulently taken, when the fraudulent taking is punishable as theft, or with transportation, is transportation for a term not exceeding fifteen years, nor less than seven years, or imprisonment not exceeding three years, with whipping (if a male); and for receiving property fraudulently taken, but where the original offence is not punishable as theft, transportation for seven years, or imprisonment not exceeding three years, with whipping (if a male).

OF CHEATING. See Appendix, Note N, pages 163—167.

575. The authors of the Code have explained at large their views regarding the offences which are brought under this head.

576. They shew that while there are many deceptions committed for the sake of gain which ought to be punished, there are many such deceptions which however immoral are not offences within the scope of this chapter. The line they have drawn is "to make it cheating to "obtain property by deception in all cases where the property is fraudu-"lently obtained, that is to say, in all cases where the intention of the "person who has by deceit obtained the property was to cause a distribu-"tion of property which the law pronounces to be a wrongful distribu-"tion, and in no other case whatever." "It appears to us," they say, "that the line which we have drawn is correct in theory, and that it is "not more inconvenient in practice than any other line which can be "drawn while the Civil Law of India remains in its present state, and "that it will be unexceptionable whenever the Civil Law of India shall "be ascertained, digested, and corrected."

577. "Whether the principle on which this part of the law is "framed be a sound principle," they proceed to remark, "is a question "which will be best determined by examining, first, whether our defini- "tion excludes any thing that ought to be included, and, secondly, "whether it includes any thing which ought to be excluded." They think "it can scarcely be contended that their definition excludes any thing that ought to be included." And we do not find any objection to the definition on that ground. But they anticipate objections on the ground that the definition includes much that ought to be excluded. "It certainly includes," they observe, "many acts which are not punish- "able by the law of England, or of France," for instance, they say, "we "propose to punish as guilty of cheating a man who, by false represent- "ations, obtains a loan of money not meaning to repay it; a man who, "by false representations, obtains an advance of money, not meaning to "perform the service, or to deliver the article for which the money is "given; a man who, by falsely pretending to have performed work for "which he was hired, obtains pay to which he is not entitled." "In all "these cases," they observe, "there is deception. In all the deceiver's "object is fraudulent. He intends in all these cases to acquire or retain "wrongful possession of that to which some other person has a better "claim, and which that other person is entitled to recover by law. In all "these cases therefore the object has been wrongful gain, attended with "wrongful loss. In all therefore there has, according to our definition, "been cheating. We cannot see why such acts as these should be treated "as mere civil injuries, why they should be classed with the mere non- "payment of a debt, and the mere non-performance of a contract."

578. The above observations have reference particularly to the illustrations (*g*), (*h*), (*i*) subjoined to Clause 392, upon which Sir H. Seton has a note questioning the propriety of "the conversion of so many civil "injuries into criminal offences, and this without any reservation of the "civil remedy."

579. The observations we have quoted shew good cause, in our opinion, for bringing the cases in question within the scope of the Penal Law. Although the civil remedy is not in express terms reserved, there is nothing which appears to us to imply that it is taken away, and we do not understand that this was intended.

580. Mr. Norton is one of those who think that the definition in Clause 392 includes too much. "A host of trivial illegal acts," he conceives, "may be brought within the vortex of this text, and many in no sense criminal."

"The illustrations in most instances," he observes, "are cases of deception in respect to the parties' *future intentions* which of course are in- "capable of proof, and are, many of them, of a quality so little allied to "criminality as to excite ridicule, such as cheating by obtaining money "under a *deceptive promise to repay it.*"

581. Here, as in other places, Mr. Norton hazards general remarks which will not bear the test of examination. Every one who reads the illustrations will see that they are not in *most instances* "cases of deception in respect to the parties' *future intentions.*" Strictly speaking there is not one such case, and out of ten illustrations of cheating there are only two in which *the deception is prospective*, relating to something which the party deceived is led to expect will be done in future by the party deceiving him. In these cases the offence turns upon its being the *present* intention of the latter not to do what he deceitfully leads the other party to expect he will do. The cases referred to are the illustrations (*g*), (*h*), particularly adverted to in the remarks above quoted. Of these the illustration (*g*) is the one which Mr. Norton points out as an example of the "many" which he describes as "of a quality to excite ridicule."

582. With regard to this illustration of the definition in Clause 392, the authors of the Code make the following further remarks :—

"Some persons may be startled at our proposing to punish, as a cheat, "every man who obtains a loan by making promises of payment which "he does not mean to keep. But let it be considered that a debtor, "though he may have contracted his debts honestly, though it may be "from absolute inability that he does not pay them, though his mis-"fortunes may be the effect of no want of industry, or caution, on his "part, is now actually liable to imprisonment. Surely it is unreasonable "to detain in prison the man who, by mere misfortune, has involuntarily "violated the rights of property, and to leave unpunished the man who "has voluntarily, and by wilful deceit, attacked those rights, if only he "is lucky enough to have money to satisfy the demands on him."

583. After giving an example to illustrate their views they proceed as follows :—

"It would be improper for us here to discuss at length the question of "imprisonment for debt. But it seems clear that whether it be or be "not proper, that a debtor, as such, should be imprisoned, a distinction "ought to be made between the honest and dishonest debtor. We are "inclined to believe that the indiscriminate imprisonment of all debtors "would be found to be unnecessary if this distinction were made." In conclusion they say, "We are satisfied that the only way to get rid of "imprisonment for debt, as debt, is to extend the penal law on the "subject of cheating in a manner similar to that in which we propose to "extend it."

584. The sentiments here expressed by the Indian Law Commissioners are in accordance with the views of the Commissioners on the Courts of Common Law in England set forth in their 4th Report, relating to imprisonment for debt. "Whilst we recommend," they say, "that alterations should be made in the law "of arrest favorable to the personal liberty of the honest debtor, we also "think it essential that provision should be made for the more effectual "punishment of dishonest and fraudulent debtors." They observe that the power with which the Insolvent Court is invested of punishing such frauds is limited, and, constituted as that Court is, they think it ill calculated to act as a Court of Criminal jurisdiction. Their conclusion is that "a debtor ought to be liable to a *criminal prosecution*" "in the "following among other cases, namely, where he has obtained credit by "means of any false act, pretence, or representation, whatsoever."

Page 43.

585. This in effect is just what is proposed in the Indian Code as explained in the Note,* and exemplified by the illustration which Mr. Norton deems ridiculous.

586. The recommendations of the Common Law Commissioners were adopted by the Commissioners on Bankruptcy and Insolvency in a Report

* See Appendix, Note N, pages 167 and 168.

Newspaper report of Speech of Lord Cottenham in House of Lords, 30th April 1844.

made by them in 1840; and the Chancellor, Lord Cottenham, in 1844, brought a Bill before the House of Lords to give effect thereto, in which, His Lordship stated in his speech, was a provision that persons guilty of fraud should be proceeded against criminally and tried by a Jury.

587. It appears from the report of the Debate on this occasion that the Bill was approved in principle by all the Law Lords, but it would seem that some impediment afterwards arose owing to which it has not yet passed into a law.

588. In the Digest of the English Criminal Law Commissioners the provisions on the subject-matter are distributed under two distinct heads, viz:—

1st. "Obtaining property by false pretences." 2nd. "Cheats and other like fraudulent practices," the latter including "false personation," which is defined as a mode of cheating in Clause 393 of the Code with a specification of the ways in which the offence may be committed.

Chapter XVIII, Sec. 4-5.

589. The definition under the 1st of these heads, viz., "Whosoever "shall by any false pretence obtain any moveable pro-"perty from any other person with intent to cheat or "defraud any other person," differs little apparently from that contained in the first sentence of Clause 392 of the Code, viz., "Whosoever by in-"tentionally deceiving any person fraudulently induces the person so "deceived to deliver any property to any person."

Sec. 4, Art. 1.

590. Upon the illustration (*k*) to Clause 392, Sir H. Seton observes—"Here the criminality of the act is made to depend upon the meaning of "fraud; the meaning of fraud is made to depend upon the meaning of "wrong; and the meaning of wrong is made to depend on the decision "of a civil tribunal."

591. An explanation is subjoined to the illustration intimating that if the deception practised upon A were such that Z has a legal right to have back the price paid by him, there is wrongful loss and wrongful gain, (that is, according to the definition in Clauses 15 and 28, a loss which the loser may recover, and a gain which the gainer may be compelled to yield by a civil action,) and if A *intended* to cause such wrongful loss and wrongful gain he has acted fraudulently (Clause 16) and has cheated. It is to this explanation that Sir H. Seton alludes. But his remark is not strictly accurate that the meaning of wrong is made to depend on the decision of a civil tribunal; it rather depends upon the rule by which the civil tribunal must decide.

Clause 394.

592. The punishment of "cheating" is imprisonment of either description which may extend to one year, or fine, or both.

593. It is properly treated as an aggravation of "cheating" when the person cheated is one whose interest the cheater was bound to protect, and the punishment is double.

Clause 395.

594. "Cheating by personation" is also liable to double the punishment for "cheating."

595. We are not satisfied that "cheating by personation" is an offence of so much more importance than "cheating" committed in some of the ways indicated in the illustrations to Clause 392, for example in the manner described in the illustration (*a*), that it ought to be made liable to a degree of punishment so much greater.

596. In the Digest of the English criminal law cheating by personation* is liable to a less punishment than cheating by false pretences generally.† The punishment for both however exceeds the punishment for simple theft.‡ Whereas the Code makes the punishment of theft§ three-fold of that prescribed for cheating.

597. It appears to us that the punishment for "cheating" should be increased to two years at least, which is now proposed for "cheating by personation," and that the latter offence should not be distinguished from the former in the degree of punishment. We would leave the aggravation described in Clause 395 liable to double the punishment for simple cheating, that is if our last suggestion should be adopted, to imprisonment which may extend to four years.

OF FRAUDULENT INSOLVENCY, Clause 398.

See Appendix, Note N, page 168.

598. The authors of the Code remark that the provisions under this head "are necessarily imperfect and "must remain so, until the whole of this important part "of the law has undergone an entire revision."

599. The offence defined in Clause 398‖ is provided for, among others, by Section 57 of the Insolvent Act for India, 9 Geo. IV, Clause 73, by which it is made punishable by protracted confinement, for such a period not to exceed three years in the whole, as the Insolvent Court shall direct, to be computed from the date of the Insolvent's petition for relief. The punishment proposed in the Code is imprisonment which may extend to seven years, and must not be less than one year, to which fine may be added.

600. It appears to us that the offence in question is properly made subject to the Penal Law on the principle advocated by the Common Law Commissioners in the Report to which we have already referred, and which has been actually adopted in the latest Act of Parliament on the subject in force in England.

7 and 8 Vict. Chap. 96, Sec. 39.

601. Of the other fraudulent acts described in the section of the Indian Insolvent law we have referred to, some appear to be punishable under different heads of this Code. Thus the falsifying of books for the purpose therein mentioned seems to fall under Clause 189, which provides for "fabricating false evidence," and the withholding of the books, &c., under Clause 156. The fraudulent destroying of books, &c., by an insolvent for the same purpose we conceive may be brought under "mischief" as defined in Clause 399.

602. We are not aware why the provision in this clause of the Code is confined to traders, nor why the punishment is extended beyond what is authorized by the present law for the government of Her Majesty's

* Imprisonment not exceeding three years, Chapter XVIII, Section 5, Article 1.

† Transportation for seven years, or imprisonment not exceeding three years, Section 4, Article 1.

‡ Imprisonment not exceeding two years with whipping (if a male), s. 1, Art. 54.

§ Imprisonment not exceeding three years, Clause 364.

‖ An insolvent removing, concealing, or otherwise disposing of property in order to prevent the distribution of that property according to law among his creditors.

Courts in India, and what, we observe, is authorized in the late Act of Parliament just adverted to. We would make Clause 398 applicable to all insolvents, and limit the punishment to imprisonment for a term not exceeding three years, which is the punishment for stealing.

OF MISCHIEF. Chapter XX. Cls. 399 to 417.

603. This title corresponds to that of "malicious injuries to property" in the Digest of the English Criminal law.

604. In the 4th Report of the English Criminal Law Commissioners it is explained that "This class of offences is characterized by malice as contradistinguished from fraud." Again by Article 4, Section 3, Chapter I of the Digest it is explained that "an act is maliciously done or omitted to be done, where being "prohibited to be done it is wilfully done, or being commanded to be "done it is wilfully omitted to be done" "without lawful justification "or excuse." And by Art. 5 that "Malice in fact or express malice "consists in some actual intention to cause hurt, damage, or injury."

Art. 100, p. 84.

605. It appears to us that the definition of "mischief" in Clause 399 agrees essentially with what is meant by the phrase "malicious injuries to property" according to the above explanations.

606. Mr. Norton however strongly objects to the definition in Clause 399 on account of the wide scope which it gives to the offence of doing mischief, so wide, he remarks, that "it includes arson and the scuttling of ships." So wide also, we observe, is the chapter of "malicious injuries to property" in the Digest, the first article of which provides for the offence of "arson,"* and the fifth article "for the scuttling of ships," or damaging ships otherwise than by fire, with intent to destroy or render them useless.

607. Upon the illustrations of "mischief" in the instances (*e*) and (*f*) under Clause 399 of ships being cast away voluntarily, Sir H. Seton remarks that "by the English law these are capital offences *where life is endangered.*" This is true, but then the offence with this aggravation falls under a different chapter, that of "offences against the person." The arrangement is the same in the Code, and where death is caused by casting away a ship, the same having been done with the intention of causing death or with the knowledge that death was likely to be caused thereby, we apprehend that the offence is capital under Clause 294. It is not capital where death has not been caused, in which the Code differs from the English law. We conceive that if the circumstances were such that the offender would be liable to capital punishment under Clause 294 if the death of any person had been caused by the casting away of the ship, he would be liable at any rate to transportation for life under Clause 308. On the most lenient view of death caused by the wilful casting away of a ship, the offender would be liable under Clauses 304, 305 and 415 to imprisonment for a term extending to sixteen years.

Digest, Chapter XV, Section 5, Art. 4.

By cl. 415, 14 years
" 304, 2 "
16

608. In laying down the punishment for different degrees of the offence of mischief, the gradation observed refers to the amount of loss sustained, a mode of distinction not admitted in estimating the degrees

* See also note, p. 88, 7th Report.

of criminality in other offences against property. Clause 400 we conceive applies to cases in which the loss is under five rupees,* cases in which the loss amounts to five rupees and upwards being provided for in Clause 402,† and cases in which the loss is one hundred rupees or more in Clause 403.‡ We think there is no sufficient reason for the distinction between Clauses 400 and 402. We would modify the latter clause so as to comprehend the cases for which the former was intended, and omit Clauses 400 and 401.

609. Referring to Clause 404, Sir H. Seton puts the case of "A, a "collector, having a duplicate specimen, and destroying it in order to "enhance the value of the remaining one," and asks "is he to be punished"? We think not, for there is no "mischief" committed, since the collector does not destroy the duplicate specimen "intending thereby to cause wrongful loss to any party." Mr. Norton points to Clause 405 as exemplifying two objections taken by him to the provisions of the Code under this head—which he characterizes as "extending criminality to acts of mischief not involving other specific crimes,"—namely, that they "can only be defended on the principle of making every species of civil "injury a public crime," and that "the punishments are out of all reason "severe." This clause, he observes, "enacts to the possible extent of "rigorous imprisonment for two years for committing any 'mischief' "(which may be by diminishing the value of any property intending to "cause wrongful loss to any party) with the deliberate intention of "*annoying* the person to whom the wrongful loss is intended."

610. He refers to Clause 408 as another example liable to the same objections. This clause he describes as "enacting to the possible extent "of like imprisonment for an attempt to commit mischief on any road "intending to render it less easy to travel by it." It is surprising that Mr. Norton should cite this as an instance of a mere private civil injury converted into a public crime, it being obvious that the essence of the offence is the injury caused by it, not to an individual but to the public, and it surely is a public injury to do such mischief to a road as "to make it less safe or easy to travel, or to convey property by it." With respect to Clause 405 it is to be observed that the annoyance is an aggravation of mischief committed in some way within the definition in Clause 399. We have already remarked that this definition corresponds in essential points with the characteristics of "malicious injury to property" in the law of England.

611. The provision made by Statute for the offence of destroying or damaging trees or shrubs in parks or pleasure-grounds, is analogous to that in Clause 405 objected to by Mr. Norton. In both cases there is injury to property and wrongful loss thereby, but the gravamen is the annoyance to the individual, to which his *loss* is nothing in comparison.

612. It is objected to Clause 406, that by determining that the value of the animal or animals, the destruction or injuring of which constitutes the offence here provided for, must be 10 rupees or upwards, there will be excluded a multitude of cases which ought to be included, as a large proportion of the animals belonging to the poor and of importance to them, are of less value than 10 rupees. The value ought to be 4 or

* Fine simply to ten times the loss.
† Imprisonment to six months, or fine, or both.
‡ Imprisonment to two years, or fine, or both.

5 rupees, says one officer, for half the tattoos and cows, to say nothing of the sheep and goats in India, are not worth more than 5 to 10 rupees each. Mr. J. F. Thomas, one of those who urge the objection here noticed, observes that the specification of cattle in Clause 406, and the absence of all reference to animals in the illustrations to Clause 399, have given rise to a doubt in his mind whether poisoning cattle is included in Clauses 400 and 401, and if not, the question arises, is the offence of poisoning cattle under 5 rupees value provided for at all?

613. We see no reason for the doubt entertained by Mr. Thomas, as the definition in Clause 399 is so general, that the destruction or injury of any animal, being property, by *any means* by which it was intended to cause wrongful loss to any party, and of course by means of poisoning, must by every rule of construction be held to fall within it. The offence being within the definition will be punishable as the Code stands, if the value of the animal is less than 5 rupees under Clauses 400 and 401,—if it amount to 5 rupees or upwards but less than 10 rupees under Clause 402,—if it be 10 rupees or upwards under Clause 406.

614. Under Clauses 413 and 414 which provide for "mischief by fire to buildings," Mr. J. F. Thomas observes as follows :—" The "grass or mat huts of the lowest classes are placed on a level with the "substantial, secure, and valuable dwellings of the better classes. The "penalty, considering the injury in the case of these frail dwellings, is "altogether disproportionate, and if, as in Clause 415, a limitation is "made to decked vessels, so I conceive a limitation similar in its charac- "ter should be made in the case of houses."

615. It is obviously proper that in the case of mischief by fire a distinction should be made between the huts described by Mr. Thomas and substantial houses, but there is sufficient room for such a distinction between the maximum of 14 years and the minimum of 1 year, and between rigorous and simple imprisonment, under cl. 413, and we think it best that the distinction should be left to the discretion of the Judge.

616. Upon Clause 414, which makes it an aggravation of mischief by fire to buildings, that the person committing the mischief "intended or "knew it to be likely that buildings ordinarily used as human dwellings "*to the number of not less than* 5, may be consumed," Mr. G. W. Bacon says: "In the close-built and combustible villages of this country, fire "rarely contents itself with the destruction of one house, and whatever "may be the intention of an incendiary, and whatever he may know to be "likely, the man who puts fire to one house will in all probability burn "half the village, and his crime is the same whether he meant to stop at "one house, or to go on to not less than 5. I would extend the punish- "ment in Clause 414 to all malicious burning of dwellings, or out-houses, "or vessels, and proportion the punishment to the probability of exten- "sive mischief."

617. It certainly appears to us unadvisable to make the conviction of the incendiary under Clause 414 depend upon his intending, or knowing it to be likely, that five houses at the least may be consumed in consequence of his act. As Clause 413 applies to mischief by fire committed with the intention of destroying a single house, Clause 414 might be worded so as to apply to mischief by fire committed by a person intending, or knowing it to be likely, that *more than one* house may be consumed.

618. The Sudder Court for the North-Western Provinces observe, with regard to Clauses 413 and 414, that they do not see any notice of occasions in which death may be caused in the commission of mischief by fire, though the proper punishment is perhaps provided for by some other clause in the chapter of "offences against the human body." This conjecture is right. The remarks we have made with respect to death caused by the casting away of a ship, or in the commission of any offence under Clause 415, apply equally to death caused in the commission of the offences defined in Clauses 413 and 414.

619. With reference to 415, Mr. G. W. Bacon observes that "A great "proportion of the vessels in this country are not decked, and mischief "may be as easily committed in these as in the others;" and Mr. Pyne, Judge of the Bombay Sudder Court, states that "the chief part of the coasting trade, also the Mocha trade, is carried on in vessels not decked." This is an important fact, for we imagine that Clause 315 was intended to embrace all sea-going vessels. In the Bay of Bengal, the dhonies or native coasting craft, we believe, are for the most part decked, but if, as appears from Mr. Pyne's statement, the native craft of the Western Coast of India, and that which navigates the northern part of the Indian Ocean to the Red Sea do not come under that description, it is fit that the definition should be enlarged so as to comprehend them as well as the larger river craft, to which probably Mr. Bacon's remark is meant to apply. In the corresponding article in the Digest of the English Criminal law the words are "any ship or vessel."

620. The Sudder Court for the North-Western Provinces suggest that there should be a provision corresponding with Clause 414 in regard to vessels, but it does not appear to us to be required.

621. In Clause 416 the aggravation is the same as in Clause 367 relating to theft, namely, preparation to cause death, &c., but the punishment in the former is imprisonment of either description limited to three years, whereas by the latter the imprisonment is rigorous and may extend to seven years. We see no reason for this difference, and would suggest that Clause 416 be altered to agree with Clause 367, both as to the extent and the nature of the imprisonment.

622. We are not aware of the intended application of Clause 417. It seems to us, as far as we can see, unnecessary.

623. While Mr. Norton exclaims against the severity of the punishments for mischief as out of all reason, several of the officers in the mofussil object to them as inadequate from their leniency. We are not prepared to suggest any alteration except what we have just proposed, and that for the offences defined in Clause 410, and in Clauses 412, 413 and 415, the imprisonment be rigorous.

OF CRIMINAL TRESPASS.

624. Clause 418 contains a definition of "trespass," which, as explained in the Note N, "is the name given "to every usurpation however slight of dominion over "property."

625. Exception is taken to the term "dominion" as it is used in this definition. Sir H. Seton questions "whether in any of the cases put (by way of illustration) dominion can be properly said to be exercised." Mr. Norton says, "I know not what is meant by *dominion;*" "can dominion," he asks, "be exercised without any actual meddling with, or personal ingress upon property, as by making sale of it for instance?" Mr. Hudleston says, "I think this is a bad definition; with reference to "the illustration (*a*) I think walking into a building is ill described as "exercising dominion over it."

626. To exercise dominion over any property, is to do in respect of that property what can only be lawfully done by the *dominus*, or by authority derived mediately or immediately from him. This we presume is what was meant by the expression as it is employed in Clause 418, and it seems to us that the illustrations are all just examples of the "exercise of dominion" in this sense. But we must admit that these words go as far as Mr. Norton's question implies, and that to sell a house would be to exercise dominion over it, which is clearly beyond the intention.

627. It seems to us therefore that it will be better to abandon the term "dominion" in this place, and to modify the definition of "trespass" by specifying the sorts of acts which we understand to have been meant. We would propose that the definition should stand as follows:—

Whoever enters or causes any animal or thing to enter upon or into any property, or who makes use of any property, not having a legal right independent of the consent of any other party, and not having the consent express or implied of any party legally entitled to give a consent, is said to "trespass."

628. "Trespass" is not an offence by the Code except when it is committed in order to the commission of some offence by which it is intended to injure, or in order to intimidate, insult, or annoy any possessor of the property on which the trespass is committed, or any person exercising any dominion over such property by permission of such possessor, which is designated in Clause 419 as "criminal trespass."

629. The aggravations of "criminal trespass" are "house-trespass" (Clause 420), "lurking house-trespass" (Clause 421), "lurking house-trespass by night" (Clause 422), "house-breaking" (Clause 423), "house-breaking by night" (Clause 424).

630. With respect to these aggravations the authors of the Code offer the following remarks:—

See Appendix, Note N, page 168.

"There is no sort of property which it is so desirable to guard against "unlawful intrusion, as the habitations in which men "reside, and the buildings in which they keep their "goods. The offence of trespassing on these places, we "designate as house-trespass, and we treat it as an aggravated form of "criminal trespass."

"House-trespass again may be aggravated by being committed in a "surreptitious or a violent manner. The former aggravated form of "house-trespass we designate as lurking house-trespass, the latter we "designate as house-breaking. Again, house-trespass in every form "may be aggravated by the time at which it is committed. Trespass of "this sort has, for obvious reasons, always been considered as a more "serious offence when committed by night than when committed by day. "Thus we have four aggravated forms of that sort of criminal trespass "which we designate as house-trespass, house-breaking, lurking house-"trespass by night, and house-breaking by night."

631. These forms of criminal trespass "aggravated by the way in

Clauses 426, 431, 435, 427 to 430, 432 to 434, 436 to 438. which they are committed," are punishable as distinct substantive offences; they are punishable again with increased severity when they are committed in order to the commission of other offences, or are "aggravated by the end for which they are committed."

632. We have already noticed an objection taken under the head of "theft" to the separation of that offence from "house-trespass" when the two actions appear to be parts of an integral crime, an arrangement which it is supposed will prove inconvenient in practice, from the references which will be necessary from one part of the Code to another. We have said that we do not think it likely that there will be any real inconvenience in the practical application of the law, owing to the arrangement in question, when the new way is once perfectly understood. In theory we are inclined to think the arrangement in the Code,* by which the trespass is treated as the primary and simple offence, and theft and other offences following upon the trespass as complications and aggravations superadded extrinsically, to be the more just and methodical. There is as much reason for treating "house-trespass" as an aggravation of any other offence in order to which it is committed, as for treating it as an aggravation of theft; but if the principle were followed out generally, it is obvious that there would be a great deal of needless and unseemly repetition, and also, we apprehend, much practical inconvenience.

Vide para. 505.

633. We observe that the English Criminal Law Commissioners have expressed an opinion in favor of the same arrangement as that which has been adopted in the Code, intimating that it is the arrangement which, if their object had been to reconstruct the law instead of merely digesting it, they would have been disposed to follow. "The "proper course as it appears to us," they say, "would "be to consider breaking a dwelling-house as in all "cases the simple offence; and then to classify the circumstances of "stealing or committing any other offence therein, of night time, and of "alarm or injury to inmates, as so many aggravations, to each of which, "when added to the crime of house-breaking, an appropriate place in the "scale of punishments should be assigned. We apprehend that an arrange-"ment of the law upon this principle, would obviate many of the most "embarrassing difficulties by which the subject is at present attended."

5th Report, p. 9.

634. For "house-trespass," "lurking house-trespass" and "house-breaking," and "lurking house-trespass" and "house-breaking by night," in order to the committing of any other offence, which offence is actually committed, the offender is liable to both the punishment for "house-trespass" (or as the case may be) and the punishment of the offence actually committed in addition.

Clauses 427, 432, 436.

635. For "house-trespass" in order to the committing of an offence punishable with death or transportation for life, but which offence is not committed, the offender is liable to transportation for life as the maximum punishment.

Clause 428.

636. There is no corresponding provision for "lurking house-trespass" or "house-breaking" by day, or by night, with the same object.

---

* The same arrangement obtains under the head of "hurt," "assault," &c.

637. When the object is the committing of an offence punishable with imprisonment, the maximum punishment is imprisonment not exceeding one-third, half, or two-thirds of the longest term of imprisonment for such offence, in addition to one year, two years, or three years, as the primary offence may be "house-trespass," "lurking house-trespass," or "house-breaking," or "lurking house-trespass," or "house-breaking by night."

Clauses 429, 433 and 437.

638. We have remarked above in commenting upon Clause 367, that there is no provision under the head of "criminal trespass" similar to that contained in the said clause, for cases in which the offender has made preparation for causing death to any person, and we have suggested that such a provision be inserted in Clauses 430, 434 and 438. The maximum punishment should be proportionately increased in each clause.

Para. 50.

639. Clause 423 defines "house-breaking" to be "house-trespass" committed in any of six ways therein described. The essence of the offence of "house-breaking" (which becomes "house-breaking by night" when it is committed "after sunset and before sunrise") therefore consists in effecting an *entrance* into "any building, tent, or vessel, used as a "human dwelling, or any building used as a place for worship, or as a "place for the custody of property"—1st, by a passage *made* for the purpose; 2nd, by a passage not intended for human entrance; 3rd, by a passage *opened* for the purpose by means not intended to be used for opening it; 4th, by opening a lock with a key not found in it, or with a key left in the lock for the purpose; 5th, by committing assault, or shew or threat of assault; 6th, by a passage known to have been fastened against such entrance, unfastened from within for the purpose.

640. These ways of entry all appear to be recognized in the definition of burglary in the Digest of the English Criminal Law Commissioners. In framing this definition the Commissioners have pursued the same course as was taken in the Code. "According to the common law definition," they observe, "an *actual breaking* as well as an entry was essential "to the offence, but the Courts had found it necessary to construe breaking "to include invasions of the dwelling-house effected by stratagem, or "fraud, or by intimidation, as well as by actual force." To avoid giving occasion for such constructions, "instead of defining the offence to be a "*breaking* and entering, &c., we have," they say, "described it as consist-"ing in an entry by any of the means which either in popular language, "or by construction of law, have been held to amount to a breaking."

Chapter XVII.

5th Report, p. 10.

641. The definition in the Code appears to fall short of that in the Digest by not including an entry effected "by means of "any stratagem, trick, or device fraudulently practised "for the purpose of obtaining admission," of which instances are given in the Note to Article 6 under the head of Burglary in the 5th Report of the English Criminal Law Commissioners. It does however provide for entrance obtained by collusion "with other persons unlawfully affording or facilitating such entry," which is provided for in the same Article of the Digest.

Chapter XVII, Art. 6.

Page 11.

642. It is explained in the Code in agreement with the Digest that the introduction of any part of the body is a sufficient entering to satisfy the definition, but there is no provision to correspond with that of Art. 10 in the Digest, by which the introduction of any engine, or instrument, or the discharge of any missile into a dwelling-house is to be deemed such entering.

643. The offence of burglary in the Digest can only be committed in a *dwelling-house*, whereas "house-breaking" by the Code can be committed wherever "house-trespass" can be committed, that is in a tent, or vessel, as well as in a building, and in a building used as a place of worship, or for the custody of property, as well as for a "dwelling."

644. In noticing above the suggestion of Mr. J. F. Thomas that in providing for offences against property a distinction ought to be made between mat and bamboo huts and such like fragile dwelling places incapable of being secured against intrusion, and substantial houses sufficiently protected from invasion, we observed that if any such distinction were required the proper place for it would be where provision is made for the offence of "house-trespass," &c. Upon further consideration of the subject on this occasion it appears to us that the provisions regarding that aggravation of the offence of "house-trespass" which is designated as "house-breaking," ought not to be applied to any buildings but such as are of a construction to admit of their being firmly secured against invasion, that is to say, buildings with substantial walls and roofs, and furnished with doors and windows having locks and bolts, or other means by which they can be effectually closed. Other buildings we would except from Clause 423. We would likewise except "tents" from the dwellings to which the provisions of Clause 423 are to be applicable. It does not appear to us to be necessary or expedient to make like exceptions from the other provisions touching "house-trespass" and the aggravations thereof.

Vide para. 509.

645. According to the definition given in the Digest of the English Criminal Law, a dwelling-house must be a "*fixed and permanent building*." The Commissioners observe, in a note on this definition in their 5th Report, that "although the authorities do not supply any precise description of the "building which, if inhabited, may be the subject of "burglary, they exclude by instances and illustrations "enclosed grounds and all erections of a merely moveable and temporary "nature, such as booths or tents."

Chapter XVII, Art. 13.

Page 12.

646. The definition of burglary in the Digest includes expressly an entry made into some *inner part* of a dwelling-house as well as an entry into a dwelling-house, but taking the definitions of "house-trespass" and "house-breaking" in the Code together, it seems to us that only the first entry into the house by any of the ways indicated in Clause 423 is provided for. We are inclined to think that a person entering as a house-trespasser (Clause 420), remaining as a lurking house-trespasser until night (Clauses 421 and 422), and then breaking or making an entrance into a closed and fastened inner chamber by any of the ways described in Clause 423, ought to be regarded as a house-breaker equally with the man that makes an entry into the house from without by any such way. This is immaterial, however, as the punishment is the same for "lurking house-trespass" and for "house-breaking."

Clause 431.

647. Referring to Clause 440 which provides for the offence of fraudulently opening a closed receptacle by a person intrusted with the keeping of it by law or in pursuance of a contract, Mr. J. F. Thomas suggests that it would perhaps avoid difficulties if the words express or implied were inserted after the word "contract." These words, we observe, are introduced in the manner proposed, to qualify the term "contract" in Clause 386 relating to criminal breach of trust, and it appears to us equally proper that they should be introduced in this place.

648. Some objections have been made by one or two officers to the punishments for the more serious offences falling under the general head of criminal trespass, but it does not appear to us that they are of sufficient importance to call for any modification thereof.

CONCLUSION.

649. Recurring now, on the conclusion of our review of the chapters which principally form the subject of this Report, to the statement made in the preliminary part of it, of what we conceive to be the practical questions regarding the Code upon which the Government desire to be advised, we think it proper to say, that it is our deliberate opinion with respect to the portion to which we have given our more particular attention in detail, that it is sufficiently complete, and, with such slight modifications as we have suggested, fit to be acted upon, and that if it be brought into operation it may be reasonably expected to work an important improvement in the administration of Criminal Justice. We think it might be brought into operation in the Company's Courts with little if any alteration of procedure with the help of a few plain and simple directions as to the manner of laying the charges, and some rules to define the offences falling to the jurisdiction of the several Courts, with reference to the punishments they are respectively authorized to inflict. It does not appear to us, as at present advised, that there would be any great difficulty in adapting the procedure of Her Majesty's Courts to the new system. Of the two Judges of Her Majesty's Courts who have expressed opinions on this point, one it will be seen has declared that he could act upon the Code immediately, while the other thinks it could not be acted upon without some change in the system of criminal pleadings.

650. In submitting this our first Report on the Indian Penal Code, we have only further to state that, pending the orders of your Honor in Council, we shall proceed with the examination of the remaining chapters of the work in the same manner as we have examined those upon which our observations are now submitted for the consideration of Government.

C. H. CAMERON,
D. ELIOTT.

INDIAN LAW COMMISSION,
The 23rd July, 1846.

POSTSCRIPT.

651. After the foregoing Report was finished the 2nd Report of Her Majesty's Commissioners for revising and consolidating the Criminal Law came into our hands, and finding that in some important points modifications of the existing law are proposed, in order to render the Penal Code of England "suitable to the present state of society, and conformable to the enlightened principles of jurisprudence," which if adopted will bring the law of England into a closer correspondence with that proposed in the Indian Penal Code, we deem it proper to add a brief notice of some of the proposed modifications affecting matters treated of in the chapters of the Indian Code which we have reviewed.

652. First we have to point out that in the chapter of Preliminary Declarations and Enactments in the Schedule prepared by the Commissioners, the first article of the section treating of incapacity to commit crimes, in agreement with Clause 66 of the Indian Penal Code, recognizes the state of idiotcy distinctly, as excepting a person from criminal responsibility. The agreement on this head stops here, for while the Indian Code declares simply, in separate clauses, that nothing is an offence which is done by a child under seven years of age, or by one above seven but under twelve years of age, who has not attained sufficient maturity of understanding to judge of the nature and consequences of his conduct, or by a person mad or delirious at the time of doing the thing, the Schedule has an article declaring generally that no person shall be criminally responsible for any act or omission who "by reason "of unripeness or weakness of mind, or of any unsound-"ness, disease or delusion of mind, wants *the capacity "of discerning that such act or omission is contrary to the law of the land.*" This definition, which is quite new, is strongly objected to by one of the Commissioners, Mr. Starkie.

Chapter I, Section 1, Art. 1, page 9.

Clauses 64 and 65.

Clause 67.

Chapter I, Section 1, Art. 2, page 9.

653. We conceive that the Indian Law Commissioners meant to include "weakness of mind" under the general term "idiotcy." This word is not in Johnson's Dictionary, but the equivalent term "idiotism" is interpreted by him as signifying "natural imbecility of mind."

654. The simple enunciation in Clause 67 of the Indian Code that "nothing is an offence which a person does in consequence of being mad "or delirious at the time of doing it," is in accordance with Mr. Livingstone's Code and with the Code Penal of France on the same point. In Article 35 of the former it is declared that "no act done by a person in a state of insanity can be punished as an offence." The following is the declaration of the French law—"Ié n'y a ni crime ni dèlit lorsque le prévenu était en état de démence au tems de l' action."

Article 64.

655. The next article in this section of the Schedule, providing that "no person shall be exempted from criminal responsi-
Art. 3, page 11. "bility by reason of any temporary incapacity which he "shall have wilfully incurred by intoxication or other means," agrees substantially with Clause 68 of the Indian Code. We would refer here to the remarks we have made in para. 119 of the foregoing Report on the distinction between delirium in Clause 67, and the temporary incapacity of mind arising from intoxication by the use of narcotic drugs, &c.

656. The article relating to Duress (p. 12) in the Schedule differs from that in the Digest cited in para. 104 of our Report, by the omission of the words "of grievous bodily harm," thereby limiting the excuse on this ground to cases in which the party acted under a present fear of death as proposed by us in para. 169.

657. The Schedule agrees with the Code in excluding the excuse of marital coercion in the case of a woman charged with
See note to Article 9, page 12. the commission of a criminal act, adverted to in paragraphs 173 and 174 of our Report.

658. In Article 2 of the 2nd section of the same chapter of the Schedule there is an explanation of the term "unlawful,"
Sec. 2, Art. 2, page 14. which will be found to agree with the explanation of the term "illegal" in Clause 28 of the Code, noticed by us in para. 91 of our Report in reference to an objection which had been made to the application of it "to every thing which furnishes ground for a civil action." According to the above article "an omission shall be deemed to be unlawful whensoever it gives cause for civil action." In explaining their reasons for rendering persons criminally liable for the consequences of omissions which they were bound by contract to have avoided, Her Majesty's Commissioners quote the remarks of the Indian Law Commissioners on the subject, in which they express a general concurrence.

659. The word "injury" is used in the Schedule as a general term, in the same way as it is used in the Code, and the definition of it agrees with that given in Clause 29 of the latter.

660. Article 6 of the same section lays down that "an injury shall "be deemed to be accidentally caused whensoever it is
Sec. 2, Art. 6. "neither wilfully nor negligently caused," and that "accidental injuries do not subject the persons causing them to punish- "ment," except as elsewhere mentioned in the Act.

661. The Commissioners explain that they intend here to depart from the principle of the present law, and following the
Second Report, pages 17 and 18. principle advocated by the Indian Law Commissioners, whose arguments they quote at length, as having their general concurrence, to make it the general rule that "where a person "does an unlawful act, and a consequence follows which has no probable "connexion with it, and can neither be imputed to wilfulness or want of "caution, the agent should be dispunishable, except for the unlawful act
Paras. 310 to 312. "in which he was engaged." We beg to refer to the observations on this head in our Report.

662. With reference to our observations in paras. 176 to 185, upon the provisions of the Code compared with the English law of Principal and Accessory, we have now to point out that in the Schedule under consideration Her Majesty's Commissioners propose to abolish the difference of punishment between principals in the first and second degree and accessories, and the technical distinction between principals in the first and second degrees, and to make the offence of being an accessory a substantive offence. By the change proposed the law of England will correspond with the Indian Code on these points.

Chapter I, Section 3, Article 1, Note (*a*), p. 19.

663. In para. 327 of our Report it is remarked that there is no limitation of time in the Indian Code, corresponding with that of the English law in respect to the cognizance of homicide. This limitation of time "confining prosecutions for murder to cases where the party injured dies within a year and a day after the cause of death," Her Majesty's Commissioners have not inserted in their Schedule.

Note (*a*), Art. 1, Sec. 1, Chap. II, p. 21.

664. Referring to the observations in our Report (paras. 242 to 249) upon the definition of "voluntary culpable homicide" in the Code, as including cases in which death is caused by an influence on the mind, and the exception of such cases in the Digest contained in the seventh Report of the English Criminal Law Commissioners, we have to note that this exception is maintained in the Schedule under consideration, the Commissioners observing that they "do "not feel justified in abandoning a principle which has "been sanctioned by long usage and high authorities," though they "conceive that there is great weight in the reasoning "urged by the Indian Law Commissioners in support of their adoption "of a different course."

Chap. II, Section 1, Article 4, Note (*d*), p. 22.

665. The Commissioners have given a new definition of "murder" agreeing in principle with that suggested by Mr. Livingstone, and to explain the advantages of it they submit the observations by which Mr. Livingstone recommended his definition to the Legislature of Louisiana. The definition is as follows: "Homicide is murder whensoever the killing is wilful, and is neither "extenuated within the provisions of Section 3, nor justifiable within the "provisions of Section 5 of this chapter." Under the explanation before given of the term "wilful," which agrees substantially with that quoted by us in para. 103 from the Digest, the above definition corresponds very closely to that contained in Clauses 294 and 295 of the Code. "Extenuated homicide," it is to be observed, includes that which is termed "manslaughter" in the Code, and also that which is designated as "voluntary culpable homicide by consent." Under the head of "justifiable homicide" are contained some provisions similar to those which in the Code find place in the chapter of "Exceptions."

Chap. II, Section 2, Art. 2.

Chap. I, Sec. 2, Art. 3.

Chap. II, Sec 3, Art. 2.

Sec. 3, Art. 3.

666. With reference to our observations upon the question of treating a person who has caused the death of another by bearing false witness against him before a Court of Justice, as guilty of murder, and making him liable to capital punishment, as provided by the Code, we have to mention that the Commissioners have decided to except this offence from the definition of murder in their

Paras. 258 to 266.

Chap. II. Sec. 2, Art. 3. Note (*b*), p. 5.

Schedule, though they observe, "the act seems to be attended with many of the bad consequences, and to have the general features of a murder of the most malignant "description," and though "there appear to be strong grounds for apprehending "that it is murder by the law of England, as it is by several other Codes." They propose to provide for the crime in the chapter relating to offences against the administration of justice, as we have advised in para. 266, in regard to the Indian Code. The terms of the definition of murder plainly embracing this offence, the Commissioners have thought it necessary to declare the exception expressly in a separate article, and perhaps it will be proper to introduce an "explanation" after Clause 294 of the Code, to notify that this offence is to be dealt with under Clause 191 of the chapter of offences against public justice.

See paras. 268 to 271.

Page 25, Note (*b*), Art. 2, Sec. 2.

Chap. II. Sec. 3, Art. 2, page 25.

667. In para. 269 of our Report we have remarked, that under the English law the plea of provocation is not available to reduce homicide from murder to manslaughter, when the provocation has arisen from mere words or gestures, but that there is no such restriction in the Indian Code. Her Majesty's Commissioners in their present Report observe, that the rules of the existing law of England on this point "appear to be unreasonable, when the principle is considered upon which "extenuation is admissible; viz., the want of self-control, occasioned by means "which, according to the constitution of human nature, ordinarily produce this "effect." They quote at length the remarks of the Indian Law Commissioners on the subject, which, they say, "seem to be very deserving of attention." Their definition of "extenuated homicide," therefore, is not restricted by any such exception as that which, following the existing law, their predecessors thought them-

19. O 3 selves

Report on the Indian Penal Code.

Digest, Chap. XV. Sec. 12, Art. 34. Explan. to Cl. 297.

selves obliged to introduce into their Digest. It does not, however, exactly agree with the Code on this point, inasmuch as the latter explains "grave provocation" to be "such as would be likely to move a person of ordinary temper to violent "passion;" whereas, by the definition in the Schedule, the gravity of the provocation is left to the judgment of the jury in each case. The Commissioners say, "It has been thought by some jurists that the criterion in these cases ought "to be, what would take away the self-control of a person of ordinary temper. "But we have thought it better to abide by the present law, according to which "the circumstances of the individual accused are relevant to the question of "extenuation."

Chap. II. Sec. 3, Art. 6, page 27.

668. As in the Code, the explanation subjoined to Clause 297, declaring what is meant by "grave provocation," such as will reduce "voluntary culpable homicide" to "manslaughter," has a proviso that such provocation was not given by any thing done in obedience to the law, or by any thing authorized by the law of civil or criminal procedure, or by any thing done by a public servant in the exercise of his lawful powers, so Her Majesty's Commissioners have introduced into their Schedule an article, declaring that homicide is not extenuated on the plea of provocation, where any officer or other person lawfully executing any writ, &c., civil or criminal, or lawfully acting in obedience to the command of a magistrate, or otherwise lawfully acting under authority for the advancement of the law, is wilfully killed.

Art. 7, page 28.

669. Again, they have an article declaring that homicide is not extenuated in such a case, although the writ, &c. be not sufficient in law, or the command be unlawful, or the officer have no authority, or the manner of executing the writ, &c., be unlawful, provided the officer believed himself to be acting lawfully as aforesaid, and provided the party killing had notice that the officer proposed to act under such writ, &c.

670. As we understand the last article, it appears to us that the effect of it, for the declared object of protecting officers of justice in the execution of their duty, will be much the same as that of the proviso to Clause 297 of the Code just adverted to, construed with reference to the declaration in Clause 75, that there is no right of private defence against an act done by a public servant, who is legally competent as such public servant to do that act, though that act may be an offence in that public servant, &c. The reasons which induced Her Majesty's Commissioners to frame the article in question, as it stands in their Schedule, are stated in pages 27 and 28 of their Report.

671. After stating those reasons, the Commissioners add, that they "also think "that where an officer believing that he is executing legal process, commits "homicide, such homicide should, notwithstanding the process is erroneous in the "frame of it, be *extenuated*." "In such case," they observe, "he will still "remain liable to severe punishment." A provision to this effect is inserted accordingly in Article 8.

Page 28.

Report, paras. 115 and 116.

672. By Clause 62 of the Indian Code, as we have interpreted it, an officer committing homicide in executing what he believes in good faith to be legal process, but which is not so, being led to the belief of its legality by a *misconception of facts*, would be wholly excused. The words of the clause, indeed, as we have observed, admit of a wider construction, and have been understood to *excuse* an officer acting under an erroneous impression of his duty, arising from a misconception of the *law*, under such circumstances as would *extenuate* the offence under the article of the Schedule which we are now considering; as, for example, an officer acting for the advancement of the law, erroneously believing himself to have authority by law so to act, and in that belief, and in prosecution of that object, committing homicide. We have advised that qualifying words be introduced into Clause 62, to prevent the wide construction here adverted to, of which some have thought it susceptible.

673. Though we are not prepared to agree to such a latitude of indulgence to officers acting *bonâ fide* for the advancement of the law, as to *excuse* them entirely from penal responsibility for homicide committed, under such circumstances as are described in Article 8 of the Schedule, when they have erred from a misconception of the *law*; yet we think that such circumstances ought to be regarded as *extenuating* the homicide. Sometimes the incidents of the case may bring homicide

Report on the Indian Penal Code.

cide so committed under the provisions for "voluntary culpable homicide in "defence," in Clause 299 of the Code. But this will not be generally applicable, and we are inclined to recommend the introduction of a new provision to correspond with the said article.

674. It appears to us to be advisable to add to Clause 75, and to the explanation annexed to Clause 297 of the Code, a proviso corresponding with that contained in the articles of the Schedule we have just been considering, requiring it to be notified that the officer is acting under a writ, or in obedience to command, or otherwise, for the advancement of the law.

675. We have observed that under the head of "extenuated homicide" in the Schedule is included what is designated in the Code as "voluntary culpable homicide by consent." In support of the provision which distinguishes such homicide from murder, the Commissioners cite the observations of the Indian Law Commissioners on the subject, which, they say, "appear to them to have great weight." Further, they distinctly provide for homicide in duelling as "extenuated homicide," and vindicate the provision upon grounds similar to those upon which we have advocated the dealing with this offence as "voluntary culpable homicide by consent" under Clause 298 of the Code, as we believe was intended by its authors. In the Schedule is a separate article declaring that homicide in duelling is not extenuated when the death of the person killed is caused by unfair means. We do not think such a proviso necessary in the Code, as the terms of Clause 298, we conceive, exclude any case of death caused by other means than those to which the person killed gave his "intelligent consent." The punishment for homicide in duelling by the Schedule is transportation for life or for any term not less than seven years; by the Code it is imprisonment of either description for a term not exceeding fourteen years, nor less than two years, to which may be added fine at discretion.

Art. 14, page 29.

Art. 16, page 30. First Report, para. 290.

Art. 17.

676. The Schedule provides specially for "negligent homicide," the definition of which in Article 2, Section 4, Chapter II, together with that in Article 5, Section 2, Chapter I, therein referred to, agrees essentially with Clause 304 of the Code. The punishment is imprisonment not exceeding three years by the former, not exceeding two years by the latter.

677. The Schedule in many cases treats as "justifiable homicide" what under the chapter of Exceptions in the Code is held to be no offence, as when the homicide is committed by a person acting lawfully under a lawful authority, in various ways, for the advancement of the law, and giving notice of the authority under which he acts. We think it advisable to add the proviso regarding notice to Clauses 62 and 63 of the Code, as well as to Clause 75, and to the explanation annexed to Clause 297, as above recommended. Particulars, it is to be observed, are given in the articles of the Schedules here referred to, which the framers of the Code left to be specified under the head of procedure, to which they appear more properly to belong. Her Majesty's Commissioners, it appears, contemplate a revision of their work when the whole Digest is completed, with a view to generalization and the systematical adjustment of the several portions, and probably there will then be a more distinct separation of the provisions which belong to procedure.

Chapter II, Sec. 5.

Compare Art. 1 to 11 with Clauses 62 and 63 of the Code.

2nd Report, p. 7.

678. Again, homicide is treated as "justifiable" in the Schedule

Chapter II, Section 5, Arts. 12 to 18. when it is committed in the lawful defence of person or property, the provisions not materially differing from those under the head of the "right of private defence," Clause 74 to 84. in the chapter of Exceptions in the Code, which are however much more full and explicit.

679. The last article in the Schedule under the head of "justifiable Art. 19. homicide," appears to correspond with Clauses 70 and 72 of the Code, except that the consent of the sufferer is not required by the former as it is by Clause 70, when the party is able to signify consent.

680. Her Majesty's Commissioners agreeing to the sentiments expressed by the Indian Law Commissioners in Note B, Page 36. Vide paras. 165 to 168. quoted in para. 166 of our Report, have resolved to omit any provision "justificatory of the homicide of an "offending party committed in order to save the life of "the accused, or rather because the accused reasonably thought that the "homicide was indispensable for preserving his own life."

681. The offence of aiding in, or abetting the commission of self-murder, which by the present law of England is murder, Chapter II, Section 6, Art. 2, page 37. the Commissioners propose to make punishable with transportation for life, or for not less than seven years, which is the punishment they provide for homicide by consent. By Clause 307 of the Code also, this offence is punishable with the penalty therein provided for homicide by consent, viz., imprisonment for fourteen years, or not less than two years, except (Clause 306) the person who commits suicide is a child, or of unsound mind, &c., when the punishment may be death, or transportation, or imprisonment for life.

682. The Schedule provides that attempts to commit murder by poisoning, or by any means causing bodily harm, or by Chapter II, Section 7, Arts. 1, 3. setting fire to, or casting away a ship, &c., shall be punishable capitally, (the Commissioners however expressing a wish to reconsider their recommendation on this point when they present a general chapter on the subject of punishments) and that attempts to commit murder otherwise than by poisoning, although no Arts. 2, 4. bodily harm shall be caused, shall be punished with transportation for life, or for any term not less than 7 years, or with imprisonment not exceeding three years. Again, the maliciously putting the life of any person in danger, by any means not before specified, is punishable with imprisonment not exceeding three years, or fine, or both.

683. Attempts to commit murder are by the Code liable to be punished Clauses 308, 309. with transportation for life; attempts to commit homicide which under the circumstances would be culpable homicide less than murder, with imprisonment which may extend to three years.

684. The term "grievous bodily harm" is used in the Schedule to designate "all the serious personal injuries, short of Chap. II, Section 7, Art. 6. Page 39, Note (e). "death, the commission of which and the attempting "to commit which should be visited with severer pun- "ishment than other personal injuries." Upon the Chap. III, Art. 1. definition of this term the Commissioners say "they "have endeavored to include within its meaning the "more serious kinds of personal injury, without reference to pugnacity "or other principle than the damage and suffering occasioned." They appear to have aimed at giving in a condensed form the substance of the detailed definition of the kinds of "hurt" designated as "grievous" in the Indian Code, which, with the remarks of the Indian Law Commissioners, they cite at length in their note. "The limitation of twenty days," in their definition, they observe, "is "taken from the French Code, and was adopted from that Code by "the Indian Law Commissioners." Upon this subject we would refer to the observations in our Report, and particularly to the observations in para. 374 on the point last mentioned. We observe that Mr. Starkie objects, as we do, to the limitation of twenty days in the definition of "grievous bodily harm" or "grievous hurt."

Clause 314.

First Report, paras. 356 to 386.

685. The punishment proposed for "grievous bodily harm" in the Schedule is transportation for life, or for a term not less than seven years, or imprisonment not exceeding three years, nor less than one year. By the Code the maximum punishment for "grievous hurt" simply is imprisonment for ten years, to which fine may be added; the minimum is imprisonment for six months. Attempts to cause "grievous bodily harm" are punishable by the Schedule in the same manner as the completed offence, except that there is no minimum limit to the imprisonment. The punishment for an attempt, by the Code, is half of that which may be inflicted for the completed offence.

Clause 319.

Chap. II, Section 7, Art. 7.
Clause 329.

686. A subsequent article of the Schedule in the same section, but separated from that relating to "grievous bodily harm," provides for other "bodily harm" (answering to simple "hurt" in the Code) or "violence," caused or done "maliciously or negligently." The punishment is the same as is prescribed by the Code for "hurt"—imprisonment not exceeding one year, or fine, or both, except that in the Code the fine is limited to Rupees 1,000.

Chap. II, Sec. 7, Art. 38, page 43.

687. Article 40 of the same section contains a provision corresponding to that of Clause 70 of the Code, justifying any harm arising from any thing not intended to cause death, which was done with the consent of the party suffering.

Art. 40, page 45.

688. The definition of assault in the Schedule differs from that contained in the Digest and quoted in our Report, by the addition of the words "or menace by gestures," by which it is made to comprehend what in the Code is designated as "shew of assault."

Art. 43, p. 45.
Vide para. 398, First Report.
Clause 341.

689. The Statute Law* of England, which we apprehend is the only law upon this subject which is enforced, differs from the Indian Code on the subject of abortion, in that the former does not punish the woman who voluntarily causes herself to miscarry, whereas by the latter she is punishable. We find that it is now proposed that "every woman being "with child, who with intent to procure her own mis-"carriage, shall maliciously administer to herself any "poison or other noxious thing, or use any instrument

Chap. II, Sec. 7, Art. 15.

* Note.—By the old Common law it seems that "if a woman be quick with child and by a potion or otherwise killeth it in her womb it is a great misprision." We ought to have noticed this at para. 347 of our Report.

or other means whatsoever," shall be liable to transportation for life, or for any term not less than seven years, or imprisonment for a term not exceeding three years.

690. The punishment proposed in the Code is imprisonment not exceeding three years, or fine, or both. By the Schedule of Her Majesty's Commissioners, and also by the Indian Code, a person causing, or using means to cause the miscarriage of a woman is liable to the same punishment as is prescribed for a woman causing her own miscarriage. By the Code a person causing a woman to miscarry without her consent is liable to additional punishment for any hurt that may ensue.

Clause 312.

Clause 313.

691. The above article in the Schedule is followed by a proviso that the Act intended to procure miscarriage was not done in good faith with the view of saving the life of the woman, which corresponds with the terms of Clause 312 of the Code.

692. The article defining "rape" in the Schedule contains, in addition to the words used in the definition given in the Digest, the words following, "or whilst she is insensible," which correspond with the second description of "rape" in Clause 359 of the Code.

Digest in 7th Report, Chap. XV, Sec. 15, Art. 20.

693. The Code includes under "rape" sexual intercourse with a girl with or without her consent when she is under nine years of age. By the present law of England this offence is punishable as rape when the girl is under ten years of age. By the Schedule it is proposed to be so punishable when the girl is under twelve. By the Statute for India the age is eight years.

First Report, para. 446, p. 290.

694. The punishment for rape by the present law of England is transportation for life absolutely. In the Schedule it is altered to transportation for life, or for not less than seven years. By the Statute for India it is death. By the Code the maximum punishment is imprisonment for fourteen years.

Report, para. 447.

695. In the Schedule there is a new provision for the offence of administering drugs, &c., to a woman to render her insensible, or otherwise to affect her so as to facilitate the object of obtaining carnal knowledge of her. There is no similar provision in the Code, but it seems to be worthy of consideration whether this offence, which we apprehend is not uncommon in India, should not be included in it. The proposed punishment is imprisonment not exceeding two years.

Chap. II, Sec. 7, Art. 24, page 43.

696. By Clause 296 of the Code it is provided that when a person intending to cause death kills a person whom he did not intend to kill, he shall be held guilty of the same degree of homicide as if he had caused the death which he intended. There are similar provisions in the Digest of the English law prepared by the late Commissioners. In the Schedule under consideration instead of those provisions limited to homicide, there are general provisions making a party liable to punishment for any injury caused by him to a person not intended to be injured, by means by which he intended to injure some person, in the

Chap. XV, Section 2, Art. 5.

Chap. II, Sec. 7, Arts. 45 and 46, page 46.

same manner as if the person injured had been intended to be injured. In explanation the Commissioners say—"If these rules be applicable to "homicide they seem equally to apply to other severe personal injuries; "as for example, if A were attempting to put out B's eye, and by accident "C intervened, whose eye was put out by the thrust intended for B."

697. We have lastly to remark that the present Commissioners have abandoned the classification of crimes as "treasons," "felonies," and "misdemeanors" according to the Digest of their predecessors, in which a new signification was given to the two latter terms; the term "felonies" being used to denote crimes punishable with death or transportation, also the crime of self-murder, and the term "misdemeanor" all other crimes except "treasons." The present Commissioners have avoided the use of these terms altogether in the Schedule. In the 7th section of the Draft of the Act to which the Schedule is proposed to be annexed, it is prescribed that offences liable to the penalties of the 6th or any higher class shall be tried in the same manner and under the same procedure as if such offences were by the said Schedule declared to be felonies; and offences liable to lower penalties as misdemeanors.

Chap. IV. Of Penalties—Transportation for seven years, or imprisonment not exceeding three years.

C. H. CAMERON,
D. ELIOTT.

INDIAN LAW COMMISSION,
The 5th November, 1846.

SECOND REPORT

ON THE

PENAL CODE

BY THE

INDIAN LAW COMMISSIONERS.

FROM

THE INDIAN LAW COMMISSIONERS,

TO

THE HONORABLE THE PRESIDENT OF THE COUNCIL OF INDIA, IN COUNCIL.

1. We have the honor to submit our second and concluding Report on the Indian Penal Code.

2. Our First Report consisted of a review of the chapters of a general nature governing the whole Code, namely, the chapter of "General Explanations," the chapter of "General Exceptions," and the chapter of "Abetment," and of the important chapters treating of "Offences affecting the human body," and of "Offences against property;" to which was added a brief notice of some modifications of the English Criminal law, affecting matters treated of in those chapters, which are proposed in the Second Report of Her Majesty's Commissioners for the revision and consolidation of that Law.

Report, dated 23rd July 1846.

Chaps. I, III, IV, XVIII, XIX.

Postscript, dated 5th Nov. 1846.

Submitted to Her Majesty, 14th May 1846.

3. In this Report we begin with the chapter of "Offences against the State," and proceed through all the chapters of offences not before examined in the order in which they stand in the Code, and finish with the chapter of "Punishments," which stands second in the Code, but which we have purposely reserved to the last.

Chapter V.

Chaps. VI to XVII and XX to XXVI.

Chapter II.

CHAPTER V.

OF OFFENCES AGAINST THE STATE.

See Appendix, Note C, page 117.

4. This chapter provides only for offences against the Government of India, and not for offences against the General Government of the British Empire, for reasons stated in the Note to the chapter, which appear to us to be good and sufficient.

See pages 118 and 119.

5. It may be well on this occasion to advert to the suggestion offered in that Note, as to the expediency of the interposition of the Imperial Legislature to pass a Law of High Treason for the Territories of the East India Company, on the ground that though "it is highly improbable that any English King will "visit his Indian dominions, or that any plot having for its object the "death of an English King will ever extend its ramifications to India, it "is by no means improbable that persons residing in the territories of "the East India Company may be parties to the levying of war against "the British Crown, without violating any local regulation. If any "insurrection were to take place in any of the British dominions in the "Eastern seas, in Ceylon, for example, or in Mauritius, it is by no means "improbable that persons residing within the Company's territories might "furnish information and stores to the rebels. And if this were done by "a person not subject to the jurisdiction of the Courts established by "Royal Charter, we are satisfied that there would be most serious diffi-"culty in bringing the criminal to legal punishment."

Clauses 109, 110 and 111.

6. The principal offence provided for in this chapter is waging, or attempting to wage war against the Government, or abetting the waging of such war; after which is the offence of concealing a design to wage such war; next is the assaulting, or wrongfully restraining, or overawing by means of a riotous assembly, the Governor-General, or any Governor or Deputy-Governor, or Member of the Council of any Presidency, in order to induce or compel him to exercise, or refrain from exercising, any of his lawful powers.

7. Mr. Norton thinks that "the Law of High Treason as expressed "in the Statutes of England in respect of levying war, &c., would with "a little concentration of their language, have more clearly defined the "offences intended to be created by these clauses."

Digest in 7th Report of Criminal Law Commissioners. Chap. II, s. 1.

8. If the plain and simple terms of the clauses in question be compared with the articles of the Digest of the English Law on the same topics, we rather apprehend that the general opinion will be contrary to that of Mr. Norton.

Arts. 11 to 13.

25 Edward III, Statute 5. 6th Report, p. 13.

9. The English Criminal Law Commissioners, it will be observed, have given definitions of the terms "levying war," both as regards the manner of it, and as regards the objects intended thereby, which they deemed necessary in order to put a stop to a latitude of construction beyond what in their opinion the Statute of Treasons contemplated, but which has been sanctioned by high judicial authority. "The "crime," they say, "is in plain and unambiguous terms "declared by the Statute to consist in a levying of war. There is nothing "to indicate that these terms were intended to be used otherwise than "according to their literal sense, and indeed the context, as well as the "history of the times antecedent to the declaratory Act, confirm the "position that they were meant to be used in that sense." After much reasoning on the subject they say in conclusion, "under "these impressions we are inclined to recommend that the "use of all constructive interpretations of the Statute of Treasons, both in "the article of levying war and of compassing the King's death, should be "abolished by the Legislature; and we have accordingly inserted in the "Digest provisions which will have the effect of excluding them."

6th Report, p 17.

10. In another place the Commissioners say, "The terms of the Statute "seem naturally to import a levying of war by one who "throwing off the duty of allegiance arrays himself in "open defiance of his Sovereign in like manner and by the like means as "a foreign enemy would do, having gained footing within the realm." So also we conceive the terms "waging war against the Government" naturally import a person arraying himself in defiance of the Government in like manner and by like means as a foreign enemy would do; and it seems to us, as we presume it did to the authors of the Code, that any definition of terms so unambiguous, would be superfluous.

Page 6.

11. The reasons assigned in the Note for making the abetment of hostilities against the Government an offence specially, instead of leaving it to the operation of the General Law of Abetment in Chapter IV, appear to us satisfactory. But we do not see that but for such a provision "a conspiracy for the "subversion of the Government which should be carried "as far as the gunpowder treason, would be punishable very much less "severely than the counterfeiting of a rupee." It appears to us that under Clause 96 such a conspiracy carried so far, acts being done in pursuance thereof and in order to the committing of the offence contemplated, would be punishable with imprisonment for six years. It is true however that under the General Law of Abetment "a conspiracy for "the subversion of the Government would not be punished at all, if the "conspirators were detected before they had done more than discuss "plans, adopt resolutions, and interchange promises of fidelity."

Page 28.

Page 29.

12. Mr. Hudleston suggests that "the condition of owing allegiance to the British Government ought to be added" to the definition in Clause 109. Mr. R. N. C. Hamilton says "ought not words fixing "some definitive individuality to be used," as "whoever *being a British* "*subject* (or subject of British India) wages war, &c., shall be punished "with death?" "The rulers of foreign Independent States (he observes) "any more than those of France or Russia, cannot be declared liable to "death for waging war. Yet the clause as it stands comprehends them."

13. The Statute of Treasons recited in the Digest is not more specific than this chapter of the Code in regard to the persons subject to its provisions. It says simply "if *a man* do levy war against our Lord the King in his realm," as the Code says, "*whoever* wages war against the Government," &c. The laws of a particular nation or country cannot be applied to any persons but such as owe allegiance to the Government of the country, which allegiance is either perpetual, as in the case of a subject by birth or naturalization, &c., or temporary as in the case of a foreigner residing in the country. They are applicable of course to all such as thus owe allegiance to the Government, whether as subjects or foreigners, excepting as excepted by reservations or limitations which are parts of the laws in question. The specification proposed by

Mr. Hamilton would exclude foreigners resident in the country. Now when foreigners enter a country it is supposed that they are allowed to do so only upon this tacit condition that they be subject to the laws. "The "public safety, the rights of the nation and the prince," says Vattel, "necessarily require this condition, and the foreigner "tacitly submits to it, as soon as he enters the country; "as he cannot presume that he has access upon any "other footing. The sovereignty is the right to command in the whole "country, and the laws are not simply confined to regulating the conduct "of the citizens towards each other, but also determine what is to be "observed by all orders of people throughout the whole extent of the "State."

Book II, Chapter VIII, Section 101.

"In virtue of this submission, foreigners who commit faults, "are to be punished according to the laws of the "country."

Section 102.

So the Statute 3 and 4 William IV, Chapter 85, empowers the Government of India to make Laws and Regulations for all persons whether British or Native, *foreigners* or others, *within* and *throughout the whole and every part of the Territories under the Government of the East India Company;* and if this Code should become the Law it would of course be understood as applicable to all persons thus subject to the Legislative authority of the Governor-General of India in Council, unless it were otherwise specially provided in the Act by which it was promulgated. Farther as the Legislative authority of the Governor-General in Council is expressly declared to extend to "all *servants* "*of the said Company within the dominions of Princes and States in* "*alliance with the said Company*," the Code would embrace them likewise.

14. The authors of the Code considered it very desirable that it should be made to extend also to British-born subjects of the Queen and to Native subjects of the British Government within the dominions of such Princes and States, but in their letter to the Governor-General in Council, under date the 2nd May 1837, they said they had serious doubts whether the Legislative authority of the Government of India went so far. Upon this point and also upon the power of the Government of India to apply the Code to offences committed on the high seas by Natives of the British Territories, they recommended that a reference should be made to the Home authorities. In the answer of the Secretary to the Government of India it was notified that a reference would be made to the Court of Directors in order that the doubts which had been suggested might be cleared up. A reference was made accordingly to the Court of Directors who took the opinion of the Attorney and Solicitor-General, and of their own Counsel on the subject, which they communicated to the Government of India in a despatch, dated 19th February 1839. The Law Officers say that in their opinion "The Legislative Council has power to pass Laws "enacting and declaring that crimes and offences committed in the "Territories of Princes or States in India adjacent to the British Terri-"tories, by persons, the *Native* subjects of and owing obedience to the "Laws of such British Territories shall be liable to be tried and pun-"ished as if committed within the local limits of the British Territories;" and also "that the Legislative Council has power in the same manner to "provide for the trial and punishment of crimes and offences committed "upon the high seas, enacting and declaring them to be offences of the "same quality and triable and punishable as if they had been committed "on land, as has been done, as to offences committed at sea, by British "Statutes." They add that "it would of course be proper to limit the

Dated 5th June 1837.

39 George III, Chapter 37. "application of such a Law to persons Natives and "subjects owing obedience to the Laws of the British "Territories. For Piracy, &c., provision has been made "by existing Laws." It is to be observed that this opinion does not touch the question of the power of the Indian Legislature to make Laws binding on *British-born* subjects of the Queen residing in the dominions of Princes and States in alliance with the East India Company, which appears to be still doubtful.

15. In the communication from the Secretary to the Government of India above referred to, it was also intimated that the Governor-General in Council fully concurred in the principle advocated by the Commissioners in the letter above mentioned, "that the Penal Law should "extend to all inhabitants of India without distinction of rank, though "from Treaty, and more perhaps in form of procedure than in actual "liability, exceptions would no doubt be found more necessary in this "than in any other country."

16. If the Penal Code shall be adopted, it may be presumed that the Act by which it is promulgated will declare to what places and to what classes of persons it shall apply generally, and will notify any reservations or limitations which may be resolved upon.

17. Mr. Hudleston referring to a suggestion of Mr. Blane, that the provision contained in Clause 111 should be extended to all constituted authorities, observes for himself that the clause as it stands "appears to be a strange provision with an inadequate penalty." It would be strange, we conceive, to magnify an assault of the nature described in this clause, committed upon an inferior officer of the Government, as a "constituted authority," into an offence against the State; and equally strange *not* to make it an offence against the State when it is committed upon the Governor-General of India, or a Governor, or a Member of the Government of any Presidency, with the view to deter him from exercising any of his lawful powers as Governor-General, &c. It appears to us that Clauses 184 and 185 sufficiently provide for the punishment of attempts to overawe other public officers or "constituted authorities," when such attempts are not made by a "riotous assembly;" when they are made by a "riotous assembly," the provisions of Clause 127 and the following clauses of the chapter of Offences against the public tranquillity apply.

18. With reference apparently to Clause 113 and the explanation subjoined to it, Mr. Norton makes the following remarks:

"As regards the object of defining the *mode* of slandering Govern-"ment—'as by words either spoken or intended to be read, or *signs, &c.*,' "and of defining what shall *constitute* slandering, namely, 'the exciting "*feelings* of *disaffection*,' as contrasted with the exciting only feelings "of such a '*disapprobation* of measures of Government as is *compatible* "with a *disposition* to render obedience *and* to support its *lawful* "authority against unlawful attempts, &c.' I conceive the composers "of this Code are as unfortunate as all others have been in that effort. "Words *spoken* and *signs* made, and words *written*, with a view to sedi-"tion or of exciting disaffection, are of very different effect and crim-"inality, and the vagueness in the definition of slander, is such, that no "two persons would probably agree in their sense of it. But the greatest "objection appears to me to be the enormous severity with which the "most trivial slander against Government, by the most trivial sign of "communication, *may* be visited—extending as it may to banishment "for life added to unlimited fine."

19. Mr. Cochrane in commenting upon Clause 113 says, "I think "that as a mere matter of public policy, every Government should avoid "punishing mere words, unless such be accompanied by acts injurious "to the interests of the State. But this clause does not only apply "to words, but is in fact a direct attack on the public press. The ex-"pression 'as is compatible with a disposition to render obedience,' "which is the qualification of the clause, appears to me of a very dan-"gerous tendency, and calculated to place men's rights and liberties in "the discretion of each particular Judge." He objects to the clause also on the ground of the injustice of inflicting such severe punishments as are authorized by it.

20. Mr. Hudleston considers the clause to be "wholly indefensible," but he does not state his reasons for this opinion.

21. The offence which the clause is intended to punish is that of attempting to excite feelings of *disaffection* to the Government; and to guard against too wide a construction of this term, and to give free scope to that kind of temperate discussion and criticism of public measures which is conducive to the public good, an explanation is subjoined declaring that by disaffection is not meant "such a disapprobation of "the measures of Government as is compatible with a disposition to "render obedience to the lawful authority of Government against unlaw-"ful attempts to subvert or resist that authority." It seems to us that by this explanation the discretion of the Judge is pretty well guided and limited, and that there is by no means so much danger of his transgressing the just line as Mr. Cochrane apprehends.

22. As to the ways in which the attempt to excite disaffection may be made "by words either spoken, or intended to be read, or by signs, or by visible representations," the terms expressing them are the same as are used in the definition of defamation, and we presume that the same reasons which determined the authors of the Code not to make a distinction between written and spoken defamation, determined them likewise not to make a distinction between seditious words spoken in order to excite disaffection in the hearers, and seditious words written and intended to be read, the object being the same. These reasons are ably stated in the Note to the chapter on "Defamation." As to sedition, there can be little question, we conceive, that the object of exciting feelings of disaffection to the Government may be effected more easily, more suddenly, and therefore more dangerously, by an inflammatory declamation on a popular topic, addressed to a multitude by a skilful orator, than by the circulation of written or printed papers. Mere vague words spoken at random ought not indeed to be brought within this clause; but as in the Digest of the English Criminal Law Commissioners it is laid down that words spoken shall not be deemed to constitute an overt act of any treason, *unless they be words of advice, direction, or persuasion*, tending to effectuate some traitorous act or design, so here must be understood significant words of advice, direction, or persuasion, tending to excite the people to whom they are addressed to a degree of disaffection incompatible with a disposition to render obedience to the lawful authority of the Government, &c., and spoken under circumstances indicating a

See Appendix, Note R, page 175.

Digest in 7th Report, Art. 18, Sec. 1, Chap. II.

design to cause such excitement, or under circumstances from which the speaker must have known it to be likely that the words spoken by him would cause such excitement.

23. It seems that by the Common Law of England, "generally "speaking, any words, &c., tending to vilify or disgrace "the King, or to lessen him in the esteem of his "subjects, even in common and unadvised discourse, amount to a "misprision punishable by fine and corporal punishment," as well as by imprisonment, and by special Statutes persons advisedly speaking against the constitution on certain points, are liable to punishment by forfeiture of lands and goods, and imprisonment "at the King's pleasure, or as other authorities have it during life," which the Criminal Law Commissioners propose to change into imprisonment for a term not exceeding 3 years, (the maximum term of imprisonment specified in the clause under consideration as the alternative for banishment,) and fine at discretion.

Russell 1, p. 221.

Blackstone 4, page 123.

Articles 11 & 12. Sec. 3, Chap. II of Digest.

24. By Article 5, Section 3, Chapter II of the Digest of the English Criminal Law Commissioners "public speaking" is specified together with "the exhibiting of flags, inscriptions," &c., as means of "exciting in the minds of the subjects of the "realm hatred or contempt of the person of Her Majesty, or of her "Government, or of the Constitution of the United Kingdom," &c. The "exhibiting of flags" is a mode of using "signs or visible representations" within the scope of the definition in Clause 113.

7th Report.

25. With regard to Mr. Cochrane's objection that the provisions of this clause, (touching "words intended to be read," we presume,) are an attack upon the public press, we have only to observe that the objection appears to apply equally to the Law of England by which the "composing, printing, or publishing" a seditious libel tending to bring into contempt the person of Her Majesty, or her Government, &c., is a penal offence. "Publications tending to degrade and vilify the constitu"tion, to promote insurrection, and circulate discontent through its "members, would," says Russell, "without doubt be "considered as seditious and criminal." Such publications only, under the explanation subjoined to Clause 113, would we conceive be liable to punishment by the provisions thereof.

Vol. 1, p. 220.

26. In England in cases of this nature the first offence it appears is punishable at Common Law. For a second offence the punishment is, by Statute, the same as in cases of high misdemeanors, that is, we apprehend, by fine and imprisonment at the discretion of the Court. Formerly the offender might be sentenced to *banishment* for such term of years as the Court should award, but this part of the law has been repealed. The punishment proposed by the English Criminal Law Commissioners in their Digest, is imprisonment for a term not exceeding 3 years.

Note to Art. 46, p. 33, 6th Report of Commissioners on Criminal Law.

Blackstone 4, p. 122-3.

Chapter II, Section 3, Art. 4.

27. Upon the propriety of the punishment of banishment for the offence in question, we shall be better prepared to deliver a positive opinion when we have maturely considered the chapter of Punishments, which we reserve for examination ultimately.

Vide post.

28. We have only further to notice in this chapter Clause 115, which provides for the punishment of persons "using any place within "the territories of the East India Company for the purpose of making "preparations to commit depredations on the territories of any power at "peace with the Government of the said territories, *or for the purpose "of taking refuge after committing such depredations.*"

29. Objection is made by several of the Officers whose reports we have had under consideration to the latter part of this clause which proposes to punish persons taking refuge in the Company's territories. This may include subjects who have gone out to commit depredations on other territories, and have returned for refuge, and persons, not subjects, who have come in for the purpose of taking refuge, after having committed depredations on another territory. It appears to us that all that it is proper for the Government to do when the refugees are not subjects is to refuse protection to them. The Magistrates might be empowered, on the applications of the proper Officers of the State on whose territories the alleged depredations were made, to enquire into the cases, and if the charges shall appear to them to be well founded to deliver the accused to be tried and punished by the laws of the country in which they committed the offences complained of. With respect to subjects it appears to us proper to make them liable to punishment in the manner proposed. Colonel Sleeman approves of both parts of this clause, in substance, but suggests the following alteration in the form of expression—"Whoever taking advantage of his position within the East "India Company's territories shall commit depredations within those of "any power at peace with the Government of the said territories; or "shall take refuge within those territories after having committed such "depredations shall, &c., &c." He says, "This is a very important enact-"ment, and will supply the place of Regulations V of 1809, I of 1822, "and VIII of 1829. The Native Chiefs should be required to observe the "same rule in their relations with each other, that we here observe in our "relations with them all; and when we make them do so our supremacy "will be really a blessing. In nothing have we so much neglected our "duty as in the licence we have virtually given them to prey upon each "other—or to allow their subjects to prey upon the subjects of others."

30. Before we conclude our remarks upon this chapter we wish to advert again to the suggestion made by the framers of the Code as to the expediency of the interposition of the Imperial Legislature to pass a Law of High Treason for the territories of the East India Company. We conceive that offences of a treasonable nature committed against the Government of India, must in contemplation of law be considered as offences against the Crown. And we have consequently very grave doubts whether the Council of India is not excluded from all Legislative power on the subject, by that part of the 43rd section of the Charter Act which provides that they shall not "in any way repeal, vary, suspend "or affect any part of the unwritten laws or constitution of the United "Kingdom of Great Britain and Ireland, whereon may depend in any "degree, the allegiance of any person to the Crown of the United King-"dom, or the sovereignty or dominion of the said Crown over any part "of the said territories."

CHAPTER VI.

OF OFFENCES RELATING TO THE ARMY AND NAVY.

31. The provisions of this chapter are intended for the punishment of persons who, not being themselves subject to Military law, exhort or assist those who are subject to Military law, that is to say, soldiers or sailors in the Army or Navy of the Queen, or of the East India Company, to commit Military offences.

32. The Note to the chapter explains the necessity of having provisions of this nature, because the general law respecting the abetting of offences will not reach persons abetting Military delinquencies, such delinquencies not being punishable by this Code. It is also shewn that from the severity of Military penal law, justified by the circumstances of those for whom it is intended, the principle of the general law of abetment which punishes the abettor with a penalty equal or proportionate to that to which the person who commits the offence is liable, could not with propriety be followed in cases of this kind. The design is to provide for the punishment of offences of this sort, in a manner more consistent with the general character of the Code.

Note D, p. 120.

33. Mr. Cochrane objects to the punishments for abetting mutiny and assaults upon Officers as extremely severe. They are not however more severe than the punishments for the same offences by the English law.

34. Mr. Cochrane further objects to there being no distinction between assaults upon Officers in execution of duty, and assaults upon them off duty; upon which we have only to observe, that the Code in this respect agrees with Article 6 of the new Articles of War contained in Act XX of 1845.

35. Mr. Hudleston observes that a distinction is made between mutiny and assaulting a superior, for which he does not see the ground. He might have discovered that the Code here follows the Articles of War for both the Queen's and Company's Forces.

36. It is asked are common soldiers and sailors only intended, and if so is it sufficiently clear? It appears that in the Articles of War for the Land and Sea forces of Her Majesty and the Company, respectively, the terms "officers and soldiers," and "officers and seamen," are used in contradistinction, and we presume that when the terms "soldiers and sailors" or "seamen" are used by themselves, as well as when, as in Clauses 118 and 119 of this chapter, a superior officer is referred to, they are meant to signify common soldiers and sailors. In the Digest of the English Criminal law, in the Section of offences relating to the Army and Navy, the expression is "Any *person* serving in Her Majesty's forces by sea or land," which we conceive includes officers as well as common soldiers and sailors.

Chap. II, Sec. 6, Art. 1.

37. We have supposed that by the terms "soldiers and sailors," are meant persons in the Army and Navy, considering the latter term to signify exclusively ships of war, but this term is not used in the text, and we doubt whether the expression "sailor in the service of the Queen or of the East India Company," by itself, can be held to denote only a sailor employed in a ship of war and subject accordingly to Military law; for the East India Company have ships which do not belong to the Indian Navy and are not ships of war, and we imagine that not all the vessels employed as Packets, Revenue Cruisers, &c., in H. M.'s Service, are deemed to be ships of war, and navigated under the laws applicable thereto. It may be better to substitute for the words "in the service," the specific words "in the Army or Navy" of the Queen or of the East India Company, which are mentioned in the title of the chapter, or to enlarge the expression as follows—"Any person employed in the Army "or Navy of the Queen or the East India Company, and subject to the "Laws and Articles of War for the Government of the Military or Naval "Forces of Her Majesty or the East India Company,"—if it should be thought proper to include officers as well as common soldiers and sailors.

38. We have to remark that in the "Exception" to Clause 124 the word "husband" has been inserted, apparently through inadvertence, by transcribing *verbatim* the "Exception" to Clause 107, which otherwise is appropriate, and which was evidently intended to be adopted in this place *mutatis mutandis*. If the exception to Clause 107 be altered as we have suggested in our former Report, this exception will need to be altered in the same manner, as well as by the omission of the word above mentioned.

First Report, para. 232, p. 244.

CHAPTER VII.

OF OFFENCES AGAINST THE PUBLIC TRANQUILLITY.

39. There is no provision in this chapter for the offence of "riot" unless where *twelve* or more persons are assembled riotously, whereas by the Law of England the offence of "riot" may be committed by an assembly of *three* or more persons.

40. By the first printed Draft an assembly of *four* or more persons might be a "riotous assembly." In the original manuscript Draft the number of persons specified is *three* or more, according to the English Law.

41. By the Law of England when twelve or more persons riotously assembled, being commanded by proclamation to disperse, disobey such command by remaining together riotously for the space of an hour, it is an aggravated offence punishable by transportation for life. By the Bombay Code it is rebellion, punishable by imprisonment for 10 years, or fine, or both, when twelve or more persons assemble for riotous or rebellious purposes not amounting to treason. By the Madras Code twelve or more persons assembling for such purposes, or for the purpose of interfering with or obstructing the collection of the public revenue, and refusing to disperse, are punishable by imprisonment for a like period. It is an offence for *any number* of persons to assemble in a manner indicating an intention to commit an unlawful act, &c., if they refuse to disperse upon the order of the Magistrate, but it is lightly dealt with, the punishment being a fine not exceeding Rs. 50, or imprisonment not exceeding one month.

Reg. XIV of 1827, Section 3.

Regulation III of 1831.

42. The objects specified in Clause 127, any of which being designed by an assembly of twelve or more persons, gives the assembly the character of "riotous," are, 1st, the overawing the Government of India, or of any Presidency, or any public servant or body of public servants; 2nd, resisting the execution of any law; 3rd, committing any assault, mischief, or criminal trespass; 4th, wrongfully restraining any person; 5th, putting any person in fear of hurt or assault; 6th, wantonly insulting or annoying any person; lastly, an assembly is to be deemed "riotous" if it is attended with circumstances which may reasonably excite apprehensions that its object is one of those aforesaid. Now, excepting the first object which it may be admitted is not likely to be attempted by an assembly which does not number more than twelve persons, it appears to us that there is none of those mentioned which may not probably be attempted riotously by a number of persons less than twelve, and we cannot but think that the law will be inefficient for the purpose of repressing riots if the number which shall be held to constitute a riotous assembly be not reduced. We would suggest in accordance with the English Law that *three* or more be substituted for *twelve* or more persons. We would then introduce into Clause 130 the words "of twelve or more persons," after the words "riotous assembly." The offences would by this alteration be, simple rioting, the offender being one of three or more persons constituting a "riotous assembly;" rioting, the offender being one of twelve or more persons constituting a "riotous assembly," with the aggravation of disobedience to a lawful command to disperse; rioting, the offender being armed; rioting, murder

Clauses 128 and 129, 130, 132.

Clauses 133, 134. being committed by one of the rioters. In addition to the punishment for "rioting," according to the circumstances, the offender will be liable to the punishment of any other offence committed by him while "rioting."

43. Mr. Norton says that this chapter appears to him "uncertain and "imperfect." As an instance he remarks that "rioting cannot be com-"mitted unless persons *are aware* of the *facts* making an assembly "'riotous and unlawful,' as detailed in Clause 127, and intentionally "join or continue in it. Now this knowledge and intention are very "difficult to *prove*, and yet to make a party liable under Clause 130 they "would have to be proved, even though there be a refusal to disperse "after proclamation, for it is only those who commit the offence of "rioting (as above *defined* and *qualified*) who are punishable by Clause 130 "for such refusal. A simple going and continuing with a riotous as-"sembly after such a proclamation is only punishable by one month's "imprisonment, or fine, or both, by a different Clause (135)." We have first to observe that Mr. Norton has misunderstood the clause last mentioned, which applies *not* to a "*riotous* assembly," under Clause 127, but to "any assembly of twelve or more persons," whose design may not have been overtly shewn to be riotous, but which from the apprehension of danger arising from it has been commanded to disperse. With respect to a "riotous assembly," certainly to bring a person who joins it within the definition of a rioter in Clause 128, it must be proved that he was aware of facts which gave it the character of "riotous," that is of facts shewing that its object was one of those specified in Clause 127, or that he was aware of circumstances reasonably tending to the apprehension that such was its object. But we do not perceive that there would be any extraordinary difficulty in proving the necessary facts and circumstances. It would be sufficient, we conceive, to give proof of significant overt acts, or of language used by the leaders, or passing among the members of the assembly, manifesting the object, so as to make it obvious to every observer. Where such acts had taken place, or such language had passed, the proof of them we should rather think would be easy. The intention of the party joining the assembly is to be inferred of course from his cognizance of facts characterizing the assembly as "riotous." By the Law of England to constitute a riot there must be a "common purpose of executing some unlawful and violent act," or of executing any act whatever with violence, &c., which common purpose is a matter of inference from the overt acts of the assembly, their language and gestures, as proved by evidence. The proof would be of the same character under both laws.

44. Mr. Cochrane objects to the qualification, "reasonably exciting apprehension," "as allowing the opinion of the Judge to be his rule of action," but this is an objection applicable to every case in which it is necessary to infer the intention from the manner of proceeding and the concomitant circumstances. We need hardly say that every system of law admits of such inferences more or less, particularly the Law of England, as we have just noticed in this very instance of riot.

45. Mr. J. F. Thomas approves generally of the provisions of this chapter, but thinks that they should not be applied to *ryots* assembled to resist unusual or heavy imposts, as it is the only way by which they can influence the public authorities. He is of opinion that unless the ryots are armed and use violence to individuals, they should not be held guilty of rioting. Mr. Thomas refers to Regulation III of 1831 of the Madras Code which was intended specially for the suppression of such assemblies, as an enactment unwise, and a great source of oppression. He says, "The tendency of the law in this Presidency, where the "Collector and Magistrate is the judge in his own cause, as to what does "or does not overawe him, is to prevent all expression of public feeling, "an evil of great magnitude, and there can be no medium whilst this "oppressive law exists, between unlimited submission on the part of the "ryot, and rebellions such as we have lately seen in Canara."

46. We think it would be altogether inexpedient and improper to except a particular class of subjects from the operation of this law, or to make it applicable to them conditionally, as Mr. Thomas suggests. An assembly of ryots may be as dangerous to the public tranquillity as an assembly of other men, and we believe that in fact the Regulation mentioned by Mr. Thomas was enacted in consequence of multitudinous assemblages of ryots in the very district named by him, which attempted to constrain the authorities rather by the mere demonstration of numbers than by show of arms—by passive rather than active resistance. It is obvious that whatever be the object or purpose of such assemblages, however peaceable the first intention, the very fact of the combination of masses of men is pregnant with danger, as must always be the case where there is a great aggregation of physical force, easy to be set in motion by any exciting influence, without any adequate means of checking or controlling it, ready to be applied on the instant.

47. Mr. Cochrane objects to the punishments in Clauses 130 and 132 as beyond the measure of the offences, while exception is taken to them, by some persons, on the other hand, as too lenient. It appears to us that the punishments are justly meted. They are greatly more lenient than those which may be inflicted under the Law of England; for example in the case provided for by Clause 130, viz., continuing in a riotous assembly after a command to disperse has been given in the manner prescribed by law, without any other aggravation, the punishment by the Code is imprisonment for a period not exceeding two years, whereas by the Law of England the offender may be transported for life. If the offender is armed, the Code makes him liable to imprisonment for an additional term not exceeding 2 years. The aggregate appears to us adequate, but not more than adequate to the offence.

Clauses 131 and 132.

48. Mr. Cochrane "protests against the enactment contained in Clause 133," which, when murder is committed in a riot by one of the rioters, makes "every other person who at the time of the committing of "the murder, is committing the offence of rioting, as a member of the "same riotous assembly," liable to imprisonment for a term which may extend to 5 years, with or without fine. He says he "cannot see on what possible principle it can be supported." He puts the case of a riot by 500 persons for the purpose of annoying some person, in which one of the rioters murders another, "can it be maintained for a moment," he asks, "that the 498 remaining rioters are each to be liable to 5 years' imprisonment with unlimited fine?" On the other hand Mr. Norton says, "If a riotous assembly have the object of overawing the "Government, and in pursuance of that criminal object one of the party "commits murder, the others engaged in that common cause are only "liable to the punishment of 5 years' imprisonment and fine. I leave to "the judgment of others whether the English Law making this high "treason and murder in all, is not the more reasonable of the two, even "if the latter be too strictly severe." Again Mr. Bacon says, "the "punishment should extend even to death (to all engaged in the riot,) "when homicide has been committed, and to imprisonment for life in "atrocious cases attended with wounding."

49. The punishment of imprisonment for 5 years under the clause in question may be enhanced to 7 years if the rioters shall have continued in assembly in spite of a command to disperse. By Regulation II of 1823 of the Bengal Code, imprisonment for 5 years is the minimum to which a person convicted of affray attended with homicide may be sentenced by the judge trying the case, the maximum being 7 years; but the Nizamut Adawlut may enhance or mitigate the sentence at the instance of the judge. Possibly Mr. Cochrane contemplates the case of one rioter murdering another from some motive unconnected with the riot and not in prosecution of the object of it. If this is his meaning we agree with him that "the 498 remaining rioters" ought not to be liable to punishment as implicated in the offence of murder. But we do not understand that they would be so liable under Clause 133, which we conceive is to be construed, as Mr. Norton has construed it, as applicable only to a case in which murder is committed by a rioter in pursuance of the object of the riotous assembly; we think this is implied in the words "while committing the offence of rioting." If it should be deemed proper to make the intention more clear, for the words last quoted might be substituted the following, "in prosecuting the object of the riotous assembly of which he is a member."

Clauses 130 and 131.

50. Before we pass from this chapter, we have to consider the question noticed in para. 122 of our former Report, whether an affray should be made an offence independently of consequences. An affray according to the Law of England is committed when two persons or more fight in *public*, so as to cause terror and alarm among the Queen's subjects; it is distinguished from assault in that the latter offence may be committed in private, where it cannot cause terror or alarm; the latter therefore is regarded more especially as an offence against the person of an individual, the former as an offence against the public peace. It appears to us that neither the law of assault as touching two persons, nor the law of rioting as touching three or more persons (if amended as we propose) sufficiently provides for this offence as respects the public tranquillity especially, and we are inclined to think it advisable to introduce into the Code an express provision corresponding in substance with that contained in Article 222 of Mr. Livingstone's Code. This may be done by adding to this chapter two clauses in the following or other terms: "When two or more persons "by quarrelling or fighting, or otherwise conducting themselves in a "tumultuous manner in a public place, disturb the peace of the inhabi- "tants of the place, they are said to commit 'an affray.'"

"Whoever commits 'an affray' shall be punished with imprisonment "of either description, for a term which may extend to one month, or "fine which may extend to two hundred rupees, or both."

51. It will be seen that we propose to transfer to this chapter the clauses which now stand as Clauses 275 to 282 in Chapter XV of Offences relating to religion and caste, to be placed after Clause 137.

Vide post.

CHAPTER VIII.

OF THE ABUSE OF THE POWERS OF PUBLIC SERVANTS.

52. The propriety of the title of this chapter is questionable, with reference to Clauses 139 and 150, which provide for offences which are not abuses of the powers of public servants, and which may be committed by persons not being public servants, and to Clauses 147 and 149, which provide for offences by public servants, which are not abuses of their powers as such. It is stated in Note E that "this chapter is "intended to reach offences which are committed by public servants, "and which are of such a description that they can be committed by "public servants alone," but this statement requires qualification with respect to the two clauses first mentioned above. The following, adopted from the Digest of the English Criminal Law Commissioners, would seem to be a more suitable title for the chapter,—"of offences by and concerning public servants."

Chapter V, Section 2. "Offences by "and concerning "judicial and "other officers of "justice."

53 "It will be seen," say the Commissioners, "that we propose, "under Clause 138, to punish with imprisonment for a term not exceed- "ing 3 years, or with fine, or both, the corruption of public function- "aries." Mr. Norton says, "I offer my humble tribute to the substantial "merit of Clause 138." The principle of this clause and of the chapter generally, is, however, strongly objected to by many persons.

54. The objection seems to be mainly this, that to render high functionaries liable to prosecution before the Criminal Courts, for imputed malversation, will tend to degrade such functionaries generally, and to diminish the respect of the public for them. Mr. J. F. Thomas has stated the objection most fully and distinctly. The following are his observations on the subject:

"The provisions of this chapter as made applicable to men placed "in offices of the highest trust and responsibility, are questionable. I "doubt the policy of subjecting such men to any further penalties for "malversation than dismission with censure and disgrace.

"It must, I conceive, degrade the office and the whole class of officers, "and lower the standard of public character, if they are to be restrained "by penalties like those here provided.

"The ample remuneration, the estimation of society, and the loss of "these, can, it is admitted, alone maintain the standard of public charac- "ter; and nothing, I am satisfied, will be added to these sanctions, unless "the penalties are very severe.

"The removal of a British Resident at a Foreign Court guilty of "malversation, from his high post as representative of the British Govern- "ment, to the common gaol, (see illustration (*c*) at page 26,) will only "prove injurious to the public interests by degrading the office. It "would be better, I should say, that he be dismissed with public "ignominy, and his degradation and punishment left solely to society. "In like manner it will not uphold the judicial character, but on the con- "trary must tend greatly to its deterioration, both in the European and "Native, if, as provided in Clauses 142 and 143, Judges presiding over "Courts of great trust and power, may be brought *as criminals*, on charges "of the nature contemplated in these clauses, and sent to the common "jail for one or two years.

"The arguments the Commissioners have used, respecting penalties "which consist in degrading exposure, &c., (vide Note E, p. 121,) appear "to me to apply to the cases under consideration. For the imprisonment "provided in these clauses, of but one or two years, would be a mere "subject of mockery to 'shameless and abandoned men'; but when inflicted on men, 'who have filled the highest stations, and maintained "respectable characters, would be so cruel, that it would become more "odious to the public than the very offence which it was intended to "repress.'

"This, I am induced to believe, would be realized, especially in the "case of natives of family and great respectability, who might be taken "from their seats as judges, and imprisoned for some even trifling ir- "regularity, to the favor or disfavor of a party before them.

"The result would, I fear, be, that such men would avoid offices which "might subject them to such degradation, for acts which would indeed "be culpable, but which would be amply provided against by simple "dismission."

55. Mr. Thomas adds, "These observations I intend to apply almost "entirely to the imprisonment provided for several of the offences de- "scribed in this chapter. Fine not commutable by imprisonment but "recoverable at any time, lies open only in part to the same objections." This qualification seems to be rejected by some of those gentlemen who concur generally with Mr. Thomas. Mr. Hudleston, for example, says, "I hope that no such provisions will be enacted in this country. The "power of Government to dismiss from office, and of the Home authorities "to dismiss from the service, with general rules such as are contained in "the Regulations, render such provisions as those of this chapter uncalled "for." It is to be gathered from Mr. Hudleston's remark that he had in his mind only the Company's Covenanted Servants. And it would seem that this class of public servants is, at least, chiefly regarded in the remarks of others to the same effect.

56. It is more especially with regard to Judges that it is urged by some, chiefly by Mr. A. D. Campbell, that to render them liable to punishment, and particularly the punishment of imprisonment, by sentence of a Criminal Court, for malversation, will tend to degrade the judicial office. Mr. Livingston thus notices a similar objection to the provisions of his Code on this subject—"There are some who think that with respect to "the judicial office, it would be degraded by enactments which suppose "the possibility of its high functionaries being influenced by such induce- "ments as would bias other men. Confidence, they argue, produces "integrity, suspicion provokes to guilt; leave the high characters of "your Judges to be sustained by their own sense of honor, and do not "fetter them with any of the degrading restrictions and penalties that "you devise to bind other men." "I acknowledge," says Mr. Livingston, "the force of the maxim that confidence in generous minds begets a dis- "position to merit it, but I deny the propriety of its general application. "The penalties of the law are founded on a supposition that without them "its precepts would not be fulfilled. Could we count on that generous "disposition which the objection supposes, there would be no need of any "sanction to our laws. The Legislator need only point out his will and "express his confidence in the integrity of those to whom it was directed, "and the work of legislation would be done. But the argument is not "pressed so far; it is acknowledged that penalties are necessary to ensure "obedience in ordinary cases; but it is said the Judges form an honorable "exception; restrain all the world by the fear of punishment—trust to "the integrity of the Judge for the performance of his duty." Not seeing the reason of any such distinction, Mr. Livingston, however, makes Judges equally with other public functionaries liable to criminal prosecution for misconduct in office, and subjects them to the punishment of imprisonment as well as fine.

57. In England, if in any country, the Judges of the superior Courts might, on grounds such as are noticed by Mr. Livingston, be exempted from responsibility under the criminal law, and left "unfettered by the degrading restrictions and penalties devised to bind other officers." But though, as justly observed by the Criminal Law Commissioners, corruption in the exercise of a judicial office is an offence "which in this country, as regards the higher Courts "may be said to exist in theory only, so rare are the "instances, in modern times, in which that high authority has been "abused for unlawful purposes;" nevertheless, the Judges of England have been ever since the time of Edward III, and are now liable to criminal prosecution for default or malversation in office, and to punishment for the same by imprisonment and fine or forfeiture. So it is declared in Section 2, Chapter V of the Digest of the English Criminal Law that "Justices (that is to say Judges of the superior Courts,) who shall be found in default on any of "the points contained in the oath required to be taken by them by a "Statute of the 18th year of King Edward III"—and "whosoever being a judicial officer shall abuse his authority by doing or omitting to do any act or thing, wilfully or corruptly, or "with the malicious intent to oppress or injure any other person in violation "of his duty as such officer"—shall incur the penalty of "imprisonment "for any term not exceeding three years, and fine at discretion."

5th Report, page 22.

Art. 1.

Art. 3.

58. Blackstone says, "In Judges, especially the superior ones, bribery "hath been always looked upon as so heinous an offence, "that Chief Justice Thorpe was hanged for it in the "reign of Edward III." "This," say the Criminal Law Commissioners, "appears to have been a mistake, and we have been unable to discover any ancient authority by which such "an offence was ever punishable capitally by the law of "England. It was, however, a misdemeanor at common law punishable "by fine and imprisonment." Accordingly in the Digest it is declared to be punishable by fine at discretion and imprisonment not exceeding three years.

Vol. IV, p. 140.

5th Report, page 20.

Art. 5.

59. As to the manner of prosecuting Judges the Criminal Law Commissioners say, "We conceive that although the ordinary "mode of proceeding against Judges has been by impeachment, an indictment may be maintained against "them as well as against inferior judicial officers."

5th Report, page 48.

60. With regard to public functionaries, not judicial, the restrictions and penalties of the Law of England are applicable to all without exception or distinction. The Prime Minister is liable to a criminal prosecution for the corrupt sale of an office at his disposal, for bribery, &c.,

Chap. IV, Section 4, Art. 1. equally with a meaner functionary; for the former offence the punishment according to the Digest is imprisonment not exceeding two years, or fine, or both; Art. 7. for the latter, imprisonment not exceeding one year with or without fine.

61. It is true that Mr. Hudleston and those who agree with him do not argue for the impunity of public servants who may commit offences such as are provided for in this chapter, but for exempting them, particularly the Covenanted servants of the Company, from amenability to the Criminal Courts, leaving them to be dealt with by the Government and the controlling authorities in England, who have the power to punish them by suspension or dismissal from office, or from the service. Note E, p. 122. This kind of punishment as observed in the Note to the chapter is one which bears with peculiar severity upon persons circumstanced as are the Covenanted servants of the Company; moreover it is one which will probably be inflicted, in the higher or lower degree, upon any servant who may commit an offence which is punishable under the Code, notwithstanding he shall be sentenced to the penalty prescribed therein. Thus, it is represented, the culprit will be liable to a double punishment.

62. But the same may be said of any functionary who holding a valuable appointment, by misconduct forfeits it, and by the same misconduct renders himself obnoxious to the criminal law; of Lord Bacon, for instance, who was dismissed from the highest and most valuable office under the Crown, being at the same time fined £40,000, and sentenced to imprisonment during the King's pleasure. It may be said indeed, in a measure, of every servant who lives by his employment, and who for misconduct which brings him under the cognizance of a Criminal Court, and subjects him to a penalty by its sentence, is liable also to be dismissed by his employers. The reason of dismissal is the same in the case of the humble servant and in that of the high public functionary—the offender has proved himself unworthy of trust.

63. Further it is well observed by Mr. Greenhill that dismissal would be a penalty altogether inadequate in the case of a man who had made a fortune by official corruption. "The punishment of fine," say the Commissioners, "will, we think, be found very efficacious in cases of this "description, if the Judges exercise the power given them, as they ought "to do, and compel the delinquent to deliver up the whole of his ill-"gotten wealth."

64. We proceed to consider the provisions of this chapter more particularly with reference to the remarks made upon them in the reports which are before us.

65. The first clause provides at once for what in the Digest of the English Criminal Law is divided under several heads, Clause 138. Digest, Ch. IV, Sec. 4, Arts. 1, 2, 7. Sec. 5, Art. 3; Ch. V, Sec. 2, Arts. 10 to 13. as selling public offices, taking reward for recommending to office, &c., taking of bribes by ministerial officers, extortion by officers, taking undue fees, &c. It applies exclusively to persons being or expecting to be public servants, accepting, obtaining, or attempting to obtain, any gratification, for doing or forbearing to do any official act, favoring or disfavoring any party in the exercise of official functions, or serving or disserving any party with Government, or with any public servant. The next clause applies generally to any persons accepting, &c., any gratification for inducing public servants so to act. This clause is much more comprehensive than the English Law, which appears to punish private persons taking reward for influencing public Officers, only when their influence is used to procure office for a party. We think the generality of Clause 139 of the Code is expedient.

Clause 139.

Digest, Chapter IV, Section 4, Art. 2.

66. Objection is made by several officers to including in Clause 138 persons "expecting to be public servants." But if a person expecting to be appointed to a public office obtains money from another as the price of favor to be shewn to that other in the exercise of his functions in that office, he is surely as corrupt as one who does the same being actually in office. It must be proved of course that he gave the other party reason to believe that he was about to obtain the office, it must be proved also, as appears by the first "explanation," that he himself expected to obtain it. In practice the provision would probably be brought into action only against persons who after having obtained the expected office are found guilty of the previous corrupt transaction, and generally only against persons who having obtained the expected office have acted officially in the corrupt manner previously promised.

67. Mr. Greenhill commenting upon Clause 138 puts this case—"A has done the Prince some service, and the Prince makes him a "present *for the past*—has A committed an offence?" He asks, "is "reward for *past service* not included? if not, the law would seem to "be defective, for it could seldom be shown that the reward was not "for some past service, and the motives could hardly ever be proved." If the present falls within the terms of the definition of legal remuneration subjoined to Clause 138, if, for example, it is what A as a public servant is permitted by the Government which he serves to accept "from the Prince," whoever *he* may be, for such service as A has rendered to him, it is obviously no offence in A to accept it. But if the service rendered by A to the Prince was such as he was bound to render officially without any remuneration, or if it was such as he ought not to have rendered, his acceptance of a present at any time "as a reward" for rendering such service would certainly be an offence. The term reward is manifestly intended to apply to a "past service." What is forbidden speaking generally is the receiving any gratification "as a motive" to do, "or a reward" for having done any such thing as is described in the definition. It is explained that "a person may "receive a gratification as a motive for doing what he does not intend "to do, or as a reward for doing what he has not done." This explanation appears to be intended to guard against such a plea as to refer again to that well-known case, was set up as an excuse for Lord Bacon; "It is pretended," says Mr. Hume in his history, "that Bacon had "still in the seat of justice, preserved the integrity of a Judge, and had "given just decrees against those very persons from whom he had "received the wages of iniquity."

68. Mr. Norton who, as we have observed, approves of Clause 138, finds fault with Clause 139. He says, "I conceive Clause 139 is of a "far too general application. It may be very praiseworthy in a party "in some instances to exercise personal influence in obtaining a favor "for a friend, such as an appointment from an official person. The "thing itself being so, the *criminality* should hardly depend on the "meanness of the motive. It may be very mean to accept of any "*previous hire* in *any* case of this kind—but a subsequent *reward* may "possibly be a mere token of gratitude, and such as there may not be "even a shadow of meanness in accepting. It is carrying the principle "of excluding all shadow even of corruption somewhat too far to visit "such an occurrence as a crime punishable by imprisonment.

69. We think that Mr. Norton is wrong in his surmise that the criminality here "depends on the meanness of the motive." "It *may*," as he says, "be very praiseworthy in some instances to exercise personal influence in obtaining a favor for a friend from an official person," in bringing, for example, a meritorious individual to the notice of an official person, and recommending him for an office at the disposal of that person, for which he is well qualified; but it *may* be very much the reverse, as, if the friend recommended is unworthy. The man who has used his personal influence with a public functionary to induce him to give an appointment to a friend, merely because he is a friend, who is unfit for it, may be as culpable as one who has exerted his interest to obtain an appointment in like manner for a person, merely for the sake of something he has obtained or expects to obtain from him, which falls within the definition of the term "gratification" in the explanation subjoined to Clause 138, but the motive in the one case is sufficiently palpable for the law to deal with it, while in the other it is not so.

70. The selection of fit persons for the discharge of public functions is of so much importance, since upon the faithful execution by the officers employed in the public service, of the various powers entrusted to them, must the due working of the state machine for all practical purposes depend, that it is necessary to make every possible provision to prevent abuse in this respect, "but it is a duty which," as observed by the English Criminal Law Commissioners, "is "so dependent on the exercise of a discretionary power "of judging as to fitness and qualification for office, as in a great measure "to exclude the possibility of restraining by penal laws any abuse of the "confidence reposed in those who are by law invested with the power of "selecting persons. In an important respect however the law interferes "to prevent a practice fraught with temptation to the parties invested "with patronage, and with mischief to the public, namely, the sale of "public offices, by punishing those who offend in this respect." It interferes also by punishing those who receive, or have any reward or profit for any interest, &c., made concerning or relating to any nomination or appointment to a public office. The English Law herein agrees with the Code in the clause in question. It appears to us that Mr. Norton's observation as to a subsequent reward being possibly a mere token of gratitude applies with as much force to Clause 138, which he approves, as to Clause 139 which he disapproves; to a public servant receiving such a reward in gratitude for an appointment bestowed by him at some previous time, as to a private person receiving it in gratitude for the exertion of his influence through which such appointment was obtained.

5th Report, page 15.

Digest, Chapter IV, Section 4, Art. 2.

71. We come now to the provisions particularly affecting Judges. The first relates to the accepting of a gift by a Judge from a party whom he knows to be a plaintiff or defendant in any proceeding in his Court, which is punishable

Clauses 141 to 143.

by imprisonment which may extend to 2 years, or fine, or both. The Commissioners say, "The mere taking of presents by a "public functionary, when it cannot be proved that such "presents were corruptly taken, we have made penal "only in one particular case," that is the one we are now to consider. "We have not made the taking of presents by public functionaries "generally penal," they continue, "because though we think it is a prac- "tice which ought to be carefully watched and often severely punished, "we are not satisfied that it is possible to frame any law on the subject "which would not be rendered inoperative either by its extreme severity "or by its extreme laxity."

See Appendix, Note E, page 123.

72. They proceed to explain distinctly the grounds on which they "have thought it advisable to leave this matter to the "Executive Government which will doubtless promul- "gate from time to time such rules as it may deem proper, and will en- "force submission to those rules by visiting its disobedient servants with "censure, with degradation, or with dismissal from the public service, "according to the circumstances of every case." They then explain their reasons for making the one exception contained in Clause 141 in the case of a Judge, remarking by the way that the prohibition therein "does not "extend to the taking of food in the interchange of ordinary civilities." "It appears to us," they say, "that the objections we have made to "a general law prohibiting the receipt of presents by public functionaries "do not apply to this clause. The rule is clear and definite. The practice "against which it is directed is not a practice which ought sometimes to "be encouraged and sometimes to be tolerated. It ought always and "under all circumstances to be discouraged. It appears therefore to "unite all the characteristics which mark out a practice as a fit object of "penal legislation."

Page 125.

73. Sir J. Awdry delivers his sentiments on the question whether the prohibition of receiving presents should be general, or limited as proposed in the Code, as follows: "One more observation I will make on a "point which though not very prominent in the Code goes to the root of "the unsuspected purity of our administration of justice, and government "in general. It is proposed to put an end to the prohibition of taking "presents. That prohibition has been most beneficial, and I cannot see "that the reasons for it have ceased. The difficulty of providing that it "shall not operate harshly on native magistrates, should be grappled "with, instead of abolishing the whole law. The difficulty of drawing a "satisfactory line is no doubt considerable, but much may easily be done. "To receive a portion with an Asiatic bride is no more illegal than to "hire a house of an Asiatic—either may become so, if colorable—neither "is so in itself. In all cases of kindred and affinity presents might be "allowed. This would at once provide for the majority of cases in which "they ought so to be, and would be attended with no danger, because "the kindred or affinity would be a warning to the public. The situation "of a disinterested functionary who was at liberty to receive presents "would be very painful, knowing (as he must know) that their real "object would be inconsistent with his integrity, yet that their rejection "would be an insult. The reasons assigned for not making bribery in "this country punishable in the giver of the bribe are most satisfactory.

"They are in substance that from the habits and circumstances of the "country he is the victim of what has to him the effect of extortion. "That pressure must and will operate on his mind as long as the person "whom he desires to propitiate is known to be ready to receive, and ready "he usually must be unless the Government by its prohibition will relieve "him from discourtesy in refusing."

74. Upon the provision contained in Clause 141, Sir J. Awdry makes the following observations: "As regards a Judge's taking a gift "from one whom he knows to be a plaintiff or defendant in a suit before "him, this is still to be forbidden. But this (while it appears to me to "concede the principle) is totally inadequate. A Judge knows not one-"tenth of the causes which are on the files of his Court, still less can he "bear in mind who are all the parties to each—still less, who, without "being nominal parties, are interested. But all these persons them-"selves, and all their enemies, know; and important as the matter "is to them, they cannot conceive that it escapes the notice of the "Judge. His character therefore suffers—and that of the administra-"tion of justice with it. But what is worse, this will most frequently "happen to the most impartial Judge. He whose attention habitually "fixes itself on the merits of the cause, not on the persons of the "litigants, except as prominent on the evidence, will most frequently "receive in ignorance a present which was intended for and will be "understood as a bribe."

75. With regard to Sir J. Awdry's general observations we have to remark that the authors of the Code by no means intend absolutely to put an end to the prohibition of taking presents, but to leave the matter to be regulated discriminatively by the Executive Government. The general rule would still probably be prohibitive, with exceptions suggested by a liberal consideration of circumstances which render a relaxation of the rule expedient.

76. With such a rule and such exceptions discreetly permitted there would clearly be no ground for some of the objections urged by the learned Judge, as he appears himself to admit. We think, indeed, with respect to public functionaries in general, that every advantage that arises from the existing law would be secured under such regulations as it may be supposed would be passed by the Executive Government, enforced by the very efficacious means of punishment which the Government can employ. With regard to Judges the reasons assigned by the authors of the Code for the distinction they have made, appear to us sufficient to vindicate it. The terms of the clause so nearly correspond with the terms of the oath required to be taken by the Justices of Her Majesty's Courts in England, on the same matter, viz., "Ye take not by yourself or by "other, privily nor apertly, gift nor reward of gold or "silver, nor of any other thing which may turn to your "profit, unless it be meat or drink, and that of small "value, of any man that shall have any plea or process hanging before "you, as long as the same process shall be so hanging, nor after for the "same cause," that it may be presumed the Commissioners had the oath before them when they framed the clause. The argument of Sir J. Awdry as to the impossibility of a Judge bearing in mind who are all the parties in the causes before him, it is obvious to remark, applies equally to the

Statute 4, 18 Edward III.

responsibility arising from the oath, as to that which is imposed by the clause in question. The oath required to be taken by the Company's Judges in like manner is directed against the receipt of presents from parties in suits in the Courts in which they sit.

Bengal Reg. V of 1793, Clause 2.

77. Mr. Norton appears to approve of Clause 141 in principle, but considers it "far too lenient to meet some cases." The punishment as before remarked is imprisonment not exceeding 2 years with or without fine. The punishment proposed in the Digest of the English Law is imprisonment not exceeding 3 years and fine at discretion. Considering that this provision is intended to meet cases where a corrupt motive cannot be proved, we think it is severe enough.

78. The next Clause 142 provides that "whoever being a Judge "pronounces on any question which comes before him in any stage of "any judicial proceeding a decision which he knows to be unjust, shall "be punished with simple imprisonment which may extend to 2 years, "or fine, or both." Objections to this clause are made by many officers, which may be summed up in the question of Sir H. Seton, "who is to decide what is unjust, and how is the knowledge of it to be proved?" Her Majesty's Justices are required by their oath to "do equal law and execution of right," that is, as it is expressed in the margin, "to do justice" to all Her Majesty's subjects, and it is provided in the Digest that all who shall be found in default in any of the points contained in the oath shall be punished with imprisonment not exceeding 3 years and fine, with a saving clause that "no judicial officer shall be criminally liable in respect of any error in giving judgment." It seems to us that a Judge, who by his decision, does injustice, *not* by error of judgment, is in other words a Judge who pronounces a decision which he knows to be unjust. We apprehend that the expression "which he knows to be unjust" was adopted purposely to exclude the excuse of an error of judgment, and that the meaning is that a Judge who pronounces a decision which is unjust without the excuse of an error of judgment, must be presumed to have pronounced the decision conscious of its injustice, and shall be liable to punishment accordingly. So understood, the clause appears to us no more exceptionable than the English Law in the same matter as it is expressed in the Digest. Mr. A. D. Campbell suggests that the words "contrary to law" should be substituted for "unjust," "as it is not intended that the Code should "meet individual opinions of justice, except as these may coincide with the "sentiments of the Legislature;" but such a substitution would narrow the provision to a degree that would greatly impair its efficacy, for many a decision may be "unjust," which cannot be said to be contrary to any law, except the general law which requires justice to be done.

Statute 4, 18 Edward III.

Chap. V, Sec. 2, Art. 1.

Art. 4.

79. Again of Clause 143, which provides for the punishment of a Judge who "for any purpose of favor or disfavor to any party disobeys "any direction of the law of procedure," Sir H. Seton observes, that all "laws of procedure must be occasionally dispensed with, or become "intolerably oppressive, as in the case of sickness, &c., and every dis- "pensation must be matter of favor." To this we answer, that it must be presumed that the Code of Procedure will itself authorize such dispensing, and therefore in such case there will be no disobedience—it will be a lawful exercise of discretion, not an act of favor, to grant a dispensation when there is such cause for it.

80. Sir H. Seton questions the policy of the provisions in both these clauses as "exposing persons in office to vague and vexatious criminal charges." Mr. Norton and others also observe that the provisions in these clauses would let in all sorts of vague and vindictive charges. Mr. E. Maltby speaking of Clause 142, particularly says—"this will give rise to criminal accusations instead of appeal." Mr. A. D. Campbell to the same purpose observes as follows: "The present law giving to the "unsuccessful suitor the right of appeal, has hitherto operated here as a "sufficient practical check against judicial decisions contrary to law or "justice; but as here proposed, to convert this simple *civil* remedy "against the *suitor*, into a criminal proceeding against the Judge himself, "will put an entire stop to the administration of justice. Judges, like "all men, are extremely fallible; and their errors are ever liable to be "attributed to wrong motives—all independence and self-confidence will "therefore be entirely lost, and the Judges completely paralized, if the "vindictive passion of the disappointed, amongst the most litigious people "in the world, are let loose to inundate the tribunals with a flood of peti-"tions against the Judges themselves, instead of against the suitors." "Be the punishment of judicial corruption what it may," he says again, "it is absolutely necessary to the independence of the Bench that every "Judge should be irresponsible to his suitors." Mr. Casamajor says "much depends on the Code of Procedure;" "before what tribunal," he asks, "are the offences in Clauses 141, 142 and 143, to be prosecuted?"

81. Mr. F. N. Maltby makes the following general observations which appear to us worthy of attention—"I believe there are few who have "watched the actual working of our Government in the provinces, who "have not found reason to doubt whether, in our endeavors to protect "the people from oppression on the part of the servants of Government, "we have not gone too far; and weakened the power of our native "servants. It is as necessary that they should be supported in the honest "discharge of their duties as that those under them should be protected "from oppression. Although, therefore, I do not venture to offer any "remarks upon the punishment to be awarded when delinquency is "proved, I would beg to observe that it will depend upon the Code of "Procedure whether this chapter is an useful or a most prejudicial one. "It must be most prejudicial if the form of procedure should allow of "public functionaries being dragged before the *Criminal Tribunal*, upon "charges, preferred in the usual form, of offences under this chapter. "I am sure that not a native functionary will feel confident in the dis-"charge of his duties if this chapter is enforced by the ordinary tribunals. "It is necessary that the form of procedure should be such as shall, as "far as possible, protect the Officer of Government from annoyance, "until delinquency is proved; and I need hardly add how necessary it "is that false charges should be severely punished. Should it be so "arranged that a mere charge of these offences, preferred before a Magis-"trate, shall put the accused on his defence before that tribunal, the "provisions of this chapter must have a most prejudicial effect. The "principle of the Madras Code of making the public officer amenable to "his superiors under rules differing in this respect from the ordinary "course of criminal procedure, appears to me to be best adapted to the "purpose."

82. The suggestion contained in the last sentence of the above extract from Mr. Maltby's Report is one which we think ought to be taken into consideration in framing the rules for giving effect to this chapter, unless the general system of criminal procedure shall embrace the institution of a public prosecutor. If such an office should be established it would be sufficient to make it the general rule that charges founded upon the provisions of this chapter should be received by the criminal tribunals only at the instance of the public prosecutor. The authors of the Code themselves propose to withhold from the cognizance of the criminal tribunals offences such as are provided for in Clause 149, namely, neglect of duty, disobedience of orders, &c., by public servants, which they think should be dealt with by the official superiors of the offender. In this opinion we agree with them.

See Appendix, Note E, page 125.

83. Clause 145 is very comprehensive, including, apparently, offences separately provided for by several Articles of the Digest, as Articles 1 and 2, Section 5, Chapter IV, and Article 3, Section 2, Chapter V, respecting the abuse of official authority, and Articles 14 to 16, Section 2, Chapter V, regarding officers omitting to arrest offenders and suffering prisoners to escape, so far as the offence is voluntary, and in general any breach of official duty, by which it is intended, or which is known to be likely to injure any party, or to save any person from legal punishment.

84. Clause 146 again provides specially for public servants charged with the preparation of documents, violating their duty in this respect, with the like intention, including among others the specific offences in respect to judicial records defined in Articles 8 and 9, Section 2, Chapter V of the Digest. Mr. Norton observes that this clause "incorporates in "too general and vague language a variety of specific crimes which may "be construed to fall within it." The clause is comprehensive, but not indefinite. It appears to us that nothing can be brought within its terms which ought not to be punished as it prescribes.

85. Mr. Norton thinks that such "breaches of contract" by public servants as are specified in Clauses 147 and 148, are not proper objects of criminal law. They are not however breaches of contract, that is breaches of conditions privately arranged between the party to be served and the party engaging to serve, which appear to be intended here, but breaches of conditions imposed by law upon public servants. These provisions are analogous to that contained in Article 12, Section 2, Chapter IV of the Digest for the punishment of persons "doing any matter or thing prohibited (by Statute) to be done." The punishment is the same, viz., imprisonment not exceeding 3 months, or fine, or both.

86. It remains for us to consider the reasons assigned by the Commissioners for not making bribery punishable in the giver of the bribe when he gives it in compliance with a demand, however signified, on the part of a public servant; the person who, without any demand express or implied, volunteers an offer of a bribe to a public servant and induces him to accept it, being punishable under the general rule contained in Clause 88 as an instigator. The reasons are that "corruption "does prevail to a great extent among the lower class "of public functionaries (in India), that the power "which those functionaries possess renders them formid- "able to the body of the people, that in the great majority of cases the "receiver of the bribe is really the tempter, and that the giver of the "bribe is really acting in self-defence." "Under these circumstances," say the Commissioners, "we are strongly of opinion that it would be "unjust and cruel to punish the giving of a bribe in any case in which it "could not be proved that the giver had really by his instigations cor- "rupted the virtue of a public servant who, unless temptation had been "put in his way, would have acted uprightly." Sir J. Awdry, as appears above, thinks that the reasons assigned by the Commissioners "are most satisfactory." Mr. Norton on the contrary says, "I cannot concur in the "reasoning of Note E by which the criminality of giving bribes is omitted "from the Code. It assumes that the administration of justice and of "public functions is so corrupt that a man cannot attain his fair right "but by bribery. If this be true I do not think the end sanctifies the "means, and I consider it a very inexpedient principle to avow and act "upon."

Note E, pp. 126 and 127.

87. Mr. G. W. Bacon says, "With reference to the Note on the "impunity of bribers (pages 126 and 127) I must submit my opinion, "that the Commissioners altogether mistake the state of the case. There "is very rarely if ever occasion for extortion on the part of the receiver "or for self-defence on the part of the giver. All act in strict conformity "with the immemorial custom of the country, that no inferior shall "approach a superior, more particularly a public functionary, without "a present in his hand to obtain favor generally, without any particular "object. No Police Darogah or Moonsiff, and very few of the higher "natives possessing power, ever pay for any thing, and are fed and clothed "by the people. If an individual require a particular boon, such as a "decree in his favor, he has only to outbid his antagonist, and this not "at the request of the officer, but as a matter of course. How could "he expect favor, when the other party paid higher? Nothing is more "common than for an appellant to state in his petition that the Sudder "Ameen or Moonsiff decided against him, notwithstanding the payment "of such a sum, or that the decree against him was given in conse- "quence of a higher bribe administered by the opposite party. Now the "appellant does not mean to state that there is any thing extraordinary "in this, or that the Native Judge has acted wrong or irregularly in "taking his money, or that of the other party, but merely that it is hard "he should have got nothing for his present, and the giving which was a "matter of custom, and an unquestionable and well-known fact. It is to "be remarked, that this is never given as a cause of dissatisfaction in "appealing from the decree of an English Judge, because it is neither "the native custom to bribe those officers, nor theirs, to receive. In the "eyes of the natives there is no crime either in giving or receiving bribes, "and if we are desirous of impressing them with a different notion, we "must punish both giver and receiver, for both are only acting in com- "pliance with the customs of their ancestors, and one is not more guilty "than the other."

88. It appears to us that Mr. Bacon's observations go to confirm the accuracy of the reasoning of the Commissioners. If, as he says, "when "an individual requires a particular boon, such as a decree in his favor, "he has only to outbid his antagonist, and this not at the request of the "officer, but as a matter of course," what is this but to say that "men "give bribes because no man can without a bribe obtain "common justice." In such a state of things the Commissioners "think that the giving of bribes is not a proper subject of punishment." By punishing the receiver they endeavor to strike at the root of the evil. If they rested here we should not think they had done enough, for in India as in England there are situations in which "the giver is generally the tempter, the receiver is the tempted." We may instance cases in which a Moonsiff or a Darogah, for example, is stationed in the heart of a large Zemindary, the Zemindar of which is rich and powerful, and whose ambition is to make his will predominant within its bounds. It is an object to him with this view to gain over the Moonsiff and the Darogah, or the Civil Judge and the Officer of Police, and he will be ready to tempt them with bribes to serve his purpose, making occasion by bringing a suit against one man before the Moonsiff, and against another laying a criminal charge before the Darogah. The Commissioners intend the general provision in Clause 88 regarding abetment by instigation to meet such cases. By Clause 138 a public servant receiving a bribe is liable to imprisonment for 3 years. So also under Clause 88 is the person instigating him to receive the bribe. We are inclined to think with the Commissioners that this provision will answer the purpose sufficiently.

See Appendix, Note E, page 126.

CHAPTER IX.

OF CONTEMPTS OF THE LAWFUL AUTHORITY OF PUBLIC SERVANTS.

89. In the Note upon this chapter are the following observations, which explain the manner in which it was prepared, and the principles of the classification observed in it.

See Appendix, Note F, page 127.

"We were at first disposed to have one chapter for contempts of "the lawful authority of Courts of Justice, another for "contempts of the lawful authority of Officers of Rev- "enue, and a third for contempts of the lawful author- "ity of Officers of Police. But we soon found that these three chapters "would be almost the same word for word. It appeared to us also that, "in the existing state of the Civil Administration of India, the separa- "tion which we were at first inclined to make would produce nothing "but perplexity. The functions of Magistrate and Collector are very "frequently united in the same person: and that person is perpetually "called upon, both as Magistrate and Collector, to perform acts which "are judicial in their nature, to try offenders, and to decide litigated "questions of civil right. While the division of labor between the "different departments of the public service is so imperfect, it would "be idle to make nice distinctions between those departments in the "Penal Code."

"In order to frame this chapter we went carefully through the "existing Regulations of the three Presidencies, and extracted the "numerous penal provisions which are intended to enforce obedience to "the lawful authority of different classes of public servants. Having "collected these provisions, and discarded a very few which we thought "obviously unreasonable, or superfluous, we proceeded to analyse the "rest."

"It is possible that our analysis may be imperfect; and it is highly "probable that the punishments which we propose may require some "modification. It will be seen that we propose the same punishment "for all the offences which fall, in our analysis, under the same head. "For example, one head is the omitting to obey the lawful summons of "a public servant. For this offence we have only one punishment; and "this punishment will be applicable alike to the witness who omits to "obey the lawful summons of a Moonsiff, to the Putwaree who in Bengal "omits to obey the lawful summons of the Collector, to the ryot who in "the Madras Presidency omits to obey the lawful summons of the Col- "lector, to the trader who in the same Presidency omits to attend a "meeting lawfully convened for the distribution of the Vizabuddy. In "the same manner we propose one punishment for the Captain of a ship "in the Hoogly who illegally refuses to admit a Custom House Officer "on board, for a landholder who refuses to admit a Surveyor lawfully "commissioned by the Collector to measure land, for a distiller who "refuses to admit the proper Officer to examine his distillery. Again, "we propose the same punishment for the person who resists the taking "of goods in execution under a decree of a Court of Justice, for the "person who resists the taking of property by way of distress for arrears "of revenue, for the person who resists the seizure of salt by lawful "authority, for the person who resists the seizure of a boat in default of "toll by lawful authority, for the person who resists the seizure of "smuggled goods by lawful authority."

90. "We are sensible," the Commissioners proceed to say, "that "there may be reasons which have escaped us for making distinctions in "punishment between offences which in our classification fall under the "same head. But it is impossible to find in any person, or in any small "body of persons, so extensive and minute a knowledge of every pro- "vince of India, and of every department of the public service, as would "be a security against errors of this description. We have no doubt "that if His Lordship in Council directs the Code to be published for "general information, valuable suggestions will be received from "servants of the Company in different parts of India, and that those "suggestions will enable the Government to modify the provisions which "we propose, by introducing proper aggravations and mitigations."

91. Referring apparently to the observation last quoted, Mr. Norton remarks that "the Commissioners seem themselves to distrust the policy "of many of the provisions in this chapter, and they are conscious of the "need of some modifications." He then offers particular criticisms. First, he observes, as regards the "instances of obstructing public officers "in the execution of their duty enumerated and provided against in "Clauses 153, 164, 166, 168, 171 and 173, it might be enough to say "that these clauses display a needless and perplexing list of qualifying "circumstances, and gradations of criminality, instead of a plain denun- "ciation of a substantive offence."

92. Such a denunciation as Mr. Norton suggests might be perplexing because of its generality, as involving under one head and subjecting to one penalty, instances of obstruction to public officers in the execution of their duty capable of being distinguished, and of different degrees of importance, but we cannot perceive how any perplexity can arise from the particularization which Mr. Norton here objects to, even if it be not absolutely necessary.

93. "But," he proceeds to remark, "these clauses offend also, in "common with almost all the others, in another respect of far greater "importance." This it seems is the "almost unlimited latitude afforded "to arbitrary constructions." He refers particularly to Clause 182, touching disobedience to local orders promulgated by public servants, and to other clauses, as Clause 155 regarding persons not attending in obedience to the orders of a public servant, Clause 152, regarding persons absconding to avoid service of a summons or notice from a public servant, Clause 157, regarding persons not furnishing information to a public servant when they are legally bound to do so, Clause 170, regarding persons bidding at a sale ordered by a public servant, not intending to fulfil the obligation incurred thereby, as being especially liable to such arbitrary construction. "It appears to me," he says, "that under such "clauses as these a number of acts may be ranged as offences punish- "able by imprisonment which I can hardly suppose to have been intend- "ed to be visited as crimes at all. It may be asked, if letting judgment "go by default by not appearing by Attorney or in person to answer a "bill in Equity or to plead to an action at Law is a crime? It may be "asked what is 'absconding' to avoid process? Is a debtor turned "into a criminal for keeping out of the way of arrest, or out of the way "of even any notice by any public servant by whatever means?"

"What is the criterion of bidding without *intention of performing all the* "*obligations*, &c. To proceed in multiplying such instances would be "endless."

94. Mr. Norton thinks that all the clauses in question are liable to arbitrary construction, especially from the excessive latitude of Clause 14, which describes "public servants." We have noticed this objection to Clause 14 before. We shall only observe here in general, that if Clause 14 with all its particularity affords room for arbitrary constructions of the penal provisions touching contempts of the lawful authority of public servants, it must at any rate be less objectionable in that respect than the article which defines the corresponding term "officer" in the Digest of the English Criminal Law, as follows: "The term "'officer' shall be deemed to signify any person invested "with authority to execute, and legally bound to execute "any public duty." The speciality of the definition in Clause 14 of the Code in effect restricts it, but here there is no restriction at all.

Chapter IV, Section 1, Art. 1.

95. We shall consider the clauses noticed by Mr. Norton in the order in which they stand in the chapter, and first we have to consider Clause 152, which provides for the punishment of a person *absconding* in order to avoid being served with a summons or notice proceeding from any public servant *legally competent as such public servant* to issue such summons or notice. The first remark that occurs to us on this clause, with reference to Mr. Norton's suggestion of its liability to arbitrary construction from the indefiniteness of the term "public servant" is that there is a precision in the words of the clause adjective to that term, which to our apprehension fixes the meaning so as to prevent any mistake in that respect at least. There appears to us to be no room at all for arbitrary construction when it is positively declared that the summons must proceed from *a public servant legally competent as such*, to issue it.

96. The same qualifying terms are used in Clause 155, to which this remark therefore equally applies. In the other clauses also to which Mr. Norton adverts, it appears to us that the public servant intended is so distinctly indicated, that on this point but one construction is admissible.

97. With regard to the term "absconding" in Clause 152, the signification of which Mr. Norton thinks questionable, we have to observe, that it is frequently used in the same connection in the existing Regulations, and we are not aware that there has ever been any misunderstanding about it. We do not think it likely, as Mr. Norton apparently does, that any person who might have to apply Clause 152, when he read that "whoever absconds in order to avoid being served with a "summons proceeding from any public servant legally competent to "issue such summons" is liable to punishment, would have reason to ask "what is absconding to avoid process?" any more than the Magistrates who have had to apply Section 4, Regulation XI of 1796 of the Bengal Code, for example, have found reason to question what is meant in the first clause thereof, by a person "absconding" "so that upon a "process issued against him" "he cannot be found."

98. As to the generality of the provision in this clause which Mr. Norton seems to object to, there can be no question, we conceive, that any person who being aware that a Court, for example, has issued a summons or notice of any kind to be served upon him, absconds in order to avoid being served with it, is guilty of a contempt of the lawful authority of the Court, of the same kind as if having been served with the summons he disobeys it. It is futile to give a Court or any public servant authority to issue a summons if no penalty is provided for the evasion of it; as well as for the neglect of the requisition contained in it, when it has been served. Of course the evasion must be proved to have been wilful, and the evasion being wilful, implies that the party knew of the issue of the summons. The clause in question goes beyond the existing Regulations, but it is understood that their inadequacy on this point has been productive of considerable inconvenience and impediment to the course of justice, particularly in regard to witnesses. To remedy this defect so far, a clause was introduced into the Civil Code compiled by Mr. Millett, providing for the punishment of witnesses absconding to evade a summons, in the same manner as witnesses not attending after having been summoned.

Part III, Section XXXI, Clause 2.

99. It is with reference to Clause 155, we presume, that Mr. Norton says it may be asked, "whether letting judgment go by default in an Equity suit or an action at law is a crime." We think that such a question could not be asked reasonably, for it is obvious that it is only disobedience to a positive order absolutely requiring the attendance of a party that is punishable under Clause 155, which is not the case in the instances put by Mr. Norton, in which it is optional with the defendant to answer, or plead, subject to judgment by default if he fail to do so.

100. The same punishment, viz., imprisonment of *either* description which may extend to one month, or fine which may extend to 500 rupees, or both, is prescribed in Clauses 152 and 153 and from 155 to 157, the object in all being similar, that is to enforce the forthcomingness of persons, and of documents, and the rendering of information requisite for the public service according to law. It has been observed by several officers that this punishment, though it might be generally adequate, would be insufficient in some cases, as, for instance, to prevent the absconding or to enforce the attendance of a principal witness in a civil or criminal proceeding of importance, in which it might be the interest of a party concerned to give the witness a reward for absenting himself, such as would more than compensate him for the imprisonment of one month and the fine of 500 rupees to which he would thereby be liable. With reference to Clause 156, respecting the non-production of documents, Mr. Greenhill puts the following case: "A sues B for an estate. "C has the title-deeds or a document by which A's claim would be "proved. C omits to produce it on the order of the Court, and pays the "fine of 500 rupees—has A no other remedy? Again, "A has the "custody of survey papers and accounts, and deeds of great value to "Government, and refuses to deliver them up"—"can A be punished "only as above?" Mr. Pyne says, "A Mamlutdar or Koolkurnee is "legally bound to deliver up a public paper to the Collector," "but which "he may decline to do. By our Revenue Law (Bombay) such refusal "subjects the detainer of these papers to imprisonment till he delivers "them up. To substitute one month's imprisonment in lieu of the existing penalty is not only to render the records of Government very "insecure and liable at all times to be withheld, but to create serious "inconvenience if not positive evil to the community, particularly the "agricultural portion of it." Mr. A. D. Campbell, also referring to Clause 156, suggests that the imprisonment should, as in the Madras Code, endure until the culprit conforms with the conditions of the law; a suggestion which is supported by others. Mr. Pycroft thinks that a larger term of imprisonment should be authorized, and the fine unlimited, on the principle explained in the Note to the chapter on Punishments.

Chap. IV, Section 3, Article 1; Section 2, Article 14.

Chap. V, Section 4, Art. 1.

Note A, p. 97.

101. The provisions in the Digest of the English Criminal Law applicable to the offences described in Clauses 153, 155 and 156, authorize a much severer punishment, viz., imprisonment for 1 year, or *fine at discretion*, or both— and we are inclined to think that to make Clauses 155 and 156 effectual, it is necessary to leave the amount of fine unlimited. In the Note to the Chapter on Punishments the case of a man suborned to commit perjury by a great bribe is given to prove the expediency of not imposing a limit to the fine. The principle is that "no man ought ever to gain by breaking the law." This principle appears to us applicable to a party bribed not to appear upon a summons or order, or not to produce some document of importance, as well as to a party bribed to give false evidence, since justice may be defeated by a witness failing to appear to give evidence which is essential and which he alone can give, or by failing to produce an essential document, as well as by a witness giving false evidence. We see no greater probability of the power being abused in such cases than in many others in which the fine is unlimited. We would also extend the maximum term of imprisonment under these two clauses to a period not exceeding 6 months. The punishment would then be the same as is provided for persons refusing to take an oath, &c., or to answer after having taken an oath in Clauses 159 and 160.

Chap. IV, Section 6, Art. 1.

102. Clauses 158 and 163 provide for the punishment of persons who wilfully give false information to public servants. It is proposed in the Digest of the English Law to punish offences of this kind under the head of "Deceits on public Officers," with imprisonment not exceeding 2 years, or fine at discretion, or both. The punishment prescribed in these clauses is imprisonment of either description, which may extend to 6 months, or fine which may extend to 1,000 rupees, or both. When false information is given upon oath, the offender is punishable under Clause 162 with imprisonment not exceeding 3 years, and not less than 6 months, and is also liable to fine. When the false statement amount to false evidence as defined in Clause 188, the offender is punishable more severely under Clause 190. We propose, as explained in a subsequent para., to omit the minimum in Clause 162.

103. It is objected to Clauses 159 and 160 that they will be less effectual than the provisions of the existing Regulations by which recusants are liable to be imprisoned until they consent to answer, &c. But the existing law limits the fine which may be imposed upon persons so offending to 500 rupees. The Code proposes to limit the imprisonment and to leave the fine unlimited, which seems to be preferable. Under the present law, we apprehend, it would be deemed a great stretch to protract the imprisonment of a recusant witness beyond 6 months; which is the maximum prescribed by these clauses.

104. It has been suggested that there should be a provision of "*toties* *quoties*" till the order is executed. Mr. Greenhill puts the following case: "A sues B; C only can prove the claim, but refuses to answer, "and is imprisoned 6 months. Does A lose his suit without remedy? or "may C be called up and on refusal again committed to prison, and "so on till he answers?" It may be presumed that there will be rules on this subject in the Code of Procedure, to which it properly belongs. We conceive that there should be provisions for treating continued recusancy after punishment has been inflicted, as a fresh offence, making the offender liable to a repetition of punishment, when such recusancy is calculated to defeat the ends of justice. These clauses leave the matter as it is left by Article 1, Section 4, Chapter V of the Digest.

105. With reference to Clause 157, which provides for the punishment of a person intentionally omitting to give notice or to furnish information to any public servant in the manner and at the time required by law, Mr. Pyne observes that by the Bombay Regulations specific penalties are provided for non-compliance with requisitions of public officers for information, and suggests that it is not consistent that both should continue in operation. We apprehend that the general provision in this clause is intended to supersede all special provisions of the same sort, as the Code generally is intended to supersede all the existing penal laws. We are at a loss to discover any ground for Mr. Norton's apprehension that this clause will afford scope for arbitrary constructions.

106. Clause 161 provides for the punishment of a person refusing to sign any statement made by him when required to do so by a public servant, with imprisonment of either description which may extend to 3 months, or fine to the amount of 1,000 rupees, or both. Upon this Mr. J. F. Thomas observes as follows:—"In practice it has always "appeared to me that the signature to a statement made before any public "authority is almost an unnecessary form when the statement is attested "by the public officer. I should hold it quite unnecessary to impose any "penalty beyond a very trifling fine for the refusal to sign, and should "declare the attestation alone of the public officer accompanied by a note "*in his own hand* that a party refused or declined signing the statement "to be a sufficient authentication, and that the statement so attested "should have the same validity as if it had been duly signed by the party. "This would take away the necessity of a penal enactment." Mr. A. D. Campbell concurs with Mr. Thomas. The existing Regulations for the Company's Courts, require the depositions of witnesses to be subscribed by them, and provide the same punishment for the refusal of a witness to subscribe his deposition, as for refusing to give evidence. On this point we would follow the suggestion of Mr. Thomas. But in every such case the officer attesting the statement should be bound to express the reason given by the party for refusing to sign it.

107. Of Clause 164, for the punishment of a person preventing or obstructing a search by a public servant, Mr. Hudleston observes that it is "too wordy—too particular." He objects to the provisions here and elsewhere for punishing "annoyance," observing that the term "is too vague to be properly used in a Criminal Code." His Colleague, Mr. A. D. Campbell, on the other hand, says, "I do not see any valid "objection to these Clauses (163 and 164) 'annoyance' is perhaps "rather a vague term; but it is easy to object to a particular word, yet "very difficult to suggest a preferable one."

108. A practical objection made to this clause is that the punishment is inadequate. We think that the fine should be limited, but it appears to us that the maximum may properly be extended from 500 to 1,000 rupees. The punishment for this offence under the general article respecting "Obstructions of Officers" in the Digest, is imprisonment not exceeding 1 year, or fine at discretion, or both. But the Code has a Clause, 165, for the infliction of additional or cumulative punishment for any other offence, as an assault, which may be committed in committing the offence described in Clause 164.

Chap. IV, Section 3, Art. 1.

109. The Code provides likewise for similar aggravations in committing the following offences, obstructing the taking, or the sale of property, resisting arrest, rescuing from custody, escaping or assisting escape from custody, insulting or interrupting a public servant in the discharge of his duty, acting in disobedience to the lawful order of a public servant in a matter affecting the public safety, &c., holding out threats to prevent a public servant from performing his duty, or to prevent a person from applying to a public servant for protection.

Clauses 166—169, 171—176, 179, 180, 182—187.

110. Clause 170 makes it penal to bid at a public sale for property on account of a party who is under a legal incapacity to purchase it, or to bid for it not intending to complete the purchase, or as it is expressed to perform the obligations under which the bidder lays himself by such "bidding." Considering such proceeding as a contempt, and as an obstruction to the public service, it appears fit to punish it, but we see no reason for the fine being unlimited. In Clause 168, which provides for the punishment of a person obstructing a public sale, the fine is limited to 500 rupees, the term of imprisonment being one month as in Clause 170. We would limit the fine in Clause 170 to 500 rupees. By Clause 3, Section 14, Regulation II of 1822 of the Bengal Code now rescinded, a person bidding at a public sale and not concluding his purchase was liable to a fine of 100 rupees, or imprisonment for 15 days. By the existing law at Madras, persons bidding who are legally incompetent to purchase, are liable for the second offence to fine and imprisonment without limitation. Mr. Norton upon this clause, as we have observed above, asks, "what is the criterion of bidding without intention of performing all the obligations, &c." We can only say that we see no need for any peculiar criterion. The fact that the bidder did not intend to complete the purchase must of course be proved by such evidence as is ordinarily admitted in similar cases.

Reg. XXVI of 1802, Sec. 21.

111. In Clauses 171, 173, 175, 177 and 178 are provisions for the punishment of resistance to arrest, the rescue of prisoners, escape of prisoners from custody, and the harbouring of persons ordered to be taken into custody or who have escaped from custody. In the next chapter, under the head of Offences against public justice, are further provisions for the punishment of prisoners *under sentence* escaping from custody, &c. The punishment for resisting an arrest, and for rescue, is imprisonment which may extend to six months, or fine, or both. The punishment for escaping from custody is imprisonment which may extend to three months, or fine, or both. For harbouring a person ordered to be taken into custody the punishment is imprisonment to one month, or fine which may extend to 200 rupees. For harbouring a person who has escaped from custody the imprisonment may extend to two months and the fine to 500 rupees. Many experienced officers have objected to these punishments as too lenient. In the case of a state prisoner, or a murderer, or a dacoit, for example, it is thought that the punishment denounced in Clauses 171 and 173 respectively, will be inadequate to deter the friends of the offender from resisting an attempt to take him into custody, or from rescuing him from custody. Again it is observed that imprisonment for three months under Clause 175, would not deter a person apprehended for a serious offence, whose punishment might be imprisonment for 14 years, from attempting to escape.

112. By the Digest of the English Criminal Law persons resisting apprehension or escaping from custody not under sentence are punishable with imprisonment which may extend to 2 years, and in felonies to 3 years; the rescue of prisoners not under sentence is punishable with imprisonment which may extend to 3 years, and in cases of felony and treason with transportation for 7 years or imprisonment not exceeding 3 years.

Chap. V, Sec. 5, Arts. 1 to 4.

Arts. 9, 10 and 11.

113. The terms of imprisonment thus authorized are very long compared with those of the Code, but it is to be considered that by the Code the amount of fine, which may be added to the punishment of imprisonment, is unlimited, and that when the offence is aggravated by the commission of an assault or any other offence at the same time, the offender is liable to additional punishment. Thus in a case of rescue, for example, if an assault were committed attended with hurt, the offender would be liable to imprisonment for 6 months for the rescue and for 1 year in addition on account of the hurt, and to fine at the discretion of the Court. It has been suggested that there should be a gradation with reference to the nature of the charge against the person whose arrest is resisted, or who has escaped, or been rescued from custody, and we are inclined to think it advisable to follow the Digest on this point. The Digest prolongs the term of imprisonment when the offence charged is a felony, that is an offence punishable with transportation. We would provide in the Code for an extension of the term of imprisonment from 6 months to 1 year when the offence charged is punishable by imprisonment which may extend to 7 years.

114. The same modification we think advisable in Clauses 177 and 178 respecting "harbour;" we would suggest that the punishment in these Clauses be doubled when the offence charged against the person harboured is punishable by imprisonment which may extend to 7 years. It is to be observed that when harbour is given to one who has committed an offence punishable with imprisonment for 7 years or upwards, with the intention of screening him from justice, it is called subsequent abetment, and is punishable under Clause 107 with imprisonment which may extend to 6 months, or fine to 1,000 rupees, or both. We have already suggested a modification of the exceptions to these clauses in commenting upon the exception to Clause 107 to the same effect.

See First Report, paras. 226 to 232, page 244.

115. Of Clause 179, which provides for the punishment of persons insulting or causing interruption to public servants in the discharge of their public functions, Mr. Hudleston observes that it is open to enormous abuse, and in the case of the lower native servants would lead to false charges. Mr. A. D. Campbell would strike out the words "offers any insult," or insert "above the rank of a common Peon or Chuprassie." Colonel Sleeman suggests that there should be one clause for the offering of insult to be punished as here proposed, and another for the mere causing of interruption, to be punished with fine, and imprisonment only in default of payment of the fine. He thinks that this distinction is much wanted.

116. We think that the objections to the provision regarding insult in this clause are overstrained. Clause 485 provides generally for the punishment of any person intentionally offering insult to another, and we see good reason as regards the public peace for this provision. But if it is properly made an offence to insult a private person going about his own business, *a fortiori* it ought to be made an offence to insult a public servant while he is in the discharge of his public functions, as it is by Clause 179, and still more to insult a public servant while he is holding a Court of Justice as by Clause 197. We would provide distinctly for the offence of causing interruption to a public servant in the discharge of his public functions as proposed by Colonel Sleeman, subjecting the offender to a fine not exceeding 200 rupees, and of course to imprisonment in default of payment under the general rule. We shall propose a similar arrangement with respect to the offences described in Clause 197.

117. Mr. Hudleston objects to Clause 181, which provides for the punishment of a person who, knowing himself to be directed by law to give assistance to any public servant in the execution of his public duty, intentionally omits to give such assistance, with imprisonment which may extend to 1 month, or fine to the amount of 200 rupees, or both. This provision appears to him calculated to lead to much abuse, and he thinks the principle of doubtful propriety and the penalty too severe. His Colleague, Mr. A. D. Campbell, expresses his dissent from this opinion, and we agree with him. The Digest of the English Criminal Law has a general article under which a person wilfully doing what is prohibited, or "omitting any matter or thing commanded to be done by any Statute" is punishable with imprisonment which may extend to 3 months, or fine at discretion, or both. The Commissioners observe that this is "an enactment which is essential for the enforcing of general laws in the absence of any particular penalties annexed to disobedience." The penalties, they observe, may be incurred although the offender is not apprised by the Digest by what acts or omissions he will incur them. This, they admit, is an inconvenience, but a necessary one, for some means are absolutely essential for compelling obedience to the direct and peremptory precepts of the law, and one who is wilfully guilty of disobedience may be regarded as having acted criminally. These observations appear to be applicable to the provision in Clause 181.

Chap. IV, Section 2, Art. 12.

7th Report, p. 11.

118. We come now to Clause 182, the reasons of which are fully explained in the Note to this chapter. What is proposed "is to empower the local authorities to forbid acts "which those authorities consider as dangerous to the "public tranquillity, health, safety, or convenience, and to make it an "offence in a person to do anything which that person knows to be so "forbidden, and which may endanger the public tranquillity, health, "safety, or convenience." The clause does "not give to the local author-

See Appendix, Note F, page 129.

"ities the power of arbitrarily making any thing an offence. For unless "the Court before which the person who disobeys the order is tried shall "be of opinion that he has done something tending to endanger the pub-"lic tranquillity, health, safety or convenience, he will be liable to no "punishment. The effect of the order will be merely to deprive the "person who knowingly disobeys the order of the plea that he had no "bad intentions. He will not be permitted to allege that if he has caused "harm, or risk of harm, it was without his knowledge."

119. We think it is satisfactorily shewn in the Note that the proper local officers should have power to issue orders for the purpose indicated, to have force without the sanction of the Legislature, so far as is provided in the clause in question; and with such a check upon the punishment of persons disobeying the orders as the clause contains, in requiring it to be proved that the disobedience, by act or omission, caused or tended to cause any of the evils against which the order was meant to guard, it does not appear to us that it is liable to abuse; nor do we see that there is such room for arbitrary constructions as Mr. Norton finds in it.

120. Mr. Hudleston says, "The intention of this clause appears "good, but I think it badly worded. Power to remove nuisances should "be given. I object to punish for causing 'any annoyance,' 'risk of "annoyance,' or 'risk of rioting.'" Mr. Hudleston does not explain what he understands by the term "nuisance." By the definition of it in the Digest of English Criminal Law it includes any act or unlawful omission which causes or tends to cause "any public calamity, mischief, "or disorder, or any common injury, damage, inconvenience, or *annoy-"ance* to the Queen's subjects," (generally, or any class of them,) in "respect of their habitations, personal safety, health, or comfort and "convenience, or property." So that according to the English Law, which Mr. Hudleston generally approves of, in giving power to order the removal of a nuisance, and, as we apprehend Mr. Hudleston means, to enforce the order by a penalty, power would be given virtually to punish for annoyance, which he objects to.

121. It has been suggested that the authors of the Code have been overcautious against abuse of the authority which they deem to be necessary in this respect, in providing, for the reasons stated by them, "that no person should be punished merely for disobeying a local order "unless it be made to appear that the disobedience has been attended "with evil or risk of evil" intending thus to secure that no person shall be punished "for disobeying an idle or vexatious order." Mr. H. C. Tucker says, "No one should be allowed to plead that an order was "'foolish' as his reason for disobeying it; until reversed on appeal the "order of every public servant should be binding, and be enforced. "Officers should be warned against issuing vexatious orders (under "liability to suit for damages in the Civil Court) and they might be "prohibited from issuing any general orders without the previous "sanction of the controuling authority."

122. The Commissioners themselves say, "we see some objections "to the way in which we have framed this part of the law. But we are "unable to frame it better." We suppose they had some apprehension that the power they felt to be necessary would be apt to be neutralized when the punishment of disobedience to it was made contingent on the judgment of another authority as to the effect of such disobedience—

that the order would not be likely to meet with the prompt obedience requisite to make it effectual for the end intended on an emergency if disobedience could not be punished summarily by the same authority which issued the order. We have some such apprehension; but we are not prepared at present to suggest any modification of the clause, which while it should make the power more effectual should leave it equally safe from abuse. We are the more content to leave the clause untouched when we find that only one officer employed in the internal administration has offered a practical objection to it.

123. Clause 184 provides for the punishment of a person holding out a threat of injury to a public servant to prevent him from doing his duty, and Clause 186 for the punishment of one who holds out such threat to any person to prevent him seeking protection from a public servant empowered as such to give him protection. In both cases the punishment is imprisonment of either description, which may extend to one year, or fine, or both. Mr. Hudleston (Mr. A. D. Campbell agreeing) objects to the former clause as liable to great abuse. "Threats," he observes, "are often effusions of passion unattended with any formal intention of wrong." The observation is true—but it is for the Court to distinguish between empty threats of this kind for which the punishment should be merely nominal, and threats calculated to cause the person to whom they are held out to be in fear of the injury threatened, which it is proper to punish with more or less severity, within the limit prescribed, according to the nature of the injury threatened and the probable efficacy of the threat. For a threat of "grievous hurt," delivered in a manner calculated to make the person threatened believe that it would be inflicted, and terrifying him with the apprehension of it to a degree likely to induce him to fail in his public duty, the maximum punishment authorized would not be too severe; still less for a threat of murder, to which the clause equally applies. Indeed, we cannot think it severe enough, when reference is made to Clause 483, which provides the punishment of imprisonment which may extend to two years, or fine, or both, for the offence of criminal intimidation, (Clause 482,) committed to induce *any person* to do what he is not legally bound to do, or to abstain from doing what he has a right to do, or merely to cause distress or terror to him. It is to be observed, that this Clause 184 applies to judicial officers as well as others, there being no special provision regarding threats to judicial officers in the next chapter of Offences against public justice. We are of opinion that the penalty should be the same as is denounced in Clause 483.

124. With reference to Clause 187 and others to the same effect, Sir H. Seton questions first, generally, the propriety of making offences cumulative; secondly, the propriety of making them so to the extent proposed in this chapter. Mr. Norton observes that double or cumulative punishments abound in this chapter with less need for them than in any other. We shall consider the general question in reviewing the chapter of Punishments. We have above suggested a reason for cumulative punishments being so frequent in this chapter, namely, to provide discriminately for aggravations which the English Law provides for indiscriminately by allowing a much greater latitude in the punishments for the primary offences, and we cannot but think the method of the Code as it limits discretion is more conducive to exactness in the apportionment of punishment.

See paras. 108, 109 and 113.

125. Mr. Pycroft observes that there is no adequate punishment in the Code for preferring false complaints, a very common practice in India. We conceive that Clause 163, upon which we have remarked in para. 102, sufficiently provides for this offence.

126. Sir H. Seton asks "are the offences contained in this chapter "to be the only contempts liable to punishment? If so what is to be "the provision for enforcing decrees, orders, &c.? Is any party to be "at liberty to set the law at defiance who is willing to submit to a "limited fine and imprisonment?" We have already offered a suggestion on the point touched by the last question. To promote the enforcement of decrees, &c., there are some further provisions in the next chapter. The penalties prescribed for the particular offences obstructive of judicial procedure which are defined in the Code must be taken as exclusive of other punishment. But it would seem not to be intended to meddle with any other coercive power the Courts possess for the enforcement of decrees, &c., as by attachment and sale of property, and so forth.

Para. 104.

Clauses 193 and 194.

CHAPTER X.

OF OFFENCES AGAINST PUBLIC JUSTICE.

127. This chapter is intended to provide for offences that interfere with the administration of justice, which do not fall within the provisions of the preceding chapter relating to contempts of the lawful authority of public servants, or of other chapters, or which appear to call for more severe punishment when committed for the defeat of justice.

128. The first five clauses in this chapter which relate to false evidence are very important. The first of them, Clause 188, defines the offence of "giving false evidence" on oath or under a sanction tantamount to an oath, distinguishing it from the offence of making a false statement to a public servant under the like sanction in Clause 162, by the circumstance that it is given in some stage of a judicial proceeding touching a point material to the result of such proceeding. The next Clause 189 defines the offence of "fabricating false evidence." Clause 190 provides for the punishment of the offence of giving or of fabricating false evidence simply; Clauses 191 and 192 aggravate the punishment when the offence is committed with the intention of deceiving a Court of Justice so as to procure a wrongful conviction of a capital offence, or of some grave offence not capital.

Clauses 188 to 192.

129. The English Criminal Law Commissioners in their 5th Report expressed an opinion "that the distinction between the "offences of false swearing in a judicial proceeding and "mere false swearing is judicious and proper." After pointing out some statutory provisions regarding "mere false swearing," they observed that the great objection to such provisions is that "they confound the aggra- "vated offence of judicial perjury with the inferior crime of false "swearing." "It appears to us," they said, "that the object of the law "may be much more effectually attained by a general clause, such as "will be found in the Digest, making it criminal in any person lawfully "required by any competent authority to declare the truth upon his oath "in any proceeding not judicial, wilfully to state a falsehood, and we "propose to place this offence in a lower degree than judicial perjury in "the classification of punishments." This is exactly the course taken by the Indian Law Commissioners in framing the Code. We find however that the English Criminal Law Commissioners took a different view in framing the Digest appended to their 7th Report. In this the Article defining perjury includes false swearing on any "other occasion where an oath is imposed, required or sanctioned by law," as well as "in some judicial proceeding." We think the arrangement of the Code is preferable for the reasons given in the 5th Report, as above cited.

P. 23, 26.

Chap. V, Section 4, Art. 5.

130. Mr. Hudleston commenting on Clause 188 says, "I do not see "why the word 'perjury' which is perfectly intelligible to the people of "India, and has been so long in use, is discarded." Mr. A. D. Campbell answers, "The reason why the word 'perjury' as well as the English "Law regarding it has been entirely discarded in this Code, has been most "satisfactorily explained in Note G." He adds, "it is gratifying to find "so many officers in the interior bearing testimony of that admiration "which I agree with them is justly due to the Law Commission for the "vast improvement they have suggested in this important branch of the "Criminal Code." The authors of the Code thought it inexpedient to use the technical terms of the English Law where they did not adopt its definitions, and so materially departed from it in substance. The reason is general, and applies to the whole body of the Code, as well as to this particular article of it. As to the people of India, although the word "perjury" is used in the English Regulations, we apprehend that the offence is better known to the generality by words of similar import to those used in the Code "expressing "the nature of the crime in the most current local "language."

Bengal Regulation II, 1807, Section 3, Clause 1, corresponding with Madras Regulation VI, 1811, Section 3, Clause 1.

131. There are "*explanations*" annexed to Clause 188 which, for the purpose of it, include as judicial proceedings certain investigations for judicial objects which do not take place before a Judge or a Court of Justice, as those terms are defined in Clauses 12 and 13. Mr. Hudleston questions the propriety of empowering such an officer as is indicated in one of the "illustrations," viz., an officer deputed by a Court to ascertain boundaries, to take evidence on oath, but we do not see any valid objection to it. The offence is the same essentially whether the oath be taken before the Judge or the officer, the intent being "to mislead the Judge on a point material to the question" before him, in order to the decision of which the investigation is directed to be made. It is to be observed that another explanation makes an Interpreter who gives a false interpretation on oath to a Court of Justice guilty of "giving false evidence" within the meaning of this clause.

Illustration (c).

132. It will of course be necessary to modify the wording of Clause 188 and of Clause 162, so as to make them consistent with Act V of 1840 and Act XXI of 1837, in respect to the affirmation substituted for an oath in judicial proceedings by the former, and to the declaration allowed to be substituted for an oath on other occasions by the latter. The punishment authorized by Section IV, Act XXI of 1837 for a false declaration is less than is authorized for a false statement on oath by Clause 162. The latter we think should not be altered.

Imprisonment not exceeding 1 year, or fine, or both.

Imprisonment not exceeding 3 years, or fine, or both.

133. Mr. Fagan proposes an additional provision for the case of a person "stating that to be true, which he could not possibly know to be "true, or stating his belief in the truth of a fact touching any point "material, &c., which he knows to be false or in the truth of which he "could not possibly have any belief." The Digest of the English Criminal Law declares a person guilty of perjury who "swears affirmatively or negatively as to some fact or thing, &c., knowing that which he swears to be false or *not knowing it to be true.*" We think it is worthy of consideration whether words similar to those in italics should not be introduced into Clause 188, making it "false evidence" when a person "states that to be true which he does not know to be true," as well as when he "states that to be true which he knows to be false" according to the present definition. According to Mr. Livingstone's Code, perjury is a *falsehood*

Chap. V, Sec. 4, Art. 5.

asserted under the sanction of an oath, &c., it being explained that "falsehood in this definition refers to the belief of the party attesting," by which explanation the party would be guilty of the offence, if, although he did not know what he stated as true to be false positively, he stated it to be true when he did not know, and therefore could not believe it to be true.

Note (x), p. 51, 5th Report of Commissioners on Criminal Law.

"The Prussian Code, (it appears,) affixes the punish-"ment of perjury 'to any person who upon his oath "denies his knowledge of any matter or occurrence "with which he is in truth acquainted.' The same "law also inflicts a penalty upon persons who from "thoughtlessness and want of care, swear falsely to facts of the true "state of which they might and ought to have been acquainted." If the alteration here suggested should be made in Clause 188, it would be proper to make it also in Clause 162.

134. Mr. Greenhill observes—"a plaintiff who voluntarily takes oath "to the truth of his claim, might come under the definition in Clause 188, "although by the Note it does not appear to be intended. By the "Bombay Code, a plaintiff is in such a case liable to the punishment of "perjury, and an instance of its infliction has occurred."

Bom. Reg. IV, 1827, Section 22, Clause 2.
Bengal Reg. IV, 1793, Section 6; Reg. XXIII, 1814, Section 28.
Madras Reg. III, 1802, Section 6; Reg. VI, 1816, Section 27.

135. It is clear, we think, that this clause is applicable to a plaintiff taking an oath to the truth of a claim which he knows to be false, under any system of civil procedure which permits such an oath to be taken, as that of Bombay does, and as do also the Regulations of Bengal and Madras on the consent of the parties. The Note which appears to be referred to by Mr. Greenhill, relates to the assertion of falsehoods in pleading, not on oath.

Pages 130, 131.

136. The observations in Note G in support of the provision contained in Clauses 189 and 190 regarding the offence of "fabricating false evidence," are quoted with approbation in the 5th Report of the Commissioners on the English Criminal Law. And in the Digest annexed to that Report, under the head of offences against the administration of justice, there is an article on the subject in the following terms: "Whosoever shall "fraudulently and deceitfully *cause any* fact or *circum-"stance to exist*, in order that such fact or circumstance may after-"wards be proved in evidence against any other person, with intent "to procure such other person to be unjustly charged or convicted "of any offence, shall incur the penalties of the ——class." The words here printed in italics appear to have been adopted from the Penal Code, and so far as the article goes it agrees with Clause 189 of the Code, but the latter is more comprehensive, applying to a civil judicial proceeding as well as to a criminal one, to which the above article is confined, and to cases in which the essence of the offence may be the deceit put upon the Court without any intention of injustice to another, as in the illustration (*c*). In the General Digest submitted with the 7th Report of the English Criminal Law Commissioners, the corresponding article is altered in terms, but it would seem to be intended to have the same effect.

Art. 119, p. 62.

Sec. 5, Art. 26, p. 169.

137. Mr. Hudleston observes of the definition in Clause 189, the leading words of which, as we have remarked, are introduced into the article just quoted, that it appears to him "an instance of a definition "not intelligible in itself made so by illustration." He is not supported in this criticism by any other officer, and it appears to us unfounded.

138. Mr. Norton says, "I agree in the expediency of the clauses "against '*fabricating* false evidence,' and its logical distinction from "giving false evidence."

139. By an "*exception*" under Clause 190, it is declared that "a "person who fabricates false evidence intending thereby to save himself "from conviction for an offence, and not intending nor knowing it to be "likely that the false evidence so fabricated may cause any injury to any "other party, is not within the penal provision of this clause." This exception the Commissioners consider to be in strict conformity with the principle of their rule. "We propose to treat the giving "of false evidence and the fabricating of false evidence "in exactly the same way. We have no punishment for "false evidence given by a person when on his trial for "an offence, though we conceive that such a person ought to be interro-"gated." "As we do not propose to punish a prisoner for lying at the "bar in order to escape punishment, so we do not propose to punish him "for fabricating evidence with the view of escaping punishment, unless "he also contemplated some injury to others as likely to be produced by "the evidence so fabricated. If A stabs Z, and afterwards on his trial "denies that he stabbed Z, we do not propose to punish A as a giver of "false evidence. And on the same principle if A, after having stabbed "Z, in order to escape detection, disposes Z's body in such a manner as "is likely to lead a jury to think the death accidental, we do not propose "to punish A as a fabricator of false evidence."

See Appendix, Note G, pp. 130, 131.

140. Sir H. Seton questions the propriety of this exception. "Why," he asks, "should a just punishment be evaded by fabricated evidence "any more than a just demand. The English Law (practically at least) "treats a defence supported by perjury as an aggravation of the offence. "Why depart from so sound a principle and surrender all the moral "considerations so forcibly insisted on in the Note?" Sir R. Comyn objects to the exception "unless the word 'fabricates' be meant to be "restricted to such acts of the party himself as are indicated by the "illustration (*a*)." "Fabricating evidence," he observes, "may include "the procuring of other men's false testimony, and a party who evades "conviction by such a proceeding, ought not to escape from the conse-"quence of one crime by the successful commission of another." Mr. Pyne says: "The very recognizing the right of fabricating false evidence "seems to be holding out somewhat an encouragement to it. The right "of pleading not guilty can never be denied to a prisoner, nor exception "be taken at a negative declaration, but when in aid and support of his "denial another substantive offence is committed, I cannot think it "should have the sanction of the law in support of it."

141. To Sir Henry Seton's question, Why should a just punishment be evaded by fabricated evidence any more than a just demand? we answer, that the evasion of a just demand is an injury to the plaintiff, and the temptation to cause that injury is like the temptation to commit any other crime *lucri causâ*. But the temptation to escape from death or infamy though deserved, by means of a fraud which injures no individual, is greater than the weakness of human nature can in general resist,

To punish a man for doing so would be to punish the want of heroic devotion. "Ignoscendum enim ei," say the Civilians, "qui sanguinem "suum qualiter qualiter redemptum voluit."

142. We do not agree with Sir R. Comyn, that "the procuring of other men's false testimony" can be considered as "causing a circumstance to exist" within the meaning of Clause 189. It is abetment of the offence of giving false evidence, and is punishable under Clause 88, notwithstanding the "*exception*" to Clause 190. It does not appear to us that any act to which the exception applies can properly be called the commission of *a crime*, seeing that to fall within the exception it must be done "not intending or knowing it to be likely" that it "may cause any injury to any other party." The kind of acts intended, is indicated in the illustration (*a*) subjoined to the exception, and in that given in the Note as quoted above, namely, acts harmless in themselves, but which being done with the intention of misleading a Court of Justice fall within the definition of "fabricating false evidence." We can hardly think that any of the objectors to this exception would deem it right to punish a person who "to save himself from conviction for an offence" did what is supposed to be done in the illustration (*a*), or in that referred to in the Note, intending that it might appear in evidence in his favor when be came to trial, any more than to punish him for a false assertion made by him in his defence.

143. The authors of the Code say: "The giving of false evidence "must always be a grave offence. But few points in "penal legislation seem to us clearer than that the law "ought to make a distinction between that kind of false "evidence which produces great evils and that kind of false evidence which "produces comparatively slight evils." "As the ordinary punishment of false evidence, we propose imprisonment for a term of not more than seven years nor less than one year. "If the false evidence is given or fabricated with intent to cause a person "to be convicted of a grave offence not capital, we propose that the "person who gives or fabricates such evidence may be punished with the "punishment of the offence which he has attempted to "fix on another. If the false evidence be given or "fabricated with the intention of causing death, we propose to punish it "in the same manner in which we propose to punish the worst attempts "to murder," that is, with transportation for life, or rigorous imprisonment which may extend to life, and must not be less than seven years, and with fine at discretion.

See Appendix, Note G, page 131.

Clause 190.

Clause 192.

Clause 191.

144. On this subject in their 5th Report, the English Criminal Law Commissioners say: "We think it a question worthy "of great consideration whether the crime of perjury "ought not to be marked by some gradations. It is "strongly remarked by the Indian Law Commissioners that 'the English "Law makes no distinction whatever between the man who has attempt"ed to take away his neighbour's life by false swearing and the "man who has strained his conscience to give an undeserved good "character to a boy accused of petty theft; the former is punished far "too leniently, the latter perhaps too severely.' We shall recur to "these considerations when we have occasion to suggest the different

5th Report, p. 27.

"classes of punishments." Accordingly in the Digest submitted with their 7th Report, there is an article providing for the punishment of a person who by perjury or subornation of perjury procures or endeavors to procure the conviction of another of a capital offence, and a further article for the punishment of one so procuring or endeavoring to procure conviction of a transportable offence. The penalties under the former of these articles are transportation for life, or for any term not less than seven years, or imprisonment for any term not exceeding three years; under the latter transportation for a term not exceeding fifteen years, nor less than seven years, or imprisonment not exceeding three years.

Chapter V, Section 4, Art. 14.

Art. 15.

7th Class.

12th Class.

145. Upon the provisions of the Code on the subject of false evidence, Mr. J. F. Thomas says—"The modification of the previous Law proposed "in the Code, by which perjury is dealt with on its own merits, and which "annexes even transportation for life to certain grades of the offence, is "a great and valuable improvement in principle. But it does not appear "to me, that the principle is carried by any means far enough in the "descending scale."

"The crime appears still to be viewed with English eyes, and visited "accordingly with heavy penalties, though in the Notes (page 130,) it is "acknowledged, that direct perjury does little harm in India, compared "with what may be effected by it in England. It is not apparently suffi"ciently borne in mind, that we have no oath by which we can bind the "conscience of the Hindoo. He does no violation therefore to his con"science, in forswearing himself; and he neither does nor can he "perceive, and feel with us the enormity of perjury. By this Clause "(190) the heavy penalty of the old Law, is in a great measure retained, "(with the very valuable addition of fine,) whether the perjury has been "committed in the *most trivial*, or, in a very important case; and the "natural and necessary consequence is, that the convictions will always "be extremely limited, and the prosecutions, as heretofore, few; perjury, "therefore, it may be predicted, will continue unabated, under a Code, "which annexes these high penalties."

"The interest of the community would, I conceive, be better served "by lowering the penalty of the offence, and enjoining frequent prose"cutions. A beneficial result has, I believe, always followed, whenever "this experiment has been tried. Captain Pottinger states, that he had "by this means so completely repressed the offence, 'that he did not "recollect a single instance of perjury having occurred before him in "six months.'—Judicial Selections, vol. IV, page 451."

146. Mr. Thomas's argument we think is valid against the minimum prescribed in Clause 190. By the Digest of the English Criminal Law the punishment for perjury, without the aggravations separately provided for as above, is transportation for the term of seven years, or imprisonment not exceeding three years, or fine at discretion, or both. Here when imprisonment is the punishment to be inflicted, the discretion of the Judge is not limited by a minimum term, and we would recommend that the above clause be modified so as to make it agree on this point with the corresponding article in the Digest. We would omit the minimum likewise in Clause 162.

Chap. V, Sec. 4, Art. 4.

10th Class.

147. In our former Report we have recommended that Clause 191 should be declared applicable generally to the offence of giving false evidence with the intention of causing a person to be convicted of a capital crime, as well when the object intended is effected, as when it is not, rather than that when the object is effected the offender should be dealt with as guilty of homicide, as intended by the authors of the Code. In Clause 192 it appears to be necessary to introduce after the words "punishable with" the words "transportation for life, or" to make the clause agree with the illustration, and to express what is obviously intended.

Para. 258 to 266 and para. 666.

148. Mr. Thomas observes that the Code does not include the offences provided for by the Madras Regulations I of 1832, and XIII of 1832, Section 7,—"the first punishing false allegations in petitions to the "Judicial Courts; the other, prevarication or other gross contempt of "Court." These provisions he considers "of great *practical* importance. "They confer upon the Courts a power essentially necessary in the "present state of society, to check the attempts hourly made to impede "the due administration of justice, and whatever may be the objections "to them on general principles, they are, I am satisfied from experience, "necessary, and peculiarly well adapted to the exigencies and circum-"stances of South India."

149. Mr. Strange says—"It is remarked in page 133 of the Notes, that "'The law on the subject of false evidence will render unnecessary any "'law for punishing the frivolous and vexatious preferring of criminal "'charges.' This ought undoubtedly to be the result of a penal provi-"sion against perjury, but so much is the law now in force cramped by "restrictive rules inessential to the determining whether the evidence "which is the subject of the charge be false or true, that the degree of "proof upon which a suitor may be punished for a false suit, or a com-"plainant before the Police for a false complaint under (Madras) Regu-"lation IX of 1832, would be considered wholly insufficient to lead to a "conviction of perjury or subornation of perjury."

150. Mr. Strange notices two points as requiring full and careful illustration, observing at the same time that they are perhaps more "connected with the Code of Procedure than with the Penal Code," viz., 1st, "What constitutes a question material to the result of a judicial "proceeding. 2nd, What is to be considered sufficient evidence of the "falsehood stated." The first of these points only appears to require attention in this place with reference to Mr. Strange's remarks, and the suggestion founded on them. His remarks are as follows:—"A prisoner "pleads that the prosecution brought against him is the result of a "conspiracy, and wishes to expose the fact that the witnesses are related "to the prosecutor. At his instance the witnesses would assuredly be "questioned on the subject of the relationship, but if they gave false "answers it is very doubtful whether an indictment for perjury could "be maintained against them, under the existing system, although their "depositions were calculated to defeat the prisoner's plea and therefore "to affect the issue of the trial." To remedy the supposed defect, he suggests that "the giving a false statement under an oath, or a declara-"tion substituted for an oath, in relation to any fact connected (in any "way) with the merits of any matter undergoing judicial investigation, "with intent to deceive, should be considered to constitute the crime of "perjury."

151. We do not think there is room for the doubt expressed by Mr. Strange upon the case here put. If the false depositions "were calculated to defeat the prisoner's plea, and therefore to affect the issue of "the trial" as he avers, we conceive that there would be sufficient ground for an indictment of perjury both under the law of England and under the law at present observed by the Company's Courts, and that an indictment would be sustainable equally under Clause 188 of the Code. As to English law, Russell says, "if the false oath has *any* "*tendency* to prove or disprove the matter in issue, "though but circumstantially; as if the party wilfully mistake the colour "of a man's coat or speak to the credit of another witness, it will amount "to perjury." This we apprehend holds good equally as applied to the definition of false evidence in the clause under consideration. It appears to us that with the "*explanation*" on the point in question annexed to the clause, the definition is as comprehensive as it ought to be. It will be an important object in framing rules of procedure applicable to the penal provisions on this subject, to take care that they are not frustrated by unnecessary restrictions as to proof.

Russell 2, p. 541.

152. With respect to false allegations in petitions to the Judicial Courts, Clause 163 will suffice for their punishment if they are not supported by false swearing, when they are so supported Clause 188 becomes applicable. It does not appear therefore that any further provision is requisite on this head.

153. But we are inclined to concur with Mr. Thomas in thinking it advisable to introduce into the Code a provision for the punishment of prevarication, which when committed before a Court of Criminal Jurisdiction is now punishable, under Clause 7, Regulation XIII of 1832 of the Madras Code, with a fine not exceeding 50 rupees, commutable, if not paid, to imprisonment not exceeding one month. We have noticed above on the authority of the English Criminal Law Commissioners, that the Prussian Code "inflicts a penalty upon persons who from thoughtlessness and want of care swear falsely to facts, of the true state of which "they might and ought to have been acquainted." We are disposed to think that a clause for the punishment of persons who being on oath, &c., in any judicial proceeding, shall prevaricate or make contradictory or inconsistent averments in a manner indicating a deliberate intention to conceal the truth, would have a very salutary effect. The punishment we would recommend is imprisonment of either description for a term which may extend to six months, or fine, or both.

154. By Regulation III of 1826 of the Madras Code, a person wilfully and deliberately giving two contradictory depositions on oath is liable to be convicted of perjury, and to suffer the punishment prescribed for that offence. It has been decided that under the law of England "perjury cannot be legally charged and "assigned by shewing that the defendant did on two different occasions "make certain depositions contradictory to each other, with an averment "that each of them was made knowingly and deliberately, but without "averring or shewing in which of the two depositions the falsehood "consisted;" and we apprehend that under similar circumstances the offence of giving false evidence could not be so charged under Clause 188. We are strongly of opinion that "whoever in any stage of a judicial "proceeding being bound by an oath or by a sanction tantamount to an

Russell 2, p. 542.

"oath, to state the truth, gives a statement touching any point material "to the result of such proceeding, which directly and positively contra- "dicts a statement touching the same point, given by him on oath, or "under a sanction tantamount to an oath, in any stage of a judicial "proceeding, at another time," should (failing any satisfactory explanation of the contradiction to negative the inference of a corrupt intention) be liable to punishment. Under such circumstances it is morally certain that the party has given a false statement on one or other of the two occasions, though it may be impossible to shew positively which of the contradictory statements is false. Both statements may perhaps be false, but one only can be true. It is possible indeed that the first statement may have been false through an error or mistake which has been corrected by subsequent information, and that the second contradicts the first because it contains the truth which had come to the knowledge of the party in the meantime. But when there is no such allegation, nor any explanation of the contradiction to negative the inference that the party at one time or the other has been guilty of stating on oath (or as it may be) as true what he knew to be false in order to deceive a Court of Justice, on a point material to the question to be decided by the Court, we think the law should be so framed that he should not be able to escape from the punishment he would well deserve. In the case in question, we do not see why the party who has given the contradictory statements might not be charged with the offence of false evidence upon each of them successively, first upon that which from the circumstances there is reason to think is most probably the false one, giving the other in evidence against him, which would throw upon him the onus of proving it to be false, and if he succeeded in defending himself against that charge by means of such proof, then upon that other statement as proved to be false by the evidence he had himself adduced. By this mode of proceeding a really guilty person could hardly escape. And a person who had such a defence as before supposed, being able to shew, for instance, that his second statement differed from the first because he had ascertained in the meantime that the first statement was incorrect, would have an opportunity of clearing himself by giving proof to that effect. If necessary a special rule might be enacted to sanction this mode of procedure.

155. Mr. Norton makes the following remarks upon Clauses 193, 194 and 196. "I conceive that Clauses 193, 194, making it criminal "to '*conceal*,' or claim with a knowledge of 'having no *rightful* claim,' "property—for the purpose of preventing its seizure for a fine, are "scarcely calculated for *fair* application from the uncertainty of the "cases falling within such terms. But they are open at the same time "to great abuse, by *unfair* application. The principle seems borrowed "from the Bankrupt and Insolvent Laws—but I think there is much "difference in the duty of bankrupts to *disclose* and surrender, and the "*obligations* of culprits to *submit* to a sentence to be *enforced* by others. "The making it criminal to sue *without probable cause* (which is the effect "of Clause 196) labours under the same objection, and I conceive it very "inexpedient to punish such conduct as a *crime*, and particularly by so "severe a possible punishment as one year's imprisonment."

156. Sir H. Seton also questions "the making a wrongful claim "to property a criminal offence" as in Clause 194. Again, he asks "whether the consequence of such an enactment" as is contained in

Clause 196, "would not be that every unsuccessful civil suit might be "connected with a criminal prosecution"? and "whether costs are not a "sufficient preventive" of the evil which the clause is intended to provide against, "or might not be made so?"

157. On the other hand, the Company's Judges and Officers who have noticed these clauses approve of them in principle, that is they think it proper that the acts described therein should be dealt with as offences, though they do not entirely agree to the provisions proposed.

158. Mr. J. F. Thomas referring to those parts of Clauses 193 and 194 which relate to civil cases, observes that they "provide only a "penalty where the fraudulent claim is set up to prevent property being "taken in execution of a *decree* of a Court of Justice." He says, "I see "no reason for confining the rule to decrees—the clause should provide "alike, for cases where property is taken in execution of a decree, or, "*in pursuance of any order of a Court of Justice.* In cases, where "orders are issued on motions, not on decrees, for taking property into "the possession of the Court, parties who may prevent the due execu-"tion of such orders by wrongful claims, or deceptious practices, impede "the due administration of justice, as much as those who so act after a "decree has been passed. It is advisable, I think, that provision should be "made for the one class of cases, as for the other." Mr. A. D. Campbell supports this suggestion, while Mr. Hudleston objects to it.

159. Of Clause 196 Mr. J. F. Thomas says—"This clause is of the "first importance to the due administration of civil justice, in the "present state of society in South India. But to be effective, it must "be enlarged. It was an evil of frequent occurrence in Tanjore, for "parties to introduce into *just* suits as regards the chief litigant, the "names of parties, as defendants, and even as co-plaintiffs, who had no "concern in the suit, placing all their property for the time being in "litigation, greatly to their detriment and annoyance. This case does "not appear to be provided for by the rule. Neither does this clause "provide for those cases in which the suit is wholly fictitious, not insti-"tuted for the purposes of annoyance."

"In Tanjore, for instance, it is not unfrequent, for an individual pos-"sessing landed property, on entering into partnership in trade, to set "up some dependant, or a near relative, to institute a suit for the whole "of his property. The claim of the plaintiff is admitted by the pro-"prietor, the defendant in these fictitious suits. No one at the time is "either injured or annoyed. It is only in the course of years, when "unsuccessful in his speculations, and at the time his creditors press "their claims against him, that the original plaintiff, the man of straw, "appears, not with a naked claim, but with a decree in his favor, adjudg-"ing him the whole of the defendant's property. This property, he will "acknowledge, he has nevertheless left the whole time in the defendant's "possession; but he pleads his right under a decree of Court."

"To put down this, and similar abusive use of the Courts of Justice, "I would strongly recommend, that the clause should be so framed, as "to include all cases of fictitious and fraudulent litigation. It might "run thus—'Whoever fraudulently institutes, *or becomes a party* to any "'fictitious suit whatever, shall be, &c.,' as in Clause 196, or thus, "'Whoever for the purposes of annoyance, or fraud, institutes, *or wil-*"'*fully becomes a party to any suit*, knowing that there is no just ground "'for such suit, shall be punished with imprisonment, &c.,' as in the "clause."

"To the explanation I would add a note that 'although a suit may be "'just as respects some of the parties, yet, if it is clearly fraudulent in "'regard to others—it may be dealt with as fraudulent.'"

160. Mr. A. D. Campbell says, "I have been Principal Collector in "Tanjore where Mr. Thomas was Zillah Judge, and I think the exten- "sion of the clause proposed by him of vital importance, not only to "check evil in Tanjore, but to impede its progress into other districts. "In the Law of Procedure this should be made a criminal offence, sum- "marily cognizable by the Civil Court in which the suit is filed."

161. Of Clause 196, Mr. G. W. Bacon says, "This is much to be "admired. I would give the power of punishing to the Civil Judge, "but limit the fine because it is a species of contempt. I also entirely "concur (he adds) in the remarks on the subject of false pleading in "the Notes, page 132. The punishment for this offence, for offence "undoubtedly it is, is perhaps more necessary in this country where "there is so much falsehood."

Imprisonment which may extend to one year, or fine, or both.

162. We are of opinion that the acts, described in Clauses 193 and 194, are properly considered as offences against public justice and fit subjects for punishment, and we think that the penalties are suitable, except that we would substitute "simple imprisonment for imprisonment of *either* description." Mr. Norton supposes that the principle is borrowed from the Bankrupt and Insolvent Laws, and he appears not to object to it in cases to which they apply. But if it be a right principle in such cases, we cannot see why it should not be right to follow it where the object is to enforce the process of the Courts for the recovery of property in *civil suits*. Indeed Mr. Norton does not suggest that there is any difference here. But he thinks there is much difference in the duty of bankrupts to disclose and surrender, and the obligation of culprits to submit to a sentence to be enforced by others. But if, as we presume, Mr. Norton will allow that it is an offence against justice in a culprit to escape from custody in order to avoid execution of a sentence of imprisonment, and an offence to harbour or assist him, and that such offences are fit subjects of punishment, we think he ought to allow upon the same grounds that the removal or concealment of property, or any dealing with it in order to prevent the execution of a sentence, of fine, for example, instead of imprisonment, is an offence against justice and a fit subject of punishment.

163. In considering Sir H. Seton's question upon Clause 194 as to the propriety of "making a wrongful claim to property a criminal offence," it is to be observed that it is not a wrongful claim simply that is punishable, but a wrongful claim made with the intention to defeat the process of a Court of Justice, which intention it is that brings it within the scope of the Penal Law.

164. In order to judge aright of the provision contained in Clause 196, it is necessary to advert to the observations upon false pleading in the Note to this chapter.* For the reasons there forcibly stated, the

---

* See Appendix, Note G, page 133.

Commissioners came to the conclusion that "a law for punishing false "pleading is indispensably necessary to the expeditious and satisfactory "administration of justice," and they only refrained from proposing such a law "because while the system of pleading remains unaltered in the "Courts of this country, and particularly in the Courts established by "Royal Charter, it will be difficult, or, to speak more properly, impossi-"ble, to enforce such a law." Therefore they went "no further than to "provide a punishment for the frivolous and vexatious instituting of "civil suits, a practice which, even while the existing system of proce-"dure remains unaltered, may without any inconvenience, be made an "offence."

165. The English Criminal Law Commissioners in their 5th Report recite a provision against deceitful practices by advocates and others, which was made in the 3rd year of the reign of King Edward I: and though they appear to be on the whole adverse to any penal enactment on the subject, in regard to advocates at least, they say, "it cannot however be doubted that the practice of special "pleading is so unlimited and unrestricted as to be the "subject of much abuse, and to afford a wide field for "the practice of chicanery, and the causing of useless expense, vexation "and delay;" they then "subjoin some of the observations made by the "Indian Law Commissioners on this subject, as entitled to general atten-"tion."

P. 27.

Note, p. 28.

166. We cannot agree with Mr. Norton that the effect of Clause 196 is to make it criminal to sue *without probable cause*, merely, nor with Sir H. Seton that the consequence of such a provision would be that every unsuccessful civil suit might be connected with a criminal prosecution; for it is expressly laid down that the suit must have been instituted "*fraudulently or for the purpose of annoyance*" to warrant a criminal prosecution against the suitor. Nor could costs be made a sufficient preventive of the evil which the clause is intended to provide against, as suggested by Sir H. Seton, for it is explained, that "it is not neces-"sary that the party to whom the offender intends to cause wrongful "loss or annoyance should be the party against whom the suit is insti-"tuted," and a case is given by way of illustration, in which it is obvious that the proposed remedy would be inapplicable. In that case the offender by the supposition has secured success in his suit, and the wrong supposed to be intended to a party not included in the suit is expected to flow from that success.

167. The Indian Law Commissioners have always entertained the opinion that much may be done in the way suggested by Sir H. Seton for the repression of vexatious litigation, and in a Report addressed to Government on the 9th November 1838, certain suggestions were offered with this view, which afterwards met with the approval of the Court of Directors. The plan was, that after the determination of a suit a fee should be levied on the losing party, proportioned, when payable by the plaintiff, to the amount claimed, when payable by the defendant, to the amount decreed, the Judge being allowed to remit the fee upon special cause shewn, and that the power of inflicting a fine, *that is punishment properly so called*, should be held in reserve for flagrant cases of malice and falsehood. The fee it was observed might be regarded partly as a compensa-

From the Indian Law Commissioners to the President of the Council of India, 9th November 1838.

From the Court of Directors, No. 22, 27th May 1840.

tion to the State for having wasted the time of its judicial functionaries, and partly as a means of discouraging suits which, though not tainted with bad faith, are open to the more venial imputation of temerity; while the fine was to be viewed entirely in the light of a punishment for an offence against justice, to be inflicted for such offence committed at any period of the suit, and whether the party committing it were ultimately successful or unsuccessful. The same principle has since been sanctioned by the Government of India in the Act for establishing a subordinate Civil Court at Calcutta, which has been read a first time.

168. The provision contained in Clause 196 is intended to include cases beyond the scope of the rule here adverted to, which had respect only to the parties in the suit, and was intended to be applied immediately at the termination of the suit, whereas the said clause, as appears by the explanation and illustration annexed to it, may be brought into operation after the termination of the suit, at the instance of one who was not a party to the suit, and not within the knowledge of the Court while it was pending, for wrong which has arisen to him from the deceit put upon the Court in that suit.

169. It is proper we think that such an offence against justice as is described in Clause 196 should have place in the Penal Code. It is a matter to be settled in framing rules of procedure by what authority the offence is to be tried and the penalty adjudged. We see no reason why the cognizance of the offence should be reserved to the Court in which the suit was instituted, when that suit shall have been previously determined, although there might be convenience in authorizing the said Court to inflict the penalty when the offence is proved in the course of the proceedings before it.

Bengal Reg. III, 1793, Sec. 12.
Madras Reg. II, 1802, Sec. 9.
Bombay Reg. IV, 1827, Sec. 54.

170. It is not an innovation in India to punish a person who has brought a suit for the purpose of annoyance. The Regulations in force in the Company's Courts authorize the Judge when a suit shall appear to him "frivolous, *vexatious*, or groundless," to fine the plaintiff, and to commit him to close custody till he pays the fine. The rule in Clause 196 is more strict, as it does not authorize the imposition of a penalty when the suit is merely frivolous or groundless, but where it has been instituted "fraudulently or for the purpose of annoyance." What is new is the extension imported by the "*explanation*" annexed to the clause.

171. Reverting to the instances of abuse of the process of the Courts mentioned by Mr. Thomas, we have to observe that Clause 196 as it stands, appears to cover some of them, as the introducing "into *just* "suits *as regards the chief litigants*, the names of parties as defendants "who have no concern in the suit," "greatly to their detriment and annoy-"ance." The introducing of parties not concerned, as co-plaintiffs against their will, is a proceeding we never heard of, and we are at a loss to conceive how it can take place with proper strictness in the admission of suits, without at least the party committing some other offence to bring him within the cognizance of the penal law. A fictitious suit such as Mr. Thomas describes for the purpose of securing the property of the defendant by anticipation against future creditors, that is against persons to whom he may in the course of business become indebted, can hardly be considered a fit subject of punishment either as respects the fictitious plaintiff or the defendant. Such a suit, however, brought for the purpose of defeating existing creditors of the defendant, we apprehend, would bring the plaintiff within the scope of Clause 196. We are not prepared to recommend the extension proposed by Mr. Thomas in order to make it include the defendant. But where the defendant is the instigator of the fictitious suit, as in the case supposed, he would be amenable under the law of abetment.

172. Many persons have asked what sort of declaration it is that is contemplated in Clause 195. We presume that declarations of the nature of certificates are intended, such for instance as are mentioned by Blackstone under the head of trial by certificate "allowed in such cases "where the evidence of the person certifying is the "only proper criterion of the point in dispute;" such again as the certificate of a former conviction of felony, by the Clerk of the Court where the offender was convicted, which is to be taken on the face of it as sufficient evidence of the first conviction. (Statute 9, Geo. IV, Chapter 74, Section 24.)

Com. 3, p. 333.

173. The provision contained in Clause 197 is an extension of Clause 179, subjecting the offences therein defined to a severer punishment when they are committed against a Court of Justice. We need add nothing to the remark we have already made on the principle of the provision regarding insult, in commenting upon Clause 179. We propose to provide for the offence of causing disturbance in a separate clause, as suggested by Col. Sleeman, subjecting the offender to punishment by fine to the extent of 500 rupees.

174. Clause 201 extends the provision of Clause 175 to the escape of a person from custody in which he is detained under a sentence, the punishment being increased to imprisonment for two years as the maximum. There is no provision corresponding with that in Clause 173 for the *rescue* of a prisoner under sentence.

175. From the Note to Clause 177, which refers to the chapter under consideration for provisions regarding "*rescue*" as well as "escape, and harbour *after sentence*," we are inclined to think that this omission was not intentional. At any rate it appears to us proper that it should be supplied. The punishment for rescue in Clause 173 is double of that for escape in Clause 175. We would suggest that the punishment for "rescue" in the case of a prisoner under sentence be the next higher grade above that for "escape" in Clause 201, viz., imprisonment which may extend to three years, or fine, or both, with a cumulative clause as in the case of escape.

176. In Note A, on the chapter of Punishments, the Commissioners say, "It will be seen that throughout the Code wherever "we have made any offence punishable by transportation "we have provided that the transportation shall be for "life." Accordingly we find no provision in the Code for transportation for a term of years except in Clause 43, as a commutation for imprisonment in the case of a person who is "not both of Asiatic birth and of Asiatic blood," and in Clause 205 for the punishment of a person sentenced to banishment returning before the expiration of the term fixed by his sentence, in which case banishment for life is to be added. Clause 203 provides for the punishment of a person transported for a term of

See Appendix, Note A, page 94.

years, *not* by way of commutation, returning before the expiration of the term, while Clause 204 provides for the punishment of a person transported under a sentence of commutation so returning. The former of these clauses we apprehend applies to a person sentenced under Clause 205.

177. Mr. G. W. Bacon says, "I do not find any mention of returning from transportation for life." The reason is, that the Law Commissioners did not think it proper to subject this offence to the penalty of death. Therefore as there is no secondary punishment higher than transportation for life it was unnecessary to mention it. The sentence of transportation for life still subsisting, the escaped convict will of course be sent back; but the regulation of this matter belongs to procedure.

178. Clause 206 in extension of Clause 178, provides for the harbouring of persons under sentence who have escaped from custody, or have returned from transportation or banishment. The punishment is simple imprisonment which may extend to 6 months, or fine to the amount of 1,000 Rupees, or both. This penalty may be fit when the offenders to whom harbour has been given is punishable under Clause 201. But we would recommend that the maximum be doubled when the person harboured is punishable under Clauses 203, 204, or 205.

179. Clause 46 declares that the Government may remit the whole or any part of a sentence absolutely or conditionally, and Clause 207 provides for the enforcement of the original sentence when the condition of remission is violated.

180. Sir R. Comyn observes upon Clause 201 for the punishment of a convict escaping from custody, that there is no punishment for the more guilty officer permitting the escape, further than by a reference to the chapter of Abetment. It seems to us that Clause 97 relating to abetment by aid, by which the abettor is liable to the punishment of the offence, is sufficient. The punishment under Clause 201 is imprisonment which may extend to two years, to which the officer permitting the escape of a convict would be liable as well as the escaped convict himself.

CHAPTER XI.

OF OFFENCES RELATING TO THE REVENUE.

181. In order to frame this chapter, the Commissioners say they "went "carefully through the Revenue laws of the three Presi- "dencies, extracted the penal clauses, analysed them, "and reduced them to a small number of general heads."

See Appendix, Note H, page 133.

182. The first head is "Smuggling," which is defined to be importing or exporting into or from the Territories of the East India Company, or conveying property from place to place within the said territories *in contravention of any law.*

Clauses 208 to 211.

183. Then follow provisions for punishing breaches of the laws which have been framed for the protection of the Revenue derived by Government from Opium, Salt, Spirituous Liquors, &c. Afterwards provisions for punishing breaches of the laws concerning Stamps from which the Government derives a revenue, and of the laws relating to the Public Post. And lastly, a provision for punishing persons licensed to do any thing with respect to any article for the doing which a licence is required by law, for breach of the licence.

Clauses 212 to 215, 217 to 224, 225 to 227, 228.

184. Mr. Norton describes this chapter "as an effort to place a vast "variety of breaches of the Revenue laws under the jurisdiction of a few "short and general provisions denouncing their criminality." Generally speaking, it denounces penalties without denoting the acts by which the penalties will be incurred, further than that they are acts in contravention of some law. To know what acts will make men liable to the penalties, reference must be had to the laws relating to the Revenue derived from Customs, Opium, Salt, &c. We think there is force in the following observations of Mr. Norton on this subject. "The only just and "only efficient course appears to me to be to make specific enactments for "specific breaches of the Revenue laws. Some may be highly criminal— "some may be better visitable by mulct. Almost all take their character "from the subject-matter and peculiar circumstances."

185. Mr. Casamajor, a Judge of the Madras Presidency, makes the following remarks upon the provisions regarding Smuggling. "The "first thing that strikes one is, that the penalties are a good deal severer "than those of the Madras Regulations. The highest penalty for smug- "gling in these, is confiscation of the thing smuggled, or treble duty. "For other frauds on the Customs there is fine (unlimited), and in case "the fine is not paid, imprisonment with or without hard labour accord- "ing to the rank of the culprit. Imprisonment is in no case adjudicable "as an original penalty for smuggling, or any other fraud on the Customs, "by the Madras Regulations, nor is it by the 3rd and 4th of William IV, "Chapter 53, which with a few subsequent modifications, contains (I "believe) the present law of England respecting smuggling. Confiscation "or fine is the punishment in every case; and no mention at all is made "of imprisonment, except in one or two cases attended with violence. "But in this chapter we have the offence of smuggling punishable in "every case with imprisonment which may extend to three months, or "fine which may extend to an amount equal to five times the market "value of the thing smuggled added to 500 rupees, or both, and this too, "besides confiscation (see Clause 229). I doubt the propriety of impri- "sonment as an original punishment for smuggling in any but a few "very aggravated cases. The remarks upon this subject in Chapter 33 "of Beccaria (who evidently does not underrate the criminality of smug- "gling) appear to me very much to the purpose. There is one strong "argument against making imprisonment the stated punishment for "smuggling; viz., that the offence is very frequently committed in this "country by traders upon whom imprisonment inflicts a much more "serious evil than is contemplated by the law, in the derangement of "their concerns consequent upon their personal management being with- "drawn, and loss of credit."

186. We consider these remarks to have great weight, but we shall forbear to enter upon a particular examination of the clauses to which they apply, and of the other clauses of this chapter, many of which are the subject of criticism in the papers before us, being strongly of opinion that it will be better to omit them all from the Code, and to leave all transgression of the Revenue laws, which are offences purely as breaches of positive enactments for special political objects of a fiscal character, to be provided for by appropriate penalties in the laws which contain the rules, the observance of which is intended to be enforced thereby.

187. In recommending this course, it appears to us that we are only following out the principle on which the authors of the Code thought it proper to omit from the chapter the provisions for confiscation which are to be found in the Revenue laws.

See Appendix, Note H, page 133.

188. The acts which are specified and defined in the clauses relating to Stamps are indeed of a character which might unobjectionably give them a place in a Penal Code, but as the specific object contemplated is the protection of the revenue derived by Government from Stamps, and the penalties appear to have been devised and determined on considerations referring to that object peculiarly, we think it advisable to omit them as well as the other clauses.

189. Mr. Norton says of the principal offences defined in these clauses, that "in his construction they fall distinctly within another more serious species of criminality, namely, forgery or uttering forgeries." We understand him as speaking of what in his construction *ought* to be comprehended under forgery—not as intimating that in his opinion those offences do fall within the definition of forgery in this Code. Possibly however the offence described in Clause 223 might be construed to fall under forgery with reference to the 4th Article of the definition in Clause 441.

CHAPTER XII.

OF OFFENCES RELATING TO COIN.

190. Coin is defined in Clause 230 as "metal used as money, and "bearing some mark that it is issued by the authority of some Government in order to be so used."

191. It is made an offence to counterfeit any coin. When the coin counterfeited is the Queen's, or the Company's, the punishment of the offence is aggravated. The distinction between the Queen's and Company's coin and other coin, is maintained all through the chapter, except in Clause 236 and Clause 242, the latter relating to the wilful uttering of counterfeit coin as genuine, the former to the possession of implements or materials for counterfeiting coin. These clauses apply indifferently to coin of all descriptions. Clause 237 makes it an offence to abet the counterfeiting of the Queen's or Company's coin *without* the territories of the Company, a provision which is confined to those coins specially.

192. An important distinction is made in regard to the uttering of counterfeit coin, between the utterer by profession, that is one who utters false coin which when he received it he knew to be false, and the casual utterer, who having heedlessly received a counterfeit coin in the course of his business, takes advantage of the next person with whom he deals to pay it away.

193. Objections have been made to providing for offences relating to the Queen's coin in this Code, to which the following remarks extracted from Note I appear to us to furnish a sufficient answer, as far as considerations of utility and convenience are concerned, though they may leave some technical grounds untouched. "It may "perhaps be thought that in proposing laws for the protection of the King's coin we have departed from the principle which "we laid down in our Note on the law of offences against the State, and "that we should have acted more consistently in leaving the British "currency to the care of the British Legislature. It appears to us, "however, that the offence of coining, though, in an arbitrary classification, it may be called by the technical name of treason, is in substance "an offence against property and trade, that it is an offence of very "nearly the same kind with the forging of a Bank Note, and that it "would be an offence of exactly the same kind if the Bank Note, like "the Notes of the Bank of England formerly, were in all cases legal "tender, or if the coin, like the Company's Gold Mohur at present, were "not legal tender. We do not therefore conceive that in proposing a law "for punishing the counterfeiting of the King's coin we are proposing a "law which can reasonably be said to affect any of the royal prerogatives."

See page 134.

194. We have no doubt of the propriety of providing for the punishment of persons counterfeiting the Queen's coin in these territories on the ground stated, but considering that such coin can hardly be said to have currency here in the course of business, we think it questionable whether for the main object in view, the protection of the public against fraud in money dealings, it should be put on the same footing with the coin of the local Government which forms the general circulating medium. The reason of the thing seems to require that it should be put on the same footing with other coins which come casually into circulation. With this observation we leave the point for the consideration of Government.

195. We have had the advantage of perusing the observations of the Chief Justice of the Supreme Court at Calcutta upon the Draft Act relating to the coin, read in Council on the 26th April 1845, which is almost entirely a transcript from the chapter under consideration.

Letter to the Governor-General of India in Council, dated 28th July 1845.

196. The Chief Justice objects to the offence of counterfeiting coin being punishable with imprisonment only, as intended by the proposed Act, while the offence of forgery would remain punishable with transportation for life. But there will be no such disproportion in the punishment of these two species of the *crimen falsi* if the proposed law be passed as a part of the general Code, since the punishment for the offence of forgery also is confined to imprisonment by the chapter of offences relating to documents. And perhaps the Chief Justice will not be opposed to this mitigation when it appears that in England the punishment of transportation is not likely to be applied in future to persons guilty of offences of this nature, and that the longest term of imprisonment to be substituted is intended to be less than the maximum authorized by the Code in respect either to the forgery of documents or counterfeiting coin.

197. Sir Laurence Peel observes that the English Law visits with the same punishment the complete and the unfinished act of counterfeiting, which he considers reasonable and expedient. We concur in this opinion. The English Statute declares that the offence of counterfeiting "shall be deemed to be complete although the coin so "(falsely) made or counterfeited shall not be in a fit "state to be uttered, or the counterfeiting thereof shall "not be finished or perfected." We would add an explanation to Clause 232 in corresponding words, or introduce into Clauses 232 and 233 respectively, after the word "counterfeits," the words "or performs any part of the process of counterfeiting," as in Clause 217 respecting Stamps. We observe that these words were used in this clause of the Code as it was first printed.

2 Wm. IV, Chapter XXXIV, Section 8.

198. Sir Laurence Peel points out that while the English Statute punishes the possession of implements, &c., for counterfeiting, equally with counterfeiting, the proposed Act (Section 10) establishes a distinction, making the possessor of implements, &c., liable to imprisonment for three years, while a person counterfeiting coin is liable to imprisonment for seven years. It is to be observed that imprisonment which may extend to seven years is the punishment for counterfeiting the *Queen's or Company's* coin, and that the punishment for counterfeiting coin in general is imprisonment which may extend to three years, the same as the possessor of implements, &c., for counterfeiting coin is liable to.

Clause 236.

Clauses 232 and 233.

199. Further, Sir Laurence Peel observes that "the 8th, 9th and "10th section of the Draft Act are too limited. The "8th and 9th apply to the making one only of many "instruments for coining and to the maker only. The "English Statute is more extensive, and embraces the mending as well

Clauses 234, 235 and 236.

"as making and the progress of the work of mending or making, and "the buying or selling of such instruments. The 10th section does not "embrace the case of one who is knowingly a possessor of any imple- "ments or material for the use of another who intends to employ the "same for the prohibited purpose. It would not meet the case of a "vendor of such instruments not being the maker of them. The "English Statute meets these and all cases which are likely to arise."

200. It is the making a *die* for counterfeiting coin that is specially punishable by Clauses 234 and 235 of the Code corresponding with Sections 8 and 9 of the Draft Act, with the same penalty as the act of counterfeiting. We conceive that the *die* is specially provided for in these clauses as the instrument by which the metal is marked so as to represent a coin, that is to say the instrument by which the act of counterfeiting is completed. But we think that any instrument used in the process of coining falling within the same category as the die, as an instrument "upon which there shall be made or impressed, or which will make or impress, or which "shall be intended to make or impress the figure, stamp, "or apparent resemblance of both or either of the sides" of any coin, that is to say any instrument which bears on its face such mark as evidently signifies that it is designed to be used in the process of counterfeiting a particular coin, considering the making of the die to be a part of such process, ought to be included. We would also provide in the same clauses for buying and selling, mending, and having in possession any such instrument. We would therefore alter Clause 234 as follows: "Whoever makes, mends, buys or sells, or has in his possession any die, "or other instrument, appearing by any mark on the face of it to be "adapted for the purpose of counterfeiting coin, intending or knowing it "to be likely that it may be employed for the purpose of counter- "feiting coin, shall, &c." The same alteration of course to be made in Clause 235 designating the coin as the Queen's or the Company's.

Section 10 of the Statute.

201. Clause 236 would then apply to implements, &c., not so significantly marked as adapted for counterfeiting particular coins, found in the possession of any person, regarding which there may be independent proof, circumstantial or positive, that he had the intention of employing the same for the purpose stated.

202. Sir Laurence Peel remarks that "knowledge of the coin being "counterfeit contemporaneous with the first reduction "of such coin into possession is treated throughout the "Act as a test of the criminality of such possession." The clauses which require such contemporaneous knowledge to be established are those directed against the professional dealers in false coin; their having received the false coin found in their possession, or which they have delivered or attempted to deliver to any other, knowing at the time they received it that it was false, is made the test of their being such dealers. The reason of distinguishing such dealers from the casual utterer, is well stated in Note I, and it appears to us satisfactory.

Clauses 240, 241, 243 and 244, corresponding with Sections 14, 15, 17 and 18 of the Draft Act with respect to counterfeit coin; Clauses 249 to 252, corresponding with Secs. 24 to 27, respecting coins of which the weight has been wilfully diminished or the composition altered.

203. To meet objections made by Sir Laurence Peel to the phraseology of Clauses 240 and 241 and of Clause 242 which appear to us to be valid, we would alter them, the two former by substituting "intending "or knowing it to be likely that such counterfeit coin may pass as "genuine," for "with the intention that such counterfeit coin shall pass "as genuine," and the latter by substituting the same words for the words "as genuine."

204. This alteration of Clause 242 will not cause it to embrace such a fraud as that adverted to by Sir Laurence Peel, termed "ringing the changes," but it seems to us that the practice which he describes should be dealt with as a cheat rather than as a case of uttering or putting off false coin. It consists apparently in sleight of hand by which a man exchanges a bad coin for a good one, and deceives the person from whom he has just received the good coin into believing that the bad one is that which he gave; in such a case if the former succeeds in obtaining from the latter a good coin for the bad one which he pretends to return, it will be cheating under the definition of that offence in Clause 392 of the Code.

205. By the words proposed to be introduced into these three clauses by which they will be made so far to correspond with Clauses 243 and 244, we think the offender could scarcely escape conviction in any of the other cases mentioned by the Chief Justice. If it could not be proved that the person uttering false coins had knowledge that they were false at the time he received them, he would be charged under Clause 242, and by the alteration he would be liable not only if he put them off as genuine, but if, as in the case mentioned by Sir Laurence Peel, he sold them to a common utterer, without representing them to be genuine, knowing his character, and well aware that his purpose was to pass them as genuine, a case which the clause as it stands would not reach.

206. We think that an alteration should be made in Clauses 249 to 252, corresponding with that which we propose to be made in Clauses 240 to 242, and we would describe the object intended by the same words in Clauses 251 and 252 as in Clauses 249 and 250.

207. We agree with the Chief Justice in the objection he takes to the punishment of the offence defined in Clause 242 by fine only, we would add "or with imprisonment for a term which may extend to six "months, or both."

208. Sir Laurence Peel observes that the 14th and 15th sections of the Draft Act corresponding with Clauses 240 and 241 of this chapter "would not reach one common case of dealing with counterfeit "coin as selling by one not being the coiner, and after the coin is made, "who has not the coin at the time of sale, and who does not deliver it." But as the seller must order delivery, he would fall under the Law of Abetment as instigating the person having possession to commit the offence defined in the said clause, and would be liable to the punishment of the offence by Clause 88 of this Code. The objection therefore will not hold if the provisions of this chapter be passed as a part of the Code.

209. Sir Laurence Peel remarks that the sections of the Draft Act from the 24th to the 27th corresponding with Clauses 249 to 252 of the Code are "apparently in conflict with the law as to currency in force here" (within the jurisdiction of Her Majesty's Courts,) that is the Common Law, by "which debased coin not counterfeit did not lose its currency as money nor could it be refused as a tender." "The Act," he adds, "seems to proceed on the assumption of the existing law forbid-"ding the circulation by an innocent holder of debased coin not coun-"terfeit. But it does not in terms enact this; and it would be the sub-"ject of doubt whether by implication from its provisions the law as to "currency be altered or not."

210. It is to be observed that Act XVII of 1835 makes certain silver coins of the Company's Mints a legal tender in satisfaction of all engagements, provided they are not diminished more than a certain proportion in weight, and are not clipped or filed or defaced otherwise than by use; and such as are so diminished, &c., of course may be refused. But the Code does not make the circulation of debased coin by an innocent holder an offence, any more than the circulation of coin which has been reduced below the proper weight by use; it is an offence to pass debased coin only when the party passing it knew when he became possessed of it that it had been diminished in weight, or altered in composition, against the provisions of the Code making such diminution or alteration an offence.

Clauses 246 and 247.

211. Sir Laurence Peel points out that the proposed law differs from the English law in not making a distinction between counterfeiting gold and silver coin and counterfeiting copper coin. He thinks the distinction reasonable. There has been no such distinction hitherto in the laws regarding coinage contained in the Regulations of the several Presidencies. The Act 9 Geo. IV, Chapter LXXIV in force in Her Majesty's Courts in India, provides only for offences relating to gold and silver coin, and so does the Code of Louisiana. The Penal Code of France makes the same distinction as the law of England between gold and silver money and copper money. It seems to us to be worthy of the consideration of Government whether the distinction observed by the English law should not be introduced into the Code.

212. Sir Laurence Peel also points out that the proposed law disregards the distinction between current coin and coin not current which is observed in the English law and the existing law here within the jurisdiction of Her Majesty's Courts. Coins absolutely uncurrent, that is not used as money, are excluded by the definition in Clause 230. The currency, speaking generally, may be said to consist of the Company's coin, and the proposed law provides by more severe penalties against the falsification thereof, as an offence highly injurious to the public, while lesser penalties are provided against the falsification of other coins which enter into the circulation in an inconsiderable degree comparatively, excepting the Queen's coin which, though not entering largely into the circulation, *honoris causâ* is put on the same footing as the Company's.

213. Objection is taken by Sir H. Seton, and also by Mr. G. W. Bacon, to the words "knowing it to be likely" in Clauses 243 and 244. Sir H. Seton says, "A gets possession of counterfeit coin with a view "to destroy it, knowing it to be likely that such counterfeit coin may "pass as genuine if left in the possession from which he takes it—must "he be imprisoned for not less than two years?" (Clause 244.) Mr. Bacon illustrates his objection by the following case—"A, a collector "of curiosities, purchases counterfeit coins knowing them to be such, and "not intending but *knowing it to* be likely from the goodness of the "counterfeit that such coin *may* be passed as genuine." "A is guilty," Mr. Bacon observes, "of the offence in Clause 243." We do not think that under the construction of the phrase "knowing it to be likely," which by a comparison of the many places in which it is used in this Code it is manifestly intended to bear, the party possessing counterfeit coins could be convicted in either of these cases. In order to a conviction there must be circumstances leading fairly to the inference that the party kept the coins in his possession contemplating it as a likely result that they might pass as genuine, not as what might possibly happen, but as what was likely to happen. We beg to refer to the citations in paras. 105 and 106 of our first Report on this point.

214. Adverting to Clause 241, Sir H. Seton says—" A wins a pool at " commerce in which he finds a bad shilling which he puts into the next " pool as his stake—must he be imprisoned for not less than two years?" It does not appear to us that A could be charged under Clause 241 with having received the counterfeit shilling knowingly, and therefore, we take it, he would not be liable to this punishment. We are inclined however to think it expedient to omit or reduce the minimum in this and the following clauses of the chapter, as we propose with respect to some of the clauses of the chapter relating to the analogous offence of forgery, &c.

Vide post.

215. Mr. Norton adverting to those clauses which make the possession of counterfeit coins an offence, observes that he "does not think the " reasoning sound for fixing the proof of the *object* and *intent to utter* on " the prosecutor in cases where numerous counterfeit coins are found in " the possession of a party. The *knowledge* and intent of uttering coun- " terfeit coin, where the *actual* uttering takes place, may be required in " substantive proof, because the circumstances of it are extant on which " a judgment can be formed. But where *no act* is done at all, there is " scarce a possibility of proving any secret object and intent—though " pregnantly suspicious circumstances are, in such a case as this, a legi- " timate ground for a party to prove, what he alone can prove, the lawful " excuse, or account for such possession of numerous articles of base coin " —and *such is the principle of the English Criminal Law on this* and other " similar subject-matter, *had it been thought worth the inquiry to ascertain* " *it*." In answer to these observations, so far as the authority of the English Criminal Law is concerned, and with reference particularly to the words we have put in italics in the last passage, it is only necessary to mention, what it seems strange Mr. Norton did not ascertain, that on the point in question the Code is in accordance with the English Statute, the latter running thus—" If any person shall have in his " custody or possession three or more pieces of false or " counterfeit coin, &c., *knowing the same to be false* " *or counterfeit, and with intent to utter or put off the same*, every such " offender shall," &c. Under the Code however conviction will be easier by reason of the words " or knowing it to be likely that such counterfeit coin may pass as genuine."

2 Wm. IV, Chapter 34, Section 8.

216. We have noticed that Clause 237 makes it an offence to abet the counterfeiting of the Queen's or Company's coin, but not of other coin, *without* the Territories of the East India Company. It has been suggested that excluding Spanish dollars and other coin which in some places are largely current may be found "highly prejudicial to commerce." Referring particularly to the Settlements in the Straits, in which we believe the Spanish dollar is the coin most current, and in which there is much complaint of the introduction of counterfeit coin of that description made without the Settlements, probably at the instigation of persons within the Settlements, it may be thought advisable to insert before Clause 237 a clause corresponding to it against persons abetting the counterfeiting of coin without the Territories of the East India Company *intending that such coin may be imported into the Territories of the East India Company*. The words in italics which are not in Clause 237 appear to be necessary to constitute an offence properly punishable by this Code, whereas to abet the counterfeiting the Queen's or the Company's coin is an offence which when committed by persons residing under the Government of the Company and owing allegiance to Her Majesty is properly punishable without reference to the intention as to the disposal of the counterfeit coin.

217. It appears to us advisable to substitute for the explanation annexed to Clause 232, a definition of what is meant by counterfeiting coin, including the substance of that explanation, as follows:—"A person is said to counterfeit coin who "makes a false coin to resemble a genuine coin, or a genuine coin to "resemble a different coin, intending to deceive by means of that re-"semblance."

See Clause 20.

218. It seems to us also that a definition should be given of the coin designated as the Queen's coin, as well of that which is designated as Company's coin, which should be in accordance with the definition in Section XXI of the Statute 2, Wm. IV, Chapter XXXIV, viz., "any "coin coined in any of Her Majesty's Mints and lawfully current in any "part of Her Majesty's dominions, whether within the United Kingdom "or otherwise."

CHAPTER XIII.

OF OFFENCES RELATING TO WEIGHTS AND MEASURES.

219. Mr. Norton observes that "there are redundancies of language in this chapter from which misconceptions may possibly arise," as for instance "*fraudulently* using weights *known* to be *false*," and with reference to the word "dealing" particularly, he says, he is doubtful whether by using this word rather than *selling* it is meant "that *all* persons *using in any manner false weights*, &c., are to be brought within the chapter." We apprehend that *not* "all persons using in any manner," but "all persons *fraudulently* using in any manner false weights, &c." are meant. The word "dealing" is used instead of "selling" obviously as being more comprehensive. We do not agree with Mr. Norton that there is any redundancy in the set of words cited by him as above—every word appears to us to be necessary.

220. With reference to Clause 255, Mr. Norton suggests that the possession of a false balance, &c., would be enough to shew guilt without evidence of intention to use them fraudulently. The intention however must be alleged in laying the charge, though it may be matter of inference only, from the fact of the possession, and the attending circumstances as manifesting the purpose, and the inference may of course be rebutted.

221. Mr. Blane suggests that the provisions in Clause 253, &c., ought not to apply to scales but only to weights and measures, as Indian scales are generally of the rudest construction, seldom correct, and the incorrectness always visible to the purchaser. "No doubt," he remarks, "the "intent of fraud is specified, yet it appears doubtful how that intention "is to be ascertained." But where the incorrectness of the scale is so visible, and there is no attempt to cover or conceal it, there can be no ground for imputing fraud from that defect alone; the circumstances negative the intention of fraud, and no charge would lie against the party using such a balance. On the other hand a false balance artfully contrived to elude detection in the use of it, carries with it a presumption of fraudulent intention, which properly brings it within the scope of the chapter.

222. It has been suggested that it may be expedient to provide in this chapter for the fraudulent use of a true balance. This it appears to us is an offence which falls within the definition of "cheating," under which head it will be liable to the same punishment as the offence of using a false balance under this chapter.

CHAPTER XIV.

OF OFFENCES AFFECTING THE PUBLIC HEALTH, SAFETY AND CONVENIENCE.

223. This chapter comprehends provisions on subjects which in the Digest of the English Criminal Law are distributed in two chapters under the heads of "Offences against public health, comfort, and convenience," and "Common nuisances."

Chapters XII and XIII.

224. The first clause in the chapter (257), for the punishment of persons doing what is likely to spread the infection of any disease dangerous to life, corresponds with Article 6, Chapter XII of the Digest, but is more comprehensive, the said article being limited to the offence of exposing in public places persons labouring under infectious and contagious diseases. What is wanting in this article appears to be supplied by the generality of the definition of common nuisance in Article 1 of Chapter XIII. The punishment in the Digest is imprisonment which may extend to one year, or, if the offence fall under nuisance, to two years, or fine, or both, whereas in the Code the term of imprisonment is limited to six months. We think that the word "human" should be inserted before "life" in Clause 257, as it is in Clause 265 and elsewhere, for though in Clause 33 it is explained that the word "death" denotes the death of a human being unless it be otherwise expressed, there is no such explanation in regard to "life" as denoting human life exclusively.

4 and 6.

225. Clause 258 provides for breaches of the law of quarantine, limiting the penalty to imprisonment for six months, or fine, or both. For the greater breaches of the quarantine law the penalty in the Digest is transportation for seven years or imprisonment not exceeding three years. For the minor offence of quitting a vessel liable to quarantine before it is discharged the penalty is imprisonment for six months and fine of 300£.

Chapter XII, Arts. 1 and 4.

226. Many gentlemen have expressed an opinion that the limitation of the term of imprisonment in Clauses 257 and 258 renders the penalty inadequate. Mr. Pyne, Judge of the Bombay Sudder Court, particularly observes that *malignantly* committing the offence defined in Clause 257 appears to be deserving of the penalties provided for the offence described in Clause 294, voluntary culpable homicide. He asks "could a person malignantly propagate plague in a populous town without believing it to be likely to cause death." If any person died of the plague and his death could be traced to infection so caused maliciously, the person who caused it, we apprehend, would be chargeable with homicide under Clause 294. It is contrary to the principle of the Code to punish acts which the doer when he committed them knew to be likely to cause certain evil results, if in fact such results were not produced, in the same manner as if such evil consequences had actually flowed from them, but we are inclined to think that the term of imprisonment in these clauses, which is the same as for adulteration of food or of medicines, is too limited.

227. There are two Clauses (259 and 260) regarding the adulteration of food or drink, one for adulterating, and the other for selling and offering for sale adulterated food or drink, and two Clauses (261 and

262) as to the adulteration of medicines, with an additional Clause (263) for selling, &c., any drug as a different drug. The term of imprisonment in all these clauses is limited to six months, but the fine, which in the clauses respecting food is limited to 500 rupees, is extended to 1,000 rupees in those relating to medicines.

228. In the Digest there is an express provision for *selling* unwholesome food or provisions, but not for adulterating food, &c., but it would seem that there are statutory provisions prescribing penalties for the adulteration of both food and drink. The punishment laid down in the Digest for selling unwholesome food is imprisonment which may extend to one year, or fine, or both.

Stephens' Summary of Criminal Law, p. 100.

229. The adulteration of drugs, &c., and the selling of adulterated drugs does not appear to be provided for specifically in the Digest of the English Criminal Law.

230. Clause 264 provides for the punishment of any person who "voluntarily causes the atmosphere in any public way to be in a state noxious to health or offensive to the senses." It has been asked why is this provision confined to "a public way?" We are not aware of the reason for this limitation. In the Digest there is a provision for this kind of offence as affecting the *neighbourhood*, and another corresponding with the one under consideration, as affecting the Queen's subjects "using any public highway or thoroughfare, or frequenting any market or other place of public resort." It appears to us that the former provision is as much required as the latter. Exception has been taken to the term "offensive to the senses" as "likely to give rise to capricious prosecutions." The word "offensive" is used in the corresponding article of the Digest in the same sense apparently. The punishment in the Code is limited to imprisonment for one month, or fine to the amount of 500 rupees, or both. The punishment provided in the Digest is imprisonment not exceeding one year, or fine at discretion, or both. It seems to be worthy of consideration whether the punishment in the Code should not be extended.

Chapter XIII, Arts. 8 and 12.

231. Clause 265 provides for the offences of driving or riding in a public way in a manner so rash or negligent as to indicate a want of due regard for human life. The English law does not distinctly provide for this offence except when some injury has been caused by it, and then the provision is limited. The Digest contains a special provision taken from the Statute Law for injury caused by the furious driving of *a stage coach or any public carriage*, except a hackney carriage.

Chapter XV, Sec. 5, Art. 40.

232. We think it highly expedient to punish the offence defined in Clause 265, which is always dangerous and terrifying, irrespectively of actual mischief caused by it. If grievous hurt is caused, the offender will be liable to additional punishment for it under Clauses 327 and 328. If death is caused, his punishment will be cumulative under Clauses 304 and 305.

233. Perhaps the terms of the definition of "nuisance" in the Digest of the English law, may be construed to include this offence as "tending to cause common injury, damage, inconvenience or annoyance to the Queen's subjects,"

Chapter XIII, Art. 1.

"in respect of their personal safety;" in which case the offender will be liable to the same punishment as is provided for the offence in Clause 265 of the Code, namely, imprisonment not exceeding six months, or fine, or both, except that the fine, which is limited in the Code to 2,000 rupees, is left to discretion in the Digest.

Art. 18.

234. Mr. Norton says, "As regards those criminal acts—such as "driving violently, negligently using fire or combustible matter, leaving "buildings in a dangerous state—the criminality of which is made to "depend on 'want of regard to human life,' it appears to me that such "want of regard is hardly capable of proof except from the result. At "the same time other acts, such as 'rash and negligent dispensing "poisonous substances' are such as by their inherent nature indicate such "want. The mere doing of such acts, I consider to be offences of a "greater or minor shade—and if actual death does follow thereby, of "course the offence becomes of a different quality."

235. We cannot agree with Mr. Norton that want of regard for human life is hardly capable of proof, in the instances he specifies, except from the result. Supposing, to take the first instance, that a person driving a vehicle in a crowded thoroughfare urges the horses to such speed that it is impossible for him to stop their course suddenly, and that a passenger is knocked down by them and killed on the spot, no doubt under the law of England the driver would be found guilty of manslaughter, because of the reckless manner in which he drove. Now if the passenger was just saved by the timely effort of another person pulling him out of the way, would not a want of due regard for human life on the part of the driver be as justly inferred from the manner of his driving, proved as we may assume by the evidence of those two persons, the one who had been in imminent peril of his life and the other who happily saved him, as if the result had been a fatal accident? So in the other instances the want of due regard for human life upon which the criminality depends, is a matter of inference from the circumstances, and wherever the circumstances proved are such that if loss of life had ensued the party committing the act would be answerable for it criminally, the same circumstances will sufficiently warrant a conviction of the simple offence where no injury has resulted. The certainty of punishment, though it be small, for the acts or omissions dangerous to life, specified in the clauses from 265 to 273 of this chapter, will be far more efficacious, we conceive, in restraining men from such acts, and preventing such omissions, than the distant apprehension of severe punishment in the event of an accident resulting therefrom, by which a life may be lost or some serious injury suffered. The Code combines both.

236. Mr. Norton remarks that the words "knowing" and "knowingly" "seem to be used in this chapter indiscriminately and without "any ruling principle," that they are "inserted where they had better "have been spared," and omitted "where *the guilty* knowledge is of the "substantive essence of the offence," "for I imagine," says he, "that the "adulteration of food or drugs can hardly be criminal unless shewn to have "been of wilful knowledge." This criticism appears to us to be quite gratuitous. With respect to the adulteration of food or drugs a guilty knowledge is plainly implied in the definitions in Clauses 259 and 260.

237. Mr. Fagan proposes a general clause for acts, such as are described in Clauses 265 to 273, done so rashly and negligently as to indicate a want of due regard for the safety of *property*, rendering persons so acting punishable with imprisonment to the extent of one month or fine to 500 rupees. We are of opinion that the Commissioners exercised a sound discretion in making the want of due regard for human life the criterion of criminality in such acts.

238. Mr. Fagan also proposes a clause for the punishment of a person keeping a house of entertainment for travellers refusing to entertain any traveller without reason. There is a provision to this effect in the Digest, in which the offence is declared to be a common nuisance, but it does not appear to us that such an enactment is called for in this country, where there are so few establishments to which it would be applicable.

Chapter XIII, Art. 16.

239. Again, Mr. Fagan suggests that there should be a provision for the punishment of any person who in any public way pursues any means of livelihood or performs any act which is repugnant to the religion, subversive of the morals, or opposed to the feelings of the public. Partly, and perhaps as far as is necessary, the purpose intended appears to be provided for between Clause 274 of this chapter, Clause 282 of Chapter XV and Clauses 486 and 487 of Chapter XXVI.

CHAPTER XV.

OF OFFENCES RELATING TO RELIGION AND CASTE.

240. The principle on which this chapter has been framed is stated and explained in Note J. "It is this, that every man should be suffered "to profess his own religion, and that no man should be suffered to "insult the religion of another." The Commissioners have well said that this is a principle "on which it would be desirable that all Governments "should act, but from which the British Government in India cannot "depart without risking a dissolution of society." "There is perhaps no "country in which the Government has so much to apprehend from "religious excitement among the people. The Christians are numerically "a very small minority of the population, and in possession of all the "high posts in the Government, in the tribunals, and in the army. "Under their rule are placed millions of Mahomedans, of differing sects, "but all strongly attached to the fundamental articles of the Mahomedan "creed, and tens of millions of Hindoos, strongly attached to doctrines "and rites which Christians and Mahomedans unite in reprobating. Such "a state of things is pregnant with dangers which can only be averted "by a firm adherence to the true principles of toleration."

241. Though objections have been made to this chapter by many persons, it does not appear to us that the general principle has been impugned. We understand the objections to apply mainly to the special provisions contained in Clause 282 and the following clauses to the end.

242. With respect to Clause 282 we shall quote the words of the Commissioners—"In framing Clause 282 we had two objects in view. "We wish to allow all fair latitude to religious discussion, and at the "same time to prevent the professors of any religion from offering, "under the pretext of such discussion, intentional insults to what is held "sacred by others. We do not conceive that any person can be justified "in wounding with deliberate intention the religious feelings of his "neighbours by word, gesture, or exhibitions. A warm expression "dropped in the heat of controversy, or an argument urged by a person "not for the purpose of insulting and annoying the professors of a "different creed, but in good faith for the purpose of vindicating his "own, will not fall under the definition contained in this clause."

243. Mr. J. F. Thomas submits the following observations:—"It "appears to me a dangerous novelty liable to extensive abuse, that a "man should be subject to a criminal prosecution for every gesture or "sound that he may utter, offensive to the religious feelings or preju- "dices of another. There can be no limit to criminal prosecutions, nor "to the variety of sentences under Clause No. 282. One Judge may, in "his charity, assume, that there could be no 'deliberate intention' of "wounding the feelings, and so absolve all offenders—another may "adopt the maxim, that the act itself indicates such intention. And if "the Criminal Courts are to be at all times open to the zealots of differ- "ing sects, on every trifling occasion, the result must be to foster bigotry, "and to keep the religious animosity of sects at its height, as well as to "interfere with individual security and peace. I give, as an instance of "the evil which might result from the law, a fact at one time constantly "under my notice. The old Saivite Pundit, Sudr Ameen of the Com- "baconum Court, in his daily public lustrations in the Caveri, poured

52

"abuse on Vishnu, and might consequently have been brought before "me as a criminal, for an act, little regarded by any but a few zealots "like himself, and which he deemed a religious duty."

"My experience also of the bigotry, and keen hatred of the opposing "Vaishnava Sects of Srerungham, the Tengala and Vadagala, of the "opposing Mahomedan Sects, Soonees and Sheeas, of Masulipatam, and "elsewhere, and their ready recourse to the Courts of Law as a means "of mutual annoyance, would lead me strongly to deprecate this provi-"sion. I greatly doubt its justice also, for under it, both the Christian "and Mossulman would be subject to penalty for the undisguised, and "natural expressions of their views of the evil and folly of idolatry."

244. Mr. Norton says:—"I know not how to construe acts as "'wounding religious or other feelings' and insulting 'religion.' It is "impossible to say to what absurdities the criminality of 'uttering any "word, or sound, or making any gesture in hearing or sight of a person, "with the intention of wounding his religious feelings' (Clause 282) "may be carried out."

245. The Judges of the Sudder Court in the North-Western Provinces would prefer the phrase "insulting" to "wounding" in Clause 282, or would prefix to "wounding" the word "wantonly." A Missionary, they observe, must necessarily, if he be in earnest, use such arguments as are calculated to "wound" the religious feelings of his hearers, without meaning wantonly to insult them.

246. Mr. Giberne, Judge of the Bombay Sudder Court, says—"This "clause might, I think, be excluded, for it almost amounts to a pro-"hibition to preaching the Gospel."

247. Mr. Sharkey suggests that an explanation should be annexed to this clause to the same effect as that given by the Commissioners in the last sentence of the passage quoted above from Note J.

248. The "Missionaries of various Protestant Societies, both of the "Establishment and Dissenting Bodies, labouring in "Calcutta and its vicinity," have remonstrated against Clause 282 and some other parts of this chapter. They say they "consider Clause 282 as specially calculated to "operate injuriously to themselves and disastrously on "the spread of Divine Truth—Deliberate and wilful "intention will surely be as strenuously, and honestly too, disclaimed by "the zealous Missionary, as it will be attributed to him by those who "deem their religious feelings wounded or insulted, when their under-"standings are simply reasoned with. If it be establishable at all, it can "only be by inference. But inference may be variously drawn from the "very same overt acts, according to the light in which they are beheld "by the adjudicators—so, 'any word or sound,' will include all discus-"sion or announcement whatever: 'any gesture,' all ordinary animation "in the advocate of truths the most interesting. Assuredly, if tried by "these rules, there is not a discourse or expostulation of Prophet or "Evangelist in the New or the Old Testament, nay, not of our Divine "Saviour himself, which would not be thought to wound, and keenly to "wound, the feelings of a zealous Jew, Mussulman, or Idolater, and "which, if so, must not be held forbidden, under the new Code, to be "either recited or imitated in the discourses of the Missionaries." What "an inlet, then," they proceed, "to an incessant imputation of 'deliberate

To the Secretary to Government, Legislative Department, not dated, received 24th March 1838.

"and wilful intention to wound or insult the feelings of 'Hindus,' would "be opened by the passing of Clause 282 of Chapter XV! *A fortiori* "may this be said in the case of Mussulmans, a fiercer and more vindic-"tive people, proud of a supposed superiority, and possessed with a "rancorous hatred of and contempt for Christianity—justly may it be "apprehended that the passing of Clause 282 into a law, would ere long "prove a prolific source of vexatious law suits, at once harassing to the "most unoffending Missionary, and largely adding to the burthen of "business in the Courts."

249. The Commissioners on the Criminal Law of England in their
P. 85. 6th Report observe that "the course hitherto adopted "in England respecting offences of this kind has been "to withhold the application of the penal law, unless in cases where "insulting or contumelious language is used, and where it may be fairly "presumed that the intention of the offender is not grave discussion, but "a mischievous design to wound the feelings of others, or to injure the
P. 82. "authority of Christianity with the vulgar and unthink-"ing by improper means." In the laws of the other European nations, offences of this class, it is remarked by the Commissioners, are invariably made to consist in the use of indecent railing or scurrilous language on the subject of religion and matters connected therewith. The reasons for distinguishing such offences and rendering them penal, viz., the preservation of religious peace and the protection of all men in the free exercise of that particular form of religion which
P. 81. they profess, the Commissioners observe, depend upon principles of general policy and toleration too obvious to require special notice.

250. It seems then to be by no means a novelty to punish persons who, transgressing the bounds of legitimate discussion, give utterance to railing and contumelious language with the deliberate intention of wounding the religious feelings of any person.

251. The Missionaries "readily acknowledge that insults may and "ought to be prohibited." "But," they contend, "if the feelings of the "weaker, i.e., the losing party in a discussion, conducted though it may "be upon the most equitable terms, be admitted to decide, then argu-"ments the fairest and the most moderately expressed, will certainly "always be deemed wounding; nay, they will be regarded as insults; "and may even be represented to be designed insults, by simply shewing "that their wounding tendency must not only have been perceived, but "anticipated as unavoidable by him who presses them; while yet, in "truth, they are the only rational and moral means furnished by our "common Creator, of opening the understanding and leading to reflec-"tion; even sarcasm itself is often the only answer that can be given to "positions too absurd to be gravely argued."

252. The authors of the Code declare that "a warm expression "dropped in the heat of controversy, or an argument urged by a person "not for the purpose of insulting and annoying the professors of a "different creed, but in good faith for the purpose of vindicating his "own, will not fall under the definition contained in this clause." We understand these instances to be mentioned as indicative of the strictness with which the definition is to be construed, so as not to make a person criminally liable for words, &c., wounding the religious feelings of another, unless a deliberate intention so to wound his feelings be unequivocally manifested, as it would be by mere railing and abuse, and by offensive attacks upon his religion under the pretext of discussion, without any argument which an impartial arbiter could reasonably believe to have been addressed to him in good faith merely for the purpose of convincing him of the truth. It is here to be observed that it is not the impression of the offended party that is to be "admitted to decide" whether the words uttered deserve to be considered as insulting, and whether they were uttered with the deliberate intention of insulting; these are points to be determined upon cool and calm consideration of the circumstances by the Judge. The intention to wound must be *deliberate*, that is, not conceived on the sudden in the course of discussion, but premeditated; it must appear, not only that the party, being engaged in a discussion with another on the subject of the religion professed by that other, in the course of the argument consciously used words likely to wound his religious feelings, but that he entered into the discussion with the deliberate purpose of so offending him. In other places in the Code a party is held to be guilty if he causes a certain effect the causing of which is an offence, intending to cause that effect, *or knowing that his act was likely to cause it.* Here there is a marked difference. Although the party uttering offensive words might be conscious at the moment of uttering them that they were likely to wound the feelings of his auditors, yet if it were apparent that he uttered them on the spur of the occasion, in good faith, simply to further his argument—that he did not take advantage of the occasion to utter them in pursuance of a deliberate purpose to offend—he would not, we think, be liable to conviction under Clause 282. If however a party were to force himself upon the attention of another, addressing to him, an involuntary hearer, an insulting invective against his religion, he would, we conceive, fall under the definition, for the reasonable inference from his conduct would be that he had a deliberate intention of wounding the religious feelings of his hearer.

253. But we agree with those who think that there would be a difficulty in drawing the line, and that different men would be apt to take very different views of what ought to be considered as evidencing a deliberate intention of "wounding the religious feelings." And under our view of the construction intended to be given to the clause, we agree with the Sudder Court for the North-Western Provinces that it would be better to change the expression by substituting "insulting" for "wounding." When a man in the course of an argument uses insulting words to another it is impossible to suppose that he does so without the intention of insulting him—it is not to be believed that he uses them in good faith simply for the purpose of convincing or persuading the person with whom he is arguing. In such a case the intention is to be inferred from the character of the words. Again when words not positively insulting in themselves are used in a manner clearly evidencing a deliberate intention to insult the religious feelings of another, the case will fall within the clause. But it will not be an offence when any person arguing with another on the subject of his religion says what is likely to wound his religious feelings, in good faith, simply for the purpose of convincing the person with whom he is arguing of what he believes to be the truth.

254. We are, though not without hesitation, inclined to think that in the very peculiar circumstances of this country, discourse addressed to any person with the intention of converting him from the faith he

professes, which, however it may wound his religious feelings, is not couched in insulting language, nor forced upon him in an insulting manner, should not be considered a crime.

255. In England an attempt to convert any one from the religion of the country by the most gentle and dispassionate address, is by law an offence; to attempt the same thing by contemptuous or vituperative language is an offence which would be severely punished in practice. But the reason is that conversion is not recognized as a legitimate object. The law assumes the truth of Christianity. But it is manifest that the Law and the Legislature of this country cannot assume the truth of any religion. And, as free discussion, or, in other words, attempts at conversion, is the best criterion of the truth of any thing the truth or falsehood of which is not already assumed by law to be beyond controversy, it seems to follow that a *bonâ fide* attempt to convert ought not in this country to be treated as a crime, even though the intention to convert be an intention to do so by wounding the religious feelings of the person addressed. We apprehend it is almost impossible to convert a sincere or ardent votary of any faith without wounding his religious feelings in the early stages of the process. And if that be so, and if it is admitted that attempts at conversion from one faith to another ought not to be punished in British India, then the wounding of religious feelings ought not to be punished when the wound is inflicted with that legitimate object.

256. The following passages from Sir T. More's Utopia, appear to us instructive with reference to the existing state of things in regard to religion in this country.

257. The founder of the Commonwealth of Utopia, it is stated, "made a law that every man might be of what religion he pleased, and "might endeavour to draw others to it by the force of argument, and by "amicable and modest ways, but without bitterness against those of "other opinions; but that he ought to use no other force but that of "persuasion; and was neither to mix with it reproaches nor violence; "and such as did otherwise were to be condemned to banishment or "slavery." He made this law seeing that "there were several sorts of "religion not only in different parts of the island, but even in every "town"—"not only for preserving the public peace which he saw "suffered much by daily contentions and irreconcileable heats, but "because he thought the interest of religion itself required it." He did not give a sanction by law to any particular religion as the true one, but "supposing that only one religion was really true, and the rest false, he "imagined, that the native force of truth would at last break forth "and shine bright, if supported only by the strength of argument, and "attended to with a gentle and unprejudiced mind; while, on the other "hand, if such debates were carried on with violence and tumults, as the "most wicked are always the most obstinate, so the best and most holy "religion, might be choaked with superstition, as corn is with briars and "thorns; he, therefore, left men wholly to their liberty, that they might "be free to believe as they should see cause."

258. The propriety of the provisions in the clauses of this chapter preceding Clause 282, for the punishment of persons intentionally destroying or defiling places of worship, or objects held sacred by any class of persons, and for the

Clauses 275 to 281.

purpose of protecting assemblies held for religious worship and for guarding places of sepulture, and protecting persons engaged in funeral rites, &c., appears to us to be sufficiently manifest. We have to notice, however, objections made by the Missionaries to two of these clauses.

259. They observe that in Clause 276, "a similar inlet to that "before remarked upon is opened for a litigious zeal to expend itself in "vexatious accusation of the Missionary who should, as heretofore, deem "it his duty to address the natives of this country at *Melas* and other "places of resort for religious observances, such as Jugurnáth, Gungá "Ságar, &c. He may as now, but quietly commence the reading of an "inoffensive tract, and when curiosity or some other motive has gathered "around him a small number of persons, may proceed to proclaim the "message of the Gospel of God our Saviour, and thereby become liable "to what hitherto he was not, an accusation of wilfully causing disturb-"ance to an assembly lawfully engaged in the performance of religious "worship." The answer to these observations is that no person can be prosecuted under Clause 276 except on an allegation that in causing disturbance to an assembly lawfully engaged in the performance of religious worship or religious ceremonies, he *assaulted* or *made shew of assaulting* or *threatened to assault* some person engaged in such worship or ceremonies.

260. "So too," the Missionaries represent, "by Clause 278 might "the most legitimate act be misconstrued into 'wilfully causing dis-"turbance in a place of worship, &c.,' though in truth such disturbance "should have proceeded altogether from the aggressions of the accusing "party." Here it is to be observed that the clause applies to an act done *in a place of worship* whereby a person *voluntarily* causes disturbance, that is to say, according to the explanation in Clause 26, to an act whereby disturbance is caused by him, *he having intended to cause disturbance by that act, or having known it to be likely to cause disturbance.* We think that no one can be convicted by the terms of this clause, under the circumstances supposed by the Missionaries; and we think at the same time that so cautiously is the clause worded, that no body can be convicted under it who has not been guilty of an aggression, which, being committed *in a place of worship,* where, by the supposition, a Missionary, that is an adversary of the worshippers, as regards their faith, has no right to enter, where by entering he is in truth trespassing, makes him highly deserving of punishment. Let us only consider what would be the sensation caused by a Mahomedan or Hindoo entering a Christian place of worship when the congregation are engaged in worship, and then and there openly impugning their faith. Supposing him to speak with all the calmness and moderation ascribed to the Missionary, would not the whole assembly be moved with indignation? would not the mere fact of his raising his voice in such an assembly on such an occasion and to such purpose be justly felt as an aggression, an insult? and would it not be thought that there was a defect in the law which did not provide for the punishment of the aggressor?

261. Before passing from these clauses we would suggest a slight verbal alteration in Clause 280. It seems to us that the word "sepulture," the proper meaning of which is burial or interment, is not sufficiently comprehensive to express what is intended in this place, for it is clear that what is contemplated is any place in which are performed the last offices for the dead, of what nature soever they may be, or in which the remains of the dead are deposited. Instead of a "place of sepulture" we would propose "any place set apart for the performance of funeral rites, or as a depository for the remains of the dead."

262. Referring to Clause 283 and the following clauses, Mr. Norton observes, "surely it may be enough to protect religious faiths, and ceremonies, by repressing the ordinary outrages against them, without "attempting to put down one species of superstitious imposture, such as "sitting in Dhurna, or conjuring—by visiting it as a crime, for the purpose of *accrediting another*, under which a weak ignorant mind is "induced to give way to such imposture. And upon the same principle "I conceive the real interests of the people are better consulted in "omitting from a Criminal Code the temporal protection of superstitions "even in regard to the preservation of caste, and in leaving pernicious "prejudices to clear away as civilization advances. A contrary course, "as it appears to me, would have greater operation in encouraging and "perpetuating, than in repressing, what is pernicious."

263. Mr. M. Lewin remarks that "Clause 283 tends to confirm the "ignorant in principles of belief which operate to their prejudice; the "power to injure is believed to exist, because its pretended application "is met by heavy punishment—people will not believe that the Govern- "ment have denounced under heavy penalties, the exercise of a power "which is only imaginary. In England sorcery was punished, as it was "in France, as long as the Government believed in its existence."

"In those districts where the pretended power of imprecating the "vengeance of the Deity, has been punished by the Magistrate, the "practice and belief have extended; where pains have been taken to "expose the cheat, and where the public authorities have openly dis- "countenanced the belief, it has declined."

264. Sir J. Awdry observes that the offences which are here thrown together are almost all capable of being included clearly, but in general tacitly, under some other head, so that when a wrong had really been committed the Magistrate would be at no loss to visit it, and he advises that they be thus distributed. The form of the law as it now stands he thinks is likely to suggest modes of annoyance to persons of adverse sects against each other. Mr. M. Lewin and others take a similar view of the subject. With respect to Clause 283, Mr. Lewin observes that a threat founded on the species of imposition described in this clause ought to be viewed with reference to its object; as criminal intimidation (Clauses 186, 483), as an attempt at extortion (Clause 370), or as an abetment (Clause 88); and punished according to the injurious tendency of the act instigated; but the punishment should not be made to depend on the name of the Deity being invoked, nor should any absurd alarm or belief be held to excuse an act in itself wrong.

265. Notwithstanding the precedents that are to be found in Regulations XXI of 1795 and VII of 1820 of the Bengal Code, and Sections 34 and 35, Regulation XIV of 1827 of the Code of Bombay, we are inclined to the opinion that it is advisable to omit the specific denunciation in Clause 283, and to extend Clause 482 which defines "criminal intimidation" so as tacitly to include the species of intimidation against which Clause 283 is directed, by a general expression. We observe that an article against false denunciations of Divine judgment which appeared in the Digest of "Offences

Art. 5, p. 90.

against Religion" in the 6th Report of the English Criminal Law Commissioners, is omitted in the General Digest submitted with their 7th Report. The article was as follows :—" Whoever shall falsely pretend " to an extraordinary commission from God, or shall terrify or abuse the " Queen's subjects with false denunciations of Divine judgments, shall incur the penalties of the —— class."

266. With reference to the provisions relating to caste in Clauses 284 and 285, the Commissioners offer the following explanation. " The " intentional depriving a Hindoo of his caste by assault or by deception " is not at present an offence in any part of India, though it may be a " ground for a civil action. It appears to us however that an injury so " wanton, an injury which indicates so bad a feeling in the person who " causes it, and which gives so much pain and excites so much resent- " ment in the sufferer, is as proper a subject for penal legislation as most " of the acts which are made punishable by this Code. We have there- " fore made it an offence. The rendering the food of a Hindoo useless to " him by causing it to be in what he considers as a polluted state is an " injury of the same kind, though comparatively venial. We propose " to make it an offence, but not to deal with it severely, unless it should " be repeatedly committed by the same person."

267. Mr. J. F. Thomas says :—" Clauses 284 and 285 are not, I think, " matter for a Criminal Code. It would be far better to leave parties " to seek redress for any damage they may sustain by a civil action. What " end, I would ask, is answered, so far as the public is concerned, by " upholding the injurious and unnatural Brahminical privilege of caste. " Suppose a Brahmin does lose caste, he may have his remedy by a civil " action, to recover the amount necessary to procure his reinstate- " ment and indemnification for his temporary loss. Who also is to " define what will cause the loss of caste. Swallowing beef-broth " may be supposed to do it in Bengal, but is such the fact—and is " not this an infringement only of caste rules, to be atoned for by " temporary penances and ceremonial observances (Mantrams). In " practice, is loss of caste incurred by any act, short of conversion " to another faith or cohabiting with a Pariar ?" In another place Mr. Thomas argues more at large against the policy of such enactments, which he characterizes as affording the protection of penal provisions to what is in itself injurious to society. Mr. Norton, as we have shewn, takes a similar view. And we find observations to the same effect made by other gentlemen. Mr. H. Frere in particular remarks that to make public officers take cognizance of offences against caste is to make them conservators of a bad system, and greatly to impede the desirable object of its gradual abolition. Mr. Pelly thinks that the provisions might be merged (as suggested by Sir J. Awdry and Mr. M. Lewin) in other chapters of the Code, if retained he considers it necessary that caste and what constitutes the loss of it should be clearly defined.

268. It appears to us that the first provision in Clause 284 against an assault by which one person intentionally causes another to lose caste is included in Clause 348, by which whoever assaults any person intending thereby to *dishonor* that person is liable to punishment, for to cause a person to lose caste is emphatically to dishonor him. Again it appears to us that the offence defined in Clause 285, causing food belonging to any person to be in a state in which according to the rules of his caste he cannot use it, if the effect is produced by any positive action upon

the food which has made a change in it, or in its situation, as by mixing any substance with it, or by overturning the vessel in which it is placed, is causing a wrongful loss to him within the meaning of the definition of "mischief" in Clause 399, and therefore that it is covered by Clause 405, as a case of mischief committed with the deliberate intention of thereby insulting or annoying the person to whom the wrongful loss involved in the mischief is intended. When the effect is produced otherwise, for example by a person intruding into the place where the food is being prepared, the offence might be brought under the general provision for the punishment of wanton annoyance in Clause 487 by the addition of a few words, the introduction of which we shall propose when we come to that clause.

269. We are not aware that there is any clause in the Code which can be construed to embrace the second provision contained in Clause 284, or can be conveniently altered so as to embrace it. We do not think the object of sufficient importance for a separate enactment regarding it.

270. It seems then that the clauses of this chapter from 283 to 286 may be omitted altogether from the Code. The clauses from 275 to 282 we think ought to be retained. But we do not think it necessary to place them in a separate chapter. We conceive that the clauses from 275 to 281 would be properly placed in the chapter "of offences against the public tranquillity" after Clause 137, changing the present order of the clauses from 275 to 279, making 275 to stand last and 276 and 277 after 278 and 279. Clause 280 would then follow Clause 275. We would place Clause 282 in the chapter "of criminal intimidation and annoyance" after Clause 486.

CHAPTER XVI.

OF ILLEGAL ENTRANCE INTO AND RESIDENCE IN THE TERRITORIES OF THE EAST INDIA COMPANY.

271. Exception has been taken to this chapter on the ground that it does not make provision for punishing the illegal entrance and residence of foreigners. The reason appears to be that the law gives authority for the summary removal of the subjects of foreign States residing or sojourning within the British Territories against the consent of the Government.

55 Geo. III, Cap. 84, Section 6.

272. The exclusive object of this chapter is to comply with the requirement of Section 84 of the Act of Parliament 3 and 4 Wm. IV, Cap. 85, in regard to subjects of the Queen not Natives of the Territories of the East India Company, entering into or residing in the said territories.

273. Mr. Norton considers that Clause 287 is "decidedly too general "to be safely acted upon." "*How soon* a person is to register his arrival "by sea, in what manner he is to 'make it known,' what is meant by "'his destination' or 'his object of pursuit,' he observes, is left altogether "uncertain." Mr. Hudleston says, "I agree with those who think the word 'intentionally' should follow the word 'Territories,'" in this clause, that is to say, that a person should not be liable to punishment for omitting to report his arrival in the Company's Territories unless the omission were intentional. Mr. Pelly suggests that a time should be given for making the required report.

274. This clause being intended to correspond as near as can be with the proviso in Section 81 of the Statute, we think that the words "from any port or place not within the said Territories," which are found therein, should likewise have place here. We think also that a certain time should be fixed, the lapse of which without complying with the condition specified in the said proviso and expressed in this clause, should subject the party omitting to comply with it to the penalty. We do not think it necessary to introduce the word "intentionally." The party is bound to make himself acquainted with the law, and his omission to comply with what it requires in this behalf in a reasonable time may be taken to be intentional. We would suggest that the time be thirty days.

275. The clause modified, as we think advisable, might run as follows: "Whoever, being a subject of the Queen, and not a native of "the Territories subject to the Government of the East India Company, "arrives by sea in any place within the said Territories from any port "or place not within the said Territories, and does not, within thirty "days thereafter, make known in writing his name, place of destination, "and object of pursuit in India to the Chief Officer of Customs, or other "Officer authorized for that purpose at the place at which such subject "of the Queen has arrived, shall be punished with fine which may "extend to One Thousand Rupees." The phrases which Mr. Norton objects to as indefinite it will be observed are retained. They are taken from the Act of Parliament, and we do not perceive how there can be any question as to what is meant by "place of destination" or "object of pursuit in India" or as to "*the manner*" in which a person is to make

known his name, &c., when he is expressly directed to make it known *in writing*.

276. Mr. Blane observes with reference to Clause 290, that "it is "not clear what will constitute the offence of again residing. If a person "convicted under Clause 289 does not quit the territories, is this a "repetition? If so the time for departure should be defined, or a power "of deportation given to the public authority." The question asked by Mr. Blane is no doubt to be answered in the affirmative. In the Act 53, Geo. III, Cap. 155, Sec. 101, there is a similar provision for the case of a person being convicted a second time of the offence of residing in the East Indies without a licence, without any explanation as to the time within which a party once convicted must depart to avoid a second prosecution, and it does not appear to be necessary to define this any more in regard to the particular offence in question than as to any other by persisting in which the offender renders himself liable to a second prosecution. A prosecution under Clause 290 we conceive could not be sustained, unless it were shewn to the satisfaction of the Court that there had been sufficient time for the party prosecuted, since his former conviction, or, if he was sentenced to imprisonment, since his release from prison, to take his departure, and there could be no defence against such a prosecution unless the party could prove that he had been making preparations to depart, and that the time had not been sufficient, or that his departure had been prevented by some impediment which it was not in his power to remove or overcome. We apprehend that with respect to persons in the circumstances described in Clause 289 the power of deportation given to the Indian Government by Section 104 of the Act 53, Geo. III, Cap. 155, is still left to the Government.

CHAPTER XVII.

OF OFFENCES RELATING TO THE PRESS.

277. It is explained in the Note to this chapter that the penal provisions contained in it are taken from the Indian Press Act No. XI of 1835.

278. Mr. Norton has taken occasion to comment at some length upon the Act here referred to, observing that "there is the less reason "for considering such remarks impertinent, as this law is in a manner "engrafted into this Code," "and it may, at all events, answer an "useful object to call the attention of Government to the necessity "of its revision." We do not consider ourselves called upon to follow Mr. Norton in this digression, as he himself terms it. But his remarks may be found worthy of attention should the Government find it expedient to review the Press Law.

CHAPTER XX.

OF OFFENCES RELATING TO DOCUMENTS.

279. "Forgery" is defined in the first clause of this chapter (441). Afterwards provision is made for the *offence* of "forgery," first, as regards *any document;* 2ndly, as regards any document which is or purports to be a *valuable security;* 3rdly, when it is committed for the purpose of *cheating;* 4thly, when it is committed for the purpose of *harming the reputation* of any party. The same clauses provide for the offence of "using as genuine" documents known to have been "forged" or "falsified by forgery," which terms as applied to documents are explained in Clause 442. The terms "document" and "valuable security" are explained in Clauses 21 and 22.

Clauses 443, 444, 445 and 446.

280. The definition of "Forgery," in Clause 441, consists of five articles, all which relate to documents, except the fifth, which relates to something which is not a document or part of a document, because it contains no word, or letter, or mark, in handwriting, or meant to appear so, but which is intended to become a document by the addition of handwriting. Though the fabrication of this inchoate document is a forgery, it is not an offence in itself; but whoever has such a thing in his possession intending that it may be made a document purporting to be a valuable security, is guilty of an offence under Clause 450.

Clause 450.

281. The first article declares that a person commits forgery who makes or marks any document so that it may be believed that it was made or marked by some other person, or at some other time, or by some authority by which it was not made or marked. By the second a person commits forgery who voluntarily omits to insert in a document which he has engaged to make by the authority or according to the direction of another, any thing which he is directed to insert in it, intending it to be believed that the document is made according to the direction of that other. By the third it is forgery to cancel a document intending it to be believed that the cancellation was made by another person, or at another time, or by some authority by which it was not made. By the fourth it is forgery to cause any part of a document or any mark for identifying or authenticating a document to disappear, intending it to be believed that such part or mark never existed, or was caused to disappear by another person, and at another time, or by some authority by which it was not caused to disappear.

282. It is an *offence* to commit forgery in any of these ways with intent to injure any party, or to render any illegal act easier or safer, or to obtain employment for any person in public or private service. It is an aggravation when the document forged or falsified by forgery purports to be a valuable security. It is an aggravation also when the object is to cheat, or to harm the reputation of any person. For forgery without any of these aggravations, or using a "forged document," or a "document falsified by forgery" as genuine, the punishment is imprisonment of either description, which may extend to two years, or fine, or both. When the document purports to be a valuable security, the punishment is imprisonment, with or without fine, for 14 years as the maximum and two years

Clauses 443, 444.

Clauses 445, 446.

as the minimum; when the object is to cheat, the maximum is seven years and the minimum one year; when it is to harm the reputation of any person, the maximum is three years and the minimum six months.

283. Mr. Hudleston says:—"To this laboured, wordy definition "(Clause 441) I prefer the English one of forgery, namely, 'the fraud- "ulent making or alteration of a writing to the prejudice of another "man's right.'" This is the definition given by Blackstone. The definition of the English Criminal Law Commissioners is as follows: "Forgery consists in the false and fraudu- "lent making of an instrument with intent to prejudice "any public or private right." They say in the 5th Report—"The general definition of the offence is in "substance that which is given by Sir W. Blackstone, "which we have adopted, and which is recommended by its conciseness, "accuracy and generality. We have, however, for the sake of compari- "son, stated those of several other very eminent Judges. We have also "introduced various articles for the purpose of more particularly defining "and explaining the nature and extent of the offence." It will be observed that the definition of the Criminal Law Commissioners omits the word 'alteration' which is contained in that of Blackstone, and adds the word 'public' in connection with right. Sir E. H. East's definition, cited in the 5th Report, explains that a "false making" is to be understood as "including every alteration of or addition to a true instrument," and so, it appears, the Commissioners intend the word "making" to be understood in their definition.

Vol. IV, p. 247.

Digest, Chapter XXI, Art. 1.

P. 67.

Art. 6.

284. It is to be observed that the articles in Chapter XXI of the Digest, under the head of "Forgery and other offences connected therewith," comprise a part only of the forgeries recognized and provided for by the law of England. The English Criminal Law Commissioners in their 5th Report observed that "there can be no doubt that "the crime of forgery is capable of being defined and "expressed in a manner much more general and concise "than that in which it now exists according to the law of England," but that they "had not considered themselves warranted in making alterations which would amount to an entire reconstruction of this branch of the law." In preparing the Digest under the above heading which is contained in the same Report, their plan was this, "after defining "the general rules applicable to the common law offence of forgery, they "proceeded to arrange and classify the several statutory enactments "relating to the offence." The Digest thus framed they described as consisting, "so far as the Statute law is concerned, of a great variety of "special provisions left unrepealed by the Statute 11th "of King George IV, and 1st of King William IV, "Chapter 66, (the Forgery Consolidation Act), of the larger number "of the clauses of the last mentioned Act, and of the different "forgery enactments passed since that Act." The Commissioners abandoned this arrangement in preparing the general Digest of the law submitted with their 7th Report, and excluding from the chapter of Forgery almost all the special statutory enactments, distributed those enactments in different chapters under the heads denoting the subjects with which they are respectively connected. Thus the provision relating to the forgery of written instruments of justice appears under the head of "offences tending to defeat or pervert justice." The offence of forging

P. 67.

P. 68.

Digest, 7th Report, Chap. V, s. 5.

a transfer of public stock, and other cognate offences, come under "offences relating to public chattels, funds, &c." The forging of stamps is provided for under "offences relating to the stamp duties;" the forging of registers of baptisms, &c., under the head of "offences relating to public records;" the forging of Exchequer bills, promissory notes, bills of exchange, &c., under "offences relating to negotiable securities;" and so forth.

Chapter VIII, Sections 1 and 6.

Chapter X.

Chapter XIV, Section 2.

285. The articles introduced in the Digest to explain the general definition of forgery are more numerous than those of which Clause 441 consists, which Mr. Hudleston characterizes as "laboured and wordy." The latter we think comprehend all that is essential in the former, and they appear to us to be expressed with clearness and precision. The only question we have remarked that seems to require notice as implying that a part of the definition in the Code is too comprehensive, refers to the second article of Clause 441, according to which a person commits forgery who having engaged to make a document by the authority and according to the direction of another voluntarily omits to insert something he was directed by that other to insert, intending it to be believed that it is made as directed. The question is put thus—"A is engaged "by B to collect certain dues, and is directed to make a faithful account "of his collections. A makes a false account, omitting to insert all. "Has A committed forgery?"

286. We apprehend that this case does not fall within the definition, which we conceive refers to a document made by one person as by the authority and according to the direction of another, and intended to pass as the act of that other, not to a document made by one man by the order of another for the use of that other. We are inclined to think, however, that the article in question, as it stands, may be construed to comprehend more than we presume was meant, and we consider it advisable to introduce words restricting it to documents intended to be taken and received as the very acts of the party who directed them to be made. We would therefore insert after the words "according to the direction of another," the words "which document is intended to pass as the act of that other," and at the end the words "and is entirely his act."

287. Generally in the provisions relating to forgery the term "written instrument" is used in the Digest where "document" is used in this chapter of the Code. In the Note upon the definition of the term "instrument" in the 5th Report of the English Criminal Law Commissioners it is observed that "as applied to writing generally the term "must mean a writing constructed for the immediate purpose of effect-"ing some moral result, such as belief or knowledge; in a legal and "technical sense it means a writing by which some such moral result is "to be effected for a legal purpose." In the Report it is explained that "as regards the subject-matter, the offence (of forgery) extends to every writing used for the purpose of authentication." The meaning which is attributed to the term "instrument" as applied to writing generally, we conceive, is what is intended by the term "document" when it is used absolutely in the Code. This wide signification is however restricted by the determinate application of the term in the penal provisions of the chapter under consideration.

288. The Digest differs from the Code in declaring that the term "written" shall be deemed to apply "whether the words or figures of "the instrument or any of them be expressed by means of writing, "printing or otherwise;" whereas the Code limits the term "document" to matter which is wholly or partly in handwriting or which is meant to appear to be in handwriting: but while by the Code handwriting is thus made essential to the constitution of a document, "a single word or a single letter or significant mark in "handwriting is sufficient to make the whole of the matter connected therewith a document."

Clause 21.

289. In our first Report we observed that it might be expedient to place the definition of document in the chapter we are now considering, for which it seemed to have been framed. We referred to the restriction in regard to handwriting, and to the objection taken to it as arbitrarily assigning a meaning to the word short of what it has in the popular sense. We thought that this restriction was intended to meet the penal provisions regarding forgery, and it seemed to us that consistently with this view the definition might be extended so as to include papers not in writing authenticated by a seal or stamp instead of a written signature, as suggested by Mr. Greenhill. It is certain that the definition was originally intended to have place in this chapter, in which it actually appeared in the first impression of the Code, but being referred to also in the definition of cheating in the chapter "of offences against property" it was afterwards properly transferred to its present position in the chapter of "General Explanations." Having now considered the definition more particularly in connection with the penal provisions of this chapter and with the clauses relating to cheating in Chapter XIX, to which exclusively it appears to have reference, we are led to the conclusion that the alteration we formerly contemplated is not required practically. In the definition of cheating in Clause 392, the word document is used as it is used in Clause 444 in this chapter in connection with the term "valuable security," which as defined in Clause 22, denotes a class of documents that we believe are always, or almost always, so made as to be within the definition in Clause 21, that is to say, documents which are wholly or partly in writing, or which are authenticated by a written signature of some kind. We do not recollect any examples of documents made without handwriting in any part, and authenticated merely by a seal or stamp instead of a written signature.

Para. 88, p. 210.

Chapter XIX, Clause 392.

290. Of Clause 443 Mr. Hudleston says, "Offences very different "in criminality are here brought together, and the special provision for "any of them I consider unnecessary." Mr. A. D. Campbell expresses his concurrence in this remark. We cannot suppose that Mr. Hudleston means that it is unnecessary to provide for forgery committed with any such intention as is expressed in this clause; but what he does mean is not clear, and Mr. Campbell does not elucidate it. It seems to us that forgery committed with any such object as is here specified, ought to be punished, and that the range of punishment prescribed affords sufficient room for the exercise of discretion on the part of the Judge in apportioning the penalty to the degree of criminality which attaches to the offender according to the circumstances of each case. At first sight it would seem that the general definition of forgery in the Digest which we have cited above does not go to the full extent of this clause, but when the explanations of the Commissioners are considered, it may be thought that there is not much difference. For the offence of forgery, it is said, "extends to every writing used for the purpose of authentication, and a "certificate by which an officer or other authorized person assures "others of the truth of any fact" is mentioned as an example of such writing. Again a case is cited in which "it was determined that the "crime extended to all written instruments by the forgery of which a "party might be prejudiced," and in Article 4, Chapter XXI of the Digest, it is laid down that "an instrument shall be deemed to be *falsely* "made when it is not really the instrument or mean of authentication for "which it is intended to be taken; but is *fraudulently* made with intent "to obtain that credit which would be due to it if it were genuine." Under these explanations the definition in the Digest may perhaps be construed to include, as Clause 443 does specifically, the forgery of a certificate "with the intention of obtaining employment for any person," also forgery committed with the intention of facilitating "any illegal act," that is to say, according to the definition in Clause 28, "any act which is an offence or which is contrary to any direction "of the law, or which furnishes ground for a civil action, as well as "forgery committed with the intention of causing any injury to any "party."

291. With respect to Clauses 444 and 445, Mr. Sharkey observes that "while they make a difference in punishment they do not discriminate "the particular classes of forgeries intended by them respectively; in "the former the term 'valuable security' only being used, and the latter "speaking merely of forgeries for cheating, while the "article 'of cheating' contemplates forgeries of equal "value with those referred to in Clause 444 of the "present chapter; and indeed the object of all forgeries "being to cheat, these different terms alone could never "be a sufficient distinction, while a distinction is absolutely necessary."

"Vide illustration (a) of Clause 392 of the article 'Cheating.'"

For the forgery of any document not a valuable security and not intended to be used for cheating, the offender is liable to punishment under Clause 443; if the document was intended to be used or was used for the purpose of cheating he is liable to enhanced punishment under Clause 445; and to a further enhancement under Clause 444 if the document be a valuable security. This all seems to be sufficiently clear. The case put in the illustration (*a*) of Clause 392, as an example of cheating by means of a forged bill of exchange, that is a document classed as a "valuable security," might be put also under Clause 443 as an example of using a forged document as genuine with the intention of injuring any party; under Clause 444 as an example of so using a forged *valuable security* with the same intention; and under Clause 445 of so using a forged document with the intention of cheating; but practically as the minor offence merges in the major the offender would be prosecuted under Clause 444.

292. Mr. Sharkey, who has written at some length upon the subject of forgery, among other things observes that the principle upon which the penalties for this offence are proposed does not appear. He says, "There should be some certain data for regulating the measure of punish-"ment, and a more uniform and fair one than the amount of the property "attempted to be defrauded I do not think there can be."

293. Mr. J. F. Thomas appears to hold a similar opinion as to the propriety of making the value of the property affected by a forgery a standard for determining the punishment. Referring to Clause 444 relating to the forgery of a valuable security and to Clause 449 relating to the possession of a forged document of that description, he says, "These clauses, &c., "would render any party who had in his possession a forged receipt to "the value of five rupees or other trifling sum, liable to two years' im-"prisonment at the least. I think, in such cases of frequent occurrence, "a penalty to this extent altogether uncalled for by the wants of society. "If such document were even uttered as genuine, a fine of ten times the "amount, commutable to imprisonment for a few months, would probably "be sufficient to check the offence in these trifling cases, and afford "ample security to property, especially if that fine, or a part of it, were "made over to the party intended to be defrauded."

Clauses 444 and 449.

294. As to what is here said of possessing a forged document, it is to be observed that the mere possession of the document is not punishable under Clause 449 unless the possessor knows it to be forged and intends or knows it to be likely that it may be used as genuine, a knowledge and intention which make the possession justly penal. The having a forged document in possession appears to be punishable by the law of England only when the document is a bank note or bank bill of exchange or bank post bill. The possession of a forged document of that description without lawful excuse, the proof whereof lies on the accused, is made highly criminal. The English Commissioners observe that "this law inverts the general principle of criminal jurisprudence that a man is presumed to be innocent till his guilt be proved." The provisions in the Code do not appear to be liable to this reproach since they require proof of a certain guilty intention. They are confined to forged documents representing valuable securities (Clause 449) or to what are intended to be made such, (Clause 450), as blank bank notes marked by forgery, the possession of which is punishable by the law of England.

Digest, Chapter XIV, Section 2, Art. 6.
5th Report, p. 67.
Art. 6 as above.

295. Mr. Thomas, in whose opinion Mr. Hudleston concurs, has adverted only to cases in which the value of the property affected by the forgery of a valuable security is inconsiderable. These gentlemen do not say whether they would follow the same principle in cases of magnitude, as where a lac of rupees is concerned. We may take it for granted that in such cases they would not recommend "a fine of ten times the amount," but what they would recommend is left to conjecture.

296. Mr. Sharkey refers to the provisions regarding "Mischief" as recognizing the principle of value. We remarked in our first Report that "in laying down the punishment "for different degrees of the offence of mischief the "gradation observed refers to the amount of loss sus-"tained, a mode of distinction not admitted in esti-"mating the degrees of criminality in other offences against property." It is to be considered however that the reference to value in cases of that description is not observed for the purpose of distinction where the loss amounts to more than 100 rupees. We are inclined to agree with Mr. Thomas that for the forgery of a receipt for 5 rupees or other trifling sum, the minimum punishment under Clause 444 of imprisonment for two years is more severe than such cases call for. Either the minimum

Clauses 400 to 403.
See para. 608, page 320.

might be omitted as we have proposed with regard to perjury; or it might be reduced to imprisonment for one year which is the minimum fixed in the Digest of the English Criminal Law; or the principle of value might be adopted to the extent that it is observed in the provisions regarding mischief modified as proposed in our first Report, making the forgery of a valuable security where the amount is less than 100 rupees punishable with imprisonment which may extend to two years, or fine, or both, and when the amount is 100 rupees or more with the penalty prescribed in Clause 444, and modifying Clause 449 in like manner. So with respect to Clause 445 either the minimum might be omitted, or the clause modified on the same principle, confining the punishment, for cases in which the amount is less than 100 rupees, to imprisonment for one year. We would recommend that the minimum be omitted in both these clauses. We would omit the minimum also in Clause 446.

297. Mr. Greenhill asks "under which clause does forging a will come?" it does not appear to come under 'valuable security' as the "destruction and concealment of one and the other are provided for separately." Notwithstanding this pertinent observation we are of opinion that the forgery of a will was intended to come under Clause 444; a will, that is the last will and testament of a person deceased, being considered a valuable security under the definition in Clause 22, as "a document whereby a legal right is created." We observe that in the first impression of the Code the word "will" was inserted in the clause corresponding to Clause 444, together with "valuable security," seemingly as signifying a thing distinct, and that on the revision of the Code when it was put into its present state, that word was struck out, apparently because it was thought to be included in the term "valuable security."

Clauses 451 and 452.

With respect to the separate provisions for the destruction and concealment of a will, and for the destruction and concealment of a valuable security, from which Mr. Greenhill infers that a will is not a valuable security, we understand merely that a will is singled out as the only kind of valuable security, the destruction or concealment of which it is deemed fitting to punish with the same punishment as the forgery of it. And there is a special reason for this distinction of a will from other valuable securities, as there is a chance of such a document falling into the hands of one whose interest it may be, to a greater degree than can apply to any other document, to suppress it; for example when one expecting to be the heir, being in the house of the Testator at the time of his decease in circumstances which give him access to his papers, finds among them a will by which he is disinherited;—the temptation to destroy would be great, the act of destruction easy, and the risk of legal conviction small. It appears to us however that as a will can only become a valuable security by the death of the Testator, the clause relating to the forgery of valuable securities would not be generally applicable. It would not apply for instance to the case stated in the illustration (*g*) under Clause 441. We are of opinion therefore that it is expedient to make Clause 444 applicable specially by introducing the words "or a will" after the words "a valuable security" in both the third and the fifth line.

298. While for the destruction or concealment of a will we do not think the punishment authorized by Clause 451, of imprisonment which may extend to 14 years, excessive, we are inclined to agree with the Sudder Court, North-Western Provinces, and with Mr. Pyne of the

Bombay Sudder Court, in thinking that the punishment in Clause 452 for the destruction or concealment of other valuable securities, viz., imprisonment which may extend to three years, may be found inadequate. Mr. Pyne in questioning the adequacy of the proposed punishment refers to the unlimited confidence reposed by Native Merchants in their Gomastahs who by this offence might cause extensive mischief to their employers, and also to the great interest in respect of valuable securities deposited in public offices. We conceive that the punishment should be the same as is provided for the forgery of a document for the purpose of cheating. We think that the same modifications as to the minimum limitation are required in these two clauses as in Clauses 444 and 445.

299. Mr. Fagan suggests that special provision should be made by a new clause to follow Clause 452, for the punishment of any public servant fraudulently destroying or defacing or secreting any document, meaning, we presume, any document which has been placed in his charge or entrusted to his keeping as a public servant. We think this suggestion worthy of attention. The offence we suppose is punishable under Clause 145, but the penalty appears inadequate. The punishment for such an offence when the document is not a valuable security we conceive should be the same as in Clause 146, for a public servant preparing a document incorrectly for the purpose of causing injury to any person. When the document is a valuable security, the punishment perhaps should extend to imprisonment up to 14 years, as for forging, or falsifying by forgery, a valuable security.

300. Clause 447 provides for the offence of making "any *apparatus* or *material* for engraving or any seal intended to be used for committing forgery, and Clause 448 provides for having in possession "any *plate* or *material* or *implement* for engraving, or any seal" intended for the same purpose. The punishment proposed is the same as for the offence of forging a valuable security, viz., imprisonment which may extend to 14 years and must not be less than two years, with or without fine. The principle of making a person *thus* accessory to the offence of forgery liable to the punishment of that offence is observed in the corresponding provisions regarding the counterfeiting of stamps (Clauses 218 and 219), it is observed also in the provision regarding the making of a die for counterfeiting coin (Clauses 234 and 235) and partly in that regarding the possession of instruments for coining, &c., (Clause 236). But as in the provisions relating to the counterfeiting of coin there is a distinction between the Queen's and Company's coin and other coin, the offence of counterfeiting the former being liable to a heavier punishment than the offence of counterfeiting the latter, and as there is a similar distinction between the forging of valuable securities and the forging of other documents, so, as there is a corresponding gradation in the punishment of the accessory offence of making the instrument as respects coining, it would seem that there should be a gradation likewise in the accessory offences as respects forging. As the forgery of a document *not* a valuable security is punishable with imprisonment which may extend to two years, while the forgery of a valuable security is punishable with imprisonment which may extend to 14 years and must *not be less* than two years, it is scarcely consistent to make the preparation of the apparatus for forging the former, the document of less importance, liable to the same punishment as the actual forging of the latter, the document of greater importance. We think that there should be one punishment for these accessory offences as regards forgeries such as are contemplated in Clause 443, and another as regards forgeries such as are contemplated in Clause 444, viz., for the former the punishment specified in Clause 443 and for the latter the punishment specified in Clause 444. We do not perceive why there is a variation in the wording of these clauses in regard to the subject-matter, which, it seems to us, should be described by the same terms in both. The same modification should be made regarding the minimum in these clauses as shall be made regarding the minimum in Clause 444.

In Clause 447. "Any apparatus or material for engraving."
In Clause 448. "Any plate, material or implement for engraving."

301. The offence described in Clause 453, namely, *a servant of the Post Office* opening a letter or packet containing a document, without authority to do so, differs from that in Clause 388 inasmuch as the latter involves a fraudulent misappropriation which need not be alleged and proved in order to a conviction under the former. Clause 454 makes it an offence for *any person* to open a fastened letter or packet. The provisions seem to be proper. It has been suggested that the punishments are too light, but they do not appear so to us.

CHAPTER XXI.

OF OFFENCES RELATING TO PROPERTY MARKS.

302. Mr. Hudleston says he thinks this chapter an instance of over-legislation; an opinion which we do not understand, for we cannot suppose that he deems the offences which the chapter provides for venial. Mr. A. D. Campbell, his colleague in the Madras Sudder Court, in reply to his observation, remarks as follows:—"This chapter I conclude refers to *land* marks, as well as to marks for other property, and "is highly necessary, particularly under the ryot-war system, where the "boundaries of fields define the rights of individual ryots, as well as "under the village or zemindary systems, where, in addition to the "boundaries of fields, which the ryot-war system requires, the boundaries of villages, and even of Zemindaries, must be maintained. It is "also, I consider, essential to the Stamp and Post Office Revenue."

303. We apprehend that Mr. Campbell is not right in considering the chapter applicable to land marks. The words "for the purpose of distinguishing the property marked from other property" might indeed apply to a land mark, but only by understanding them in a sense inapplicable to other marks. A stone distinguishes A's field from B's in a sense quite different from that in which a brand distinguishes A's sheep from B's. All the offences relate to counterfeiting marks none to removing marks. But the common offence touching land marks is the removal of them. It would seem to be gratuitous to provide for the offence of counterfeiting a land mark.

304. Mr. Norton says, "Of this chapter, to which I have to offer "no very material objection, I shall merely say, that agreeing in the "expediency of extending criminality to the counterfeiting private marks "on private property, even though no fraud may be thereby actually "effected, yet it appears to me that the '*using*' such counterfeits as "genuine, knowing it *likely* or *intending* that injury may be effected "thereby—or 'for the *purpose* of cheating' is more open to doubtful con-"struction, and other objections, than the plain law against the *obtain*-"*ing* money or goods by false tokens or pretences."

305. But it is obvious to remark that the plain law against the *obtaining* money or goods by false tokens or pretences (which is provided for under the head of "cheating") would not answer for the object here intended, the expediency of which Mr. Norton himself acknowledges.

Clause 392, et seq.

306. Mr. F. N. Maltby observes that this chapter does not provide any penalty for removing property marks. "The offence," he remarks, "is perhaps included under other heads, but it is under this that it would "naturally be looked for." As respects land marks, this offence is provided for under the head of mischief in Clause 411. As respects marks for distinguishing property such as appear to be intended in this chapter, the removing of them may perhaps come under "mischief" as "causing a change in the property" "by which its value is diminished," or it may come under "criminal trespass" as defined in Clauses 418 and 419 as they stand in the Code; or within the modified definition of trespass proposed in a subsequent part of this Report.

Vide post Chapter XXVI.

307. We think with Mr. Maltby that it will be more proper to provide generally for the offence of removing, destroying, or defacing property marks, in this chapter, and we would suggest that the following clause be added to it accordingly :

" Whoever removes, or destroys, or defaces any property mark, intend-
" ing or knowing it to be likely that he may thereby cause injury to any
" party, shall be punished with imprisonment of either description which
" may extend to one year, or fine, or both."

CHAPTER XXII.

OF THE ILLEGAL PURSUIT OF LEGAL RIGHTS.

308. It is explained in Note O that "this chapter is intended to "prevent the enforcing of just claims by means which are so liable to be "abused that, even when used for an honest end, they ought not to be "tolerated. A creditor, for example, who has repeatedly in vain urged "his debtor to pay him, finds that he has no chance of recovering "his money without a troublesome and expensive law suit. He accord-"ingly seizes on property belonging to the debtor, sells it, keeps only "just as much as will satisfy the debt, and sends back the surplus to the "debtor. This act is distinguished from theft by one of the broadest "lines of demarcation which can be found in the Code. It is not a "fraudulent act. It is intended to correct a wrongful distribution of "property, to do what the Courts of Law, if recourse were had to them, "would order to be done. Public feeling would be shocked if such a "creditor were called by the ignominious name of a thief."

"At the same time it cannot be doubted that it would be most "dangerous to allow men to pronounce judgment, however honestly, in "their own favour, and to proceed to take property in execution, for "the purpose of satisfying that judgment. A specific thing, indeed, "which a man has a right to possess, it is no offence in him to take "wherever he finds it." "This license, as it appears to us," say the Commissioners, "must be confined to cases in which specific things are "taken. In such cases the chance of abuse is very small. But where "one thing is due, and another is taken, where a man seizes on another's "furniture in satisfaction of a promissory note, or drives away another's "cattle by way of paying himself for a suit of clothes, the case is very "different." "In such cases, we think it absolutely necessary to provide "a punishment for the illegal pursuit of legal rights."

309. Mr. Norton says, "This whole chapter appears to me so "obviously open, on the very face of it, to every species of objection "arising from uncertainty of meaning and application, to say nothing "of its utter inexpediency in principle, that I do not feel occasion to "expend much observation upon it. It appears to me to be a law whose "operation depends altogether upon proof of the *belief* and *secret* and "*future intentions* of a party, whose act, *in itself* gives no proof or "indication of what such belief, or intention, or object may be. If a "man takes property under circumstances proved, which shew he did "so under *color*, or in assertion, *of right*, I should suppose that, under "any law but this, he would be guiltless of *crime*. But under this law "the question of criminality in taking the property under these circum-"stances is made to depend on what he may *happen afterwards* to do "with it—or rather upon *what intention* he may be supposed to have, or "subsequently to form, about the property. So, on the other hand, if he "clearly takes the property *without any color of right* whatever—yet "the criminality of the act is under this law made to depend on the "result of some inquiry, or of some impression on the part of those who "try him, as to what he *intended* at the time to do with the property—"and even upon the intention he may subsequently conceive."

310. These observations appear to us to be by no means just. First, we can scarcely suppose Mr. Norton to mean that if a man takes *not* the specific thing to which he has a right, but something which he considers to be of equal value, in lieu of it, or that, in a case of debt, if A owes B a thousand rupees, and B being unable to get the money from him, takes from the possession of A, without his consent, goods of his to the same value, B "would be held guiltless of crime under any law but this." But as explained in the passage cited above from Note O, "a "specific thing which a man has a right to possess, it is no offence in "him (under this law) to take wherever he finds it." "He may com-"mit other offences in order to take it. But the mere taking is no "crime at all."

311. Next, under this law the question of criminality in taking the property is *not* "made to depend on what he (the party taking) may happen afterwards to do with it." It depends simply on the intention with which he took it, as evidenced either by his expression at the time, or by the manner and circumstances of the taking, or by both together, as in all other cases in which the intention or animus determines the question of guilt or innocence.

312. Under Clause 460 a man taking property under such circumstances that, if his intention were fraudulent, he would be guilty of theft, escapes from the imputation of that crime, if by the evidence it appears that he took the property, not fraudulently but in good faith, in order to obtain summary satisfaction of a debt, but he is amenable to the law for pursuing his right in an unlawful manner. As the ordinary discovery of the *animus furandi* is where the party commits the fact clandestinely, or upon its being laid to his charge denies it: so, to apply with some variation words used originally to distinguish trespass from theft, if a man takes away the goods of another openly before him or other persons, otherwise than by apparent robbery, this carries with it an evidence negativing fraudulent intention, because done openly in the presence of the owner, or of other persons who are known to the owner; and this negative evidence will be strong where a person having possessed himself of the goods of another, avows the fact before he is questioned, or if at the time of taking the goods or before he is questioned he declares his object to be the recovery of a debt due to him by the sale of them, and his intention to return any surplus there may be from the proceeds of the sale, and if his acts correspond with such declaration. Again, it can only be discovered by means "of some inquiry" such as is always made before a man is put upon his trial for any offence, whether the property was taken "without any color of right," and where this appears, and where the taking appears to have been clandestine, and concealment to have been practised subsequently, there will be a strong presumption of a fraudulent intention such as will bring the taking under the definition of theft. It is obvious to remark that where there is not "a color of right" in the taking the plea of "good faith" must be excluded, so that such a case could not be brought under Clause 460.

Russell 2, p. 96.

313. By Clause 461, although it may appear that property was taken at first in good faith without a fraudulent intention for the purpose merely of enabling the party who took it to recover a debt, yet if the whole or any part of it is *kept* fraudulently, the party so keeping it is made liable to the same punishment as if the taking had been fraudulent. This is the case which Mr. Norton appears to allude to as one in which the criminality appears to depend "upon the intention he (the party taking the property) may subsequently conceive." We can see no objection to the provision. The party is punished not for his first offence, the *taking*, in which there was no fraudulent intention, but for the subsequent distinct offence of *retaining*, in which there is a fraudulent intention, a retaining with the intention of causing thereby a wrongful gain to one party, and a wrongful loss to another party from whom the property is kept.

314. Of "the utter inexpediency on principle" which Mr. Norton imputes to the whole chapter, we can only say, as generally, that we are unable to perceive any reason for the imputation.

315. Mr. Giberne, a Judge of the Bombay Sudder Court, observes that this chapter is much required. Mr. Bannerman, a Judge of the Madras Presidency, says, "such cases," that is cases comprehended by the provisions of this chapter, "form a great portion of the wrong which goes unredressed."

316. Mr. Greenhill puts the following question:—"A lends B his "horse, owing B money, B refuses to return the horse till paid. Under "what clause does this come? B does not take the horse from A's "possession in the manner punishable by the letter of this clause. It "does not tally with any of the illustrations of Chapter XIX, and it "does not come under the head of criminal breach of trust, because it is "not fraudulent."

317. The question here is, would A be guilty of the theft under the circumstances stated if his intention were fraudulent? which we think may be answered by help of the illustration (*w*) under Clause 363. From this illustration it may be inferred that if A took the horse lent to him by B, fraudulently, intending to carry it away altogether, or to sell it and appropriate the price of it, he would be guilty of theft; and if so it follows that taking the horse intending at the time, not to return it, as implicitly promised by his receiving it on loan from B, but to appropriate it for the satisfaction of the debt due to him by B, he is guilty of the offence defined in Clause 460.

CHAPTER XXIII.

OF THE CRIMINAL BREACH OF CONTRACTS OF SERVICE.

318. In Note P upon this chapter, the Commissioners say, "We "agree with the great body of Jurists in thinking that, in general, a "mere breach of contract ought not to be an offence, but only to be "the subject of a civil action."

"To this general rule there are however some exceptions. Some "breaches of contract are very likely to cause evil such as no damages, "or only very high damages, can repair, and are also very likely to be "committed by persons from whom it is exceedingly improbable that "any damages can be obtained. Such breaches of contract are, we "conceive, proper subjects for penal legislation."

319. The Commissioners observe that the law they have framed on this subject applies only to cases in which the contract is lawful. "The "traveller, therefore, who resorts to the highly culpable, though, we "fear, too common practice of unlawfully compelling persons against "their will to carry his palanquin or his baggage will not be protected "by it. If they quit him, it is what they have a legal right to do, "nor will they be punishable whatever may be the consequence of their "desertion."

320. Clause 463 contains the general law on the subject. Clause 464 contains a special provision for the punishment of seamen in merchant vessels for breaches of the contract by which they are bound to their employers. "The insubordination of seamen during a voyage," it is observed, "often produces fatal consequences." "Their desertion "in port may cause evils such as very large damages only could repair. "But they are utterly unable to pay any damages for which it would be "worth while to sue." Clause 465 provides specially for the punishment of persons engaged to take care of infants, of the sick, and of the helpless, who omit to discharge their duty. The reason of this special provision is that "the misery and distress which their neglect may cause "is such as the largest pecuniary payment would not repair," and that "they generally come from the lower ranks of life, and would be unable "to pay any thing."

321. Sir R. Comyn remarks, that this chapter introduces a novelty in our criminal jurisprudence, but the reasons for it, in Note P, he considers satisfactory.

322. Of the many other persons who have offered remarks on this chapter, all but Mr. Norton appear to approve of it as far as it goes. Mr. Norton says, "There may be no sound objection to the rendering "*some sorts* of contract of service criminal, but I conceive those particu- "lar breaches of service should be specifically designated, and that a law "making *all sorts* of breaches of contract to *convey* persons or property, "all sorts of illegal *disobedience* or leaving of a vessel *by a seaman, all* "sorts of omission in attendance or *supplying wants of helpless* persons "by their servants, criminal, and punishable by various degrees of "imprisonment, or fine, or both, is carried to a preposterous extent."

323. On the other hand many think the law ought to be more comprehensive. Mr. A. D. Campbell, Judge of the Madras Sudder Court, says, "For the reasons given by the officers in the interior, I would "extend this chapter to the punishment of servants quitting their "masters without giving a month's previous warning. It is a great "evil to individuals, and when troops are ordered suddenly to march, "becomes a public evil."

324. The Sudder Court, North-Western Provinces, "think that some "provision might justly be made to meet the contingency of servants "quitting their master's service without notice, while on a march or "during a journey—their sudden departure on such occasions must "almost necessarily involve much embarrassment and inconvenience."

325. Mr. Giberne, Judge of the Bombay Sudder Court, says, "con-"sidering the state of society in the East, I think a law is required "to protect both masters and servants. Often are the former put to "painful inconvenience and annoyance by servants refusing to go to a "distant station, on the very eve of departure, although they have "received sufficient notice and were before inclined to go. Servants "on the other hand may be turned off, at a moment's warning. I "would have recommended that a month's pay be given, or a fine "imposed to that amount."

326. Mr. F. Lewin observes that "whole sets of servants constantly "desert young officers after a few marches to join Regiments, after they "have cheated him out of all his ready cash; and the misconduct of "servants generally to ladies is often just as distressing as that of "palanquin bearers," (referred to by the Commissioners by way of illustration) "when they are unprotected." Mr. Blane and Mr. E. C. Monckton likewise strongly insist upon the evil arising from servants engaged for a journey or a march suddenly deserting their employers at the time of setting out or on the road, as rendering such a breach of contract a proper subject for penal legislation, on the ground stated in the 2nd para. of Note P.

327. Several of the gentlemen who argue for an extension of Clause 463, or an additional provision to include servants deserting their employers in breach of an engagement to proceed with them on a journey, would go further than this, to the length of punishing every menial servant who before the expiration of the term for which he is hired, or without a certain notice, quits his employer, which is authorized by Section 6, Regulation VII of 1819 of the Bengal Code, and some to the length of punishing such servants generally for omission or negligent performance of their duty, which is authorized by Section 18, Regulation XII of 1827 of the Bombay Code and by the Police Regulations of Calcutta and Madras. A Native Officer, *v.* Sreenavasiah, Naib Sherishtadar of Chinglepnt in the Presidency of Madras, in reference to the remark of the Commissioners that it does not appear that good masters are in much danger of being voluntarily deserted by their menial servants, observes that though this may be true as regards European masters, it is not the case with Natives, where each man must be served by the lower orders of his own caste; meaning we conceive that this limitation to one class narrows the market so much as to make their servants careless of pleasing their masters as being sure of employment.

328. With reference to Mr. Norton's censure we have to observe, that the proposed law does *not* "make *all sorts* of breaches of contract to convey persons or property criminal," but only a breach of such a contract by a person intending or knowing it to be likely that his illegal omission to fulfil it will cause injury to some person. Again with respect to the clause regarding seamen, it appears to us that the terms "*illegally* leaving a vessel," and "*illegal* disobedience of orders," are sufficiently definite, and that there cannot be many *sorts* of illegal leaving or illegal disobedience to perplex a Magistrate or Judge who might be called upon to apply the law.

329. We are inclined to agree with those who consider that the extension of Clause 463 to menial servants engaged for a journey is recommended by the same reasons as induced the Commissioners to propose the provisions now contained in it. We are not prepared to punish as a criminal every menial servant who quits his employer without a certain notice upon the expiration of the term for which he is hired, under ordinary circumstances. But we conceive that Clause 465 may be improved in one respect. It seems, as it stands, not to be applicable to any but those servants who have contracted specifically to attend upon the sick, insane, &c., but we think it should be made to apply to servants who are or ought to be in attendance upon a sick or insane master, though they may have only contracted with him in the ordinary way, while he was of sound body and mind, and to servants, whether engaged specifically for the purpose or not, who by the lawful command of their employers have been ordered to take care of young children and have not objected to do so.

330. Sir R. Comyn considers the provision contained in Clause 464 for offences committed by seamen inadequate to enforce subordination on board a ship, and observes that the leniency of it is a contrast to the severity of existing Acts of Parliament relating to Shipping. Acts of insubordination, especially when accompanied with violence, he thinks ought to be viewed in a more serious light than criminal breaches of contract. He suggests that there should be a separate chapter for offences on board ship. We think it proper to mention the views thus expressed by Sir R. Comyn for the consideration of Government, but we are not prepared to recommend any alteration in the clause, which of course would not prevent a seaman from being subject to punishment for any act or omission which is an offence.

CHAPTER XXIV.

OF OFFENCES RELATING TO MARRIAGE.

331. By this chapter it is made an offence in a man by deceit to cause a woman to believe that she is lawfully married to him and in that belief to cohabit with him, when the marriage is not lawful. It is an offence also in a woman so to deceive a man. Here the essence of the offence is the deceit operating injury, but as the injury is much greater when the woman is the sufferer, the punishment is made much more severe in the former case than in the latter. Again it is made an offence for any man or woman with any fraudulent intention to go through the ceremony of being married knowing that such marriage is not lawful. Here there may be no deceit as between the parties, but there must be an intention to defraud, within the meaning of Clause 16, as when the pretence of a lawful marriage may enable the parties to obtain possession of property settled to come to one of them on marriage.

Clause 466.

Clause 467.

Clause 468.

332. Under these provisions bigamy is punishable, where the law of the parties forbids a second marriage while the first is undissolved, but only when a deception is practised, or fraud is intended. "We do not," say the authors of the Code, "at present propose any law for punishing a person who, "without practising any deception, or intending any fraud, goes through "the forms of a marriage which he knows to be invalid. The difficulty "of framing such a law in this country is great. To make all classes "subject to one law would, evidently, be impossible. If the law be made "dependent on the race, birth-place, or religion of the offender endless "perplexity would arise. Races are mixed; religion may be changed or "dissembled. An East Indian, half English, half Asiatic by blood, may "call himself a Mahomedan, or a Hindoo, and there exists no test by "which he can be convicted of deception."

See Appendix, Note Q, page 172.

333. In not providing for the punishment of bigamy not aggravated by deception or fraud, the Code differs materially from the law of England as it now stands, but not as it stood before the reign of James the First. On account of this omission the Code has been severely censured, and, as Mr. Norton remarks, "much public abuse has been expended upon it."

Blackstone 4, 163.

334. The authors of the Code apparently anticipating that its provisions would be regarded as defective on this point, and admitting that from the deep interest which society has in the sacredness of the matrimonial contract, it may be justifiable to punish those who go through the forms of that contract for the purpose of imposing on the public, without deception *between the parties* or any *fraudulent intention*, suggest for the consideration of Government whether, pending inquiry into the various laws of marriage prevailing in India, "it might not be, on the "whole, better to retain the existing law applicable to "Christians in India, objectionable as that law is, than to allow absolute "impunity to bigamy."

See Appendix, Note Q, page 172.

Page 173.

335. They consider the English law objectionable because being "framed less for the purpose of preventing people from injuring each "other than for the purpose of preventing the profanation of a religious "ceremony," "it makes no distinction between bigamy which produces "most frightful suffering, and bigamy which produces no suffering to "individuals," as instanced in the two cases stated in the Note.

336. We do not see why Christians should not be made subject to the provisions of this chapter as it stands, for bigamy aggravated by deception or fraud, by which what is considered objectionable in the English law would be avoided, even should a new provision be introduced retaining the English law, with respect to them, for bigamy without such aggravation.

337. The present law applicable to Christians in India is contained in Section 70 of the Statute 9, Geo. IV, Cap. 74. The punishment is transportation for seven years or imprisonment not exceeding two years. The punishment might be confined to imprisonment not exceeding two years, if cases of aggravation were left to be dealt with under the provisions of Clauses 466 to 468. The new provision might run thus—"Whoever, professing the Christian religion, being married, shall marry "any other person during the life of the former husband or wife, whether "the second marriage shall have taken place within the Territories of "the East India Company or elsewhere, shall be punished with simple "imprisonment for a term which may extend to two years, and shall also "be liable to fine." Then might follow the exceptions specified in Section 70 of the said Act.

338. We believe that such a provision would satisfy most of the objectors to this chapter, who do not find fault with the proposed law so far as it goes, but find fault with it for not going farther—who think with Mr. Giberne, Judge of the Sudder Court at Bombay, that by this chapter as it stands "Polygamy is so far allowed to the English in India that provided no deceit is practised no penalty is enacted for the crime." Sir R. Comyn and others particularly express assent to the suggestion of applying the existing law relating to bigamy to Christians in India.

339. For ourselves we must say that we do not perceive that the difficulty adverted to by the authors of the Code as an impediment to a general law for punishing a person who without practising any deception or intending any fraud goes through the forms of a marriage which he *knows to be invalid*, is of more force in this case than in the cases provided for by Clauses 466 to 468, particularly where, as by Clause 468, the guilt of the party depends on his *knowing that he is not lawfully married* by the forms he goes through.

340. We are of opinion that the maximum punishment authorized by Clause 466, viz., imprisonment which may extend to 14 years, is excessive. We would limit it to seven years, the maximum term of transportation under the Statute 9, Geo. IV, Cap. 74. And we would extend the punishment to be awarded under Clause 467 to two years, to correspond with the new provision above suggested.

341. With reference to the minimum fixed by Clause 466, Sir H. Seton puts the following case:—"A believing his former wife to be dead "marries B. He afterwards discovers that she is alive, but conceals the "fact from B." "Must A," he asks, "be imprisoned for not less than "two years?" Under such circumstances A would no doubt be liable to conviction by the terms of Clause 466, and he must of course be sentenced to punishment accordingly. Under the English law, A having married a second wife believing his first wife to be dead, but the period of seven years not having passed since he knew she was alive, would be liable to punishment for bigamy, if it appeared she was not dead at the time of the second marriage, but it would be at the discretion of the Judge to pass a light sentence if he thought the case did not call for severity. The case put by Sir H. Seton certainly is one not calling for severity. It may be advisable not to fetter the discretion of the Judge by prescribing a minimum—or it may be reduced to one year.

342. Mr. F. N. Maltby points out what he considers "an important omission under the head of offences relating to marriage" that it does not provide for the "very serious crime of marrying a party without the "intelligent consent of the party, or of guardians competent by the laws "of their religion, to act for the party." He mentions a case which had lately occurred, in which "a Hindoo girl of 6 or 7 years old was left for "a few days by the father and mother at the house of a relation. This "relation, without the consent of either party, married the child to a "relation of his own, a man of about 30 years old."

343. It seems to us that such a case as this amounts to the offence of "kidnapping from lawful guardianship" defined in Clause 354, as it might be alleged that the child had been *conveyed out of the keeping of the lawful guardian* under a *consent obtained by deception or concealment as to the future treatment of the child, for a purpose of injury to the child*, that is for the purpose of marrying her improperly. We conceive that the relation who gave the child in marriage under the circumstances stated would be liable under this law as principal, and the man who married her as an abettor. We are not prepared to recommend a more express provision to punish a party marrying a woman child who is under the age at which the law makes her responsible for her actions, and of course assumes her to be capable of giving an intelligent consent, without the consent of her guardian. When a party marries a woman above that age without her consent, he will probably have done something which will make him liable to punishment under some of the provisions regarding assault, or "wrongful restraint," or "wrongful confinement," or "criminal intimidation."

Clauses 31 and 65.

344. Adultery, which is recognized as an offence by the existing laws for the administration of criminal justice in the Company's Courts in all the Presidencies, and for regulating the punishment of which in the Territories under the Presidency of Bombay an Act was lately passed by the Government of India, is not made an offence by this Code. The reasons for omitting it are thus stated in the Note upon the chapter under consideration.

Act II, 1845.

Note Q, p. 173.

"We considered whether it would be advisable to provide a punish- "ment for adultery, and in order to enable ourselves to come to a right "conclusion on this subject we collected facts and opinions from all the "three Presidencies. The opinions differ widely. But as to the facts "there is a remarkable agreement."

"The following positions we consider as fully established, first, that "the existing laws for the punishment of adultery are altogether "inefficacious for the purpose of preventing injured husbands of the "higher classes from taking the law into their own hands; secondly, that "scarcely any native of the higher classes ever has recourse to the Courts "of law in a case of adultery for redress against either his wife or her "gallant; thirdly, that the husbands who have recourse in cases of "adultery to the Courts of law are generally poor men whose wives have "run away, that these husbands seldom have any delicate feelings about "the intrigue, but think themselves injured by the elopement, that they "consider their wives as useful members of their small households, that "they generally complain not of the wound given to their affections, not "of the stain on their honor, but of the loss of a menial whom they "cannot easily replace, and that generally their principal object is that "the woman may be sent back. The fiction by which seduction is made "the subject of an action in the English Courts is, it seems, the real gist "of most proceedings for adultery in the Mofussil. The essence of the "injury is considered by the sufferer as lying in the '*per quod servitium* "*amisit.*' Where the complainant does not ask to have his wife again, he "generally demands to be reimbursed for the expenses of his marriage."

"These things being established, it seems to us that no advantage is "to be expected from providing a punishment for adultery. The popu- "lation seems to be divided into two classes—those whom neither the "existing punishment nor any punishment which we should feel ourselves "justified in proposing will satisfy, and those who consider the injury "produced by adultery as one for which a pecuniary compensation will "sufficiently atone. Those whose feelings of honor are painfully affected "by the infidelity of their wives will not apply to the tribunals at all. "Those whose feelings are less delicate will be satisfied by a payment of "money. Under such circumstances we think it best to treat adultery "merely as a civil injury."

"Some who admit that the penal law now existing on this subject is "in practice of little or no use, yet think that the Code ought to contain "a provision against adultery. They think that such a provision, though "inefficacious for the repressing of vice, would be creditable to the "Indian Government, and that by omitting such a provision we should "give a sanction to immorality. They say, and we believe with truth, "that the higher class of natives consider the existing penal law on the "subject as far too lenient, and are unable to understand on what "principle adultery is treated with more tenderness than forgery or "perjury."

345. Upon these points the Commissioners observe as follows: "That "some classes of the natives of India disapprove of the lenity with which "adultery is now punished we fully believe, but this in our opinion is a "strong argument against punishing adultery at all. There are only "two courses which in our opinion can properly be followed with respect "to this and other great immoralities. They ought to be punished very "severely, or they ought not to be punished at all. The circumstance "that they are left altogether unpunished does not prove that the Legis- "lature does not regard them with disapprobation. But when they are "made punishable the degree of severity of the punishment will always "be considered as indicating the degree of disapprobation with which "the Legislature regards them. We have no doubt that the natives "would be far less shocked by the total silence of the penal law touching "adultery than by seeing an adulterer sent to prison for a few months "while a coiner is imprisoned for fourteen years."

"Nobody," they proceed, "proposes that adultery should be punished "with a severity at all proportioned to the misery which it produces in "cases where there is strong affection and a quick sensibility to family "honor. We apprehend that among the higher classes in this country "nothing short of death would be considered as an expiation for such "a wrong. In such a state of society we think it far better that the "law should inflict no punishment, than that it should inflict a punish- "ment which would be regarded as absurdly and immorally lenient."

346. Lastly, the Commissioners advert to "some peculiarities in the "state of society in this country which they observe may well lead a "humane man to pause before he determines to punish the infidelity of "wives. The condition of women of this country is unhappily very "different from that of the women of England and France. They are "married while still children. They are often neglected for other wives "while still young. They share the attentions of a husband with several "rivals. To make laws for punishing the inconstancy of the wife while "the law admits the privilege of the husband to fill his zenana with "women, is a course which we are most reluctant to adopt."

347. Colonel Sleeman opposes the reasoning of the Commissioners on this subject. The backwardness of the natives to have recourse to the Courts for redress in cases of adultery he asserts "arises from the utter hopelessness on their "part of ever getting a conviction in our Courts upon any evidence that "such cases admit of," that is to say in Courts in which the Mahomedan Law is observed. "The rich man," he proceeds, "not only feels the "assurance that he could not get a conviction but dreads the disgrace "of appearing publicly in one Court after another, to prove, by numerous "witnesses, male and female, his own shame and his wife's dishonor. "He has recourse to poison secretly or with his wife's consent; and "she will generally rather take it than be turned out into the streets a "degraded outcast. The seducer escapes with impunity—he suffers "nothing, while his poor victim suffers all that human nature is capable "of enduring. Many instances of this have come within my own know- "ledge. The silence of the Penal Code will give still greater impunity "to the seducer, while their victims will in three cases out of four be "murdered or driven to commit suicide. Where husbands are in the "habit of poisoning their guilty wives from the want of legal means of "redress, they will sometimes poison those who are suspected upon in- "sufficient grounds, and the innocent will suffer."

Letter, 18th February 1840.

"At present I believe no Magistrate could hope to get a conviction "in a Court of Sessions against any person charged with adultery under "Regulation XVII of 1817 in one case out of a hundred that might "take place in his district. His only resource would be in Regulation "VII of 1819, which authorises him to punish a person convicted of "enticing or taking away a wife or unmarried daughter for the purpose "of rendering her a prostitute. But this law which provides for another "class (pimps) can seldom be so strained as to reach this class of offender, "the seducer, and few Magistrates feel disposed so to strain it for the "purpose. That men do not seek redress in our Courts for the seduction "of their wives and daughters arises from the defects of the law, and "these defects may easily be remedied. It is an error to suppose that "the natives of India want a heavier sentence—all they want is a fair "chance of conviction, and such a measure of punishment as shall make "it appear that their rulers think the crime a serious one, and are dis- "posed to protect them from it.

"Sometimes the poorest persons will refuse pecuniary compensations; "but generally they will be glad to get what the heads of their caste or "circle of society may consider sufficient to defray the expenses of a "second marriage. They dare not live in adultery—they would be out-"casts if they did—they must be married according to the forms of their "caste, and it is reasonable that the seducer of the wife should be made "to defray these expenses for the injured husband. The rich will of "course always refuse pecuniary compensation, and for the same reason "that they would never prosecute the seducer in a Civil Court. The "poor could never afford so to prosecute in such a Court; and, as I have "said, the silence of the Penal Code would be a solemn pledge of "impunity to the guilty seducer, under an efficient Government like ours "that can prevent the husband and father from revenging themselves "except upon the females."

Letter, 6th March 1840.

348. In support of his opinion as to the causes which deter the people from applying to our Courts in general, Colonel Sleeman observes that in the Sangor and Nerbudda Territories where those causes did not exist he did not find that the injured husband was unwilling to prosecute the seducer of his wife. "In the Nerbudda Territories," he says, "the Regulations were not in "force, and the husband had to prosecute the seducer of his wife in our "Court only, that of the European officer in charge of the District, and "in that Court there was no Mahommedan Law officer, or Mahommedan "Law of Evidence to be considered. The maximum of punishment "amounted to two years' imprisonment, or fine, or both." He infers that "when the impediments to redress of such wrongs shall be removed in "the same manner in all other parts of India by diminishing the punish-"ment to such a minimum measure as the Magistrate's Court may be "competent to award, and by doing away with the necessity of a "Mahommedan Law officer in such trials, the people will in all parts "be found ready to seek redress through the constituted tribunals, and "the seducer will then, and not till then, share danger with the seduced."

349. The following are the observations of the Sudder Court, North-Western Provinces, on this chapter: "With reference to the arguments "of the Commissioners and to the difficulty so clearly set forth in the "Notes, the Court have no objection to the exclusion of penal provisions "for adultery from the Code; which does not, however, appear to "contemplate any punishment for enticing away females, married or "unmarried, from their legal protectors, and that seems to them a defect. "The Court believe that Regulation VII of 1819 has been found in "practice to be a very useful enactment, and well suited to the feelings "of the lower classes of the community, who, in cases of wives leaving "their husbands, can by its provisions, get the crime of seduction "punished without their dishonor being brought prominently forward, "the female being induced by fair promises, on the seducer being sent "to jail, to return, and domestic harmony restored."

350. The following remarks we notice as coming from a Bramin, v. Streenevasiah, Deputy Sherishtadar under the Collector and Magistrate of Chingleput. Dissenting from the opinion of the Commissioners that it is not advisable to provide a punishment for adultery, he says, "The chief ground of this opinion is the prevalence of polygamy "in this country, but it is doubtful whether the Commissioners have "taken into their consideration under what circumstances and restric-"tions polygamy is allowed. The Hindoo Law permits it only in cases "where a wife first married was proved barren after a trial of 12 years, "or is afflicted with an irrecoverable disease, or addicted to irremediable "unvirtuous habits, provided these qualities have been established to the "satisfaction of society in which the parties move. It must also be "remembered, that it is not only in cases where a man has more than "one wife that adultery is committed, but women who are the only "wives of their husbands, and to whose comfort and happiness all "possible attention is paid, often corrupt their chastity in consequence "of immoderate lust, or any defect in the graces or qualities of their "husbands, or from want of reciprocal affection, or such other causes not "less forcible than that of having rivals; which cannot therefore justify "the commission of adultery. Offences of this kind are inexcusable "under any circumstances, and whatever may be their inherent causes."

351. As to the alleged reluctance of the natives to prosecute in cases of adultery, he says, "If the higher classes of natives shew little or "no desire to bring their corrupt wives to justice, and if the lower class "content themselves with a compensation which would enable them to "re-marry, it is partly owing to the indignation which a public prosecu-"tion causes, and the helpless condition of the poor, and partly to the "implied indifference with which the unchastity of females is understood "to be viewed by European Judges."

352. We have observed that adultery is recognized as an offence by the existing laws of all the Presidencies, and that an Act has been lately passed by the Governor-General of India in Council for regulating the punishment of the offence in the Bombay Territories. Adultery is punishable by the Code Penal of France. It is provided for in the Code of Louisiana. The following are Mr. Livingstone's observations on the subject: "Whether adultery "should be considered as an offence against public morality, or left to "the operation of the civil laws, has been the subject of much discus-"sion. As far as I am informed, it figures in the penal law of all nations, "except the English; and some of their most celebrated Lawyers have "considered the omission as a defect."

Act II of 1845.

"Neither the immorality of the act, nor its injurious consequences on "the happiness of females, and very frequently on the peace of society "and the lives of its members, can be denied. The reason, then, why "it should go unpunished, does not seem very clear. It is emphati-"cally one of that nature to which I have just referred, in which the "resentment of the injured party will prompt him to take vengeance into "his own hands, and commit a greater offence, if the laws of his country "refuse to punish the lesser. It is the nature of man, and no legislation "can alter it, to protect himself where the laws refuse their aid; very "frequently where they do not; but where they will not give protection "against injury, it is in vain that they attempt to punish him who supplies "by his own energy their remissness. Where the law refuses to punish "this offence, the injured party will do it for himself; he will break the "public peace, and commit the greatest of all crimes, and he is rarely "or never punished. Assaults, duels, assassinations, poisonings, will be "the consequence. They cannot be prevented; but, perhaps, by giving "the aid of the law to punish the offence, which they are intended to "avenge, they will be less frequent; and it will, by taking away the "pretext for the atrocious acts, in a great measure insure the infliction "of the punishment they deserve. It is for these reasons that the "offence of adultery forms a chapter of this title."

353. Having given mature consideration to the subject, we have after some hesitation come to the conclusion, that it is not advisable to exclude this offence from the Code. We think the reasons for continuing to treat it as a subject for the cognizance of the Criminal Courts preponderate. We conceive that Colonel Sleeman is probably right in regarding the difficulty of proving the offence according to the requirement of the Mahomedan Law of Evidence, which demands an amount of positive proof that is scarcely ever to be had in such a case, as having some effect in deterring the natives from prosecuting adulterers in our Courts, although the Regulations allow of a conviction upon strong presumption arising from circumstantial evidence. This difficulty, if it has had the effect supposed, will be removed should the Code be adopted. Colonel Sleeman's representation of the actual consequences of the present system, which while it recognizes the offence renders it in the opinion of the natives almost impossible to bring an offender to justice, it will be observed, coincides with, and confirms practically, Mr. Livingstone's view of the result to be expected when the law refuses to punish this offence. The injured party will do it for himself—great crimes—assassinations—poisonings—will be the consequence. The law here does not refuse, but it fails to punish the offence, says Colonel Sleeman, and poisonings *are* the consequence.

354. Colonel Sleeman thinks that the Commissioners have wrongly assumed that it is the lenity of the existing law that is complained of by the natives, and believes that they would be satisfied with a less punishment for the offence than the present law allows, viz., imprisonment for seven years, if it were certain to follow the offender. He proposes that the punishment of a man "convicted of *seducing* the wife of another" shall be imprisonment which may extend to seven years, or a fine payable to the husband, or both imprisonment and fine. The punishment of a married woman "convicted of *adultery*" he would limit to imprisonment for two years. We are not aware whether or not he intends the difference in the terms used to be significant of a difference in the nature of the proof against the man and the woman respectively.

355. While we think that the offence of adultery ought not to be omitted from the Code, we would limit its cognizance to adultery committed with a married woman, and considering that there is much weight in the last remark in Note Q, regarding the condition of the women of this country, in deference to it we would render the male offender alone liable to punishment. We would however put the parties accused of adultery on trial together, and empower the Court in the event of their conviction to pronounce a decree of divorce against the guilty woman, if the husband sues for it, at the same time that her paramour is sentenced to punishment by imprisonment or fine. By Mr. Livingstone's Code the woman forfeits her "matrimonial gains," but is not liable to other punishment.

356. We would adopt Colonel Sleeman's suggestion as to the punishment of the male offender, limiting it to imprisonment not exceeding five years, instead of seven years allowed at present, and sanctioning the imposition of a fine payable to the husband as an alternative, or in addition.

357. The punishment prescribed by the Code of Louisiana is imprisonment not more than six months, or fine not exceeding 2,000 dollars, or both. By the French Code, the maximum term of imprisonment is two years with fine in addition, which may amount to 2,000 Francs.

358. If the offence of adultery is admitted into the Penal Code, there should be a provision in the Code of Procedure to restrict the right of prosecuting to the injured husband, agreeably to Section 2, Act II of 1845.

359. Colonel Sleeman conjoins the offence of seducing the daughter of any person with that of seducing a married woman, and proposes to render it liable to the same punishment. We conceive that this offence so far as it is proper to treat it as penal, falls within the definition of "kidnapping a child from lawful guardianship" in Clause 354, which applies to any child under 12 years of age. We observe that Colonel Sleeman proposes that in the clause here referred to, the age should be extended to 14 years, but seeing that 12 years is the age at which by this Code every person is assumed to have attained sufficient maturity of understanding to judge of the nature and consequences of his or her conduct and to give an intelligent consent, such extension does not appear to us to be expedient. Whoever conveys a female above the age of 12 years out of the keeping of her lawful guardian without her "free consent," will be liable to punishment as guilty of "assault or wrongful restraint," &c., according to the circumstances.

CHAPTER XXV.

OF DEFAMATION.

360. Defamation is defined in Clause 469 as follows:—"Whoever, "by words either spoken or intended to be read, or by signs, or by "visible representations, attempts to cause any imputation concerning "any person to be believed in any quarter knowing that the belief "thereof would harm the reputation of that person in that quarter, "is said, except in the cases excepted in the nine clauses next following, "to defame that person."

361. It is explained that no imputation "is said 'to harm a person's "reputation' unless that imputation directly or indirectly lowers the "moral or intellectual character of that person, or lowers the character "of that person in respect of his caste or of his calling, or lowers the "commercial credit of that person if he is engaged in trade, or causes it "to be believed that the body of that person is in a loathsome state, or "in a state generally considered as disgraceful."

362. In the Digest submitted by the English Criminal Law Commissioners with their 7th Report, under the head of Libel, are the following definitions:

Chapter XVI, Libel.

Art. 1.—"A libel consists in some matter or meaning injurious to "individuals or to the public, as in this Act defined, "and expressed or signified by any written, printed, "painted or other representations, characters or signs, "or by effigies, dramatic performances or other visible devices."

Art. 2.—"A personal libel is one which expresses or signifies any "contumelious, defamatory or opprobrious matter or meaning designed "to insult or injure any living person, or to disgrace the memory of one "who is dead, and thereby to excite any person to wrath."

Art. 3.—"The terms 'defamatory matter or meaning' as used in the "last preceding article, comprehend any matter or meaning which tends "to injure the reputation, character, or credit of any person, or to render "him odious, contemptible, or ridiculous; or to injure him in his office, "profession, or occupation; or to exclude him from the benefit and "comfort of society."

363. An essential difference between the definition given in the Indian Code and that contained in the Digest of the English criminal law is that the former recognizes "words spoken" as a mode of defamation, and the latter does not.

See Appendix, Note R, page 176.

364. Upon this point the authors of the Code say:—"We considered "whether it would be advisable to make a distinction "between the different modes in which defamatory "imputations may be conveyed: and we came to the "conclusion that it would not be advisable to make any such distinc- "tion."

"By the English law, defamation is a crime only when it is commit- "ted by writing, printing, engraving, or some similar process. Spoken "words reflecting on private character, however atrocious may be the "imputations which those words convey, however numerous may be the "assembly before which such words are uttered, furnish ground only for "a civil action. Herein the English law is scarcely consistent with "itself. For if defamation be punished on account of its tendency to "cause breach of the peace, spoken defamation ought to be punished even "more severely than written defamation, as having that tendency in a "higher degree. A person who reads in a pamphlet a calumnious reflec- "tion on himself, or on some one for whom he is interested, is less likely "to take a violent revenge than a person who hears the same calumnious "reflection uttered. Public men who have, by long habit, become cal- "lous to slander and abuse in a printed form, often shew acute sensibili- "ty to imputations thrown on them to their faces. Indeed defamatory "words spoken in the presence of the person who is the object of them, "necessarily have more of the character of a personal affront, and are "therefore more likely to cause breach of the peace, than any printed "libel."

"The distinction which the English criminal law makes between "written and spoken defamation is generally defended on the ground "that written defamation is likely to be more widely spread and to be "more permanent than spoken defamation. These considerations do "not appear to us to be entitled to much weight. In the first place it "is by no means necessarily the fact that written defamation is more "extensively circulated than spoken defamation. Written defamation "may be contained in a letter intended for a single eye. Spoken defam- "ation may be heard by an assembly of many thousands. It seems to "us most unreasonable that it should be penal to say in a private letter "that a man is dissipated, and not penal to stand up at the Town Hall, "and there, before the whole society of Calcutta, falsely to accuse him "of poisoning his father."

"In the second place it is not necessarily the fact that the harm "caused by defamation is proportioned to the extent to which the "defamation is circulated. Some slanders, and those slanders of a most "malignant kind, can produce harm only while confined to a very small "circle, and would be at once refuted if they were published. A malig- "nant whisper addressed to a single hearer, and meant to go no further, "may indicate greater depravity, may cause more intense misery, and "may deserve more severe punishment than a satire which has run "through twenty editions. A person, for example, who, in private "conversation, should infuse into the mind of a husband suspicions of "the fidelity of a virtuous wife, might be a defamer of a far worse "description than one who should insert the lady's name in a printed "lampoon."

"It must be allowed that, in general, a printed story is likely to "live longer than a story which is only circulated in conversation. But "on the other hand it is far easier for a calumniated person to clear his "character, either by argument, or by legal proceedings, from a charge "fixed in a printed form, than from a shifting rumour which nobody "repeats exactly as he heard it. In general, we believe, a man would "rather see in a newspaper a story discreditable to him which he had "the means of refuting, than know that such a story, though not pub- "lished, was current in society."

6th Report, p. 48, et seq.

365. The English Criminal Law Commissioners very freely admit that considered abstractly there is no reason for the distinction in question between words spoken and words written. They say, "The truth of the general abstract "proposition is undeniable that when the subject of publication is in its "own nature noxious and offensive, any mode of publication must be "objectionable, and can be material only as regards the extent and degree "of the mischief likely to be occasioned by it." "If a slander conveyed "in writing be injurious to reputation the same must be injurious when "published orally, the more especially if that be done before a great "number of hearers." They allow that "slanderous and abusive lan-"guage may be much more likely to provoke the party to whom it is "applied when spoken in the presence of many others than if addressed "to him by letter, where an interval was allowed for the subsidence "of sudden resentment." Also that a law which "with a view to "the public peace, merely prohibited written insult, would be incom-"mensurate with its object, viz., the preservation of the peace, which "is quite as likely to be broken in consequence of an oral as of a "written insult."

366. "Each mode of publication," they observe, "may, in truth, "be more pernicious than the other when the comparison is made of "different injurious consequences." They remark however that in ordinary cases there is this marked distinction between oral and written communication, as regards the mind and intention of the publisher and the effect of the thing published, that "the committing of injurious and "defamatory matter to writing evinces a more determined and deliberate "purpose than is ordinarily to be inferred from mere words spoken. "Communications by writing are therefore likely to make stronger "impressions than such as are merely oral. They are permanent and "capable of wider diffusion."

367. Conceding that "distinctions founded merely on a consideration "of the particular mode of communication must be in a great measure "arbitrary and artificial, and dependent on reasons of collateral policy "and convenience," they say, "when, however, considerations of extrinsic "policy are taken into the account, and allowed to operate in restraint "of criminal liability, it is obvious that a distinction founded on the "mode of publication, including within its scope such modes as, by their "capability and facility of diffusion and their permanency, must or-"dinarily be considered as the more dangerous, and excluding such "as are merely oral, may well consist with general convenience."

368. In conclusion they observe, that "Whatever distinction as "concerns the civil remedy, may be made between oral and written "slander, there are several reasons for confining penalties in respect of "personal defamation to written publications. In the first place, to "extend the offence to oral defamation would be inconvenient." "In "the next place, the proof of an offence committed by the writing and "publishing of illegal matter is far more definite and complete than "where the offence is merely oral, when so much depends on tone and "manner, the situation of the speaker, the circumstances under which "he spoke, the understanding and memory of the hearers." The inconvenience referred to is that "to make mere oral communications penal "when they reflected on the characters of individuals, would be a heavy "restraint on the ordinary intercourse of mankind, and would neces-"sarily and unavoidably occasion much and vexatious litigation, and "would weaken the great securities for the discharge of legal as well as "moral obligations, the love of reputation, and the fear of public censure "and disgrace."

369. By the Bill brought into the House of Lords by Lord Campbell in 1843, founded on the Report of a Select Committee of that House it was intended to put oral slander on the same footing as written slander. But this alteration was not agreed to by Parliament, and the Act passed to amend the law respecting defamatory words and libel (6 and 7 Victoria, Chap. 96) was clipped of the sections which provided for it. The grounds of the proposed alteration are thus stated in the Report. "At present, while for "many words reduced into writing which in any way tend to injure reputation, though communicated to only one individual, the law gives a "remedy, there is no remedy, without proof of special damage, for mere "words, however injurious to reputation, and however publicly spoken, "unless they impute an indictable offence, or apply to a man in his "business, or import that he is labouring under an infectious disease, so "that falsely and maliciously to impute, in the coarsest terms and on the "most public occasion, want of chastity to a woman of high station and "unspotted character, or want of veracity or courage to a gentleman of "undoubted honesty and honour, cannot be made the foundation of any "proceeding, civil or criminal; whereas an action may be maintained "for saying that a cobbler is not skilful in mending shoes, or that any "one has held up his hand in a threatening posture to another. The "Committee conceive that those distinctions, which are quite peculiar "to the law of England, do not rest on any solid foundation, and that "wherever an injury is done to character by defamation there ought to "be redress by action."

Law Magazine, August 1843.

370. We have quoted the foregoing passage because we think the reasons contained in it are equally valid against maintaining a distinction between words spoken and words written in regard to criminal proceedings. We concur in the remark made by the English Criminal Law Commissioners that "it is difficult to suggest any "good reason for making penal restraints for the protection of property or for the safety of the person, which would not be "equally applicable to the providing for the protection of reputation." And it seems to us that their reasoning on this point applies indifferently and with equal force to every mode in which imputations injurious to reputation can be conveyed to defamatory words spoken as well as written.

6th Report, p. 48.

371. We have to mention that Sir R. Comyn though inclined to agree in many of the arguments adduced in the Note (R) to this chapter, is not able to arrive at the same conclusion on all the points, particularly as to verbal slander, which he thinks should not be put on the same footing as that which is written or printed. Sir H. Seton has the same opinion on this point, considering that the law of England in denying criminal redress to verbal slander affords a specimen of practical wisdom.

372. The definition of "defamation" in the Indian Code it will be observed is subject to nine exceptions, which are specifically set forth in the clauses from 470 to 478.

373. The first exception introduces a new principle, by declaring that "it is not defamation to attempt to cause any thing which is true to be believed in any quarter concerning any person."

374. In the Digest submitted by the English Criminal Law Commissioners in their 6th Report they provided for the punishment of any person publishing a personal libel *which should be false*, if the falsity of it were alleged in the indictment, by a heavier penalty than that prescribed for the publication of a personal libel *not* alleged to be false, allowing the truth of the libel to be proved by the defendant in bar of the prosecution in the former case, but not in the latter.

375. "We recommend," they said, "that in respect of personal libels, "two distinct classes of offence should be constituted.

P. 70.

"That one of these should be founded on the general "principle of protection to private reputation against such defamatory "imputations as are false as well as malicious. That the second should "be founded on the principle already established, of protection to the "public peace by preventing the publication of libels on private persons "tending to the disturbance of the peace."

"That in respect of the former class, the truth of the matter published, when it either directly or by implication contained a charge of "misconduct, should be a bar to the prosecution. That in cases within "the latter class, the truth of the matter published should in no case be "available by way of defence to the publisher of the libel."

"But that in either case, and generally evidence of the truth or falsity "of the matter published should be admissible where the occasion of the "publication was a privileged one, such as legally to raise the question "as to the actual intention of the defendant, whether he acted *bonâ fide* "in reference to the particular occasion, or with an actually malicious "intention independently of the occasion."

376. A provision to the latter effect is inserted in the Digest contained in the 7th Report, but the provision for the aggravation of punishment in the case of a libel proved to be false is omitted, and the exculpation of the defendant by proof of the truth of the matter published is not permitted. The Commissioners still thought that the laws should be extended so as to admit proof of the truth, but they inclined to the opinion that it would be preferable to visit the offence of publishing a personal libel with a specific penalty, with a proviso that the defendant should by proving the truth be enabled to reduce it to a lower limit, on the principle that a libel must be taken to be false until the truth be proved, and that it therefore lies on the publisher to allege and prove the truth where he insists that the charge is true. Until it should be determined whether the law should be extended, and if extended whether according to their former or their latter suggestion, they adapted the articles in the Digest to the present state of the law.

Art. 16, p. 239.

7th Report, p. 112.

377. The Statute 6 and 7 Victoria, Chapter 96, provides distinctly for the offence of *maliciously publishing a defamatory libel knowing it to be false*, and for the offence of maliciously *publishing a defamatory libel.*

Sections 4 and 5.

378. It does not, as proposed in the 6th Report, allow the truth of the imputation to be inquired into *only* when the indictment alleges the imputation to be false, but to entitle the defendant in a trial for a defamatory libel to give evidence of the truth of the matter charged it is made necessary for him to allege the truth thereof in the manner now required in pleading a justification to an action for defamation, and further that the publication was for the public benefit, and it is enacted that the truth of the matters shall not be inquired into without such plea or justification.

379. The authors of the Indian Code have stated fully in Note R the reasons upon which they came to the conclusion that the truth of an imputation prejudicial to character ought in all cases to exempt the author of that imputation from punishment as a defamer. They consider these two propositions to be established by their argument; "first, that in some cases of prosecution for "defamation the truth of the imputations alleged to be "defamatory ought to be a justification; secondly, that in the vast "majority of such cases, if not in all, truth, if it be not a justifi-"cation, ought to be a mitigation." From these two propositions they deduce a third "that in all cases of prosecution for defamation, if the "defendant avers that the imputations complained of as defamatory "are true, the Court ought to go into the question of the truth of those "imputations."

See Appendix, Note R, page 179.

"This ought to be done, not only in justice to the public, and to the "defendant, but in justice to the innocent complainant. It must not be "forgotten that one of the most important ends which a person proposes "to himself in prosecuting a slanderer is the refuting of the slander. "He generally considers the punishment of the offender as a secondary "object; and, when there is no circumstance of peculiar aggravation in "the case, is often willing to stay proceedings after obtaining a retracta-"tion and apology. To clear his fame is his first object. It is, we con-"ceive, an object for the attaining of which he is entitled to the assistance "of the law. But it is an object which cannot be attained unless the "Courts go into the question of truth."

380. "But," they proceed, "if in all cases the Courts allow the "question of truth to be gone into, we are satisfied that no respectable "person will venture to institute a prosecution for defamation in a case "in which he knows that the truth of the defamatory matter is likely to "be proved. He will feel that by prosecuting he should injure his own "character far more deeply than any libeller can do. However disa-"greeable it may be to his feelings that a discreditable story concerning "him should be repeated in society and should furnish paragraphs "for the newspapers, it must be much more disagreeable that such "a story should be proved, in open Court, by legal evidence. By "prosecuting he turns what was not at most a strong suspicion into an "absolute certainty. While he forbears to prosecute, many people will "probably disbelieve the scandalous report, many will doubt about its "truth. The mere circumstance that he abstains from prosecuting is no "proof of guilt. It is notorious that slanders are often passed by with "silent contempt by those who are the objects of them. Indeed, in a "country where the press is free, a man whose station exposes him to "remark would have nothing to do but to prosecute, if he should "institute legal proceedings every time that he might be calumniated."

381. They say "it has been suggested to us from quarters entitled "to great respect, that it would be a preferable course "to admit in every case the truth of matter alleged to be "defamatory to be given in evidence, for the purpose of "proving that the accused person had not acted maliciously; but not to

See Appendix, Note R, page 180.

"allow the proof of the truth to be a justification if it should appear that "reputation had been maliciously assailed."

382. This suggestion very nearly corresponds to the provision in Article 387 of Mr. Livingstone's Code, viz., "Allegations in writing "made with respect to all other than official acts (elsewhere provided for) "which would if they were false, be defamation, shall, although true, "constitute that offence, if they are made from motives of revenge, "hatred, or ill-will of any other kind, entertained by the party making "them, or to gratify either of those passions in any other, and they "shall be deemed to have been made from such motive in all cases in "which the defendant cannot show that he was actuated by some motive "of public good or private duty in making the allegation." It will be observed that the resemblance is close between this provision and that contained in Section 6 of the new Libel Act mentioned above.

383. The authors of the Code remark upon the suggestion abovementioned that "if a provision of this kind were adopt-"ed, it would, for the reasons which we have already "given, be in practice nugatory. For no respectable "person would prosecute the author of an imputation which could be "proved to be true. And we take it for granted that the law of "procedure will not be framed in so cruel and unreasonable a manner as "to permit a prosecution for defamation to be instituted in opposition to "the wishes of the person defamed."

See Appendix, Note R, page 181.

384. "But," they continue, "if the provision which we are consider-"ing were not certain to be in practice nugatory, we should think it a "highly objectionable provision. When an act is of such a description "that it would be better that it should not be done, it is quite proper to "look at the motives and intentions of the doer for the purpose of de-"ciding whether he shall be punished or not. But when an act which is "really useful to society,—an act of a sort which it is desirable to "encourage, has been done, it is absurd to inquire into the motives of "the doer for the purpose of punishing him if it shall appear that his "motives were bad."

385. Pursuing their argument they maintain that "no act ought to "be made punishable on account of *malicious intention*, unless it be in "itself an act of a kind which it is desirable to prevent," and consequently that "malice is not a test which can with propriety be used for the "purpose of determining what true imputations on character ought to "be punished, and what true imputations on character ought not to be "punished."

386. It seems to us that all this may be admitted, and that the principle of the provision contained in Section 6 of the new Libel Act may be maintained notwithstanding, namely, the principle that the truth of the imputation complained of shall amount to a defence if it was for the public benefit that the imputation should be published, but not otherwise. The Select Committee upon whose Report the Bill for amending the law of libel was founded expressed their sentiments on this point as follows:

"The Committee are of opinion that the truth ought not to amount "to an absolute defence in a criminal or civil proceeding for libel, but "that it ought to be received as an ingredient in the defence, to enable "the Jury to determine whether upon the whole the publication is "justifiable. A difficulty arises as to the question to be submitted to "the Jury beyond the truth of the imputation. Some witnesses suggest- "ed that it should be the motive of the defendant; but the just consider- "ation seems to be, whether the public have an interest in the truth "being made known to them. It is only in such a case that private "offences ought to be made the subject of public comment, and in such "a case, for the good of the community, the publication must be tolerated, "though prompted by spite. The Committee think that admitting "evidence of the truth under this limitation will remove a scandal from "the administration of justice, and will have a strong tendency to put "down the infamous libellers, who, living by deliberate calumny, when "prosecuted complain of the existing law of libel by which all inquiry "into truth is forbidden, assert that if permitted they could justify all "their fabrications, and thus sometimes succeed in creating public "sympathy in their favor against those whom they have so cruelly out- "raged."

387. Recurring to the argument of the authors of the Code it seems to us that the publication of the private history of individual members of society is scarcely "an act of a sort which it is desirable to encourage" absolutely. We are inclined to agree with the Select Committee that there are many cases in which a wrong, for which a remedy should be given, may be done to an individual by making public what may be proved to be true concerning that individual,—"as where the imputation "refers to some personal defect, or an error of conduct long atoned for "and forgotten;—and that the justification equally in criminal and civil "proceedings, ought not to be complete without showing to the satisfac- "tion of the Jury," (or the Judge, as it may be,) "that the community had an interest in the truth being known," or in other words, "that the publication was calculated to prevent some detriment to the community, or to serve some purpose by which the community would be benefited."

388. The authors of the Code admit that the throwing of true imputations on character "may be a very pernicious act." They say, "We are sure that it is often a great "public service; and we are sure that it may be very "pernicious when it is not done from malice, and that it may be a great "public service when it is done from malice. It is perfectly conceivable "that a person might from no malicious feeling, but from an honest "though austere and injudicious zeal for what he might consider as the "interests of religion and morality, drag before the public frailties which "it would be far better to leave in obscurity." From which it appears to us to follow, that the law should not indeed inquire into the motive of the defendant, but should inquire into the question whether what he has done be for the public good or not.

See Appendix, Note R, page 181.

389. Again it is said, "It is also perfectly conceivable that a person "who has been concerned in some odious league of villainy and has "quarrelled with his accomplices, may from vindictive feelings publish "the history of their proceedings, and may by doing so render a great "service to society." True—but here the publication would be justifiable under Section 6 of the Libel Act by the public benefit it was calculated to produce.

390. On the whole we are led to conclude, that the first exception ought to be qualified so as to make the admission of the truth as a defence to a prosecution for defamation depend upon conditions such as are prescribed by the English Statute.

391. We think that the opinion above quoted, that no respectable person would prosecute the author of an imputation which can be proved to be true, is not to be admitted without qualification. We can conceive a person who has rendered himself respectable by a long course of good conduct in a certain sphere, whose reputation has been maliciously attacked by some one raking up and publishing a transgression of an earlier period, long since "atoned for and forgotten," prosecuting the author of the attack under a law which like the new Statute obliges the party who makes a defamatory imputation to prove not only the truth of the imputation, but also that it was for the public benefit to publish it. We can imagine such a person ready to prosecute, and willing if need be to admit the truth, that he may have at the same time the opportunity to prove by the testimony of those among whom he has lived for years, and who have known him intimately, how amply he has atoned for the transgression; grieved and hurt at the revival of a passage of his life's history of which he felt ashamed, but conscious that he had made amends by his subsequent career, he would, we imagine, be impatient to counteract the poison by setting off the long course of virtuous conduct against perhaps the single error, or it may be the deviation of a season. He would not let the bane work when he could, with a little moral courage, supply an antidote. And we conceive he would have the sympathy of the better part of the public with him.

392. In the opinion we have expressed against the unqualified adoption of the first exception, we concur with Mr. J. F. Thomas, whose observations upon the subject are highly deserving of attention; and with Mr. Greenhill, who has offered some pertinent remarks to shew the inexpediency of admitting the truth as a defence without reserve.

393. For reasons which are sufficiently explained in the Note, the Code makes defamation an offence "without any reference to its tendency to cause acts of illegal violence."

See Appendix, Note B, page 176.

394. Upon this Mr. Norton says, "Defamation in most people's "estimate will, I believe, be considered purely as a civil wrong, when "directed against individuals—except in so much as its tendency may "be to create open commotion or violence from the irritation thereby "created. Those who do not concede any such tendency, or, conceding "it, doubt (as the Commissioners do) the propriety of such tendency "being considered a criterion of criminality, would find it difficult to "assign a sound reason for distinguishing an injury done by personal "defamation from any other civil injury."

395. We may cite by way of answer to Mr. Norton, the following observations of the English Criminal Law Commissioners: "It has appeared to us, after attentive consideration, "that the law of England, in making the criminal branch of the offence "to depend on the tendency of the libel to provoke to a breach of the "peace, is constructed on too narrow a basis. And we apprehend that

6th Report, p. 54.

"some incongruities which are to be found in the practical application "of this branch of the law are attributable to this defect."

"Although it be true that the danger to the public peace is one ground "for penal restraint, it is not, we think, an exclusive one. The injury "to private reputation is beyond all doubt a sufficient ground of legal "interposition for the protection of reputation, by giving a remedy in "damages, and there seems to be no satisfactory reason why that protec- "tion should be so limited to civil reparation any more than there is in "the case of mere spoliation of property. The law which gives a remedy "in damages in respect of trespass to property, is confessedly insufficient "for the protection of proprietors against the fraudulent abstraction of "property; and in many instances severe penal restraints against mali- "cious destruction or damage are deemed to be necessary to the extent "even of subjecting offenders to the penalty of transportation. Although "it be not necessary to punish a malicious libeller in respect of the de- "struction of private reputation with so much severity, the law might "justly be regarded as inconsistent and defective which thus carefully "protected property, but afforded no more than the mere civil remedy "in respect of wilful injuries to reputation. In the former case the "injury is made penal, simply because the giving a remedy by action "affords no adequate protection against injuries of a fraudulent or mali- "cious nature perpetrated, it may be, by offenders unknown, or where "known, irresponsible through poverty or other circumstances. But "precisely the same reason, viz., the inadequacy of the civil remedy, "suggests the expediency of also affording protection by the like means "against malicious attacks so easily and frequently made by otherwise "irresponsible authors."

396. We need hardly say after citing the above remarks, which appear to us to be perfectly just, that we do not see the force of Mr. Norton's observation, that "when the Commissioners avow that the truth of "defamatory charges is a legal excuse for the permanent dissemination of "them, and at the same time disallow the tendency to irritation and "consequent breach of the peace as any criterion of criminality, they "appear to overthrow all foundation of *criminality* whatever in defama- "tion." We shall only observe that it would be more proper to describe the Code as disallowing the tendency to irritation, not as any criterion, but as *the sole* criterion of criminality in defamation. It makes defamation an offence independently of any such tendency, "because defamatory "imputations of the worst kind may have no tendency to cause acts of "violence;" but the tendency of calumnious imputations to provoke breaches of the peace is undoubtedly one of the reasons for making defamation an offence.

397. The Indian Code, it is to be observed, agrees on this point with that framed by Mr. Livingstone, in which it is declared that the offence of defamation "consists in the injury offered to reputation, not in any probable breach of the peace or other consequence that may result from it."

398. Mr. Norton considers that the chapter "errs throughout as well in principles as in details." As to principles, we have seen that he thinks it errs in making defamation an offence without reference to its tendency to provoke breaches of the peace. He thinks it wrong also in the exception which admits the truth to be pleaded. As to details, he says, "I think all impartial persons versed in the English law of libel, "or unversed in any law, will be ready to exclaim against the involved "and perplexing definition of defamation, with its accompanying explan- "ations and exceptions as detailed in this chapter. Such phrases as "'*attempting* to cause it to be *believed*,' instead of the term '*publishing*' "and designating the matter published as 'an imputation which would "harm reputation' in 'the quarter' where 'believed,' but which is not "to be defamation if published '*in good faith* respecting the conduct of "a public servant in the discharge of his functions,' or if published of "'any person respecting his conduct touching any public question,' or "being censure of the 'conduct of a person in *matters* to which the "publisher's *lawful* authority over another *relates*'—and so on, appear "to me to give the widest latitude of construction."

399. The phrase "attempting to cause it to be believed" taken by itself might be obscure, but it is not to be taken by itself, and when it is considered together with the words which are intended to determine the meaning it appears to us to be perfectly intelligible, and to make the definition sufficiently precise. We venture to say this in the face of Mr. Norton's assertion that "the various *modes* which may be adopted of "publication or 'attempting to cause it to be believed' by no means help "out the vague generality of the phrase adopted." The term "publishing," which he seems to prefer, it is obvious, would not suit the definition, without other words to qualify and apply it, for it is not the mere general promulgation of an imputation that is aimed at, but the notification of it in such a way that it may reach a particular quarter and cause an unfavorable impression in that quarter, it being explained that "an "imputation which is defamatory when intended to be believed in one "quarter is not necessarily defamatory when intended to be believed in "another quarter."

400. Respecting the modes of defamation specified in the definition, Mr. Norton observes "they are all obvious methods of publication but in "all qualified by reference to the ulterior intention of the parties in so "issuing the libel." Again he says "the gloss put by one of the illus- "trations upon the meaning of 'attempting to cause it to be believed' "under which all publishers of libels are to be held guiltless unless their "*intention* appears of causing the imputation to be believed" "gives a "general franchise of libelling." He appears to allude here to the illustration (*h*) under Clause 469, which admits of a *defence* against a charge of defamation on the part of a person who has been unintentionally an agent in the publication or circulation of defamation. A charge of defamation must impute to the party accused the intention described in the definition of the offence, as inferrible from the circumstances to be given in proof. It will be for the party accused to allege and prove any special circumstances by which that inference may be avoided, or to shew that the alleged intention is not justly inferrible from the circumstances proved by the prosecutor. The English Criminal Law Commissioners say "ignorance of the contents of "the matter published by a party, or to the publication of which he was "instrumental, must in principle be regarded as a sufficient legal excuse, "provided the want of knowledge be not in itself wilful with a view to "impunity, or otherwise culpable. In such cases the total absence of all "criminal design or neglect ought to exempt from penal consequences."

6th Report, p. 51.

401. With reference to the illustration (*h*) we have to remark, that it seems to apply to the explanation which intimates that "it is not "necessarily defamation to repeat or circulate an imputation which it "was defamation originally to make." The journeyman printer may be acquitted of defamation on the ground that in setting the types for printing defamatory matter and so aiding towards the circulation thereof, he had not the intention described in the definition, and had therefore not aided voluntarily, according to the definition of that term in Clause 26, to harm the reputation, &c., while the person who wrote the defamatory matter, for printing which the journeyman ignorantly set the types, may be convicted, because it may be clear that his purpose was to defame. Though the journeyman printer may be acquitted of defamation because of his unconsciousness of the tendency of the matter printed, the possessor of the press is not allowed this plea when the press has been used for printing a defamatory imputation, unless he can prove that the printing was purposely concealed from him—in this case, and also if the printing was contrary to his directions, he is exempted from punishment, otherwise he is liable to the same punishment as for defamation.

Clause 480.

See Libel Act, 6 and 7 Vic., c. 96, s. 7.

402. It seems to us that the exceptions which Mr. Norton represents as "giving the widest latitude of construction" are really not liable to this reproach. We cannot see the vagueness which he attributes to them. Having well considered the terms in which the exceptions are expressed, they appear to us, indeed, to be remarkably free from ambiguity. We cannot discover whether Mr. Norton considers these exceptions, that is to say, the exceptions contained in the clauses from 471 to 478 to be objectionable in substance as well as in the form of expression, further than that he says of one of them, the fourth, (Clause 483) that "the liberty given of expressing in *good faith any opinion* whatever "respecting the conduct or character of any party, witness, or *agent* in "any case brought before a Court, or their *character* as far as it appears "in such conduct, excites my astonishment."

403. Upon this exception the authors of the Code remark as follows:

"By Clause 473 we have allowed all persons freely to discuss in "good faith the proceedings of Courts of law, and the "characters of parties, agents, and witnesses, as connect- "ed with those proceedings. It is almost universally "acknowledged that the Courts of law ought to be thrown open to the "public. But the advantage of throwing them open to the public will "be small indeed, if the few who are able to press their way into a Court "are forbidden to report what has passed there to the vast numbers who "were absent, or if those who are allowed to know what has passed are "not allowed to comment on what has passed. The only reason that the "whole community is not admitted to hear every trial that takes place "is that it is physically impossible that they should find room, and by "Clause 473 we do our best to counteract the effect of this physical "impossibility."

See Appendix, Note R, page 183.

404. We cannot account for Mr. Norton's "astonishment" at the exception which allows free comment in good faith on the conduct of any person as a party, witness, or agent, in any case before a Court of Justice, or on his character as it appears in such conduct. We can hardly believe that he would disallow such a comment as that instanced in the illustration (*a*); nor with respect to an *agent* in a case in which the evidence brought forward by him

Clause 473.

was proved to be entirely false, that he would refuse protection to the reporter if he remarked that the conduct of the agent in trumping up such a case was scandalous.

405. The exceptions from the 5th to the 9th appear to be embraced in Articles 11 and 14 of Chapter XVI of the Digest of the English Criminal Law Commissioners, in which are described the publications that are held to be "justifiable either absolutely or in a qualified manner in respect of the occasion." Article 14 would seem also to cover the 2nd and 3rd exceptions, as it justifies publications "made *bonâ fide*" "for the benefit of any party or of the public," or "with a view to the discussion of any acts, measures, or proceedings affecting the public," "or otherwise howsoever, any party or the public having an interest in the making or receiving of such communication." This article it may be observed admits of much wider "latitude of construction" than the exceptions in the Code.

Clauses 474 to 478.
7th Report, p. 238-9.
P. 471-2.

406. We have seen that the first exception in the Code makes the truth a defence. In the eight following exceptions it is not required that an imputation should be true. "We require only," say the authors of the Code, "that it should be made in good faith. For to require in these cases that the imputation should be true would be to render these exceptions mere nullities." So by the above articles of the Digest "a publication is justifiable in a qualified manner in respect of the occasion whensoever it is made *bonâ fide* concerning any other person" for any of the purposes therein described.

See Appendix, Note R, page 183.

407. The authors of the Code observe that "whether an imputa- "tion be made or be not made in good faith is a ques- "tion for the Courts of law. The burden of the proof "will be sometimes on the person who has made the imputation, and "sometimes on the person on whom the imputation has been thrown. "No general rule can be laid down. Yet scarcely any case could arise "respecting which a sensible and impartial Judge would feel any doubt. "If, for example, a public functionary were to prosecute for defamation "a writer who had described him in general terms as incapable, the "Court would probably require the prosecutor to give some proof of bad "faith. If the prosecutor had no such proof to offer, the defendant "would be acquitted. If the prosecutor were to prove that the defendant "had applied to him for money, had promised to write in his praise if "the money were advanced, and had threatened to abuse him if the "money were withheld, the Court would probably be of opinion that the "defendant had not written in good faith, and would convict him."

Page 184.

"On the other hand, if the imputation were an imputation of some "particular fact, or an imputation which, though general in form, yet "implied the truth of some particular fact, which, if true, might be "proved, the Court would probably hold that the burden of proving "good faith lay on the defendant. Thus if a person were to publish "that a Collector was in the habit of receiving bribes from the Zemin- "dars of his district, and were unable to specify a single case, or to give "any authority for his assertion, the Courts would probably be of "opinion that the imputation had not been made in good faith."

408. "It will be necessary" they further observe, "to provide in "the Code of Procedure rules for pleading in cases of defamation, which "may give to an innocent man who has been calumniated the means of "clearing his character. It will be proper to provide that a defendant "who is accused of defamation, and who rests his defence on the truth "of the imputation alleged to be defamatory, shall be held strictly to the "proof of the substance of the imputation if the imputation be particular, "and shall be compelled to descend to particulars in his plea, if the "imputation be general."

409. Upon the explanation annexed to the definition of defamation, that "a collection of persons cannot, as such, be defamed," Mr. Norton remarks that he does not know on what principle libels against public bodies, &c., are exempted from criminality. Such libels are not however exempted from criminality, as the same explanation intimates that a defamatory imputation thrown on a collection of persons is an offence against each one of those persons—Thus "it may be defamation of every Judge of the Sudder to say—'The whole Sudder Court is corrupt.'" We may note that the chapter of the Digest under the title of Libel, like the chapter of Defamation in the Code, is confined to defamatory imputations upon individuals.

Illustration (*i*), Clause 469.

410. As Clause 480, as above observed, makes the possessor of the press by which defamatory matter is printed liable to punishment without proof of his having had the intention described in Clause 469, so also, by Clause 481, the person who first sells or offers for sale any printed or engraved substance containing defamatory matter is made liable to punishment without proof of such intention.

411. Sir H. Seton suggests that a question may arise as to who is the first seller, &c., when a work is first advertised for sale at different places at the same time.

412. Generally, we apprehend, when a work is so advertised for sale at different places, there is one principal or original seller at the place of publication, who supplies copies of the work to the appointed sellers at the other places by wholesale. In such cases we conceive that this wholesale dealer from whom the others purchased will be the first seller within the definition. Some works however are published as a joint stock concern by several parties residing at different places, and they probably receive their shares direct from the printer, and dispose of them partly by wholesale to other dealers, and partly immediately by retail at their own shops. Each of these parties we think is to be considered as a first seller, that is to say, as selling at first hand within the meaning of the definition. If this view is held to be correct, it may be advisable to subjoin to Clause 481 corresponding illustrations.

413. We have to remark that by the Code the maximum punishment for defamation, which implies a false imputation, is simple imprisonment which may extend to two years, or fine, *or both*. By the Libel Act the maximum punishment for a *false* libel is the same except that fine is prescribed positively in addition to imprisonment. The punishment for a person convicted of a defamatory libel without reference to its truth or falsity is imprisonment not exceeding one year, or fine, *or both*.

414. We have only further to observe upon this chapter, that

Mr. Hudleston, one of the Judges of the Madras Sudder Court, is "decidedly of opinion that its omission is more advisable than its retention in a Criminal Code for this country." While Mr. Giberne, one of the Judges of the Bombay Sudder Court, remarks that "the provisions and principles upon which the law of defamation has been framed appear most excellent, and all that can be said has been said in that very interesting Note R." Mr. Hudleston says more particularly, "The explanations are highly artificial—out of place in a Criminal Code—the definition an over-refinement—the whole calculated to do harm rather than good; to lead to groundless prosecutions, and to involve the tribunals in investigations, tending to no practical advantage." With respect to the first explanation in Clause 470, he says "I would not carry the principle of legislation on this subject further than it is in England." Again he says, "The libel punishable should be such only as is malicious and intended to provoke to rage, or expose the libelled to public hatred, contempt and ridicule."

CHAPTER XXVI.

OF CRIMINAL INTIMIDATION, INSULT AND ANNOYANCE.

415. This chapter is in some sort supplementary to the chapter "of Defamation." It is observed in Note R on that chapter, that an imputation which is not defamatory under the definition, explanations and exceptions in that chapter, may, under certain circumstances, be punishable on other grounds. For example, "an imputation which is not defamatory may be uttered "in the hearing of the person who is the object of it for the purpose of "wantonly and maliciously annoying that person. If so, it is punishable "under Clause 485 (487). There are many cases in which it is fit that "unpleasant truth should be told respecting an individual. But there "is no case in which it is desirable that such truth should be told in "such a way that the telling of it is a gross personal outrage. A person "who has detected, or thinks that he has detected, a dishonest misrepre-"sentation in a book, has a right to expose it publicly. But he cannot "be allowed to intrude into the presence of the author of the book, and "to tell him to his face that he is a liar. A person who knows the "mistress of a female school to be a woman of infamous character, de-"serves well of society if he states what he knows. But he cannot be "allowed to follow her through the streets calling her by opprobrious "names, though he may be able to prove that all those names were "merited. A person who brings to notice the malversation of a public "functionary deserves applause. But a person who hangs a public func-"tionary in effigy at that functionary's door with an opprobrious label, "does what cannot be permitted even though every word on the label, "and every imputation which the exhibition was meant to convey, may "be perfectly true."

See Appendix, Note R, page 185.

416. Mr. Hudleston, Judge of the Madras Sudder Court, who so decidedly objects to the chapter of Defamation, questions the expediency of this chapter also, considering that "the enactment of its provisions, "among other mischievous consequences, would bring the administration "of criminal justice to a stand, and that the Magistrate would in vain "attempt to dispose of the work which these provisions alone would "probably create." Mr. Giberne, Judge of the Sudder Court at Bombay, on the other hand, expresses approbation of this chapter, as he does of the chapter of Defamation.

417. Mr. Norton says, "There seems to me much propriety in "making provisions against crimes classing under 'intimidation'—but "as regards the mode in which that object is accomplished in this "chapter, it appears to me sufficient to point out that, without strain-"ing constructions beyond the legitimate meaning of the language, any "person who shall *threaten* to kill his neighbour's cat which trespasses, "intending to 'distress' the owner of it by such *threat* (no act being "done) may (under Clause 482) be punished by two years' imprison-"ment." We are obliged to remark on this criticism that it does appear to us to savour of a "strained construction." Distress is a term of strong signification, rendered by Dr. Johnson by the words "calamity, misery, misfortune," it is used as synonymous with affliction, and in this place its connection with the word "terror" denotes clearly that it is not a trifling pain which will pass as fulfilling the definition. It may be however that a person has that degree of attachment to or value for a cat that a threat to kill it would cause real distress to that person; and if any person from a malignant desire to distress his neighbour deliberately threatens to kill his cat which he knows him to value so highly, it does not appear to us to be ridiculous that he should be liable to punishment under this clause. It is we conceive a "strain" to suppose that the punishment might be imprisonment for two years, that is to say, the maximum punishment authorized by the clause for the gravest form of criminal intimidation, namely, a threat of murder.

418. We have said that it appears to us that the object of Clause 283 may be met by extending Clause 482 which defines "criminal intimidation" so as tacitly to include the species of intimidation against which the said clause is directed. We propose to insert before the words "with the intention of causing," the words "or holds out to any person a threat of any injury or misfortune to be brought upon that person directly or indirectly."

419. There are special Statutes in the English law for offences of this nature. The offences to which those Statutes apply, according to Russell, are, "I.—The sending or delivering any letter or writing
Russell 2, p. 579. "threatening to kill or murder, or to burn or destroy "houses, &c. II.—Demanding property with menaces, "with intent to steal. III.—Accusing or threatening to accuse of an "infamous crime, with an intent to extort or gain, and thereby extorting "or gaining. IV.—Sending or delivering any letter or writing demanding "with menaces, and without any reasonable cause, any chattels, &c. "V.—Accusing or threatening to accuse any person of any of the crimes "mentioned in the Act, with an intent to extort, &c. VI.—Sending or "delivering any letter or writing, accusing or threatening to accuse "any person of any such crimes with a like intent." In the Digest of the English Criminal Law Commissioners the provisions relating to offences of this description seem to be distributed under the heads of "Offences against the public peace" and "Extortion by threats." The punishments are transportation for life, or for a term not less than seven years, or imprisonment for a term not exceeding three years. Except in the case of sending a letter threatening to kill or murder or to burn or destroy houses, &c., it must be alleged that the offence was committed with a view to extortion, in order to bring the offender within the reach of the law. By the Code the offender will be liable if his object was to cause distress or terror to the person to whom the threat was conveyed, or to induce that person to do what he was not legally bound to do, or to omit what he had a legal right to do. The Code is therefore more comprehensive in regard to the intention, as it is also in regard to the nature of the threats.

420. The punishment prescribed by the Code is much more lenient than that ordained by the English law. For the offence of criminal intimidation in ordinary the maximum punishment is imprisonment which may extend to two years, with or without fine; when the offender has taken precaution to conceal the quarter from whence the threat comes the imprisonment may extend to three years.

421. A good deal of objection has been made to Clause 485 and the clauses following, relating to insult and annoyance by a person "uttering "any word, making any sound, making any gesture, or exhibiting any "object intending that such word or sound shall be heard, or that such "gesture or object shall be seen by any person" intending thereby to

insult* or annoy† that person, or intending specially to insult the modesty of a woman‡ by word, sound, gesture, or exhibition.

422. Mr. Norton makes the following observations:—"It appears "to me that all the clauses against 'insult' and 'annoyance' by *words*, "*gestures* or *sounds*, must (where they deserve criminal punishment at all) "more appropriately rank under 'defamation' or contempts of Judicial "authorities. And it appears to me that nothing can more forcibly "corroborate the observations I have made regarding the exemption "of true defamation from criminal cognizance than the necessity of these "extraordinary enactments (as they seem to me) against *insulting* "words, *gestures* and *sounds*—which, if they are not too trivial for any "legal cognizance whatever, can only be criminal as creating irritation, "and tending consequently to occasion acts of open violence."

423. Mr. Hudleston says, "I consider this clause quite preposterous, and "I entirely concur in opinion with those gentlemen, who recommend the "omission of it and of the two clauses which follow. The second para-"graph of the explanation to Clause 485 is not very clear—the illustra-"tion (*b*) seems to suppose the absence of the power of punishing for "contempt of Court."

424. Sir R. Comyn points out the extreme vagueness of the words "insult" and "annoy." He observes that "the offence is made to "depend almost entirely upon the sensitive feelings of the person com-"plaining of the annoyance, and not upon distinct definition. A private "offence is converted into a matter for public prosecution."

425. It seems to us that the observation of the learned Judge as to the offence depending upon the sensitive feelings of the person complaining is not well founded. It depends surely upon the calm dispassionate opinion of the Judge whether the act complained of was from its nature and the circumstances attending it calculated to insult, and was done with the intention of insulting the complainant. We have elsewhere noticed the objection to the words "insult" and "annoy" on account of their alleged vagueness. We do not think that as they are here used there is any probability of their being misunderstood.

426. We are not sure that Mr. Norton is positively of opinion that the offences against which these clauses are directed are too trivial for legal cognizance. It will be observed that his expressions are doubtful. We are ready to concede to him that the tendency of such insults and annoyances as are contemplated in these clauses, to create irritation and to provoke acts of violence, is an influential reason for treating them as criminal, but we do not think that this is the *only* reason for so treating them. For example, we think it a perfectly legitimate object of penal legislation to provide, as in Clause 486, for the protection of a woman against insult to her modesty, in consideration especially of her inability to protect herself, and of course without respect to any risk of a breach of the peace from her attempting to avenge herself.

427. We conceive that the object of the law is properly twofold, on the one hand to defend the weak by holding out punishment to those who shall disturb their peace by insult and annoyance, and on the other hand, to restrain those who have strength to avenge themselves from resorting to violence when they are provoked by such offences offered to them, by giving them redress at the hands of the Magistrate.

* Clause 485. † Clause 487. ‡ Clause 486.

428. From the manner in which Mr. Hudleston and some others speak of these clauses regarding insult and annoyance by words, &c., and of the additional work which they suppose such enactment would bring upon the Magistrates, it might be thought that there was nothing of the kind in the existing Regulations for the guidance of the Magistrates in the Provinces. Whereas by the Regulations of all the Presidencies the Magistrates are expressly empowered to take cognizance of complaints of abusive language and calumny and other such petty offences, and to punish the offenders, in the Bombay Presidency by imprisonment to the extent of six months, or fine, or both; in the Presidencies of Bengal and Madras by imprisonment not exceeding 15 days, or fine to the amount of 50 rupees in ordinary, and to the amount of 200 rupees when the offender is of superior condition.

Bengal Reg. IX, 1793, Sec. 8. Madras Reg. IX, 1816, Sec. 34. Bombay Regulation XIV, 1827, Section 29, Cl. 2.

429. The illustration (*b*) under Clause 485 noticed by Mr. Hudleston is obviously intended to exemplify the 2nd explanation subjoined to that clause which Mr. Hudleston finds fault with as "not very clear." The explanation intimates that although the making of an imputation may not amount to the offence of defamation, and may therefore not be punishable under Chapter XXV, it may however be an offence under Clause 485, as being made with the intention of insulting. In the case stated in the illustration the offender would be punishable under Clause 197 if the Magistrate were sitting as a Court of Justice.

430. We propose to introduce into Clause 487 the words "or who intrudes upon the privacy of any person," and to make the same addition to Clause 486 substituting "any woman" for "any person." This modification of the two clauses we think advisable on general grounds. And it will make Clause 487 serve instead of Clause 285, as far as appears requisite, in the case of a person wantonly approaching a place where another is preparing his food, or where it is kept ready for use, intending thereby to make it unfit for his use according to the rules of his caste.

431. Colonel Sleeman proposes that a clause be added to this chapter against combinations to prevent any person following any trade which he is by law authorized to follow, &c. It appears to us that this offence is sufficiently provided for by Clause 95, concerning abetment by conspiracy, by which all engaged in the combination would be liable to the punishment provided for criminal intimidation.

432. We have had occasion in considering the terms of Clause 482 in this chapter, to recur to the definition of "trespass" proposed in para. 627 of our First Report, and upon this revision it has appeared to us advisable to give the definition a wider scope. We would recommend that it be modified as follows, and that it be substituted, as modified, for Clause 418:

"Whoever enters, or causes any person, animal, or thing, to enter "upon or into any property, or does any thing to any property affecting "it corporeally, by his own direct act, or by the intervention of another "person involuntarily impelled by him, or by means of any animal or "thing caused by him to act upon it, not having a legal right independ-"ent of the consent of any other party, so to enter upon or into or to "act upon such property, and not having the consent, express or implied, "of any party legally entitled to give a consent, which would authorize "such entrance or action, is said to trespass."

CHAPTER II.

OF PUNISHMENTS.

433. The punishments provided by the Code are:

First.—Death.

Second.—Transportation.

Third.—Imprisonment, rigorous and simple.

Fourth.—Banishment from the territories of the East India Company.

Fifth.—Forfeiture of property.

Sixth.—Fine.

434. The forfeiture of *all property* is a punishment confined to one class of offenders, that is, to persons waging or attempting to wage war against the Government, or previously abetting that high offence (Clause 109). The forfeiture of *specific property* is authorized by one clause only (115) for the offence of using the Company's territory for the purpose of making preparation to commit depredations on the territory of a power at peace with the Government, &c. The punishment of banishment is also confined to special cases. There are only three Clauses (113, 114 and 290) in which it is authorized primarily as the proper punishment of the offence. These two kinds of punishment may therefore be considered *extraordinary*.

DEATH. Clauses 300, 306, 380.

Clause 109.

435. Of the punishments which may be considered the *ordinary* punishments of the Code, the first is death. It is confined to cases in which murder has been committed (including the case of a person who aids a child, or one who is of unsound mind, or in a state of intoxication, to commit suicide, and the case of murder in dacoity, which being committed by one of a gang of dacoits, every member of the gang is liable to the punishment of murder,) and the highest political offence, that of waging war, &c., against the Government.

TRANSPORTATION.

Clause 43.

436. The second punishment, transportation, may be substituted for death in all the capital cases. It is not allowed for any term short of life, except in one instance under Clause 205, in the case of a person returning from banishment, and then banishment for life is to be added. It is also permitted as a commutation, under the orders of Government, in the case of European offenders condemned to long terms of imprisonment. It is the specific punishment for persons returning from transportation for a term of years before the expiration of the term (Clause 203), or returning from transportation and banishment, the sentence not having been remitted (Clause 204). It is the primary punishment for the offences specified in the following Clauses, viz., 117, 123, 191, 308, 311, 320, 322, 343, 356, 379, 391, 414, 428.

IMPRISONMENT.

437. The third mode of punishment, imprisonment, is of two kinds, rigorous and simple. Under this head we may distinguish 25 classes.

NOTE.—In the following enumeration of the offences liable to imprisonment, where the imprisonment is rigorous it is denoted by the letter R, where it is simple by the letter S. Where there is no mark the imprisonment may be of either description.

438. The first four classes comprise offences, which are liable to imprisonment which must be for life, or which may extend to life, but may be limited to shorter periods, viz :—

Class 1. Imprisonment for life.

„ 2. May extend to life, and must not be for a less term than 7 years.

„ 3. May extend to life, with a minimum of 3 years.

„ 4. May extend to life, without a minimum.

439. In all the capital cases but one, imprisonment to endure for life (1st class) may be substituted for death; in that one (Clause 380) the imprisonment may be for a term not less than 7 years (2nd class).

(Clauses 109 R., 300 R., 306 R., 380 R.)

440. In all cases but one, in which transportation is the primary punishment, imprisonment for life, or for a term of years, may be substituted. In that one, Thuggee, the imprisonment must be for life. In seven cases the imprisonment may be for life, or for a term not less than 7 years (2nd class). In four cases, the minimum is 3 years (3rd class). In one case there is no minimum (4th class).

Clauses 311, 191 R., 308 R., 320 R., 322 R., 343 R., 356 R., 414 R., 117, 379 R., 391 R., 428 R., 123.

441. There appears to be one case only in which imprisonment which may extend to life is the specific punishment for the offence—in this case the minimum is 7 years.

Clause 363.

442. The remaining 21 classes comprising offences liable to imprisonment for terms of years, or shorter periods, are exhibited in the following Table :—

Class.	Terms of Imprisonment.	Clauses in which the Offences are specified.
5	May extend to 14 years and must not be less than 2 years.	110, 115, 302, 307, 357, 360, 361, 371, 373, 377 R., 415, 444, 447, 448, 449, 450, 451, 466.
6	May extend to 14 years and must not be less than 1 year.	321 R., 324, 413.
7	May extend to 14 years without a minimum.	301, 303.
8	May extend to 10 years with a minimum of 6 months.	319.
9	May extend to 7 years and must not be less than 2 years.	233, 235, 237, 239, 241, 244, 245.
10	May extend to 7 years and must not be less than 1 year.	111, 116, 119, 122, 190, 217, 218, 219, 220, 221, 275, 355, 367 R., 372, 374, 378 R., 381 R., 398, 445.
11	May extend to 7 years and must not be less than 6 months.	412, 438.
12	May extend to 5 years..................	133.

Class.	Terms of Imprisonment.	Clauses in which the Offences are specified.
13	May extend to 3 years and must not be less than 1 year.	247, 250, 252.
14	May extend to 3 years and must not be less than 6 months.	118, 162, 232, 234, 236, 238, 240, 243, 276, 346, 365 R., 366 R., 385, 388, 416, 446, 452, 457, 468, 484.
15	May extend to 3 years and must not be less than 3 months.	484.
16	May extend to 3 years	94, 113 S., 114, 121, 138, 140 S., 146, 309, 312, 323, 364 R., 369, 387, 390, 406, 407, 408, 409, 410, 435, 440.
17	May extend to 2 years.....................	130, 132, 141 S., 142 S., 144 S., 195, 199, 201, 291 S., 292 S., 293 S., 304, 334, 347, 348, 349, 384, 395, 396, 403, 404, 405, 430, 431, 439, 443, 453, 458, 479 S., 480 S., 481 S., 483, 486.
18	May extend to 1 year and must not be less than 3 months.	246, 248, 249, 251.
19	May extend to 1 year	108, 120, 136, 143 S., 145 S., 184, 186, 193, 194, 196, 253, 254, 255, 256, 278, 280, 282, 283, 290 S., 318, 326, 333, 338, 350, 370, 394, 397, 411, 426, 456, 459, 460, 467 S.
20	May extend to 6 months	105, 107, 125, 129, 139 S., 158, 159, 160, 163, 166, 171, 173, 197, 206 S., 222, 257, 258, 259, 260. 261, 262, 263, 265, 266, 267, 268, 269, 270, 271, 272, 273, 284, 327, 401, 402, 454, 465.
21	May extend to 3 months	124, 126, 147 S., 148 S., 150, 161, 164, 175, 179, 209, 210, 212 S., 213 S., 214, 223, 224, 225, 288 S., 289 S., 342, 364, 485.
22	May extend to 2 months.....................	178.
23	May extend to 1 month.....................	135 S., 152, 153, 155, 156, 157, 168, 170, 177, 181, 182. 264. 286, 325, 332, 351, 352, 358 S., 425, 463, 487.
24	May extend to 24 hours.....................	488 S.
25	Imprisonment—the duration of which is to be determined proportionally with reference to that which is authorized or prescribed for another connected offence.	90, 93, 101, 102, 106, 329, 335, 336, 337, 344, 345, 429, 433, 437.

Fine.

See Appendix, Note A, p. 97.

443. "Fine," say the authors of the Code, "is one of the most "common punishments in every part of the world, and "it is a punishment the advantages of which are so "great and obvious, that we propose to authorize the

"Courts to inflict it in every case, except where forfeiture of all property "is necessarily part of the punishment." Thus in every penal clause, except Clause 109 which involves forfeiture, fine is prescribed positively as the punishment, or authorized as an alternative or additional punishment.

444. The following are the clauses specifying the offences for which fine is the sole punishment, the fine being limited in all but one (Clause 226,) viz., 149, 211, 215, 216, 226, 227, 228, 242, 274, 285, 287, 400.

445. In 170 cases fine may be inflicted as the *alternative* for some other punishment; in most of these it may be *added* when the other punishment is adjudged as the principal one. In all other cases, except Clause 109 which involves the forfeiture of all property, fine may be *added* at discretion to the principal punishment, whether that be death, transportation, banishment, or imprisonment.

Clauses 291 to 293, 265 to 273, 107, 158, 161, 197, 206, 225, 261 to 263, 283, 318, 327, 333, 350, 426, 485.

446. The number of cases in which the fine is limited appears to be 70. The maximum is Rs. 5,000 which is authorized in three cases only, of offences relating to the Press. In nine cases the fine may extend to Rs. 2,000, the offences being such as indicate a want of due regard for human life. In sixteen cases the limit is Rs. 1,000. The lower gradations are Rs. 500, Rs. 200, and Rs. 100.

Clauses 161, 225, 485.

447. In the cases in which the maximum fine is 5,000 rupees the alternative imprisonment may extend to 2 years. In all cases in which the maximum fine is 2,000 rupees the alternative imprisonment is limited to 6 months. In five cases in which the maximum fine is 1,000 rupees the alternative imprisonment may extend to 1 year, in eight cases it may extend to 6 months, in the rest it is limited to 3 months.

PUNISHMENTS IN THE DIGEST OF THE ENGLISH CRIMINAL LAW.
Article 8, Chapter XXIV.

448. The Commissioners on the Criminal law of England in the Digest, submitted with their 7th Report, propose a scheme of penalties consisting of 45 classes to be substituted for the numerous varieties of punishment which now obtain. These may be reduced to four principal heads, viz., death, transportation, imprisonment, and fine.

P. 96.
Article 7, Chapter XXIV.

449. The Commissioners in their Report recommend the abolition of forfeiture, but there is a proviso in the chapter of Penalties which continues it by declaring that the classes of penalties therein set forth "shall not be deemed "to affect any law concerning forfeiture or any other "collateral consequence to which an offender is now liable on a conviction "of any offence which is an offence under this Act," which proviso is retained in the Draft Act relating to offences against the person appended to the 2nd Report of the present Commissioners on the Criminal Law.

P. 108.
5 & 6 Vic., c. 51.
Discharging or aiming fire-arms, &c., with intent to injure or alarm the Queen.

The Commissioners in their 7th Report, express an inclination to reject altogether the punishment of whipping except in the instance in which it has lately been imposed by the Legislature as constituting a signal mark of ignominy. It still appears however in some of the classes of penalties as a punishment which may be added to the principal one if the Court shall think fit.

450. "Capital offences below the degree of treason," say the English Criminal Law Commissioners, "are now founded almost "wholly on the principle that they involve either the "wilful destruction of human life, or the wilful exposing "it to peril." Such are the following which the English Law punishes with death :—

DEATH. 7th Report, p. 96. Treason, Class 1. Murder, &c., 2.

1. Murder.
2. Attempting to commit murder by administering poison or by wounding, &c.
3. Burglary aggravated by assault with intent to murder, &c.
4. Robbery with wounding.
5. Piracy aggravated by assault with intent to murder any person on board the vessel in respect of which the piracy is committed.
6. Setting fire to a dwelling-house any person living therein.
7. Destroying vessels with intent to murder.
8. Exhibiting false lights, &c., with intent to bring a vessel into danger, &c.

451. The only offences not falling within the above category which are punishable with death are,

9. Destroying Ships of War, Royal Arsenals, &c.
10. Unnatural offences.

TRANSPORTATION. **452.** The classes of transportation are as follows :—

Class 3. For life positively.
„ 4 to 8. For life, or any term not less than 7 years.
„ 9 to 12. For a term not exceeding 15 years, and not less than 7 years.
Classes 13 and 14. For a term not exceeding 10 years, and not less than 7 years.
Class 15 to 17. For the term of 7 years.

453. In all but one class (the 4th) imprisonment for a term not exceeding 3 years may be inflicted as the alternative in lieu of transportation for life or for any shorter term. In two classes (5th and 9th) the imprisonment must not be for less than 1 year. In three classes (8th, 11th, 16th,) fine may be substituted for transportation, instead of imprisonment; in two of these (11th and 16th) fine may be added to imprisonment. In four classes (6th, 10th, 13th and 15th,) the offender may be sentenced to whipping in addition.

IMPRISONMENT. **454.** The longest term of imprisonment as a substantive punishment is 3 years. The classes are as follows :

Class 18. For a term not exceeding 3 years, and not less than 1 year.
„ 19. Not exceeding 3 years, and not less than 6 months.
„ 20 to 22. Not exceeding 3 years.
„ 23 to 26. Not exceeding 2 years.
„ 27. Not exceeding 18 months.
„ 28. For 1 year.
„ 29 to 31. Not exceeding 1 year.
Classes 32 and 33. For 6 months.
„ 34 and 35. Not exceeding 6 months.
Class 36 to 38. For 3 months.
„ 39 to 41. Not exceeding 3 months.

455. In four classes 20th, 32nd, 36th and 37th, fine must be added to imprisonment; in the first of these classes the fine is unlimited, in the rest it is limited. In several classes 31st, 24th, 25th, 27th, 29th, 34th, 39th, fine may be substituted or added; in one only of these classes (25th) the fine is limited; in two classes fine may be substituted but not added, (31st and 41st) the fine being limited.

FINE.

456. There are four classes of penalties consisting of fine simply, viz:—

Class 42. Fine at discretion.
„ 43. Fine of 500£.
„ 44. Not exceeding 100£.
„ 45. Fine of 40£.

457. With the classes in which fines are authorized as alternative or additional to imprisonment, there are altogether twenty-one classes in which fine is prescribed or authorized as a punishment. In ten the amount of fine is limited, in eleven it is left to discretion.

PUNISHMENTS OF THE CODE.
DEATH.
See Appendix, Note A, page 93.

458. With respect to the punishment of death, the authors of the Code anticipated that many persons might think they had erred in restricting it to cases in which either murder or the highest offence against the State has been committed, and might be of opinion that gang robbery, the cruel mutilation of the person, and possibly rape, ought to be liable to capital punishment. We find the extension of capital punishment to gang robbery advocated by several Officers of the Madras Presidency, particularly by Mr. Kindersley, Mr. F. M. Lewin, Mr. S. Scott, Mr. J. J. Cotton, and Mr. E. Maltby, and by an experienced and intelligent Native Officer, Tambusawmy Moodily. Mr. J. F. Thomas would extend the penalty of death to convicts returned from transportation. Mr. E. Maltby would include under the punishment of death, besides gang or torch robberies at night accompanied by wounding, the offences of setting fire to dwelling-houses, and the pollution of mosques for the purpose of creating popular disturbances, as loss of life is generally a consequence of such acts. In the last suggestion Mr. F. N. Maltby concurs.

459. Mr. A. D. Campbell states that "the gravest doubts have arisen "in his mind of the efficacy of death as a punishment, especially in "India." After mentioning general grounds for these doubts, he observes that in 1830 the Madras Sudder Foujdaree Adawlut issued an order requiring the Officers executing death-warrants to record the impressions made by the execution in every case, in order to assist a judgment of the effect of such examples, and that having examined these records for several years, their perusal has strongly confirmed him in the doubts he before entertained. He notices particularly some remarkable reports by the Native Judge of Vizagapatam of executions superintended by him, as exemplifying the power of superstition in annihilating the dread of this punishment, observing that "where superstition prevails "to such a lamentable extent as this, death, the last sentence of the law, "is robbed of all its terrors. The people collected by idle curiosity, or "by that inclination for spectacles of any kind which characterizes "Indians, sympathize with the expiring criminal, as a sacrifice to fate— "purified by the extreme unction of the ruling power—and the lamentable "scene exhibited (by the Native Judge) with a truth which none but a "Native was capable of portraying, closes with an interchange of civili- "ties between the spectators and the dying culprit." "The apathy ex-

"hibited by the spectators," he remarks, "is greatly exceeded by that displayed by the culprits themselves." On the whole however Mr. Campbell says, "I am not prepared, on this subject, to recommend any alteration in the law itself; but its administration should I think be greatly modified. The Executive Government should take the punishment of death more into its own hands with the view of gradually diminishing the number of capital executions, increasing their solemnity and effect, and organizing a system for the occasional revision of capital sentences."

460. The Officers who propose to extend capital punishment, as abovementioned, entertain generally a lighter opinion of the efficacy of the punishment of transportation than that which is expressed by the authors of the Code. Mr. Kindersley observes that "the feeling of horror for it is beginning to wear off, from the accounts of Sepoys and escaped Convicts, a fact best proved by the general emigration to Mauritius and the Eastward." Tambusawmy Moodily has observations to the same effect, adding that "the mystery is gone by." Mr. Vaughan says, "With regard to the 'Black Water' which the Commissioners view as so terrible to the Native, I believe that they will find that the march of intellect and of Troops to the Eastern Settlements has extended the information of those of the Madras Presidency (at any rate) on these matters considerably. Still I believe it is more dreaded than death by men of high caste, while others may hear of the ease and independence which (Officers who have been to the Eastward have described it to me) afford quite a burlesque on severe punishment." Mr. F. N. Maltby mentions that "two Regiments lately returned from the Eastward have been stationed in this district (Canara), and have brought information of the manner in which the prisoners in the penal settlements live, and of the wages they receive as private servants, which must deduct from the terrors of the punishment, especially in a maritime province."

Report to the Governor-General of India in Council, dated the 8th January 1838. Para. 216.

461. The Committee upon Prison Discipline while they recommended the retention of the punishment of transportation, as a punishment which "in this country and at the present time, while it causes less pain excites among the great mass of the people greater terror than imprisonment for life," admitted, however, that "at the capital of the Presidencies where transportation for terms of years is a common punishment, the feeling is not the same." "Probably also," they observed, "in the neighbourhood of all sea-ports the feeling is generally less strong than it is with the mass of the people. Seafaring people have undoubtedly none of this peculiar feeling. But those who fall within these exceptions form but a small portion of the population of British India. Nevertheless," they continued, "they are sufficiently numerous to prevent our arguments" (in favor of this mode of punishment in comparison with imprisonment for life) "from applying with their full effect universally. Yet our arguments apply to their full extent so generally, that if the Government should coincide in our views, in order to make the most use by way of example of the same actual infliction, the penalty of transportation for life ought to be generally preferred to that of imprisonment for life for the most heinous

Para. 217.

offences not punished with death." Adverting to communications received from Madras by the Indian

Law Commissioners "complaining of the laxity of discipline amongst "the prisoners in the Straits, and stating that in consequence of the "agreeable life which the convicts there lead, the terror of transporta-"tion has greatly diminished in some maritime parts of the country," the Committee observed that "this is a great evil, but that it arises "chiefly from the mismanagement of the convicts, and the remedy is "very simple."

462. We think that the authors of the Code have given very cogent reasons for not punishing with death any crime against the person which stops short of murder. They argue that "to put robbers, "ravishers and mutilators on the same footing with "murderers is an arrangement which diminishes the "security of life." Offences of this kind they observe, "are almost "always committed under such circumstances that the offender has it in "his power to add murder to his guilt. They are often committed under "such circumstances that the offender has a temptation to add murder "to his guilt. The same opportunities, the same superiority of force "which enabled a man to rob, to mangle, or to ravish, will enable him "to go further and despatch his victim. As he has almost always the "power to murder he will often have a strong motive to murder, "inasmuch as by murder he may remove the only witness of the crime "which he has already committed. If the punishment of the crime "which he has already committed be exactly the same with the punish-"ment for murder, he will have no restraining motive."

See Appendix, Note A, page 93.

463. It is probably true that the punishment of transportation is less dreadful to some classes of the Natives than it was, for since multitudes of free persons have been in the habit of shipping themselves to Mauritius, and even to the West Indies, and returning from time to time, it is to be supposed that the horror of the "black water" which principally made it awful, has greatly abated. It is true too that the people who are most apt to engage in gang robberies are among those who have learnt to regard this incident in the punishment of transportation which formerly had so powerful an effect, with comparative indifference. Still there is reason to believe that with the many who have not been in the way to become familiar with the idea of passing the sea as a common event, the dread of it still prevails to a degree that makes a sentence of transporta-tion a terrible punishment. And even without this aggravation there is enough we conceive in a perpetual exile in a foreign land and a perpetual separation from all persons and things which have been through life the objects of interest to a man, with perpetual privation of all indulgences, under a rigid discipline such as ought to be maintained in a penal settle-ment, there is enough we conceive in these essential incidents of the punishment of transportation to make it always very formidable and of powerful efficacy. But were it less so than we suppose, and were it evident with respect to gang robberies in particular, that men are not to be deterred by the fear of it from committing this kind of offence, which is unquestionably a very atrocious one, and extremely alarming to the peaceable people liable to be victims of it, we think it would not be justi-fiable to try the experiment of putting it down by resorting to capital punishment, for even supposing that the experiment should be partially successful, that the number of gang robberies should be diminished, which is a matter of speculation, there would be a great risk of the offence being aggravated by acts of greater atrocity whenever it should be committed, the offenders being rendered desperately reckless, and their ferocity exasperated, by the consciousness of their liability to death at all events.

464. This objection does not apply to visiting with capital punishment convicts returning from transportation for life; and considering the importance of keeping up the impression that this punishment absolutely precludes the hope of returning, that it cuts off the criminal from any chance of future intercourse with his kindred and connections, and re-appearing on the scene of his former active life, as effectually as if he were removed by death, especially in the case of notorious Dacoits who have been the terror of a country, we see some reason for hesitating with respect to such heinous criminals at least, to abolish the powerful bar which the fear of death opposes to their attempting to escape from transportation. At present a convict returning from transportation is liable to suffer death by the law in force in the Supreme Courts in India, (though the offence is no longer capital in England) and by the Regulations of Bengal and Madras, but not by the law of the Bombay Presidency.

465. But though what appears to us a very strong, indeed a conclusive objection, to punishing such crimes as gang robbery with death, does not apply to the case of a convict returned from transportation, and we recognize a reason of some force for making that offence capital in respect to convicts *under sentence for such crimes*, in order to give the utmost efficacy to the punishment of transportation, yet on the whole we are of opinion that the line drawn by the framers of the Code, by which the punishment of death is confined to cases where either murder or the highest offence against the State has been committed, ought to be maintained.

TRANSPORTATION.

466. With respect to transportation, from the absence of objection it may be concluded that there is a general consent to the principle that this punishment shall be invariably for life.

IMPRISONMENT. Note A, p. 95.

467. The authors of the Code express a hope that it will shortly be found practicable to reduce the terms of imprisonment proposed by them through the introduction of an improved system of prison discipline. They seem to have anticipated that the terms might be reduced to about one half, that one year's confinement under a good system of discipline would generally prove as efficacious as confinement for two years under a lax one. Mr. J. F. Thomas recommends that the terms of imprisonment be reduced at once. He says, "To a people who, in nine cases out of ten, "cannot compute time; who know not whether their children were "born ten, twelve, or fourteen years back, nor their own age—when the "friends and associates of a prisoner cannot tell, in the majority of cases, "whether he has been respectively 6 or 7, or 10 or 14 years in jail— "the long terms of imprisonment provided for by the Code, appear to "me the infliction of so much needless pain—and except in the case of "notorious offenders, as leaders of gangs, or persons detained on security "for the peace of the district, an useless expense entailed on Govern- "ment. The only notion of the punishment the criminal can now form, "is, that it has been a long separation from his home; and that idea is "as strong, when the imprisonment has been ten, as when it has been "fourteen years. I almost think it indeed demonstrable in the case of "offenders of the uneducated classes, who probably constitute nine-tenths "of the criminals, that 6, 8, and 10 years are respectively, as effective "penalties, as 7, 10, and 14 years; and that the terms of imprisonment "now provided, should therefore be reduced." Mr. Thomas would leave the present terms only in the cases of suborners of perjury or forgery, leaders of dacoits, and similar offenders of great criminality, or more raised in society. Mr. Vaughan also recommends that the terms of imprisonment be reduced, with greater rigour during imprisonment.

468. We agree with the authors of the Code that whenever a Code of prison discipline shall be brought into operation which, without shocking the humane feelings of the community, may yet be a terror to the most hardened among them, it will be advisable greatly to shorten many of the terms of imprisonment.

469. We have noticed that it is only in one case that imprisonment which may extend to life is prescribed positively as the specific punishment of the offence. In all other cases imprisonment which may extend to life, is authorized as the alternative for transportation for life. In awarding punishment in these cases, we are of opinion, with the Committee on prison discipline, that the penalty of transportation for life ought to be generally preferred to imprisonment for life, indeed that this alternative should not be resorted to but for special reasons, referring to age, sex, infirmities, &c., rendering transportation an unfit punishment in particular cases.*

Para. 216.

470. While imprisonment for life, or which may extend to life, is the alternative for transportation for life by the Code, the Digest of the English Law fixes three years as the maximum term of imprisonment to be inflicted in the alternative for transportation for life, or for any term of years. The Commissioners observe that "were the "alternative terms of imprisonment to be regarded as "equivalents, to be substituted at discretion for another "species of punishment, our recommendation would involve inconsis- "tencies; for, if imprisonment for three years were to be regarded as a "proper equivalent for fifteen years' transportation, the same term of "imprisonment could not be a proper equivalent for either a higher or "lower maximum of transportation. Such terms of imprisonment, how- "ever, are not meant as equivalents, but simply as alternatives to be "adopted at the discretion of the Court. Upon this subject it is proper "to observe, that where imprisonment may be inflicted as a lower and "alternative punishment, it is by no means necessary, but that on the "contrary it would be inconvenient, that the highest alternative punish- "ment by imprisonment should be proportioned to the highest alternative "of transportation. It is desirable that whatever be the extremes of "punishment, there should be no such chasm as might exclude the inflic- "tion of any such intermediate degree of punishment as the exercise of "discretionary authority might require. If, for example, the extremes "of punishment were in one case to be transportation for life and "imprisonment for one year, but, in another instance, transportation for "fifteen years and imprisonment for one year, it is obvious that, as it "was in common to the two offences that the punishment should be

7th Report, p. 103.

* Act XIV of 1844 directs that whenever a Sudder Court shall sentence an offender to imprisonment for life, it shall at the same time sentence such offender to transportation for life, unless there be special reasons inducing the Court to think he is not a proper subject for transportation.

"varied at discretion from fifteen years' transportation to one year's "imprisonment, the discretionary power within those limits should be "the same in both cases. This, however, could not be, if in the one case "imprisonment for four years might be inflicted, whilst in the other the "highest alternative of imprisonment was restricted to three years. A "common maximum of the intermediate alternative punishment is not "only proper for the purpose of preserving a continuity in the scale of "punishment between two extremes, but is also advisable for the purpose "of affording a wider discretion as to the kind of punishment in reference "to the circumstances of each particular case."

471. We confess we are not satisfied by this reasoning, that there should be one maximum term for imprisonment when it is inflicted in the alternative for transportation for life, and when it is inflicted in lieu of transportation for 7 years. And we do not know how the argument is to be reconciled with what is stated in the following paragraph, in which the Commissioners say "the terms of imprisonment proposed as alter- "natives for the shorter terms of transportation are not, we feel assured, "of longer duration than is necessary for affording room for the exercise "of a sound discretion," but "the length of the highest alternative term "of imprisonment might, we think, have been conveniently extended." Here they seem to intimate an opinion that when imprisonment is substituted for transportation the term of it should bear some proportion to the term of transportation, at least that the term should be longer when it is substituted for transportation for life, or a long term of years, than when it is substituted for transportation for a short term of years. The reasons which they give in this place for not extending the highest alternative punishment is simply that they regard certain late enactments "as a legislative declaration, that no alternative term of imprisonment "ought to exceed three years."

472. In the Indian Code imprisonment as a substantive punishment occupies the place of transportation for terms of years in the English law. The Digest, as we have seen, limits the term of imprisonment when it is inflicted as a substantive punishment as well as when it is substituted for another penalty, to 3 years. By late intelligence from England, it would seem to be intended to substitute imprisonment for transportation to a great extent, without prolonging the maximum term.

BANISHMENT.

Ante para. 27.

473. We have remarked that there are only three Clauses (113, 114, and 290) in which banishment from the Territories of the East India Company is authorized as the primary punishment of offences. In commenting upon Clause 113 we reserved our opinion upon the propriety of the punishment of banishment for the offence of "attempting to excite feelings of disaffection to the Government" therein defined, until we should have maturely considered the chapter of Punishments. We have now to submit our opinion that it would be an unwarrantable severity to inflict the punishment of banishment for life upon a Native of the Territories of the East India Company constantly domiciled there from birth, for the offence in question. Probably the extreme penalty of banishment *for life* was not intended to be applied to persons of this description, but to temporary inhabitants. It might perhaps be sometimes politically expedient to banish a temporary inhabitant, convicted of attempting to excite disaffection to the Government, for life. But we do not think it consistent with the principles upon which the penal provisions of the

Code have been constructed generally, to extend the punishment beyond the measure of the offence upon any such consideration. We think the punishment of banishment is a fit punishment for the offence, but we would recommend that the term be limited to 5 years, as the term of simple imprisonment, which may be inflicted in the alternative, is limited to 3 years.

FINE. See Appendix, Note A, page 97.

474. Upon the subject of fine, the authors of the Code observe that in imposing it as a punishment "it is always necessary "to have as much regard to the pecuniary circumstances "of the offender as to the character and magnitude of "the offence." "It is impossible to fix any limit to the "amount of a fine which will not either be so high as to be ruinous to "the poor, or so low as to be no object of terror to the rich. There "are many millions in India who would be utterly unable to pay a fine "of fifty rupees; there are hundreds of thousands from whom such a "fine might be levied, but whom it would reduce to extreme distress; "there are thousands to whom it would give very little uneasiness; "there are hundreds to whom it would be a matter of perfect indif-"ference, and who would not cross a room to avoid it. The number of "the poor in every country exceeds in a very great ratio the number of "the rich. The number of poor criminals exceeds the number of rich "criminals in a still greater ratio. And to the poor criminal it is a "matter of absolute indifference whether the fine to which he is liable be "limited or not, unless it be so limited as to render it quite inefficient as "a mode of punishing the rich. To a man who has no capital, who has "laid by nothing, whose monthly wages are just sufficient to provide "himself and his family with their monthly rice, it matters not whether "the fine for assault be left to be settled by the discretion of the Courts, "or whether a hundred rupees be fixed as the maximum. There are no "degrees in impossibility. He is no more able to pay a hundred rupees "than to pay a lac. A just and wise judge, even if entrusted with a "boundless discretion, will not, under ordinary circumstances, sentence "such an offender to a fine of a hundred rupees. And the limit of a "hundred rupees would leave it quite in the power of an unjust or "inconsiderate judge to inflict on such an offender all the evil which can "be inflicted on him by means of fine."

"If, in imitation of Mr. Livingstone, we provide that no fine shall "exceed one-fourth of the amount of the offender's property, no serious "fine will ever be imposed in this country without a long and often a "most unsatisfactory investigation, in which it would be necessary to "decide many obscure questions of right purposely darkened by every "artifice of chicanery. And even, if this great practical difficulty did "not exist, we should see strong objections to such a provision in a very "large class of cases. Take the case of a corrupt judge, who has accu-"mulated a lac of rupees by his illicit practices. A fine which should "deprive such a man of the whole of his fortune would not appear to us "excessive. And certainly we should think it most undesirable that "he should be allowed to retain 75,000 rupees of his ill-gotten gains. "Again: take the case of a man who has been suborned to commit "perjury, and has received a great bribe for doing so. Such a man "may have little, or no property, except what he has received as a bribe. "Yet it is evidently desirable that he should be compelled to disgorge "the whole. No man ought ever to gain by breaking the law; and if

"Mr. Livingstone's rule were adopted in this country, many would gain "by breaking the law."

"We have never seen any general rule for the limiting of fine, which "we are disposed to adopt. The difficulty of framing a rule has evidently "been felt by many eminent men. The authors of the Bill of Rights, "with many instances of gross abuse fresh in their recollection, could "devise no other rule than that excessive fines should not be imposed. "And the authors of the constitution of the United States, after the "experience of another century, contented themselves with repeating "the words of the Bill of Rights."

"It will be seen that in cases which are not very heinous we propose to "limit the amount of fine which the Courts may impose. But in serious "cases we have left the amount of fine absolutely to their discretion; "and we feel, as we have said, that, even in the cases where we have "proposed a limit, such a limit will be no protection to the poor, who "in every community are also the many. We feel that the extent of the "discretion which we have thus left to the Courts is an evil, and that "no sagacity and no rectitude of intention can secure a Judge from "occasional error. We conceive, however, that if fine is to be employed "as a punishment, and no judicious person, we are persuaded, would "propose to dispense with it,—this evil must be endured. We shall "attempt in the Code of Procedure to establish such a system of appeal "as may prevent gross or frequent injustice from taking place."

475. Blackstone observes on this subject "that the quantum of "pecuniary fines neither can nor ought to be ascertained "by an invariable law. The value of money itself "changes from a thousand causes; and, at all events, what is ruin to "one man's fortune, may be matter of indifference to another's." "Statute law has not therefore often ascertained the quantity of fines, nor "the common law ever."

Comm. 4. 377.

476. The English Criminal Law Commissioners in their 7th Report remark, that "the inequality and injustice in some cases, and the inefficacy in others, of resorting to *fixed and absolute* fines as a mode of penal "restraint confine its adoption within narrow limits, principally to instances of minor delinquencies punishable by virtue of a summary "jurisdiction, and in some particular instances of higher magnitude "where the condition of the class of person on whom the restraint operates, is such as to remove, or at least greatly to reduce the probability "that it will operate either with unequal severity, or will be ineffectual "from the inability of those who offend to pay the fine, and where, in "addition, such a mode of punishment is appropriate to the nature of "the offence, and does not afford room for invidious comparison with "other instances in which corporal punishment is inflicted in respect of "less heinous transgressions."

477. With respect to the discretionary power of punishment by fine, they observe that it does not admit of a limit, "the magnitude of a fine must in justice be proportioned to the offender's means."

P. 107.

478. In respect of the few offences for which by the Code fine is the sole punishment, (none being very serious) the amount of fine is limited in all but one, and while for every other offence in the Code (except one which involves the forfeiture

Supra para. 444.

of all property) fine *may* be imposed either as a substitute for other punishment, or in addition, the number of cases in which the amount is limited is no more than 70, the maximum being 5,000 rupees, and there being only 12 cases in which the amount exceeds 1,000 rupees, and 28 in which it is above 500 rupees.

Para. 446.

479. In the Digest, as we have before remarked, out of 4 classes in which fine is the sole punishment, the fine is limited in all but one; while out of 21 classes of penalties in which fine is an ingredient, in 10 the amount of fine is limited, in 11 it is left to discretion. The 25th class is the highest in which the fine is limited, the maximum being 500£—it is alternative for imprisonment not exceeding 2 years. This class we believe is applicable to a single offence. The next highest class of limited fine is the 31st, in which the maximum is 100£, alternative for imprisonment for 1 year. This also appears to be applicable to a single case. Other classes in which the fine is limited appear likewise to have a special application to particular offences.

Para. 456.

Art. 14, Sec. 5, Chapetr V of Digest.

Art. 7, Sec. 4, Chapter VIII of Digest.

480. Sir J. Awdry says, "As regards fine I agree that the only "just rule is the indefinite one of the 'Bill of Rights.'" "The investi-"gation of the amount of a man's property is impossible. The fining to "the whole extent of property acquired by crime is not excessive."

481. Mr. Sharkey has attempted to controvert the reasoning which led the authors of the Code to leave the amount of the fine unlimited in the great majority of the cases to which that punishment is applicable. The conclusion he comes to is that "it will be more expedient and "consistent to do away with it (the penalty of fine) altogether, and "substitute some other penalty for it, than that the measure of the "penalty should be left to the arbitrary and discretionary power of a "Judge, especially so 'an unjust and inconsiderate Judge.'" It appears to us that he has not made out more than is admitted by the authors of the Code, namely, that "the discretion left to the Courts is "an evil." They contend that if fine is to be employed as a punishment this evil must be endured. Rather than it should be endured, Mr. Sharkey would dispense with the punishment of fine altogether, a measure which *they* were persuaded no judicious person would propose. Mr. Sharkey has not suggested any substitute for this punishment, being satisfied of the feasibility of limiting the fine in every case; and "the fine "being once apportioned to the offence must be considered as founded "on its legitimate basis, and like every other limited punishment be "awarded without any hesitation, whatever the circumstances of the "offender might be."

482. Mr. Vaughan "protests against the high estimation of the "great and obvious advantage of fine expressed by the Commissioners "in page 5 of their notes," and "wonders how they came to the resolution of proposing fines in every case, &c." It is to be observed here that fine is not *proposed* but *authorized* in every case, an observation which obviates the objection that Mr. Vaughan appears to ground upon the extreme poverty "of the millions" in India. Mr. Vaughan would narrow the application of fine very considerably—"I would propose," he says, "fine commutable (if not paid) to private but rigorous "imprisonment for cases of offence of a slight and palliable nature "committed by those not previously convicted of any, and for those "only." He extends this afterwards by suggesting that "heavy fines "at the discretion of the Court should also be adjudged for the use "of Government in cases of extortion, corruption, forgery, and all "offences relating to coin, gang robbery, considerable thefts, and "receiving stolen property, such being cases arising from cupidity, "beyond the petty theft which proceeds from sudden temptation or "idle habits." "In all cases below those which demand transporta- "tion or death and confiscation of property," he thinks "rigorous "imprisonment should be imposed, and fine should be added (without "reference to the means of the offender) for reimbursement to the "prosecutor for the loss of property sustained, or for remuneration on "account of damage to his person." In the slight cases for which he thinks fine the fitting punishment he would limit it, "*not to exceed* two "rupees in the case of any living by daily labour or as a petty cultivator; "five rupees on any petty farmer or shop-keeper; half a month's pay "for any one receiving wages; and in no case whatever to exceed 500 "rupees; drawing out the gradation even more minutely." "Offences "which Zemindars and other men of property are likely to commit in "contempt of authority, &c., may be distinctly stated, and the punish- "ment fixed in fines to a large amount." Further he says, "Let fine "stand as a part of the punishment which *may* be imposed for theft, but "let it be declared that the Courts should sentence to fines *for the use "of Government*, those only who may be reputed to have made large "gains by dishonest means. Let claims to *their* property be rigidly "scrutinized; but as to the mass of offenders, I hold that general fining "and power to levy within six years is most inexpedient, cruel to the "families, and mischievous to the general peace."

483. Mr. J. F. Thomas observes, that "the penalty of unlimited "fine so frequently provided gives the Courts enormous power open "to great abuse over the wealthy classes, who would suffer any thing "rather than the degradation of imprisonment in the Common Gaol." This objection seems to us to be hardly tenable, for if oppression were the object (and we do not see what other there could be in the wilful imposition of an excessive fine which must be accounted for) that object could be better accomplished by sentencing the party at once peremptorily "to the degradation of imprisonment in the common gaol" so much dreaded by the wealthy classes. Mr. Thomas points out as an example of possible abuse, in another direction, of the discretionary power of fining, that under Clause 390 an habitual receiver of stolen property might be let off with "a very trifling punishment, a fine possibly of trifling amount." He thinks that "in such cases the law should specifically provide for the infliction of the highest penalties, not leaving it to individual judgment." The offence in question, it will be remarked, is one of those "arising from cupidity," which Mr. Vaughan would have visited with heavy fine at the discretion of the Court. Certainly if a limit should be set to the fine by law it must be a high one. The clause now authorizes imprisonment which may extend to 3 years or fine or both. The fine could not be limited to less than 1,000 rupees, an amount which every one must acknowledge to be utterly inadequate in the case of one proved to have gained, it may be, tens of thousands, by his dealings with gangs of robbers, and equally in excess in the case of a petty dealer, who on some occasion may have received stolen goods from the hands of a thief, the value being a trifle. We cannot think that Mr. Thomas on reflection would desire that the law should not leave it to the discretion of the Court to inflict any but *the highest penalty* of imprisonment or fine, that is, imprisonment for 3 years, or fine, say to the amount of 1,000 rupees, in such a case.

484. Mr. G. W. Bacon objects to Clause 50, because "it leaves too "much to the discretion of the Judge, like the English law regarding the "punishment of manslaughter, and also because under the Code fines are "limited and unlimited in amount without any reason whatever, and "without any reference to the nature of the offence. Examples of the "kind are innumerable." In another place he says, "In page 6 of the "Notes, I find it was intended that serious cases alone called for un-"limited fine, but I have found many instances of it being made the "punishment of very trifling offences."

485. Certainly reasons are not given in every case in which the fine is limited, for applying a limitation, nor in every case in which it is unlimited, for dispensing with a limitation; to have done so would have been both cumbrous and inconvenient: but it is not to be concluded because reasons are not assigned, that the arrangement was made arbitrarily. In the instances cited by Mr. Bacon, the arrangement appears to us evidently systematic and referrible to principle. As to unlimited fine being authorized for very trifling offences, as Mr. Bacon alleges, we apprehend it will be found that though the offences may ordinarily be not very heinous, yet they are occasionally aggravated to a degree that renders it necessary to give power to the Courts to enhance the punishment by adding fine at discretion to the primary penalty, which is probably imprisonment limited to a short term.

486. We do not pretend to affirm that the authors of the Code have always been successful in drawing the line in the matter of fines. We have ourselves suggested amendments here and there, sometimes to remove the limitation proposed by them, sometimes to introduce a limitation where they did not think it necessary, sometimes to extend the limitation. But after a very close examination of the whole Code the instances in which we have seen reason to suggest alterations are far from numerous.

487. Having explained their provisions for the imposition of fines, the authors of the Code proceed to state the arrangements they propose to be observed in default of payment. "We propose," they say, "that "at the time of imposing a fine, the Court shall also fix a certain term "of imprisonment. In fixing this term, the Court will in no case be "suffered to exceed a certain maximum, which will vary according to the "nature of the offence. If the offence be one which is punishable with "imprisonment as well as fine, the term of imprisonment in default of "payment will not exceed one-fourth of the longest term of imprison-"ment fixed by the Code for the offence. If the offence be one which, "by the Code, is punishable only with fine, the term of imprisonment "for default of payment will in no case exceed seven days."

"But we do not mean that this imprisonment shall be taken in full "satisfaction of the fine. We cannot consent to permit the offender to "choose whether he will suffer in person or in his property. To adopt "such a course would be to grant exemption from the punishment of "fine to those very persons on whom it is peculiarly desirable that the "punishment of fine should be inflicted, to those very persons who "dislike that punishment most, and whom the apprehension of that "punishment would be most likely to restrain. We therefore propose "that the imprisonment which an offender has undergone shall not "release him from the pecuniary obligation under which he lies. His "person will, indeed, cease to be answerable for the fine. But his "property will for a time continue to be so. What we "recommend is that, at any time during a certain limited "period, the fine may be levied on his effects by distress. "If the fine is paid or levied while he is imprisoned for default of pay- "ment, his imprisonment will immediately terminate, and if a portion "of the fine be paid during the imprisonment, a proportional abatement "of the imprisonment will take place."

Clauses 55, 56, and 57.

488. The limited period during which the fine may be levied on any effects of the offender that may be found available is 6 years, a period which we apprehend has been adopted from the English Statute of limitations, and the corresponding provision regarding simple debts in the Bombay Code, and it is provided that the death of the offender (if it takes place within 6 years we presume) does not discharge from liability any property which would after his death be legally liable for his debts. It is to be observed, in considering this provision, that the authors of the Code contemplate an arrangement to enable every person who is injured by an offence to obtain reparation for the injury, by making it competent to the tribunal which has tried the offender to award the whole or part of the fine to the sufferer, provided that the sufferer signifies his willingness to receive what is so awarded in full satisfaction of his civil claim for reparation, and if he prefers to sue for damages in the Civil Court, to make the fine answerable as far as it will go in satisfying those damages.

Clause 57.

See Appendix, Note A, page 101.

489. Objections have been made to the proposed provisions on this head in regard to two points chiefly, viz. the limitation of the period of imprisonment in default of payment of a fine when the offence is punishable with fine only, to 7 days, the imprisonment being simple; and the keeping the fine hanging over the offender when he has suffered imprisonment in default of payment, during 6 years, and making it recoverable after his death from any property left by him which would be liable for his debts.

490. With respect to the first point it is observed in the Note, that "if the offender has not the means of paying the fine "while he is subject to it he will be quit for his impri- "sonment." So also, however, an offender having the means of paying the fine, but his property not being tangible, might be quit likewise for simple imprisonment during 7 days, setting at nought the provision for levying the fine on his effects at a future time, by removing from the place. This would be likely in such a case as is provided for by Clause 287, in which the fine may amount to 1,000 rupees. It is true that the number of offences punishable with fine only as set forth in para. 444 is small, and that the offences are not of much importance, and not in general involving moral guilt. And with respect to some it is probable that the offenders will generally be in circumstances to enable them to pay the fine, and persons who will rather pay the fine than go to gaol for the shortest period. But it may be otherwise. And we cannot but

Note A, p. 100.

think that a discretion should be given to extend the imprisonment. With respect to two of the offences which the Code makes punishable with fine only (Clauses 242 and 400) we have recommended that they be liable to imprisonment also.

491. On the second point the authors of the Code have anticipated the objection that the proposed rule will operate harshly. They take the case of an offender who, being really unable to pay his fine, lies in prison for a term, and within 6 years after his sentence acquires property, as the only case in which the objection can be made with any plausibility. "Even in this case," they remark, "it is evident that the "proposed law will operate far less harshly than a law which should "provide that an offender sentenced to a fine should be imprisoned till "the fine should be paid. Under both laws imprisonment is inflicted, "under both a fine is exacted. But the one law liberates the offender "on payment of the fine, and also fixes limit beyond which he cannot be "detained in gaol whether the fine be paid or no. The other law keeps "him in confinement till the money is actually paid. It is therefore at "least as severe as ours on his property, and is immeasurably more "severe on his person." They then observe that by the English law in the case of an insolvent not a trader, where his person is liberated his future acquisitions still continue to be liable to the claims of his creditors. They consider an offender who has been sentenced to fine, "as a debtor, and as a debtor not entitled to any peculiar lenity," and they conclude that "if a temporary imprisonment for debt ought not to cancel the "claim of the private debtor, neither ought a temporary imprisonment "in default of payment of a fine to cancel the claims of public justice." The analogy of the private creditor will be the more apt and perfect if the arrangement contemplated by the authors of the Code for giving reparation for injury out of the fine imposed upon the offender be adopted.

492. Mr. W. B. Anderson says, "The difficult question, when a fine "has been imposed, what measures shall be adopted in default of pay-"ment? appears to me to have been ably argued by the Law Commis-"sioners. I think they have clearly shewn why the imprisonment which "an offender may have undergone, should not release him from the "pecuniary obligation under which he lies—and that the offender who "has been sentenced to fine must be considered as a debtor, and as a "debtor not entitled to any particular lenity."

493. Sir J. Awdry thinks that the plan proposed of a limited additional imprisonment and a right still to levy the fine, is better than the indefinite imprisonment of the English law; but he prefers the power of increasing the rigor to extending the term. He conceives that the power of changing simple into rigorous imprisonment would be a very desirable mode of enforcing in many instances the payment of fine, "dwelling on the importance of making him who pays in person because "he cannot pay in purse, work out his liberation within the term of his "original sentence."

494. Mr. Casamajor says, "I do not see on what principle the "liability is here limited to six years; nor is it explained in the Notes. "In the parallel case of civil debtors there is no such limitation. "Quære, might not that parallel be still further applicable to fines? "And when the imprisonment substituted for the fine has been under-

"gone, might not the party fined be allowed, like an insolvent debtor, as "a condition of his liberation, to enter into proof that he had *bonâ fide* "given up all his property. In case he did satisfactorily prove this, "he might be liberated, in case he did not he should be still detained, "nor could this well be complained of as a hardship, because the deten- "tion would be voluntary."

495. On the question of making fines a means of reparation, as suggested in the Note, Sir J. Awdry says, "I am clear that the Commis- "sioners are right both in the holding that civil satisfaction should not "be lost because the crime is a great one, and that the suffering inflicted "by requiring that satisfaction should go in part of the punishment." "Mr. A. D. Campbell considers "the admirable principle of involving "compensation to the injured in the punishment of crimes, especially of "those against property, as quite invaluable." He "hails the proposed "enactment as a long-needed and most welcome blessing, particularly "if the law of procedure is, as promised, so framed that one trial should "do the work of two." Mr. M. Lewin says: "Hitherto there has been "neither vengeance nor compensation in the law. The Code proposes "to unite these principles—though the merit of the invention does not "belong to its framers; it is to be found in some of the Regulations of "the Local Government, and also in the Mahomedan law. The principle "obtained in the country before it came under British rule, and its "disregard has been a fruitful source of complaint against all its arrange- "ments." "In a country such as India, where the great majority of the "people are poor, and unable to sustain the ordinary expense incident to "the maintenance of their rights,—where cheap justice is the only "justice—the principle should be carried to its utmost limit, it should "be prompt and complete justice at the least possible cost to the injured "party." Mr. Vaughan, Mr. Anderson, Mr. Casamajor, Mr. J. F. Thomas, and others, also approve of the principle, and consider the object highly desirable. Mr. F. N. Maltby, on the other hand, points out the danger of leading to false charges in order to transfer a true cause from the civil to the criminal file, and to charges actually false, a consideration which is referred to also by the Commissioners on the English Criminal Law.

496. But while Mr. Campbell and Mr. Casamajor approve of the principle of involving compensation to the injured in the punishment of crimes, they think it should not be carried into effect in the manner proposed. The following are the observations of Mr. Casamajor, in which Mr. Campbell expresses his concurrence. "*Fine* should be distinguished from *restitu-* "*tion*. The corrupt judge and the perjurer, in page 6, and every other "illegal gainer, should be made to disgorge the whole of their illegal "gains so far as they were within their power, as *restitution*, and be "fined besides. For the restitution, imprisonment should not be allowed "as a substitute; the culprit should not be set free till he had accounted "satisfactorily for the whole of his illegal gains, and shewn what portions "of them were really and truly within his power, and what portions "irrecoverably and *bonâ fide* beyond his control, or the possibility of "recovery; for the fine, imprisonment should be allowed as a substitute, "because the fine is simply penal and so is the imprisonment in lieu of "it."

7th Report, p. 94.

497. Mr. Casamajor appears to mean actual restitution of property wrongfully acquired or as much of it as is recoverable, and nothing more.

Mr. Campbell would seem to mean actual restitution as far as possible, and making good the value of what cannot be restored, for he says it is only when the Court is satisfied that the offender's "means of repaying "the value of the remainder (after restitution of what property is forth-"coming) are quite exhausted" that the period of imprisonment ought to be limited.

498. The term "restitution" implies that something has been wrongfully obtained which is to be restored, and this appears to be the meaning attached to it by both these gentlemen generally; but Mr. Campbell speaks also of "remuneration for damage committed" as comprehended under this head, and we presume that in such a case, as there is nothing to be restored, he would have the damage assessed in money to be levied on the effects of the offender and paid to the party injured. Mr. Campbell proposes that "in cases of restitution where the money is due by the act "of the culprit himself it should be recoverable from him by distraint at "whatever time means may accrue."* "I see no reason," he says, "why the period for its recovery should be limited to 6 years only."

499. It seems to us that there is no substantial difference in effect between the imposition of a fine upon an offender and awarding a certain portion thereof, or the whole if need be, to the party whom he has injured, and the awarding of "restitution," including under that term reparation for damages as Mr. Campbell appears to intend, and the imposition of a fine, as separate acts. It appears to us that there would be inconvenience, in a case of theft, for example, in making an award of restitution absolutely, and that as a practical measure it would be necessary to provide that if the goods stolen cannot be restored the offender shall pay the value. It seems to be a simpler and more easy arrangement to impose a fine, and to order a certain portion of it to be paid to the party who has suffered loss or damage, providing in cases of theft, &c., that if the goods stolen are restored wholly or in part, the restitution shall discharge, or shall be credited in part satisfaction of so much of the fine as is awarded by way of reparation. A rule to this effect should form a part of the Code of Procedure. In every case we apprehend the process of distraint will be allowed for the recovery of fines where there is tangible property. This is a mode of "levying by process of law," such, we presume, as is meant in Clause 55. The Code of Procedure will of course give the necessary powers, and make such provisions as may be deemed proper regarding the reservation of tools, seed, &c., as suggested by Mr. Vaughan and Mr. A. D. Campbell.

500. We think there is some force in the distinction between imprisonment in default of payment of a fine which is strictly penal, and of one which is partly penal and partly compensative, upon the ground of which Mr. Casamajor and Mr. Campbell would let so much of the fine as is penal be *satisfied* by the endurance of imprisonment for a certain time where there is no property presently available for the discharge of it, while they would make future acquisitions of property answerable for the purpose of "restitution," or for the payment of so much of the fine as is intended for reparation. But, with a view to this distinction, if it

* Colonel Sleeman suggests that "when a fine is imposed for compensation to "another the person fined should be required to pay the whole amount, or to pro-"duce an application for his release within the period fixed, by the injured person, "or his or her heirs."

should be thought proper to establish it, there would be no necessity to separate the award of reparation from the fine, as under the provision intended by the Code, the portion of the fine awarded as compensation would be distinctly specified in the sentence. Some modifications of details would be requisite, and we should be rather inclined, in pursuance of Mr. Casamajor's suggestion, to make it a condition of the entire release of a person who has suffered imprisonment in default of payment of a fine that he should enter into proof that he had given up all his property without reserve, failing which, though liberated in person, the fine should still be leviable according to Clause 57.

501. It is to be observed that by an Act passed by the Government of India since the Penal Code was presented by the Indian Law Commissioners, Magistrates are empowered to levy fines imposed by them, by distress, and if no property is forthcoming to commit the offender to prison, there to be kept to hard labour for any term not exceeding 2 months where the fine does not exceed 50 rupees, and for any term not exceeding 4 months where the fine does not exceed 100 rupees, and for any term not exceeding 6 months in any other case.

Act II of 1839.

502. When fines are imposed by superior Criminal Courts in the Presidencies of Bengal and Madras, by the present laws they are required "to fix a definite period of imprisonment to be held as equivalent to the fine, at the "expiration of which the persons convicted shall be "discharged although they should have omitted to pay "the fine." The law is the same in the Bombay Presidency, except that the term of imprisonment is limited to 5 years.

Bengal Regulation XIV, 1797, Section 3.
Madras Regulation VII, 1802, Section 29.
Bombay Regulation XIV, 1827, Section 9.

503. The Regulations of Bengal and Madras above referred to, specially prohibit the imposition of fines by any Court of criminal jurisdiction save and except to the use of Government, and ordain that no pecuniary compensations, &c., shall be recoverable in any criminal prosecution. But with respect to Madras, Act XXX of 1845 makes it competent to Session Judges "in adjudging a sentence of fine to award such "fine, or any part of such fine in compensation to the party who may "have been injured, in like manner as it is competent to Magistrates to "award fines under Clause 2, Section 39, Regulation IX of 1816 of the "Madras Code." There is a similar provision for the Presidency of Bombay in Act IX of 1838. The principle of compensating prosecutors out of fines levied by the Supreme Courts is sanctioned by the Statute 9, Geo. IV, Cap. 74, Section 52. And the Act of the Government of India, No. XXXI of 1839, Section 29, following 7 and 8, Geo. IV, Cap. 29, Sections 41 and 42, and Cap. 30, Section 24, authorizes Justices of the Peace on summary convictions to award a fine over and above the value of property injured, &c.

504. The authors of the Code, after vindicating the punishments provided in it, proceed to explain why some others were omitted. They state particularly their reasons for omitting public exposure and flogging from their list of punishments. We are inclined on the whole, though not without hesitation, to agree with them, but there are many who are of a different opinion.

See Appendix, Note A, page 103—105.

505. Sir J. Awdry says, "I greatly doubt the expediency of totally "abolishing the punishment of public exposure. It should be very "sparingly used—should be confined to crimes really scandalous, and to "which we wish to teach the people that we attach a particular "opprobrium. The more atrocious species of the *crimen falsi* have this "character. They have moreover this characteristic, that whilst exposure "is, as the Commissioners justly remark, the most unequal of all punish-"ments, the severity varies, if restricted to this class of crimes, in a "great measure with the circumstances of aggravation of individual guilt "and public mischief." Mr. A. D. Campbell, Mr. Vaughan, Mr. A. W. Begbie, and others, think this kind of punishment should be retained for perjury and forgery, and crimes against nature.

506. A considerable majority of officers of the Madras Presidency express strong objections to the abolition of flogging as a punishment. It is to be remembered that the law, which abolished corporal punishment in the Territories subject to the Presidency of Fort William, was not extended to Madras and Bombay.

Regulation II, 1834.

507. The Commissioners thus conclude their observations on the subject:—"Being satisfied, therefore, that the punishment of flogging "can be proper only in a few cases, and not being satisfied that it is "necessary in any, we are unwilling to advise the Government to retrace "its steps, and to re-establish throughout the British Territories a practice "which, by a policy unquestionably humane, and by no means proved "to have been injudicious, has recently been abolished through a large "part of those Territories." Neither are we prepared to recommend to Government to recede from the position taken in 1834 on this subject. We believe that though corporal punishment is still legal in the Presidencies of Madras and Bombay, it is much more rarely resorted to than it used to be.

508. It is observed in Note A that the moderate flogging of young offenders for some petty offences is not open, at least in any serious degree, to the objections stated against the general use of this mode of punishment. On the contrary, it is admitted that in countries where a bad system of prison discipline exists, the punishment of flogging has in such cases a great advantage over that of imprisonment, namely, that the young offender is not exposed even for a day to the contaminating influence of an ill-regulated gaol. It was upon this ground we believe that the Magistrates were authorized by Act III of 1844, to punish offenders of tender age with stripes. At the same time, professedly as a temporary measure, until adequate improvement in prison discipline can be effected, the Magistrates were authorized to sentence to corporal punishment persons convicted of petty theft. By a later Act XVIII of 1845, on the ground that offences committed by convicts sentenced to imprisonment for life should be punished with greater severity than such offences are punished with in other cases, such convicts are made liable to corporal punishments. This may be considered a measure of prison discipline.

See page 104.

509. By Clause 59 it is declared that "where it is provided that "punishment shall be cumulative, that provision does "not authorize the combining in any case of the punish-"ments provided by more than two penal provisions of "this Code."

CUMULATIVE PUNISHMENT.

510. Sir J. Awdry commends "the expressly providing for cumulative punishment" as "very good." Sir H. Seton as we have already remarked, questions the propriety of this arrangement which runs through the Code and is a distinguishing feature of it. Mr. Norton says, "I conceive the doctrine of cumulative "punishment to be unjust in principle and calculated to perplex, as the "illustration to Clause 60 may serve to indicate. I conceive the plain "law of one punishment for one offence without breaking substantive "offences into separate offences is the best law." We have before mentioned what we take to be the principal reason for the arrangement in question, namely, to provide discriminately for aggravations which the English law provides for indiscriminately, by allowing a much greater latitude in the punishments for the primary offences. It will be found we think that the arrangement does not consist, as Mr. Norton imagines, "in breaking substantive offences into separate offences," but in prescribing appropriate punishments for the substantive offences, according to the definitions of them, without extrinsic aggravations, and providing that where an extrinsic aggravation does occur which amounts to an offence under any clause of the Code, the penalty of that offence may be added to the penalty of the primary offence. For example the penalties for house-trespass are laid down in Clause 426, and it is provided in Clause 427 that "if any person commits house-trespass in order to the committing "of another offence and actually commits that other offence the "punishment shall be cumulative," that is, the offender shall be liable to the punishment of that other offence as well as to the punishment of house-trespass. The punishment of either offence intended to be applied where there is no extrinsic aggravation, would be insufficient by itself; but the addition to be made in consequence of the extrinsic aggravation is not left to arbitrary discretion, the nature of the aggravation determines it, the Judge has to consider whether it amounts to an offence, and if it does, he will add the punishment of that offence. The Commissioners on the English Criminal Law remark that "one of the principal imperfections incident to the "system of punishment adopted by the law of England, is the want of "regular gradations of punishment corresponding with the aggravations "incident to large classes of crimes." "At present," they say, "such aggravations, though not defined, do in "fact enhance the punishment, yet the malefactor is not only without "notice of the intention to prove the circumstances which operate in "aggravation, but is without warning that they will be regarded as "aggravations." Under the arrangement adopted in the Code, the offender will have the most precise information both of the primary charge, and of the secondary charge alleged by way of aggravation, which if proved will subject him to a certain additional punishment. We repeat that we cannot but think that the method of the Code as it limits discretion is conducive to exactness in the meting of punishment, while it will tend to the advantage of the offender by apprizing him specifically of the aggravation he has to answer for.

Supra, para. 124.

Ibid.

7th Report, p. 97.

P. 99.

511. We have now to notice the provisions for the commutation of sentences—"It will be seen," say the Commissioners, "that we have given to the Government a power of "commuting sentences in certain cases without the

See Appendix, Note A, page 95.

"consent of the offender. Some of the rules which we have laid down "on this subject will be universally allowed to be proper. It is evidently "fit that the Government should be empowered to commute the sentence "of death for any other punishment provided by the Code. It seems to "us also very desirable that the Government should have the power of "commuting perpetual transportation for perpetual imprisonment. Many "circumstances, of which the executive authorities ought to be accurately "informed, but which must often be unknown to the ablest Judge, may, "at particular times, render it highly inconvenient to carry a sentence of "transportation into effect. The state of those remote Provinces of the "Empire, in which convict settlements are established, and the way in "which the interests of those Provinces may be affected by any addition "to the convict population, are matters which lie altogether out of the "cognizance of the tribunals by which those sentences are passed, and "which the Government only is competent to decide.

512. Mr. Norton, we believe, stands alone in objecting to these arrangements. He says, "the arbitrary authority (Clause 42) to change "transportation for life into imprisonment for life, which may be pos-"sibly rigorous, and which may be far the severer punishment is, in my "opinion, uncalled for, and may be unjust." Considering that imprisonment for life is made generally the alternative for transportation for life, and adverting to the circumstances referred to in the Note, which may sometimes render it inexpedient to carry a sentence of transportation into effect, we are not surprised that there is none who agrees with Mr. Norton in pronouncing the provision for this commutation "uncalled for," or in surmising that it "may be unjust." Sir J. Awdry says, "the power of the Executive Government to commute transportation, as "distinct from the general prerogative of mercy, is, I think, grounded "on sufficient reason." This power of commutation is practically exercised in England under Section 10, 5 Geo. IV., Cap. 84, by which it is lawful for the Secretary of State to order convicts, under sentence of transportation, to be confined in any place appointed for the purpose by Her Majesty, in England, until, it may be, they "shall become entitled to their liberty."

513. By Clause 42, a sentence of transportation may be commuted also for banishment from the Territories of the East India Company. Mr. Norton says this is a mode of punishment, which "appears almost impracticable." "How it is to be enforced is not provided." Mr. Norton must have overlooked Clause 205, which provides that a person returning from banishment "shall be punished with transportation for a term "which may extend to seven years, to which banishment for life shall "always be added."

514. The authors of the Code anticipated objections to Clauses 43 and 44. In the latter of these they provide that "whenever a person not both of Asiatic birth and of Asiatic "blood commits an offence so serious that he is sentenced to two years of simple imprisonment, or to one year of rigorous "imprisonment, it shall be competent to the Government to commute "that punishment for banishment from the Territories of the East India "Company." In the former they provide that if a person of the same description commits an offence so heinous as to be visited with a sentence of imprisonment for seven years or more, the Government shall have "the power of substituting an equal term of transportation for

See Appendix, Note A, page 96.

62

"that term of imprisonment, and of excluding the offender, after the "expiration of the term of transportation, from the Territories of the "East India Company." "We are satisfied," they say, "that both "humanity and policy require that those provisions, or others very similar "to them, should be adopted." Their reasons for this opinion they state as follows:—"the physical difference, which exists "between the European and the Native of India, renders "it impossible to subject them to the same system of prison-discipline. "It is most desirable, indeed, that in the treatment of offenders convicted "of the same crime and sentenced to the same punishment there should be "no apparent inequality. But it is still more desirable, that there should "be no real inequality, and there must be real inequality unless there be "apparent inequality. It would be cruel to subject an European for a "long period to a severe prison-discipline, in a country in which exist-"ence is almost constant misery to an European who has not many "indulgences at his command. If not cruel it would be impolitic. It is "unnecessary to point out to his Lordship in Council how desirable it is "that our national character should stand high in the estimation of the "inhabitants of India, and how much that character would be lowered "by the frequent exhibition of Englishmen of the worst description, "placed in the most degrading situations, stigmatized by the Courts of "Justice and engaged in the ignominious labor of a gaol." The reasons they give for not suffering Europeans who have been convicted of serious crimes and have suffered punishment, afterwards to reside in this country, are of a similar character to those last stated. It would be impolitic, for their degradation and vicious habits tend to reflect disgrace on the Government. Parliament, when it threw open a large part of India to British subjects, directed the local legislature to provide against dangers which might be expected from the influx of men of lawless habits and blasted character. No regulation can promote more effectually, or in a more unexceptionable manner, the end which Parliament had in view than that now proposed.

Note A, pp. 95, 96.

515. Sir J. Awdry says, "the observations (of the Commissioners) "on transportation appear just as regards this country, but they have "properly qualified their application to Europeans" (in allowing the term of transportation to be short of life.) "The banishment from "India of foreign criminals seems to me most properly made a part of "the Code." On the other hand Mr. Cochrane and Mr. Norton make objections to those clauses. Mr. Cochrane indeed protests against them as containing "terrible enactments," "in his view wholly unjustifiable." He objects in principle to the interference of Government for the purpose of superadding punishments to those affixed by Courts of Justice, which he thinks is within the scope of these provisions, as both impolitic and unjust. Notwithstanding the explanations offered in the Note, he cannot see that transportation involving imprisonment with labour in some British Colony situated in a temperate climate is to a European a favorable commutation for imprisonment with labour in an Indian gaol. He says, "The observations of the Commissioners on the subject of the "imprisonment of Europeans, would apply rather to the regulating such "imprisonment than furnish any reason for vesting the Government with "a power so terrible as that which the 43rd and 44th Sections seek to "confer." "I know of no such physical difference, which should in "any degree entitle such provisions to be passed." He contends that the provisions in these clauses allowing banishment for life do in effect produce inequality of punishment between Europeans and Natives, that the so-called commutation involves really additional punishment.

516. Mr. Norton says, "I think both Clause 43 and Clause 44, "under which after part of a sentence of imprisonment may have been "endured by a person not of Asiatic birth or blood, that imprisonment "may be arbitrarily changed to transportation in some cases, and to "banishment for *life* in others; and, that, although possibly but a few "months of imprisonment may have to be undergone—authorize the "*power* to confound and overthrow all justice, equality, and humanity, in "sentences." Upon this we must remark that instead of a *few months*, there must remain under Clause 44 two-thirds of the whole term of imprisonment, which ranges from one year, when the law requires that it shall be of the description termed "rigorous," and two years when the description is not specified, to any period short of seven years; while under Clause 43, the remaining term must be at least five years.

517. Mr. Vaughan conceives that "punishment may be provided "for Europeans under the rules for rigorous imprisonment, and labour "may be enforced against them, with no more danger to health than it "is now voluntarily performed by Soldiers, Artificers, &c." "Small "European jails may be established at healthy European Stations, and "European attendants may be selected from steady men not fit for "active service, to whom it would afford an extra provision."

518. Mr. Hudleston and others offer objections, which we need not particularly notice; Mr. A. D. Campbell thus refers to them—"To "Clauses 43 and 44, not only Mr. Hudleston, but many other officers in "the interior, object, I think, on insufficient ground. For under the "explanation given, banishment from the Company's Territories, even "for life, is plainly intended in mitigation, not in enhancement of the "sentence specified, when passed on Europeans, and transportation as "regards them is not to be perpetual. But though the policy and "humanity of these enactments seem to be vindicated, I doubt their "impartiality; and, on this point, would direct attention to the strong "opinion given by a Native, V. Sreenavasiah, Naib Serishtadar in "Chingleput—who, with reference to the desire of the Law Commission, "'to save Englishmen of the worst description from being placed in "'degrading situations, and engaged in the ignominious labour of a gaol "'equally with the Natives of India' compares such exemption with the "indulgence of the Hindoo Law in favor of Bramins, 'ridiculed by the "'European nations,' and concludes that 'any distinction made in the "'punishment of Englishmen and Natives' will, instead of upholding, "lower, the British character in the eyes of the public."

519. On the point last adverted to by Mr. Campbell, Mr. Vaughan says, "As for exposure of the European character, one would think that "the writers had never seen those which, unhappily are too frequent "wherever an European Corps appears. The Natives have not such a "high opinion of red and white faces, as to suppose all who possess them "to be immaculate; and I should think it well to let them see that "justice is administered equally to all."

520. These clauses, as stated in the Note, are intended primarily to admit of the Government relieving *European* offenders from a mode of punishment, which in general, it is conceived would, from the influence of the climate, be a more severe infliction upon them than upon Natives. But the expression used to designate the class of persons to whom they are to apply "is not both of Asiatic birth and of Asiatic blood." Referring to Clause 32 it will be found, that "the words 'a person of "Asiatic blood,' denote a person whose father, or mother, or grandfather, "or grandmother, was of Asiatic birth, and as far as can be discovered "of pure Asiatic extraction." The expression, no doubt, was widened as above to admit of persons natives of temperate climates out of Europe being put on the same footing as Europeans in this respect.

521. Mr. Norton says, "I do not understand the difference meant "between persons of Asiatic *birth* and of Asiatic *blood* (*both* of which "qualities are to combine to bring parties under Clause 43) if a person "born of an Asiatic father or mother *is* of Asiatic blood, Clause 32." Though several other persons have commented on the definition in Clauses 43 and 44, of the parties affected thereby, none but Mr. Norton has failed to perceive that by a person of "Asiatic birth" in contradistinction from a person of "Asiatic blood," is meant one who was born in Asia.

522. Mr. Vaughan objects to the definition as rendering persons liable to be transported, who, though they could not be proved to be of Asiatic blood strictly according to Clause 32, are presumably of Asiatic extraction. How "hardly would these clauses operate," he says, "against any with even a tinge of Asiatic blood, which ought to be "sufficient to give them a claim to residence till *sentence* of transporta-"tion is passed by a *Court*, and even in the case of an European in "regard to such offences as are intended in Clause 44, can there be any "necessity to banish him from the Territories of the Company, to tear "him away from landed property and a family partly of Asiatic blood." Mr. Greenhill puts the case of the son of Indian parents born at Malta or Constantinople, who, though he may have been all his life resident in India, not being of Asiatic *birth*, would he apprehends be liable to transportation and banishment, at the pleasure of Government, under Clauses 43 and 44 respectively.

523. Mr. G. W. Bacon objects to these clauses because by the definition "a child of an Englishman born in wedlock is deprived of his father's "rights, and vested with those of his maternal grandmother, if she be a "native of any part of Asia;" and because a person "whose grand-"mother was a native of India is (erroneously as he conceives) presumed "to be so physically different from a pure European as to feel little "annoyance from confinement for seven years and upwards in the Jails "and under the climate of this country."

524. We must say that Mr. Bacon's objection appears to us well founded. For clearly a person who was merely born in Asia, but who was brought up from infancy and educated in England, whose mother was of English birth, and whose father and paternal and maternal grandfathers were both of English birth and English blood, could not be relieved by Government under these clauses, if his maternal grandmother were of Asiatic birth, that is, born somewhere in Asia, it may be on the confines of Europe, and were, "as far as could be discovered, of pure Asiatic extraction." Again, a Native of Siberia, being both of Asiatic birth and Asiatic blood according to the definition, could not be relieved under these clauses, though confinement in an Indian gaol would, no doubt, cause as much suffering to him as to an European.

525. These appear to us to be very strong objections to the definition in question, and to the terms employed, subject to that definition, in Clauses 43 and 44. But we are unable to suggest an amendment which would remove the difficulty, and be otherwise unexceptionable. We do not attach a great degree of importance to any of the considerations which suggested the introduction of the clause we are examining into the Code, except the first mentioned, the consideration that a long imprisonment in an Indian gaol is a much more severe punishment to an European to whose constitution the climate is unfavorable, than to a native. For the end in view on this consideration, namely, the relief of parties who from their constitution and habits are unfitted to endure such punishment, it appears to us that the provision in Clause 45 empowering the Government to commute the punishment to which an offender has been sentenced, *with his own consent*, for any other punishment provided by the Code, except death, may be sufficient. Under this general provision the Government would be empowered to give the relief of transportation to a more temperate region to all to whom the commutation would be welcome.

526. We have lastly to consider the provision contained in Clause 61, "intended to prevent an offender whose guilt is fully "established from eluding punishment on the ground "that the evidence does not enable the tribunals to "pronounce with certainty under what penal provision his case falls." For example, in a case of murder, when it may be certain that either A or B murdered Z, and that whichever was the murderer was aided by the other in the commission of the murder, it is meant that the Court shall record its finding according to the literal truth, namely, that A has either murdered Z, or aided B to murder Z, and that B has either murdered Z or has aided A to murder Z, and upon this finding shall sentence A and B respectively to some punishment common to both offences, that is, a punishment which might be inflicted if the parties were convicted positively either of murder, or of the previous abetment of murder by aid. In this instance the punishment happens to be the same. Again "it will often be certain that there has been a fraudulent appropriation "of property; and the only doubt will be whether this fraudulent appro-"priation was a theft or a criminal breach of trust." In such a case it is intended that the finding shall be in this form—that the accused has committed either theft or criminal breach of trust, and that sentence shall pass thereupon awarding some punishment which may be inflicted for either theft or criminal breach of trust. The difference between the punishments for these offences is merely that for theft the imprisonment *must be* rigorous, while for criminal breach of trust it may be rigorous or simple at discretion. We cannot but agree with the authors of the Code that in the former case "to suffer both offenders to go unpunished "though it is certain that both are guilty of capital crimes merely because "it is doubtful under what clause each of them is punishable, would be "most unreasonable," and equally absurd in the latter case to allow the offender clearly guilty of a fraudulent misappropriation to escape unpunished because of a doubt as to the precise designation of the offence, as theft or criminal breach of trust. The offender ought not to be subjected to a penalty to which he would not be liable if the conviction were positive for the minor offence, which is ensured by the rule that the punishment is to be one common to both offences; this being provided for, justice as it appears to us will be satisfied by the provision in Clause 61.

See Appendix, Note A, page 105.

527. Sir J. Awdry observes that "the principle of punishment "on conviction in the alternative is just. It does directly what the Law "of England professes not to do, but does indirectly, and subject to "defeat by technical accidents, as where the crime is laid differently in "different Courts." Mr. Norton says, "The last Clause 61, appears to "me in point of reason the most objectionable of any. It provides for "the punishment of parties where either the law or the fact is so doubtful "that the Judge cannot say what offence has been committed." But it is to be remembered that according to the supposition the main facts which constitute the *corpus delicti* are proved, and that the doubt relates to some incidental point which is of a quality important only as determining whether the offence falls technically under one designation or another, as for example in the case already put, where a man is charged with theft, and the fraudulent appropriation is proved, but a doubt is raised by the evidence whether the party had not the property in trust. Without determining this point the Court convicts him in the alternative, and sentences him to a punishment equally warrantable whether the offence technically were theft or breach of trust. We do not see that the party is any way wronged by this proceeding, while public justice is vindicated. Mr. Hudleston says, "A Judge should be bound to make up his mind as "to the particular crime for which he holds the prisoner guilty." "The "accused is entitled to know precisely of what he is accused in order to "defend himself," and "a decision of guilty or not guilty of a specific act "must be passed." It is proper that the accused should know precisely of what fact he is accused, and it is proper that there should be a decision of guilty or not guilty of a specific act, but all this is compatible with Clause 61. The *corpus delicti* may be set forth and the accused may be pronounced guilty or not guilty of it, although the offence be not positively designated by a specific term. It does not appear to us to be essential that the Judge should make up his mind to convict positively of theft or breach of trust, or else to acquit, if he finds the *corpus delicti* to be proved, and is satisfied that it is theft if it is not breach of trust, and breach of trust if it is not theft, certainly either the one or the other. Mr. A. D. Campbell says, "in all cases of doubt, giving the prisoner the benefit of it, I would convict of the minor crime alone." This would be doing exactly what the authors of the Code wish to avoid, making the Court affirm what is not literally true; it is surely better to adhere to the literal truth by finding in the alternative, and passing a sentence which would be appropriate if the conviction were for the minor offence.

528. Mr. Bacon suggests a difficulty with reference to the case stated in the illustration (*a*) to Clause 98. He supposes the Court to find it doubtful what "A considered likely" to be "done by B," and to be therefore "at a loss whether to convict A of abetting murder or only abetting robbery." "As there is no punishment common to both crimes," he asks, "what sentence is to be passed on A? B being convicted of robbery and murder." The question is easily answered. Under the circumstances of the case as stated in the illustration, it is clear that A was guilty of abetting robbery, possibly he was guilty of abetting murder also, but that not being clear, the Court would of course convict him of the former offence only, and sentence him accordingly.

CONCLUSION.

529. Having now accomplished a detailed review of the whole Penal Code, and of the criticisms, objections, and suggestions, contained in the

Reports upon it, which appeared to us most proper to be presented to the notice of Government, or which seemed to call for remark from us in the way of answer or explanation, in the prosecution of which review we have fulfilled the instruction of Government to "direct our attention to "the act of crimes and punishments contained in the seventh Report of "the Commissioners on the Criminal Law of England with a view to "comparison, and the detection of any omissions, or other imperfections "that may exist in the Code," and having distinctly expressed our sentiments upon the definitions and penal provisions of the Code as they have severally passed in order under our examination, we have only in conclusion to say, in general, that the opinion we delivered in our former Report, with respect to the portion to which he had then given our more particular attention, is that which we would now offer as our mature judgment on the whole work.

Para. 649.

530. As to the manner in which we have performed our part, we cannot but entertain a fear that in spite of the pains and care we have taken to present fully and fairly for the consideration of Government the criticisms upon the Code the most deserving of attention, we may have omitted observations well worthy of notice, and creditable to the sagacity and judgment of those who offered them, and may have imperfectly stated the views of some whose remarks we have adverted to. Comprising as the Code does 488 Clauses, upon almost all of which we have had occasion to comment, we cannot flatter ourselves that we have entirely escaped from error in our own interpretations of it, nor in the constructions we have put upon the criticisms of others. Some inaccuracies and oversights, we doubt not, may be detected in the comments we have made both upon the Code and upon the remarks of its critics. We hope however that none will be found of any great importance; and for any errors or omissions that may be discovered, our apology must be the extensiveness of the subject we had to treat, and the voluminousness of the Reports containing the criticisms we had to examine and digest.

531. Should the Government on the whole concur in the judgment we have expressed as the result of a very searching examination of the Penal Code in all its parts, and in our general estimate of it as a body of law, in a practical view, we would beg very earnestly to recommend the enactment of it for all the Territories subject to the Government of the East India Company, except what is comprised within the local limits of the Criminal Jurisdiction of the Courts established by Her Majesty's Charter. *

532. The strange anomaly in the jurisprudential condition of British India, which consists in the three capital cities having systems of law different from those of the countries of which they are the capitals, cannot, we imagine, be permitted to exist much longer. The year 1854,

* We have already recommended in our Report, dated the 4th November 1843, that British Subjects should be made subject to the jurisdiction of the Company's Courts. But we did not think, and do not now think, it desirable that such persons should be made subject to the existing penal law of the Mofussil. If however, the Penal Code is adopted there can be no reason for excepting British Subjects from its operation. We are now preparing a scheme of pleading and procedure with forms of indictment adapted to the provisions of the Code, in conformity with the instructions conveyed to us in Mr. Secretary Bushby's letter, dated the 20th March last, and in submitting it to Government, we shall take the opportunity to suggest the mode of proceeding which appears to us the most expedient for the trial of British Subjects by the Company's Courts, especially in capital cases.

will probably put an end to it, if it should be permitted to endure till that epoch.

533. But the question arises, should the assimilation be brought about by extending the law of the Presidencies over India, or by extending the law of India over the Presidencies, or by an amalgamation of the two?

534. In our opinion, if the penal law of India consists of this Code, and the civil law of India consists of portions of the Hindoo and Mahomedan law, and that system of English law, which our commission have recommended as the *lex loci*, which may be described as the English system of rules for accomplishing the ends of universal Jurisprudence, there can be no doubt that these laws should be extended over the Presidencies in preference to either of the other schemes.

535. But at the present moment we do not recommend the enactment of this Code for the Presidencies, unless the Judges of any of the Supreme Courts should express a wish to that effect.

536. We do not advise the general repeal of the penal laws now existing in the Territories for which we have recommended the enactment of the Code.

537. We think it will be more expedient to provide only that no man shall be tried or punished (except by a Court Martial) for any facts which constitute any offence defined in the Code, otherwise than according to its provisions.

538. It is possible that a few actions which are punishable by some existing law and which the Legislature would not desire to exempt, may have been omitted from the Code. And, in addition to this consideration, it appears to us that actions which have been made penal on special temporary grounds ought not to be included in a general Penal Code intended to take its place amongst the permanent institutions of the country.

539. The law, for example, which prevents the Natives of India, of the labouring classes, from exercising the ordinary right of freemen by contracting to carry their labour to any market which may seem to them advantageous, though it may be a useful and necessary law while a large part of the population is in a state of ignorance which unfits it for the discreet exercise of such a right, is yet obviously a law marked out for abolition when advancing civilization shall have rendered it unnecessary and consequently vexatious, and such a law should not, we think, be suffered to intrude into a Code intended to endure, we will not say for ever, but until more ample experience and the reflections of Jurists and Statesmen may bring to light new principles more effectual for the prevention of crime.

540. Any existing penal law, not virtually superseded by the Code, which the Legislature does not approve of, ought, in our view, to be specifically repealed.

541. If the Legislature adopts our recommendation to enact the Code, we beg to point out the expediency of immediately making it a subject of study in the Government Colleges, and of requesting the Council of Education to introduce questions framed upon its provisions and upon the Notes appended to it, into the examinations for carrying into effect Lord Hardinge's Resolution of 10th October 1844.

542. It is not the least of the many advantages of a Penal Code of which the principles are purely rational, and of course always consistent with each other, that a student may become thoroughly master of it without the aid of any extrinsic learning.

543. The English Criminal Law cannot be fully understood without a considerable share of historical and antiquarian knowledge. Knowledge of that kind is no doubt an elegant and even a useful accomplishment. But it is no more necessary to the comprehension of a penal law founded solely on principles of Morality and Jurisprudence, that an acquaintance with the biography of Euclid is necessary to the comprehension of the problems and theorems of Geometry.

544. The study of the Code will require no such foreign illustration, and will on this account and also on account of its systematic form, be a task incomparably easier than the study of the criminal law administered by the Supreme Court. And the consequence will be, that in a few years the penal law of India will be familiarly known to a great number of young men of the middle classes, who, besides furnishing recruits to the judicial service, will constitute a public prepared to criticise the proceedings of the Criminal Courts in a fair and enlightened spirit.

C. H. CAMERON,
D. ELIOTT.

INDIAN LAW COMMISSION,
The 24th June, 1847.